PRACTICAL CHRISTIANITY

PRACTICAL CHRISTIANITY

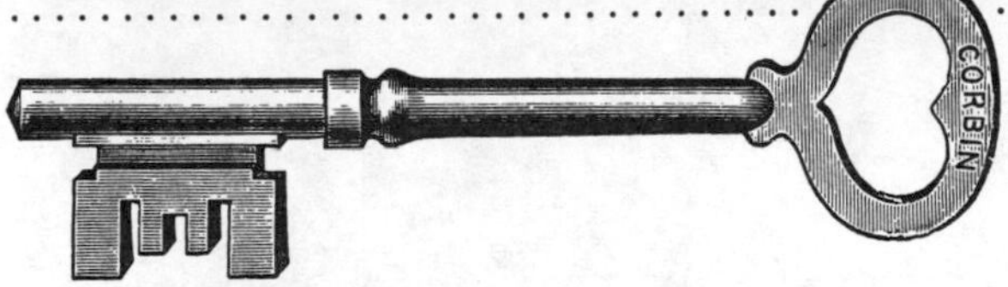

Compiled and edited by:

• LaVONNE NEFF • RON BEERS
• BRUCE BARTON • LINDA TAYLOR
• DAVE VEERMAN • JIM GALVIN

Tyndale House Publishers, Inc.
WHEATON, ILLINOIS

CREDITS

General Editors
Bruce Barton
Ron Beers
James Galvin
LaVonne Neff
Linda Taylor
David Veerman

Editorial Director
Ron Beers

Managing Editor
LaVonne Neff

Editorial Assistant
Linda Taylor

Topic Development
Bruce Barton
David Veerman
James Galvin

Other Special Editors
Ann Himmelberger Wald
Marilyn Thompson
Nancy Stetson
Isabel Anders Throop
Linda Krause
Betsy Elliot
Ellen Parks
Ken Petersen

Design
Tim Botts

Unless otherwise noted, all Scripture is taken from *The Holy Bible,* New International Version.

First printing, June 1987
Library of Congress Catalog
Card Number 87-50140
ISBN 0-8423-4957-X

Printed in the United States
of America

CONTRIBUTORS

Dr. Hudson T. Armerding
Wheaton College
Wheaton, Illinois

Drs. David and Cheryl Aspy
Carkhuff Institute of Human Technology
Amherst, Massachusetts

Mrs. Pamela Barden
Youth for Christ/USA
Carol Stream, Illinois

Dr. Bruce Barton
Youth for Christ/USA
Carol Stream, Illinois

Mr. Thomas A. Bassford
Youth Ministry Services
Topeka, Kansas

Mr. David M. Bastedo
Youth for Christ of San Gabriel/Pomona Valley
Covina, California

Dr. V. Gilbert Beers
Books for Living, Inc.
Elgin, Illinois

Dr. James Montgomery Boice
Tenth Presbyterian Church
Philadelphia, Pennsylvania

Dr. William R. Bright
Campus Crusade for Christ, International
San Bernardino, California

Rev. and Mrs. Stuart Briscoe
Elmbrook Church
Waukesha, Wisconsin

Mr. Trent Bushnell
Greater Lansing Youth for Christ
Lansing, Michigan

Kathy Callahan-Howell
Epworth Free Methodist Church
Cincinnati, Ohio

Dr. Anthony Campolo
Eastern College
St. Davids, Pennsylvania

Mrs. Evelyn Christenson
Evelyn Christenson Ministries
St. Paul, Minnesota

Rev. Larry Christenson
International Lutheran Renewal Center
St. Paul, Minnesota

Dr. Gary R. Collins
Trinity Evangelical Divinity School
Deerfield, Illinois

Mr. Charles Colson
Fellowship Communications
Washington, D.C.

Rev. John Crosby
First Presbyterian Church
Glen Ellyn, Illinois

Mr. Gary Dausey
Youth for Christ/USA
Carol Stream, Illinois

Mr. Ken Davis
Speaker
Arvada, Colorado

Mrs. Betsy R. Elliot
University of Chicago Press
Chicago, Illinois

Mr. Ajith Fernando
Youth for Christ/Sri Lanka
Sri Lanka

Dr. Richard Foster
Friends University
Wichita, Kansas

Dr. James C. Galvin
Youth for Christ/USA
Carol Stream, Illinois

Dr. Norman Geisler
Dallas Theological Seminary
Dallas, Texas

Dr. Vernon Grounds
Denver Seminary
Denver, Colorado

Dr. Richard Halverson
Senate Chaplain
Washington, D.C.

Senator Mark O. Hatfield
United States Senate
Washington, D.C.

Dr. James C. Hefley
Hannibal-LaGrange College
Hannibal, Missouri

Dr. Howard G. Hendricks
Dallas Theological Seminary
Dallas, Texas

Mr. Oswald C. J. Hoffman
Lutheran Hour Speaker
St. Louis, Missouri

Miss Hannah Hurnard
Author
Salem, Oregon

Dr. Jay Kesler
Taylor University
Upland, Indiana

Mr. Larry Kreider
Youth for Christ/Adult Ministries
Houston, Texas

Mrs. Madeleine L'Engle
Author
New York, New York

Mr. Richard Lovelace
Writer
South Hamilton, Massachusetts

Dr. Martin E. Marty
University of Chicago/ Divinity School
Chicago, Illinois

Mr. Josh McDowell
Josh McDowell Ministries
Dallas, Texas

Dr. David L. McKenna
Asbury Theological Seminary
Wilmore, Kentucky

Mr. Dean Merrill
Christian Herald
Chappaqua, New York

Rev. Calvin Miller
Westside Baptist Church
Omaha, Nebraska

Mr. Tom Minnery
Christianity Today, Inc.
Carol Stream, Illinois

Mr. Harold Myra
Christianity Today, Inc.
Carol Stream, Illinois

Mrs. LaVonne Neff
Youth for Christ/USA
Carol Stream, Illinois

Mrs. Janette Oke
Author
Alberta, Canada

Dr. J. I. Packer
Regent College
Vancouver, British Columbia

Luis Palau
Luis Palau Evangelistic Team
Portland, Oregon

Mr. John B. Pearrell
Atlanta Youth for Christ
Decatur, Georgia

Rev. John M. Perkins
The Foundation for Reconciliation and Development
Pasadena, California

Rev. Eugene H. Peterson
Christ Our King Presbyterian Church
Bel Air, Maryland

Dr. Clark H. Pinnock
McMaster Divinity College
Hamilton, Ontario

Rev. John C. Pollock
Rose Ash House
Devonshire, England

Mr. Terry Prisk
Detroit Metro Youth for Christ
Detroit, Michigan

Mr. Richard Owen Roberts
Author and Speaker
Wayne, Illinois

Mr. Shawn A. Robinson
Youth for Christ of San Gabriel/Pomona Valley
Covina, California

Rev. Adrian Rogers
Bellevue Baptist Church
Memphis, Tennessee

Mr. Thomas R. Sanders
Albuquerque Youth for Christ
Albuquerque, New Mexico

Rev. Robert Schuller
Robert Schuller Ministries
Garden Grove, California

Dr. David A. Seamands
Asbury Theological Seminary
Wilmore, Kentucky

Mrs. Luci Shaw
Harold Shaw Publishers
Carol Stream, Illinois

Dr. Lewis Smedes
Fuller Theological Seminary
Pasadena, California

Pastor Howard Snyder
Irving Park Free Methodist Church
Chicago, Illinois

Dr. R. C. Sproul
Ligonier Valley Study Center
Altamonte Springs, Florida

Mr. Kenneth Steinken
Freelance Writer
Rapid City, South Dakota

Mrs. Isabel Anders Throop
Freelance Writer
Shaker Heights, Ohio

Rev. John R. Throop
Christ Episcopal Church
Shaker Heights, Ohio

Dr. and Mrs. Roger Tirabassi
Robert Schuller Ministries
Garden Grove, California

Mrs. Ingrid Trobisch
Author
Springfield, Missouri

Dr. David Veerman
Youth for Christ/USA
Carol Stream, Illinois

Dr. Larry Ward
Food for the Hungry, Inc.
Scottsdale, Arizona

Dr. Robert Webber
Wheaton College
Wheaton, Illinois

Dr. Earl D. Wilson
Lake Psychological & Counseling Services
Milwaukie, Oregon

Mrs. Joan H. Young
West Shore Youth for Christ
Scottville, Michigan

CONTENTS

HOW TO USE THIS BOOK

Practical Christianity is a reference book containing the collected wisdom of scores of Christian leaders. This has been compiled into hundreds of articles on specific subjects. Our goal is to help people understand the Christian faith and to mature in their walk with God, so this book has both information and problem-solving advice. Above all, it contains invaluable counsel for applying biblical principles to life—making faith real and putting it into practice.

There are several ways to use *Practical Christianity.* You may wish to find a specific problem or topic of interest in the index and then read the articles that relate to it. Another approach would be to choose a general subject, like prayer, and then study it in depth individually or in a group. But you can also read *Practical Christianity* from cover to cover—the subjects are arranged in an order that leads you from understanding the nature of Christian growth, followed by *how* we grow, and concluding with specific areas and arenas for growth. Whatever approach you choose, you will find *Practical Christianity* to be an invaluable resource for maturing in your relationship with God.

CHAPTER

1

Christian Growth Begins at Christian Birth

- ✓ Why would I want to become a Christian?
- ✓ How do I become a Christian?
- ✓ In what areas will I grow?
- ✓ Will I ever be perfect?
- ✓ What is the difference between maturity and perfection?

How Does a Person Become a Christian?

LUIS PALAU

Millions of people claim something has happened that has changed their lives, brought them profound peace of mind, and assured them about the future. People have faced death singing, entering eternity with confidence.

Some with this unusual confidence say they have been "saved," others use the term "born again," and still others say that they have "found eternal life."

All these terms are synonymous, for they each have to do with three aspects of life: being saved from past guilt, being delivered from present thought patterns, and gaining assurance for the future and for eternity. All these mean that a person has become a Christian.

At this point, let us look at some things that do not guarantee a person is a Christian. Being born in America or the British Isles, living a decent life, thinking positively, going to church, giving to charity, taking the sacraments, praying—none of these is a guarantee. Not even believing in God makes a person a Christian—many people of other religions believe in God.

What is a real Christian? First, a real Christian has been born into the family of God. Just as we are born into our human family, so we have to be born into God's family. The Gospel of John puts it this way: "Yet to all who received him, to those who believed in his name, he gave the right to become children of God—children born not of natural descent, nor of human decision or a husband's will, but born of God" (John 1:12, 13). In other words, we are all created by God as his creatures, but we only become members of God's family when we open our hearts to Christ, believe in him, and receive him into our hearts.

Second, a true Christian is walking in the way of life. Jesus said there are two roads: the broad road leads to destruction, and the narrow road leads to eternal life (see also Deuteronomy 30:19; Jeremiah 21:8). The narrow road leads to a clear conscience and liberation from habits that destroy us. We do not have to walk under clouds of guilt—real or imagined. When you have found Jesus Christ and have been forgiven for your sins, you have absolute peace with God. You know that your sins were dealt with on the cross and taken away. You are free to live a new life of moral cleanliness—this does not mean perfection, but it does mean walking in the light and desiring to be pure.

Third, the true Christian has eternal life. Such a promise comes into its fullness when we die, but we can enjoy it now, here on earth. Eternal life lives in our hearts, convincing us that we need never feel alone or empty. Jesus said, "I have come that they may have life, and have it to the full" (John 10:10). You can have the assurance of eternal life because Christ lives in your heart. John Calvin called this the inner witness of the Holy Spirit.

Now that we have a clear picture of what a Christian is, how does one become a Christian? There are three basic steps. Step one is to admit that your sins keep you away from God. The Bible says there is no difference among people because we all have sinned and fallen short of God's perfection (Romans 3:9-23). We can deny how we miss the mark, but as the apostle John put it, "If we claim to be without sin, we deceive ourselves and the truth is not in us. . . . If we claim we have not sinned, we make him out to be a liar and his word has no place in our lives" (1 John 1:8, 10).

Step two is to believe that Jesus Christ died on the cross to lead us back to God. We do not have to understand it all, but we do need to believe it. I do not understand how electricity or radios work, but I trust that they work and enjoy their benefits. "For what I received I passed on to you as of first importance: that Christ died for our sins according to the Scriptures, that he was buried, that he was raised on the third day according to the Scriptures, and that he appeared to Peter, and then to the Twelve" (1 Corinthians 15:3-5).

Step three is to receive the Lord Jesus as Savior by making a personal decision. The individual must take a step of faith, which is receiving based on believing. It is not enough merely to believe; the gift of eternal life must be grasped. When I travel and bring home a present for my wife, all she has to do to enjoy the gift is to take it and say thank you. To receive Jesus Christ is similar. By faith you say, "Thank you, Lord. I receive you into my life." At that moment the gift of God, which is eternal life in Jesus Christ, is yours.

This last step demands a personal decision. It is an act of the will, for we can either reject or receive Christ. Too many people depend on inherited faith—a second-hand faith. But only authentic faith leads to life eternal.

♦ TWO WOMEN, ONE SAVIOR / LUIS PALAU

One night in November 1971, I was preaching in the capital city of Lima, Peru. In the crowd was a woman who was a guerrilla fighter and had killed policemen and civilians alike. She heard the Word of God and before the next sunrise had knelt by her bed and, with little knowledge of the Bible, received the Lord Jesus as her Savior.

That woman's life has been completely transformed by Christ. Now she is taking care of two thousand poor children by feeding them a full breakfast. She has built schools for them in the slums of Peru and started churches too.

I also know of one of the wealthiest women in the British Isles. Despite her breeding and education, she was filled with fear of the occult and of death. She is now living a life of peace and freedom from fear—belief and trust in Christ have brought her this. She is now leading many others to the Lord.

In the worst slums of Latin America or the wealthy circles of Great Britain, people are experiencing eternal life—promise for the future and hope for today.

WHO CAN BECOME A CHRISTIAN?

✍ Clark H. Pinnock

Who can become a Christian? The answer in a nutshell is that anyone can. Anyone who wants to can "take the free gift of the water of life" (Revelation 22:17). Whosoever will may come. Everyone has an invitation to the marriage supper of the Lamb (Matthew 22:9).

The Bible's teaching about God's gracious desire to save everyone is too strong and clear for us to accept the notion—which many hold—that God is free to give and to withhold salvation as he pleases, and that he gives it only to special individuals whom he has selected.

Paul said that God wants everybody "to be saved and to come to a knowledge of the truth" (1 Timothy 2:4). Peter added that God is "not wanting anyone to perish, but everyone to come to repentance" (2 Peter 3:9). Through Ezekiel, God announced: "I take no pleasure in the death of the wicked, but rather that they turn from their ways and live. Turn! Turn from your evil ways!

Why will you die, O house of Israel?" (Ezekiel 33:11).

Jesus told us who can become a Christian. "Come to me, all you who are weary and burdened, and I will give you rest" (Matthew 11:28). It seems that God quite sincerely wants everyone to be saved. "Look, the Lamb of God, who takes away the sin of the world!" (John 1:29). On another occasion Jesus said, "I, when I am lifted up from the earth, will draw all men to myself" (John 12:32).

So strong indeed is the scriptural teaching about God's universal saving will that people have sometimes even concluded that all will in fact be saved, that no one at all will be lost. As Paul said, "As in Adam all die, so in Christ all will be made alive" (1 Corinthians 15:22). Because of Paul's teaching elsewhere—as when he warns about God's wrath that is coming (1 Thessalonians 1:10)—we know there will be wicked who perish and are banished from God's presence. But we should not lose the marvelous scope of Scripture. God's intention is to save the human race, not a pathetic little segment of it. "Just as the result of one trespass was condemnation for all men, so also the result of one act of righteousness was justification that brings life for all men" (Romans 5:18).

According to this kind of theology, we ought to think of being saved as the normal outcome and being rejected as the exception, and not the other way around. I think we have erred in thinking of condemnation as the ordinary and salvation as the extraordinary outcome of the history of divine redemption.

Who can become a Christian? According to the New Testament, anyone can. It is certainly true that not all do make the decision to give their lives over to God. Some stubbornly insist on going their own way. "Whoever rejects the Son will not see life, for God's wrath remains on him" (John 3:36). Such people will not enjoy the salvation God has for the world. "Yet to all who received him, to those who believed in his name, he gave the right to become children of God" (John 1:12).

But a difficulty comes to mind—not on God's side, who is on record as desiring the salvation of the race, but on man's side. Has not sin affected human nature so as to make it impossible for individuals to save themselves and even to turn to God for salvation? Are people not so hopelessly alienated from God and dead in their sins that they have no ability and no desire to turn to God for help? Is it perhaps true that anyone may but no one actually can become a Christian?

If we focused only upon man's lost condition, we might very well suppose that bare invitations to eternal life would be useless and would fall upon deaf ears. But we must remember God's powerful Word. His invitation to save sinners carries with it all the resources necessary to see it happen. God's grace creates within humans the power to respond to or resist his love. He works in their lives to draw them to himself. When God calls a sinner to turn to him, he gives the sinner the strength to do what he requires.

God does not abandon sinners in their depravity, but visits them with his grace and goodness. He gives them good gifts out of his abundant creation and sends his Spirit to draw them back to himself. Stephen made that clear in his last sermon: "You stiff-necked people, with uncircumcised hearts and ears!

You are just like your fathers: You always resist the Holy Spirit!" (Acts 7:51).

God works in sinners to draw them to himself. It does not follow that they will return. His drawing of them, being the call of love, is not irresistible. Love which did not leave the option of refusal would not be love. God deals with us as persons. We are saved not by force, but by faith, the free decision to trust in God.

Who can become a Christian? Anyone can, because God's grace closes nobody out. There are no limits to his grace except those that sinners impose upon themselves. Jesus Christ, our Advocate, has become "the atoning sacrifice for our sins, and not only for ours but also for the sins of the whole world" (1 John 2:2). Salvation is so broad as to encompass potentially the entire human race. So let us enter in, and let us invite others to enter the kingdom of God.

♦WHAT IS A CHRISTIAN? / YFC EDITORS

A Christian is one who . . .

- *has faith*
  John 3:16
  Romans 6:23
  Ephesians 2:8, 9
  Hebrews 11:1
- *has commitment*
  Luke 9:57-62
  Romans 12:1, 2
  Matthew 10:37-39
  Proverbs 3:5, 6
- *demonstrates by example*
  Galatians 5:22, 23
  James 1:22-27
  James 2:17, 20
  Romans 2:15
  1 John 2:5, 6
- *shares God's Good News*
  Matthew 10:32, 33
  Matthew 28:19, 20
  Mark 16:15
  Romans 10:9, 10

The Marks of a Christian

✍ CALVIN MILLER

Francis Schaeffer called love the mark of a Christian in a book of that title. This simple wondrous truth is the theme of the popular chorus, "They Will Know We Are Christians by Our Love." This truth, according to 1 John 4:12, is the mortar of all relationships in the Church: "No one has ever seen God; but if we love each other, God lives in us and his love is made complete in us." When God lives in us, we cannot help but love him and each other.

As love marks our lives in Christ, so does the inner control of the Holy Spirit. Thus Christians differ from non-Christians at this very crucial issue of inner direction and guidance. When we are controlled by God's Spirit, we begin to care about the things that he cares about. And what are they? The Spirit's first concern is the exaltation of Christ. Jesus said, "He will remind you of everything I have said to you" (John 14:26), and "He will bring glory to me" (John 16:14). Thus, whichever way he points our individual destiny or careers, the

Holy Spirit will direct each of our lives to exalt Christ.

As others look at us, they will of course not be able to see this invisible controller, but over a period of time they will observe that our life-styles are marked by directions greater than our own values, ethics, or willpowers could ever explain.

These two marks of a Christian—love and Spirit-control—work hand in hand. As the Holy Spirit directs our lives, we become less abusive and more loving to others. People soon learn they can approach us, trust us, and feel secure around us. They then feel as though they can come to us, confide in us, and feel good about being with us. The Christ in us becomes near and touchable, a resource for those who desire his counsel and love.

A third mark that characterizes Christians is the overwhelming desire to please Christ. Jesus yearned to please the Father on earth: "I always do what pleases him" (John 8:29), and at Jesus' baptism, God made it clear he was pleased with him: the voice over the river said, "You are my Son, whom I love; with you I am well pleased" (Mark 1:11).

As the Father and Son find pleasure in each other, so we seek the pleasure of Christ. Paul wrote, "So we make it our goal to please him" (2 Corinthians 5:9). This desire to please Christ, then, is shown in our continual willingness to submit ourselves to God's will, to take up our crosses daily and follow him (Luke 9:23). This desire to please means Christ should permeate our whole life-style. Proverbs 3:6 says, "In all your ways acknowledge him, and he will make your paths straight."

Part of pleasing Christ means we joyfully enter into God's redemptive plan. Paul said in 2 Corinthians 5:19, "God was reconciling the world to himself in Christ, not counting men's sins against them. And he has committed to us the message of reconciliation." Because Christ is in us through his Spirit, we enter God's wonderful reconciling work, and through love we help to draw people toward God.

When we have all these marks of a Christian, what will other people see in our lives?

First of all, they will see joy. A Christian martyr once observed that "joy is the most infallible proof of God's presence!" People want to look at Christians and see happiness in our walk—joy in our lives! Isaiah 3:9 says, "The look on their faces testifies against them." If a Christian looks sad all the time, his very face testifies that he doesn't contain much of God. People want to see the abundance of our great spiritual wealth reflected in our positive spirits. Jesus likened the kingdom of God to a treasure hidden in a field: this hidden treasure is the wonderful sense that God is working in us to make us complete in abundance and joy.

When we have the marks of a Christian, people will see personal stability in our lives. In our hassled age, everyone is looking for inner peace and freedom from the stress that often characterizes even Christian lives. Isaiah 26:3 says, "You will keep in perfect peace him whose mind is steadfast, because he trusts in you." And when we fail, they want to see us handle our disappointments in the way Paul described in Philippians 4:11: "I have learned to be content whatever the circumstances."

People will readily see the good works we do in Christ's name. In the Sermon on the Mount, Jesus said, "Let your light shine before men, that they may see your good deeds and praise your Father in heaven" (Matthew 5:16). Others want to see us triumph over our need to serve ourselves, to turn outside ourselves and reach out to help others. They continually watch to see what we will do when other people are wronged; they do not observe just how we treat other Christians, but whether or not we show concern for those who don't know Christ.

Those around us seek those who are more interested in serving than in being served. Although Christians should never do good works in order to be seen, the Christian life is so different from the world's that a person who is really following Christ will be immediately visible. Jesus said, "By their fruit you will recognize them" (Matthew 7:16). The fruit of the Spirit, as Paul pointed out, is quite different from the fruit of the sinful nature (Galatians 5:19-24).

When we let our negative characteristics show through, they will eradicate our witness. Others may say, "You can't be much of a Christian or you wouldn't be doing that." We don't want to be hypocritical and pretend to be something we aren't, but we want to work awfully hard at showing others the positive, consistent, and joyful Christian we want people to see. If people ask us about our struggles and problems, we should always be honest and confess that we do have them. At the same time, we want to be constantly purifying our lives and moving toward our better selves.

What do I mean by "work awfully hard"? You can't obtain the marks of a Christian simply by trying to act as if you are loving or at peace. When you try to please Christ, character results. When you try to obey Christ, you end up serving others because that's what he motivates you to do. Still, it is not as though you are straining to produce lots of good works; rather these good works are the natural response of your life because you have a new love and allegiance.

When a man and woman fall in love, they do not measure every little act of courtesy. They don't try to be good to each other. Their desire to please each other is so overwhelming that a life-style of mutual love and service flows from that desire. All people who come to know Christ have this same need to serve him. Christian character develops and results in serving Jesus naturally.

It's natural, therefore, once Christ comes into our lives, to set spiritual goals for ourselves, making time to study and pray. We do this because we love him. It is natural for young lovers to dine together every evening at seven. They do this because they love each other. By observing this "seven o'clock" discipline, they will increase the amount of time they have together.

We will never develop the marks of a Christian by trying hard. We can, however, set up forms of discipline for ourselves that will help us grow. And as we grow, the Holy Spirit will transform our lives and make our Christianity visible.

Paul said in Romans 12 that we don't want to be conformed to this world, but we do want to live in such a way that sooner or later we will be conformed to the image of Christ. Phillips translates verse 2 in a beautiful way: "Don't let the world around you squeeze you into its mold." Instead, our minds are to be transformed. God is in the process of bending us and molding us into the image of Christ as we yield to him moment by moment. This momentary yielding is how we grow in obtaining the marks of a Christian.

♦GOODNESS IN ALL PEOPLE / CALVIN MILLER

One of the wonderful things about God is that he gives all of us, whether we follow him or not, a temperament that includes many strengths. Many non-Christians are charitable and kind and gracious. I believe that all good qualities ultimately derive from God's goodness. As James said, "Every good and perfect gift is from above, coming down from the Father" (1:17). So there is goodness in many people—not just Christians. But the Holy Spirit does a refining work. He continually purifies our lives and makes us better than we would be without him.

♦WHAT IS CONVERSION? / YFC EDITORS

Conversion or "accepting Christ" is a matter involving action on the part of two persons—you and God. In a sense conversion is a continual process. We become more involved with Jesus day by day.

However, the act of deciding to change course in mid-life, so to speak, is what is normally referred to as conversion. It is this act that is cited as the beginning of being a Christian. When a person becomes converted, he by faith in Christ (putting his whole trust and reliance upon, confidence in, utter dependence upon him), turns *toward* God and away from his life of isolation and rebellion against God (Hebrews 11:1, 6; Acts 26:20).

Sin brings

- alienation from God
- rebellion toward his control
- activities, attitudes, actions done without reference to him

God asks us to accept

- his guidance and management of our life
- his point of view
- his source of strength

You must turn your mind

- away from sin
- toward God

♦BECOMING A CHRISTIAN / J. I. PACKER

How does a person become a Christian? The process is not difficult to understand. It can be explained as easily as *ABC:*

A represents the truth that all have sinned. It calls me to *admit* my sins. To be a Christian, I must acknowledge my sins.

B stands for *belief* in the Lord Jesus Christ. I must call on him, receive him, trust him, and worship him, recognizing who he is and what he has done for me.

C stands for something Paul requires in Romans 10:9—I must *confess* that the risen Christ is my Lord and Savior. That seals the transaction.

When I have admitted my sins, believed in Jesus, and confessed Christ as my Savior, I am a Christian, ready to "grow in the grace and knowledge of our Lord and Savior Jesus Christ" (2 Peter 3:18).

What It Means to Be Born Again

RICHARD OWEN ROBERTS

Many people use the term *born again* carelessly. Nicodemus, they say, is the first New Testament example of a converted man. In saying this, they show that they have misread John 3.

To understand John 3, the account of Jesus' conversation with Nicodemus, it is crucial to look also at the last three verses of John 2: "Now while he was in Jerusalem at the Passover Feast, many people saw the miraculous signs he was doing and believed in his name. But Jesus would not entrust himself to them, for he knew all men. He did not need man's testimony about man, for he knew what was in a man" (vv. 23-25).

The ending of chapter 2 does not seem to relate to the rest of the chapter, which tells about the marriage at Cana and the cleansing of the temple. Until you go on and read chapter 3, those three verses appear to be just dangling. But John carefully constructed his Gospel, and he didn't let odds and ends dangle without relationship or meaning. The story of Nicodemus makes the meaning of those verses clear.

In chapter 2, verses 23-25, John is making a generalization: A large number of people in Jerusalem believed in Jesus because they saw his miracles, but Jesus refused to commit himself to those people. He knew what was in their hearts. He didn't need their affirmation.

Then immediately in chapter 3 we move from this general statement to a particular example. Jesus selects an individual out of the larger group—Nicodemus.

Nicodemus comes to Jesus by night and declares his belief in exactly the terms we would expect from one of the Jerusalem believers: "Rabbi, we know you are a teacher who has come from God. For no one could perform the miraculous signs you are doing if God were not with him" (3:2).

In spite of the way evangelists and a great many others use this passage, Nicodemus is not here a converted man. Jesus didn't commit himself to the larger group, who believed in him as a result of his miracles, because he knew what was in their hearts. Nicodemus comes as their spokesman, and it is sensible to suppose that Jesus would not here commit himself to Nicodemus either.

Instead, he challenges Nicodemus's thinking and announces a great truth: "I tell you the truth, unless a man is born again, he cannot see the kingdom of God" (3:3).

Nicodemus's responses are not positive, believing responses, but the words of a man who doesn't understand what is being said: "How can a man be born when he is old?... Surely he cannot enter a second time into his mother's womb to be born!... How can this be?"

The telling words that indicate most clearly how this passage must be understood are verses 11 and 12: "I tell you the truth, we speak of what we know, and we testify to what we have seen, but still you people do not accept our testimony. I have spoken to you of earthly things and you do not believe; how then will you believe if I speak of heavenly things?" So Jesus ends the conversation by verifying the fact that the individual, Nicodemus, is like the larger crowd in Jerusalem—he doesn't believe what he's told about Jesus and salvation.

We aren't given exact details about Nicodemus's life after his talk with Jesus, but later passages indicate warm sympathy on his part with Christ and the disciples (see John 7:50, 51; 19:38-40). It may be that he eventually became a very real believer, but in this John 3 passage it is plain that he has not yet been born again.

Here's the key: the crowd believed what they saw Jesus do, but they didn't believe what they heard Jesus say. Nicodemus believed what he saw, but not what he was told. Yet nowhere in Scripture are we told that people come to faith in Christ through the eyegate. Instead, we are told that "faith comes from hearing the message, and the message is heard through the word of Christ" (Romans 10:17). Anyone who professes to be a Christian solely because of what he has seen is in the same category as the Jerusalem group and as Nicodemus, when they had not yet heard the word in faith and believed.

If the new birth, then, is not simply seeing miraculous deeds and being impressed by them, what is it? Jesus' words in John 3 need to be taken literally. Regeneration is like physical birth. Here is an important question to ponder: What part did I play in my first birth, my physical birth?

Obviously we didn't give birth to ourselves. We didn't dictate who our parents would be. We didn't even suggest the time at which we were to be born. We in no way participated in making decisions leading to our conception or in managing the events of our birth.

It would seem incongruous to suppose that we, who had nothing to do with determining the events of our first birth, would have a great deal to do with bringing about our second birth. It seems perfectly logical to assume that, if it is the parents who are responsible for the physical birth of a child, there must be someone other than ourselves responsible for our spiritual birth.

Being born again, or regeneration, is not something I do; it's something God does. I can't enter the kingdom through sight—through seeing miraculous works. I must be born again to enter it, and the new birth is something that God must bring to pass. God is the initiator of this glorious work of salvation.

If we pay close attention to New Testament stories and terminology, we will see God's part and our part in the whole glorious process of salvation. God does the initiatory work: he awakens us and brings us to life. When he has done this, we must believe what we hear in his Word and repent of all that has displeased and grieved God. Then God will justify us through the work of Christ, the Redeemer, and we will be in the midst of the work of salvation. We will be new persons in Christ, "born not of natural descent, nor of human decision or a husband's will, but born of God" (John 1:12).

What Do All Those Words Mean?

RICHARD OWEN ROBERTS

A lot of New Testament words are being thrown around loosely and used interchangably as if they all mean the same thing—words like *new birth, conversion, salvation, regeneration, justification, sanctification, glorification.* What exactly do these words mean?

It is helpful to think of an umbrella and to call the umbrella *salvation.* Under the umbrella term of salvation a whole series of biblical concepts can be arranged sequentially in order of appearance in life.

As far as the individual believer is concerned, the work of salvation begins with the *new birth* when God quickens the person, replacing deaf ears with those that hear, blind eyes with those that see, and a heart of stone with a heart of flesh. The gospel then has meaning and the cross of Christ can be and is responded to in repentance and faith. In repentance there is a turning away from sin and in faith a turning toward the Lord Jesus Christ. In response to believing faith, God then *justifies* the believer and makes him legally as if he had never sinned.

At the same time he receives the spirit of adoption and knows himself to be a child of God. This inner work of God takes on outward visible aspects in a *conversion* or turn-around in life. In 2 Corinthians 5:17 Paul writes, "Therefore, if anyone is in Christ, he is a new creation; the old has gone, the new has come!" Obviously that can be seen. A process of growth and development then begins that is called *sanctification.* This is like a plant that in time produces a bud and eventually a beautiful flower is seen. Daily the Christian is to grow in the grace and in the knowledge of Jesus Christ until the very beauty of Jesus is seen in the life. This process must continue from the point of justification until glorification.

The process of salvation is magnificently concluded in *glorification,* when the person dies and enters glory, or when Christ returns in glory and gives his people their incorruptible spiritual bodies (1 Corinthians 15).

It is important to remember that all of these words are part of a single process called salvation. Jesus Christ is our Savior, "the source of eternal salvation for all who obey him" (Hebrews 5:9). He is our justification, our sanctification, and our glorification.

♦ SALVATION—PAST, PRESENT, AND FUTURE
RICHARD OWEN ROBERTS

Salvation begins with the new birth, but it does not end there. It is a continuing process. I was saved when God quickened me in the new birth and justified me. I am being saved as I live a life of holiness in obedience to Christ. I will be saved when I receive my glorified body and live in the presence of Christ for eternity.

How Is a Christian Different from a Non-Christian?

J. I. PACKER

The difference between a Christian and a non-Christian has two focal points: One is allegiance, and the other is a change of heart at the very center of a person's being.

Let's first discuss allegiance. I use this word because no modern word is quite as strong. In the middle ages, if a man swore allegiance to the king, he was making an absolute commitment. He was putting himself entirely at the king's disposal. That is the kind of relationship to Jesus Christ that I want to talk about.

Allegiance means that the one to whom you are committing yourself is absolutely in command of you and can dispose of you in any way he wishes. This is a foreign concept to the modern person. Even in marriages nowadays, people's commitment is so weak and conditional that it doesn't make an adequate illustration of allegiance. Commitment to the Lord Jesus Christ is much stronger, not stronger than the marriage commitment ought to be, but stronger than the marriage commitment often is.

A person who is a Christian is connected to Jesus Christ—that is the point of allegiance. That is what it has meant to be a Christian ever since the days when Jesus was ministering in Galilee. The disciples actually followed Jesus in his travels. Wherever he went, they went. He was poor; they had to accept not knowing from one day to another where they were going to sleep at night. And yet, out of loyalty to him, they followed uncomplainingly wherever he went.

That pictures the kind of relationship that marks you when you become a Christian. As a Christian, you realize that Jesus is more powerful than any mere human being. You can trust him with your soul. You know what he can do for you, and you put yourself into his hands. Out of that comes allegiance.

You live as the Lord's person, subject to his command. Your commitment is motivated by love and gratitude. You know he loves you; you know he died for your sins. And you know that if you put yourself in his hands, in his love he will forgive your sins, watch over you, and bring you to glory. Your allegiance is thus a glad and joyful thing.

The other focal point of difference between a Christian and a non-Christian is that the Christian has a renewed heart. In Scripture the heart is not the organ that sends blood around the body, but rather the center of identity, the source of all motivation, purpose, and drive. That's why Scripture says, "Guard your heart, for it is the wellspring of life" (Proverbs 4:23). On the conscious level, a Christian's allegiance is drawn out by the knowledge of God's love and an understanding of his personal need. At the same time, on the unconscious level, God is at work changing the heart.

This change of heart causes a discernible difference. In John 3:8, Jesus said to Nicodemus, "The wind blows wherever it pleases. You hear its sound, but you cannot tell where it comes from or where it is going. So it is with everyone born of the Spirit." You're aware the wind is blowing because you see its effect; but it remains a mystery. Likewise, everyone born of the Spirit shows a new purpose and direction in life. This is a mystery to the unbeliever.

A changed heart is absolutely basic to becoming a Christian. It is easy to profess faith and not be a real believer, but if a person claims to be a Christian and yet continues to live as he did before, I would doubt that the profession of faith is real. The difference is discernible if the heart, the very core of life, has been changed.

One difference in the Christian's life is that he has new attitudes. These are spelled out in Galatians 5:22, 23: "The fruit of the Spirit is love, joy, peace, patience, kindness, goodness, faithfulness, gentleness and self-control." That is the character profile of the Lord Jesus, and it is to be reproduced in believers. Each of these qualities is a way of responding to situations, and none can be there as a consistent reality unless a person's heart is changed.

Another difference is that a person with a renewed heart has changed motivations. Paul said in 1 Corinthians 10:31, "Whether you eat or drink or whatever you do, do it all for the glory of God." The Christian behaves in a way the non-Christian can't understand because he doesn't have the Christian's motives. The non-Christian's heart is self-regarding and self-absorbed. He only understands those motives that spring from self-centeredness. The Christian has a heart after God, a love for worship, a love of praise, and a desire to be with God's people and share with them about divine things. He is a child of God, his heavenly Father, and like any normal child, he is interested in what his Father is doing.

Third, the Christian has an interest in finding out Bible truth. He wants to learn as much as he can about his heavenly Father, and he knows in his heart that Scripture is God's Word; so he gets much joy from reading and studying it. In that way too he perplexes his unconverted friend, who again and again will say, "I don't know what makes this fellow tick."

A fourth observable difference is mentioned in 1 John 3:14: "We know that we have passed from death to life, because we love our brothers." We find it natural to love our fellow Christians. Something has happened within our hearts, something that gives us a new love for God's people as an extension of our love for the God we all serve.

Finally, what marks the Christian is the desire to make the Lord known. A Christian is ready to be a witness to him.

A Christian, then, is observably different from a non-Christian. His allegiance is to God rather than to himself. His heart has been changed; he has new attitudes, motives, interest in Scripture, love for other Christians, and desire to witness. Everything in his life is in the process of being reshaped and refocused around the new center, Christ.

I'm always struck by Paul's words in Philippians 3:13, 14, "Forgetting what is behind and straining toward what is ahead, I press on toward the goal to win the prize for which God has called me heavenward in Christ Jesus." Paul did many things in his life, but they were all integrated around Christ. In that, he is a model for every believer. We too can have lives that are integrated around the Lord—loving him, pleasing him, and glorifying him in everything we do.

◆ WHO AND WHAT AM I SUPPOSED TO BELIEVE? / J. I. PACKER

A Christian should believe everything he reads in the Bible because the Bible is the Word of God—he is the true, divine author. The Bible is God's instructions to his people. The applications change, but the essential truth of the message remains the same.

As for Christian teachings you hear in other places—at church, in books, from friends—take Paul's advice in 1 Thessalonians 5:21: "Test everything. Hold on to the good." He means you are to check everything you hear by the Scriptures, the Word of God. See if what is being said is a faithful echo of what the Bible says. If it isn't, don't believe it.

You can be a Christian by just believing the basics, even if you are ignorant of or mistaken about other truths God has revealed. You become a Christian on the basis of the essentials: admitting sin, believing in Jesus, and confessing that Jesus is your Savior. But every new Christian ought to acknowledge the Bible's authority and begin to feast on its words. They are food for his soul.

If you do not do this, ignorance and error will eventually weaken your Christian life. Soak yourself in the Scriptures, then, to make sure that mistaken notions and ignorance don't have any place in your mind. They can only do you harm.

What It Means to Repent

✍ CHARLES COLSON

All my life I thought I was a pretty good guy. I did everything I thought good people did. I gave money to charity. I took care of poor people when they needed help. I was always careful to tell the truth—when I was young, my dad had lectured me that a person should never lie.

In politics, I played the game hard—it was dog eat dog—but I liked to tell myself I wasn't doing anything other than what others had done before me. Actually, I thought I was especially good: in the White House, when I was counsel to the president, I received Christmas gifts as everybody did—everything from cases of whiskey to crates of fruit—and I never kept any of them. I sent them to the limousine drivers, or the switchboard operators, or other White House staffers because I wanted to be incorruptible. When I went to the

White House, I left a six-figure law practice to go to work for forty thousand dollars a year. I put everything into a blind trust so that I couldn't be corrupted.

So I looked at my life and thought, When I die, if there is a God [and I wasn't sure there was, but I figured there must be], I won't fare too badly because I'm not much different from anybody else. I reckoned God was like a college professor—he would grade on a curve.

Then I encountered an old friend, Tom Phillips, and he had changed. He told me about Jesus Christ and what he had done in his life. And, as Tom talked, I saw I wasn't so good after all. I saw that I was full of pride, that I had done some ugly things in politics, that I had hurt people, and that I hadn't felt any remorse over it. I came to realize that I was cold and hard and tough. By the time I reached Tom's driveway to leave his house that night in August 1973, I felt unclean for the very first time in my life. And I wanted to be clean, to live by different standards, to be pure. It was no longer enough that I wasn't any worse than anybody else. I sincerely wanted to know what it was to have a pure heart. I wanted to be cleansed, forgiven, to have a new start.

I had never heard the phrase "regeneration in the Lord." I'd never heard of being "born again." I was simply convinced that I was a sinful person who needed to be forgiven by God. I was, for the first time, under the conviction of sin.

I don't believe it is possible for a person to be regenerated until the Holy Spirit has convicted that person of sin. Man can't be moral on his own. Given a choice, we will always choose the sinful way. I thought I was a moral person, but it wasn't until the moral person died that the Spirit of God could come to work in me. I love what William James said: "The death of a moral man is his spiritual birthday."

This is gravely misunderstood in the Church today. We preach about a new birth without mentioning the death of the old self first. What brings about the death of the old self is the awareness of sin. Aleksandr Solzhenitsyn writes about this in the second volume of *The Gulag Archipelago,* where he speaks of reflecting on his life and realizing all of the things he had done that were really evil when he thought he was doing good.

The conviction of sin by the Holy Spirit is the beginning. Without it, we cannot understand our need for God, and we cannot understand God's grace. We must not ever leave that out of our preaching, teaching, or understanding of Christianity. To omit it is to trivialize the work of Christ on the cross.

Conviction of sin leads to repentance. If I were asked today to name the one doctrine of the Christian faith being preached about the least, I would have to say repentance. Repentance means change, and we don't want to threaten people with the need to change.

Repentance is commonly thought of as breast-beating, but it is not that at all. The Greek word used in the New Testament is *metanoeo,* which means, very simply, "change of mind." When you come to God, you have a change of mind, from exalting yourself to exalting Christ. Repentance means turning from man's ways to embrace God's ways. It means a desire to be different, to belong to Christ and to live as he commands us to live. Repentance, then, is the flip-side of conviction of sin—it is the longing to turn away from the old self and to live a new life in Christ.

In my own life, repentance meant that I wanted to adopt new values. I wanted to be forgiven of what I'd done in the past and not continue doing those things, but rather be led by the Spirit to the kinds of things that God wants from my life. There is a certain sorrow that goes with repentance, a sorrow over your sins, a desire to restore where you have done harm in the past. One thing I did was to apologize to some of the people I had hurt in politics. I went to them to seek their forgiveness because I realized that God had forgiven me and I should seek to restore my relationships with people I had injured. Some of them remained cynical about me. They had been political enemies, and they thought my seeking forgiveness was some sort of ploy. Some did not understand it. Others were deeply affected by it. And some people had trouble accepting my repentance. They would say, "Sure, I forgive you," but they were very uncomfortable because it convicted them as well.

A prime case of repentance leading to restoration is the well-known case of Cathleen Webb, who falsely accused Gary Dotson of raping her. When she came under the conviction of sin—six years later—she realized that she had to recant her story and tell the truth. You can just imagine the pain that was involved for that young girl in coming forward with the truth. I met with her, and I know that her decision was a moving of the Spirit. She was left with no choice but to confess.

That's what happens when the conviction of sin leads to repentance. The yearning for God's cleansing is so strong that we cannot find peace until we have accepted that "change of mind" and begin to walk in the new life with the Lord.

♦ HOW CAN I BE SURE I'M A CHRISTIAN?
EVELYN CHRISTENSON

How can I be sure Jesus is my Savior and Lord?

One way is through the explosion of joy and excitement I feel when I read Scripture. That happens when God is speaking to me through Scripture. It could not happen if I didn't know Christ.

Another way I know is by the sense of God's presence I have when I'm alone. When I travel overseas and the bed is empty, God is there. In the hospital room, God is there.

Christians who have never felt God speaking to them and putting his arms around them in the lonely times may not really know him. Walking with God is not a theological matter; it is experiential. It is a response, a feeling, an emotion. There is emotion in every other relationship I have, and there is also emotion in my relationship with God.

◆ HOW CAN I BE SURE I'M SAVED? / YFC EDITORS

The question arises because we don't always *feel* saved. There will be times in our Christian walk when we don't *feel* close to God, when we don't *feel* like being Christians, when we just *feel* the Christian "blahs."

But our salvation is not based on feelings. We didn't need strong faith to be saved; we just needed faith. We don't need warm feelings to be sure God is with us; we just need faith.

When you feel this way, ask yourself two questions: (1) Do I really believe what God says it takes to be saved (John 3:16)? (2) Was I sincere when I asked Jesus to come into my life? If you can say yes, then you're ready to look into God's Word and find assurance for your faith.

You have salvation and eternal life because of what Jesus Christ did for you (1 John 5:11, 12). God has shown his love for you by giving eternal life (Romans 5:8). Your sins are covered and you have his Holy Spirit (1 Peter 3:18).

If you received him, you are his child (John 1:12). When you believe in Jesus Christ you have eternal life and you stand guiltless before God (John 5:24). No one can take you away from him (John 10:27-29).

You have begun a new life (2 Corinthians 5:17). You may not always *feel* new and different, but you can trust in God's promises to you.

How Long Does Conversion Take?

CHARLES COLSON

Regeneration happens in a moment. The process of becoming a Christian, however, may take a long time. I deal with many people in prison who have made professions of faith, and I know God has regenerated them, but they live in agony, subjected to every kind of pressure and temptation. They struggle and fight back, and they get up again and keep going. They are prayed over and they pray; they fall back into sin and they get up. Their conversion is taking a long time, and a lot of pain and struggle go into it.

Some other conversions happen on a modern-day Damascus Road. But don't forget that Paul went off for three years after his Damascus Road experience to be taught by the Lord. Although people think of his conversion as a blinding flash, that experience was the moment of regeneration. His conversion took years.

We become Christians when God's regenerative Spirit moves in our lives. Conversion means we are changing from one thing to another, and the process of change is not instantaneous. Sanctification goes on all of our lives. If you encounter people who think they have arrived at a spiritual plateau where they have become fully sanctified, you'd better stay clear of them; they're usually very dangerous.

Some people grow up in the faith in Christian homes. They've never known anything different. God regenerates them and their conversion is painless. Other people go through very difficult, tormenting experiences. I don't think that one experience is more significant than the other. My own conversion was rather dramatic, but that is only an advantage to me because, in a sense, I have lived two lives. In the secular world, I felt what life is like without Christ. I saw the corruption of power and success. Today I can look at the secular world I was once part of and critique it from a Christian perspective. I can also look at the Christian world as a relative newcomer and see what some brothers and sisters, who don't really know what it means to surrender all to God, are missing. I pray God can use my two lives to challenge other believers and to challenge nonbelievers to see the bankruptcy of life without Christ.

How Much Do I Have to Believe?

JAMES BOICE

I was talking with a missionary doctor once who said that in his judgment good work was being done on the mission field, but there was one serious lack. "We want so much to win people to Christ," he told me, "that we water down the gospel. We make it too easy to become Christ's follower. People don't see the need to change their lives."

Not only is that a problem on the mission field. It also describes much of Christianity in America. Often what passes for Christianity isn't real Christianity at all.

But how much does an individual have to believe to become a Christian? That's an honest question. Obviously no one understands everything about the faith. Since we can be saved by understanding only a part of faith, which part is necessary?

People have been saved with very limited knowledge of Christian truth. That's because salvation depends on a person's being born again. If God has done a work of grace in the heart, even in the heart of a very young child or in the heart of someone who is mentally retarded, the person is still saved.

I heard a story that illustrates this. Years ago an orphanage in Scotland catered to mentally retarded children. Along with Bible stories, the children were taught a little nursery rhyme with hand motions. It went like this: "Three in one and one in three, the one in the middle he died for me." To signify the three persons of God in one, the children held up one finger followed by three fingers. Then the children would put their hand around the middle finger for "the one in the middle he died for me."

One youngster couldn't even talk. He would listen to the Bible stories and these rhymes, but no one knew if he understood. Then one night, the orphanage caught on fire. After the fire had been put out, this child was found dead, asphyxiated by smoke. But the child was found clutching his middle finger.

So how little does a person have to understand to be saved? Perhaps it is as minimal as that—to know that you are a sinner and that Jesus Christ, the Second Person in the Trinity, the Son of God, died for you.

That is a perfectly valid answer. Millions of people have been saved by understanding precisely that. But although Jesus begins where we are, he's never satisfied with the minimum. If we're to be real followers of Christ, we must give up everything. We must follow him wholeheartedly. We cannot hold back a single portion of ourselves.

Some people say that as heirs of the Reformation, all we need to understand is the simple gospel. But the simple gospel is really not all that simple. The three principles of the Reformation, *sola scriptura* (the Bible alone), *sola fides* (faith alone), and *sola gratia* (grace alone), are quite rigorous.

1. *Scripture alone.* To stand for Scripture alone, we stand for the Word of God over and above human opinion, especially when human opinion is contrary to what the Scripture teaches.

We must subordinate our thoughts and inclinations to the authority of the Word of God. We must "demolish . . . every pretension that sets itself up against the knowledge of God," and we must "take captive every thought to make it obedient to Christ" (2 Corinthians 10:5). We must hold all our thoughts and beliefs up to the standard of Scripture.

2. *Faith alone.* Faith alone is not mere intellectual assent to certain doctrines. It is personal trust in the One who is our Savior and Lord. We have to give up confidence in ourselves in order to trust him. We must reorient our entire lives.

3. *Grace alone.* To live by grace alone is to give up our own self-righteousness. We cannot rely on our own goodness. We have to relinquish the pride we have in our own works.

When we think through the implications of the faith, we see there is a tremendously high price to pay. Christ requires absolutely everything from us.

Some people will still want to know what they have to do to be a Christian. As a Christian I can no longer count myself as a good person. I have to see myself as a person that has broken all of God's laws and is under his just wrath and condemnation. I have to pay the price of my self-righteousness. I can't cling to the sins I cherish. But in their place I gain the holiness that Christ gives, and "without holiness no one will see the Lord" (Hebrews 12:14).

As I have studied all of Christ's sayings in the Gospels about what it means to be his follower, I've been impressed that when people came to him, he did not treat them the way most of us treat inquirers today.

Take his interview with the rich young man (Mark 10:17-25). The rich young man was earnest and moral, and he knew the law. If most of us were confronted by an individual like that, we would tell him salvation is simple: you recognize you are a sinner, and you trust Christ.

But that's not what Jesus did. Jesus challenged the man's conception of God and brought him up against the law. He exposed the young man's sin and pressed commitment upon him. Jesus did this to the point that the man's wealth became a barrier. He had to give it all up if he wanted to follow Christ.

Jesus wasn't interested in making it easy to follow him. He didn't minimize what it took to enter the kingdom of God. He did the exact opposite. He made sure people understood they were getting into a whole new way of life, a whole new way of thinking. He wanted them to know that if they followed him, they would never be the same.

♦ LIP SERVICE OR LIFE SERVICE? / JAMES BOICE

We are afraid of making it so difficult to become a Christian that people will reject Christianity. But what is the greatest danger? To show how difficult it really is or to tell people they are saved when they are not? I think the second is worse.

This is happening today. People give lip service to the faith. We accept their faith even if we don't see differences in their lives. We tell them, "As long as you believe these things, you are going to go to heaven." But what if they have not been born again? Then we're telling them they are all right when they are on their way to hell.

So how can we have an assurance of salvation? It is only by a change of life. It is by faith's fruit. Real faith will produce a new attitude toward sin, and as we become conformed to Christ's image, we will grow in our assurance that we are saved.

♦ HONEST STRUGGLES / JAMES BOICE

Some people submit their lives to Christ but still struggle with biblical doctrines. Are they Christians?

When we don't understand something in the Bible we can choose between two different approaches. One approach is to admit that we don't understand it and ask God to show us if and where we are wrong. If that is our attitude, we are saved, but questioning.

A person taking the other approach says, "Well, that's what the Bible says, but it is just the Bible. I can believe something entirely different." That person probably does not have the mind of Christ.

If we are born again, the Holy Spirit lives in our hearts. The Holy Spirit has also inspired the Bible, so the Spirit within us ought to testify to the Spirit that speaks from its pages.

♦ WHAT YOU KNOW vs. HOW YOU GROW J. I. PACKER

In order to become a Christian, one must believe in the saving power of Jesus Christ. The Gospels make it impossible, however, to equate this with precise knowledge of specific doctrines. When Jesus was ministering on earth, people became Christians with very little understanding. They believed Jesus was from God; they recognized him as the One who leads his followers to glory, they loved him, and they wanted to be his people. Their lives were changed by their relationship in Christ though they had no deep understanding of all the truths about him. This shows that we have to be careful before we say, "You can't become a Christian unless you understand all the doctrines."

Nevertheless, the doctrines need to be explained. For example, the human heart is inclined to believe you can become a Christian by your own works. Therefore most of us will never get clear what it means to trust ourselves to Christ until we are taught justification by faith. We need to understand that Jesus took our place under God's judgment, and that because of this, and only this, our sins are forgiven, and without this we should be lost.

The idea of salvation by works has such a strong hold on most people's minds that they won't understand what it means to commit themselves to Christ until this truth about the atoning death of Jesus and God's acceptance of them for his sake becomes clear to them. Only those who know that without Christ they are "guilty, vile, and helpless" (as the hymn says) will ever trust him wholeheartedly.

◆HOW A CHRISTIAN GROWS / YFC EDITORS

1. God begins his work in an atmosphere of complete trust.
   Ephesians 2:8-10
   Philippians 1:6; 2:13
   Colossians 2:19
   John 14:21
2. You yield (confess, commit, obey).
   Romans 6:11-19; 12:1, 2
   1 Peter 3:15
   Luke 9:23
   2 Corinthians 7:1
3. Jesus becomes Lord.
   Colossians 2:6, 7
   Ephesians 4:15
   Hebrews 5:8, 9
   Philippians 2:5, 11
4. The Holy Spirit gives you power.
   Ephesians 3:16, 17
5. You become sensitive to the Holy Spirit's guidance.
   Galatians 5:16-21
   Ephesians 4:30
   John 14:26; 16:13

This produces

- power to acknowledge Christ as Lord (1 Corinthians 12:3)
- power to witness (Acts 1:8)
- improved character (Galatians 5:22, 23)
- feeling of being loved (Romans 5:5)
- direction (Acts 13:2)

Disobedience brings

- guilt
- rebellion against lordship
- lack of the Holy Spirit's power
- lack of feeling of warm love

Christians—Freed to Lead

ROBERT SCHULLER

I became a Christian when I realized I had a to make a decision to either accept or reject Jesus Christ. I realized then that just being a member of the family didn't make me a Christian, and being born and baptized into a church didn't make me a Christian either. I had to make a personal decision and no one else could do it for me.

In that process of deciding, I probably experienced one of my first leadership acts. I soon discovered that being a Christian is a wonderful way to become a genuinely free person, a leader and not a timid follower.

Becoming a Christian gives a person individual identity. When I accept Christ, in the here and now, I become a person. I cease to be a puppet.

As I become a Christian I have an authentic experience of grace—that is, I experience total acceptance even though my imperfections and faults are clearly exposed. And the person who accepts me is the ideal One—Jesus Christ, God's representative to humanity.

When I have the experience of being accepted genuinely, honestly, and affectionately by Someone I look up to in awe and profound admiration, I also experience a birth of inner self-worth and self-dignity. And to a limited degree I begin to experience the emotional and mental state of health that Adam experienced prior to the Fall. Paradoxically I recover my lost pride and, at the same time, learn authentic humility.

I no longer need to play games, wear masks, or lean upon cultural crutches to try to prop up a faltering and feeble ego. Instead, my sense of human dignity is profoundly and authentically satisfied in a wonderful new relationship with the God who is my ultimate source.

Reconciliation is complete. Now I know I am somebody. This gives rise to an awareness that I can do something. Self-esteem produces possibility thinking: the I Am produces the *I can.* When I become a Christian I truly know for the first time that I can do all things through Christ who strengthens me (Philippians 4:13). As a result, I become a leader, for what is a leader but an individual who has the power and the responsibility of reviewing all the possibilities in a given situation?

Becoming a Christian means I will stand out from the crowd. Paul, quoting Isaiah 52:11, said, "Come out from them and be separate, says the Lord" (2 Corinthians 6:17). That can be read as a call to become a positive, inspiring leader, a bright light in a dark world. I am now a light in the world set on a hill; I cannot hide being a Christian (see Matthew 5:14-16).

As a Christian, I'm walking a new road. I no longer see myself as a doormat. I'm not letting society make my decisions for me. I'm not going to be just a member of a commune. Instead, I'm going to be a solitary, single, thinking, praying, soul-searching person. And in this process I acquire a quality of character: integrity.

I can now make decisions. I do not need to be manipulated, nor do I need to surrender to intimidation. I can be a unique person making my own choices, coming to my own decisions under God. That's leadership. And it is possible only when I know that I have value, that I am related and connected to a sovereign God who will sustain me. So in becoming a Christian I acquire the freedom to lead.

Becoming a Christian means becoming a decisive, choice-making, choice-selecting creature. It means becoming a leader, and it means achieving real freedom.

How Do I Submit to Jesus Christ?

DAVID AND CHERYL ASPY

Very few people know the power of surrender. Most of us know only the power of resistance. We derive a kind of negative energy from holding out.

For example, we may resist our parents. We feel strong when we break the family's rules or defy our parents' admonitions. If they tell us not to stay out too late, we assert ourselves by coming home later than they advised. In a similar manner, we may defy spouses, teachers, bosses, the police, and even God.

God asks us to love him and obey his commandments (John 14:15; the book of 1 John), but we find power in "doing it our way." I remember one physically large person who stood on a chair in my office so he could get closer to God. Then he shook his fist and yelled, "I dare you, God!" Most of us choose more subtle ways to defy God, but we defy him nonetheless.

Defying God is a way of drawing negative energy from him. It's like the person who flirts and darts just far enough to both attract and elude the pursuing lover. Somehow we feel powerful when we think God is chasing us. What a pathetic way to react to his love!

There seem to be at least two valid ways to submit to Jesus Christ. First, there is an intellectual route. A person who comes to Christ this way asks questions such as, "What are the possible ways to live my life?" After delineating the alternatives, this person rates the relative merits of each according to her own values. Finally, she concludes that among the possible ways to live, one is the best for her. If she chooses the Christian way, she surrenders to Jesus Christ and lives according to his teachings.

It is important to realize that the choice to become a Christian can be derived from purely intellectual considerations. Some people suspect this kind of detached, intellectual choosing, but they should realize that God created the mind as well as the emotions. A person can love God's intelligence and relate to him through her own cognitive powers.

This kind of conversion is often seen in engineers and scientists who are awed by the physical mysteries of the universe. To them, a process like photosynthesis is elegant and superbly wonderful. Frequently scientists will say they believe in God because they can see his universe. They think its formation required a God. Thus they infer that God exists from what they can see. Quite probably, this kind of surrender happens only among those who value and use their intellects.

A second route for submission to Jesus Christ is based on emotion. In this type of conversion, the person "falls in love" with Jesus Christ in the best and fullest sense of that expression. He learns about the love of Christ for him; perhaps he hears descriptions or sees pictures of the crucifixion. He experiences directly and openly the tremendous divine love that made such a gift.

People who follow this route to Jesus ask no hard questions, because their experience is emotional rather than logical. All of us who fully love another person know exactly what it means to "just love someone" without being able to explain why. Our responses in love are not rational. This does not mean they are irrational; as Pascal said, "The heart has its reasons that reason knows nothing about." Love does not follow logical patterns of reasoning, but it is not crazy.

An emotional conversion is a leap of faith. Because of that, some people find it more beautiful than a logical conversion. Perhaps we are all attracted to the innocence of a child who blindly leaps into our arms with complete faith that we will catch him or her. But when we submit to Jesus Christ, the intellectual route is just as beautiful as the emotional route in his eyes.

Surely God looks the same upon all those who submit to him. God knows he made people in different ways: some short, some tall; some outgoing, some reflective; some emotional, some intellectual. The blessed part is that God made all of us, and he knows we will come to him in different ways. What is important is that we arrive.

When I surrender to a purpose I gain power, because once I surrender I am freed from the conflict of indecision. After I surrender to Jesus Christ, no longer is part of me resisting his call. I am able to be twice as forceful, because all of me is now headed in the same direction.

Can I trust Jesus enough to surrender to him? Is Jesus trustworthy? I cannot know until I put him to the test. But whether I surrender to him or not, I will put my trust in something. Many of us trust money, and we surrender our lives to accumulating it. We have to make a choice—am I going to submit to Jesus Christ, or is something or someone else more worthy of my devotion?

Once we make a choice, we proceed toward eternity on faith. I shall never forget Paige Patterson shouting from the pulpit of the First Baptist Church in Dallas: "I have planted my feet squarely on the promise of Almighty God and his Son, Jesus Christ. I believe he has saved my soul, and I will be in eternity with him!"

I don't know whether Paige's conversion was intellectual, emotional, or both, but I cried at the beauty of the vision his words evoked—Paige and all the other people I love gathered around Jesus. It doesn't make any difference to me whether these people thought their way to submission or loved their way there. The fact is that they all submitted to Jesus Christ, and the joy that followed is the heart of the matter.

How I Know God Has Accepted Me

✍ ROBERT SCHULLER

To some people, the gospel sounds too good to be true. Maybe God will save others, they think, but surely he won't save me; I'm not acceptable. But God doesn't want us to think that way. He wants us to know he has accepted us.

I find my assurance that God has accepted me by looking at the contract. The sacred Scriptures are God's covenant, or contract, with me. There I find what God has promised to do for me if I will do certain things. It's clearly written that if I accept Jesus Christ as my personal Lord and Savior, he'll accept me. Any friend of Jesus is considered a friend of the almighty heavenly Father.

Jesus said, "Whoever comes to me I will never drive away" (John 6:37). To me, that's one of the most beautiful passages in the Bible. When I fall into times of inner insecurity, I fall back on that verse. It steadies me again so I can stand up straight without trembling.

So one way to have assurance that God has accepted us is to go back to the contract. "For it is by grace you have been saved, through faith—and this not from yourselves, it is the gift of God" (Ephesians 2:8).

Another way to know God has accepted us is to listen to him speaking to our hearts. The Scriptures say that the Spirit bears witness within us "that we are God's children" (Romans 8:16). There is an inner knowing that is from the presence and reality of the Holy Spirit.

Jesus gives me an abiding sense of serenity and peace. Gone is any fear of divine judgment. I am no longer subject to the wrath of God; I no longer have a neurotic fear of him. Instead, I have a profound sense of gratitude that defies verbalization because of this inner sense of peace of soul and mind. "Since we have been justified through faith, we have peace with God through our Lord Jesus Christ" (Romans 5:1).

A third way we can have assurance of God's acceptance of us is to look at our lives and see how we have changed. Jesus said, "By their fruit you will recognize them" (Matthew 7:16). We can know we're in tune with God's will if we are reflecting his light and our salvation through a life of sacrificial service. We will know we are his if we are continually growing in the process of holiness.

God wants us to feel accepted. That is why he has given us his assurance, through his Word, through his Spirit, and through his work in our lives, that indeed he has accepted us for all eternity.

Keys to a Dynamic Christian Life

✍ WILLIAM BRIGHT

Understanding the attributes of God—his holiness, love, sovereignty, wisdom, grace, and power—is the greatest thing that ever happened to me, because a dynamic Christian life begins with one's view of God. As I travel the world, visit many countries, and have contact with many religions, I find that individuals, societies, and even nations are influenced by their view of God. If I believe in the sovereignty of God, I am not upset when things go wrong. If I believe God works in the affairs of nations, if I believe he has a plan for man, then even when adversity, sorrow, and tragedy come, I can handle them, because I know that the God who rules my life will provide for me as he promised.

The most important thing I can communicate to a believer is that God is trustworthy. But if we don't understand who God is, we can't trust him. The Bible says, "The just shall live by faith" (Romans 1:17, KJV), that "whatsoever is not of faith is sin" (Romans 14:23, KJV), and "without faith it is impossible to please him" (Hebrews 11:6, KJV). I can't demonstrate faith if I don't know and understand the object of my faith, which is God and his holy Word.

The key, then, to a dynamic Christian life is to understand God and to master his Word. That knowledge cannot be superficial, shallow, and legalistic. In fact, many people who are given a list of dos and don'ts give up and say, "There's no way I can live the Christian life." In order to understand the keys to a dynamic Christian life, one needs to realize that the Christian life is a life of relationship—a supernatural relationship. Man cannot live the Christian life alone.

That brings us to a second key to a dynamic walk with God, which is to understand that the Christ of the Scriptures lives in us. Jesus Christ is God incarnate, perfect God, perfect man, the visible expression of the invisible God, the One in whom dwells all the fullness of the Godhead, the One who said,

"All authority in heaven and on earth has been given to me" (Matthew 28:18). And yet he, in his resurrection power, is closer to us than our hands, our feet, our very breath.

Everything about the Christian life involves relationship to Jesus, the incomparable, peerless, matchless Son of God. The first thing I do every morning is to get on my knees and acknowledge Christ's presence within me and his lordship of my life. I invite him to walk around in my body, to be with me all day long. I ask him to think with my mind, love with my heart, speak with my lips, and to continue seeking and saving the lost through me. That's what Jesus wants to do in each of our lives.

Prayer is the lifeblood of a vital relationship with Christ. Through prayer we have been given the power of attorney. "I will do whatever you ask in my name" (John 14:13). One cannot possibly experience the dynamic Christian life apart from the power and privilege and exercise of prayer.

Prayer is not just talking to God. It is communion. It's listening. As a matter of fact, I probably spend more time asking God questions and communing with him and meditating upon his Word than I do talking at him. One has to be careful, of course, because many people have said that God told them to do all kinds of weird things. For example, God didn't tell half a dozen fellows to marry a particular girl who happened to be very beautiful as they claimed. God doesn't say, "Kill your wife." When God speaks to us in our innermost beings, his voice is consistent with Scripture. "For it is God which worketh in you both to will and to do of his good pleasure" (Philippians 2:13, KJV). God never contradicts through impressions what he has written in his Word.

It is a sad fact that, despite the privilege of prayer, in spite of our knowledge of God and relationship with him, we often fail in our attempt to live the Christian life. We take surveys all over the world, and 95 percent of the people in the Christian body indicate that they are not doing the things they know they should do. In 1 Corinthians 3, Paul describes three kinds of people in the world—the natural man, the spiritual man, and the carnal Christian. The carnal Christian is a believer who has experienced the new birth but is living, as Paul describes it, as a baby Christian, sometimes acting as though he or she doesn't even know Jesus Christ at all.

Why do Christians experience this conflict? Why is there this failure to live what we know? I see three reasons: the world, the flesh, and the devil. As we read in 1 John 2, we're not to love the world or the things that are in the world. I like the *Living Bible* passage: "Stop loving this evil world and all that it offers you, for when you love these things you show that you do not really love God; for all these worldly things, these evil desires—the craze for sex, the ambition to buy everything that appeals to you, and the pride that comes from wealth and importance—these are not from God. They are from this evil world itself. And this world is fading away, and these evil, forbidden things will go with it, but whoever keeps doing the will of God will live forever" (1 John 2:15-17).

In Galatians 5:16, 17, we read: "Live by the Spirit, and you will not gratify the desires of the sinful nature. For the sinful nature desires what is contrary to the Spirit, and the Spirit what is contrary to the sinful nature. They are in conflict with each other, so that you do not do what you want." As long as we live, warfare with the flesh will go on. Paul speaks of this in Romans 7: "For what I do is not the good I want to do; no, the evil I do not want to do—this I keep on doing.... What a wretched man I am! Who will rescue me from this body of death?" (Romans 7:19, 24).

Along with the flesh, Satan is also a very real foe. Ephesians 6:12 says, "For we are not fighting against people made of flesh and blood, but against persons without bodies—the evil rulers of the unseen world, those mighty satanic beings and great evil princes of darkness who rule this world; and against huge numbers of wicked spirits in the spirit world" (TLB). There are demonic powers in the world. We need to recognize that apart from the strength and the enabling of our Lord, living within us through the Holy Spirit, we cannot possibly resist the attacks and the temptations of Satan. He is a formidable enemy. It is not possible to be a victorious Christian, to live the dynamic life, apart from the enabling of the Holy Spirit. Jesus said, "You will receive power when the Holy Spirit comes on you" (Acts 1:8). The person who tries to serve God in the flesh without the Holy Spirit is doomed to failure.

The only one who can help me to live a Bible-obeying Christian life is Jesus Christ himself, through the enabling of the Holy Spirit. John 16 records what Jesus said to his disciples on the eve of his crucifixion: "It is expedient for you that I go away: for if I go not away, the Comforter will not come unto you; but if I depart, I will send him unto you. And when he is come, he will reprove the world of sin...he will guide you into all truth: for he shall not speak of himself;...he shall glorify me" (verses 7, 8, 13, 14, KJV).

When we understand that the Holy Spirit dwells in us and draw upon his special power by faith, we can live victorious, dynamic Christian lives. But the average person does not understand that. Our surveys indicate that at least 95 percent of the Christian world does not understand the role of the Holy Spirit in their lives.

Through all of our lives, the old flesh wars against the new nature. We have to decide whom we are going to serve—whether we are going to allow Satan through the old nature to influence our lives, or if we are going to draw upon God's strength through the new nature to live according to the Word of God. It is an act of the will—a decision that determines our destiny.

The Path to Perfection

RICHARD HALVERSON

It was perhaps the very first temptation—offered by the serpent to Adam and Eve in the Garden of Eden—a chance to achieve perfection. The story is recorded in Genesis 3. Our first parents, who were created in God's image, were tempted to doubt their completeness and to believe there was something they had to do to achieve perfection and holiness. The serpent tempted them to disbelieve God, to disobey him, and thus to frustrate God's purposes for them.

They gave in to this temptation because they lacked faith. Paul wrote in Philippians concerning the true route to Christian perfection: "Not having a righteousness of my own that comes from the law, but that which is through faith in Christ—the righteousness that comes from God and is by faith" (3:9). He was a successful, gifted person, but he acknowledged his dependence on God for righteousness and fullness. "If anyone else thinks he has reasons to put confidence in the flesh," he said, "I have more"—but after listing his religious credentials and achievements, he concluded, "I consider them rubbish, that I may gain Christ and be found in him" (3:4-9).

Perfection is not something we achieve, but rather something we receive as a gift of grace through Jesus Christ. Christ is our perfection. It is important that we live on this basis. The minute we try to achieve perfection ourselves, we depart from walking in faith through the Spirit. This is the simplest of facts. It is clearly presented throughout the Bible—but Christians still struggle with it.

Despite all the "victorious life" movements, the Keswick Movement, the modern charismatic movement—an authentic visitation of God in the world—many Christians still lack an understanding of our relation to holiness, righteousness, and perfection.

Instead of Christ-centered teaching on this crucial topic, we see instead the how-to syndrome: the hundreds of books that play right into the hands of the Adversary because they tell us how we can achieve these goals. Thus the goals themselves become idols, and human effort is glorified.

In Romans 7 Paul tells us that the flesh actually lusts against the Spirit—that the two are in conflict. The idea that man can and should achieve his own perfection comes from the flesh. Perfection is not a product of my own effort; I am already perfect in Christ by virtue of his sacrifice on the cross.

Perfection is a gift to be received, and as we believe and appropriate it more and more, it is increasingly ours. I not only have that perfection; I am also growing in it, becoming more and more Christlike as I use the means of grace available to me. I grow as I live by faith in God and trust Christ and walk in the Spirit. Christ comes to live in me more and more. As John the Baptist said, "He must become greater; I must become less" (John 3:30).

The only way we can "work" at holiness or perfection is by learning the means of grace, as Jesus explained in John 6. It is recorded that when people asked Jesus, "What must we do to do the works God requires?" Jesus said, "The work of God is this: to believe in the one he has sent" (vv. 28, 29). That is the hardest work we have to do, because the enemy, who began to tempt man in the Garden, continues to say to us, "It is not enough to believe God." He wants us to believe a lie instead of the truth. Our first parents chose to believe his lie, and thus it was that they sacrificed their Godlikeness (though not completely). God's image in them was marred by their lack of faith.

Whenever we deny what God said and disobey him, we recreate the essence of the Fall. We can't seem to accept the simple word of the gospel that we cannot achieve our salvation by working at it or by trying to be pure and virtuous—because pride goes along with any attempt at works.

This certainly applies in the area of the spiritual disciplines. We can't achieve righteousness by our own goodness or works, however good our intentions. I have been through the whole legalistic aspect in private devotions—reading my Bible thirty minutes a day, praying thirty minutes—and if I missed I felt guilty. What I really needed was just to walk and talk with Christ every moment, every hour, as I would with a friend.

We certainly cannot measure our own growth into perfection. Paul said that "what is seen is temporary, but what is unseen is eternal" (2 Corinthians 4:18). How can we measure something that has invisible results? Yet Scripture is clear that we can know God's will concerning the Christian virtues, morality, and obedience toward God's law. We can tell by our conduct whether or not we are walking in faith.

Oswald Chambers said that if I'm truly growing in grace, all my progress is in humility. Paul said in Romans 5 that "where sin increased, grace increased all the more" (v. 20). Then he gave the reason: "Just as sin reigned in death, so also grace might reign through righteousness to bring eternal life through Jesus Christ our Lord" (v. 21). Through sinning I learn the adequacy and availability of grace. Now, I don't sin in order to enjoy grace, but I inevitably fall—and thus I learn what grace truly is.

Everything God offers us we have in Jesus Christ. He is our wisdom, our justification, our sanctification, our redemption. In him all truth is stored up, and in him "all the fullness of the Deity lives in bodily form" (Colossians 2:9). All of God's promises—including our perfection in faith—are bound up in Christ (see 2 Corinthians 1:20). When we have Christ, we have everything. We grow in Christ by learning to take his offer of salvation seriously—by continuing to believe and live in his power.

RELATED ARTICLES
Chapter 3: **From Slave Trader to Hymn Writer**
Chapter 9: **The Kind of Love God Has for Us**
Chapter 17: **Responding to God in Prayer**
Chapter 18: **Dealing with Doubt**
Chapter 27: **The Powerful Effect of Being Saved**
Chapter 28: **Making Spiritual Changes That Last**

CHAPTER

2

Growing Toward Spiritual Maturity

- ✓ What do I have to give up to become a Christian?
- ✓ How can I tell where I'm at spiritually?
- ✓ Can you become a Christian and not grow spiritually?
- ✓ If we are Christians, is growth really necessary?
- ✓ Discouragement is part of growing

The Meaning of Surrender

✍ CALVIN MILLER

It seems to some a fearsome proposition: Should I become a Christian or not? I don't want to give up everything in life I now enjoy. This fear of surrender comes because they have not begun to understand the great love of Jesus Christ. Once they come into contact with Christ's love, they no longer see conversion as a surrender, but rather as the beginning of a truly worthwhile life.

Discipleship based on the "giving-up syndrome" thinks too much of self and needs to be replaced by a preoccupation with Christ. Once we're really involved with Christ we never notice our sacrifice, having been overwhelmed by the glory of his own.

Certainly the Bible mentions things that must be surrendered, but surrender is not its primary emphasis. Scripture doesn't give us a list of things to give up so that we can measure our spirituality. Instead it talks about such positive things as involvement with Christ or loving one another or evangelizing or discipling.

There are things a Christian must give up if those things are prone to get in the way of a relationship with Jesus. Some churches traditionally preach against tobacco, alcohol, and dancing. We need to ask ourselves to consider larger issues than these. What we should emphasize as surrender are those things that exalt themselves against God, "every pretension that sets itself up against the knowledge of God" (2 Corinthians 10:5). We must be prepared to surrender anything in our lives that is standing in the way of his mercy and compassion. Eating is good, but if we can sit before the television and eat a big meal while watching newsreels of starving people, we are on the way toward being callous and uncaring. We may decide to sacrifice a meal here and there if by doing so we can help those who hunger elsewhere in the world.

I don't think it is possible for a psychologically healthy person to give up too much. Jesus said in Luke 6:38, "Give, and it will be given to you. A good measure, pressed down, shaken together and running over, will be poured into your lap. For with the measure you use, it will be measured to you." I don't especially like to hear the video evangelists saying that if we give to them, God will give back to us fourfold. It all sounds so calculating. On the other hand, I admire Mother Teresa, who believes that no one can outgive God.

Whatever we give, we should consider that we are giving it to Jesus alone. Never give money to a particular ministry without considering it a gift to Jesus. Then you won't need to measure your gift, because Jesus already owns everything you have, even as he owns you.

The first and most important thing for us to give is ourselves. Jesus said, "The man who loves his life will lose it, while the man who hates his life in this world will keep it for eternal life" (John 12:25). Once we give up our old narcissistic selves, it gets easier to abandon the little things.

♦ BEING A CHRISTIAN vs. JUST BEING RELIGIOUS / YFC EDITORS

There is a chasm of difference separating the true Christian from the person who just considers himself religious.

Being religious focuses on man's search for God. It emphasizes *doing* in order to please God—living right and morally, going to church, giving money to Christian causes. Being religious focuses on the individual, and salvation depends on what the person does.

Being a Christian focuses on what God has done for you. You cannot be *doing* things in order to please him. You must simply love and believe in him because your salvation is based on your faith. When you are a Christian, you do good things, love God's Word, love fellow believers, but you do those things out of love for God. You know they do not save you. Christ saves you. "For it is by grace you have been saved, through faith—and this not from yourselves, it is the gift of God—not by works, so that no one can boast" (Ephesians 2:8, 9).

Being a Christian means you both worship God and desire a relationship with him. Your love focuses on God, not you, and what God has done for you.

Does the Lordship of Christ Demand Sacrifice?

✍ STUART BRISCOE

What do I have to sacrifice to be a Christian? To answer this question, we have to address two things: becoming a Christian and being a Christian.

What do I have to give up when I become a Christian? The biblical emphasis is not so much on what you sacrifice, but on what Christ has sacrificed for you. In Philippians 2:6-8 we read that Jesus, "being in very nature God, did not consider equality with God something to be grasped, but made himself nothing, taking the very nature of a servant. . . . He humbled himself and became obedient to death—even death on a cross!" That's sacrifice.

Clearly, if we are touched by the immensity of his sacrifice, we're going to be moved by the realization of what we have done to make that sacrifice necessary. If we begin to love the Lord Jesus, we begin to hate the things that cost him his life. Instead of worrying about how much we have to sacrifice, we want to walk away from our sins and be done with those things.

To answer the question specifically, I would say that to become a Christian you have to be willing to sacrifice anything that's going to hinder God's work of grace in your life.

Then what do I have to give up once I am a Christian? Christians have been introduced to a servant life-style, to the concept of the lordship of Christ. Unavoidably, this new life-style confronts us with the need for new priorities. The apostle Paul put it in very graphic terms in Philippians 3:7, 8. He said quite frankly that Christ is the one for whom he has "lost all things." But he did not seem to consider this a great sacrifice: "I consider them rubbish," he continued, because of the great gain of knowing Christ.

As we become more and more enamored with Christ, as we have more and more a sense of privilege in being his followers, then I think we are less and less likely to consider the things we give up as sacrifices. But, let's face it, some things will change.

There will need to be a reorganization of time. If we're going to serve, if we're going to worship, then we're not going to have as much time for goofing off—or maybe even for making money. A proper devotional life doesn't just happen; it needs regular time.

If we are going to be involved in the work of the church, then we'll need a disciplined use of financial resources. This means we're not going to have as much money to spend on frivolous, expensive, or extravagant things—or even on things we have always considered necessities.

If we are going to dedicate our lives to Christ's service, we will need a careful use of energy. We will not be able to do much for God if the hours we set aside for him are the tired leftovers. An important part of our spiritual life is our physical well-being. For the sake of our spiritual well-being, we're going to have to build in care for our physical body as well. And that is going to mean some discipline in time and energy use.

Being a Christian is, in part, a life-style. It requires us to determine a suitable standard of living, one that will permit us to make time, resources, and energy available for God. Many people today are caught in the upward mobility track. As soon as they have the opportunity of a promotion, they take it without sitting down and thinking to themselves, What will this promotion do to my family? What will it do to my ministry? What will it do to the commitments I've made? Sometimes we may need to sacrifice promotions for the sake of our more important commitments.

Some people look at sacrifice negatively. They concentrate on the things they have to give up, never stopping to ask, What kind of life would I lead if I kept those things? For Christians, however, sacrifice should be nothing more than a discipline that permits them to live the kind of life they have chosen. This life is abundant in the present world, and it promises eternal rewards. As Paul understood, the things we are sacrificing are really "rubbish."

♦ TURNING A NEGATIVE WORD INTO A POSITIVE ACT / STUART BRISCOE

My big question for the girl who led me to Christ concerned the sacrifices I would have to make to become a Christian. The gospel as she presented it sounded attractive and exciting to me. But I asked her, "What do I have to give up if I become a Christian? What do I have to sacrifice?"

After a moment of silence, she answered, "Only your sin."

She went on to explain that God would require repentance for sin. I would have to turn away from things that would harm me or make me less than the person I should be. That made sense to me.

If she had said I'd have to give up pleasure, or tennis, or friends, I might have thought twice about becoming a Christian. But when she said I had to sacrifice only the things that would do me harm and mar my life—and certainly sin would do that—then sacrifice was not a negative word but a very positive act.

Growing As a Healthy Christian

✍ EUGENE PETERSON

It is both natural and appropriate to be excited about a person's conversion. It is the most significant event in life—to be born anew, to be a new creature in Christ. But that significance and the excitement accompanying it do not excuse ignorance and indifference to the complex process of growth into which every Christian is launched via this new birth. Because growth involves so much—so much detail, so much time, so much discipline and patience—it is common to dismiss it and turn our attention to something we can get a quick handle on: the conversion event. Evangelism crowds spirituality off the agenda. But having babies is not a vocation; parenting is. It is easier, of course, to have babies. But a church that refuses or neglects the long intricate, hard work of guiding its newborn creatures into adulthood is being negligent of most of what is in Scripture.

The Bible is full of references to growth and growing. Luke, for example, describes both Jesus and John as growing. John "grew and became strong in spirit" (1:80), and Jesus "grew in wisdom and stature, and in favor with God and men" (2:52). The word *grew* is the last word on both John and Jesus before their public ministries are narrated. Both the greatest of the prophets and the unique Messiah grew into the fullness of their ministries.

The apostle Paul used growth words frequently as he urged people to enter into the full implications of their life in the Spirit. When we become mature in the faith, he said, "we will no longer be infants, . . . [but] we will in all things grow up into him who is the Head, that is, Christ" (Ephesians 4:14, 15). "Your faith is growing more and more" is his commendation to the church at Thessalonica (2 Thessalonians 1:3).

Peter urged believers to "grow in the grace and knowledge of our Lord and Savior Jesus Christ" (2 Peter 3:18). Comparing them to newborn babies, he said, "crave pure spiritual milk, so that by it you may grow up in your salvation" (1 Peter 2:2).

Growth is the basic metaphor in several parables that involve us in participation in the kingdom. The most dramatically placed growth image is at the center of the Gospel of John (12:24). Jesus said that unless a seed falls into the ground and dies, it does not grow, but if it dies, it grows. Growth is a major concern of John's Gospel—maturing into everything that God does in Christ, gathering all the parts of our lives and all the details of Jesus' life into a single whole. John arranges his Gospel into two almost equal parts: this growth image in 12:24 is the hinge that holds the two halves together.

When we live the life of faith biblically, growth is the most natural thing in the world—or, in reality, the most supernatural thing in the world. We can't keep a child from growing, yet we know of parents who try to keep their children immature all their lives, and sometimes succeed. Some Christian leaders do that too. But when leaders in the Christian community get out of the way and let the Spirit have his way, growth takes place and believers come into the full possession of the Spirit's gifts as he develops his life in us.

It is in the nature of what God is doing in us that we grow. But this "naturalness" does not mean that growth is painless. Growth calls into action new parts of our minds, our emotions, our bodies. What we experience at these times often feels like pain. We are not used to stretching ourselves in these ways. But the pain should not surprise us—our muscles ache when we take up any new activity. Athletes expect to get sore muscles when they begin training.

A commitment to Christ and obedience to his commands stretch us beyond ourselves, and that hurts. But this is a very different pain from that inflicted by torture or punishment. Growth pain is the kind we don't regret; it leads to health and not disease or neurosis.

Most growth takes place unconsciously. Biological growth and spiritual growth are analogous here. We can't see it happening, only that it has happened—and those closest to it are often least aware of it. There are things to do that promote and aid growth in ourselves and others, but the actual growth takes place at a mysterious level, far beyond our ability to observe or control it. Everything we do is significant, but none of it is determinative. Christian growth is the Spirit's work; he gives the direction and form. The Christian community can only stand back in awe at what goes on. Too often, though, it complains, like resentful parents, of the mess and inconvenience.

Introspection is ill-advised here. The spiritual masters in our faith consistently discourage introspection. Growth takes place in quietness, in hidden ways, in silence and solitude. The process is not accessible to observation. Constantly taking our spiritual temperature is bad for our health. When we are introspective about our growth, what we are actually doing is examining our feelings—and feelings are notorious liars, especially in matters of faith.

Attentiveness to spiritual growth that does not become introspectively neurotic is only accomplished by participation in a worshiping community. Healthy spiritual growth requires the presence of the other—the brother, the sister, the pastor, the teacher. A private, proudly isolated life cannot grow. The two or three who gather together in Christ's name keep each other sane.

God gives us various means to grow: prayer and Scripture, silence and solitude, suffering and service. But the huge foundational means is public worship. Spiritual growth cannot take place in isolation. It is not a private thing between the Christian and God. In worship, we come before God who loves us in the presence of the others whom he also loves. In worship, more than at any other time, we set ourselves in deliberate openness to the action of God and the need of the neighbor, both of which require us to grow up to the fullness of the stature of Christ, who is both God and man for us. Regular, faithful worship is as essential to the growing Christian as food and shelter to the growing child. Worship is the light and air in which spiritual growth takes place.

◆MEASURING OUR GROWTH / CALVIN MILLER

It is encouraging to know we are improving all the time in any area, even in our walk with Christ. But measuring our growth can cause problems. If we feel we're not growing, we can become frustrated. If we feel we are, we can become arrogant. It would make a child neurotic if her parents shoved her up against a wall every two days and made another little mark above her head. If you measure that often, a child doesn't seem to grow. What we need to do is not to measure the child but to feed her. The best kinds of growth seem to occur automatically in response to good nourishment.

♦ MEASURING MY BROTHER'S GROWTH
EUGENE PETERSON

It is possible to become a Christian and then not to grow. There are cases of arrested development and laziness, or of growth that is perverted and distorted. I'm wary, though, of looking at a person and saying, "He's not growing." I don't know what's going on inside him. There may be subterranean influences there that I'll never be aware of, battles that never get reported, beauties and glories that I am not trained to see. Everybody is subject to influences toward growth; we can't see how they are being worked out.

A person can, I suppose, say, "I've changed my mind; I'm not going to grow," and stubbornly withdraw from the life of faith. But my basic conviction is that the Spirit never quits working with that person no matter how that person's spiritual life may look to outsiders.

There are common patterns for growth, and we need to be aware of those, but much harm is done when we try to push people into a mold. We have no right to set a certain standard for where believers should be during their stages of growth. Patterns that we force on others are often cruel and actually inhibit growth because they don't allow for individuality. Children grow at different rates; so do Christians. Some of us take much longer to learn to do something than others. The task of the Christian community is not to measure Christian growth and judge it, but rather to be attentive so growth can be encouraged, stimulated, and enabled.

How Important Is Spiritual Growth?
GARY DAUSEY

For two Sundays in a row I got a different count, so I would have to try again next Sunday. What I was counting were the large bricks that made up the wall of our church behind the pulpit. What made the task so difficult was that many of them were covered by a large framed oil painting of Christ in the Garden of Gethsemane, and I had to guess how many were behind the painting.

What really troubled me was that I was counting at all. Why was my mind wandering during the sermon? Not many months before, as a new Christian, I sat glued to every word our pastor said. Everything was so fresh, so new, and I was intensely interested in every concept being taught.

I had so much to learn. I didn't know the difference between 1 Chronicles and 1 Corinthians. I'd look up the sermon text in advance and mark it in my Bible to save the embarrassment of fumbling for it during the service. It took me literally six months of churchgoing before I figured out that "Gloria Patri" was not our church organist.

Each church service, each Christian radio broadcast, each book I read yielded some new insight into the Christian life. Slowly, almost indiscernibly that was all changing. Now the pastor could speak for twenty or thirty minutes without ever intercepting my wandering mind. The romance of my new faith was slowly fading. I began to see creeping into me the complacency and near indifference I had observed in older Christians.

I wanted desperately to maintain the freshness of my early experience, but it seemed I had to continually seek some new spiritual high to do it. Was this normal Christian growth or was my faith deteriorating? What about some of my new friends who had grown up in the church and never had the opportunity of experiencing a new life in sharp contrast to an old one? What was growth for them?

Without a doubt, one of the most recurrent questions we Christians ask ourselves is, Am I growing? What we are really asking is, Am I further along today in my relationship with God than I was a month or a year ago?

For the believer, spiritual growth is crucial for several reasons:

1. *It tones our spiritual muscles* for the stresses we find in the "real world." God never promised that Christians would be free of problems, but he has provided the resources with which we can confront them. He helps us find the resources necessary when we are thrust into the stress of a marriage that is falling apart, or a situation with one of our children who has become rebellious, or a loss of employment, or the loss of someone very close to us. The person without a deep well of spiritual resources is apt to give in quickly to despair. The Christian with a firm and growing faith will still have the problem, but will also have the inner strength to deal with it.

2. *It puts a wall around us to protect us from sin.* Sin is insidious—it creeps in a little at a time. It is easy for us to become comfortable with things we have no business becoming comfortable with. Satan is often throwing his fiery darts at us and, if we are spiritually immature, those darts can often penetrate and cause us to do those things that displease the Lord. Those who have a firm and solid faith can fend off those attacks of Satan. When Christ was tempted by Satan (Matthew 4), he used the Word of God to repel the attacks, and he was successful. Any Christian with a solid foundation in the Word of God can claim the same resources on a daily basis.

3. *It helps us as we model Christ to others.* Whether we like it or not, others are constantly watching us to see how we live. It may be a person in our office or a neighbor or perhaps even the little eyes of our children. A spiritually immature person may, through daily actions, do more to hurt the cause of Christ and discourage others from following him than to point people to him. It is so easy for our humanity to raise its ugly head and, before we know it, we've said or done something we regret. If we are growing spiritually, the Lord is taking control of all areas of our lives and it is he who helps us become better models to others.

Spiritual growth is an important dynamic for all believers. It is not related to how I feel, it is related to where I am with the Lord. You may also discover that what you needed to do to grow at one stage of your Christian development may not be the same as what you need now. For instance, perhaps what you needed at the earliest stage of your Christian experience was to sit and soak up truth. But now perhaps the most helpful ingredient in your growth is some form of service or sharing that truth.

Growth takes various stages, has different needs at different times, and is often a slow process. But we should not be discouraged and fall into the trap of boredom in our Christian walk—boredom that causes us to count bricks instead of listen to sermons! We must pray for God to help us grow, understand the need for growth, and use with enthusiasm the tools God gives to help us grow. And with such stimulus, we can't be bored in this new life.

Transformed

EVELYN CHRISTENSON

Growth is a never-ending process for us Christians. Although we are complete in Christ at salvation, we are not finished. In fact, becoming a Christian is just the beginning. Having accepted Christ, we are to be transformed by the renewing of our minds (Romans 12:2), by getting a new mind-set from God.

We can become so much more than we were before we met Christ. That's what the word *transformed* means. We change into another form as Jesus Christ did on the Mount of Transfiguration. (*Transfiguration* and *transformation* mean the same.) This change starts when we come to know Christ, and it continues as we come to know him better.

There are two reasons we know we are not done growing. First, in Romans Paul is writing to the saints, "to all in Rome who are loved by God and called to be saints" (1:7). Saints are people who have been justified in Jesus Christ; their sins are gone, and they are on their way to heaven. But Paul is telling these saints (and that includes us) to be transformed and renewed in their minds.

The second reason is the tense of "to be transformed." In the previous verse Paul said, "Offer your bodies as living sacrifices" (12:1). That happens once and for all. You do it and it's done. Salvation is not a process; it is a moment in time when we pass the threshold from death to life and our names are written in the Lamb's Book of Life. Before that moment we were eternally damned; after that moment we are eternally bound for heaven. But in verse 2, Paul switches tenses, saying we are to be transformed. Transformation is a continuous, ongoing process.

God initiates the process of change, but we supply the willingness by praying, "I will be transformed, I will let God change me." God does the changing—I am not capable of that by myself. My part is to discipline myself and take the steps so I am in the place where God can work. I stay in the Word, in prayer, in obedience.

I have been a Christian since I was nine. Throughout my life I had studied the Bible and tried to let God change me, but I didn't have a goal. I didn't know what I was supposed to be changed to. In 1968 I cried, "Lord, change me," and I asked God what my goal should be. I found my goal in Romans 8:29, "For those God foreknew he also predestined to be conformed to the likeness of his Son." That is the goal of our changing, to become like Christ. It is not changing for the sake of change.

The more I read Scriptures, the more I see of Jesus. The more I apply Scriptures to my life, the more like Jesus I become. The more like Jesus I become, the more I realize how I fall short. I will never achieve my goal until I see Jesus, because he is "the radiance of God's glory and the exact representation of his being, sustaining all things by his powerful word" (Hebrews 1:3). "We know that when he appears, we shall be like him, for we shall see him as he is" (1 John 3:2). In the meantime, I participate in the process of transformation.

If we allow ourselves to stagnate in our faith and don't grow, we will have regrets when we finally see Jesus. We will see all of our lost chances to be like Jesus, and we will say, "If only I had grown."

Recognizing the Inadequacy of Self

RICHARD HALVERSON

Have you ever looked at Jesus, at Scripture, or at other Christians and said, "I feel so inadequate"?

If so, congratulations! If you recognize that you need the grace of God, and that it is offered to you in Jesus Christ, you are rich indeed. Your sense of need is an asset rather than a liability.

It is lukewarmness, not inadequacy, that God finds intolerable. As he tells the Laodicean church in Revelation 3:16, "Because you are lukewarm—neither hot nor cold—I am about to spit you out of my mouth." It is wishy-washiness, not an honest admission of need, that God find deplorable. If a person needs nothing, he is dead. I am alive; therefore I get hungry and thirsty and need rest.

There is a parallel to this in the Christian life. If your spiritual life is alive, you will be challenged to grow, and you will feel a need to be fed. A cadaver doesn't need food and drink and clothing. Neither does a spiritually dead person know he needs to be nurtured.

The rich Laodicean church had a surplus of goods. They felt they didn't need God because of their wealth. Remember the warning Moses gave the children of Israel before they entered the Promised Land: "When you eat and are satisfied, be careful that you do not forget the Lord, who brought you out of Egypt, out of the land of slavery" (Deuteronomy 6:11, 12).

By contrast, the very heart of growth is the recognition that you need God's grace and that it has been provided in Jesus Christ. Now that I'm sixty-nine years old, my deepest longing is to live in God's grace. The greatest desire of my life is to think Christ's thoughts. I feel my own neediness. I know that the only life I have is Christ—and I discover this often by failing and sinning. Then I allow him to live his life in me. Without him I can do nothing.

If you truly desire to have Christ live in you, it requires a deep commitment to his way of life. Peter talked big at the Last Supper and said he would never forsake his Lord, but minutes later he denied him with cursing. Later he repented and went out and wept, realizing he hadn't fulfilled the verbal commitment he had made. He had to learn that he could not depend on himself to live up to his decision.

When Christ restored Peter (the story is recorded in John 21), he asked, "Do you love me?" Peter said, "Lord, you know I love you." What he was really saying was "Lord, I know I haven't proved it. My actions look like I don't love you at all. But you know what is in my heart." We need to bring our outer actions up to our inner conviction, and we can do this only through the power of Christ.

Even with the best of intentions, we all—like Peter—fail. But every time we fail, we learn that we can't trust ourselves, that we can put no confidence in the flesh. So each time God brings us again to the place of trust and dependence on him.

Oswald Chambers said that if our trust is in anybody but Christ, we're going to be disillusioned over and over. Part of the process of maturing spiritually is to go through the stages of disillusionment, of doubt in ourselves, and of feeling great need. All this turns us—like Peter—back to Christ.

So if you feel inadequate, turn to Christ. Confess your need, and find restoration through his grace. This is the heart of his redemption—he heals us and gives us new life.

◆ WEAR ME LIKE A GARMENT
RICHARD HALVERSON

Each day before I leave my study I ask God to "wear me like a garment." My clothes are nothing in themselves—they are inanimate, and when I take them off they can't stand up or walk or do anything on their own. They collapse. I want to be like that in relation to Christ. I want my only animation to be Christ who lives in me, who thinks his thoughts, desires his will, and loves his love through me.

Another way to say this is, "I have been crucified with Christ and I no longer live, but Christ lives in me. The life I live in the body, I live by faith in the Son of God, who loved me and gave himself for me" (Galatians 2:20).

Do You Need a Personality Change?
J. I. PACKER

The ancient Greeks distinguished between four basic temperaments: sanguine—cheerful and optimistic; choleric—passionate, emotionally up and down; phlegmatic—supercool; and melancholic—tending toward gloom.

Your personality will shape your Christian growth, because out of your personality are likely to come your besetting sins, weaknesses, or problems. If you're naturally sanguine, you'll be in danger of being irresponsible in your optimism. If you're naturally choleric, your danger will always be impatience (I'm pretty sure Simon Peter was choleric). If you're phlegmatic, your besetting sin is likely to be detachment—you sit on the fence in relation to everything. The melancholic is likely to lack joy and perhaps peace, being beset with doubts and complaints that produce bitterness. Christ, by his grace, must deal with such weaknesses and teach us better habits.

Spiritual growth, growth in grace, is essentially two things. It's a matter of your moral character, and it's a matter of your relationship with the Lord. Paul said in 2 Corinthians 3:18, "We, who with unveiled faces all reflect the Lord's glory, are being transformed into his likeness." In other words, we are becoming like what we look at. We look at the Lord Jesus, and—as we see him—new habits of Christlikeness are formed in us. That's character change.

There is also a relational aspect of growth toward Christian maturity. Those who have walked with God through thick and thin are further along the road than those who haven't yet learned to do that. They have grown in grace; their faith has become firmly anchored. They are more mature in the faith than are Christians who wobble under pressure.

Growth in grace is especially apparent when people are put under pressure. The testing situation brings out the best and the worst in them. In it the Lord challenges them, and they have to decide how to respond. Their reaction to pressure does two things: it shows whether they've been growing in grace, and it also points out where they need to grow. If they have developed bad habits because of their personality type or because of bad company, pressure will show these up. Once they have found out what their bad habits are, they can ask the Lord for help to break them.

All of us have temperamental handicaps, but I don't think one temperament type is more resistant to spiritual growth than another. What hinders growth is slipping back into carelessness, sin, and compromise—letting our first love grow cold. It is a spiritual issue, not a personality problem.

Say, for example, a person has a stubborn personality. This person is naturally thoughtful and questioning, and he spends a long time mulling things over before he can commit himself to any new idea. Thus he is slow to respond to the Lord's calls. In fact, he quite resolutely clings to his own way of doing things.

Now stubbornness, though it may be associated with certain temperaments, is actually a habit of mind. It is an expression of fallen human pride. It is a sin—and God knows how to work with sin. He works with us wherever we are, gradually leading us to a better way of responding. He starts with the person in his stubbornness and teaches him to open his mind and listen to God.

In some of us stubbornness seems to be very strong, and we are very conscious of it much of the time. But if we can say, "Though I'm stubborn, I can thankfully testify that I'm not as stubborn as I used to be," that is a sign we have been growing in grace.

The important thing is that we be able to look back and say, "Well, I'm not where I hope to be someday, but thank God I am different from what I was." We ought to have a conscious testimony to being changed. Thank God for what he's done in you by his grace. Don't start comparing yourself with others, or you may get discouraged. Just keep before your mind the ways the Lord has changed you already. That will encourage you to believe he can deal with all the rest of your sins and problems—even stubbornness.

It's important to look honestly at our emotions, to pinpoint the patterns that need to be changed, and to ask the Lord specifically to do something about those patterns. He is faithful, and there will be changes. Everybody has habits and attitudes that need to be changed. In some people it's habitual resentment of others; in others it's habitual ingratitude. From the start of your Christian life, you ought to identify those things that need changing and ask the Lord to change them. When he does, you will have a testimony to change; you will be able to tell others what the Lord has done for you.

Different temperaments may have different needs, but all Christians need to grow in faith, in hope, and in love—the three dimensions of our fellowship with Jesus. If we're moving ahead in those areas, our other struggles will fall into line.

If we're going to grow, whoever we are and whatever our temperament, we all need to use the means of grace: prayer, Bible study, and fellowship in the church, including the Lord's Supper. Prayer is keeping in touch with our Lord. It is as vital to the Christian life as air is to physical life. Reading and studying God's Word is just as vital. It is food for our souls. Fellowship is vital too. We need each other's help and encouragement, for none of us can walk well alone. And nowhere shall we appreciate Jesus' love and power more vividly than as we share in the Supper.

Whatever our temperament and wherever we are in the Christian walk, we have to accept the discipline of all our circumstances as they come. New circumstances are always developing, putting pressure on us in different ways. We have to remember that they come from God. Illuminated by Romans 8:28—"We know that in all things God works for the good of those who love him, who have been called according to his purpose"—we practice the discipline of walking faithfully with God in good times and bad, learning what he means us to learn in each set of situations as it comes. In order to grow, we need to pray each day, "Lord, walk with me and my temperament through today's circumstances." Then we, for our part, must seek to walk through the day consciously with God.

Although there are principles in Scripture that apply to all of us, each person's experience will be shaped individually. God has a different growth program blocked out for each of us. He knows my weaknesses; he knows where I am especially vulnerable; he knows where my temperament can get me into trouble. He will order things so that I am built up where I most need help. God's training program is like an individual course in a gymnasium. The first thing the trainer does is find out which muscles are weak; then he plans exercises and disciplines to make those weak muscles strong. Personal training is slightly different for everybody.

Our temperaments need not stand in the way of our spiritual growth. God created each of us unique, and he will guide each of us to grow in our own unique way.

♦ DISCOURAGEMENT: THE PAIN OF GROWTH
EUGENE PETERSON

Anyone involved in growing in the Christian faith soon understands that we are in a lifelong process of becoming mature and realizes that discouragement is part of the pain of growth. There is no way to live the Christian life in a growing way without times of discouragement. Discouragement is not foreign to the life of faith, but part of it.

We get discouraged when we evaluate our lives in terms of what we are doing rather than what God is doing. Instead of letting him do what he wants to do and take as much time as he wants to do it, we set an agenda for ourselves. We want to follow our own schedule. If we are successful, we become proud and self-satisfied. So God doesn't let it work. He doesn't reward us for doing the wrong thing. Naturally, we get discouraged. Discouragement then becomes a prod to move us through arrested development into continuing growth. Persons who mask their discouragement with a false bonhomie, or seek for diversions that lessen its impact, never mature.

Discouragement that is resented or denied can be seized by the Tempter and used as a lever to pry us loose from faith in Christ. But when it is welcomed as the Spirit's gift, it wakes us up: we realize that we are going about things the wrong way, trying to perpetuate an immature faith life—and we are motivated to open ourselves again to the new thing that the Spirit wills to do in us.

Resolutions Become Realities with God
✍ BRUCE BARTON

Lose weight. Work out. Finish homework earlier. Witness to someone every day.... It's amazing how many of us have difficulty keeping even one New Year's resolution. Whether it involves cleaning our rooms or making life-changing decisions, we struggle and feel guilty about our inability to keep these personal promises.

Many times we fail because our approach is wrong. We ensure our own failure in one of these ways:

1. We make trivial resolutions just to prove we can keep them, but there are no consequences to doing them or not.

2. We make resolutions that are totally impossible to keep. Idealism is great, but some things are way out of reach. For example: "I'm never going to get angry again."

3. Deep down inside we wear a "failure" label. We really want to succeed, but we have already concluded that we are not capable of controlling our behavior.

4. We become sidetracked easily. That is, we never keep going in one direction long enough. We are enthusiastic about a goal only until something more exciting comes along.

Maybe you can identify with one of these approaches. As a person who knows what it's like to blow it totally with resolutions, let me share some suggestions that worked for me.

First, realize that God is far more concerned about your personal growth and success than you could ever be.

Then learn that there is a vast difference between doing something in your own strength and doing it in the power of the Holy Spirit.

With these truths as your starting point, analyze your relationship with God. Is he in control? Have you given every area and desire to him? God can do anything, but he wants to work through individuals who are totally committed to him. If this is the case with you, then you're ready for his guidance.

Next, check out his Word, the Bible. There God has set out guidelines for developing values that are both worthwhile and reasonable.

Finally, pray. Ask God to show you what—in light of his values—he wants you to do to glorify him with your life. Talk this over with respected Christian friends.

Now that you have looked at your relationship with God, checked the Bible, and prayed, you are ready to set goals and objectives. It is important to continue praying as you set them. Paul said, "Pray continually" (1 Thessalonians 5:17), for every step of our lives must be given to God for his direction.

Because you have yielded your life to Christ and are living under his control, the Holy Spirit is able to release his power in you. And when you receive the Spirit's power, you are ready to act. This time you aren't trying to keep human resolutions. Instead, you are carrying out Spirit-led goals in the power of the Spirit. The difference is enormous.

The Importance of Spiritual Exercise

CALVIN MILLER

Growth, whether physical or spiritual, is always related to two things: nutrition and exercise.

Nobody grows without eating. Psalm 119:11 says, "I have hidden your word in my heart that I might not sin against you." Our growth is directly related to consistently ingesting the Word of God.

Regular exercise is also important. If a child only lies in bed and eats all the time, he may grow but he won't be of much use. But as he learns to walk and exercise, his muscles grow strong. Spiritually, we can't just study the Bible all the time and expect to grow. We must turn from study to ministry, taking the principles of the Bible and applying them in the world.

Although all Christians should grow, we won't grow in the same areas and at the same speed. Nonetheless, every Christian should grow in the knowledge of the Bible and in prayer.

Since not all Christians will grow in every area of ministry and service, a Christian should expect to grow only in whatever area he or she is specially called to serve. Three times in his letters (in Romans 12; 1 Corinthians 12; Ephesians 4), Paul talks about the fact that each Christian has an area of calling. In 1 Corinthians 12:28, he names seven different callings that God puts in the Church—apostles, prophets, teachers, miracle workers, healers, helpers, administrators, and those who speak in other tongues. This list is not meant to be all-inclusive, but it is meant to show the diverse ways God uses us all.

We get in trouble when we fail to understand how God meant to use our lives. My area of calling is not musical performance. I don't believe I could ever grow in that area no matter how hard I worked at it. But some people are uniquely called and equipped to be great musicians. Still, even the gifted never receive a gift from God that is fully developed. Even the musically gifted, at some time in their lives, couldn't have found middle C on the piano. But they learned, little by little, until one day they could play Tchaikovsky. They could grow in the area of musical performance because this was the calling God gave them. Similarly, all Christians can grow in those areas of God's calling.

But in order to grow we must exercise. This is obvious in the physical life. If an infant just lay in his crib and never moved a muscle, eventually he would not be able to move at all.

To say we need spiritual exercise is not to advocate righteousness by works. No real righteousness can ever be by works. The best goodness is not what we contrive on our own, but what Jesus did when he was in this world and what he now imputes to us. It is as if God pinched off Christ's goodness and placed it in the center of our lives.

A growing Christian isn't straining and struggling to make the Christ-life happen. That would only build tension into his life. It would take away his peace and make him absolutely neurotic, always inspecting his own growth and asking, "Am I getting better?" or "Why don't I get better?"

Most of us as Christians are troubled by the fact that long after we became Christians we are still asking God's forgiveness for some of the very sins we sinned when we first gave our lives to Christ. It is frustrating! We would like to order God to rip these sins out of our lives. Still, it is better to realize that these sins are still in our lives because the process of getting them out is so gradual. We must grow patient with a gradual cleansing. We don't have to despair. We know that Jesus is in our lives and that, bit by bit, he is remaking us in his image.

An apple tree doesn't decide it's going to produce apples and then stand and grunt until they pop out. It is the very nature of apple trees to produce apples. Sooner or later—given nutrition, sunshine, and water—it happens. Similarly, the Christian who emphasizes the bases of growth will grow. He doesn't have to measure his works or strain until good deeds pop out of him. He has but to focus on Jesus, nutrition, and exercise, and sooner or later growth happens.

♦ DECIDING LIFE'S PRIORITIES
OSWALD HOFFMAN

In deciding my life's priorities, I should keep three things in mind—my relationship to God, my relationship to other people, and my relationship to myself.

Priority 1: Glorifying God. The old

Heidelberg Catechism said that the chief purpose of mankind is to know God and to glorify him forever. The first commandment says, "You shall have no other gods before me" (Exodus 20:3). God should come first in everything. This does not mean our faith should be a fanatical pursuit of heaven to the detriment of everything else in the world. But the first question we should always ask is, Does this glorify God? If it doesn't glorify God, don't do it.

Priority 2: Loving others. God cares for the world so much that he gave his only Son to save it (John 3:16). Because of this, we can serve him by caring for the people around us. This means living the life of Christ. How do we do that? By being gentle, humble, kind, and forgiving (Colossians 3:12-17).

Priority 3: Living in the light. Paul said, "Let the peace of Christ rule in your hearts, . . . [and] let the word of Christ dwell in you richly" (Colossians 3:15, 16). We should choose activities that enable us to be conscious of God all the time. We don't have to walk around with our hands folded. But we should worship God on Sunday and carry the experience with us into Monday.

In deciding what to do in our everyday lives, these three priorities should guide us. But we have to use our judgment, which we can develop through education, practice, and experience. Then, like Jesus, we will grow in wisdom and stature (Luke 2:52).

Guidelines to Spiritual Maturity

HANNAH HURNARD

For sixty years I have lived an adventurous and exciting life as a disciple of the Lord Jesus. There have been many tests, joys, and miracles of God's grace and loving-kindness, with never a dull moment or any possibility of feeling bored.

These are the principles I have followed:

1. Yield to God everything that seems impossible to surrender. Then God becomes real.

2. Remain in contact with God by means of an early morning quiet time. During this time, listen to him talking to you in your thoughts, explaining the things you read in the Bible, and giving you guidance for the day.

3. Keep building altars of self-surrender by practicing real faith. Real faith is the willingness to obey God's will and the things he teaches you, with no compromise at all.

4. Share with others the light God gives you, or you shall lose it. Always keep open to new light. Realize that light rejected brings darkness, and light responded to brings more light.

5. Don't let fears frighten you away from where all God's best blessings await you. Rejoice that God is compassionate toward the fearful. Realize that fearful people are fortunate, for they have more opportunities to develop faith than do fearless people.

6. Learn to love others as yourself, because you are members in the one body of God's creation. What you do to others, you do to yourself also.

7. Give all your love to God. Then God's divine, unpossessive love will flow

into you and enable you to love everyone with his love and not with your own earthly, possessive love.

8. Learn to forgive and forget wrong things that others do to you. Never talk about the things you forgive, but act as though they had not been done. Then they will drop out of your memory altogether. If wrong things continue to be done to you, you shall be able to forgive continually. Great blessing will be the result.

9. Go through each day praising and thanking God for everything that happens, including the not good and even seemingly very bad things. Your spirit of thanksgiving waves a wand of heavenly love over these things and transforms them into blessings.

10. Let God transform all your negative thoughts and cleanse your lips, so that you think and talk only about good, lovely, true, and helpful things. Learn Philippians 4:8 by heart. When you concentrate on calling attention to what is good, you help cause evil things to destroy themselves. That is the one good things about evil—by its very nature it must destroy itself. When you protest against evil things and talk about them to others, you only strengthen them and prolong their existence.

11. Never pray about or say anything concerning other people behind their backs that you would not say if they were present and could hear you. Always speak in a way that will cause everyone to be "amazed at the gracious words that [come] from [your] lips" (Luke 4:22), just as they were when Jesus spoke.

12. Be absolutely honest in all things, like a crystal clear window through which people can look without your wanting to hide anything shameful from them.

13. Thank God for your handicaps, which are blessings in disguise. God's strength is made perfect in your weakness (2 Corinthians 12:9), and so your greatest infirmities become the things for which you learn to thank him most of all.

14. Truly repent. This means loathing the things you do wrong and asking God's grace to keep you from ever doing those things again.

15. Realize that everything you sow, you will reap (Galatians 6:7). You will experience in some way all that you say and do.

16. Obey as far as you can see. When you are bewildered and seem utterly unable to get guidance from God, you should take the first step by obeying what you think is most in harmony with Jesus' teaching. You can ask God to confirm this by opening the way ahead or by blocking it so that you shall not go wrong.

17. Intercede with God for others. Intercession is the Bible's word for contacting God's power, by obedient faith, and contacting those who need that power, by praying for them. Pray with the loving desire that they may be helped in the way God sees best. Intercession is like a power cable along which God can transmit his grace and help to those who need it.

18. Test your beliefs. Jesus taught that you can discern the true from the false by the results that follow the teachings (Matthew 7:15-20). If greater love for God and for others floods into you as a result of a teaching, then you can be

sure it is at least partly true, even if it is not yet the full truth. If, however, you become more impatient and critical of others, you need to beware of the teaching.

19. Always long to press onward to higher levels of God-consciousness and love. Never be content with something less than the highest possible.

20. Always picture living with Jesus. Think, speak, and act as you would if you could see him visibly present with you. Then you shall be able to fulfill the royal law of love (James 2:8) and do unto others what you would like done to you (Matthew 7:12).

◆ CHRISTIAN CHECKPOINTS / YFC EDITORS

How can a Christian know he or she is on the right track in the Christian life? Are there any checkpoints along the way?

A believer always needs to recheck his or her focus. Is it centered on Christ, or has it shifted to self and personal needs and desires?

Another set of checkpoints are the Ten Commandments. Are you careful to follow these and the subtleties underlying them described by Jesus? For example, you may not commit adultery, but is lust a problem? You may not steal, but do you waste time at work? Checking against these can help you get back on track in your Christian life.

Love is a vital checkpoint. The Bible says love is the mark of a Christian. Do you love God with all your heart and soul and mind (Matthew 22:37)? Do you love God's Word and read it in order to learn and obey (Psalm 119)? Do you love God's people (1 John 4:11, 12)?

◆ WHAT IS TRUE HOLINESS? RICHARD OWEN ROBERTS

Some people see holiness as *not* doing a group of forbidden things. In truth, that is about as far removed from the central issue as anything could possibly be.

We have to understand that the requirements of holiness may differ for different individuals. What may be perfectly acceptable for one may not be acceptable for another, for the will of God is not in every single small point universal.

True holiness is doing the will of God, whatever that may be.

Called to Holiness

✍ RICHARD OWEN ROBERTS

As Christians, our goal is perfect obedience to all God requires. Our desire is to exercise faith in all its reaches, to obey God in absolutely everything. This life of perfect obedience is known as holiness.

The term *holiness* scares people. Most Christians tend to shy away from it, letting particular denominational groups specialize in it. To many of us, holiness seems to be an extreme condition—we can't really be expected to be holy, can we?

I've talked with individuals who suggest that there is no real hope of arriving at any degree of holiness. For example, I once talked with a man who was living in adultery. I confronted him with his sin and sought to bring him to repentance. His response was, "This just happens to be my weakness. God understands. In fact, he's more understanding than you are!"

Insincere people say things like that as a coverup, but some sincere people also hold that belief because they have been defeated time after time. Thinking there is no solution for their sin, they have grown used to it.

I think we've given the wrong impression to many sincere believers. We say to them, "Don't expect to grow or to develop too much. You should grow some, but don't count on an awful lot." But surely the Lord's teaching is plain. Holiness, in the biblical view, isn't an option; it's mandatory. "Be holy because I, the Lord your God, am holy," God says repeatedly (see, for example, Leviticus 19:2).

Jesus put tremendous emphasis on holiness. He was holy, and he called his followers to holiness. The Beatitudes and the Sermon on the Mount clearly indicate Christ's view. In Matthew 5:8, Jesus declared, "Blessed are the pure in heart, for they will see God." This purity of heart in this passage is not freedom from impure thoughts, but singularity of heart. The pure in heart are those whose hearts are not divided. Sin occurs in the Christian when he allows himself to be torn between two positions and gives in to the evil. A life of victory requires a mind single to God's glory. This is the very point Jesus makes in Matthew 6:22-24: "The eye is the lamp of the body. If your eyes are good, your whole body will be full of light. But if your eyes are bad, your whole body will be full of darkness. If then the light within you is darkness, how great is that darkness! No one can serve two masters. Either he will hate the one and love the other, or he will be devoted to the one and despise the other." Holiness means having a single focus, an undivided loyalty.

Jesus was as thoroughly and deeply tempted as any of us, yet he never sinned. It wasn't his divinity that kept him from sin, but the singleness of his purpose. He had only one commitment—to do God's will. He at no point allowed a secondary thought or a lesser purpose to grip him. Therefore, when he was tempted to evil, he could not even consider the temptation.

That is real holiness: singularity of mind and purpose.

The Key to Holiness

RICHARD OWEN ROBERTS

If a believer is to progress in sanctification, he must have a goal. That goal ought to be none other than the one Jesus himself was gripped by: the goal of doing God's will. If we commit ourselves to that one goal, then we can lay hold of the biblical helps and the help of the Holy Spirit and make very real progress in holiness.

God is holy, and his will for us is holiness. We are to be as he is. As we reflect soberly on God's holiness, it becomes more and more astonishing. I've lived relatively few years—only fifty some—and I have not had a single year of absolute holiness and perfection. Not even a month or a week. Probably not even a day. God has lived not fifty or a hundred years, not even a few thousand years. God has lived for an eternity, billions and billions of years plus, and not for one single moment has he been anything less than absolutely holy.

It's God's will that I be holy too. Now God wouldn't will something impossible for me. Some say, "Well, anger happens to be my weakness. God understands." Or, "I have this sin that I fall into repeatedly, but God is understanding." Where do we get that sort of viewpoint about God? That's not understanding; that's tolerance. Where do we read in Scripture that God is tolerant of sin, that he says, "Well, in your case, it's OK"? Instead he says, "I want you to be as I am." And because God wills our holiness, he—being gracious, merciful, compassionate, and endlessly loving—has made provision for it. He wouldn't have demanded it of us if he hadn't made it possible.

First Corinthians 1:30 tells how God has made holiness possible for us: "It is because of him that you are in Christ Jesus, who has become for us wisdom from God—that is, our righteousness, holiness and redemption." We know we cannot be holy in and of ourselves. But we can constantly hold onto this: Jesus Christ is my sanctification, my holiness.

When Christ died on the cross, he did not die merely to rescue me from the consequences of sin. He died to save me from sin itself. The cross of Christ deals with every aspect of salvation from sin: righteousness, justification, sanctification, and glorification. It provides the total of salvation. This is a key concept. Sadly, many don't understand this. They believe that Christ died to justify them, but that the burden of responsibility for holiness or sanctification rests on them. They think that Christ is the glorious justifier, but sanctification is their own task. But as that verse in 1 Corinthians makes so plain, Christ is our sanctifier too.

I can't think of anything more discouraging than struggling along, trying to sanctify myself. Anyone who has tried it knows how utterly frustrating it is. You say to yourself, "I absolutely won't do that again. It's sin. It displeases God. With all my heart I want to do what's right." And presto, you do it again. It's an extraordinarily frustrating thing. No wonder people say, "Well, this is my weakness. I've gotten used to it. I know eventually God will save me from it. I just have to bear with it now." This type of mentality comes from the conviction that we must sanctify ourselves.

If I were to ask someone, "What do you have to do to be justified?" he might readily say, "Believe." If I asked him what he had to do to be glorified, he might astutely say, "Drop dead," for the believer is glorified not in this life but in the next. But if I asked him, "What do you have to do to be sanctified?" he might give me a whole list of things he felt he had to do.

The key to sanctification and holiness, however, is not works but faith. That's almost too easy for some; they can hardly believe it's that simple. But that's what it says in Scripture: Christ is the sanctifier, just as he is the justifier. I am made holy in sanctification by faith, just as I am made initially righteous in justification by faith.

In Ephesians 1, Paul launched into a series of marvelous statements of the benefits that are ours in Christ Jesus. The very first of these, in verse 4, is this: "He chose us in him before the creation of the world to be holy and blameless in his sight." Some versions use the verb *elected.* Just think of it: God has elected you to be holy! That's his will. He chose you from the world, from a life of sin and selfishness. He chose you expressly and purposely to be holy.

Let's take a look at this word *elected.* Our country's president wanted to be president for a long time. First he campaigned indirectly; then the time came when he was able to lay aside the indirect approach and campaign vigorously for the office of president. All during that time of campaigning, he could have awakened any morning and said to himself, "I'm tired of this rat race. I'm weary of this whole thing. I'm not going out campaigning today. In fact, I'm not even going to try to be president." He had that option.

But the day came when he was elected president by a sufficient number of voters. Once he was inaugurated, he couldn't wake up the next morning and say, "This has been a busy season. I'm utterly tired. I don't want to be president today." He couldn't wake up and say, "I'm not in the mood to be president." Now that he has been elected, he can't help himself; he is president.

Typical earnest Christians want so badly to be holy. They yearn with great zeal to advance in sanctification. They try to live holy lives, but they fail. When they are tempted, they look at the temptation and say, "Oh, no, I mustn't do that." The trouble is, as long as they feel the choice is theirs, they leave themselves open to temptation. But if they recognize that they've been elected by God—the holy God—to be holy as he is holy, all freedom of choice is gone.

Before I was a Christian I could look at a temptation and say, "Well, let's see. If I do that, it might hurt my family. No, I won't consider it." Or I could say, "Well, I don't know. It would be a lot of fun. I think I'll do it." The choice was always mine. But when a person is a Christian, he simply needs, in faith, to lay hold of the fact that God has elected him to holiness. Therefore he's no longer free to do what he wants or what he is tempted by the devil to do. His only freedom is to do God's will.

Someone might immediately object, "This sounds great, but in actual fact I find I still can sin." I'm not talking about what we can and cannot do. I'm talking about what we are elected to do. Our president can refuse to serve as president tomorrow, but he cannot choose not to be president. He may not function as he ought, but he was elected president, and president he is. Though I have been elected to be holy, I may refuse to function as a holy man of God. Nevertheless, God's choice and election of me remains firm.

I won't make any real progress in holiness until I agree with God. When I agree that God elected me to be holy, then my only choice is to be holy. If I choose to act otherwise, I haven't acted as a Christian, but as a non-Christian.

In Romans Paul put it this way: "Count yourselves dead to sin but alive to God in Christ Jesus" (6:11). The King James Version says we should "reckon ourselves dead." That word *reckon* suggests that I must make a sound inward decision. I must say to myself, God elected me to be holy. I have been crucified with Christ, and I am dead to the old nature. I must not give place to it. I must take as a settled fact my death to sin and my resurrection to newness of life, and I must act accordingly.

Election to holiness is not a great crisis experience that suddenly overpowers a person. Rather, it's a daily reckoning. Each day I come to grips with the fact that I've been elected to be holy, that I am indeed in Christ, dead to sin. Each day I must refuse to give place to the old man who is dead, and each day I must in faith allow the new man to live for Christ.

That day-by-day reckoning is the key to holiness.

The Power for Holiness

✍ RICHARD OWEN ROBERTS

In the first chapter of Ephesians, Paul prayed a wonderful prayer that ends like this:

I pray also that the eyes of your heart may be enlightened in order that you may know the hope to which he has called you, the riches of his glorious inheritance in the saints, and his incomparably great power for us who believe. That power is like the working of his mighty strength, which he exerted in Christ when he raised him from the dead and seated him at his right hand in the heavenly realms, far above all rule and authority, power and dominion, and every title that can be given, not only in the present age but also in the one to come. And God placed all things under his feet and appointed him to be head over everything for the church, which is his body, the fullness of him who fills everything in every way. Ephesians 1:18-23

The glorious truths in this prayer undergird a great principle of holiness: None of us can calculate how much power it took to raise Christ from the dead, but Christ's resurrection took no more power than it takes to raise me from a grave of spiritual death.

In this prayer Paul suggested a series of truths that relate to our sanctification:

1. Great power was exercised in raising Christ from the grave.

2. Great power was exercised in raising Christ from earth and placing him at the right hand of the Father in the heavenly realms.

3. Great power was exercised in putting under Christ's feet all rule and authority, all power and dominion, and every title that can be given, and in making Christ head over all things.

These three truths apply to our own lives. When I was dead in trespasses and sins, the Spirit that raised Jesus from the grave raised me from spiritual death. The Power that set Jesus at the right hand of God is available to me so that even now I can live and reign with Christ in the heavenly places. The Power that put all other powers under Christ's feet is capable of putting under my feet all hostile powers in my life, so that with Christ I rule and reign victoriously.

When God elected us for holiness, he didn't just say, "I've chosen you for this role. Go to it." Instead, he tells us, "I've equipped you. Through the cross of Christ I've purchased your sanctification. Through the power of the Holy Spirit I've given you all you need to live a holy life."

Every single day we must realize that just as the Spirit raised Jesus from the grave, so he's raising us from the grave of sin. Just as the Spirit lifted Jesus' feet from earth and put him on the throne, so he's raising us from earth and enabling us to live with Christ in our minds and hearts in the heavenly realms. Just as the Holy Spirit put other powers under Christ's feet and made him victorious over all, so he's putting all our enemies under our feet. Today can be a day of victory through the power of the Holy Spirit.

Many times when I'm sorely tempted and find I have no strength in myself to prevail, I say, "Let the very Power that raised Jesus from the dead raise me from this grave of sin right now. Let the Power that transported Christ transport me to the heavenly realms right now. Let the Power that makes Christ rule victoriously enable me to be victorious right now." In that way, I lay hold of these glorious principles.

God has chosen us to be holy, and he has given us his power to make holiness possible. All we have to do is appropriate it.

Checking Up on the Inner and Outer Man

CALVIN MILLER

How can we know that God's Spirit is controlling our lives? We need to look both inside and outside ourselves to answer the question.

I think there are three basic questions we need to ask about our inner person.

First, Is my inner person always in communion with Christ? Paul said in 1 Thessalonians 5:17 to "pray continually." I don't think he meant that we are to go around constantly talking to God (or even constantly listening). A great human relationship doesn't demand constant talking or listening. When we enjoy the presence of a close friend, we feel comfortable without even saying a word. Just being with the person is a kind of communion. Paul is also speaking of that constant, continual awareness of Christ. The inner person must ever ask: Do I desire this continual communion with Christ? Am I consistently walking with him?

The second basic question is this: Do I live in continual confession? We will scarcely have peace if we dwell on every immoral act we commit. But every unconfessed transgression of our relationship with God is potentially a snag in our fellowship with him. We need to admit our sins: "If we confess our sins, he is faithful and just and will forgive us our sins and purify us from all unrighteousness" (1 John 1:9). This verse is talking about agreeing with God that we are sinners. This acknowledgment paves the way for his greatness and our humility. In the passage just cited, the substance is that if we confess any sin, he forgives every sin. This eliminates the nasty business of keeping books on our transgressions. We don't have to remember every sin to be forgiven for all sin. The very attitude of contrition before God brings not only his forgiveness but his pleasure. If we live in continual contrition, we will be continually in relationship with God.

Third, Am I living under Christ's thought-control? Am I keeping him in my mental awareness? I think that's what Paul means in 2 Corinthians 10:5: "We demolish arguments and every pretension that sets itself up against the knowledge of God, and we take captive every thought to make it obedient to Christ."

I find it easiest to stay in touch with my inner person when I'm out in God's wonderful world. I love to hike. Recently my wife and I hiked the Grand Canyon. In such a marvelous place, God's nature music surrounds me and resonates with the inner Christ. Here the glory of the Father God of nature and his inward Son celebrate each other in the center of my life.

But life in Christ is not always an inner celebration. We demonstrate that the inner life is valid only when we allow the indwelling Savior to reach out to those around us who are in need. How can we know if we are allowing him to reach through us? By asking these basic questions.

Perhaps the first question we need to ask is: Do I relate to others in a spirit of thankfulness? In our cold world, we often remain impersonal to those in need of our responses. Sometimes we don't even say thank you to the checkers at the market or to others who show us little acts of kindness.

Our responsiveness to all who interact with us or give us any affirmation of all we are is essential to the demonstration of the Christ-life. I have a motto that I often repeat: No gift is ever to be despised. Therefore, when a little child gives me a picture she's drawn of me in the pulpit (drawn sometimes during church), I celebrate the act and the child. It's a beautiful gift and it always delights me. Gratitude is a characteristic that our "outer man" should display.

Consider the second question as well: Do I identify with others? I like what Norman Vincent Peale calls "shooting prayers." Sometimes while stopped at a red light as a car whizzes by in front of me, I try to see what the driver's face is registering. I try to imagine that person with her cares and needs, and then I pray for her. I heard a preacher say that 60 percent of the people carry around with them what they think is a tremendous problem. If that's true, then more than half the people we see casually are very troubled. We Christians need to identify with them and pray for them.

Jesus, I believe, taught us to make this question primary: Do I care for my neighbors' needs? Jesus put love for one's neighbor right next to love for God when he summarized the Ten Commandments (Matthew 22:37-40). But our love for others needs to be more than an attitude. It should show itself in our actions. Paul said in 1 Corinthians 9:19, "Though I am free and belong to no man, I make myself a slave to everyone, to win as many as possible." The servant spirit is a characteristic of a person who is submitted to Christ.

Consider this question as well: Am I willing to spend time alone with God? Do I make the necessary time for God? Will I use that time to talk to him and to listen? Jesus said in Matthew 6:6 that we are to shut the closet door when we pray. When we do this we shut out the hassle and focus on him. That's a good time to organize all our inner priorities, to realize that our top priority is the kingdom of God.

Surely there can be no more important question than this: Am I winning others to Christ? Do I at least care about their salvation? If I care, sooner or later I will attempt to win people to him. If I am a person of compassion, I'll recognize that people without Jesus don't have hope. If I care about them, I'll want to bring them into relationship with God.

To grow myself, I must answer this question: Am I faithful in public worship? Do I go to church? I think it is impossible to please God or to grow in Christ without gathering together with other Christians. Hebrews 10:25 says, "Let us not give up meeting together, as some are in the habit of doing, but let us encourage one another." We need to worship with others, to learn to have fellowship with others.

Do I care about social justice? When I hear about terrorism, wars, political corruption, do I think about how the victims must feel? Once my family was accosted by an assailant and held against our will. I remember the terror in my children's eyes. When acts of violence occur all over the world, Jesus identifies with the sufferers. Do I care as he does? Do I do anything to make the world a more just place?

It is important that God fill both our inner and our outer person. We cannot hoard God and keep him all for ourselves. If we don't let his love overflow into the outer world, our spiritual life will shrivel. On the other hand, if we try to live like Christ without having his Spirit inside us, we will turn into hypocrites. If God is in our inner life, his love will pour into our outer life and our actions will gradually become more and more like his.

RELATED ARTICLES

Chapter 4: **Being Holy As God Is Holy**
Chapter 9: **Self-Love and Self-Centeredness**
Chapter 10: **The Problem of Low Self-Esteem**
Chapter 12: **The Purpose of the Spiritual Disciplines**
Chapter 15: **Responding to God in Worship**

CHAPTER

3

How People Grow

This chapter tells about various people, past and present, famous and not-so-famous, who have discovered how to grow spiritually. Although they grew in a variety of ways—through other people, experiences, or ideas—they all had the same goal, to be committed to living as God wanted them to.

From Slave Trader to Hymn Writer

JOHN POLLOCK

The hard-bitten young sailor stood grimly at the wheel as the battered vessel plunged and rose and shuddered. Her sails were gone; part of her side had caved in; great seas washed over her. Most of the crew of twelve believed that the ship must soon go down in the North Atlantic and all would drown on that terrible day, March 10, 1748.

John Newton had been the worst man among them. As a boy of nineteen he had deserted the British Navy; upon recapture, he had been flogged. Later he became a slave trader on the West Coast of Africa and then a slave in chains himself. During this captivity he had smuggled home a pitiful letter to his father, though he had offended him again and again. This battered ship, the *Greyhound,* sailing from Liverpool, had been asked to find him. By an amazing coincidence her captain had met him on a distant shore, but Newton's fortunes had turned again and he nearly refused to come.

The captain and crew soon wished they had never taken him on board. As they traded up and down the coast (not in slaves), he showed himself not only the hardest swearer, but a ribald, blaspheming atheist. Then came the storm. They were used to storms, but the ship was rotten after a long voyage in the tropics. As John Newton labored at the pumps, facing death if she broke up or foundered in the exceptional seas, a chance remark suddenly faced him with the appalling insight that God, whom he despised and denied, might exist after all. If so, John Newton was about to face judgment.

Up from the depths of his mind came the long forgotten teaching of his devout mother, who had died when he was seven years old. His terrible past, as a blasphemer who would wreck the faith of any man he met; as a lecher whose body raped the black girls in his power, although his heart was given to a pure English maiden named Polly, living in Kent, a girl he scarcely hoped to win; all this overwhelmed him until, in deep contrition, he sought forgiveness of the God he had scorned. When the storm abated and they had survived, he began to believe God might grant his request, although doubts of God's existence still assailed him.

In the days that followed, he struggled to believe. When the immediate danger had passed, his crew mates quickly forgot their prayers, but John Newton spent his off-duty hours trying to grasp the gospel. No pastor or Christian brother was present to help, but insight followed insight as the fog of unbelief gradually dispersed. When, weeks overdue, the battered ship dropped anchor in an Irish harbor, Newton had surrendered to God and believed that Christ had died for his sins. Yet so hazy was his understanding that he saw himself as a galley slave, laboring to offset the wickedness of his past.

For the rest of his life Newton honored March 10, 1748, as the "hour I first believed," when amazing grace had "saved a wretch like me." But his growth as a Christian was painfully slow. Experience, people, and insights from books and the Scriptures all played their part.

The owner of the *Greyhound,* his father's friend, offered him command of a slaver, for Newton was a skilled and experienced seaman. He asked to go first as second-in-command, and sailed from England, secure in the knowledge that Polly had not rejected him though her hand was not yet his.

He resolved to be true to her and worthy of Christ, but he had forgotten what he afterward described as "the dreadful effects of the slave trade" on the morals of those engaged in it.

With no fellow Christian on board his new ship, the *Brownlow,* he slackened in prayer, forgot to read his Bible, and cooled his gratitude for past mercies. By the time they reached the slave coast of West Africa he was "almost as bad as before," except that he no longer swore. When the slaves came on board, and he saw the lecherous grins of the sailors as they each chose a black girl to rape, his good resolutions dissolved, his blood surged, and he went down into the hold where the girls lay naked and chained.

After that he "followed a course of evil of which, a few months before, I should not have supposed myself any longer capable." Temptation proved stronger than conscience, or thoughts of Polly, or of Christ. Then Newton fell ill with a fever while staying on the very island where he had suffered as a slave but now was honored as a guest. Debauchery had weakened him and he knew he might die. His heart smote him as he recalled his solemn vows, his sincere gratitude for deliverance. Having crucified the Son of God afresh, he believed that he had shut and locked the door of hope. Then he remembered that his Judge was also his Father of infinite mercy.

Weak, almost delirious, Newton dragged himself to a remote corner of the island and cast himself on the mercy of God. No particular text or spiritual light flashed into his mind, but he was able to hope and believe in a crucified Savior. Peace returned to his conscience. Within two days he was fit again.

The experience was decisive. He never backslid violently again. All his life he would be keenly aware how often he failed his Lord, but he was now genuinely seeking to grow. When the *Brownlow* had made the "middle passage" across the Atlantic, the slaves were sold at Charleston, South Carolina, and the ship was in harbor, loading with tobacco and cotton, Newton slipped away into the woods. "My views of Christian truth were very imperfect and my conduct inconsistent. Spiritually I chiefly depended on myself. I knew I had been very bad. I had a desire to be better, and thought I should in time make myself so."

In May 1754, six years after the Atlantic storm, Captain John Newton, age twenty-nine and in command of the slaver *African* from Liverpool, brought his cargo of slaves safely to the small West Indian island of St. Kitts. Newton had commanded two earlier voyages and had transported hundreds of his fellow beings to slavery and hard labor for life. He tried to be humane but no voice had been raised against the slave trade; it was considered honorable and necessary. Newton said afterward that had he realized its wickedness, he would have stopped at once. He thought it an unpleasant occupation, like that of a jailer, but he had a wife, his adorable Polly, to support. His prayers, as he had sailed toward St. Kitts that spring, were dominated by two petitions: that he might be freed from this distasteful occupation, and that he might know God better.

At St. Kitts, Captain Newton was popular at the planters' evening parties, served by house slaves, for he was amusing, could write verse, and had a fine singing voice. At one party he met another captain who was not in the slave trade, one Alexander Clunie, a lively, cheerful Scot in his late thirties. Some "casual expressions in mixed company" revealed to both men that they, alone among hosts and guests, loved God. They walked back to the quayside together and soon became inseparable, preferring to spend their evenings in one or the other's cabin talking of the things of God rather than idling the hours away at parties.

Clunie, who lived in London, was a well-taught Christian. He opened Newton's understanding. The Bible became like a new book. Newton realized at last that the distant God whom he had served in fear and humble gratitude, but without joy or intimacy, could be a friend, walking at his side. The name of Jesus became sweet to his ear. "The knowledge of His love to me produced a return of love to Him. I now adored Him and admired Him." John Newton made an unreserved surrender to Jesus, "My Lord, my Life, my way, my end."

Back in England a few weeks later, Newton suffered a sudden illness that prevented him from taking a new command to sea. In due time he received a respectable post in the Customs Service in Liverpool. Here his faith grew fast, and when George Whitefield came to town and swayed great crowds with his glorious voice as he proclaimed the gospel, Newton determined to devote the rest of his days to preaching "amazing grace." Ten years after he had met Clunie he was ordained a clergyman, despite delays and disappointments.

Soon afterward came a fresh insight. It ensured that he would not only be one of the best-loved hymn writers of the day but a powerful influence on the age. Reading a pamphlet newly written by his friend John Wesley, his eyes were opened to the wickedness of the slave trade. He became utterly ashamed that he had engaged in it. A few more years passed before its abolition became even a remote political possibility, but when the campaign began, John Newton was the only Abolitionist with inside knowledge of its horrors.

The struggle lasted a quarter of a century. By a last, touching providence, the aged Newton lived just long enough to see the trade abolished on both sides of the Atlantic Ocean, which he had sailed with his cargoes of slaves.

Politician Turned Reformer

JOHN POLLOCK

A few years before the French Revolution, an ugly little Englishman with a delightful character and a great sense of humor sat squeezed in a post chaise that bumped and swung along the roads of France. Beside him, taking up most of the seat, was a huge, jolly bear of a man with one of the most brilliant minds in England.

The smaller of the two, William Wilberforce, M.P., was rich and of political importance, although only twenty-five years old, for he had recently won Yorkshire for Pitt, the young prime minister and his bosom friend.

Wilberforce's widowed mother and his sister had wanted to winter in the south of France, taking also a delicate cousin, Bessy Smith. As the ladies would fill the family carriage, Wilberforce sought a traveling companion for the chaise, and happened to meet his former schoolmaster, Isaac Milner, now a tutor at Cambridge University.

Unknown to Wilberforce, Milner had become an evangelical Christian. Wilberforce, when a boy, had enthusiastically followed Christ while living with an uncle and aunt after his father's death. These relatives had been Whitefield's converts and friends of John Newton, once a sailor and slave trader, now the great hymn writer and preacher. The boy had looked on the whimsical Newton, with his incredible but true tales of the sea and of Africa, as his hero. Then his mother, alarmed that her son was fast becoming a "little Methodist," removed him, and scrubbed his soul until nothing was left of his fervor except a more moral tone than usual among men of fashion. And he went to church weekly, though his choice was Unitarian.

In the chaise, a religious topic came up. Wilberforce fired off some Unitarian notions and ridiculed John Newton's views. Milner tried to explain evangelical Christianity, but Wilberforce showed little interest.

They had not been long on the Riviera when the prime minister wrote Wilberforce to return to support him on parliamentary reform. As the two travelers prepared to set out again, leaving the ladies in the sunshine, Wilberforce casually picked up a book belonging to Bessy Smith, *The Rise and Progress of Religion in the Soul* by Philip Doddridge, and leafed through it. He asked Milner's opinion. "It is one of the best books ever written," replied Milner, seizing his chance. "Let us take it with us and read it on our journey."

The effect, as they drove northward, was dramatic. By the time Wilberforce arrived at 10 Downing Street, he had reached intellectual assent to the biblical view of Christ as Son of God and Savior of man. He thrust it to the back of his mind and plunged back into politics and social life.

The next summer, 1785, he and Milner set out again to rejoin the ladies and bring them back through Switzerland. This time, for mile after mile, the two men read and discussed the New Testament until intellectual assent became profound conviction that unless Wilberforce repented and trusted Christ, he "should perish everlastingly." But evangelicals were despised and derided; coming out as a believer might ruin his political future. Struggling to yield his stubborn will, he turned gloomy and sad and decided that his only hope was to withdraw from politics and become a clergyman.

Back in England the conflict continued until Wilberforce felt that unless he could confide in a spiritual counselor he would go out of his mind. Covering his tracks, lest his fashionable friends discover, he secretly visited his boyhood hero, John Newton. Newton's own slow conversion from lecher and slaver to humble Christian made him an understanding adviser. Moreover he convinced Wilberforce that God could use him mightily in the counsels of the state.

Wilberforce walked out of Newton's study that December day of 1785 with a less-burdened conscience; yet it was not until Easter that he reached joyful assurance that he had been redeemed from the slavery of sin by a Savior who had paid the price with his own blood.

Conversion had been a long, drawn-out experience. And it was primarily through experiences that William Wilberforce grew to full stature as a Christian.

He began immediately to serve God in political life, making tentative attempts to right some of the wrongs of eighteenth-century England. Then he received a letter from one of the only two other evangelicals in the House of Commons, Captain Sir Charles Middleton, a naval administrator who later, as Admiral Lord Barham, was the supreme strategist of the Trafalgar campaign. Before the American War, Middleton had served in the West Indies, where all labor was done by slaves imported from Africa. He now urged young Wilberforce to lead a parliamentary campaign to stop the Atlantic slave trade.

Almost all England believed the slave trade to be an economic necessity. In

Parliament, a strong West Indian lobby would violently oppose any attempt at Abolition. Only a few voices, such as John Wesley's, had been raised against the trade.

Wilberforce traveled to Kent where the Middletons lived. He already knew Sir Charles and his wife, an accomplished artist and woman of great benevolence who longed to rouse the country's conscience. They took him to their rector, James Ramsay, formerly a surgeon and clergyman in the West Indies who had been forced out of his parish by irate slave owners after he had protested at brutal punishments inflicted on the slaves. Wilberforce met Nestor, Ramsay's delightful black servant, whom he had bought as a slave and set free.

The Middletons had learned much about slavery from a young Moravian missionary, Benjamin La Trobe, who now lived in London. Wilberforce paid him a visit. Fact by fact, Wilberforce learned the horrors of the slave trade; and all the time John Newton, bitterly ashamed of his own part in it, which had continued for some years after he had become a believing Christian because no one had then spoken of it as evil, urged Wilberforce to take up the cause. Wilberforce wondered whether he had the strength or the faith to change public opinion and force abolition through a reluctant Parliament. He hesitated until one night, poring over a mass of papers and statistics by the light of guttering candles, he suddenly realized how high was the death rate of slaves in the ships engaged in the trade. "From that moment, so enormous, so dreadful, so irremediable did its wickedness appear, that my own mind was completely made up for abolition. Let the consequences be what they would, I from this time determined that I would never rest until I had effected its abolition."

He soon found that he had stirred up a hornet's nest. Never strong physically, he was overwhelmed by the work of preparing his case to lay before Parliament, especially as he was also engaged in the moral reformation of England. Pitt, as prime minister, helped him by ordering an investigation of the slave trade by a standing committee of the Privy Council; this increased Wilberforce's load as he briefed counsel and members until, in February 1788, he collapsed. He fell so ill that his political opponents prepared for the by-election that his death would cause.

The doctors saved his life by prescribing opium, then considered a pure drug; but as he reached convalescence he fell into a "dark night of the soul," perhaps partly through the side effects of the medicine. He cried to God to "restore me to rest, quietness and comfort, in the world; or in another by removing me hence into a state of peace and happiness."

He dreaded the abolition battle ahead. "Give me grace to trust firmly in thee, that I may not sink under my sorrows nor be disquieted with the *fears* of those evils that cannot without thy permission fall upon me." Fears closed in from every side, but at length his experience of Christ's power outweighed them. Wilberforce slowly returned to calmness and a determination to persevere.

Physically frailer, spiritually stronger, with a deep love of the Bible, Wilberforce went back to the Commons. On May 11, 1789, in a great speech of three and a half hours, he asked the House to vote for the abolition of the slave trade.

The House refused. Thus began a parliamentary struggle of eighteen years. One opponent complained that Wilberforce "is blessed with a very sufficient quantity of that enthusiastic spirit, which is so far from yielding that it grows more vigorous from blows."

He preserved his humor and charm; he loved his enemies while never letting them forget their guilt; and throughout these long and painful years each partial success or renewed failure taught him more of the love of God, until at last, on a February day in 1807, the Commons voted by a large majority for abolition. Almost the whole House rose to its feet and cheered Wilberforce, who sat, head bowed, with tears streaming down his face.

From that night he had not only saved the slaves, but had become the moral leader of the Western world.

A Coolie for Christ

JOHN POLLOCK

Coolies dropped their baskets; women, with their bound feet, hobbled closer; even a few shopkeepers left their nearby stalls. Twenty-three-year-old Hudson Taylor climbed onto a barrel. Like all Protestant missionaries, he wore narrow trousers and a frock coat that contrasted strongly with the dress of Chinese teachers and gentlemen in their flowing robes, and the crowd was more amused than frightened by this "foreign devil."

The frock coat fascinated them. Before he could begin to preach, young Taylor had to answer questions about pleats and buttons and braid. At last he launched into a warm and simple proclamation of Jesus. As he preached he noticed that one man had moved up close and was transfixed by the message. Taylor paused and addressed him personally.

"Yes, yes," replied the man. "What you say is doubtless very true. But honorable Foreign Teacher, may I ask you one question?"

This was what Hudson Taylor had intended.

"I have been pondering all the while you have been preaching, and the subject is no clearer to my mind."

Taylor was delighted at the coming opportunity to expound the faith more fully.

Then the man asked his question.

"The buttons," he began, "in the front of the honorable garment must be for wet or windy weather, but this is what I cannot understand: what can be the meaning of those buttons *in the middle of the honorable back?*"

"Yes," chorused the crowd, "in the middle of the back!" Text and sermon were forgotten because every Victorian frock coat had three buttons in the small of the back.

Taylor left the town with that question in his ears. The useless buttons summed up the annoyance of Western dress in a Chinese setting. It marked him as a foreigner, and therefore either dangerous or funny. It made him sweat in hot weather and shiver in cold.

Hudson Taylor had already thought of making himself into a Chinese. But this would mean more than buying a robe, shaving most of his head, dyeing the rest of his sandy hair black, and weaving into it a long pigtail. The step would horrify other missionaries and enrage consuls and merchants. They regarded Western dress as an essential mark of superiority. Even his parents in England would be shocked.

But he knew he must take the step in faith as a response to a clear call of God. A few weeks later when the consul threatened him with punishment if he preached away from the treaty ports, Hudson hesitated no longer. He bought a satin robe, suitable for a teacher.

When he tried concocting a dye for his hair, an ammonia bottle exploded and threw acid into his face. His extra thick spectacles saved his eyes but the acid would have suffocated him had not the water butt been filled to the brim an hour before. He might have died of his burns had not his medical colleague, Dr. Parker, so often out, been at home. Taylor counted no less than four providences that showed the hand of God.

He recovered quickly, then endured the painful shaving of his head and acquired a pigtail. On August 23, 1855, he walked out of Shanghai in the billowing garments of a preacher. At once he found a new freedom. He could walk unnoticed. When he preached he was generally recognized as foreign, but his hearers accepted him as an honored guest wearing civilized clothes instead of "foreign devil's" contemptible dress.

The rage and disgust of fellow Westerners was nothing to his inner joy. "The future is a ravelled maze," he wrote to his parents, "and my path hath ever been made plain one step at a time. . . . I think I do love *him* more than ever, and long to serve him as he directs, more than ever."

One year later, in the summer of 1856, Hudson Taylor took another great step forward to maturity; again it was the result of an unexpected experience.

In his desire to fit himself for the arduous task of opening the forbidden inland of China to the gospel, he had been learning all the time, especially after he joined forces with a veteran Scottish missionary, William Burns. Burns, for his part, quickly noticed the advantage that Chinese dress gave to Taylor, and followed his example.

The southern treaty port of Swatow became a center for their preaching tours in a district of great beauty. Taylor would come in at night, exhausted and blistered, but a passing missionary noticed the respect in which he was held by the Chinese: "His influence was like that of a fragrant flower, diffusing the sweetness of true Christianity around him." Burns and Taylor, however, were unable to hire a preaching place in Swatow. Taylor therefore returned to Shanghai intending to bring back his surgical instruments so that he could open a healing hall (though he was not yet a qualified physician) where they would also preach.

He found the Shanghai storehouse in ashes. Almost all he possessed had been burned, to his acute disappointment and vexation. Taylor decided to go by canal to Ningpo where Dr. Parker might sell him surplus equipment.

All went well until he reached a town where the canal's level had fallen too low for boats. He decided to walk to the sea, sixteen miles away, and take a junk. He engaged coolies and told his new servant to bring them on while he walked ahead in his uncomfortable Chinese shoes.

Everything went wrong. The coolies proved to be opium addicts; the new servant absconded with the camp bed and his luggage box, including the few surgical instruments to have survived the fire. Hudson found himself alone at dusk in a strange town. A young man offered to lead him to lodging but deceived him, and he spent the night on the steps of a temple among beggars who tried to rob him and might have murdered him had he not kept himself awake by praying out loud and singing hymns, "to the great annoyance of my companions."

At dawn he slept. At sunrise he was shaken awake by the deceitful young man who damanded money and menacingly seized his sleeve. Taylor lost his temper and gripped the man's arm with such unexpected force that he withdrew a few feet. Hudson lay down again, angry, until the gun signaled the opening of the city gates. After argument, Hudson agreed to give him the price of two candles.

Walking painfully back in the heat toward Shanghai, almost penniless, his belongings lost by fire and robbery, Hudson felt perplexed and hurt. At a wayside tea shop he ate some eggs and cakes and bathed his blistered feet, then slept. He walked on refreshed, and as the tension eased he suddenly realized that his loss of temper had been un-Christlike; that he had been anxious about lost luggage rather than the lost souls around; and had resented having no place to sleep rather than remembering that the Son of man had had nowhere to lay his head. As he walked, "I came as a sinner and pleaded the blood of Jesus, realizing that I was accepted in him, pardoned, cleansed, sanctified—and oh the love of Jesus, how great I felt it to be." By the time Hudson Taylor reached Shanghai he was serene, despite hardships and uncertainties. He had committed himself and his affairs to the Lord.

The stolen goods had been worth the then considerable sum of £40. A few days later the home mail came in after its long voyage. Among his letters was one, posted months before, from a Mr. Berger, a businessman in England whom Hudson scarcely recalled. It contained a donation of preceisely £40.

This and several other extraordinary providences fostered a daring thought that had been germinating in his mind.

He had come out to China like any other missionary, as a member of a society that contracted to pay him a small quarterly salary. But the China Evangelization Society was so inefficient that his salary was never paid in full and frequently did not arrive, reducing him to sore straits.

Some years earlier in England, while a medical apprentice to an absent-minded uncle, Hudson Taylor had for a time trained himself to "live by faith." If he needed money, he asked God but never reminded his uncle about overdue salary. Thus he had simulated the conditions he might meet in inland China if cut off from supplies by brigands or floods, and he received many amazing answers to prayer.

These now came to mind and, within a few months of the robbery, he decided to cut adrift from the hopeless Society and live by faith.

He made himself banners that proclaimed in Chinese characters two of the great place names of the Old Testament: *Ebenezer* ("hitherto hath the Lord helped us") and *Jehovah-Jireh* ("the Lord will provide").

He had learned that both were true, and he built the China Inland Mission of the future on this faith: "God's work done in God's way will never lack God's supplies."

Crusader for the Oppressed

JAMES C. HEFLEY

Dorothea Dix was a frail woman. When she was only twenty-nine, she was told she probably wouldn't live many more years because of a lung disease. And even if she survived, the doctor predicted she would be an invalid.

The doctor was mistaken: this frail woman went on to become one of the great social reformers of nineteenth-century America.

To improve her health, Dorothea went to England to rest. While there she read the New Testament through several times, constantly asking herself as she read, "What would Christ have me do with my life?" Upon her return home to Massachusetts in 1841, she found the answer when a minister asked her to teach the Bible to prisoners in a local jail.

She began her classes but was constantly interrupted by wild screams from the back of the jail. A prisoner answered her question: "Those are the lunatics, ma'am. They ought to gag them."

Appalled, Dorothea went to the jailer and asked to see the "lunatics." He tried to convince her that she really didn't want to, but to no avail. She was given passage.

To her horror she found two women inside a cold stone cell, dressed in rags and chained in cages. An old woman, about seventy-five, was almost naked; a young woman, about eighteen and blue with cold, kept pleading, "Please help me, ma'am!"

Running back to the jailer, Dorothea demanded, "What have they done to deserve treatment like this?"

He replied, "Nothing, ma'am—they're just lunatics."

Dorothea hurried home and returned with clothes and blankets. She also asked the jailer and other town officials for a stove to warm their room. The authorities answered, "They're not worth it. They are just human rubbish."

She began examining the treatment of people with severe mental illness in other towns. To her dismay, she discovered that they were treated the same way all over her state, and presumably everywhere else as well. Nobody seemed to care; this was the way things had always been. Dorothea decided to take the matter into her own hands.

She meticulously gathered evidence, prepared a speech, and went before the Massachusetts legislature. "Gentlemen," she declared, "I call your attention to the state of insane persons confined within this commonwealth, in cages, closets, cellars, stalls, and pens—chained, naked, beaten with rods and lashed into obedience." She pointed out that Massachusetts' treatment of the insane was often far worse than the treatment of slaves in the South.

Her speech, which was widely reported, shook New England. It opened the eyes of people who had been blind to the appalling facts. People began to get concerned. Reform began. Prisoners were pulled from the dungeons and given adequate shelter, clothing, and food.

From Massachusetts, Dorothea then moved on to other state legislatures. She carried her reform to Canada, Scotland, and England. In Italy she found dungeons filled with the mentally ill right next door to the Vatican, so she went personally to the pope—and he enacted reforms. Slowly but surely, the wheels began turning all around the world. Hospitals were built for the mentally ill, and care and treatment became more humane.

Though she wasn't supposed to live a healthy life beyond age twenty-nine, Dorothea crusaded for reforms for the mentally ill until she was eighty years old. And it all began when a young woman asked the Lord what he wanted to do with her life.

Rescuer of the Hopeless

JAMES C. HEFLEY

The Pacific Garden Mission in Chicago has had a reputation for effectively ministering to the city's down and out. One icy night in 1897, Harry Monroe, an ex-counterfeiter who had been converted at the mission, was leading the singing when a young drunkard was ushered to a seat. Monroe stopped the singing and prayed aloud, "God save this poor, poor boy." The boy jerked his head up and listened intently to the sermon and the testimonies. His name was Mel Trotter.

Trotter had started drinking at age nineteen. Soon his drinking was out of hand, and it began to affect his performance at work. Trotter began losing one job after another. Married young, he kept promising his wife he'd straighten up. He would stay off booze for a while, but his dry times didn't last long. After a few days or weeks, he'd nosedive deeper than before. He traded his horse, his medication, anything he could get his hands on for whiskey.

His wife had a baby, a boy. He loved his son, but his behavior did not change. He kept right on drinking. One day he came home after a ten-day spree and found his baby son dead in his wife's arms. In agony, he wanted to kill himself for neglecting his child. His wife, who was a Christian, put the baby down, took Mel into her arms, and dropped to her knees in prayer. Listening to her pray,

Mel vowed, "I'll never drink another drop." But after the baby's funeral he staggered home drunk.

Finally, in despair, Trotter decided to end his life. On January 19, 1897, he headed off to Lake Michigan to drown himself. As he walked along Van Buren Street, a fellow literally reached out and pulled him through the doors of the Pacific Garden Mission.

And that was when the speaker, Harry Monroe, stopped his sermon to pray specifically for Mel. After the service, Monroe spoke to him. "Jesus loves you," he told him. "Make room in your heart for him now." And Mel, having sobered up slowly throughout the service, knelt in front of Monroe and gave his heart to Christ.

From that day on, instead of slipping out of the house to go to bars, Trotter spent his spare time at the mission. He played the guitar, led the singing, and even visited churches in the area with Monroe.

His growth in the faith advanced rapidly. Three years after his conversion, he was appointed superintendent of a rescue mission in Grand Rapids. There he spend the next forty years in fruitful ministry. He used this mission as a base to start sixty-six other rescue missions across the country, all designed to reach the hopeless and helpless for Christ.

Prisoners for God

JAMES C. HEFLEY

Corrie ten Boom lived with her sister and father over a watch shop in Haarlem, Holland. The shop had been in her family for one hundred years, and the ten Booms were pillars of the community.

After World War II erupted in Europe, the ten Booms became aware of the persecution of Jews in Germany. This concerned them, but it was too far away to affect them personally. When the Germans occupied Holland, however, the ten Booms got involved. They realized that in spite of the evil government they must do what God would have them do—protect his people. Corrie's father put their feelings into these words: "In this household, God's people are always welcome."

Hiding people would not be easy. The Dutch underground movement sent a "building inspector" (who was actually one of Europe's most famous architects) to design a secret room from part of Corrie's bedroom. A false wall was put in, and a sliding door placed in the back of a closet built into the wall. The "hiding place" was ready.

The ten Booms began welcoming Jews. Seven became permanent guests, while others came and went. These Jews lived comfortably on an upper floor of the ten Boom home. Whenever Nazi soldiers would arrive to do a search, the "guests" could dash into the secret room, close the sliding door, and stay there until the danger passed. To the soldiers, it appeared that this was simply the home of an elderly watchmaker and his two spinster daughters.

Inevitably, the ten Booms were found out, probably through an informer. Though the Jews in their home were able to stay safely hidden in the hiding place, Corrie, Betsie, and their father were arrested and taken to concentration camps.

Corrie and Betsie ended up in Ravensbruck, a women's extermination camp in the heart of Germany. The horrors they experienced there are hard for us to imagine. Eleven-hour work days, standing in formation for hours at a time in all kinds of weather, lice, dirt, humiliation, even beatings. At one point Betsie, already very weak, fell down while working and was whipped by the guards. Corrie could do nothing to help. Betsie only said, "Don't look, Corrie. Look at Jesus only."

The Germans permitted the prisoners to have worship in their barracks, though they were quite confident that they would be too tired and discouraged to do so very often. But Corrie and Betsie would gather the suffering women around them and read from the Bible. One would read in Dutch as translations were passed along to the many nationalities represented. Many women in the barracks came to know Christ because of Corrie and Betsie's ministry.

Betsie died in the prison camp. Due to a clerical mix-up, Corrie was eventually let go. The week after her release, all the women her age were put to death.

Corrie and Betsie's great courage is an inspiration to us today. They were willing to stand for what they knew was right regardless of the consequences. And though the consequences were horrible, they never stopped trusting God.

Helper of the Homeless

JAMES C. HEFLEY

Harry Holt's life was never the same after he saw a film about orphaned children in Korea.

Holt, a middle-aged Oregon farmer, knew he had to do something to help those children, some of whom had been fathered by American GIs. He and his wife, Bertha, decided at first to support one orphan for each member of their family. In 1955, Harry flew to Korea to pick up twelve orphans, four of them for other families.

On this trip, he saw hundreds of orphans. When he came back, he spoke so convincingly of the needs in Korea that within a year he had lined up six hundred Christian families to welcome new children. Congress had to pass special legislation to make this immigration possible.

Holt threw himself into his work with orphans. On one of his so-called orphan lifts, he sat up all night and nursed twenty-five children who were sick with measles, dysentery, or pneumonia. On another trip he experienced sharp pain and was told to get some rest, but he insisted on going on to another village where children needed him.

Harry Holt lived nine years after he made his first orphan lift. In those nine years this "ordinary farmer" who wanted to do something to help Korean orphans found homes for three thousand children. He founded Holt Children's Services (Post Office Box 2880, Eugene, Oregon 97402), which has expanded its services to include both adoptions and foster care for children from India, Southeast Asia, the Philippines, and Latin America.

Persevering through Tragedy

JAMES C. HEFLEY

Betty Mitchell, a long-time missionary with the Christian and Missionary Alliance, is one of the most remarkable people I've ever met in over twenty years of traveling the world to research stories for Christian books. To tell Betty's story, I must go back to 1945 and start with Archie, the man who was to become her husband.

Archie was pastoring a church in Oregon. For a special outing one day, he took his pregnant wife and five Sunday school children on a picnic in the woods. While looking for a place to eat lunch, one of the boys poked at what appeared to be a parachute. Archie's warning to get away came too late. The Japanese balloon bomb, which had drifted across the Pacific Ocean, exploded with devastating force. All the picnickers were killed except Archie, the pastor, who happened to be shielded by a large tree.

Betty Pazke, a member of Archie's church, lost two younger sisters in the blast. She and Archie were drawn together by the losses of their loved ones, and two years later they became man and wife. After their marriage, they went to Vietnam as Alliance missionaries, arriving in Hanoi in 1948 for language study. By 1962 they were serving at a leprosarium—a jungle hospital—deep in the central highlands of South Vietman. Archie served as superintendent of the leprosarium, and Betty assisted him while caring for four energetic offspring.

South Vietnam was now engaged in a bloody war with Communist Viet Cong guerillas supported by North Vietnamese regular troops. The jungle around the hospital was a kind of no-man's land in which guerillas roamed at will, making occasional raids on the local populace. The mission hospital welcomed patients without regard to politics, so the missionaries felt they were safe. Nevertheless, in 1962 a Viet Cong raiding party swept onto the grounds and took as captives Archie, the hospital doctor, and an agricultural missionary.

The morning after the raid, Betty and her four children, along with four missionary nurses, fled to the town of Banmethuot, twelve miles away, where the mission had a Bible school near a South Vietnamese army post. Betty was determined to remain in the area. First, she believed her calling was to serve the people, and second, she wanted to be there when Archie was released.

Her commitment was immediately tested when she volunteered to help in the local public hospital. The nurse told her, "Some of these people are Viet Cong. You may not want to bother with them. We understand that your husband was captured by the communists."

Betty remembered a text from the sermon given by a fellow missionary, Bob Ziemer, the previous Sunday: "Those who hope in the Lord will renew their strength" (Isaiah 40:31). She prayed, "Lord give me strength to love those who may be my enemies." He did.

She asked an orderly to take her through the ward and cough when they passed the bed of a Viet Cong. In this way she was directed to a communist couple. The man lay in a bed with a cast to the waist. They were cold at first, but when she kept coming back they became responsive. One happy day the woman told her, "You are the first person who ever told me about Christ. He is in my heart now."

Betty and her children remained in Vietnam for five more years before going home on furlough. While they were away the North Vietnamese soldiers overran Banmethuot, dynamited the mission houses, and killed six missionaries while taking two others captive. To the surprise of many people, Betty insisted on coming back when the houses were rebuilt. With her children away in school much of the year, she remained there for the next seven years. I talked with her during a trip to Vietnam to research a book on the martyrdom of missionaries. "This is where God wants me," she said. "I'll stay until he directs otherwise."

She recounted stories from tribespeople who came in from the jungle claiming they had seen her husband. "I believe them," she said. "Archie is out there, and one day, in God's good time, he will be released."

Then in 1975 the North Vietnamese attacked again. This time Betty and eight other missionaries were taken prisoner and forced to march from South Vietnam to Hanoi. Along the way she asked people if they had seen her husband. No one had.

After months of imprisonment, the captives were released. With North Vietnam now firmly in control of the entire country, the missionaries could not go back. Betty went to Malaysia.

The last we heard, Betty was still there, serving faithfully and waiting expectantly for her husband, now missing for more than twenty years, to be released. Reports continue to come of tribespeople seeing Caucasian prisoners in the Southeast Asian jungles. Betty believes Archie is among these prisoners.

Her favorite passage is 2 Corinthians 1:8-11:

I think you ought to know, dear brothers, about the hard time we went through in Asia. We were really crushed and overwhelmed, and feared we would never live through it. We felt we were doomed to die and saw how powerless we were to help ourselves; but that was good, for then we put everything into the hands of God, who alone could save us, for he can even raise the dead. And he did help us, and saved us from a terrible death; yes, and we expect him to do it again and again. But you must help us too, by praying for us. For much thanks and praise will go to God from you who see his wonderful answers to your prayers for our safety! (TLB)

Betty Mitchell continues to hope, and she continues to serve.

Triumph through Tragedy

JAMES C. HEFLEY

Christians over the age of forty remember the 1956 massacre of five young American missionaries by Auca Indians in the jungles of western Ecuador. The tragic event received vast publicity because a photographer and writer from *Life* magazine covered the story. *Life*'s circulation was huge, so the tragedy was published all over the world.

Part of the reason this story touches so many people's hearts was that these five missionaries were all married and some had children. Twenty-five years after the massacre, my wife and I visited the widows of the men killed by the Aucas.

Olive Fleming, wife of Peter, told us, "I've never really felt bitterness or resentment, mainly because I feel God prepared me for that experience. Pete had kept a diary while he was a single missionary in Ecuador, and I was reading it just before Palm Beach [as the missionaries called the area]. Several times Pete wrote that he would be willing to give his life for the Aucas, and I questioned him about it. He didn't think God was going to require that, but the possibility never left my thinking. I still don't have any idea why God let it happen. But it's enough for me to know that God can use the experience for his glory before the world." After Pete's death, Olive married Walter Liefeld, a professor at Trinity Evangelical Divinity School in Deerfield, Illinois, and they have three children.

Marilou McCully, wife of Ed, says for all the widows, "We're thankful for the results of the sacrifice of our husbands. We would like to understand what God did by that event. We want to say that the deaths of the five men was God's way to reach the Aucas or to send more Americans to the mission field, but we can't be sure why God allowed them to be killed. We have to leave that mystery to him." Marilou, who has not remarried, lives near Seattle and works in a suburban hospital. As for her own life, she says, "The Lord always takes care of his own. He has provided for me, and I have learned to look to him for help." She is thankful that her two brothers-in-law have taken her three boys under their wings, providing men for them to talk to.

Barbara Youderian, wife of Roger and mother of two children, has stayed in Ecuador all these years. She manages the guest house for the Gospel Missionary Union in Quito. I've been to that guest house, and she is the perfect hostess. Barbara says, "I've learned a lot about serving. I never thought I would be here in a guest home in the capital, but God has given me an opportunity to help missionaries and to be sensitive to their needs and problems. It's been a joyous opportunity." As she looks back she says, "I don't really have any regrets about what was called 'operation Auca.' God was there, just as he was with us after we learned the men were killed, working out his perfect will. I'm sure we'll understand it fully someday." Because of that experience, Barbara says heaven is more real. She looks forward to a joyful reunion with all her loved ones who have gone to be with the Lord.

Marge Saint, wife of Nate, a missionary pilot, was left with three children. Like Barbara, she stayed in Ecuador for many years. She told us, "The worst thing you can do in a situation like that is sit around and feel sorry for yourself. As a Christian I just don't feel I have any right to do that, so I have to look at what the Lord has done for me and what I can do for him." Marge continues, "I wouldn't say the Auca experience changed the direction of my life, but I think it confirmed the direction in which I was already going. It made me want to be sure of my priorities. It made me see the differences between the trivial and the important as never before." Marge is now married to Abe Van Der Puy, former president of World Radio Missionary Fellowship and now the missionary speaker for the "Back to the Bible" radio broadcast.

The fifth widow is probably the best known of them all. Elisabeth Elliot, wife of Jim, wrote *Through Gates of Splendor* and *Shadow of the Almighty* about the massacre. She says, "I was trying to say something about who God is, to get at the basis of faith. Do you trust God for who he is or for what he is supposed to do for you? John the Baptist was left in prison to have his head chopped off. Does God ever do things like that? The problem is that we don't know God. If we really know him we don't try to put him in a box or defend him. It's a question of authority. Are we really under his authority?"

Elisabeth Elliot has suffered two great tragedies. Her second husband, Addison Leitch, died of cancer in 1974. Now married to Lars Gren, she says, "I've always believed and I still believe that God knew exactly what he was doing in Ecuador. God was in charge just as it says in Romans 8:28—everything fits in a pattern for the good. If God had never saved an Auca and never called anyone to the mission field because of the death of these men, I would still have no question in my mind that their death was part of his pattern for good. I've never changed that belief; I've hung my soul on the sovereignty of God. That is the bedrock of my belief."

Not incidentally, there are literally hundreds of missionaries on the mission field today—my wife and I have met many of them in our travels—because of the massacre of those five men. And their five killers, Auca Indians who killed them with spears, all subsequently became Christians and leaders of the Auca church.

Finding God at Death's Door

DAVID N. ASPY

People learn about God's infinite mercy in a wide variety of ways. My way of learning about God's love for me was through my experience with triple bypass surgery. That experience taught me to savor life and the blessings God has provided. Through it and God's grace, I have learned to say quietly but firmly, "I am a Christian."

The cardiologist sat at the end of my hospital bed and said, "Let me assure you—you need to be here!" He started to explain, but I interrupted.

"Please don't give me the details," I said. "Just do what you need to do."

In a little while, the cardiac surgeon entered my room carrying a diagram. Holding it up for me to see, he began to point to various parts of the drawing in order to explain his plans for surgery. Again I didn't want to face the details. "Just do whatever is necessary," I pleaded.

I vaguely recall the next day and a half. There were apparently endless tests and pills to take. My clearest memory is of a full-body shave administered by a variety of people who seemed to wander in and out of my room. They laughed and chatted as they changed blades and continued to remove the hair from every part of my body. They seemed to be having a party.

The pills had dulled my senses, so I don't recall going into surgery Friday morning. My first recollection after the bypass procedure was my younger brother's face looking down at me. "You made it," he said. "It's all over."

Lying in intensive care, I was conscious of a tube in my throat and an IV in my arm. The electrocardiogram monitor was going *beep, beep, beep.* Once the cardiologist entered the room and asked the nurse, "What are you doing to my patient?" At one point I was placed in a frigid blanket to reduce my temperature. Finally the surgeon removed the tubes in my abdomen—an excruciatingly painful event—and told me I could go to a regular hospital room. I had reached the first plateau.

As I sat in my hospital bed, I marveled at just being alive. I had pain in my chest, and coughing was utter agony, but I was alive! Having survived both deadly heart disease and the major surgery intended to correct my weakened condition, I began to turn my thoughts to God.

I prayed every kind of prayer a person can pray. I asked for forgiveness for my sins. I prayed for strength to live more in keeping with God's will. I prayed for those I loved. But most of all I prayed for God to make his will more clear.

For a while I arrogantly thought that, having faced death and been spared, I had learned the most profound lesson in life. But as life continued, I realized there were still many lessons God had in store for me. Learning some of these lessons turned out to be as difficult as facing death.

One lesson I learned was that each moment of every day is a gift from God. Not only had he brought me through surgery; he was giving me the special privilege of life each morning, noon, and night. With my newly heightened awareness of life, I gloried at the opportunity just to breathe and to walk. I marveled at my hands and feet. I glowed at the opportunity to visit my home church and to see old friends.

Learning to appreciate the present moment had its dark side, however, that required me to learn other, more difficult lessons. It seemed that as I valued each day more and more, I became less and less tolerant of things that destroyed opportunities or frittered them away. Before my surgery, I did not know how cruel and sinful I could be. Neither did I understand how hurtful and destructive others could be. Observing my behavior and that of others brought me moments of agony and sheer disbelief. I have had to learn to forgive others and to ask them to forgive me. This has been an exceedingly difficult lesson for me to learn, and I still have not learned it perfectly.

Other lessons have been more joyous. The birth of our daughter, for example, taught me two lessons in love.

First, I learned the joy of new life. When my wife became pregnant, I prayed that God would let me live to see our child's face. As she grew in my wife's abdomen, I felt her first movements and heard her tiny heart beat. I prayed, "O God, let me see my child before I die." When her birth day arrived and I held her in my arms for the first time, I looked toward heaven and said, "Thank you, Lord." The love I felt for my daughter was a new feeling to me. It was immediate and unencumbered. She depended on me, and I felt ready to give her everything.

But just as the joy of her new life settled upon us, my wife began a short, intense battle for her life. I saw her blood spill over the delivery table and heard someone call out her blood pressure—58/27! Suddenly I was learning a lesson my wife had already learned—how it feels to be in danger of losing the one you love most. I held her hand and whispered into her ear, "I love you! I love you! I love you!"

In seconds that seemed like hours, the surgeon found the source of the hemorrhage, and replacement blood was started in her arms. She was safe. For the second time in an hour, I said, "Thank you, Lord!" Then it was over, and I went out to the waiting room to greet the rest of the family and announce that mother and baby were doing fine. But I could not speak—instead I dissolved into tears of joy and relief.

The night after our daughter's birth, I slept in the waiting room so I could be close to her and her mother. As the lights dimmed, I thought of my heart. How wonderful it was! Even though I had abused it and it had had to be repaired, it kept doing its job through this blessed event and hundreds of less dramatic ones. I put my hands on my chest and thanked God for the wonderful heart he had given me.

As often as I am in the city where I had surgery, I go to the hospital chapel. It is a sacred place to me. I kneel with my wife and child and close my eyes. In my mind's eye, we are in heaven, joined with all those who have ever loved the Lord. A bright light comes to the center of our group, and all of us smile and look toward it. I love. I cry. I laugh. I sing. I rejoice.

The joy I feel and can now express is a gift that has come to me since bypass surgery. I do not understand how this good gift grew out of such difficult circumstances, but I am positive that God does. I pray that someday I too will understand, for I know that the source of all that is good is in the very heart of God.

◆ LOOKING AGONY IN THE FACE
ANTHONY CAMPOLO

I have made several visits to third-world countries. My family isn't rich, but I was so affected by what I encountered in Haiti and in Africa that I made sure each of my family members went to a third-world country with me and stared at the agonies of those people face to face. I have actually seen starving children stop breathing and die.

I took my son with me to the Dominican Republic and Haiti and we lived among the people for a couple of weeks. We walked among the poor and the suffering. His attitude toward the affluent life-style, his perception of his goals in life, and his understanding of what our family should be about were all radically changed. One cannot help but raise all kinds of questions after experiencing that.

It becomes easier to communicate to your children that such luxuries as a VCR are not absolute necessities. They come away not so much with a sense that one should appreciate all the things one has, but that one should question all the things one has. Children should understand this and raise such questions themselves as, Why does God allow unequal distribution of wealth? The answer they often come up with is that they don't know why, but because they have so much, they need to be more responsible to those who don't have anything at all. That comes through loud and clear. Then the real question is, What am I going to do with all that I have?

There are many people who argue that those who propagate the simple life-style are creating guilt complexes. Guilt is generated not by what is said but by the healthy response of those who have so much when they confront those who have so little.

I am a strong advocate of what has been euphemistically called the simple life-style. Being among the poor in third-world countries caused me to reevaluate my life-style and change my whole value system. When I was surrounded by hopelessness and despair, the Spirit of God spoke to me. The difference between our time and Jesus' time is that in today's world, those who are affluent are segregated from the poor. It's possible, even likely, for a young person to grow up without ever having sensed the desperate situations in which most people live. It is our obligation to make sure that our kids see poverty and oppression. It is our responsibility to make sure that we see poverty and oppression. Such experiences cause unparalleled clarification of values.

A Defender of the Faith

JAMES C. HEFLEY

Justin, who was not called "Martyr" until after his death, was a young pagan philosopher who lived about one hundred years after the crucifixion of Christ.

This was a time of severe persecution for Christians in the Roman Empire. Christianity was illegal for two reasons. First, emperor worship was required by law, and Christians absolutely refused to burn the required pinch of incense in front of the emperor's statue. Second, Christians preached that Christ's kingdom would soon be established. This alarmed the Romans; they feared that a Christian kingdom would threaten the Roman Empire.

Justin knew of Christians who had been beheaded or thrown into barrels of boiling oil for refusing to say the words "Caesar is Lord." Though not yet a Christian himself, he was deeply disturbed by the persecution.

An inheritance enabled Justin to travel throughout the Roman Empire seeking truth. Wearing a threadbare cloak that marked him as a philosopher, he would ask questions: "Can a man really know God? Can you really have the longing of your soul satisfied?"

One of his encounters was with a Stoic teacher who believed that virtue is the important thing. "Don't just seek God, seek virtue," urged the Stoic.

Another teacher said, "I will teach you the truth—for a fee."

Still another teacher said Justin would first have to know astronomy and geometry before he could be taught.

Virtue, money, knowledge—if Justin had to acquire these in order to know God, he might never satisfy his soul's longings! Discouraged, he tried a Platonist philosopher. "If you flee the world," this sage told him, "you will become like God. Slough off the bodily imprisonment, and return to the world of pure spirit." Justin tried to control his bodily desires, but the emptiness was still there.

All this time he kept observing Christians who were dying for their faith. Obviously they put high value on their way of approaching God. This intrigued Justin, but it also puzzled him—he just couldn't accept their belief in a crucified Savior.

One day he went for a walk in a field near the Mediterranean Sea not far from his home in Ephesus. As he walked he noticed a bearded old man. Justin looked at him intently. The old man, aware that he was being watched, said, "Do you know me?"

"No," Justin answered.

"Then why do you look upon me this way?"

Justin answered that he simply hadn't expected to see anyone in this place.

"Why do you walk here?" asked the old man.

"I have come to think and to exercise my reason."

The old man ventured, "Do you think philosophy brings happiness?"

Justin answered in the affirmative.

The old man dug deeper. "What is philosophy, young man?"

Justin quoted the standard definition: "Philosophy is the foreknowledge of reality and the clear perception of truth. Happiness is the reward of such knowledge and wisdom."

"Well, what do you call God?"

Justin answered with another stock quote: "God is the changeless cause of all other things."

"Then can one know God without hearing from one who has seen him?"

"God can only be discerned by the mind, and then only when the mind is pure and well disposed," came Justin's platonic reply.

"Young man, I refer you to teachers more ancient than the philosophers, teachers who spoke by the divine spirit and proved themselves by their predictions and miracles." The old man continued, "Pray that they will open the gates of light to you. You cannot know these things by your understanding; you can know them only by the man, the Messiah, to whom God has imparted wisdom."

Justin never saw the old man again, but he kept thinking about this conversation. He began to study the Hebrew Scriptures and to read the letters and Gospels circulating through the Empire. Then he began to talk with Christians about their faith.

Ultimately, Justin became a Christian. He dedicated his life to traveling all over the Roman Empire as a Christian philosopher, telling people the truth.

In Justin's day, Christians were thought to be atheists because they didn't worship the emperor. In his First Apology, addressed to the Roman Emperor, Justin said: "Christians are not atheists; they worship God the Father, the Son, and the Holy Spirit. The state has nothing to fear from them. Christ's kingdom is not of this world. The empire has no better subjects than the Christians—look at the change in their character and their lives since they left the service of demons. They pay tribute, give to the poor, avoid swearing, and love everybody."

Inevitably, Justin was arrested and brought before the chief judge of Rome. According to the record of his trial, he was told to obey the gods and submit to Caesar. If he did this, he would be released.

Justin told the judge that by obeying Christ he had done no wrong. The judge only sneered.

Justin continued, "We believe in one God and in Jesus Christ his Son." This interested the judge, who asked Justin and the others on trial with him many questions about their faith.

Finally the judge asked Justin, "If you are scourged and beheaded, do you believe you will ascend into heaven?" Justin replied, "I know and I am fully persuaded of it."

At this the judge lost his temper and said, "I order you to sacrifice to the gods." Justin refused. "We will kill you if you don't."

Justin replied, "Do what you will. We are Christians and we do not sacrifice to idols." And so Justin and his companions were put to death.

Justin Martyr is remembered today as one of the greatest of the early apologists, or defenders of the faith. He wrote two Apologies and a Dialogue that remain classics in Christian literature.

The Awakening That Spanned Two Continents

JOHN POLLOCK

The attic in the Oxford college looked as cheerless as its occupant, who lay groaning on the bed, worn down by his spiritual search. Twenty-year-old George Whitefield, born the year that King George I came to the throne, was a servitor, the lowest rank of undergraduate, wearing a coarse gown and giving menial service to the noblemen and gentlemen of Pembroke.

George Whitefield had blue eyes with a squint, and a deep voice of bell-like quality and strength. But it had been heard little these past weeks of the early spring of 1735. He suppressed his laughter and merry ways. His whole being was concentrated on a struggle to be born again.

He had come up to Oxford to read for Holy Orders in the Church of England

and had been noticed by John Wesley and his brother Charles, who recruited him for their "Holy Club." Three years would pass before John Wesley's heart was "strangely warmed"; each of his little group was earnestly striving to fit himself for heaven by good works and devotions, so methodically organized that a hostile university dubbed them "Methodists."

Charles Wesley had lent George a pile of books. Among them, scarcely recalled by Charles, was one by a Scotsman of the previous century, which opened George's eyes to the need to be born again. He began at once to strive for this new birth with scant sympathy from the Wesleys, who still believed that infants were born again at baptism; and since baptism was the only means of registering a birth, they believed almost every English infant a born-again Christian.

Whitefield knew that the Wesleys were wrong. He redoubled his efforts to rid himself of his sins and become good enough for Christ: the new birth would be the reward. George pored over the New Testament; he fasted, prayed, and gave up all he enjoyed, yet even this price was not high enough. The new birth had eluded him and he neared the end of his strength. He had no ears for the birds singing outside his window, no eyes for the blossoms appearing on the trees.

Another book lay unopened on his desk. He could not remember how he had come by it, but he left his bed, picked it up, and was amazed by what he read. A calm and moving meditation on the Cross began to make everything plain. Christ himself had paid the price of sin. The new birth was a *gift,* not a reward; George had only to accept it. But he could not surrender all his efforts. Days passed until a morning came when he threw himself on his bed and uttered his first cry of utter helplessness—all previous prayers had been conscious attempts to win God's favor.

Suddenly George Whitefield realized he was happy—and knew why: he had thrown himself, without reserve, into God's almighty hands, and someone unseen had removed his burden and replaced it with the joy of God's presence. George laughed aloud at the simplicity of it, and the floodgates burst: "Joy—joy unspeakable—joy that's full of, big with glory."

As soon as the Oxford term ended, he left for his home city of Gloucester, his heart singing as the stage wagon bumped westward along the rotted tracks of the Cotswolds. At Gloucester he was rebuffed by his brother, landlord of the public house where George had been born; but when he called on a girlfriend, now married, and talked of the new birth as the unmerited gift of a gracious God, her eyes lit up. She begged him to read the Bible with her and to help her believe. At an alms house he saw an old woman weeping and spoke to her shyly about Christ. The effect astonished him: she dried her tears and went away happy.

As the Bible unfolded its treasures while he sat in the summer sunshine beside the River Severn, he began to realize that he, a plain layman, "a worm taken from a public house," understood more about "the knowledge of God's free grace and the necessity of being justified in His sight by *faith only,"* than the Reverend John Wesley, who had sailed away to the new colony of Georgia with Charles, still intent on saving their souls by doing good. George realized they were bondservants of a stern, unbending Master, not sons rejoicing in a Father's love.

A new bishop had come to Gloucester. "I have heard of your character," he told Whitefield, "and like your behaviour in church." One year later, on June 20, 1736, he ordained George Whitefield as a deacon of the Church of England, although he was under the proper age. The next week Whitefield preached his first sermon. He read from a carefully prepared script, his deep voice filling the church as he proclaimed free grace with such effect that some of the hearers complained to the bishop that the new parson had driven fifteen people mad. The bishop retorted: "I hope their madness lasts until next Sunday!"

In Gloucester, in London (where he took a friend's place as chaplain of the Tower), and in two tiny country parishes, Whitefield discovered the spiritual thirst of Hanoverian England. He tried to keep pride in check and not lose a sense of wonder that whenever he preached—lowborn, young, and squint-eyed as he was—men and women of all ages cried out for the living God.

Fresh insights came as he prayed, read the Bible and old books of divinity, and visited cottages. He learned that Christ's grace was so free that his own long struggle had been unnecessary; he rejoiced at instant conversions. He no longer confined public prayer to the words of the liturgy; he even began to preach extempore, a most daring innovation for a parson of the day. By February 1737, little more than six months after his ordination, the twenty-three-year-old George Whitefield became the means of an extraordinary revival in Bristol. "Churches are as full on weekdays as they used to be on Sundays," he wrote to a friend, "and on Sundays so full that very many are obliged to go away. Oh pray that God would always keep me humble, and fully convinced that I am nothing without Him."

A still small voice had been urging him to go abroad as a missionary to Georgia. John Wesley wrote; Charles Wesley urged in person when he returned; above all was the inner certainty that God called. Before Whitefield sailed, the revival had spread to London, and he was the most popular preacher of the day. Men begged him to stay, but the call was insistent: God must have other plans for Britain.

The day that Whitefield embarked for Georgia, John Wesley landed at the same port in Kent, a defeated missionary: "I went to Georgia to convert Indians; but oh, who will convert me?" When Whitefield reached Georgia—after a revival on board ship—he learned the sad story of Wesley's embittered chaplaincy that upset the colony with the excessive rigor of his religious demands, and by an unfortunate love affair. Whitefield saw at once that the colony needed the message of free grace. His four months in Georgia were a time of great happiness and convinced him that America should be his home. But he hurried back to England to be ordained priest and to raise funds for a much needed orphan house. The colony wept to see him go.

Back in Britain he heard that the revival had spread mightily, for the Wesleys, converted, were now evangelists. They all spent the night of New Year's Day 1739 together in London, leading the prayers and praises of converts with no hint of future differences between them. "Here seems to be a great pouring out of the Spirit," wrote Whitefield, "and many who were awakened by my preaching a year ago are now grown strong men in Christ, by the ministrations of my dear friends and fellow labourers, John and Charles Wesley."

Many clergy, however, were enraged. When Whitefield returned to Bristol, he found pulpits shut against him. It was then that a flash of insight revealed where his greatest work would lie, both in Britain and in America: the open air.

The mayor of Bristol had told him the year before that if he wished to preach to Indians, there were plenty nearby: the savage, illiterate coal miners, whose hearts were as black as their sooty faces. Whitefield determined to preach to them as they left their coal mines at the end of the day. To preach in the open air might possibly break the laws of England: Wesley warned Whitefield that it was "a mad step."

On February 17, 1739, Whitefield stood on a little hill in his cassock and pitched his voice one hundred yards to a group of miners moving toward him: "Blessed are the poor in spirit," he cried, "for they shall see the kingdom of heaven!" The miners stopped and stared. Slowly they moved nearer. Others joined, and instead of a riot he had a silent, listening audience packed close below his hillock.

He spoke of Jesus, the friend of sinners; of hell, black as a pit, and judgment; of the Cross, and the love of God. He warmed to his theme, forgetting all sense of time. And then he noticed an unforgettable sight: "the white gutters made by their tears down their black cheeks."

The Horizon Never Ends

JAMES C. HEFLEY

Rochunga Pudaite comes from the Hmar tribe in northeast India, a tribe once known as fierce headhunters. Rochunga's turning point came when he was just nine years old.

His father was a preacher, but he didn't have the Scriptures in his own language so he preached from what he had heard and remembered. The tribal elders, who desperately wanted to be able to read the Bible themselves, prayed and decided that Rochunga would be the one to do the translating. Thus they dedicated him to the task and prepared to send him to the nearest school, a Baptist mission school, for education. This nine-year-old was about to embark on a great adventure, for the school was ninety-six miles away through dense jungle.

Rochunga's father had told him that God's love extends beyond the horizon. But Rochunga asked, "What do you mean, the horizon? How far is that? If it's as far as I can see, that isn't very far, and the school is farther than that!"

Before Rochunga left for school, his father asked him to walk with him to the top of the mountain. When they arrived, they climbed to the top of a tree. His father pointed down to the valley and said, "You see, there is the Cachar Valley.

It is many days' journey across that valley. Now son, look to the long mountain range beyond. Do you see that peak where the heaven kisses the earth?"

"Yes," Rochunga replied.

"If you were to journey many weeks and reach the top of that mountain, you would see another just like it. If you journeyed for many more days to the second mountain, you would see a third. My son, the horizon never ends. There is no place in this world where the love of God cannot go with you. So when you go to school, whether you are in a mountain or a valley, God will encircle you with his love. He will protect you."

Today Rochunga Pudaite is president of Bibles for the World—a Bible-distribution ministry through which millions of Bibles have been mailed to scores of nations.

A Scientist Faces a Crisis

✍ JAMES C. HEFLEY

In the 1930s, Dr. Howard A. Kelley was a surgeon and professor of surgery at Johns Hopkins University. At that time he was probably one of the best-known evangelical scientists in America. He often spoke as a lay preacher, and he actively supported missions. Sometimes he traveled to mission fields in order to better educate himself.

Dr. Kelley, though very conservative, came to a crisis over a theological approach called higher criticism of the Bible. Higher criticism, imported from Germany in the late nineteenth century, taught that mankind could not take the Bible just as it presented itself. The Bible, according to higher critics, was a purely human book. Its prophecies were written after the things they predicted had come to pass, and its miracles were stories that became embellished in Hebrew folklore.

All of this disturbed Kelley. He knew people who believed the teachings of these higher critics. Some lost their faith entirely, while others tried to straddle the fence by believing that the Bible was the Word of God even though it was not entirely trustworthy. Kelley wanted to talk with his friends about the Bible, but he felt insufficient to the task. He did not know how to answer the arguments of the so-called experts in archeology and ancient languages.

So he decided to go directly to the Bible itself. He would find out what it said about itself and how it worked.

As he studied, he discovered that the Bible from Genesis to Revelation claims to be God's personal message to man. His next step was to accept the Bible as the "textbook" of the Christian faith, just as he accepted scientific writings as textbooks in medicine. Finally, he submitted to the Bible's condition: "If any one chooses to do God's will, he will find out whether my teaching comes from God or whether I speak on my own" (John 7:17). His conclusion: the Bible must be accepted by faith as the inspired Word of God, different from any human book.

Dr. Kelley continued to be known for his personal commitment to Scripture and became a towering witness in the scientific community. When he faced a crisis of belief, he examined his faith closely—and came out stronger than ever before.

You Have to Really Love Them

✍ JAMES C. HEFLEY

Dr. Frank Laubach tells about a turning point in his life that occurred as he worked with the Moro tribes in the Philippines.

The Moro people were Muslims, hostile to outsiders and to missionaries. In fact, they had been driven back into the mountains of the Philippines by sword-wielding Christians. Laubach entered this anti-Christian atmosphere as a young man believing that God was going to help him win the Moros to Christ.

But as he worked, he seemed to get nowhere. The Moros looked upon Frank as their enemy. As the months passed, he became very discouraged and wanted to quit.

One evening he climbed Signal Hill, which overlooked one of the Moro villages. He talked to God about his burden for the Moros and his frustration at the walls he kept running into. He said, "Lord, how can I help these people? Some of them are murderers. They're hostile. What more can I do? I've been trying so hard."

It seemed that he heard the Lord's answer: "My child, the problem is that you don't really love these Moros. You think you're superior because you're white, and they can sense your feelings. Try to forget you're white and American, and try to think of how much I love them."

Tears flowed down Frank's cheeks. He asked God to love the Moros through him.

When he came down from the mountain, he sought out the Muslim leaders and asked them to teach him about their religion. They spent several hours explaining the tenets of Islam. Then they turned to Frank and said, "Now teach us about your religion."

When Frank began to listen to the people, respect them, and love them, they responded. Some even became Christians.

♦ LOVING JESUS THROUGH PEOPLE
ANTHONY CAMPOLO

One idea that has influenced me greatly is that the Jesus I love in the abstract can become concrete for me in every person I meet. If I look at the person a second time, I can see through him or her to Jesus. And Jesus says to me, "Hey, love me in this person!" Loving Jesus through people has affected my life dramatically. Each person becomes sacred when I sense that on the other side of that person is Jesus waiting to be loved.

I want to emphasize that the person is not Jesus, the person is not

God; but I can get at God through the person, and, strangely enough, God can get at me through that person too. In reality, you cannot love God without loving people. And God loves you through people.

This understanding has revolutionized the way I relate to people. If someone treats me like dirt and I'm about to get angry, I look at that person again and—if I'm prayerful—I can sense the presence of God on the other side of that person. When I sense God coming at me through that person, no matter how rotten the person is, my attitude toward him or her is altered.

Apostle of the Love of God

JOHN POLLOCK

On a spring Saturday in 1855, six years before the Civil War, a youth of eighteen wrapped up shoes at the back of his uncle's shop in Boston.

D. L. Moody (he disliked his first name, Dwight) had come from the rural community of Northfield in upstate Massachusetts. Brought up by a strict, widowed mother, he had tired of working the family farm and had taken the railroad to Boston the year before. He was a muscular lad with a large chest, a thickset neck, dark brown hair, and merry gray eyes, who loved practical jokes and skylarking. He was also ambitious and longed to become a millionaire.

However, another influence was at work. He had been raised a Unitarian, for the First Congregational Church of Northfield had followed the trend that had extinguished much of the old Puritan fervor in New England. The Boston uncles, however, were biblical Christians, though not particularly committed; and to keep young D. L. out of mischief they insisted that he attend their church and go regularly to Sunday school. For a whole year, therefore, he had heard, in sermons and lessons, that Jesus Christ was not merely a great teacher and a good man, but the Son of God, that he had risen from the dead, and was alive and at work in the world by the Holy Spirit.

That spring of 1855 the church held an eight-day revival. By Saturday, as he wrapped and stacked shoes, Moody was admitting to himself the force of the call for commitment to Christ, but he was held back by the other clerks who might laugh, and the number of changes needed in his way of life.

Suddenly he felt a hand on his shoulder. He looked up and saw his Sunday school teacher, Edward Kimball. Moody had liked Kimball from the day of first joining the class, when Kimball had saved him from embarrassment, for Moody had been hunting for St. John's Gospel in the pages of Genesis, and Kimball had quietly handed him his own Bible, opened at the right place.

Kimball now spoke very seriously. "Moody," he said, "will you come to Christ? He loves you. He wants your love. Moody, he should have it!" And Moody noticed tears in Kimball's eyes.

Moody needed no further persuasion. "The young man was just ready for the light which broke upon him," wrote Kimball many years later when Moody was famous, "for there, at once, in the back of that shoe store in Boston, he gave himself and his life to Christ."

As Moody began, so he grew. As Kimball's influence had been decisive in conversion, so the influence of individual Christians would be the major factor at the great moments of growth.

Five years after the incident in the shoe store, Moody was in Chicago. By 1860 he was a successful traveling salesman in a shoe business, his lack of education being outweighed by the force of his personality and his almost incredible energy. He believed he was indeed on the way to becoming a millionaire, although much of his time went to Christian work in the roughest part of the city. At first he had thought he could never preach; but he could drum up boys and girls and tell them stories of Jesus, Moody's powerful voice conquering the wildest whoops of the slum lads. Soon he had the largest and most lively Sunday school in the slums, with many faithful teachers.

It was one of these, "a pale, delicate young man," who staggered into Moody's office on a hot June day, and threw himself down on some boxes.

Moody, who knew that the man suffered from tuberculosis, was sorry to learn that the doctors now gave him up: he was leaving Chicago to go home and die. But he looked so upset that Moody asked the trouble, knowing he was not afraid of death, and ready.

"I am anxious for my class," replied the man. "I have failed. Not one of my girls has been led to Jesus."

Moody recalled those frivolous girls, the worst in the school. He offered to hire a cab and take the man to call at their homes.

They drove into the slums. At the first tenement a girl listened wide-eyed as her teacher told her he was dying and begged her to put her trust in Christ. Then "he prayed as I never heard before," and the girl promised to "settle the question then and there." They called on three others, until the man's energy gave out.

Ten days later the teacher again climbed Moody's stairs. This time he was radiant. "The last one of my class has yielded herself to Christ. The great vital question of their lives is settled. They have accepted my Savior. My work is done and I am going home."

That night Moody gave a tea for all the girls to say farewell. After a last hymn had been sung and the two men had each prayed aloud, Moody "was just rising from my knees, when one of the class began to pray for her dying teacher." Moody listened, astonished, to the faltering extempore prayer of a girl who had been a scoffer. One by one the others followed. As Moody listened to these fervent, artless prayers, his business ambitions died. Overwhelmingly he wanted to spend his years as the teacher had spent the days—if courage and faith could make the break.

The struggle lasted three months. "It was a terrible battle. But, oh," he would say years later, "how many times I have thanked God's will."

Eight years later, in 1868, came another turning point in Moody's growth. Again the formative influence was an unlikely person.

Moody was now happily married to English-born Emma Revell and was already a substantial figure in the religious life of the Midwest, although only thirty-one. During the Civil War he had been a lay chaplain in the Chicago camps and at the front, where his ministry to the wounded and dying had convinced him that a man could turn to Christ in a moment. He had built up a nondenominational church on Illinois Street (later on Chicago Avenue), though he was never ordained. He was president of the Chicago YMCA, a leader in the Sunday school movement, and already a mighty, if homespun, preacher and evangelist. And he always emphasized God's wrath against sin and sinner alike. Moody's own lovable nature rather belied his message.

In 1867 the Moodys had visited the British Isles. At the close of a service in a Brethren hall he had heard someone address him in a strong Lancashire accent: the voice came at the level of his shoulder. "Ah'm 'arry Moorhouse. Ah'll come and preach for you in America."

Moody had heard of Harry Moorhouse, a converted pickpocket who was known as the Boy Preacher because he looked absurdly young. Moody turned and dismissed this beardless little man with a few kind words.

In late January 1868 Moody was annoyed to receive a letter from Moorhouse stating that he would soon be in Chicago and would preach. Moody, dashing off to a convention, told Emma to put him up and let him address a basement meeting. When Moody returned on the Saturday, Emma told him that the people had liked Moorhouse "very much. He preaches a little different from you. He preaches that God *loves* sinners."

"He is wrong," snorted Moody.

"I think you will agree with him when you hear him," replied Emma, "because he backs up everything he says with the Bible."

Next Sunday morning Moody noticed that the congregation all brought Bibles, which he had never asked them to do. Moorhouse announced his text: John 3:16. "For God so loved the world, that he gave his only begotten Son, that whosoever believeth in him should not perish, but have everlasting life." Then Moorhouse, recalled Moody, "went from Genesis to Revelation giving proof that God loves the sinner; and before he got through, two or three of my sermons were spoiled.... I never knew up to that time that God loved us so much. This heart of mine began to thaw out; I could not keep back the tears."

Moody's young brother-in-law, Fleming Revell, the future publisher, never forgot the sight of Moody drinking it in, as Moorhouse in the pulpit shifted awkwardly from one foot to another and the congregation sat riveted as text after text poured out.

From that day, Moody became the apostle of the love of God.

◆ FAITHFULNESS PAYS OFF / NORMAN GEISLER

Starting at age nine, I went to Sunday school every week while my parents slept. I wasn't a Christian, but I got up, got dressed, and rode the Sunday school bus because people from this little church had gone door to door and invited me.

I was impressed with three things about the people in this church.

First, they were faithful. They picked me up every Sunday without ever missing a week. They did this four hundred times before I became a Christian—in spite of the fact that Sunday after Sunday I kicked the other kids, threw paper wads, and generally caused a disturbance.

Second, these Christians were happy, smiling, joyous people.

Third, these faithful, happy people were truly concerned about me.

These things deeply impressed me, and after eight years of regular Sunday school attendance, at the age of seventeen, I became a Christian.

Called to Be a Servant

LARRY WARD

It may sound exaggerated, but I mean it: the most beautiful word in the English language is *servant.*

Our Lord himself set an example for us when he came to us in the form of a servant. He "made himself nothing, taking the very nature of a servant" (Philippians 2:7). If Jesus was not above serving, can any of us be too important to be servants?

Service is an important concept in Scripture—about five hundred times we find forms of the noun *servant* and the verb *serve.* When we come near the end of life, we understand why. Looking back, we realize that only the things we did in the service of God are important.

One of the greatest servants I have ever known was my mother. Her whole life was service. Her first thought was always for someone else. Her instinctive reaction was always to put the other person first. By her example, she taught us to look at the world in terms of how we could serve, and she taught us to look at every friend as someone we could help.

My mother lay in a coma for eleven days before she died. During those eleven days, I was at her bedside almost constantly. I thought back to how, years before, she had come to faith in Christ. A very shy and private person, she could never stand up and lead a group or teach a class. Whenever she was asked to take part in what we called the opening exercises in Sunday school, I ached with her. When she stood to read, the paper shook in her hand. Public speaking was almost impossible for her to do, but as she lay unconscious on her hospital bed before she was called into the presence of the Lord, people would come into her room and say—in almost the same words—"Your mother was the greatest Christian I ever knew."

One woman said, "If I had a problem, I felt free to call her. I even called at three or four o'clock in the morning, and your mother never seemed to mind. She would listen to me and counsel me and pray for me over the phone."

A mother and father and two small children said, "It is because of your mother that we came to know the Lord. She came to our house to visit and invited us to church. We didn't care anything about church, but she was so friendly we thought we ought to do it once. When we arrived Sunday morning, kind of shy and not knowing where to go, she was out in front of the church to meet us. She called us by name, and she helped the children find where they were to go. We found other friends, and we liked it. We came back, and within a couple of weeks we all came to faith in Christ. We owe it all to your mother."

I looked at this dear person, so shy about doing anything in public. God had given her an attitude of sharing and caring that was tremendously important. As God's servant, she had used this gift.

There's an old saying, "If called to be a missionary, don't stoop to be a king." I'd like to change *missionary* to *servant*. In fact, the best king, president, or other leader is the one who knows he's a servant.

In the psalms, King David referred to himself as a servant over and over again. For example, in Psalm 27:9 he pleaded, "Do not turn your servant away in anger," and in Psalm 31 he cried, "Let your face shine on your servant." David was a king, but he thought of himself first as a servant of God.

If we think of ourselves as servants, we will constantly look at other people in terms of what we can do to serve. In all we do, we will ask, What can I do to help? That's what being God's servant is all about.

A Great Man with a Servant's Heart

JAMES C. HEFLEY

Cameron Townsend founded and was the general director of Wycliffe Bible Translators, which now has more than five thousand people working in more than six hundred languages. Wycliffe is the all-time leader among translators for minority language groups. What I learned from "Uncle Cam" is servanthood.

Uncle Cam always signed his letters in his tiny, squiggly handwriting, "Your servant for Jesus' sake." This "servant for Jesus' sake" was probably the most influential private American citizen in Latin America, particularly in Colombia, Peru, Mexico, and Guatemala, for more than two decades. Often when he went to a country, the president would throw a banquet for him. Yet he was the most humble person I ever knew.

In writing Uncle Cam's biography, my wife and I talked to scores of people who shared personal experiences about him. One that really spoke to me came from my friend Hugh Steven.

When Hugh and his wife, Norma, came to Wycliffe Bible Translators, they had heard about Cameron Townsend, but they hadn't gotten to know him personally.

One evening they were having dinner when suddenly the great man just popped in. They were delighted to see him and invited him to come in and finish the meal with them. You can imagine how Norma must have scurried around to make sure everything was just right!

As they got involved in talking with him, they forgot the time. Suddenly they realized they would be late for their Bible study that night. The dirty dishes were still on the table, and they would not have time to wash them before leaving. Uncle Cam spoke up immediately. "I'll wash the dishes," he said. "It will be a pleasure."

Hugh and Norma were aghast. "Oh, no, not you, Uncle Cam! We'll wash them. We can be a little late."

But Uncle Cam insisted, "You go on to your Bible study." There was no dissuading him, so these two young members of the mission went out while the director of the mission stayed home and washed their dishes.

Hugh said later, "I've met a lot of peple who give the impression of being high and mighty. Then I met Uncle Cam. When he washed our dishes, I realized I had been standing in the presence of a true follower of Jesus, a man with real humility."

♦A MAN WHO TOOK TIME TO CARE
VERNON GROUNDS

Jacob Stem Patterson was a lawyer who befriended me when I was a young pastor. Although he was extremely busy—he was the father of seven children, involved in several Christian organizations, and served as the international president of the Gideons—he found time to care for me. He took time to pray with me once a week. He gave me space in his suite of offices. He provided secretarial help. He encouraged me. He set before me an example of efficient, godly activity. If any one human being affected my life, it was he.

Seed Planters
JAMES C. HEFLEY

I grew up in the Ozarks in a log cabin with my parents and seven brothers and sisters. My education was in one-room schools through the eighth grade. I entered high school at age nine, graduated at thirteen, and went on to college at Arkansas Tech. I was not a Christian and really did not know much about Christianity. The Bible was something to be laughed at. It made little impression on me.

In college I was a problem. I gambled so much that my nickname was Blackjack. At age fourteen, I operated my own gambling business. It was illegal at the time, and I was eventually closed down by the sheriff. At one point the dean even called a meeting of all the men at the college and told me I was the worst influence on the campus. So I returned home.

Back home, I sat on the porch of my parents' store one morning with some other local hillbilly boys and watched as an old car drove up and a couple of stylishly dressed women stepped out. One introduced herself: "My name is Florence Handyside, and this is my partner, Helen Lievie. We're missionaries from the North Arkansas Gospel Mission. We've come to hold young peoples' meetings in the schoolhouse on Monday evenings, but we need permission from the chairman of the school board. Could you direct us to that gentleman?"

My buddies and I snickered. I pointed up the street (the only one in town) to my Uncle Bill, who was dozing on the post office porch. The two women were gone and back within a few minutes. Uncle Bill had given them permission to hold their meetings, and they invited us to come. One of my buddies poked me and promised, "We'll be there." As they drove away, we grinned in anticipation of the fun we'd have.

We were there all right, but only to cause trouble. We did everything we could to cause commotion. The ladies were very patient with us, however. They kept coming back every Monday night, and we kept going so we could keep them from getting anything done.

Finally we exhausted our bag of tricks. Though I enjoyed the commotion I caused, I began to respect Florence because she had such patience and love. She kept smiling. So one evening I sat still and listened to her for the first time. "Can you imagine God becoming a man like us, a servant, a sacrifice for our sins?" she said during her Bible talk.

Of course, I was pretty tough. I had heard it all before. But Florence continued, "Some of you may think you're too good or too smart to believe in Jesus." She seemed to be looking right into my mind. That was my problem—I thought I already knew everything. "The real problem," she said, "may be that you're just too chicken to look and see if it could be true."

I was interested, but I didn't know where to begin. Besides, I wasn't sure I wanted to look into Christianity. I'd had enough of the arguing over churches and doctrines among my own relatives. Sure enough, Florence went on, "Are you asking yourself where to begin? Well, you don't start by arguing over doctrines. You ask God to show you if Jesus is all he claimed to be."

During the invitation song one night, I wanted to accept Jesus. I looked over at my buddies, hoping one of them would take the first step. I would have followed right away. But nobody did.

A few weeks later I went back to college. The next time I returned home, I found that Florence and Helen had stopped coming to our little community.

One Sunday night the following spring, a preacher came through town. He was going to preach right in our living room, and my mother invited people over. I was home from college for the weekend, and she wanted me to hear him. I slunk into the room after the service started and climbed to the top of the stairs to sit in the dark; I was there only to please my mom. But I caught myself listening. The preacher was saying the same things Florence had been saying, only more emphatically. "If you don't accept Christ," he roared, "you're on your way to hell." Even though I'd been in trouble with the law, I was still pretty self-righteous. Hell was a place for bad people, not for me. That preacher really got me to thinking. When he gave the invitation, I went forward.

A few days passed and the preacher returned to talk to me. He said, "I believe the Lord is calling you to some kind of special service, maybe to be a preacher." The words just popped out of my mouth, "Yes, I think he is." That preacher found a place for me to speak, and for the rest of the summer I went around to different churches and preached.

I owe my lifelong Christian faith to two faithful women who sowed and one traveling preacher who reaped (see John 4:34-38).

What I didn't know until years later was that Miss Handyside and Miss Lievie hadn't wanted to be in the Ozarks at all. Helen's heart was in India, where she later went as a missionary. Florence had wanted to go to Korea, but had come to work in the Ozarks instead because of the Korean War. She finally got to Korea as a clerk for the U.S. Army. She worked during the week and did her missionary work on the weekends. After eight months, she was permitted to stay as a full-time missionary. Not long after this she got sick and died.

Florence had been a full-fledged missionary for less than a month, but she had been a missionary all during her time of waiting. She never knew I became a Christian, but I will always be thankful that Florence and Helen didn't wait until they got to the mission field to be missionaries. They were missionaries where they were. In what may have looked to them like their worst failure, their ministry in the Ozarks, they were truly successes. They planted a seed in my heart.

A Right Attitude Reaps a Harvest

JAMES C. HEFLEY

Many times people can witness to others by accepting God's will in difficult situations. And they may not even realize the effects their attitude is having!

Dr. Donald G. Barnhouse was preaching at special services in a church whose pastor's wife was due to have a baby any day. One evening the pastor did not show up, so Dr. Barnhouse assumed he was at the hospital for the exciting event.

That evening the pastor came to talk to Dr. Barnhouse, but not with the excited smiles he expected. Instead he burst out, "We have had a mongoloid [Down's Syndrome] child. My wife doesn't know yet. I have to tell her."

Dr. Barnhouse softly replied, "My friend, God has a purpose for you and your wife in this. He has given you this child to love. When you talk to your wife, tell her that God has blessed you with a mongoloid child, and assure her of God's love and purpose in your lives."

The pastor, somewhat reassured, telephoned his wife and talked to her as Dr. Barnhouse suggested.

They didn't know it, but the hospital switchboard operator was listening in. She was quite skeptical of Christianity, but when she heard this couple's touching words, she was astounded at their faith. They actually believed they were blessed with a mongoloid child!

The switchboard operator shared this story with many hospital employees. The next Sunday, seventy nurses attended the pastor's church. When he gave the invitation, more than twenty came forward to accept Christ.

The Influence of Godly Parents

✍ RALPH BALISKY with JAMES C. HEFLEY

George and Nellie Balisky raised ten children. Six became missionaries, and four are active Christians supporting the family's "overseas branch." The Baliskys' oldest son, Ralph, was asked to recall some things his parents did that had an impact on the children.

"Dad had only a fourth-grade education, but he and Mother dedicated themselves to raising a Christian family.

"First, Mother and Dad gave us to the Lord before we were born.

"Second, they had family prayers every day. We didn't always like it when Dad wanted us to pray around the circle, but it did something to us I can't explain.

"Third, although Dad was our friend and we loved him, he wasn't a buddy. He was our father, the head of the family. There was no court of appeals above Dad.

"Fourth, Dad and Mother were always fair to us, and we weren't punished unless we deserved it—but we never got away with anything either.

"Fifth, Dad and Mother were committed Christian stewards. Every year they made a mission promise, even when they didn't know where the money would come from.

"Sixth, they never pressured us to become missionaries. They told us to get guidance from the Lord. Of course we knew they would be very happy if some of us should become missionaries, because they considered that a very high calling. They saw to it that every visiting missionary who came into the area stayed at our house.

"Seventh, Mother and Dad lived the way they talked. They set the ideals before us, and—maybe most important of all—they loved us."

♦ YOU MAY BENEFIT FROM YOUR WIFE'S CRITICISM! / ANTHONY CAMPOLO

I was married for at least a decade before I recognized that the greatest instrument in my spiritual growth is my wife. She knows me better than anyone else, and I find it easier to take criticism from her than from anybody else—primarily because I have never sensed any rejection in her criticism. What she says is always said in love and is intended to make me a better person.

What intrigues me is that my wife is not theologically trained. In our early days of marriage, I thought she spoke in too many "Christian cliches," but the longer I've lived with her, the more I've realized the validity of those cliches. One she uses on me most often is "It's nice to be important, but it's more important to be nice."

When I first heard that I thought, "How corny!" But she kept saying it, and I began to see its truth. In this whole game of speaking and running to conferences and being on the platform, it's so easy to be caught up in the importance of what I'm doing that I fail to be nice to the people around me. My wife has worked overtime to help correct what I think is the most negative dimension of my personality—my failure to be sensitive to ordinary people I meet every day.

Books That Make a Difference

HAROLD MYRA

In today's culture we are constantly bombarded by despair. We find it in television, books, magazines, movies, and everywhere else we turn. I'm grateful for authors who can speak to us and help us make sense of the world we live in. Books have made a big difference to me at several important stages in my Christian growth.

One might not think that the spiritual life could be influenced by fantasy novels, but certain science fiction books, some of my earliest reading, expanded my understanding of God's universe. When I was still a teenager, I started reading C. S. Lewis and was delighted to find an intellectually credible Christian author. I went to a state university, and to read someone like Lewis during those formative years was tremendously stimulating and helpful.

I started reading Paul Tournier's books early in the sixties, when psychology was making such dramatic inroads into our culture. He quoted a broad range of philosophers and medical practitioners and integrated their thoughts into a Christian framework. His perspective had a tremendously positive effect on me.

In the seventies, as I was wrestling personally with the existential despair being projected in our culture, I read the works of Helmut Thielicke. He put his faith up against those big questions, and his answers had a powerful effect on me.

I often turn to books for insights and ideas. Here is a brief overview of a few of my favorites:

Perelandra by C. S. Lewis presents a world in which the forces of good and evil are arrayed against each other. It is richly creative. This book is the second volume of a trilogy in which Lewis shows God as creator of the universe. I found his view of God much larger than my previous conception had been.

The Lord of the Rings by J. R. R. Tolkien, another trilogy, further expanded my perceptions. Although not overtly Christian, this masterwork carries the thoroughly Christian understandings of its author. Again and again I find myself thinking, "Yes, life in many ways is the same as the hobbits found it."

The Genesee Diary by Henri Nouwen is a delightful book in which the author chronicles his stay at a Trappist monastery. Looking at himself realistically, he shares some of his deepest feelings about trying to live the Christian life. I appreciate his honesty about his own failings.

Praying Hyde, edited by E. G. Carre, is the story of a magnificent missionary at the turn of the century who had an intense focus on prayer. His life had an unusual impact.

Our Heavenly Father and *The Waiting Father,* both by Helmut Thielicke, are excellent collections of sermons, the first concentrating on the Lord's Prayer and the second on Jesus' parables. Thielicke speaks powerfully to modern existential despair because he thoroughly understands it, having preached for years in the disillusioned, cynical atmosphere of postwar Germany.

The Meaning of Persons by Paul Tournier is one of many helpful books by a man who, having read widely in the literature of psychology, maintains a thoroughly Christian perspective and weds psychological principles to a biblical worldview. Each of his books is anecdotal, empathetic, and enjoyable to read. I have gained more psychological understanding of myself and others from Tournier than from any other single author.

The Knowledge of the Holy by A. W. Tozer is a distillation of the great historic creeds of the church. This book gives a powerful, persuasive new perspective on what is happening in the world today.

Prayer by O. Hallesby, a Norwegian seminary professor and evangelical leader, is probably my most popular book. It explains basic principles, such as the need to come to God in the spirit of helplessness, and thus deepens and enriches one's prayer life.

The Practice of the Presence of God by Brother Lawrence is another classic about how to pray. The new translation by Blaiklock puts this work in today's English. It also contains a fine introduction.

The Imitation of Christ by Thomas à Kempis shows a tremendous depth of perception concerning discipline, as well as keen psychological insights on topics such as accepting criticism and freeing ourselves from greed. Thomas's handling of psychological dynamics has drawn me back to this book time and time again. I've gone through four or five different editions and have underlined them all extensively.

My Utmost for His Highest by Oswald Chambers is one of his many books with marvelous depth and insight. Another of his books that I recommend is *Daily Thoughts for Disciples.* Both of these books are based on his sermons, and both are noteworthy for their dynamic phrasing and keen insights.

These books are all classics. Some were written hundreds of years ago; some are more recent. All should be readily available in a good bookstore (either on the shelves or through special order) or public library; and all would be well worth ordering for your church library as well as for your personal use.

◆BOOKS THAT HAVE INFLUENCED ME
VERNON GROUNDS

Several books have influenced my spiritual growth. I have been profoundly influenced by a relatively unknown book by Søren Kierkegaard called *Words of Love.* In it, he sets forth the meaning and the demand of

love as it is taught in the New Testament. My reading of that book many years ago helped put the concept of love at the center of my life. Emil Brunner's *The Divine Imperative* also influenced me. In it he seeks to work out in heavy theological form the simple imperative of love.

RELATED ARTICLES

Chapter 25: **Service and Spiritual Growth**
Chapter 25: **Serving the Church**

CHAPTER

4

Knowing God

- ✓ How can you be sure there really is a God?
- ✓ How does God make himself known?
- ✓ What does it mean that God is sovereign?
- ✓ How can God be three persons in one?
- ✓ If God can do anything, why isn't he doing anything for me?

Proving the Existence of God

R. C. SPROUL

The basic truth that forms the foundation for our knowledge of God is his self-revelation. The Scriptures make it clear that he has revealed himself unambiguously in nature. That revelation is so penetrating that it gets through to everyone. Romans 1:19, 20 declare that "what may be known about God is plain to them, because God has made it plain to them. For since the creation of the world God's invisible qualities—his eternal power and divine nature—have been clearly seen, being understood from what has been made, so that men are without excuse."

The confidence that we have in that knowledge, however, wavers. It is assaulted with doubts and questions from time to time. There is a process by which we need to shore up our confidence in the things of God. Our problem is not with a lack of evidence of God's existence but with our sinful disposition to suppress the knowledge that is plain to us.

In other words, our fallen natures do not want us to believe in God. We would prefer to be free from God to live our own lives. But this does not negate the fact that the proof of God is not only possible but is clear and compelling. Also, we must make a distinction between proof and persuasion. Objective proof obligates people to submit to the argument or to the evidence, but even if the proof is unassailable, not everyone submits to it or is persuaded by it. Many approach an issue with a great deal of prejudice or hostility toward a given conclusion; they give themselves a certain mind-set that, no matter how much evidence is presented, they will find ways to dodge the conclusion they fear.

To answer such prejudices, the great apologists of the church have argued that nature does in fact prove the existence of God. The oldest argument for God's existence is that something cannot come from nothing. The universe requires a cause and an intelligence to give it order. This gives the universe its coherency.

To account for the universe we have three options: (1) the universe came from nothing; (2) the universe has always existed; (3) the universe was created by something that has the power of "being" within itself.

Who is it, what is it that has this power? If I am a dependent creature—a human being with a history—I know that I do not have the power to exist in and of myself. Consequently, I know that the identification of God is not with me; I am not God. But someone, something has that power. Some skeptics want to locate such power in the universe itself, but if one part of the universe has the power of being, that would make it immediately different from any part of the universe that is dependent on that self-existent part. The self-existent part, therefore, would have to be distinguished from the other part. The self-existent part would be what we call God.

Another approach is to examine how we look at reality. Consider an everyday object—a tree, for example. There are only four alternatives for the existence of that tree. First, the tree or my experience of it is an illusion; it does not really exist. Second, the tree itself is self-existent and eternal. Third, the tree is self-created. Fourth, the tree is created by something that ultimately is self-existing.

If we take the first option, illusions, we have to account for the fact that something or someone must be having the illusion. That someone or something must be either self-existent, self-created, or created by something that is self-existent. So we can eliminate illusion as the ultimate option.

Notice that two of the remaining three options demand some kind of self-existence. The only alternative to self-existence is self-creation, which is manifestly irrational and absurd. For something to create itself, it would have to exist before it existed. It would have to exist and not exist at the same time and in the same relationship. This is a logical impossibility. To believe in self-creation is to abandon the mind and to abandon reason. Many viewpoints today embrace this concept and dress it up in terms such as *spontaneous generation* or *chance*. It remains, however, a type of self-creation.

The only alternative to account for the tree is that it has been created by something that is self-existent. I believe that something is a Someone—God.

♦THE INCARNATION IS ... / YFC EDITORS

God is the Trinity: Father, Son, Spirit. God has revealed himself to man through nature, his Word, history (particularly Israel), and Christ.

The Trinity at Creation	Genesis 1:26—"Let us make man in our image"
Jesus Christ the Creator	Colossians 1:16
Jesus Christ in the beginning	John 1:1-14
Incarnation and salvation were implied when man first sinned.	Genesis 3:14, 15—Jesus is the seed whose "heel" was bruised. Bruising the serpent's head refers to the death blow Jesus delivered to Satan's power over man.
God became man.	Isaiah 53 Isaiah 9:6 Micah 5:2 Philippians 2:6-8 John 1:14
God took on himself the frailty of a human body.	Luke 2:40—natural growth Luke 4:2—hunger Luke 8:23—sleep Luke 9:58—poverty John 4:6—weariness
God died for mankind.	Romans 5:8 Hebrews 2:9
God rose from the dead.	1 Corinthians 15:3, 4
Jesus went to the right hand of the Father to plead our case.	Hebrews 10:12
God exalted Christ.	Ephesians 1:20, 21 Philippians 2:9-11
Christ became man for eternity.	1 Timothy 2:5

God Speaks to Us Today

JAMES BOICE

A number of years ago I was in northern California for a meeting of the International Council on Biblical Inerrancy. I had a few free hours, so I turned on the radio. A program called "Have You Had a Spiritual Experience?" was on, and people were calling in to describe their experiences.

This was just after a presidential election. A woman who said she was a lifetime Democrat told about going into the polling booth fully expecting to vote for the Democratic candidate. But as she stood in front of the voting machine a strange feeling came over her, and in spite of herself she pulled the lever for the Republican candidate. That was her spiritual experience.

Is that the way God speaks to us today? Does he speak through vague feelings that come over us?

The Bible tells us that God speaks to us in four different ways.

1. *God reveals himself in nature.* Psalm 19 describes this kind of revelation: "The heavens declare the glory of God; the skies proclaim the work of his hands" (v. 1).

Romans 1:20 also speaks of the revelation of God in nature. "God's invisible qualities—his eternal power and divine nature—have been clearly seen, being understood from what has been made." Anyone who has seen nature knows enough about God to seek him out.

The revelation of God in nature proclaims that God exists and that he should be followed. But although this is a true revelation, it is limited. It doesn't tell us anything of God's moral character. More important, it doesn't tell us anything of his love. It has never led anybody to faith.

2. *God reveals himself in history.* In the Old Testament, God spoke to people personally and intervened in a miraculous way by altering the rules of nature. For example, in delivering the Jews from Egypt, he revealed his character and his moral law. He delivered the Israelites from bondage so they would follow him and obey his commandments.

The chief revelation of God in history is Jesus Christ. The book of Hebrews describes how "God spoke to our forefathers through the prophets at many times and in various ways, but in these last days he has spoken to us by his Son" (Hebrews 1:1, 2). In Jesus Christ we discover things about God we don't learn from nature. We learn that God is a person, that God is loving. Above all we find the way of salvation through Christ's death and resurrection.

3. *God reveals himself in the Bible.* God's written revelation is crucial, because whatever we say about God is based on his revelation in the Bible. The Bible is the record of what God has done, focusing on what he has done through Jesus Christ. The Old Testament anticipates Christ's coming. The four Gospels detail his earthly ministry. The Epistles and the other books of the New Testament explain the rest of the Bible for our benefit. More than nature and history, the Bible leads us to seek God.

4. *God reveals himself through the Holy Spirit.* Through the illumination of

the Holy Spirit, a person experiences rebirth. This is the most personal form of God's revelation. Without the Spirit, we cannot understand spiritual things. They are "foolishness" to us (1 Corinthians 2:14). We can't understand the revelation of God in nature, history, or the Bible. But the Holy Spirit makes us alive in Christ. He gives us a new nature. He gives us a new capacity to see God in nature and history and to read the Bible with new understanding.

A non-Christian will attend a Bible study, but nothing makes sense. Then suddenly something clicks and it becomes clear. The Holy Spirit has revealed to him in a personal way that Jesus Christ is God and that Jesus Christ is the Savior. He can now see what he couldn't see before. The person has been born again through the work of the Holy Spirit, who is constantly illuminating the truths of the Bible.

Luke 24 illustrates how this happens. The two Emmaus disciples were returning home after the resurrection of Christ. When Jesus appeared to them on the way and asked why they were downcast, they told him the whole story.

They said there was a man, Jesus of Nazareth, who was a great prophet. But he had been killed that weekend. They explained that they had been in Jerusalem when it happened. They had heard stories from certain women and men who had gone to the tomb and who said the tomb was empty. Some of the women even said Jesus had risen from the dead.

Even though the disciples on the Emmaus road had heard the testimony of witnesses to the resurrection, they didn't understand. And they certainly didn't believe it! So Jesus explained his mission and opened the Scriptures to them (Luke 24:27). Next, he opened their eyes (Luke 24:31), and they recognized him. This is illumination. He was personally doing for them what the Holy Spirit does for us when we study Scripture. Finally, he opened their minds (Luke 24:45). As they began to think about what he had said, and as they connected different passages in Scripture, their minds were opened. They became different people.

The same process is still at work today. If I want to know God, I can read the Bible and pray for the Holy Spirit to illuminate what I read. Then he will open the Scriptures, my eyes, and my mind so I can know him better.

♦ GOD SPEAKS THROUGH SCRIPTURE
JAMES BOICE

Luther, Calvin, and the other Reformers had a very strong sense of the presence of the Holy Spirit and were confident in his ability to teach and lead us. At the same time they were confident that God speaks through Scripture. To them the leading of the Holy Spirit and the teaching of the Bible went hand in hand.

They knew that without the Holy Spirit, the Bible is a dead book. On the other hand, without the Bible as an objective guide from God, a person's claim of special leading by the Holy Spirit can lead to error or excess.

Martin Luther was asked to sign the flyleaf of a Bible. Instead of just signing his name, he wrote a verse and a little message. The verse was John 8:25: "'Who are you?' they asked. 'Just what I have been claiming all along,' Jesus replied."

Then Luther wrote this little comment: "They desire to know who he is and not to regard what he says, while he desires them first to listen; then they will know who he is. This is the rule: listen and allow the Word of God to make the beginning; then the knowing will nicely follow. If, however, you do not listen, you will never know anything. For it is decreed: God will not be seen, known, or comprehended except through his Word alone. Whatever therefore one undertakes for salvation apart from the Word is in vain. God will not respond to that. He will not have it. He will not tolerate any other way. Therefore let his book in which he speaks with you, be commended to you, for he did not cause it to be written for no purpose. He did not want us to let it lie there in neglect, as if he were speaking with mice under the bench or with flies on the pulpit. We are to read it, to think and speak about it, and to study it, certain that he himself (not an angel or a creature) is speaking with us in it." (Ewald M. Plass, comp., *What Luther Says: An Anthology,* vol. 1 [St. Louis: Concordia, 1959], 81).

That is how the Word of God and the leading of the Holy Spirit interact. The opening of our eyes leads to the ordering of our lives.

♦ GOD SPEAKS THROUGH THOUGHTS
HANNAH HURNARD

I couldn't believe there was a God until he showed himself to me. Many years ago a wise person suggested, "Why don't you put an empty chair in front of you. Picture Jesus in that chair, and begin talking to him as you would if you really saw him." This helped me. When I did that, God began to make himself known to me.

The way God makes himself known to me is in my thoughts. I talk in thoughts to him about things I hear at worship services and at conferences, about everything that happens in my daily life. In my thoughts I ask him for his guidance.

He talks back in my thoughts. I can tell if the thoughts come from him or from me, because the ones that come from me are bewildered or unloving or about not nice things, and the ones that come from him are happy. They remind me of God's love. They make me want to follow him and do what Jesus taught.

I have a little notebook in which I jot down the thoughts I think come from him. The moment I say, "Please, Lord, explain this," the thoughts begin to come into my mind. At first this happened slowly and in a small way, and then his thoughts came to me more and more. I have been doing this for sixty-one years, and it's wonderful.

God in Three Persons
✍ R. C. SPROUL

To speak of the Trinity is to speak of a mystery. To say that God is one in essence and three in person describes one of the mysteries of Christian doctrine, though we can get a glimpse of its truth.

We are not being contradictory, illogical, or irrational to consider the concept of a single being with a tri-personality. We have no human reference point for it because, in our experience and from our perspective, all persons we know are singular beings. Each is one person, one being. None is one being, three persons.

Many analogies have been set forth to try to make it simple—such as a man who is at the same time a father, a son, and a brother. But this is not what the Bible is talking about when it speaks of the three persons of God. God describes himself as having three distinct personae within his essence.

The Bible speaks of the three personages of God—Father, Son, and Holy Spirit. We ask, how can that be? Logic cannot prove that something is. All that logic can do is to prove that something is rationally possible or impossible. That is, logic gives us a formal test of the possibilities of reality. The idea of a God who is at the same time three in essence and one in essence, or three persons and one person, would be impossible. It would be logically false. But there is no rule of reason that is violated by the concept of one being with three persons.

The Trinity, therefore, can logically exist. That does not mean that it does. We can conceive of many things that are consistent with logic that do not necessarily exist. For example, there would be nothing logically impossible about having a being that is one being with four persons, or five persons, or six persons. We have no reason to believe that such a being exists. But it is a logical possibility.

So, in answer to the question—How can the Trinity exist?—I respond, why not?

If we accept the mysterious existence of the Trinity, how do we react to each person of the Godhead? Some of these personal distinctions in the Bible are made economically, that is, according to the work that each performs. Specifically, it is the Father's task to send the Son into the world to redeem us, and it is the task of the Son to effect our reconciliation. The Holy Spirit applies the work of Christ to us.

As we see these roles of activities that are ascribed here to the Father, there to the Son, there to the Holy Spirit, they give us a clue as to how we are to react to each person of the Trinity. When I think of the member of the Godhead who has effected my salvation, I think of God the Son, and I respond appropriately to that. When I think of who has quickened my soul and brought me from death into spiritual life, I think of God the Holy Spirit. When I think of the one who sovereignly ordains everything that comes to pass, I think of God the Father.

Although there may be special emphasis given to one or the other members of the Godhead in these various works of creation and redemption, in all of these things we have a trinitarian involvement. The mystery continues.

Getting to Know God

TERRY PRISK

Pascal once said that there is a God-shaped vacuum within every individual. We sense he exists. But we need to know him as more than just a Creator. We need to know him intimately—what he is like, what we can do to please him. When we begin to realize who God is, we discover that we desire to be more like him, to make his character our character. Why should *we* get to know God better? Because he is light, he is love, and he is spirit.

God is light (1 John 1:5)—he offers me direction. I should get to know him better because, as a result of my character becoming more like his, I am given direction in my life. It is like the young man who was exploring a cave. With light, he could find his way; but when he dropped his flashlight down a shaft, it went out. He scrambled around and yelled for help. Someone heard his call, shined a light toward him, and this pointed him to safety. That is light. He is direction.

God is also love (1 John 4:8). I get to know God better so that I have a greater capacity to love, to reach out, to be what I need to be for other people. When I begin to identify with the purpose of why Christ came—which was to serve, not be served, to minister, not be ministered to—I realize as I try to imitate him that I will be more effective in contributing to my family relationships and relationships in society. As I learn about his nature of love, I learn how to love. "Greater love has no one than this, that one lay down his life for his friends" (John 15:13).

The greatest example of love was when Christ, hanging on the cross after being whipped and bruised and mocked, said, "Father, forgive them, for they do not know what they are doing" (Luke 23:34). As I get to know God in a more meaningful and intimate way, he gives me a capacity beyond myself to love those people who treat me in ways that are not right, suitable, or even enjoyable.

As I get to know God better, I learn that he is spirit (John 4:24). He is *not* a transcendental, meditation-type guru, but he is spirit in that he cannot be confined by space or time. He is with me to assist, to comfort, to love, to provide peace.

I am the created being, he is the Creator. I get to know God better because without him becoming a part of me, I will fall on my face along with my plans and goals. I cannot function without the instruction, guidance, and expertise of my Creator.

You may feel as if you are doing fine until you realize that you are a complicated, integral creation that needs to be developed mentally, socially, physically, and spiritually. That is not possible without knowing the Creator.

I get to know God better because I realize who I am, I realize who he is, and I realize that for fulfillment, peace, and hope I need to get to know him.

Biblical Metaphors Help Us Know God

✍ LUCI SHAW

The Bible uses numerous metaphors for God and Christ. Each metaphor gives us a different view of God; each emphasizes a different aspect or attribute of God.

God is a king with a kingdom. He has subjects, and he has enemies. He is a general with an army and a strategic plan. He's a potter who is shaping both ordinary earthen vessels and highly refined, decorated, beautiful art objects. God is a father who loves and disciplines his children.

In Malachi we see God as a refiner's fire who burns out our impurities just as molten gold is refined in a furnace, so that the surface is so pure you can see your face in it. God wants us to be like that, so he can see his reflection in us.

In Hosea we see God as an evergreen tree that provides shade and fruit all year long, no matter what the season. God, like that evergreen tree, is always there, giving us shelter and beauty and nourishment.

One of the more persistent images in the Bible is that of the suitor, or the lover, who is pursuing a very fickle woman. She is often unfaithful to him and runs off with other men, but because he loves her he keeps after her and finally makes her his bride. Christians tend to ignore it, but frank sexual imagery is strong in the Bible.

Another image is that of the vinedresser—the farmer who wants to see his grape harvest come to fruition. We're those grapes, and the grapevine is the Christian community—little individual grapes clustered together, dependent on each other, and in touch with each other. And the sap of the Holy Spirit is flowing through to each of those grapes.

The Bible gives us various images for the Holy Spirit, too. He's seen as a dove, as oil, as fire, as water, as a mediator, or a friendly lawyer. He's the unseen go-between, our comforter, the one who stands beside us in times of need.

And, of course, for Christ there's a whole list of images. He's the bread of life, he's the kernel of wheat that decays in the ground in order to sprout and produce more grain. He's the wine poured out, he's the water in a spring. He's the grapevine, the cornerstone of the building. He's the door to the sheepfold, and in that same setting the image changes, and he becomes the shepherd who leads the sheep through the door.

He's the bridegroom, the solid rock foundation, the pioneer, the morning star. He's the lion—royal, powerful, untamed, golden-maned—but he's also the white-fleeced, innocent, helpless, submissive lamb.

There are womanly images of God in the Bible. Very often they're passed over or ignored because they don't fit our traditional way of picturing God. But God is the mother hen who wants to gather us like little chicks. God is the nurturer, the comforter, the builder. God is the woman who searches for the lost coin and rejoices when she finds it. The very idea of the family of God points to God's motherly characteristics, for what's a family without a mother?

In Isaiah 66:13, God says: "As a mother comforts her child, so will I comfort you." Jesus gave that sort of feeling when he said, "Let the little children come to me, and do not hinder them, for the kingdom of God belongs to such as these" (Mark 10:14). Such closeness, intimacy, warmth, and provision are typical of mothers.

All these metaphors are pictures. God is so ineffable, so far beyond us, that we need these gifts of imagery to bring him down within our reach, so to speak. They're just touches of him. They're pointers to him. We will never totally understand him while we're restricted to finite minds and bodies—we just have to hold onto these pictures he gives us.

I think Jesus was the ultimate metaphor of God. He showed us what God looks like in daily life. The kind of life Jesus lived tells us that God understands us. Jesus was a small-town carpenter. He was often tired; his muscles ached after a day in the shop. Yet he loved people; he wept when his friend died—he was so human. He got angry; he was frustrated with all those temple tradespeople with their corruption and their commercialism. We can relate to a God like Jesus. Our God is not some far-off deity who hands down decisions without any personal contact or caring or touch.

If we don't pay attention to metaphor in the Bible, we'll miss out on a whole spiritual dimension. We'll get a flat view of God rather than a true one. Imagery makes for a much more interesting, personal, and colorful understanding. God has planned it that way; he has built imagination into the human psyche. And if we fear it, or skip over it carelessly, we'll twist ourselves into something he didn't intend for us to be. If we ignore metaphor in the Bible, we deprive ourselves and diminish our spiritual understanding.

◆ ATTRIBUTES OF GOD / INGRID TROBISCH

Fatherliness and motherliness are both attributes of God. The longer a man has been growing in his walk with the Lord, the more motherly he can be. He learns to nurture—to take care of people, to feed them physically and spiritually. Likewise, the more a woman has grown up into Christ, the more fatherly she can be. She can structure her life and make decisions; she can be creative.

Practical Atheists

DAVE VEERMAN

An atheist is someone who says that he or she does not believe in God. Agnostics say they don't know if God exists (or that no one can know whether or not God exists). According to the polls, most Americans are not atheists or agnostics: the overwhelming majority of us profess to believe in God. We are "theists."

According to these same polls, however, there is a vast gulf between our beliefs and our practices. In other words, belief in God seems to make very little difference in our lives. Whether or not we believe in God, most of us act as though he does *not* exist—we are *practical atheists.*

If we believed that God exists, we would be spending time with him, talking about and with him, and worshiping him. But church attendance is declining—instead we worship the almighty NFL on Sundays.

If we believed in God, our values would reflect his. Instead, we devalue human life, created by him in his image, through our bombs, abortions, and sexual promiscuity. And we hoard and conserve what we have, turning our backs on the poor and oppressed of the world.

If we really knew God, our focus would be heavenward, knowing that eternity looms beyond the grave. Instead, we live as though this life is all there is, grabbing all the gusto, toys, money, and pleasure that we can. We are self-centered and pleasure oriented.

If we actually *believed* in God, we would be spreading the word about his love and his justice. Instead, however, we circle our wagons, protect ourselves, and hide the light under a bushel.

If we truly knew God, our lives would show it! Our children, neighbors, relatives, and friends would see him in us.

God *does* exist and he wants to have a vital, growing relationship with us through Jesus the Christ, his Son. Trust Christ; believe God; and live for him.

Being Holy, As God Is Holy

✍ JAMES BOICE

Holiness is both important and practical. It is important because God is holy, and it is practical because we are told to be holy. But many Christians do not understand what holiness really is.

Most Christians think of holiness as a moral measuring scale like a rating on a term paper. People who are unholy are down at the bottom. People who are average are somewhere in the middle. The very good people are up near the top. But nobody is 100 percent holy except Jesus.

This explanation is misleading. Holiness involves ethics and righteousness, but that isn't the essence of holiness. The essence of holiness is to be set apart.

God is wholly other, unique to himself. God is infinitely set apart. No one is like the holy God. God's holiness has many facets. It's like a prism that reflects many colors at one time.

The first facet is *majesty.* God is majestic, like a king on his throne. The word *glory* describes this aspect of holiness. Those who catch a vision of God in his holiness are generally overcome with a sense of their own inadequacy. He is great and we are not. He is holy and we are sinners. When the writers of the Bible tried to describe the greatness of God's holiness, they had to repeat the word *holy* three times. "Holy, holy, holy is the Lord Almighty" (Isaiah 6:3).

The second facet is *will.* God is not a formula or a concept. God is will, a will that accomplishes things. God's will is predominantly set on proclaiming himself as the holy God, acting as God, and being recognized as God. That is why he is not indifferent to how men and women regard him.

The third facet is *wrath.* God's wrath is not a capricious anger. It's the natural expression of God's holiness in response to sin. God cannot coexist with evil. We know God's wrath because we are sinners. Our minds and wills are set on that which is other than and contrary to God.

The fourth facet is *righteousness.* God's moral righteousness is the will of God working out in life. God's will acts to conform the world to God's moral character. The law of God is a good expression of his moral righteousness.

These four facets of God's holiness help us understand what it means for us to be holy. "Be holy because I, the Lord your God, am holy" (Leviticus 19:2). That verse is not saying, "Be God as I am God." It's not talking about God's majesty and glory. It's not even saying, "Be as morally righteous as I am morally righteous." We cannot be holy to the same degree as God, but we can be holy in a corresponding way. As God is holy, set apart, we are to be holy and set apart.

This is what sanctification means, of course. Our words *saint* and *sanctify* come from the Latin word for holy, *sanctus. Holy* derives from old Germanic languages; *saint* and *sanctify* derive from Romance languages, but the idea behind all the words is the same. Sanctification, like holiness, means being set apart to God.

When Moses dedicated the tabernacle that the Jews carried in the wilderness, "he anointed it and consecrated the altar and all its utensils" (Numbers 7:1). In other words, he sanctified them. He didn't produce a mystical change in the nature of the stones or metal of the altar. He set them apart for a holy use.

To be holy is to be sanctified, and to be sanctified is to be a saint. Jesus was set apart for God's holy work by giving himself up to death on the cross. He wants us to be set apart for the work of God in the same way. He prayed for our sanctification in John 17:19: "For them I sanctify myself, that they too may be truly sanctified."

There are three steps in being set apart. The first is to be aware of our sin. When God begins to work in our lives, we become conscious of our sinfulness. We become aware of the things that separate us from God.

The second step is to be born again. No one can be set apart without that experience. Jesus said to Nicodemus in John 3:3, "I tell you the truth, unless a man is born again, he cannot see the kingdom of God."

The third step is to "produce fruit in keeping with repentance" (Matthew 3:8), which is turning from sin to faith. God works in our hearts to open our eyes to his truth. When he makes us aware of our sins, we can truly repent of them for the first time. In deep awareness of our need, we turn our hearts to Jesus Christ in faith.

Then we are no longer our own. Then Jesus sets us apart for the work of God, and our lives begin to bear fruit for him. Then we are on the path of holiness.

♦ SEEING GOD AT THE SHORE / LUCI SHAW

The beach is a rich source of images that speak of the Lord. All the elements are at work—above you is the sky reaching up, behind you is a whole continent, and in front of you is the sea, deep and mysterious. Earth, air, and water all meet in this one place.

I think of the waves coming endlessly to the shore. These wrinkles that continually spread out and cross each other are a picture of God's diversity, immensity, and infinity. Like God, they never stop reaching toward us. They speak of his constancy.

I'm a great shell lover. I collect shells indefatigably; I can't resist them. Picking up a shell from among a million others along the beach reminds me that God reached down and touched me; he saw value in me and chose me and picked me out as individual. It's a metaphor of election, or grace. Somehow, among millions of others, I catch his attention. He loves me with his glance and with his touch; he picks me up and brings me home.

♦ SOVEREIGNTY AND CONVERSION J. I. PACKER

When talking about God's sovereignty and personal conversion, it is important to stress two things. One is that coming to Christ really is your decision, your commitment, your action. Yet, when you entrust yourself to the Lord Jesus and receive him as your Savior, you ought to get down on your knees and thank God for leading you to him and enabling you to make the decision. Right from the start you should acknowledge God's sovereignty. You turned to him because he turned you to himself. Every Christian knows it wasn't his own wisdom or good sense that led him to God; it was God himself. So give him the praise.

God's Sovereignty at Work

✍ J. I. PACKER

God's sovereignty may seem a dry theological topic to some, but the working out of his sovereign will can be seen in practical ways in our everyday lives. Sometimes we see it even as it works; sometimes it is years before we realize what God has been doing.

The fact that I'm a professor of theology at Regent College is all because of God's sovereignty. I was sitting in my study at Trinity College, Bristol, when the principal of Regent called me from Vancouver about a post there. I did not particularly want to cross the Atlantic, and my first thought was that this job wasn't for me. But when he explained it further, I realized it was just my shape. I saw that God had created a situation where what they wanted at Regent was exactly what I could give and what I wanted to do with my life. That was sovereignty at work in a very obvious way.

I saw it again in due course. My wife came ahead to buy a house, more confident than I that there would be something waiting for her when she got to Vancouver. Sure enough, there was an ideal house—our home now.

Everything about this move seemed right except that at the time of accepting the appointment, there did not seem to be a local church with which we could identify. However, six months before we left England, my oldest friend among Canadian evangelical clergy was called out of the blue (so he thought) to a large church here in Vancouver, less than five minutes' drive from the home to which God led us. In every sense, this church has been a spiritual home. In this, too, God's sovereign providence has become evident.

That is one example of the way God's sovereignty works. God, without in any way taking from us our responsibility for making decisions, overrules in such a way as to answer our basic needs. This shows that God's lordship is not remote but is involved in our individual lives. I might add here, lest you get the wrong idea, that this divine involvement is as real when you cannot see what God is up to in your life as it is when you can.

God's sovereignty doesn't mean we are robots, that we are not free to make our own decisions and answer for them. It certainly doesn't mean we are not free to commit or not commit ourselves to other people. People misunderstand God's sovereignty because they suppose that a God who is sovereign must be a remote God.

What sovereignty means is that God is in control all the time, and nothing happens apart from his will. He is not remote or unconcerned. The God who calls us to love him is the God who cares for us. He made us with the power to make our own decisions and commit ourselves in love to others. He doesn't override our humanity in his dealings with us. He doesn't treat us like sticks and move us around at his pleasure. He comes to us person to person; he addresses our minds by his Word; he draws out of us the response of love and affection. That's always his way in dealing with human beings.

◆GOD'S WILL / YFC EDITORS

GOD'S WILL	OUR RESPONSE
Sovereign Decrees	
"All may have eternal life."	We trust him and obey.
"All may choose to accept or reject me."	
"All who reject or ignore me will be punished."	
Conditional Intervention	
"If you want my opinion, ask me. I'll be glad to help."	We pray.
"If you need a miracle, ask me. If I agree, you'll get it."	
Natural Law	
"Apple trees produce apples, not turnips."	We plan accordingly.
"Smoking produces lung damage."	

God's will actually functions on three different levels. The sovereign decrees and natural laws are nonnegotiable; there's not a whole lot we can do about them. But in the middle lies an area of human affairs in which our attitudes and actions can make quite a difference.

We sometimes don't understand which level is involved in our various questions. We often want guidance on something that has been settled by a sovereign decree or a natural law, and we just haven't done our homework. But in many other areas, our requests for guidance are legitimate.

♦ DOES GOD REALLY CARE ABOUT YOU? YFC EDITORS

God does care. He created us. He gave us other Christians to love us. He sent Christ to demonstrate his great love in terms we human beings could understand.

Some Bible people experienced times when they wondered if God really cared or if he had simply forgotten them. Joseph sat in prison for a crime he didn't commit, waiting on God, wondering what would happen. David, the anointed king of Israel, was chased through the mountains by Saul who wanted to kill him out of jealousy. Nehemiah prayed to God beside the ruins of the glorious city of Jerusalem. These men experienced what we often experience—the feeling of Where is God when I need him? Does he really care about me? But look at the results. Joseph was prepared with great wisdom and faith in God in order to run Egypt and bring his family there. David was always protected from Saul and eventually did become Israel's greatest king. Nehemiah's faith in God allowed him to supervise the rebuilding of the walls of Jerusalem.

We may go through trials and frustrations that cause us to feel as if God doesn't care, but he is *always* with us, working for our ultimate good.

♦ DOES GOD REALLY WANT GOOD THINGS FOR YOU? / YFC EDITORS

What do you mean by "good?" Yes, God wants what is good for you—but he looks at what is ultimately good. The good things he gives you are not necessarily wealth, material possessions, or happiness by the world's standards. If that's what you're looking for, then you may be disappointed.

Instead, God has given you himself. His love for you caused him to send his Son to die for you so that you could be saved. He has given you the promise of eternal life in heaven. You need never doubt God's love and care for you. He created you and knew you before you were born (Psalm 139). He delights in you as you follow him (Psalm 37:23). Nothing can ever separate you from his love (Romans 8:38, 39).

The good things he has given you are far beyond anything you could ever ask or think.

♦ WHY DO BAD THINGS HAPPEN? YFC EDITORS

If God is all-powerful, if God can do anything to bless his children, why doesn't he seem to bless you?

You are not an "only" child. God's care involves all of his children, not just you. It is a childhood fantasy to believe that God exists only to serve your needs.

There is no question about what God *can* do—he can do anything. But he lets difficult things happen to us so that we might grow up in character. If he gave us everything we wanted, he wouldn't really love us. Why? Because many of the things we want are not good for us. And he is always working for the *best,* not just good.

Difficult times build character. Not having everything we want teaches us perspective and helps us to trust. When we face hard times, we are better able to serve others. When we can go without things we think we must have, we become spiritually mature. The "good" thing may have been to not have the problem in the first place. The "good" thing may be being blessed with what we want. But the "best" thing is to grow in character and learn to trust God more. We have indeed been blessed, but in ways that are wonderfully unexpected.

RELATED ARTICLES
Chapter 2: **Called to Holiness**
Chapter 16: **Does God Speak through the Bible?**
Chapter 17: **Talking to a Holy God**
Chapter 22: **Decision Making and the Sovereignty of God**

CHAPTER

5

Becoming Like Christ

- ✓ How does Jesus live in me?
- ✓ What is the image of Christ?
- ✓ Why should Christ be in charge of my life?
- ✓ What does it mean to be crucified with Christ?
- ✓ How do we become more like him?

Jesus: Both God and Man

✍ NORMAN GEISLER

Jesus had a heavenly Father and an earthly mother. He is fully human because he was born of a human and he lived a human life—growing, eating, sleeping, dying. He is fully God because he has a divine nature and has been coequal with the Father and the Holy Spirit from all eternity.

Christ, then, has two natures—one human and one divine—in one person. The Godhead has one nature in three persons—Father, Son, and Holy Spirit.

Athanasius, a great church father, said that when Jesus became man, he did not subtract deity but rather added humanity. Jesus wasn't less than God, but he became something in addition to God, namely, man. He assumed a new nature, one he didn't have from all eternity.

I give an explanation of this eternal mystery that I call my evangelical Abbott and Costello description: in the Trinity there is one What, or nature, and three Whos, or persons. In Christ there is one Who and two Whats. Jesus never lost his divine nature when he took on his human nature; he had both Whats simultaneously.

Think of God's nature as a triangle. The top corner is the Father, the bottom left corner the Son, and the bottom right corner the Holy Spirit. Then think of Jesus' human nature as a circle attached to the bottom left corner. Jesus had both a triangular nature—because he was God—and a circular nature—because he was man. He lived within both the circle of humanity and the triangle of deity.

The Scriptures support the fact that Jesus was human. Obviously, all the passages about his birth attest to his humanity. In Galatians 4:4 we read that he was born of a woman, and in Luke 2:52 we read that he grew. In John 11:35, "Jesus wept." He hungered, he was tempted, he died on the cross. All the Gospels record that he had emotions.

The Scriptures also show that he was truly divine. John 1:1, 2 say: "In the beginning was the Word, and the Word was with God, and the Word was God. He was with God in the beginning."

Jesus is the Lord of the Old Testament. "A voice of one calling: 'In the desert prepare the way for the Lord' " (Isaiah 40:3) was fulfilled by John the Baptist, who went out to the desert to prepare the way for Jesus (Matthew 3:1-17; Mark 1:1-8; Luke 3:1-18; John 1:19-28).

"The Lord is my shepherd," wrote David about God (Psalm 23:1), and Jesus said, "I am the good shepherd" (John 10:14).

In Zechariah 12:10 the Lord said, "They will look on me, the one they have pierced," and in John 19:37 this is applied to Jesus.

We read in Isaiah 44:6, "This is what the Lord says—Israel's King and Redeemer, the Lord Almighty: I am the first and I am the last; apart from me there is no God." In Revelation 1:17, Jesus said to John, "Do not be afraid. I am the First and the Last."

There are dozens of passages in which Jesus claims to be the creator of the universe (see, for example, John 1:3 and Colossians 1:16). In Mark 2:1-12, Jesus claims the divine power to forgive sins. In John 5:21, he said he is able to give life to the dead. Several times in the New Testament, Jesus accepts people's worship (in John 20:24-29, he accepts Thomas' cry, "My Lord and my God!").

We see, then, that Jesus claimed to have God's attributes and to do his acts. Because of this, he received worship that is due only to God. Although Jesus never said "I am God" in so many words, his words and actions leave no doubt about who he was claiming to be.

This doctrine of Jesus' two natures is important, because if it isn't true, we can't be saved. If he's not God, then he can't reach to God for us, and if he's not man, he can't reach to man. 1 Timothy 2:5 says, "There is one God and one mediator between God and men, the man Christ Jesus." Jesus needs to be both divine and human in order to bring God and man together.

As believers, we need to relate to Jesus both ways—as God and as man. Jesus said, "Anyone who has seen me has seen the Father" (John 14:9). Jesus is God reflected in human flesh.

We've heard people say of children, "He's a chip off the old block," indicating that the son looks and acts like his father. Christ was the image of God. Hebrews 1:3 states, "The Son is the radiance of God's glory and the exact representation of his being." And Paul, in Colossians 1:15, wrote, "He is the image of the invisible God."

Jesus was both God and man. He lived, ate, slept, and died like a man, but we can also see in him the attributes of God. Jesus brings deity down to the level of humanity; we can identify with him. Because of Jesus, God no longer seems remote, far off, and ethereal. For good reason he was called Immanuel—"which means, 'God with us' " (Matthew 1:23).

♦ THE CLAIMS OF CHRIST / YFC EDITORS

It is well established that Jesus was a man of history. No serious scholar would dispute that. Roman, Greek, and Jewish historians attest to that fact as well as biblical historians. But that doesn't tell us whether Jesus actually is God. This is an important question since the case for Christianity rests on it. Christ made some extravagant claims about himself. His statements leave us with some definite decisions to make.

THREE ALTERNATIVES

His claims were false, and he knew his claims were false.	His claims were false, but he did not know his claims were false.	His claims were true, and he told the truth.
He made a deliberate misrepresentation.	He was sincerely deluded.	He acted in a manner consistent with his claims.
He was a liar and a hypocrite.	He was a *lunatic*.	He was not just a good man.
Conclusion: He was a fool for he died for it.	*Conclusion:* He was a fool for he died for it.	*Conclusion:* He is Lord.
Reject him.	Reject him.	Accept him.

What Is Jesus Really Like?

V. GILBERT BEERS

If we were to ask a hundred people, What is Jesus like? we would get many different answers.

One person would describe a long-remembered picture of Jesus wearing a sad, pained expression. This person might think of a Jesus who never laughed.

Another would think of a painting in which Jesus' searching eyes looked into the depths of his soul. This person might see Jesus as a divine X-ray machine, penetrating his life until he squirms with discomfort.

Another would remember Jesus with the whip, driving the money changers out of the temple. This person might see Jesus as the great punisher. I had better watch out, this person would think, or he will get me, too.

As a child growing up in a small village church, I absorbed various Sunday school materials and formed an image of a harmless character who never stepped off a four-color poster. Jesus was kind and good but somewhat static.

Many years later I began to write Bible learning materials for children and families. To do this, I read the New Testament dozens of times. I came to know the New Testament character of Jesus Christ.

I learned that Jesus was sorrowful in Gethsemane and at Golgotha, but not because he was a somber person. No, it was because he was pouring out his love for me unto death and was receiving my sins upon himself. No wonder he looked sad!

I learned also that Jesus was often joyful. He talked about the lilies of the field, the birds of the air, and the wonders of his Father's home in heaven. He went to dinners at tax collectors' houses and wedding feasts.

Not only was he joyful himself; he also brought joy to those around him. He fed hungry people. He helped blind people see the trees and flowers around them. He led his followers into a grainfield to get something to eat.

The Gospels, I learned, are a record of God's grand design for redemption, and Jesus is the one who made it possible. He is the one who specializes in taking care of broken lives and making them whole again.

Most of us have a one-sided view of Jesus. This is unfortunate, because Jesus' character is rich and complex. People who do not know this may dismiss Jesus as being too sad or too moralistic or too threatening or too boring without ever realizing that they have caught only one out-of-focus glimpse of his personality.

Happily, there is a cure for this kind of spiritual astigmatism. It's time to put down the distorted images we may have formed in our childhood from half-remembered paintings, stories, and sermons. It's time to pick up the only lens that will make it possible for us to see the real picture—the Bible. The Gospels of Matthew, Mark, Luke, and John give a well-rounded picture of a well-rounded man. The more often we read them, the clearer our vision will be.

Knowing Christ

RICHARD HALVERSON

Years ago I was flying down to Winston-Salem, North Carolina, for a meeting, and I sat next to an IBM executive. I had an opportunity to witness to him, and I spoke of knowing Christ.

Finally, with some frustration, he said to me, "You keep saying you know Christ. What do you mean?"

I tried to explain. He had told me earlier that he was going to see an old friend he had known since they were five years old but hadn't seen in twenty years. So I made this comparison: "You've mentioned the man you're going to be meeting in Winston-Salem. You've told me his name. Do you know him?"

"Of course I know him," he said. "We've been friends since we were five, and even though I haven't seen him in twenty years, I know him."

"What's the color of his hair?" I asked.

He thought about it for a minute. "Well, I can't remember," he answered.

"What color are his eyes?"

Silence.

"How tall is he?"

No comment.

"Where was he born?"

"I don't think he was born in Winston-Salem—I didn't meet him until he was five," the man said.

"But I thought you said you know him," I pressed. His answer was a classic.

"I don't know what I mean—but I know him, and I know I know him."

He knew the essence of the person, though not a sum of facts about him. From that point I was able to talk to him of knowing Jesus Christ in a personal way.

My wife and I have a one-year-old granddaughter. She knows her mother and her father and her sisters and her grandparents. She can identify us, and she responds instantly to us in a way she doesn't to strangers. But how can we measure her degree of knowing us? *Know* is a great word, but what does it mean?

You can know Christ, as you can know any person, the minute you begin a relationship with him—that is, from the very beginning of your Christian life. Then as you grow in Christ you get to know him better and better.

We can't equate knowing about Christ with knowing Christ himself. I may know a lot about Abraham Lincoln—perhaps more than his personal friends did at the time. But they knew him in a way I cannot, despite the list of facts I've gathered about him. Today there are brilliant theologians who know a lot more about Christ than his disciples did, but they don't know him.

How do we get to know him? I believe no one can respond to Christ unless there is already a work of grace in him. I believe in the sovereignty of God, election, predestination, and the divine call—that before the foundation of the world, God called us to himself.

The desire to know Christ is planted in us by God himself, but we have to act on that call. For instance, we baptize children on the basis of the faith of the parents. They commit themselves to raise and nurture their children as part of the family of God. Then when the children come to the age of accountability and are able to act on the grace that has been offered, they naturally respond to what God has been doing in their hearts all along. Getting to know Christ, then, is a matter of responding to him as he calls us—at the beginning of our Christian lives, and day by day.

Jesus Loves Me

JANETTE OKE

"Jesus loves me, this I know, for the Bible tells me so. . . ." This is probably the first song our children learn. It has become so commonplace to us within the church that perhaps we sing it without even thinking about the words.

Try to imagine for a moment what this song might mean if you were hearing it for the very first time.

Jesus? Who is Jesus?

He's the Son of God, the Creator of all things, the King of kings, the Lord of the universe, the sustainer of life.

If he is all that, why does he love me?

Because he created you for fellowship with himself, because he really knows you as a person, because you are important to him as an individual.

Aw, come on, I don't believe it.

It's true—the Bible says so.

The Bible is an old book.

The Bible is the Word of God. His Word will never pass away. It's as relevant today as when it was written, and it says he loves me. "Jesus loves me . . . the Bible tells me so."

A great theologian, known worldwide for his in-depth study of the Scriptures, was asked one day by one of his students, "What is the greatest discovery you have ever made in your extensive searching?"

He answered, "Jesus loves me, this I know, for the Bible tells me so."

This is not a trite saying. It is not a little ditty that sounds cute on the lips of our lisping babies. It is a truth. It is a fact. One we can stake our lives on.

We must never let the little song's familiarity take away from its glorious truth. I will not soon forget the experience I had a few years ago when listening to an excited new Christian who had just discovered something worth shouting about in the Scriptures. He had found a verse, and he wanted to share it with all of us because it was so special. He could hardly read it for his emotion—it was so new, so exciting, so great a discovery!

His excitement was contagious. We could hardly wait to hear what he had found. He lifted his Bible and, with a quiver in his voice, began to read: "For God so loved the world that he gave his one and only Son, that whoever believes in him shall not perish but have eternal life" (John 3:16).

I settled back in my seat thinking, "Oh, that." I had learned the verse as a child, had heard it repeated often, and had taught it to my own children and to other boys and girls in Sunday school. I had forgotten to be excited about it. I had forgotten what a fantastic discovery it is for someone who has not known it before.

"God so loved the world that he gave his one and only Son. . . ." As I watched the face of the new believer, I began to catch the excitement of that verse again. Thank God he loved us! Thank God he loved us so much he sent his Son to free us from our sin. Thank God we can be forgiven, released, made whole because God loved us enough to pay the ultimate price to redeem us.

How wonderful it is to know that Jesus loves me, Jesus loves you. It's true—the Bible tells us so, over and over and over again.

♦ GOOD MORNING, LORD / LUIS PALAU

A Christian should begin each day by thanking Jesus, for he has chosen to live within each of us.

The first thing each morning I thank him. "Thank you, Lord Jesus, that you have chosen to indwell me, that you came to live within me those many years ago. Thank you that you are alive." In a way, it is like saying good morning to the Lord and affirming that you want him to run your day.

Next, I meditate on God's revelation, especially the New Testament, so that I can search his mind to know what his desires are. Finally, I say to the Lord Jesus, "I will obey you and gladly so, because you are indwelling me, because you are God, and because you are my Savior."

Jesus Is Lord

✍ DEAN MERRILL

What does a Christian mean by saying, Jesus is Lord? The answer all depends on which century you have in mind.

If you're talking about the first Christians, those who lived under the rule of the Roman Empire, the statement "Jesus is Lord" was nothing less than a fast ticket to trouble if the local authorities chose to take you seriously. The empire already had a lord—Caesar—and he didn't take kindly to the idea of sharing his authority with some teacher from the eastern hinterlands of his domain.

In a letter to the emperor Trajan around A.D. 111, a provincial governor named Pliny double-checked to see if he was handling the Christians properly:

"I interrogated them whether they were Christians; if they confessed it I repeated the question twice again, adding the threat of capital punishment; if they still persevered, I ordered them to be executed....

"Those who denied they were, or had ever been, Christians, who repeated after me an invocation to the gods, and offered adoration, with wine and frankincense, to your image, which I had ordered to be brought for that purpose ... and who finally cursed Christ ... I thought it proper to discharge."

What did the emperor think of all this?

"The method you have pursued, my dear Pliny ... is extremely proper," Trajan wrote back.

As you can see, things have changed. Not many presidents or prime ministers have the nerve these days to proclaim themselves lord. Great Britain still has a House of Lords, but it has no power to command. It's a group of wealthy gentlemen who mainly agree to the decisions of the noisier House of Commons. They are known best for the long robes and white wigs they still wear on state occasions.

So what is a lord? We hardly know anymore.

Juan Carlos Ortiz, a former Argentine pastor who now lives in California, says, "We have an interesting problem in Spanish with the word *lord. Lord* is *señor,* the same word we use for *mister.*" In other words, Señor Lopez runs the gas station on the corner, Señor Rodriguez drives a city bus, and Señor Jesucristo listens to your prayers.

"The result in Spanish," Ortiz continues, "is that we have lost the 'lord' concept. To call Jesus the Lord (Señor) doesn't really say anything very strongly.

"But since I have come among English-speaking people, I have found that you have the same problem, even though you have two separate words, mister and lord, in your language. . . . The Bible presents Jesus as King, as Lord, as the maximum authority. Jesus is at the very center" (Juan Carlos Ortiz, *Disciple* [Carol Stream, Ill.: Creation House, 1975], 11, 12).

Yet in most English-speaking countries, there is no king, no highest authority. The United States government, for example, is based on a division of power into three equally high branches.

Perhaps the fastest way to cut through the jargon is simply to get honest and say a lord is a boss. The person in charge. The person who has the power to tell us what to do.

Jesus? He was a wonderful man who set a fine example for us all, said many wise things—but does he give us orders? Yes. The only remaining question is whether we will obey his orders or whether we will rebel. Is he the boss or not? That is the question every Christian must answer every day of his life.

My wife and I are currently in the midst of raising twin daughters. They're one another's best friend most of the time, but neither one (understandably) wants to be dominated by the other. They're very sensitive to issues of fairness and equality.

One day, when they were about six years old, Rhonda felt Tricia was taking charge of playtime a little too aggressively, making too many one-sided decisions without proper debate. Suddenly she shot back, "Look—you're not the president of me!"

A lot of us strong-willed Christians have trouble admitting Jesus is our president, our boss, the one with the right to tell us what to do. We know that he is forever a good boss, a kind and thoughtful leader who never takes advantage of his people; that he is always looking out for our good—but still, the idea of surrendering to him sticks in our throat. In that case, he really is not Lord (despite what we may recite or sing on Sunday morning).

When Jesus was on this earth he knew he was the boss, and so he took charge. He walked up to more than one total stranger, looked him in the eye, and said, "Follow me." He didn't beg or plead; he didn't offer a guaranteed salary or any other kind of "deal"—he just gave a straight directive. Then Matthew, or Zacchaeus, or the rich young ruler had to make a choice: Will I obey this man or won't I? Some did, some didn't.

One who decided to obey was John. Decades later, he put it to us bluntly in an epistle: "We know that we have come to know him [Jesus] if we obey his commands. The man who says, 'I know him,' but does not do what he commands is a liar, and the truth is not in him. But if anyone obeys his word, God's love is truly made complete in him" (1 John 2:3-5).

Not much room to weasel, is there?

The Scripture is chock-full of commands from the boss. Again, as John reminds us, "his commands are not burdensome" (1 John 5:3). But they are commands. They force us to respond, "OK, I will," or "No, I won't." In the first case, Jesus is Lord. In the second, we make him just a nice guy.

Jesus understood that we would struggle sometimes over whether to obey. He knew our stubbornness. That's why he told the story of the two sons whose father directed them to go work in the vineyard (Matthew 21:28-32). The first son said, "No way"—but later thought better of it, got his hoe, and went out after all. The second son (a smooth fellow who knew all the right answers) said, "Sure, Dad"—but never arrived.

Jesus told that story to make the point that talk is cheap. Action is what counts. The statement "Jesus is Lord" is easy to mouth; it is harder to live. The Christian life is more than a matter of believing the right things. It is doing what the Person in charge says to do.

What we must get into our minds is that the reason for doing what he says is not always apparent—but he does know what he is talking about. A ship's captain was once guiding his vessel along a rocky coast on a cloudy night. He peered ahead and saw a faint light. He ordered his signalman to send this message by radio: "Alter your course ten degrees south."

Soon a message came back: "Alter your course ten degrees north."

The captain was a little disgusted. He sent a second message: "The captain says, 'Alter your course ten degrees south!' "

A second message came back: "Seaman Third Class Jones says, 'Alter your course ten degrees north.' "

This sent the captain into full-scale fuming. "Alter your course ten degrees south—this is a battleship!" he thundered.

One more reply came back: "Alter your course ten degrees north; this is the lighthouse."

Our modern world is full of voices shouting orders into the night, telling others how to live, what to do, how to change. And there is one Voice whose directions seem opposite to all the rest. The listeners are not sure whether to pay him any attention; some are openly sarcastic.

The only trouble is, he is the one voice who knows what he's talking about. He is the Light of the world. He is the authority on this treacherous coastline. He is Lord.

How to Become Like Christ

RICHARD OWEN ROBERTS

If I want to become like Christ, I must discover what Christ is like. If I don't know what he is like, then I won't be able to make any real progress in Christian growth. I need to know what he said, who he is, and what he did.

To learn what Christ is like, I need to master his words and let his words master me. I want to know everything Christ said, and I want everything he said to affect me in the deepest reaches of my being.

I've gone very carefully through the Gospels and, on separate three-by-five cards, written down every single statement Christ made. I broke down every statement to the smallest possible thought, putting each statement on a separate card. From time to time I go through the cards, shuffling them about. I put together everything Christ said on this subject and on that subject, and I ask myself: Are you there? Are you obedient? Are you doing this? Has this affected you? How ought it to affect you?

The first step in being like Christ, then, is to come to grips with what he said. The second step is to come to grips with who he is. For that, I can't focus solely on the Gospels. I must have a broad acquaintance with all of Scripture to understand who Christ is. Christ can be found in every book of the Bible. Christ is not less than God; he is God. So when I learn who God is, I also learn to know Christ.

There are dozens and dozens of Scriptures in which God speaks and reveals something concerning himself. For example, in Malachi 3:6 God said, "I the Lord do not change." That's a phenomenal statement. Sit down with those words "I do not change" and let them lay hold of you. Come to grips with a God who has been around billions of years and is not one speck different today from what he was long, long ago. In a hundred trillion years God will still be identical to what he is now. We humans are such a contrast to that. We're in a continual state of flux. Seeing this reduces us to a proper level. A significant part of becoming Christlike is becoming aware of the difference between myself and Christ. I do this as I begin to see the majesty, power, absolute supremacy, and eternalness of Christ.

Isaiah 57:15 says, "This is what the high and lofty One says—he who lives forever, whose name is holy: 'I live in a high and holy place, but also with him who is contrite and lowly in spirit, to revive the spirit of the lowly and to revive the heart of the contrite.' " One is broken by seeing the difference between oneself and God, and only this brokenness can lead to revival.

The key to Christlikeness is humility. If I'm proud or arrogant, there's no way I'm going to see Christ. But when I'm reduced to my proper level, I will see Christ's majesty, beauty, purity, and holiness, and I will yearn to be like that. Humility comes from seeing God as he is. That in itself will take the pride and arrogance out of me. Humility is the key to personal revival.

I urge Christians to work through the Bible carefully and systematically, making note of these passages where God tells us about himself. This isn't just a week or two of study, but a lifetime pursuit.

After coming to grips first with what Christ said, and next with who Christ is (and consequently, with who the whole Trinity is), I then study what Christ did. I laboriously go over all Christ's actions, continuously seeking the application in my life. If I'm going to be Christlike, I'm going to have to learn to do what he does.

For example, take evangelism. I want to be like Christ in the realm of personal witness and sharing my faith with others, so I look at how he approached others. Did Christ go to school to study personal evangelism? Did he have a certain formula he used with each individual? Did he say the same thing to each person he dealt with? Did he make a great effort to get an immediate decision out of people, or was he content to speak the word and leave the results for the appropriate moment? By studying what Christ did, I gain insights on how to conduct myself.

Or we can look at persecution. The Gospel of John makes it plain that from the earliest days of his ministry Christ suffered severe persecution. Attempts on his life were numerous. If I want to know how to live like Christ in a world that persecutes holy men and women, I need to bathe myself in Christ's conduct in that realm in order to learn from his example.

If I want to learn how to reply to my critics, I study the life of Christ and observe carefully his behavior with each person who criticized him. Again I find immense help. As I identify with Christ in all he endured, I learn how to react as he did.

I can come directly to Christ and examine with great care every area of practical Christian living. I'm not saying that everything I would ever want to know is fully recorded. However, in the Bible we have an immense amount of material that most of us haven't begun to tap.

Most of us have never spent an hour a day meditating upon Christ's life and drawing out of his life specific, practical help for our own future conduct. But if we are to begin the lifelong process of becoming Christlike, this is what we need to do. To become like Christ, we need to dwell on what Christ said, who he is, and what he did.

Christlikeness

V. GILBERT BEERS

To be Christlike is to be like Christ, not because we are imitating him, but because he dwells within us.

We can try to imitate all kinds of people—even Jesus—but we can never become the person we are imitating. The genius of the gospel is this: we do not need to imitate Jesus, for God in his wonderful plan has made a way for Jesus to dwell within us. Living inside us, Jesus himself will cause us to be like him.

Each year at commencement, the Wheaton College graduates sing these words: "May the mind of Christ my Savior live in me from day to day, by His love and pow'r controlling all I do and say." To listen to these young people and realize that most of them will let the mind of Christ guide them as they pursue careers, choose mates, and live out their daily lives is an inspiration for all present.

How do we receive the mind of Christ so that we may let it live in us and guide all we do and say?

Reading the Gospels, seeking to understand what Jesus did and why he did it, is a good start.

It is helpful also to obtain a red-letter edition of the New Testament and read only the words of Jesus. What we say reveals who we are, and Jesus' words are no exception. I recommend taking a red-letter edition along on a trip and reading Jesus' words again and again until your mind has absorbed what he is saying.

As you read, ask these questions: (1) What is Jesus saying here? (2) What did this mean to those who heard him in the first century? (3) What does this mean to us in the twentieth century? (4) What does this mean to me personally?

Philippians 2:5-11 is a classic passage that tells about Christlikeness. I like the King James Version best for this passage. "Let this mind be in you, which was also in Christ Jesus" is the beautiful prologue (v. 5). The passage goes on to describe the unique mind of Christ, who was willing to give up everything for those he loved.

This is another gem to take on a trip and read again and again until you have absorbed its meaning. Try reading it fifty times over one weekend. Talk about it with others. Think about it as you spend some quiet time in a hotel room or on a plane, while waiting for a traffic light or for an appointment.

Just as Christlikeness is not imitating Christ and his thinking, neither is it programming our minds with his thoughts. Both these activities have their place, but Christlikeness comes from within. It is letting Christ dwell within us and live through us.

We must be sure we have invited Jesus Christ to be our Savior and dwell within us. Then we must seek to understand the mind of Christ through his life and his words. Finally we must allow him to live his life through us. Then our Christlikeness will be a genuine expression of Christ in us.

Being Conformed to Christ's Image

J. I. PACKER

The image of God in which we were created has been marred by sin. According to Genesis 1–2, when man was created he was rational, righteous, creative, and loving—all qualities of God himself. However, when Adam sinned, he lost, for himself and for us, both the righteousness and a good deal of the rationality. The creativity with which he was created now has nowhere to go. Relationships Godward and with other people are self-absorbed and self-seeking. We are far from God.

What can be done? The answer is that we have to be reconstructed—we have to be conformed to the image of Christ (see Romans 8:29).

To be conformed means to have reproduced in ourselves the character profile of the Lord Jesus. We daily increase in the fruit of the Spirit—"love, joy, peace, patience, kindness, goodness, faithfulness, gentleness and self-control" (Galatians 5:22, 23). Being conformed refers to a change in our relationship with God and other people. We humble ourselves before God to worship and serve him, and before fellow human beings to serve them.

This doesn't mean that our personal identity ceases, that we will begin to look and act like all other Christians. Individuality goes on in the Christian life. We are to look like Christ not in a physical sense, but by showing the same spirit and attitudes.

A person who is conformed to Christ's image is still unique, but in terms of motivation and purpose he or she is increasingly like Jesus. There's no point at which we can justify ourselves in not being like Jesus. We're called to be like him, and we're told that his Spirit actually changes us in this way. Our minds are renewed (Romans 12:2), and we are transformed into his likeness (2 Corinthians 3:18).

Here on earth, our physical bodies imperfectly express what is in our hearts. We use our bodies to serve God, but we do not serve him perfectly. When Christ comes again, we shall be given bodies to match our renewed hearts. Our resurrection bodies will be the perfect expression of what is in our hearts.

Part of being conformed is to "have the mind of Christ" (1 Corinthians 2:16). Having the mind of Christ means that we share in the instincts, urges, and motivations of the resurrected life. It means we have Christ's outlook. We can learn to have the mind of Christ more and more by nourishing our new nature through Bible study, prayer, and church. The mind of Christ is also formed in us by active service for the Lord—practical helpfulness and faithful witness.

We may ask, "Do we have to conform ourselves, or does Christ conform us?" The answer is both. Ephesians 5:1 says, "Be imitators of God." Thus we must learn about Christ in order to be like him. And Romans 12:2 says, "Be transformed by the renewing of your mind." "Be transformed" is a passive verb in the Greek, meaning Christ reshapes our minds. Thus, even as we seek to be Christlike, Christ makes us like himself.

◆ HAVING THE MIND OF CHRIST

YFC EDITORS

The mind of Christ is the *attitude* of Christ. Christ's attitude was being a servant. To have Christ's attitude means we must lay aside selfish desires in order to do God's work on earth.

Having the mind of Christ means having the *eyes* of Christ in order to see the world, the future, and fellowmen in a new way.

Having the mind of Christ means having the *heart* of Christ, which shows compassion and forgiveness to others.

Having the mind of Christ can only happen when we have the *spirit* of Christ, the Holy Spirit, living within and working through us.

The Quest for Obedience

CHARLES COLSON

To be a Christian is, in a sense, to be a man without a country. If you truly are obedient to Christ—if you take the Scriptures to heart and attempt to live them—you will inevitably come into conflict with the world. You belong to no one but Christ, while those in the world give themselves to people, possessions, institutions, and idols other than to Christ. To be a Christian is to stand apart and yet to remain within—to dare to be different. You look at everything through the prism of Scripture, and things look different when viewed biblically.

Success in the world means power, influence, money, prestige. But in the Christian world, it means pleasing God. This quest for obedience may lead you to do things that are wholly contrary to what the world wants and rewards.

Christianity takes sharp issue with the values of the world when they are corrupted, as they so often are. It means taking a stand when a lot of people are getting along comfortably by conforming. As Romans 12:2 says, "Do not conform any longer to the pattern of this world, but be transformed by the renewing of your mind." Putting that into practice can be a tough, abrasive, confrontive experience, but that's what being a Christian is all about.

Jesus summed up the essence of the Christian life as loving the Lord your God with all your heart, mind, and soul and your neighbor as yourself. But how does a person love God? I wrote my third book, *Loving God,* in an attempt to answer that question. Some people say that loving God means having a warm feeling inside, or going to church, or doing good things, or reading the Bible. But that isn't what Jesus said. He said, "If you love me, you will obey what I command" (John 14:15).

Obeying his commandments means reading and understanding Scripture, then determining that you are going to live exactly as Scripture teaches. I don't believe anybody can do that, because it is almost impossible not to be caught up every day in the ways of the world. But you can make an effort to live biblically. That is how the process of sanctification works—learning how to obey God, how to listen for his commands in your life. It is reading the Scripture and allowing it to soak into you. It is understanding the requirements of God's commandments and then gradually, day by day, in large ways and small, allowing that understanding to control the actions of your life.

This is a joint process. God has given man a free will so that we can say yes or no, even to what we know is right. Yet he helps us to say yes through the working of the Holy Spirit. We can't sit back and do nothing and expect God to sanctify us by the Spirit. On the other hand, we can't on our own decide to do everything right and obey the commandments. God works in our lives, and we do our very best to cooperate in what God is doing.

If I had to pick the one thing in American culture that has probably caused the most failure in obeying God, it would be that we figure God's time is our Bible study, our prayer time, the meeting with our prayer group, and Sunday morning church service. That's just not true. God's time is every moment of our lives. Bible study and church simply prepare us for the rest of the moments of our lives. Being obedient to Christ is a twenty-four-hour-a-day thing. We don't put him on and take him off like a suit of clothes. We have to live God. If we would "wear" him all day long, we would discover obedience becoming a reflex reaction.

In practical terms, we should start out each day by saying, "I want God's will for my life today." Meditate on what God is working on with us at that point. Pray. Read the Scriptures. Then during the day, we shouldn't put God aside. We can't reserve a half hour in the morning for God and the rest of the day for ourselves. God has to control the whole day. By ten o'clock in the morning we're probably off track. We have to stop and think, Lord, please lead me now. We should constantly be seeking God's strength and guidance in our lives as we use the minds he gave us to obey Christ and think about his teaching. When we're confronted with ethical and moral questions, as we will be every day, we should think, How would Christ respond? As we practice his presence in our thought processes, we'll discover that our decisions are fundamentally influenced by him.

How to Keep Your Focus on Christ

GARY DAUSEY

"Turn your eyes upon Jesus, look full in His wonderful face; and the things of earth will grow strangely dim in the light of His glory and grace."

Many of us have sung these words without fully appreciating the impact of their truth. Words to even meaningful hymns can roll out of us in a very mechanical manner at times. It is also true that often, in the times we need to focus most clearly on Christ and his place in our lives, it is the most difficult to do so.

I've observed over the years that those who seem to have the most supportive faith are those who have had their faith tested. When the difficult times in life come, some become stronger in their faith while others seem to collapse under the load. The difference appears clear. The former have learned to look upward in these times, while the latter turn inward.

Peter experienced both situations. When the Lord called to him, Peter climbed out of a boat and walked on water, but then he doubted, looked inward, and began to sink (Matthew 14:25-31).

Most of us have not had the need to walk on water, but we have faced those times when our faith has been tested just as dramatically. Have you turned out to be a walker or a sinker?

What causes us to take our eyes off of the Lord during these times? Sometimes it's the people around us. We confuse those who represent Christ with Christ himself. As long as we put our focus on people, even the best-intentioned people, we will be disappointed. Paul experienced this when he wrote, "You know that everyone in the province of Asia has deserted me, including Phygelus and Hermogenes" (2 Timothy 1:15). "Demas, because he loved this world, has deserted me" (2 Timothy 4:10). "At my first defense, no one came to my support, but everyone deserted me" (2 Timothy 4:16).

It's clear that our focus must go beyond people to Christ himself. Paul was sustained during his darkest hours, not by the tentativeness of his Christian friends, even though they are very important, but by his primary relationship with the Lord.

Another reason we take our eyes off the Lord is that we are so consumed by the problem that we don't take time to seek the solution. In short, it takes discipline and work.

I have found it easy to sit in a church service and let my mind wander, to let the problems I may be facing surface and to struggle with solutions. It has helped me to remind myself that the man in the pulpit spent the majority of the week researching and preparing the material he is presenting, and that if I focus my mind on those thoughts I can learn in twenty minutes or so what took him hours to research.

Similarly, I must read the Word of God in a planned and regular manner. This too takes discipline. But the rewards are great. If I'm not allowing the Lord to speak to me through his Word, how will he speak? The Lord often brings comfort, direction, and motivation as we read his Word. It's easier not to, but then we have only our resources to draw on, and not the Lord.

Similarly, our time in prayer is crucial to keeping our focus on the Lord. There are times in our lives when it is more difficult to pray and often that's when we need prayer the most. What I'm trying to say is captured best in the phrase, "Pray hardest when it is hardest to pray." Talking to the Lord and meditating on him in prayer will help us keep our focus on him. A regular time for prayer will give us the discipline that's needed to keep a sharp focus. Spontaneous prayer that flows when we are reminded of a specific need keeps our prayer from being mechanical and controlled.

The writer of the book of Hebrews reminded us of the importance of our focus and our need to keep our eyes fixed on the Lord. He used the illustration of a foot race when he said, "Let us throw off everything that hinders and the sin that so easily entangles, and let us run with perseverance the race marked out for us. Let us fix our eyes on Jesus, the author and perfecter of our faith" (Hebrews 12:1, 2).

♦ WHY DO I KEEP SINNING? / J. I. PACKER

There is always something every day that needs to be forgiven. If a Christian is at all self-aware, he knows that. Indwelling sin shows itself in us again and again, and we are disappointed because we thought we had killed it for good. We think we've finished with a bad habit, we think

we've put it to death, and then we suddenly find ourselves doing the thing or at least wanting to do it again. The battle has to be fought again, and it's slow going.

Galatians 5:17 says, "The sinful nature desires what is contrary to the Spirit, and the Spirit what is contrary to the sinful nature. They are in conflict with each other, so that you do not do what you want." Though we want to love and serve the Lord in everything we do, we can't achieve that. Our reach exceeds our grasp, and the flesh fights back. We never achieve that perfect service of God we aimed at.

God promises, however, that indwelling sin won't be with us after we've left this body behind. When Paul talks about being delivered from this body, he assures us that when we are out of this body we shall be finished with the conflict against indwelling sin (see 1 Corinthians 15:42-57). In our resurrection body, our hearts will be completely set on the Lord. Then we shall be able to love him with no distractions and no contrary, disruptive desires.

♦ CHOOSING THE BEST WAY TO LIVE
J. I. PACKER

Everything we need to know about living the way Christ wants is set out in Scripture. The best way to live that way in each situation is to acquire wisdom along with our knowledge of the Bible.

Wisdom is the ability to see what you ought to aim at and then to discern the best steps to take to get there. James 1:5 says, "If any of you lacks wisdom, he should ask God, who gives generously to all without finding fault, and it will be given to him." Pray for wisdom.

As you seek to live for Jesus, think things out properly. Consider the various alternatives and ask the Lord to help you choose the best course each time. One rule of Christian wisdom is never to let the good be the enemy of the best. The question in our hearts ought always to be, "Lord, what is the best I can do for your praise and the good of others in this situation?"

As you keep that question before the Lord, ask him to jog your mind and your conscience if you're on the wrong track. "Lord, if I am not doing what is best, please let me know." The Holy Spirit indwells us, and he will make us feel uneasy if we're off the road. He'll make us rethink, backtrack, or wait for further orders, all within the limits that Scripture sets.

The wisdom that comes from the Lord always leads you to God's best for you. As you listen to him, you will learn to live the way Christ wants you to.

Living in Christ
J. I. PACKER

How does Jesus live in me? How do I live in Christ?

The first thing to do is clarify what this relationship is not. It isn't a mystical affair of losing your personal identity through some kind of fusion with Jesus. Neither is it a passive state of letting your mind and limbs be moved by an outside force—it isn't a sort of "possession."

Jesus living in you and you living in Christ means simply that the Lord is united to you and you are united to him. He empowers you out of that relationship to do what he wants you to do. There are two sides to it: he shows you what you ought to do, and he sends his Spirit to indwell you. It's through the indwelling presence of the Spirit that Christ actually lives in us. He is personally and physically in heaven, but by his Spirit he's present everywhere. By his Spirit, he indwells all believers.

But that doesn't mean we're all alike. We still have our individual identities, our unique talents and gifts. Just as God made us all different, so he keeps us different when he indwells us. He loves diversity and desires to work through us with the unique gifts and talents with which we were created. These become sanctified as means of expressing our life in Christ. Before, our talents couldn't communicate anything of Christ because there was nothing of Christ in us to communicate; now they can. And as we use our talents and gifts, people see Christ in us.

Living in Christ involves constant repetition of a four-part scenario. First, we look at what God has told us to do as the Spirit has helped us to understand this from his Word, and so focus the task that faces us.

Second, we go to Jesus and tell him, "Without your help and power, I can't do any of this as I should. By myself, I don't have the resources." That's abiding in Christ—looking to him at every turn of the road, every time a fresh job has to be done, asking him to enable us.

Third, believing that our prayer for help is being answered, we go to work with high expectation. We tackle the job boldly, because we expect to be helped.

Fourth, we look back on what we have done and thank the Lord for everything he has helped us to do right (even if there were still some slips and mistakes). As we ask him to forgive our wrongs, we also ask him to enable us to do better next time.

If we spend our lives repeating that four-step formula, we are living in Christ.

The Indwelling Christ

✍ LUIS PALAU

Galatians 2:20 is a revolutionary verse in my life: "I have been crucified with Christ and I no longer live, but Christ lives in me. The life I live in the body, I live by faith in the Son of God, who loved me and gave himself for me."

This is the very heart of Christian living, for the foundation of Christianity is the cross and resurrection of Jesus Christ. The astonishing fact is that Jesus lives within the believer, and they become one in spirit. The apostle Paul described this as "the mystery that has been kept hidden for ages and generations, but is now disclosed to the saints. To them God has chosen to make known among the Gentiles the glorious riches of this mystery, which is Christ in you, the hope of glory" (Colossians 1:26, 27).

Jesus foretold this relationship in his high priestly prayer in the Upper

Room. He especially prayed that unity among believers would be a picture of the unity between him and the Father. "I pray also . . . that all of them may be one, Father, just as you are in me and I am in you. May they also be in us so that the world may believe that you have sent me. I have given them the glory that you gave me, that they may be one as we are one: I in them and you in me" (John 17:20-23).

Many Christians miss out on the thrill of Christian living because they have not understood that Jesus Christ literally lives within them—a fact they could not change if they wanted to. Throughout my teens and early twenties, although I believed in Christ, I did not realize this truth. I struggled to obey him, trying to bring fruit to the glory of God, but I did not understand that I did not have to do it on my own. I felt that Jesus was seated far away, at the right hand of the Father, and I was down here on earth.

I loved God very much and tried with all my heart to please him, but I did not understand how and lacked the strength in myself. It was at this point that the truth of Galatians 2:20 was made clear to me, particularly through a sermon by Ian Thomas at Multnomah School of the Bible. He likened Christ's indwelling to Moses' experience with the burning bush.

Moses had prided himself on his background, his adoption by Pharaoh's daughter, his education, and so forth. When he tried by his own strength to liberate the Israelites from the Egyptians, he failed miserably and ran off to the desert for forty years. In humility, he was challenged by God in the burning bush. God was trying to teach him that any old bush would do, as long as God was in the bush.

Suddenly I realized that I was like Moses: I had thought that my good education, my mind, my ability to communicate were everything it took to please, serve, and honor God. But my outlook began to change as I saw that, because Jesus lives in me, his was the strength to work through me. After this, fruit began to come of my ministry. I preached the same messages, but I began to see hundreds and later thousands of people come to Christ.

A related question arises at this point. If I am alive in Christ, what does it mean to be crucified with him? In 2 Corinthians 4:10, Paul said, "We always carry around in our body the death of Jesus, so that the life of Jesus may also be revealed in our body." Jesus painted the picture this way: "I tell you the truth, unless a kernel of wheat falls to the ground and dies, it remains only a single seed. But if it dies, it produces many seeds" (John 12:24).

These two verses express the same truth. Every time my will crosses God's will, and I choose his revealed will over my own, that is the death of Jesus at work in me. That is the grain of wheat falling into the ground and dying. That is taking up my cross and following him.

Picture a gloved hand. The glove is a limp piece of leather until the hand moves into the glove and begins to mobilize it. When the hand does something, the glove could say, "I just picked up my coffee cup," but it really is not the glove doing it. In a sense, Jesus' living in us is like the hand in the glove. Jesus Christ clothes himself and uses me for his purpose. I want to allow the indwelling Christ to mold me and use me and bend me any way he pleases, as long as he accomplishes his will.

◆THE THREE *C*s / LUIS PALAU

In describing how Christians are to live in Christ, Jesus used a vivid image. "I am the true vine and my Father is the gardener," he said. "He cuts off every branch in me that bears no fruit, while every branch that does bear fruit he trims clean so that it will be even more fruitful. You are already clean because of the word I have spoken to you. Remain in me, and I will remain in you. No branch can bear fruit by itself; it must remain in the vine. Neither can you bear fruit unless you remain in me" (John 15:1-4).

To be in Christ is to obey him gladly and to acknowledge him as Lord. My pastor used to say that we are to live in a state of constant conscious communion—the three *C*s. Christians must not take Jesus for granted, or our relationship with him will suffer—just as our marriages and friendships suffer when we take others for granted.

We must be truly in touch with him, in loving and worshipful obedience.

The Surrendered Life

AJITH FERNANDO

In the world today we can discover three basic attitudes toward the self.

The first attitude can be described as self-indulgence. Those following this path reject the whole idea of self-denial. They say, "If you want to do something, go ahead and do it." They frown upon moral restraint. Don't give temptation a second thought, they say. Give in at the first opportunity! If it feels good, do it.

This is a harmful way to live. It goes against the complete life God intended for man. It denies man's true humanity. However much a person tries to fulfill himself through self-indulgence, he can never be fulfilled. This is because he has set aside and revolted against a very important part of his humanity, his moral and spiritual self. All the pleasure in the world cannot fill the void that results from denying our complete humanity. That is why Hebrews 11:25 says the pleasures of sin are fleeting.

A second attitude, by contrast, wishes to destroy all that can be included in the self. This attitude can be found among adherents of some non-Christian religions and also among some Christians. These people say that the self and human desire are evil, and therefore we must give up all enjoyment of anything that has to do with ourselves. For them, self-denial becomes an end in itself.

This attitude is harmful because it too denies a person's full humanity. God created our ability to enjoy things, to desire what is good. This ability and desire were tainted because of sin. The answer to this problem is not to stop enjoying life, but to enjoy the right things—the things God approves of. Joy is a very important Christian characteristic. Tertullian, a great theologian of the early church, said, "The Christian saint is hilarious." Those who destroy the self do not know this joy. They become gloomy ascetics.

The biblical attitude toward the self is to surrender it to Christ and let Christ be Lord of our lives. Christ will not destroy the self that is surrendered to him. Rather he redeems it and gives it back to us so that we can live the rest of our lives in partnership with him. The person who is surrendered to Christ gives up everything that hinders total unity with him. In biblical language, he puts these things to death (Romans 8:13; Colossians 3:5).

The surrendered life is well described in Galatians 2:20: "I have been crucified with Christ and I no longer live, but Christ lives in me. The life I live in the body, I live by faith in the Son of God, who loved me and gave himself for me." According to this verse, there is a sense in which we do not live. No longer do we control our lives. Our decisions are no longer based only on what we think. Christ is now Lord of our lives.

But that does not mean we cease to exist. Our individual personalities are retained in a redeemed form. Enjoying our partnership with Christ, who is our Lord, we are fully ourselves.

In this partnership, everything that displeases Christ is crucified. Our old self often surfaces with many such desires which have to be put to death. So there is self-denial in the surrendered life. But what we deny is what is harmful to us, what destroys our life. Thus self-denial is not harmful for a Christian. It is like the removal of a cancerous tumor.

A redeemed self is not like a passive machine that does only what God wants it to do and has no will of its own. On the contrary, the will of a redeemed person is fully active. He chooses to do the will of God, not because he is forced to, but because he wants to. He realizes that this will is "good, pleasing and perfect" (Romans 12:2).

This life of doing what is good, pleasing, and perfect and of living in a harmonious partnership with God is what he intended for man when he created him. So when a person surrenders his life to Christ, he finally becomes fully human. Surrender to Christ, then, is not harmful to us. It is the only way to live a complete life.

♦ CRUCIFIED WITH CHRIST / J. I. PACKER

To be crucified with Christ is to be united to him in his death and in his resurrection. Jesus, as the Son of God, transcends space and time. His crucifixion and resurrection were certainly historical events, but they are more than that. They can be as close to us now as they were to the people in Christ's own day.

The phrase "crucified with Christ" comes from Galatians 2:20. Paul said, "I have been crucified with Christ and I no longer live, but Christ lives in me." A related text is Romans 6:6: "Our old self was crucified with him so that the body of sin might be rendered powerless." ("Our old self" is the person we were before becoming Christians, the person dominated by indwelling sin.) A third text is Galatians 5:24: "Those who belong to Christ Jesus have crucified the sinful nature with its passions and desires."

To be crucified with Christ means we're no longer slaves of indwelling sin. The other side of this is that we are risen with Christ, one with him in his resurrection. His human instincts are now our instincts, so that our deepest desire is to love the Lord, have fellowship with him, glorify him, and please him, just as Jesus loved and pleased his heavenly Father. It is out of this union with Christ's death and resurrection that our Christian lives are lived.

When we become Christians, we become new persons. "If anyone is in Christ, he is a new creation; the old has gone, the new has come!" (2 Corinthians 5:17). Our new creation is something we recognize as having already happened as we turned to Christ. The Galatians text, "I have been crucified with Christ," is in the Greek perfect tense, which expresses the present result of a past action.

If I am a Christian, then, God has put new life within me. The old me has been crucified with Christ, and I have risen with him to new life. I am a changed person—changed inside. I now have to live out the results of my crucifixion and resurrection—to negate the flesh with its affections and lusts, and to enter daily into the joy—it is joy—of living to God. This is the meaning of being crucified with Christ.

Responding to the Power of the Indwelling Christ

LUIS PALAU

How do we let Jesus control our lives? And once he is in control, do we just sit back and relax?

First, we must admit that in and of ourselves we do not have the supernatural power it takes to live life to the fullest.

Second, we must willingly and intelligently obey him. In other words, now that Christ lives in us, we are free to obey him.

The Living Bible puts this second point in direct terms: "Don't you realize that you can choose your own master? You can choose sin (with death) or else obedience (with acquittal). The one to whom you offer yourself—he will take you and be your master and you will be his slave. Thank God that though you once chose to be slaves of sin, now you have obeyed with all your heart the teaching to which God has committed you. And now you are free from your old master, sin; and you have become slaves to your new master, righteousness" (Romans 6:16-18).

Third, we must receive the power that we need to carry out his work, that is, the Holy Spirit, who comes upon us from the moment we open our hearts to Christ. This is not to say that we come under automatic pilot, that all we do is float along in the Christian life. The Bible teaches that our wills must be engaged to the point where we say, "Lord, I want you to have your way in my life. I want to know what your desires are, and I want to obey you in the power that you provide."

God gives us the desire to do his will and then the supernatural power to obey that will. Sometimes we look at ourselves and see only our weaknesses, but he can overcome that because all power in heaven and on earth has been given to him. He can conquer our selfishness, our impurity, our covetousness—but first we must submit ourselves to his will. There is no sitting back and floating downstream; rather, it is a willing cooperation with the power of the indwelling Christ.

The end result of all this is Christlikeness. Loving, obedient response to an indwelling Lord changes us. Godly character is the fruit of being molded by obedience, by constant conscious communion, and by worship.

♦ WHO IS IN CONTROL? / YFC EDITORS

When we become Christians, suddenly Someone else is in control of our lives—Jesus Christ himself. But how does that happen? How can I let him control my life?

When we yield our lives to Jesus, the Holy Spirit comes to live within us. He teaches and reminds us of Jesus' words. He helps us know what Jesus would want us to do in each situation. He helps us know what is true because he shows us only what he knows from God. He convicts us of our sin so we can repent and stay in communication with God. When we let the Holy Spirit control our lives, we are living lives that please God.

But allowing him to control doesn't mean we can sit back and relax. He shows us what is right and true and good, but we must *do* it—sometimes facing persecution, problems, and rejection by others in order to do so. Letting the Holy Spirit control our lives makes *knowing* what we should do easier, but it doesn't necessarily make *doing* it any easier.

RELATED ARTICLES

Chapter 1: **How Do I Submit to Jesus Christ?**
Chapter 7: **Jesus Christ: The Foundation of Faith**
Chapter 7: **Obedience: Faith in Action**
Chapter 18: **Our Quiet Confidence in Christ**
Chapter 22: **Obedience and God's Will**

CHAPTER

6

Living by the Power of the Spirit

- ✓ Why do I need the Holy Spirit?
- ✓ How is the Holy Spirit different from God and Jesus?
- ✓ How do I know if I am filled with the Spirit?
- ✓ What kind of power does the Holy Spirit have?
- ✓ What are the gifts of the Spirit? Do I have any?

Who Is the Holy Spirit?

NORMAN GEISLER

The Holy Spirit is the Third Person of the Trinity. We have to realize when we're talking about the Holy Spirit we're not talking about an it or a thing, but about a person. The Holy Spirit thinks, wills, and feels. He is an intelligent, directing individual who teaches and guides us. The Bible says the Holy Spirit can be grieved. It says the Spirit gives gifts according to his will. So the Holy

Spirit has all the attributes of personality—intellect, emotion, and will.

The Spirit inspired the Bible. He illuminates our minds to understand the Word as we read or hear it, and he helps us apply it to our lives.

The Holy Spirit is a very important member of the Trinity. He's coequal with the Father and the Son. There's a functional order in the Trinity: the Father plans, the Son accomplishes, and the Holy Spirit applies. Each member has his own role in the divine outworking of God's plan.

In John 16:8, Jesus said, "When he [the Holy Spirit] comes, he will convict the world of guilt in regard to sin and righteousness and judgment." The Spirit convicts us of our sin and then regenerates us, giving divine life to those who believe. When we're born again we're born of the Spirit. The Holy Spirit then indwells us; he takes up residence inside us. He instructs, teaches, and fills us as we yield our lives to him.

The Spirit differs from Christ in that he doesn't have a human body, and he has only one nature because he's a spirit. You can't see him, touch him, or smell him; the Holy Spirit isn't available to the five senses. This doesn't mean we can't get to know him, however.

What we know about the Spirit is through the Scriptures. Romans 8:16 states: "The Spirit himself testifies with our spirit that we are God's children." Some people confuse tingly feelings or shivers with the Spirit. Such feelings may or may not result from his presence. We need to "test the spirits to see whether they are from God" (1 John 4:1). Some counterfeits look very much like the real thing. We have to scrutinize what we see in order to know the difference.

In Ephesians 5:18 Paul wrote: "Do not get drunk on wine, which leads to debauchery. Instead, be filled with the Spirit." The way you become drunk with wine is by imbibing. You yield to it, taking it willfully and ingesting it. As you yield to alcohol or any other kind of drug, you become controlled by it.

If we yield our lives to the Holy Spirit we will become filled with him and controlled by him. Someone once said that when you get filled with the Holy Spirit, you don't get more of the Spirit, he gets more of you. You can't get part of the Holy Spirit. He's a spirit, and he can't be chopped into little pieces.

The verb in Ephesians 5:18 is in the present tense, and it means "keep on being filled." Being filled with the Spirit is not something that happens once and for all. It is a daily process of yielding our lives to him.

♦ THE POWER OF THE HOLY SPIRIT
YFC EDITORS

Can the Holy Spirit help us do more than is otherwise humanly possible? Yes, that's why he came. It is humanly impossible to live the Christian life. But the Holy Spirit gives us the power to do it.

- He helps us pray (Romans 8:26).
- He helps us witness for Christ and know what to say (Mark 13:11).
- He helps us love (Galatians 5:22).
- He helps us do what is right (1John 2:27).

Tasks of the Holy Spirit

DAVID McKENNA

When we consider the tasks of the Holy Spirit, we usually emphasize comforting, guiding, empowering, gift-bringing, cleansing, and sanctifying—all of which are certainly part of and essential to his work. But in John 16, Jesus defines the specific tasks that the Holy Spirit will do.

The first task of the Holy Spirit is teaching. "When he, the Spirit of truth, comes, he will guide you into all truth" (16:13). One of his major tasks is to guide Christians into all truth by reminding us of the things Christ has said.

This guidance is personal and developmental in each of our lives. The Holy Spirit is vitally involved in our growth process; he teaches us the truth so we can live out this truth. He addresses all areas of our lives, not just one, and makes all truth—personal, practical, psychological, spiritual—integrated truth. Thus, his work in our lives leads to wholeness, a vitally important characteristic if we are going to live out the Christian life in this evil world.

A second function of the Holy Spirit is convicting. "When he [the Holy Spirit] comes, he will convict the world of guilt in regard to sin and righteousness and judgment" (16:8). Jesus goes on to explain in more detail.

The Holy Spirit will convict of guilt "in regard to sin, because men do not believe in me [Jesus Christ]" (16:9). The Holy Spirit is the goad, the spiritual conscience, bringing sin to conscious awareness.

When the Holy Spirit convicts the world of sin, he keeps before us the fact that we are sinners. Anyone who downplays the nature of human sin, whether in a secular or spiritual context, is perverting the gospel, because we cannot be redeemed without an awakened consciousness of sin. The Holy Spirit keeps before us the fact that we are sinners except by the grace of God in Jesus Christ. He won't let us forget that it is God's grace, not our works, that makes the difference in our lives.

The Holy Spirit will also convict of guilt "in regard to righteousness, because I [Jesus] am going to the Father, where you can see me no longer" (16:10). This is the positive side of his task, constantly convicting us that righteousness is always reflected in the person of Jesus Christ. The Holy Spirit, then, keeps before us the model of Christ's life. Thus, when we come to a career decision, a problem, or an ethical decision, the Holy Spirit brings to mind what Jesus would do as a model for how we should act in given situations.

In addition, the Holy Spirit convicts of guilt "in regard to judgment, because the prince of this world now stands condemned" (16:11). The Holy Spirit keeps before us the fact that the world and all its works are under God's judgment. This does not excuse us from doing God's work in the world; we work to redeem, but we must not take ourselves too seriously, because the salvation of the world is not exclusively in our hands. We work, but always under the control of the Holy Spirit.

Finally, the Holy Spirit "will tell you what is yet to come" (16:13). Besides being the Teacher and the Convictor, the Holy Spirit is also the Futurist, showing us the big picture. The greatest sin of this current self-centered and narcissistic generation is the short-range, me-centered view of life. Whatever feels good now, whatever seems best for me now is the standard for action.

Christians are to be natural optimists, because the Holy Spirit keeps before us the fact that God is in control; his will is good in the long term. When the Lord spoke through the prophet Jeremiah to the exiles in Babylon, he said, "'For I know the plans I have for you,' declares the Lord, 'plans to prosper you and not to harm you, plans to give you hope and a future'" (Jeremiah 29:11).

The Holy Spirit, then, has three specific tasks: a teaching task, a convicting task, and the task of showing the big picture and long-term will of God. He brings wholeness to our lives. He convicts us of sin, shows us Christ's righteousness, and reminds us that this world has been judged. He is our hopemaker.

♦GOD COMMUNICATES / YFC EDITORS

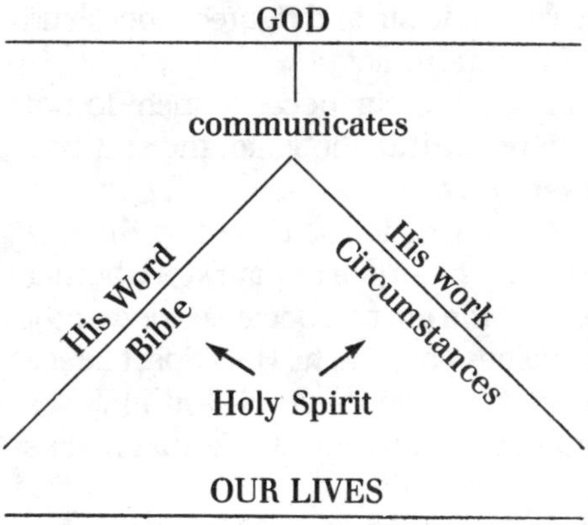

God communicates himself and his desires to us in a general way through the world around us. But when it comes to specific matters in our lives, he has promised us help. And that help comes through his Word (the Bible) and his work (his activities in our lives and in circumstances). The Holy Spirit is active in this communication process. The one thing we can know is that the Holy Spirit will not lead in a way contrary to God's will as revealed in the Bible—the objective record of God's nature and desires.

The Holy Spirit and Character Growth

✍ LEWIS SMEDES

Jesus told Nicodemus, "The wind blows wherever it pleases. You hear its sound, but you cannot tell where it comes from or where it is going. So it is with everyone born of the Spirit" (John 3:8). Like the wind, the Holy Spirit is mysterious. We cannot control him or limit him. If we could specify precisely what the Spirit has to do with character—in distinction from other influences such as genetics, culture, or parental teaching—we would be implying that these other influences are void of God.

God is not merely active in a religious context; he uses many situations, influences, and people. We should not make a line between the enablement brought by the Spirit and that from other things. He is not removed from these influences, nor is he limited by them.

For example, many say that character is developed in the first few years of life, that we are shaped only by genetics and early influences. Certainly much of what we are comes from our genetic heritage and the particular parents we had, but that is not the end of the story. The Holy Spirit takes our characteristics, dispositions, and temperaments and guides us in a new direction.

Before his conversion to Christ, the apostle Paul was an aggressive person. He was much the same after conversion—intolerant, difficult to get along with. So his temperament did not change very much, but it was put in a new direction and given a new purpose. In that sense, he received a new character.

The Spirit is a great respecter of persons. He honors the normal way people develop and does not ordinarily reject that. He uses what we are, redirects our characteristics, and gives us the freedom to grow. We can dedicate our natural gifts to new goals. We can never do this without divine help, and this is true for every person. Christians thank God for character because they know it is a gift. Non-Christians have character but pride themselves on their achievements or are at most grateful for their parents and teachers.

As Christians we are people who know what God wants and have dedicated ourselves to being the kind of people God wants us to be. Simply by following Christ, we are saying, "I want to have Christlikeness built into my character." We have dedicated ourselves to the will of God, and we have the advantage of the enablement of the Spirit. We are open by faith to the Spirit.

We have a lifetime of growth ahead. How odd it would be if the Spirit, through whom all things were created, violated everything real about life. The essence of life is to grow, to gradually become more of who we already are, not to be radically changed overnight. Sometimes we are frustrated with our progress: How do we harmonize the awesome power of the divine Spirit entering human beings' lives with the piddling growth we experience?

In the Heidelberg Catechism, I read that throughout life I make only a small beginning. I am not an overwhelmingly better person than I was ten years ago. A snippet here, a smidgen there, but I am very much the same person—same weaknesses, same failures—though there is movement of the soul toward Christian character. My theology is that the Spirit leads and enables me, but that he never violates the integrity of my will and my mind. The Spirit gives me the freedom to fail as well as the enablement to succeed. Therefore, the "filling of the Spirit" is not a displacement of my ego. Yes, Christ lives in me in a mysterious way (see Galatians 2:20), but he still makes it possible for me to be genuine.

Finally, good character grows when I cooperate with the Holy Spirit. All the gifts of character are balanced by the necessity of exercising them. I pray for discernment, for example, but it works in conjunction with very human ingredients. In order to discern the will of God, I must be aware of what is going on. I must be willing to listen to people and to let things enter my consciousness that might make me uncomfortable. My memory must be honest, not disguised, even when things are painful.

Most of all, I simply must be aware. I must realize that every human situation into which I enter—insignificant as it may seem—asks a question: What are you going to do with me? My decision will determine the road I take into new situations that call for new decisions. The decision I make at noon then determines the sort of decision I must make at five o'clock. I either have or have not discerned the will of God. Paul exhorts us with words such as *exercise* and *discipline* even as he promises the help of the Holy Spirit. There is a genuine collaboration.

Steps to Being Filled with the Spirit

✍ JOSH McDOWELL

The Holy Spirit is a person. When someone confesses Christ as Savior and Lord, the person of the Holy Spirit comes to live within him, to indwell him. This happens with every Christian. Paul said in Romans 8:9, "If anyone does not have the Spirit of Christ, he does not belong to Christ."

Once we come to know Christ personally, and he takes up his presence within us, how can we be sure we are filled with the Holy Spirit? Here are four helpful steps.

1. Desire to be filled with the Spirit. Jesus said that "those who hunger and thirst for righteousness . . . will be filled" (Matthew 5:6). We must desire to be controlled or empowered by the Holy Spirit.

2. Do not allow unconfessed sin to remain in your life. In 1 John 1:9 we read, "If we confess our sins, he is faithful and just and will forgive us our sins and purify us from all unrighteousness"—past, present, and future. By faith we can thank God that he has forgiven us our sins (see Colossians 2:13-15; Hebrews 10:11, 12).

3. Ask the Holy Spirit to fill you. This is a request God will honor, because it is according to his will. In 1 John 5:14, 15 we find this promise: "If we ask anything according to his will, he hears us. And if we know that he hears us—whatever we ask—we know that we have what we asked of him."

Now, it's certainly according to God's will that we walk by faith, filled with the Holy Spirit. In fact, he has commanded us to do so. For example, Ephesians 5:18 says, "Do not get drunk on wine, which leads to debauchery. Instead, be filled with the Spirit."

Since we are commanded to live our lives by the indwelling power of the Holy Spirit, we can be sure that God will unleash his power and fill us with the Spirit if we ask him to.

4. Thank God for filling you with the Holy Spirit. Then walk by faith, moment by moment, thanking him that you have been filled.

When I was filled with the Holy Spirit, I prayed this prayer:

Dear heavenly Father, I need you. I acknowledge that I have been in control of my life, that I have sinned against you; and I thank you that you have forgiven my sins through Christ's death on the cross.

I now ask Christ to take control of the throne of my life. Fill me with the Holy Spirit as you have commanded me to be filled, and as you promised in your Word that you would do if I asked in faith. I pray this in the name of Jesus Christ.

As an expression of my faith, I now thank you for taking control of my life and filling me with the Holy Spirit. Amen.

After this prayer, I realized I was now filled with the Holy Spirit. I began walking by faith, and I've never been the same since. If sin enters my life, I confess it, thank Christ for indwelling me, and ask him to fill me again. Then I continue to walk by faith.

I believe that is how the Holy Spirit's power is released in a person's life. It doesn't depend on one's feelings. Sometimes I feel so filled with the Holy Spirit that I'm going to bubble over. Other times I feel as if I'm here, and the Holy Spirit is in exile in Argentina. But my being filled with the Holy Spirit is not based on my feelings. It's based on the integrity of the Word of God in Jesus Christ.

Walking in the Spirit

WILLIAM BRIGHT

To be "filled with the Spirit" means to be controlled by Christ. The Holy Spirit of God came to glorify Christ. If I am filled with the Spirit, it means that Jesus Christ has an opportunity to live his life through me in all of his resurrection power—to walk around in my body, think with my mind, and love with my heart.

Just as a person receives Christ by faith, so he is filled with the Spirit by faith. In Ephesians 5:18, Paul wrote: "Do not get drunk on wine, which leads to debauchery. Instead, be filled with the Spirit." In the original Greek, the passage says, "Be ye being filled with the Spirit." This Spirit-fullness is a way of life. Christians are commanded to be Spirit-filled from the time they wake up in the morning until they go to bed at night.

God never commands us to do anything he does not give us the ability to do. He promises in 1 John 5:14, 15 that if we ask anything according to God's will, he hears us, and if he hears us, he answers us. We know it is God's will that we be filled with the Spirit.

The moment a person accepts Christ, he or she is filled with the Holy Spirit and sealed into the body of Christ. There is only one baptism into the body of Christ, but there are many fillings with the Spirit. That's the reason for the admonition we noted earlier in Ephesians 5:18: "Be ye being filled."

The Holy Spirit comes to fill us and dwell within us at the moment of spiritual birth, and he never leaves us. But if we grieve or quench the Spirit, he is no longer guiding and directing our lives. If we lie, or steal, or are prideful, or resort to anything that grieves the Spirit and violates the laws of God, we are on our own. The flesh takes over. That's when we do all the things that quench the Spirit. It's like a human relationship between husband and wife. They surrender their wills to each other "until death do us part." They love each other dearly. But one day the husband does something that makes the wife angry, or she does something that insults him, and their relationship is strained. They are still married; they are still living in the same home and sharing their lives together, but there is no communication.

The average person is so ignorant of the Holy Spirit and his role that he or she has no idea of whether the Holy Spirit is living within him or her or not. In fact, it has been said that if the Holy Spirit withdrew from the Church at large, most people wouldn't know the difference. Therefore, it is important that we understand (1) that the Holy Spirit comes within us at the moment of spiritual birth; (2) that he never leaves us; and (3) that by sin we grieve him and quench his power so that it is no longer operative within us. The way to restore the relationship with the Holy Spirit is to confess our sins, acknowledge the lordship of Christ, and hunger and thirst after righteousness. Jesus said, "Blessed are they which do hunger and thirst after righteousness: for they shall be filled" (Matthew 5:6, KJV).

To be a truly spiritual person, Christ must be absolutely, irrevocably the Lord of my life, because to be controlled by the Holy Spirit means to declare "Jesus Christ is Lord." The sad thing is that most people, after a few days of joy in their salvation, become carnal, as described in Romans 7, and spend the rest of their lives as baby Christians. They lack an understanding of who the Spirit is and how he operates. Not knowing how to deal with sin, they never enter into the joy of the Lord.

There is a vast difference between the Spirit-controlled person and the person who is carnal. The Holy Spirit came to glorify Christ. Ephesians 5 reminds us that when we are filled with the Holy Spirit we glorify him as we sing and make music in our hearts to the Lord, "always giving thanks to God the Father for everything, in the name of our Lord Jesus Christ" (Ephesians 5:20). It is impossible to manufacture joy and love in the energy of the flesh. But the Spirit within us bears fruit manifested in love, joy, peace, long-suffering, gentleness, goodness, faith, meekness, and temperance.

God works in different ways in all of us. No two snowflakes are alike; neither are any two people. Some people are very joyful and charismatic in the way they worship God, singing and dancing and making a joyful noise to the Lord. I'm not at home in that kind of meeting. By nature I am shy and reserved. I love the Lord with all my heart, and I praise him and thank him all day long. Yet I've never felt free to dance to the Lord. I don't criticize those who do. Some people like opera, some symphony, some country and western music, some rock, some classical. In the same way, we all worship God differently.

A problem develops when people come to depend on feelings instead of faith in their relationship with God. The just shall live by faith, not feelings. Feelings can be very dangerous. One of the great tragedies of the Christian church today is the emphasis on the subjective rather than the objective. We live more on emotions than by depending upon God and his Word, so that if I don't feel spiritual, I assume there is something wrong.

The fact of the matter, according to Scripture, is that all I have to do if there is sin in my life is confess it. The word *confess* means to be in agreement with God. If I agree with God, I do several things. First, I acknowledge that whatever I do that grieves or quenches the Spirit in my life is sin. These sins may be in the form of a subtle attitude of pride or self-sufficiency or lying, stealing, cheating, and other such actions. Second, I acknowledge that Christ paid the penalty for that sin or those sins on the cross. Third, I repent, which means I change my attitude toward whatever I have done that dishonors God and results in a change of action. And I begin to do what God tells me to do. When the Spirit is in control of my life, I will exalt and honor Christ in the way I think, in what I say, in my attitudes, desires, and actions.

Receiving the Holy Spirit

LARRY CHRISTENSON

Receiving the Holy Spirit is a topic of vital interest to all Christians, but it seems to be tangled with differences and misunderstandings. All believers agree that it is necessary to receive the Holy Spirit. Differences arise over when one receives the Spirit, how it happens, and what kind of results follow.

The New Testament writers spoke of receiving the Holy Spirit in different contexts. Paul talked about receiving the Spirit of adoption into God's family: "For you did not receive a spirit that makes you a slave, ... but you received the Spirit of sonship" (Romans 8:15). Luke, on the other hand, spoke about receiving or being filled with the Holy Spirit primarily in terms of power for ministry: "You will receive power when the Holy Spirit comes on you" (Acts 1:8).

We do this same kind of thing in everyday speech. Depending on context, the same word can have different connotations. For example, "He's cool!" may refer to the temperature of a man's skin, or it may describe a certain behavior style, or it may reveal how the speaker feels about the man.

Luke used the word *receive* in a particular way when he referred to the coming of the Holy Spirit. We should not attempt to impose Paul's usage on the writings of Luke. That would distort the meaning, and it would rob us of the unique emphasis the Spirit wants to bring through Luke.

Is receiving the Spirit different from receiving Christ? In Paul's writings these concepts run very close to each other, yet the element of the Spirit's charismatic manifestation is not absent. In Galatians 3:1-5, he spoke of the Holy Spirit coming in power, complete with miracles. He asked, "Did you receive the Spirit by observing the law, or by believing what you heard?... Does God give you his Spirit and work miracles among you because you observe the law, or because you believe what you heard?" The Galatians had experienced the power of the Spirit in miraculous manifestations, and Paul pointed to this as confirming the reality of the saving faith by which they received Christ. In Luke however, the focus is somewhat different. Receiving the Holy Spirit is the way that those who already believe in Christ are empowered to serve him.

People receive the Holy Spirit, in Luke's meaning of the term, in different ways. Some people receive the Spirit more or less spontaneously, while for others the response is quite conscious and deliberate; some experience dramatic manifestations of the Spirit, while with others the manifestations are more subdued. The way in which people receive the Spirit will be determined, to some extent, by the situation and by the person (his or her personality type, age, station in life, church environment). More important than the particular way that we receive the Spirit, however, is what we do after having received.

It's like the difference between a big church wedding and a small family wedding. The kind of wedding you have doesn't determine the kind of marriage you'll have. What's important is how you live out the reality of married life.

It's important that we receive the power of the Spirit for living the Christian life. Luke's message needs to come through loud and clear. But when it comes to the questions of how, it's more important to focus on how one lives the Spirit-filled life than on a rigid formula for receiving it.

Receiving the Spirit in the Lukan sense is not a one-time event, but an ongoing way of life. It is needed every day; some occasions may call for a special filling of the Spirit (see Acts 4:31; 7:55). The effects of the Spirit's filling may be dramatic, accompanied by supernatural signs; they may open up a new area of witness or ministry; they may issue in quiet growth of the fruit of the Spirit. When the Spirit controls us, he moves us to accomplish God's will in God's way.

Luke's emphasis on receiving the Spirit to empower us for ministry is a needed emphasis today, when one thinks of the enormous missionary challenge facing the church—3 billion people who haven't heard the gospel. We need to move beyond past misunderstandings and get on with the task!

How to Live in the Spirit

LARRY CHRISTENSON

One thing above all distinguishes me from a non-Christian, or from myself before I became a Christian: the indwelling life of Christ the Holy Spirit brings to me.

This is not simply an idea. It is a reality. I can know that Christ is my Savior and have perfectly orthodox ideas about him, but that is different from having his living presence within me. As a Christian I have two natures perfectly united within myself by the working of the Holy Spirit: my human nature and the living presence of Christ. To live in the Spirit means the living presence of Christ has the authority. To live in the flesh means I have taken over the rule, and Christ does not have freedom to operate in me.

How do I learn to live in the Spirit, to activate the presence of Christ within me? I must take two basic steps.

First, I must say yes to the Spirit. I must recognize him and ask for his help. The most natural way to do this is in daily prayer. It seems as if the Holy Spirit thrives on recognition. As I recognize his presence, he makes that presence effectual.

I need to recognize the Holy Spirit day by day, so that he is free to work in me. Then, as I go about the activities of my daily life, I just say, "Lord, I'm going through these outward acts, and I'm trusting you to work out their eternal dimension. The results, both in my inner life and in the lives of the people I touch, are up to you."

One way, then, to release the Spirit within me is simply to recognize him. Another way, related to the first, is to deal decisively with the flesh. The flesh has a constant desire to take over and get the authority back in its own hands. I simply must not allow the flesh that chance. Paul said, "Live by the Spirit, and you will not gratify the desires of the sinful nature" (Galatians 5:16).

Paul didn't say, "Don't have the desires of the flesh." Everyone has those desires, and it would be hypocritical to deny it. We are still of the flesh, and there's nothing wrong with the flesh—so long as it isn't in the driver's seat. But we tell the flesh, "No, you cannot have the steering wheel." Even though we have the desires of the flesh, we don't have to act them out. And when we say no to the flesh, we free the Spirit to act.

I had a disagreement with my wife one morning while we were traveling together in Europe. I was really angry with her. I felt she had been completely off base. We were going to take a train ride, and I was thinking, "If we get a compartment all to ourselves, I'm going to really straighten her out."

As we were riding down the hotel elevator, ready to check out, I sensed the Holy Spirit saying, "Don't talk about it." The message was very clear. This irritated me, and I mentally started to argue. "No," the Holy Spirit said, "don't bother. It's not worth the time." I recognized the Holy Spirit speaking, and so I didn't say any more.

The whole thing was resolved in a far different way from what I had expected. We got a compartment all to ourselves on the train. I said nothing to my wife about our disagreement. She had a real burden to pray about one of our children, and so we had a good prayer time together. When we walked off the train a couple of hours later, the little thing I had been concerned about had just vanished. It had no more importance at all.

The Spirit, you see, had really wanted us to intercede for our child. All I had to do to release the Spirit was to decline to gratify the desire of the flesh to set my wife straight. The rest just happened; the Spirit took over. But in order for the Spirit to take over, I had to be willing to say no to the desires of the flesh.

Thus when we say no to the flesh, we are saying yes to the Spirit. At the moment of saying no, we may not know precisely what the Spirit wants to do. But we can be sure he will tell us later, once we have cleared the way for him to act.

Most people today have an individualistic mentality. They may have social relationships, but they think of themselves primarily as solitary individuals. This should not be true of Christians. What makes the Christian life so exciting is that we have been removed from a life of solitariness into a life of being united with another. This union needs to be quickened day by day. Day by day we need to become more aware of the presence of Christ living within us. We can do this if every day we say no to the flesh and yes to the Spirit.

♦ EQUIPPED FOR BATTLE / DAVID McKENNA

Can the Holy Spirit fight our daily battles for us? There may be emergencies in which we see the Holy Spirit at work, and we realize that he has, in a sense, taken over when we are at the end of our resources. But the basic task of the Holy Spirit is to teach us, to convict us, and to give us a perspective that will make us more effective in fighting our daily battles. He equips us to fight, rather than taking over our battles for us.

Why Does a Church Need Spiritual Gifts?

DEAN MERRILL

When you stop to think about it, the idea of a church is rather preposterous, especially in our high-specialty age. North America is a pastiche of precise markets and interest segments: golfers don't try to associate with racquetball players; classical radio stations don't throw in a little rock 'n' roll each hour for flavor. Everybody has his own slot.

And the businesses, groups, and organizations that prosper are those that stick with the one audience they know best.

So what's the church doing trying to be all things to all ages (infants to grandparents), all income levels (welfare mothers to executives), all education levels (dropouts to PhDs), both sexes, all races and ethnic backgrounds? How can these be mixed into one pot each Sunday morning?

Did Jesus really know what he was doing in establishing the Church as "one body . . . fellow citizens . . . and members of God's household" (Ephesians 2:16, 19)? Was he realistic in asking all his followers to do more than practice a private religion the way most Buddhists do? They gather occasionally at a monastery, but each person is basically on his own to work out a balanced Karma. How can the wide variety of Christians feel at home and receive usable spiritual help while in a group?

God thought of that problem—and designed the Church in a unique way to compensate. His plan, as explained by the apostles, is that our various needs be met by a variety of input. Church is not just one voice using one tone, one approach. It is intended to be a many-splendored thing.

Not everything comes through the clergy. Granted, the ordained leadership of the church plays a crucial role in guiding the entire congregation. Pastors and other leaders are the primary conduit for truth.

But part of their assignment, says Ephesians 4:12, is "to prepare God's people for works of service, so that the body of Christ may be built up." First Corinthians 14:26 is specific: "When you come together, everyone has a hymn, or a word of instruction, a revelation, a tongue or an interpretation. All of these must be done for the strengthening of the church."

Not everything comes in the same format. Just as the most effective teachers in school were those who used a variety of techniques, so God gets through to us from the front, the "blind side," the "back door," and a number of other angles.

Here are some of his tactics, or spiritual gifts, to his body, the Church: serving others, showing mercy, healing the sick, teaching, miracles, prophecy, public speaking with tongues, interpretation of those tongues, leadership, an utterance of wisdom, an utterance of special knowledge, discerning the true source of spirits, giving to those in need, celibacy, even martyrdom! The New Testament doesn't give us an official roster of the gifts; instead it provides several informal "for-example" lists from which the above was compiled (Romans 12, 1 Corinthians 12, 1 Peter 4).

The point of all the gifts, however, is "that the church may be edified" (1 Corinthians 14:5). By using this cornucopia of gifts, the Holy Spirit is able to cover the many bases of need in a congregation, no matter how varied it may be.

The person who needs information about God can receive teaching.

The person who is out of a job can receive money and encouragement.

The person who is trying to hide something from God may have his deception exposed.

The person who is ill can receive healing.

The person who is skeptical about God's power can be confronted with something beyond his power to explain—a miracle.

The person who needs his attention drawn to a particular truth can be captivated by one of the vocal gifts (teaching, prophecy, tongues with interpretation).

The many people who have a willing spirit but aren't sure how to proceed can be mobilized by someone with the gift of leadership.

And so forth.

Christians sometimes get nervous about gifts they don't fully understand, especially if they sense the Holy Spirit nudging them to be the channel of such a gift. It is important to remember that the Spirit doesn't give white-elephant gifts. His presents are not useless, like the thing you dragged home from the last group Christmas party. We are wise not to turn up our noses at his gifts, for he knows what he is doing. And the Church is waiting to benefit from our participation.

What if we don't sense anything stirring? Have we been left out? Not according to 1 Corinthians 12:7 ("To each one the manifestation of the Spirit is given for the common good") and 1 Peter 4:10 ("Each one should use whatever gift he has received to serve others, faithfully administering God's grace in its varied forms").

So, experiment! Say yes to opportunities that come along, if for no other reason than to see if God has gifted you along a particular line. Try things. Stay open-minded. See what brings results. Don't fall for Cornford's Law, which says, "Nothing should ever be done for the first time."

Instead, opt for the perspective of Charles Schulz, creator of Peanuts: "Life is like a ten-speed bicycle. Most of us have gears we never use."

If we could scan a congregation with God's radar, we would probably spot dozens of unused gifts—spiritual capacities lying dormant in the lives of many Christians. Meanwhile, the Church as a whole is poorer.

Leonard Ravenhill tells a story about a group of tourists visiting a picturesque village. When they came to an old man by a fence, one of the tourists asked, "Were any great men born in this village?"

The old man leaned on his cane and replied, "Nope, only babies."

A frothy question brought a profound answer. Nobody starts out great. God has no instant giants of the faith. The most gifted Christian you know began tentatively, serving the Lord with butterflies inside, not sure if he or she would ever make an impact for the kingdom of God. But availability turned into ability. The Holy Spirit's gifts were welcomed and then released to help change the world.

◆ GIFTS OF THE SPIRIT / YFC EDITORS

The Bible has several lists of various gifts of the Spirit, found in Romans 12, 1 Corinthians 12, and Ephesians 4. However, these are not exhaustive lists; the gifts listed are not the *only* ones people have.

Gifts of the Spirit are special abilities given to us by the Holy Spirit when we become Christians. These gifts are used in building up the body of Christ. Each person has his or her unique gifts. These gifts are not to be used for selfish purposes, but to build up the church and bring people to Christ. And because the gift-mix of each person is so unique, there is no place for comparison or jealousy in the body of Christ. We are to rejoice in one another's gifts and thank the Lord for the great diversity of tools he has given us.

Discover Your Spiritual Gifts

✍ KEN STEINKEN

I Want to Be a Clone is the title of Steve Taylor's first album. The front cover shows the inside of a church with men and women who all look alike. Was he serious? Who would want to be an exact replica of another person? It's not a very appealing idea in an age of self-oriented individualism.

Most of us desire to have our own identity. There's nothing wrong with that. After all, it's the way God made us. Even identical twins have different fingerprints. We are as different as each snowflake that falls from heaven.

But for some reason a new Christian is seldom encouraged to discover what it means to be a "new creation in Christ Jesus." If the old things have passed away and all things have been made new, shouldn't we take time to find out what that new work is all about?

Jesus tells a story in Matthew 25:14-30 about a man who was going on a trip.

Before leaving he gave each of his servants a sum of money. After a long time the man returned. The man was delighted with the servants who had multiplied that which he had left them. He dealt harshly with the third who did nothing with the money. The master expected them to use wisely that which he had entrusted to them.

A new Christian needs to identify what the Master has given to him as part of his new creation. If you don't, you may fall to the temptation of becoming a spiritual clone instead of a new creation. Or even more serious, you may disappoint the Master when he returns or when you go to meet him.

The apostle Paul said, "We have different gifts, according to the grace given us" (Romans 12:6). Each of us is unique, and each has unique gifts with which to serve. We need godly men and women to disciple us and serve as examples for us to follow. But we should not assume that we are called to do everything they do. Many young Christians who sincerely desire to serve God become quickly discouraged when they get involved in some form of service where they have no strength, gift, or ability. There is a good chance, if you are a new Christian under forty, that you will be asked to teach Sunday school or be a youth group leader within the next few years. If you say yes, even though these positions do not match up with your gifts, then the result will be a near disaster at best.

Here are three steps you can take to help you identify your gifts so you can learn the best areas for you to serve:

1. Study Romans 12:3-8; 1 Corinthians 12:1-31; and Ephesians 4:1-13. Write down any of the gifts you might have. These Scriptures do not list all the gifts.

2. Make a list of things you enjoy doing or that you've always been good at. God gives us these natural abilities and interests to be used for his purposes.

3. Finally, talk to other Christians whom you respect. They should also know you well. Ask them what they think your gifts are.

These three steps will help you begin to understand where you fit into the body of Christ, where you should and shouldn't serve.

As a result of this self-evaluation you will gain an important fringe benefit. You will begin to see where others fit into the body of Christ. You will be less tempted to expect them to be spiritual clones of your pastor, some TV preacher, or even yourself.

When I sat down to do this, I found that I had the gift of giving and the gift of faith. I have always been critical of Christians who do not tithe or who are reluctant to take God at his Word. But when I realized that these things that came so naturally for me were gifts from God, I became aware that it wasn't right for me to expect the same behavior or attitude from someone who didn't have those particular gifts. This makes it easier for me to get along with Christians who are different from me in one way or another. If I don't want to be somebody else's clone, why should I expect someone else to be my clone?

Let's be bold in discovering our gifts. Let's dare to be new creations in Christ Jesus. Let's give others the freedom to use the gifts, talents, and abilities that God has given them to build up the body of Christ while we explore those he has given us. After all, who wants to be a clone?

Speaking in Tongues

LARRY CHRISTENSON

Paul, in his first letter to the Corinthians, spent three chapters focusing on spiritual gifts and the motivating factor behind them—love. Paul explained that although there are many gifts, all come from one Source, God; and all are to be used in love for the common good (12:4-7).

One of these spiritual gifts is speaking in tongues (12:10). *Tongues,* a technical term in the New Testament, does not refer to a learned language but to a spontaneous expression of exalted speech granted to the speaker by the Spirit. Speaking in tongues therefore does not proceed from the mind but from the spirit (14:14). This does not mean, however, that speaking in tongues is ecstatic or uncontrolled. It may contain as much or as little emotion as other kinds of speech, depending upon the speaker's emotional state.

Tongues describes a common experience in the early church, yet one that sometimes caused confusion. Paul helped the Corinthian believers put this extraordinary gift into perspective. His words may cut through some of the confusion that still surrounds the practice today.

Is speaking in tongues an essential sign of receiving the Holy Spirit? Does it always happen if you are filled with the Spirit? Some interpreters say that speaking in tongues is the evidence that one has been filled with the Spirit. But it is difficult to substantiate this view either from Scripture or experience.

There are many cases of people who are obviously moving in the power of the Spirit, yet who have not manifested the gift of tongues. Even in the book of Acts, where those at Cornelius's house spoke in tongues and extolled God when they were filled with the Spirit (10:44-46), and the disciples in Ephesus spoke in tongues and prophesied when the Holy Spirit came on them (19:1-6), it isn't altogether clear that everyone spoke in tongues. Some may have extolled God or prophesied—another form of exalted speech, but in the vernacular. Tongues may not have been the only sign of the filling of the Holy Spirit, though it was certainly a common one.

But it does seem clear in the book of Acts that to be filled with the Spirit produces demonstrable results. At the time of salvation, a person could receive the Holy Spirit in a quiet way; but wherever the Spirit is manifested in power for mission, the results are clearly evident. The most common way the Spirit initially made his presence known in the book of Acts seems to have been some form of exalted speech.

At Pentecost the believers spoke in tongues, declaring the mighty works of God in exalted speech (Acts 2:1-12). Peter's sermon which followed was likewise an inspired utterance.

Is speaking in tongues an experience all believers should seek? Both Luke 11:9—"seek and you will find"—and 1 Corinthians 14:1—"eagerly desire spiritual gifts"—indicate that the body of Christ should seek the full range of spiritual gifts. Scripture indicates that the Spirit will distribute gifts differently to one believer than to another. But the body of Christ as a whole should certainly want all the gifts to be functioning in its midst. In 1 Corinthians 14, Paul suggests that three gifts are distributed so widely by the Spirit that, practically speaking, they are universal: speaking in tongues, interpretation, and prophecy (14:5, 13, 31). If some gifts are totally absent from a community of believers, it should concentrate prayer in that area.

A major function of tongues, both in Scripture and in people's lives today, is to enhance personal devotions. Since all Christians have a personal prayer life, tongues is a gift that could be widely used in the body of Christ.

When Paul said, "I speak in tongues more than all of you" (1 Corinthians 14:18), he indicated that tongues have value for a mature believer as well as for brand-new believers like those in the household of Cornelius. Paul also said, "He who speaks in a tongue edifies himself" (14:4); that is, tongues build the person up in some part of his life in Christ.

But Paul seems to have used tongues primarily in private devotions. "In the church I would rather speak five intelligible words to instruct others than ten thousand words in a tongue" (14:19). His concern in this passage is not to downplay tongues but to criticize the use of uninterpreted language in public assemblies. Where tongues are interpreted, they are similar in value to prophecy (14:5). The final evaluation of a gift is its usefulness for edifying the church (14:12).

Was the gift of tongues for another era, or is it for today too? I can't see any place in Scripture that sets off any of the gifts for another era. The gifts were given for the last days of the church, the days announced at Pentecost (Acts 2:17). Paul said in 1 Corinthians 13 that when the perfect comes—that is, when Christ returns—the gifts will pass away. But until then, they are to be used for the edification of the church.

All gifts, including tongues, must be motivated by love. "If I speak in the tongues of men and of angels, but have not love, I am only a resounding gong or a clanging cymbal" (1 Corinthians 13:1). Spiritual gifts miss the mark if they are not motivated by love for God and for others.

What about Speaking in Tongues?

DEAN MERRILL

Among the many astounding things that happened in Scripture was the Day of Pentecost, when 120 disciples "began to speak in other tongues as the Spirit enabled them" (Acts 2:4). It turned out not to be a one-time fluke; Christians were still doing this as much as twenty years later (see Acts 19 and 1 Corinthians 14).

Those who heard these odd syllables coming from the mouths of unschooled believers were "amazed and perplexed," says Acts 2:7—an understandable reaction. The same happens in our time. The Jerusalem crowd wondered if the apostles were drunk; modern observers occasionally use terms such as *crazy* or *imbalanced.*

I've spoken in tongues as part of my devotional life for about thirty-four years now, and I can assure you the practice does not give you warts, make your hair fall out, or fry your brain. In fact, it doesn't even require working up a sweat (despite what you may have seen or heard about in some religious meeting).

It is simply an alternate way to communicate with God—a Route B that bypasses the usual patterns of stringing words together from a learned vocabulary according to certain rules of grammar. It is instead an unleashing of speech from deep within, speech that carries feelings, needs, concerns, and praises heavenward in a mystical way.

The apostle Paul described his own experience: "If I pray in a tongue, my spirit prays, but my mind is unfruitful. So what shall I do? I will pray with my spirit, but I will also pray with my mind; I will sing with my spirit, but I will also sing with my mind. . . . I thank God that I speak in tongues more than all of you" (1 Corinthians 14:14, 15, 18).

Modern neurology has learned a great deal about the human brain—and has a way yet to go. Beginning in the 1860s we found out that the two sides are not alike. The left side of the brain specializes in syntax, phonics, and the individual pieces of language, while the right side appears stronger in processing impressions, humor, emotional content, and overall structure. Might speaking in tongues simply be a form of "right-brain praying"? We don't know, but it is worth researching.

Another area worth studying is how often the words someone says in tongues turn out to be a known language. Some linguists have listened to tape recordings of tongues and pronounced them gibberish, without any identifiable language structure. But at the same time, there are too many documented cases of hearers in various parts of the world being surprised by a language they knew (French, Swahili, Vietnamese) but the speaker didn't—which is what happened on the Day of Pentecost.

One of these cases occurred in my own family. A fourteen-year-old cousin who lived in our home began to pray in tongues, the only family member to do so. My parents were skeptical—until a Brazilian visitor to our church approached my father during a prayer time and said, "Excuse me, but who's praying in Portuguese here?" The two men walked to the altar area to investigate, and the visitor singled out my cousin. She had studied no foreign language to that point.

Needless to say, my parents were more open to tongues after that.

What we know from the New Testament is that tongues occurred in Acts more than once when the Holy Spirit was poured out upon people, and that Paul warned us against trying to squelch speaking in tongues (1 Corinthians 14:39). He also said, "He who speaks in a tongue edifies himself" (1 Corinthians 14:4), which isn't a bad thing to do. It's not the only way to be built up as a Christian, for sure. But it is a way.

The New Testament also tells us about a second use for tongues: in public worship. Paul spends a full chapter (1 Corinthians 14) on that subject, specifically straightening out some problems that had developed in the Corinthian church.

His overriding point is this: Tongues alone don't do a congregation any good, for the obvious reason that they can't understand the words. Talking to God is one thing, but communicating with a churchful of people is something quite different. Therefore, public tongues must be followed, Paul said, by an interpretation in the common language of the people, both the tongues and the interpretation enabled by the Holy Spirit. Otherwise it is all a waste of time.

Why the tongues, if the real meat is in the interpretation? A fair question. Apparently the tongues serve simply as God's red flare, a way of getting everyone's attention for what follows. Tongues don't deliver the message, but they do make sure the audience is awake. In that sense, they are like God's burning bush that Moses could not ignore. He was drawn to check it out—and then came the divine words in a language he could comprehend.

Not all churches in our time are comfortable with this, and the Holy Spirit does not force it upon them. He is as gentle as a dove.

The individual used by God to convey his message through tongues and interpretation is no more a superstar than any other gift-channel in the church, whether for teaching, showing mercy, or serving. He or she is merely carrying out an assignment from above. Excessive emotionalism, pride, or an occasional contamination of the message with human distractions are not what the Lord of the Church had in mind. But he seems willing to keep working with imperfect messengers.

We may never fully understand tongues in the sense of being able to draw a schematic diagram of how they occur. But our faith was not made for scientific analysis. We serve a God bigger than our minds, a God who regularly surprises us, a God whose ways are not always our ways—and would we want it any different?

◆ TWO DANGERS CONCERNING THE GIFTS
LARRY CHRISTENSON

Some criticize speaking in tongues, saying there is pressure to fake it. There is no more pressure to fake tongues than there is to fake any other religious experience. For example, plenty of young people are baptized just to satisfy their parents. They don't believe the Christian message, but they feel pressured by the situation. This can be true of any important religious experience proclaimed by any religious culture, tongues included. In our churches, we need to maintain a healthy balance between earnest proclamation and restful trust in the working of God, so that people respond to the Spirit and not to human pressure.

Another criticism is that the gift of tongues is seen as a status symbol. Again, anything can be used as a status symbol if it is received not in thanksgiving but in pride. Consider the disciples who came back from their mission excited that even the demons were subject to them. Jesus, spotting the potential danger, said (and I've paraphrased), "That's true, they are. I gave you that power, but don't rejoice that the demons are subject to you. Rejoice instead that your name is written in heaven"

(Luke 10:17-20). There's always a danger that we will take the things of God and then consider them our property, earned by our own merit. Paul, who had an abundance of gifts, was also given a "thorn in the flesh" so that he would not glory in the abundance of his revelations.

Thus there is always the danger of succumbing to pressure or to pride, with tongues as with any other of God's gifts. The dangers, however, do not invalidate the gifts themselves.

Is the Gift of Tongues for Today?

NORMAN GEISLER

Paul said two things that persuade me that the biblical gift of speaking in tongues no longer exists today. First, in 1 Corinthians 14:22, he said that "tongues . . . are a sign, not for believers but for unbelievers." Second, in 1 Corinthians 13:8, he said that "where there are tongues, they will be stilled"—that is, they will cease.

Whenever God gave a new revelation—at the time of the Exodus, in the days of the Old Testament prophets, and at the first coming of Christ—he gave sign gifts to confirm his revelation. A prophet did not just speak for God; his words were also confirmed by God's mighty acts.

Moses supported his call to leave Egypt with the signs of the ten plagues. Elijah called Israel to repentance and backed up his words with miracles. Jesus healed the sick and raised the dead. The Word of God was always confirmed by an act of God (John 3; Acts 2; Hebrews 2).

There are three great periods of miracles in the Bible—the Mosaic era, the prophetic era, and the apostolic era. In each era, God did something new, and he always provided miraculous confirmations of his new revelation. In apostolic times, tongues were a sign gift. They told the people God was doing something special. Tongues, along with healing the sick and raising the dead, all indicated that God was giving a new revelation to his people.

In each era, the sign gifts were given for unbelievers—to show them that the new revelation was true. Then, once the revelation was accepted, the sign gifts became inactive. What happened between those eras is the same thing that's happening today: the fact of miracles continues, but the gifts of miracles cease.

What's the difference between the fact and the gifts? God heals people today—that's a fact. But no one today has the special gift of healing; that is, no one can heal anyone at any time. We have the fact of healing, but not the gift of healing.

If you have the gift of teaching, you can teach anyone who is willing to be taught anytime anywhere. If you have the gift of helps, you can help anyone anywhere who is willing. If you have the gift of healing, you can heal anyone who is willing at any time. The apostle Paul had the gift of healing. Sometimes he healed everybody in a city. But no one has that gift today. Even the so-called faith healers can't heal everyone willing on every occasion. They admit that readily. In fact, some faith healers build hospitals. If they had the New Testament gift of healing, they would be emptying them.

Ephesians 2:20 says that we are "built on the foundation of the apostles and prophets, with Christ Jesus himself as the chief cornerstone." The foundation of our faith was laid in the first century, and no other foundation can be laid. That's why there are no apostles and prophets today.

So God does heal today, and he does perform miracles, but no one has special gifts or special powers, because God isn't giving any new revelation. He's not adding the sixty-seventh book to the Bible. The Bible is complete, sufficient for faith and practice. When the canon of the Scripture was complete in the first century, the revelation ceased, and so did the special gifts that confirmed it. God didn't stop doing miracles, he just ceased giving special powers to individuals to confirm new revelations, since he had completed all he wanted to say to us.

One charismatic pastor, Neal Babcock, studied the Scriptures and concluded that his experience was not the same as the biblical gift of tongues. In the Bible, he discovered, the gift is a known language, not a nonlinguistic pattern. In Acts 2:6, for example, the people in the crowd heard the apostles preaching in their own languages. Pastor Babcock also recognized that today's tongue speaking is not a confirmation of a new revelation. Having decided that his experience was not the New Testament gift of tongues, he gave it up. (He describes this change in *A Search for Charismatic Reality.*)

I believe that most people who speak in tongues today are godly, devout Christians who are filled with the Holy Spirit. They are sincerely trying to serve God, but they are mistaken in thinking that they have what is biblically known as the gift of tongues. I think what they have instead is a Romans 8 experience, where they have "groans that words cannot express" (v. 26). What happens when you attempt to express the inexpressible? It comes out as the unintelligible.

We should never put our minds in neutral or on empty when we're talking, because we don't know then what spirit is speaking through us. We could be open to deception.

"Dear friends," said John, "do not believe every spirit, but test the spirits to see whether they are from God" (1 John 4:1). To test the spirits, we must use our understanding. As Paul said, "If I pray in a tongue, my spirit prays, but my mind is unfruitful. So what shall I do? I will pray with my spirit, but I will also pray with my mind; I will sing with my spirit, but I will also sing with my mind" (1 Corinthians 14:14, 15).

RELATED ARTICLE

Chapter 17: **The Spirit's Prayer for His People**

CHAPTER

7

Stepping Out in Faith

- ✓ What is faith and how do you get it?
- ✓ How do we know if we have faith in the right thing?
- ✓ Why is faith necessary for salvation?
- ✓ What is the difference between faith and works?
- ✓ What can hinder the growth of our faith?

The Foundation of Faith

✍ GARY DAUSEY

Hurricanes, tornadoes, earthquakes—all can strike fear in us and unleash tremendous destructive power.

Hurricanes generally give us some warning. We trace their paths as they develop from a tropical storm to their full fury. The National Weather Service plots their course and initiates warnings for evacuation. Tornadoes are less

predictable. Even though we are warned when the conditions are conducive for them, they cannot be predicted with a high level of accuracy. Tornadoes tend to skip around with much less certainty than hurricanes, but anyone who has ever been through one has great respect for their power and heeds warnings to take cover when the sirens blow.

In many ways, earthquakes do more damage not only physically but also mentally. The difference is that when the earth below you trembles and heaves, there is no place to run. There is no possible way to feel secure or protected. When earthquakes do occur those buildings with foundations firmly planted in bedrock tend to stand while others with foundations in less solid soil sway and break apart.

All of us face times when the earthquakes of life hit us hard. It's imperative that when these times come, we have a firm spiritual foundation under us to support us.

The psalmist said,

I waited patiently for the Lord; he turned to me and heard my cry. He lifted me out of the slimy pit, out of the mud and mire; he set my feet on a rock and gave me a firm place to stand. Psalm 40:1, 2

Those who have developed a strong faith have a foundation, "a firm place to stand," when the testing times of life come. Without this our lives can crumble in much the same way as an unprotected building in an earthquake.

What would it take to shake your faith?

We all have our breaking points when we just can't take any more. Where is your breaking point? Do you have a solid foundation underneath you?

Paul said to Timothy, "Nevertheless, God's solid foundation stands firm" (2 Timothy 2:19). *The Living Bible* expands this phrase to read, "But God's truth stands firm like a great rock, and nothing can shake it. It is a foundation stone."

Although philosophies may come and go and human relationships may disappoint us from time to time, we are reminded that if the foundation of our lives is based on the Word of God, we will be sustained through both the good and bad times. The Word of God becomes our pattern for establishing life's values.

When I was in my preteens, my father gave me the assignment of cutting sixty-four two-by-fours to a certain length. To assist me, he cut one board and told me he wanted them all the size of that pattern. I used that pattern to cut the first board. Then I picked up the board I had cut and marked the next board and used that board to mark the next and continued on in this manner until I was through. It wasn't until I completed the project that I saw my error: the last board was several inches longer than the pattern I was given.

I was reminded that the pattern of faith that I need for the foundation to my life must be primary, not two or three generations away. I must go directly to the source. There is no substitute for building a strong spiritual foundation on a regular and consistent time in the Word of God. It is the foundation stone for all we build in our lives.

What Is Real Faith?

JANETTE OKE

Jesus had a great deal to say about faith. He healed followers who had it (Mark 2:5; 10:52; Luke 5:20; 7:50) and rebuked those who didn't have enough of it (Matthew 6:30). Where it was absent, his miraculous works were restricted (Matthew 11:58); but faith as tiny as a grain of mustard seed, he said, was sufficient (Matthew 17:20).

In the Bible, faith is a necessity. God asks for it, and then he provides it. The faith needed for our salvation is not a blind leap into the dark; it is standing on the one thing we can be absolutely sure of—God's loving goodness to us.

Faith is needed at the beginning of our Christian walk. We come to God in faith. Believing, we confess our sins and ask for his forgiveness. God has promised to cleanse us and save us from our sins, blotting out all our transgressions and giving us new life in him. We can depend on him to do just that; there need never be a moment of doubt.

Faith is also needed as we continue to walk with Christ. After we are saved by faith we often get into areas that require difficult decision making. Although the Bible is unmistakably clear about how to come to Christ, it is not always explicit about every choice we must make afterward. We thus need to live by faith daily, knowing that God keeps us, helps us grow in him, and prepares us for heaven.

Sometimes we have difficulty sorting out when to act in faith, and when to let go and let God do the leading. Our confusion may stem from confusing the faith that saves us and the faith that keeps us. The famous text that changed Martin Luther's life, "The righteous will live by his faith" (Habbakuk 2:4) makes it clear that faith deals with our daily living as well as with our initial salvation. We must live by faith in God daily.

Faith is believing with our whole hearts that God loves us, cares for us, and has our best interests in mind. Now some people figure that because God loves us so much, he's going to give us anything we want. This is not so. He loves us far too much for that. In fact, often because of his great love, he will withhold things from us or even send us trials. Scripture bears this out in many instances. For example, the apostle Paul had his "thorn in the flesh" (see 2 Corinthians 12:7-10). In the great faith chapter, Hebrews 11, we read accounts of miraculous things done by individuals who had unbending, unwavering faith. But although some people even saw dead loved ones raised to life again, others were tortured, mocked, scourged, stoned, and killed. The faith of the Christians who were persecuted was just as strong as that of those who were rewarded, and those suffering Christians will be rewarded.

So God does not necessarily respond to genuine faith by meeting all our desires. Still, in the midst of all kinds of trials and difficulties, faith is what hangs onto God, knowing he has our best in mind and will see us through.

Great faith in God means humility, obedience, and growth. Its results are not necessarily success, good health, popularity, prestige, or financial blessing; its most obvious result is the fruit of the Spirit (Galatians 5:22, 23). Our faith, then, should not be measured by what we have but by what we are.

God's highest priority for his followers is our salvation—our safe entrance into heaven and a refined and purified nature. He works in our lives the way he sees best to achieve these goals. True faith says, "I believe God in spite of whatever the world or Satan might do. No matter what my circumstances, I still believe God loves me, has saved me, and will get me through to glory."

The three men in the fiery furnace said, "If we are thrown into the blazing furnace, the God we serve is able to save us from it, and he will rescue us from your hand, O king." Then in the next breath they added, "But even if he does not, we want you to know, O king, that we will not serve your gods or worship the image of gold you have set up" (Daniel 3:17, 18). Even though they believed totally that God was capable of rescuing them, they still left the outcome in God's hands, trusting him that whatever happened, it would be for their good and his glory.

Real faith can be the acceptance of hard things, not the demand to be delivered from them. In faith we cling to God for his grace and strength while facing our trials. In faith we say, "God, I give this—my plan, my future, my ministry, my business—to you. You take it and do with it whatever you see is best for me, for others, and for the glory of your name." Instead of asking him to bless our plans, we give them to him to do with as he wishes.

Joni Eareckson Tada has that kind of faith. She has matured spiritually a great deal in the years since her accident, and yet even with a strong faith, she is still paralyzed. Her difficulty has not been taken from her, but God has used it to open up a ministry for her.

Corrie ten Boom's faith was greatly tried before she became an attentive servant. She was not rescued from Nazi police but had to endure the tortures and privations of prison camp. When she came out, she had been molded so that she was even more usable for God and his kingdom.

Real faith in God does not give orders. Sometimes we hear people say, "I believe God can (heal me, deliver me from this financial burden, lead me forward in this venture, bless me in the business I have chosen), and therefore he will do so." Real faith says instead, "I believe, so I can leave it totally to God to do as he wills."

Jesus Christ: The Foundation of Faith

JOSH McDOWELL

The foundation of the Christian faith is a person—Jesus Christ. In this, Christianity is different from most other major religions. Almost all the others are based on a philosophical proposition—something to believe or adhere to. Christianity, by contrast, is based on the identity of its founder, Jesus Christ, and a historical event, the resurrection.

If you took Buddha out of Buddhism, you'd still basically have Buddhism; if you took Confucius out of Confucianism, you'd still have Confucianism. These are both ethical systems. If you took Muhammad out of Islam, you'd still have Islam, because it all depends upon Allah, not Muhammad. But if you took Christ out of Christianity, you would no longer have Christianity, because Christianity is Jesus Christ.

The validity of everything Christ taught is based upon his being who he claimed to be. You cannot separate the teachings of Christ from the person of Christ. With most religious leaders you can do this, but with Jesus, you can't. Everything he taught is based upon his being the Son of God. For example, look at his teaching about a person's relationship with God: "To all who received him [Jesus Christ], to those who believed in his name, he gave the right to become children of God" (John 1:12).

Few people will say to you, "Why are you a Christian?" But they will say, "Why is your life different? Why do you have so much joy? Why do you have a peace about you? Why do you have hope in a hopeless world?" The answer to this, according to 1 Peter 3:15, is Jesus Christ. I have joy, peace, and hope because Jesus is who he claimed to be. I trust him, because I know who he is.

One afternoon I arrived at the San Diego airport, and no one was there to meet me. I took my luggage out to the curb and waited. Some people who had been on my plane stopped, and one of them said, "It looks like they left you hanging." "Nope," I said.

Somebody else came by and said, "Looks like you're going to have to get a taxi." "Nope," I said.

Somebody else said, "They must not love you anymore." I said, "That's not the case."

Finally someone said, "How do you know somebody's going to pick you up?" And I said, "Because I know my wife."

I know her character, her qualifications, her qualities. She is trustworthy. My faith is based on who she is. And my faith was not disappointed—she came to pick me up.

It's the same when somebody asks, "Why do you have hope?" I say, "Because I know Jesus Christ. He is who he claimed to be." Then I tell the person about the qualities and character of Jesus Christ.

The foundation of the Christian faith is Jesus Christ. If he is not who he claimed to be, then the teachings of Christianity are all false. The credibility of our faith is based on Jesus being the Messiah, the Christ, the Son of God.

That was a big source of conflict between Jesus and the Pharisees. The Pharisees thought that observing the law was fundamental. Jesus said no. The really important thing was how people related to him. In other words, his identity is the central issue.

"Who do people say the Son of Man is?" Jesus asked his disciples. The answers he got were disappointing. "But what about you?" he asked. "Who do you say I am?"

Simon Peter gave the answer he was looking for, "You are the Christ, the Son of the living God" (Matthew 16:13-16).

♦ CHRIST, THE OBJECT OF OUR FAITH
OSWALD HOFFMAN

We often talk about salvation by faith and faith alone. But we can't forget that the power of salvation comes not from faith, but by faith in Jesus Christ. The power comes from him; the good news is about him. "I am not ashamed of the gospel [that's the good news of Jesus Christ], because it is the power of God for the salvation of everyone who believes" (Romans 1:16). So while some people say it doesn't matter what you believe as long as you believe something, that's not what God says. It is not faith that saves, but faith in Jesus Christ that saves. This makes all the difference in the world.

I often crush up a dollar bill in my hand in front of a group of children. Then I shift it from one hand to the other and ask them which hand it is in. This never fails to prick their curiosity. Some will say it is in the right hand and some will say it is in the left, but they all want to know which one it is in. If I did this with a pebble, their interest would not be as great. They are interested not because I have something in my grip, but because I have a dollar bill in my grip.

In the same way, believing in something is not what makes the difference. The important thing is believing in the right person—Jesus Christ.

A False Concept of Faith
✍ JOSH McDOWELL

People have said to me, "I don't feel as if I have enough faith to be saved."

A person who says that has a false concept of faith and Christianity. He apparently believes that one obtains forgiveness of sin and a personal relationship with God through faith. That is a lie. In fact, it is one of the greatest heresies taught today.

We cannot be saved by faith—it is impossible. I wasn't saved by faith, and believe me, I am saved; I have a personal relationship with God through Christ for the forgiveness of sin.

You may be saying, "Now, wait a minute, Josh. My whole life I've been taught that I'm saved by faith." Then you were taught wrong.

Let me share what I mean. Faith is not some magical formula. Faith is trust. It acts like an arm reaching out to receive what Christ has done. If you could be saved by faith, you wouldn't need Jesus. All you'd have to do is drum up your faith to get saved and stay saved.

You say, "Well, how am I saved?" I was saved in what I believe is the biblical way—by grace, through faith in Jesus (Ephesians 2:8). It was God's grace that brought about my salvation. The basis of my salvation is what Jesus Christ did on the cross for my sin—his death, his burial, his resurrection.

The grace of God is unmerited favor. My faith is simply an arm reaching out to receive that grace. Romans 3:22 calls God's gift to me "this righteousness from God." Now that's what we need. In order to have a personal relationship with our Creator, we need a righteousness that's the righteousness of God himself. Paul said this righteousness "comes through faith in Jesus Christ to all who believe." It is God's grace, not our faith, that provides his righteousness.

Faith must have an object. When it comes to salvation, that object is Jesus Christ. If you were to take Jesus Christ away, then you wouldn't have salvation. The object is what gives value to the faith. Remember this: The key to faith is not the one believing, but rather the one who is believed. It is not in the faithfulness of the one exercising the faith, but the faithfulness of the one in whom the faith is placed—Jesus Christ.

Let's say you see a lake with ice on it. It's only about a quarter of an inch thick, but if you really believe, the ice will hold you, won't it? Of course not. You can have all the faith in the world, but if the object of your faith, the ice, is unreliable, you will fall in the lake.

But suppose the ice is two feet thick. You, however, have little faith. You say, "Boy, I don't know if I should walk out there. But by faith, I guess I'll do it." Your faith is small, but the object is trustworthy. You go out on the ice, and even though your faith is weak, the ice holds you.

This comes back to who Jesus is. If he is who he claimed to be—the divine and human Son of God—and I exercise faith in him, placing my trust in him as Savior and Lord, then I am saved. I have a relationship with God. My salvation is not based on my faith; it is based on who Jesus Christ is and what he did on the cross. Jesus is the basis of my salvation.

And that is why I say nobody can be saved by faith. If you could, all you'd have to do is drum up enough faith and you'd be saved. But the important factor is not the amount of your faith. It is the fact that you put your faith in Jesus Christ. And that makes all the difference in the world.

When a person tells me, "I don't feel as if I have enough faith to be saved," I answer, "I don't think anybody ever feels as if his faith is adequate. Fortunately, the issue is not your having enough faith. It is this—do you believe Jesus Christ is who he claimed to be? Do you believe he can do what he claimed to be able to do? If you do, then place your trust in him. That's all he asks."

♦ PERSONALITY WORSHIP / JOHN PERKINS

Many Christians don't understand that obedience is tied up with faith. The problem lies in the way we have organized Christianity. We have highly overpersonalized it. We are making personality cults out of it.

I think some of our so-called church growth is no more than personality growth. People are going for personalities. Many people have very weak faith, but they feel good being around those personalities. And so they go to church to get a good feeling about being close to someone who seems close to God.

But we ought to be teaching people how to learn to be close to God themselves. We need to teach them how to actively be a part of collective worship, part of a fellowship of believers. We need to show people that Christianity is a body of believers, not a cult of a personality.

What Is Faith?

RICHARD HALVERSON

Years ago I had a Bible class every Thursday at the University of Southern California. After one of these classes a young woman came up to me. I could tell she was angry. She told me she had been reared in a godly home and was involved in her parents' church for some time. Then a series of misfortunes occurred in her life, and she "lost her faith." Now she was outside the church entirely.

She told me the final break she made with her previous faith was to throw away her New Testament, which she had held in a drawer for many months. This was symbolic to her of the finality of her decision.

She came to ask me, What is faith? but I put the question back to her.

She said, "Faith is believing what you can't know."

I said, "Do you trust Bill Bright?"

She answered, "I don't know him—how can I trust him?"

And I said, "Wait a minute. You just told me that faith is believing what you can't know. Now you tell me you can't trust someone you don't know. Which is true?"

Obviously the young woman was right the second time. Knowledge must come before faith. Faith is a response to truth. The purpose of Scripture is to bring us to that truth. If I respond in faith, I believe it is because the Holy Spirit is working in my life.

Faith is not something based on nothing. Nor is it acquired. Paul said in Romans 10:17 that "faith comes from hearing the message, and the message is heard through the word of Christ." I trusted my wife when I married her forty-three years ago; and if you ask me if I trust her implicitly, I would have to say yes. I've lived with her all these years, and I've learned firsthand that she can be trusted. Because it is based on knowledge, my confidence in her is total.

This is also true as we get to know God. The more I experience him, lean on him, and find that he bears my weight—no matter how much I put on him—the more I am able to trust him.

Faith always has to go through testing. Some dear friends of ours have a son with a serious form of cancer. For the last three months they have been challenged and tested beyond belief, and they still are not beyond the problem. But underlying their struggle is a deep faith and tremendous confidence that God is able to do what he says. He can bring good out of all conditions.

Romans 4:11 calls Abraham "the father of all who believe" because of his early example of trusting in God. Following God's leading to another land, he "obeyed and went, even though he did not know where he was going" (Hebrews 11:8). I read recently that a leader is one who knows where he is going. I instantly contrasted that with Abraham, who went out not knowing where he was going. That definition of leadership is an example of carnal thinking—as far removed from the Bible as the devil is from God. It is an evidence of a subtle form of worldliness creeping into many Christians' thinking, as the serpent crept into the Garden of Eden.

Instead, the Bible encourages faith in the God we know. He is our leader, and he teaches us to follow in trust. In Romans 4:18-21, Paul described Abraham's faith. "Against all hope, Abraham in hope believed.... Without weakening in his faith, he faced the fact that his body was as good as dead—since he was about a hundred years old—and that Sarah's womb was also dead." At their age, pregnancy simply was not possible. But God's promise transcended their situation.

Faith never denies the facts, no matter how bad they are. But faith recognizes the superior, overriding fact of God's integrity and his promises. Abraham faced what was humanly a hopeless situation—but, as one of my seminary professors once reminded me, "*Hopeless* is not a Christian word. It doesn't belong in our vocabulary." Rather, with God there is always a way to live. Paul reminds us that the essence of biblical faith is being persuaded that God is able to do what he promises (see Ephesians 3:20).

We need to think of faith in terms of quality, not quantity. It is not a means of exchange, such as a bill of currency, marked by its dollar value. We tend to think that if we have enough faith we can "buy" whatever we want from God. No. Faith is absolute trust—giving God our whole lives.

We are never to lay a guilt trip on others by implying that "if only they had enough faith" certain things would come true for them. Years ago the great healer Kathryn Kuhlman, in a televised interview, was asked why not everyone who came to her was healed. She answered in a beautiful way: "God is sovereign in healing, and it is he who heals some and not others. There is nothing more cruel than implying that someone didn't have enough faith to be healed. It is all up to God."

We grow in faith as we exercise it. Remember how difficult it was for Abraham and Sarah to believe in God's promise. But through each experience, as they saw his promises fulfilled, their faith was strengthened. Such strength comes only as we exercise faith in our lives.

"Faith comes from hearing the message, and the message is heard through the word of Christ." The more we know the Word, the more we know Jesus, the stronger our faith will become.

◆ SAVED BY FAITH / MARTIN MARTY

The root word for *salvation* in the Hebrew Scriptures transliterates *yasha,* which means "to give space" or "to make room." Today we would say "to make whole."

Different people at different stages of life need to be saved from different things. Some people have to be saved from a nagging sense of guilt that never leaves them. Other people have to be saved from a sense of meaninglessness. Other people need to be saved from terror at the brevity of life.

To be saved by faith means that if I place my trust in God, if I let my attention be focused on God, God will grasp me and will give me *yasha.* He will give me space, room, and wholeness.

Is Faith Blind?

JOSH McDOWELL

Most people, Christians and non-Christians alike, believe faith means believing in something whether it's true or not. But that is contrary to Scripture. For example, in John 8:32 Jesus said, "You will know the truth, and the truth will set you free." He didn't say to ignore questions of truth and simply have "faith," meaning blind faith.

In Matthew 22:34-40, a lawyer was trying to back Jesus into a corner. He asked a leading question, "Teacher, which is the greatest commandment in the Law?" Jesus answered, "Love the Lord your God with all your heart and with all your soul and with all your mind." He didn't say to turn off the mind and simply love.

In 1 Peter 3:15, Peter said, "Always be prepared to give an answer to everyone who asks you to give the reason for the hope that you have." And Paul counseled Timothy, "Study to shew thyself approved unto God, a workman that needeth not to be ashamed, rightly dividing the word of truth" (2 Timothy 2:15, KJV).

Christianity is an appeal to truth; that's what makes it different from other religions. It is based on a historical person, Jesus Christ, and a historical event, the resurrection. I have found that the more I come to understand my faith intellectually, the more faith the Spirit gives me.

Faith can be reasonable without being 100 percent certain. For example, if I fly an airplane, I cannot be 100 percent certain that it will not crash. We live in a contingent universe, and things change and go wrong. Nothing is 100 percent certain, except maybe in the area of math, but just because you can't prove something 100 percent doesn't mean you shouldn't check it out.

Sometimes when I'm in a classroom speaking on the deity of Christ, a student will say, "Can you prove to me beyond any doubt that Christ is the Son of God?" And I'll say, "No." Then the student will say, "See, you take it by faith"—and by this, he means blind faith. My answer is "Faith, yes; credulity, absolutely not."

Or I'm speaking on the resurrection and a professor will say, "Just a minute. Can you prove the resurrection with 100 percent certainty?" and I'll say, "No." The professor will chuckle and say, "See, you just take it by faith"—meaning blind faith. Again I'll say, "Faith, yes; credulity, absolutely not."

When I fly a plane, I can't prove that the flight will be safe because of the contingencies. But that doesn't mean I don't check the plane out. Blind faith would be checking nothing, just getting in the plane and taking off. That's not faith; that's sheer stupidity.

Faith is when I check the plane out. I run a pressure check; I check the gas. I come up with maybe a 99 percent probability that the plane is safe. Then I commit myself to fly it.

That's intelligent faith. I know why I am committing myself. And faith in Jesus Christ should be intelligent. Before having faith in Jesus, gather the evidence about him. Look at historical evidence, and look at what's portrayed in the Scriptures—his miracles, the resurrection, his teachings. Don't believe blindly; know the person in whom you place your faith. Paul wrote, "Faith comes from hearing the message, and the message is heard through the word of Christ" (Romans 10:17).

I believe the Holy Spirit uses evidence, both biblical and historical, to lead us to intelligent faith. Our faith is not blind. It is very intelligent. The heart cannot rejoice in what the mind rejects. I believe God has given us a mind for knowing, a will for choosing, and a heart for loving him. And all three need to be operational in a maximum relationship with God.

The Two Aspects of Faith

OSWALD HOFFMAN

People have always argued about what it means to believe. Some people think belief means having a logical, intellectual explanation for their faith. Other people view belief as spiritual vitality and emotional expression. But focusing on one aspect of belief and not the other damages a person's faith.

A university professor once told me that among the students who came to his university, even the good Christian young men and women had very little intellectual basis for their faith. Their faith had plenty of emotion, but they understood so little about it. Yet the intellectual side of belief is important.

On the other hand, if belief becomes purely intellectual, it becomes arid and dry and stale. Someone who knows all there is to know about the Bible and theology runs the risk of being so preoccupied with the intellectual side that the emotional fervor dies out. The Pharisees in Jesus' day were so concerned about the intellectual component that they lost the heart of their faith.

I remember attending a meeting of the staff of *Revelation* magazine, which is now *Eternity* magazine. An intense argument was going on between two well-known Christians about the relative importance of the intellectual and the emotional in faith. One of them was arguing heatedly for the intellectual as the most important part of faith. The other one was arguing just as adamantly for the emotional component of faith. As this continued across the table, the other people drew back their chairs to get out of the line of fire.

Finally Dr. Donald Grey Barnhouse, editor of the magazine and a great Bible teacher, interrupted. "I'm always curious about how things work," he said. "I've even investigated my coffee percolator. And I've discovered that unless you have coffee grounds on top, you're not going to have any coffee. But unless you have heat underneath, you still won't have any coffee."

In the silence that followed, a Baptist at the end of the table said, "I'd like to remind you that you also need water." The laughter didn't solve the argument, but it relieved some of the tension.

A person's whole being has to be involved in faith. A logical, intellectual explanation of faith is just as important as a vital emotional expression. The faith of the apostles was both intellectual and emotional. Through the ages,

Christian faith has involved all aspects of one's being. Faith must always be a matter not only of intellectual pursuit but also of emotional expression. The two go together. You simply can't separate them.

♦ A FAITH THAT ACTS
RICHARD OWEN ROBERTS

When we talk about having faith, we run the danger of suggesting that mental acquiescence is all that's needed. But saving faith is more than just saying, "Oh, yes, I believe that."

Our fathers had an expression for that mistake; they called it "mental assent." They insisted that genuine saving faith cannot be just giving assent to historic truth. In actual fact, Satan's mental assent may be firmer than ours (see James 2:19). We sometimes are plagued with doubts, but the devil was an eyewitness to the resurrection. He believes unshakably that Christ rose from the dead, but obviously he has not acted on what God has said through Christ.

If I have faith, I believe Christ. If I say I believe in Christ, I'm very apt to be saying I believe that Christ is God and that he died for the sins of the world, including mine. This is all well and good. But if I believe Christ, then if Christ says, "Jump," I will jump. If Christ says "Don't," I won't. If he says, "Do," I will.

The importance of a faith that acts is illustrated in Hebrews 11, where each witness summoned is described as having done something. Noah believed God and built an ark. Rahab believed God and hung out a scarlet ribbon. Abraham believed God and offered his son. In every single instance we're given the specific act that demonstrated faith in God.

Childlike Trust
LARRY WARD

"I tell you the truth, anyone who will not receive the kingdom of God like a little child will never enter it" (Mark 10:15). What did Jesus mean by these words? When I think of children, I think first of all of trust.

Childlike trust is unafraid. I was being introduced at a service club the other day, and just before the very nervous emcee was to present me, he turned around and asked, "What is your most important title?" I answered quickly, "Grandpa!"

When I think of receiving the kingdom of God like a little child, I see the upraised, trusting faces of my little grandsons, Colin and Jonathan. When this doting grandpa can be with them at mealtimes, I enjoy sitting in front of them with baby food and spoon. Those beautiful faces look up at me and the little mouths open without hesitation. They trust me, and they are ready to accept whatever is on the spoon.

This spirit of total trust communicates something about God's character and how we, his children, perceive him. In 1 John 4:18 we read, "There is no fear in love. But perfect love drives out fear." Just as my little grandsons can trust Grandpa to put the right things into their mouths, so we can trust God, who loves us more than any grandfather ever loved his grandchildren.

Various forms of the word *father* are used over a thousand times in Scripture. Jesus taught that we should come to God like children coming with trust and confidence to their father. Children are impressionable. If they have a good relationship with their father, they believe anything he tells them. This is the way God wants us to relate to him.

Childlike trust is willing to accept correction. In Hebrews 12:7 we read, "Endure hardship as discipline; God is treating you as sons. For what son is not disciplined by his father?" If we want to trust God like a child, we have to be willing to accept the correction he gives us.

Whoever heard of a child who is never corrected? If God does not discipline us when we need it, we are not really his children at all. We expect our fathers on earth to discipline us; should we not all the more cheerfully submit to God's training so that we can really begin to live? As the passage in Hebrews says, "Our fathers disciplined us for a little while as they thought best; but God disciplines us for our good, that we may share in his holiness" (v. 10).

Childlike trust is expressive. Children are spontaneous and uninhibited in the way they express their trust. Once, when with my wife and our son's family at a restaurant, two-year-old Courtney apparently decided she had had enough of the adult conversation. In her mind, it was time to sing, so she leaned back and began. The dining room quieted down as her little voice rang out—"Jesus Is the Answer." Faces filled with amazement turned toward us from all over the restaurant. I thought, God, give me that same absolute conviction that she reflects so freely. Give me a lack of inhibition so I can express those feelings regardless of where I am. Give me that kind of total confidence!

The beautiful concept of childlike faith, then, means coming to God in absolute trust. It means expecting God to shape us and train us. And it means expressing the joy that God puts in our hearts.

In chronological years, we may be children, parents, or grandparents, but regardless of the number of days or years we have spent on earth, we still need to come to God in childlike trust.

Jesus said, "If anyone would come after me, he must deny himself and take up his cross daily and follow me" (Luke 9:23). So I don't just say, "Good morning Lord, it's nice to see you," and let Christ pass on. When Christ comes to me, I crucify myself and put to death my desires, my ambitions, my wishes, dreams, and purposes. I say, "Christ, I'm coming with you, and I'm doing what you say. You can count on me now."

On What Is Your Faith Based?

LARRY CHRISTENSON

Years of parish teaching and experience have convinced me that there is a great deal of misunderstanding about faith and works. Theological writing about justification by faith seeks to make a distinction between living by faith and living by works, yet both faith and works are part of the Christian life. How can we understand this concept? How can we know if we are resting in faith or working in our own righteousness?

Faith can manifest itself in a variety of ways. It can be a silent trust in God's grace (Mark 4:40), or it can actively work for the good of others (Galatians 5:6). Faith can raise its hands in worship or reach out a hand to help somebody else. Quietly trusting in God's mercy is a way faith expresses itself, and when I reach out to a person in need, that's faith manifesting itself in love.

We have to have an adequate understanding and an adequate trust in the working of the Holy Spirit in order to look at faith and works in the right way. If either faith or works becomes something I do on my own to please God, then I'm living under the law. If either faith or works is the working of the Holy Spirit, then it's something that comes to me by the grace of God. As the Holy Spirit comes into my life and brings me the redeeming presence of Christ, he quickens faith within me—and he quickens works as well.

If I feel that faith is something I must do to be a Christian, I'm really depending upon myself rather than looking to Christ. But when I begin to turn my life and thoughts to Christ and believe in him, that is an indication that the Holy Spirit is at work in my life. As I express faith in Christ, I am at the same moment expressing confidence that the Holy Spirit is able to comfort me, aid me, and direct me in my work. That focus is different from thinking I've got to believe more or do this or that in order to be saved. After all, how much faith can I generate from within myself? I can't work up any faith, but I know that the Holy Spirit, working within me, can.

We should always ask ourselves, Who initiated this work? Is this something the Spirit gave me to do? Or is this something I'm doing on my own? I remember sitting in a discussion group in the mid-sixties when there had been race riots in Watts. Someone had received information about a group of people in the San Fernando Valley who had decided to sell their homes and move into Watts. They planned to share the life of the rioting people and try to bring about reconciliation.

The comment of a colleague in the group was very appropriate: "If they are doing this at the initiative of the Spirit, God bless them; it's going to bring a great harvest. But if they are doing this out of their own thoughts and ideas, I can only say, God have mercy on them." Righteousness based on works is something I initiate and glory in, whereas righteousness based on grace is something the Spirit initiates. When my righteousness is based on grace, I glory only in what Christ does.

So the quality of my action—whether it is vigorous working or quiet resting—does not depend on what I know or what I can do or how much faith I have. Instead of focusing on myself, I should ask, Do I rely and trust on what the Holy Spirit is bringing forth, or do I trust in doing something in my own strength that will bring about a result?

When one of my children was small, I sent him to his room for an act that required disciplinary action. I can remember walking down that hall knowing I had to go in and give him a spanking. I said, "Now, Lord, I can go through the action of giving him a spanking, and that may have some good result in his life. But unless you are at work in the midst of this whole action, nothing of significance is really going to happen. What I do is not going to touch his inner life. Your working in the midst of this situation will make the difference between my action being just a human control and its being a work of the Spirit."

In Ephesians 2:10 Paul wrote, "For we are God's workmanship, created in Christ Jesus to do good works, which God prepared in advance for us to do." In other words, when I walk into something, I say, "God, this is something you've set up. You've prepared this situation. I'm going to walk into it, but it's your working in it that will make it a work of the Spirit to bring about what you intend."

It all comes down to dependence upon the Spirit—trusting in the sovereign plan and purpose of God. Are we asking God to come along and bless what we have initiated? Or are we walking in what God has planned for us?

False Confidence and Faith in Christ

OSWALD HOFFMAN

For many people today, faith means believing something that isn't true. These people, of course, are not talking about faith but about false confidence. Since they think they know what faith is, though, it is important to make the distinction clear.

Bait-and-switch offers in advertising illustrate false confidence. In St. Louis a meat dealer offered a whole side of beef at a very good price. But when the people came to buy it, he tried to persuade them to buy more expensive meat, saying it was better. Only 70 people ended up buying their meat at the advertised price, but 406 other customers took the switch and paid three times more than the original offer. Unfortunately, our gullible nature often leads us astray. We are often more willing to trust a total stranger than God, who can be trusted and who always is faithful in carrying out his promises.

This is human nature. Our natural disposition is not toward God but away from him. We spontaneously follow our own will, not his will. As Isaiah said, "We all, like sheep, have gone astray, each of us has turned to his own way" (Isaiah 53:6).

Throughout the Old Testament, God warned his people against idols. They were forbidden to put up something or someone else in the place of God. The first commandment, "You shall have no other gods before me" (Exodus 20:3), means we should fear, love, and trust in God above all else. But we continue to go astray by placing our confidence in the age-old idols of money, power, security, and human talents rather than in Christ.

In America, the number one idol is money. We think a big bank account will solve all our problems. We hope to find security and hope in wealth.

But money is a false source of confidence. In the long run it gives us neither happiness nor security. Many rich people lead disturbing and distressing lives.

Suicide is not uncommon among the wealthy. That's because money disappoints.

The apostle Paul knew this. "The love of money is a root of all kinds of evil," he said (1 Timothy 6:10). It's not the money itself, but the love of money, that causes trouble. When money becomes the goal of our lives, it becomes destructive.

Another popular idol in this country is personal achievement. We're seduced by the phrase, "You've got to have confidence in yourself." In one sense, there's nothing wrong with self-confidence. In fact, one goal of American education is to teach young people to be self-confident and self-reliant. But like money, self-confidence does not cure all the ills of humanity.

When we place our confidence in ourselves and then experience failure, the disappointment can shake us deeply. We have nowhere to turn. But for the Christian, failure is not an impossible obstacle. Failure is only a stumbling block that leads us to higher things. And that is where faith comes in. Faith in Christ builds a genuine self-respect and a proper self-confidence.

Faith in Christ is not just knowing about Christ; it is trusting him as well. When we trust other people, they will disappoint us sometimes. We even disappoint ourselves. But Jesus never disappoints.

Faith in Christ gives us the right kind of self-confidence. It is not the boastful confidence of the self-made man or woman; this is often pure delusion. Rather, it is confidence that we are worthwhile because Jesus values us.

Our confidence in Christ comes when we look back and see what Christ has done for us. He became human and was willing to lay down his life for us. Because of his perfect life and sacrifice, he conquered death for us. His resurrection gives us tremendous confidence.

When God's Spirit touches our hearts, we are enabled to place our full confidence in Christ. This is faith, and it has nothing to do with false confidence. As Paul said, "I know whom I have believed, and am convinced that he is able to guard what I have entrusted to him for that day" (2 Timothy 1:12).

This confidence is more than passive belief. It changes lives. It enables us to follow Christ's way, the way of the cross.

♦ CIVIC RIGHTEOUSNESS AND HOLY RIGHTEOUSNESS / OSWALD HOFFMAN

Civic righteousness is living as an honorable citizen in your community. It is laudable and good. It is needed for the health of the community and for the welfare for the state.

But although civic righteousness is praiseworthy, it will not save anybody. A completely different kind of righteousness is needed for salvation—holy righteousness. It is not a righteousness based on observing the law. "This righteousness from God comes through faith in Jesus Christ to all who believe" (Romans 3:22).

Righteousness is not something God expects of a person, but something with which he invests a person through faith in Christ. This is also his gift.

The Old Testament moral laws describe civic righteousness. The New

Testament describes the righteousness that comes by faith in Jesus Christ.

Luther, writing about the Ten Commandments, explained the difference between civic righteousness and holy righteousness. "You shall not murder" (Exodus 20:13) can be interpreted to mean we should not harm our neighbor's body. That's civic righteousness. "You shall not murder" can also be interpreted to mean we should help our neighbor in all his physical needs. That's the way holy righteousness works.

The righteousness that saves goes far beyond law observance. It requires a new hope, a new trust, and a new way of doing things.

Authentic Faith Produces Authentic Works

JOHN PERKINS

Authentic Christian faith must be seen in authentic works—works of righteousness, works of justice, works of mercy. If faith doesn't work itself out in authentic works, it's dead. And works alone, without faith behind them, are dead.

As to which is more important, faith or works, there is no doubt that to the unsaved you begin with faith. With the saved, you begin with works. A person must have faith for salvation because without faith it's impossible to please God (Hebrews 11:6). For the person who has faith, the Bible says that we are created in Christ Jesus for good works (Ephesians 2:10). Faith and works really go hand in hand. One is saved by faith, and that faith produces good works. Therefore authentic faith in God is always revealed in good works.

When John the Baptist was in prison and Jesus was preaching, John was about to lose faith. So he sent some of his disciples to Jesus to ask if Jesus was truly the one who would come. John wanted Jesus to authenticate himself. Jesus had to strengthen John's faith. Jesus did not send back to John and say, "Just believe." He said, "Go back and report to John what you hear and see. The blind receive sight, the lame walk, those who have leprosy are cured, the deaf hear, the dead are raised, and the good news is preached to the poor" (Matthew 11:4, 5). His works authenticated who he was and restored John's faith.

Gideon is a good example of acting on faith. Gideon tested God until he realized God had truly called him. But after he did that, he put his faith in his army. God said, in essence, "I don't want you to put your faith in the military. I want you to put your faith in me. I want you to understand that we can win the battle with a few of you, and my presence. Then they will know that the battle belongs to the Lord."

And God acted in a mysterious way. Gideon and his men still had to be obedient. They had to light the lanterns, they had to encircle the camp, they had to break the lanterns as God had ordered. They had to believe that they would win the battle because they did what God said. Thus it was God's victory, not Gideon's.

Joshua is another good example of acting on faith. He was a mighty man of faith, willing to believe that he and the people of Israel could walk around the city of Jericho for seven days, and then on the seventh day, blow trumpets and shout and the walls would collapse. He could have just sat on his belief that God could do that. But instead he got himself and the whole army of Israel involved in acting on that faith. And God gave the victory.

And so faith without action, faith without works of love and mercy, is not faith at all. That's the weakness of a simple intellectual response to Jesus Christ. We can go to the altar or ask Jesus to come into our hearts. But we need to be willing to take our faith and trust God in the risks and needs of life. When we are willing to use our belief in God to work for him in a desperate world, then we are revealing authentic, living, vital faith.

♦ FAITH AND WORKS / OSWALD HOFFMAN

Just as you cannot separate the intellectual from the emotional in faith, you cannot separate faith from works. If we have faith, we will have good works. As we grow in faith, we also grow in good works. But it is the faith in Jesus Christ, not the good works growing out of that faith, that saves us.

Many people claim that if you just live a good life, God will accept you. But that's not what he says. He says: "Whoever believes and is baptized will be saved, but whoever does not believe will be condemned" (Mark 16:16). We have to go by his rules, not manmade rules that say good works are enough.

The world is filled with human pride, the pride that says, "I'm no worse than other people; in fact, I'm a little better than most of them." Even it that's true, such an attitude is not going to get us anywhere. When we examine ourselves honestly, our righteousness is like the dishcloth we just used for washing the dishes. When we are honest with ourselves we have to say that all kinds of ignoble emotions taint even our noblest actions. We are not as good as we like to think we are, and our goodness cannot save us.

In the Gospel of John, people asked Jesus what they should do in order to do the works of God. Jesus answered, "The work of God is this: to believe in the one he has sent" (John 6:29).

But we have to remember that the Christian life is not all faith and no works. Although we're not saved by our works, works are very important and necessary to the Christian faith. Good works are always the product of love; love that reaches out to our neighbor, love that is willing to put itself in the place of our neighbor just as Christ has put himself in our place.

In the Christian life, faith and works go together.

Obedience: Faith in Action

JOHN PERKINS

The Bible says, "Faith is being sure of what we hope for and certain of what we do not see" (Hebrews 11:1). Faith, in its classic sense, is believing and obeying the Word of God.

That's what made Abraham the father of our faith. In the biblical accounts of faith, there are many people who lived before Abraham. But Abraham became the father of our faith because, though he lived in an idolatrous world where there was faith in many gods, he believed the revelation to him that there was one God in heaven. And he walked out in obedience to what his God told him to do—to leave all the other gods and his family, and to go to a new country. And he went out in obedience. His faith—his belief in God and his action on that belief—made him the father of our faith.

A believer acquires faith from God's Word. "Faith comes from hearing the message, and the message is heard through the word of Christ" (Romans 10:17). In his letter to the Romans, Paul had just shown us that the world is in heathen darkness, but he is "not ashamed of the gospel, because it is the power of God for the salvation of everyone who believes" (Romans 1:16). It is the gospel of Christ that is the basis of our faith. That is why one must hear the Word.

And even your belief in God's Word is a divine act. Authentic faith is a mystery in the sense that it's imparted from God to us. Authentic faith doesn't start with us, it begins with God. Jesus asked his disciples, "'Who do people say the Son of Man is?' They replied, 'Some say John the Baptist; others say Elijah; and still others, Jeremiah, or one of the prophets.' 'But what about you?' he asked. 'Who do you say I am?' Simon Peter answered, 'You are the Christ, the Son of the living God.' Jesus replied, 'Blessed are you, . . . for this was not revealed to you by man, but by my Father in heaven'" (Matthew 16:13-17). Jesus is saying that the faith with which you believe that he is the Christ, the Son of the living God, is itself a gift from God.

In what form one hears the word of God is not the most important thing. That word might come through a vision, through preaching, reading, or a personal witness from another believer. It might come in a verbal, audible voice, or it might come in special revelation, but when you "hear" it, you know it's a word from God. Hebrews says, "In the past God spoke to our forefathers through the prophets at many times and in various ways" (1:1). The revelation appears in many different ways, but it is the word to you from God. And you must respond to it. Faith is taking God at his word and obeying it, believing it, living it.

Real faith rests in God and believes that God can sustain us. He that has begun a good work in us will finish it. If he loved us enough to save us, he loves us enough to provide for us. But too often we are like Peter walking on the water. We have the initial faith when we hear his Word, but when we begin to see the billows in the water around us, we take our eyes off him and put them on our own provision in the crisis.

Because our faith is sometimes weak, like Peter's, it must be nurtured. That makes worship crucial. We are worshiping a living God, and we must admire him. We know that the God we serve is a God who's still working in our lives and in the lives of others. That becomes an important element in the nurture and perfecting of our faith.

Faith has a maturing aspect—it grows by using it. The concept in the New

Testament is that faith begins as small as a mustard seed and grows as large as a mountain. You can believe more today because you exercised your faith yesterday. You can get the courage to say, "I'll make another step of faith. I see that this God I serve is trustworthy. I can rest my faith on him because he will do what he says."

Today many people have a cultural faith, a faith that leads only to a superficial, "maybe sometime" conversion. But the real believer is not only to trust God in conversion, he's to live by faith. Authentic faith is faith that obeys. It works itself out by reaching out to help other people. Faith is not just a mental agreement, "Yes, God is real." We must live out this belief.

In the book of James the question is asked, "Do you have the faith of our Lord Jesus Christ?" Then James said, in essence, "Show me your faith by your works. Show me your faith by your walk." "Religion that God our Father accepts as pure and faultless is this," he said: "to look after orphans and widows in their distress and to keep oneself from being polluted by the world" (James 1:27). Faith must work itself out in creative works.

Our faith must focus on God in and Jesus Christ his Son. We need to understand that this faith is in the God of creation, the God of provision, the God who loves and sustains us. When we recognize that and keep our faith in him, then that faith itself will grow and mature. The focus of our faith is God, and the action of our faith is obedience to his revelation. God is always revealing himself to us so we will believe him, believe that he is good, and believe he loves us and has our best interests at heart. Faith is trusting in the God of creation and provision, trusting what he has said, and living our lives according to his words.

♦ FAITH IS . . . / YFC EDITORS

The three ingredients of faith are the following:

1. *Belief* based on examination of the evidence. Your investigation of the evidence leads you to a rational decision to agree with the facts. Suppose someone says that a certain airplane is safe. The flight record of the plane (evidence) verifies the information. So you decide to believe the facts (John 20:31; John 1:12).

2. *Trust* based on personal confidence in the *object* of your belief. This act of your will says, "I believe in the facts that say that plane can carry *me.* Therefore, I trust it." The evidence has proven the object of your faith to be valid, so you exercise personal confidence in it (John 1:12).

3. *Action* that takes personal involvement. You pin all your hopes on something and relax. That would involve boarding the plane and letting it carry you to your destination (John 1:12).

Faith is not anti-intellectual, guesswork, or wishful thinking. It is rooted in fact. A person becomes a Christian when he has *faith* in Jesus Christ—the total package.

A Christian continues this process throughout his life. He looks at some area of his life that he's in charge of right now. Then he looks at Jesus to see whether he can *believe* that Jesus is trustworthy. Next he may come to the decision that Jesus can actually be *trusted* with that chunk of his life. And if he is to become like Jesus, he must *act* on his trust by yielding it to Jesus Christ, letting go, and relaxing.

♦ WILLING TO BE USED / CHARLES COLSON

The more you surrender yourself to trust God, the more you begin to see things happen that you could not possibly have done on your own. As Jesus said, "He who seeks to save his life shall lose it. He who loses his life for my sake will find it."

In my own life, God has used what was in the world's eyes my defeat to touch the lives of many people. Prison Fellowship is now active in hundreds of prisons in America and in dozens of nations abroad, with more than thirty-five thousand volunteers. It is an extraordinary demonstration of the power of God at work. I can't possibly glory in it. I did not organize it. I could not have organized it. In fact, I consciously tried not to organize it. But God has done it through my life and has raised up people around the world.

The most amazing thing is to see him work in his sovereign way. Really, all he wants from me is my availability and my willingness to be used. That's all he wants from any of us. That's all he needs to accomplish great things through his people.

♦ WHEN TO MOVE AND WHEN TO STAY
LARRY CHRISTENSON

There are times when the Holy Spirit says, "I want you to rest. This is your time not to be doing something." If rest is what the Spirit calls for, then rest is a perfectly good expression of faith. But at other times the Spirit says, "You've rested long enough. Now it's time to get up and get a move on."

I am reminded of the people of Israel in the wilderness. Sometimes the pillar of cloud would bring them to rest, and sometimes it would move them out. They had to keep their eyes on the pillar to know which to do. In our case, we need to keep our ears tuned to the Holy Spirit. We need to be conscious of when he says to move out and when he says to pitch camp.

Trusting Faith
✍ MARTIN MARTY

When we talk about faith, we need to distinguish between faith as belief and faith as trust. We may believe that God is trustworthy; that is faith as belief. Or we may put our trust in God; that is faith as trust.

Belief belongs to what Martin Buber called an I-it relation. Belief as trust is an I-thou relation. The most important aspect of our faith is trust. We may need to grow in our trust more than in our belief in God.

That doesn't minimize the importance of belief in the dogma, tenets, and content of faith. Through biblical and Christian history, however, people with strong faith have placed their confidence in God even when appearances suggest it's not the best policy.

A trusting faith looks beyond the world of sight. When I look at the human world, I see terrorism and devastating earthquakes and horrible evil. That does not give me reason to trust. If I let my eyes do all the deciding for me, I will become suspicious, cynical, weary, and angry.

On the other hand, if I look beyond what the eye of sight sees to what the eye of faith sees, I will have a different perspective. I will understand that human history doesn't exhaust God's eternal purposes. My attitude will be like Job's: "Though he slay me, yet will I trust in him" (Job 13:15, KJV). I will more likely be strong as I face the hard times and grateful when I face the good times.

The world can deceive us. It often creates the impression that things are all right when they really are quite fragile. I can achieve a good job, and the next day my company merges, and I'm out. I can achieve a good marriage, and the next day something comes along to betray it. I can achieve a sense of self-reliance and independence, and then I am tempted and discover a hidden weakness.

The world we take for granted often looks as if it merits trust, but it doesn't. When our trust is betrayed—as it will be—we feel cheated and find it very hard to trust again. And the more often we have our trust betrayed, the more difficult it is to trust. We can see this in foster children. In a new home, even if the foster parents offer good reasons for trust, the foster child is often suspicious and distrusting because of past experiences. It takes a long time to break down resistance to trusting.

When we begin our journey of faith, the first step of faith is neither a blind leap nor a logical step that can be reasoned out. It's not blind because there are reasons for believing—heart reasons, head reasons, historical reasons.

On the other hand, if it could all be reasoned out, we would no longer call it faith. Even philosophers who can prove the existence of God on rational grounds know that rationality is not enough for belief in God. To say that we can reason ourselves into faith would mean one of two things. Either we've produced a defective God, limited to our own reasoning ability, or our faith is vulnerable to the first rational assault and could easily disappear. We certainly have to use our brains when it comes to faith, but we can find as many reasons to believe as to not believe. Faith belongs to a different dimension of the mind from reason.

Anthony Kenny, a great British philosopher, was brought up Catholic. As a young priest, he studied philosophy at a British university. But somewhere along the line, his reasons for believing simply slipped away. Faith became inaccessible to him. He now teaches at a university with two other philosophers, Elizabeth Anscombe and Peter Geach, both extremely intense and articulate Catholics. The reasons for faith that Anscombe and Geach find compelling, Kenny does not.

One day I was chuckling over something in Mormonism, and an agnostic colleague said, "Well, you know, the only advantage Christianity has over Mormonism is that it is eighteen centuries older." To this law professor the Christian faith is just as implausible as Mormonism. If faith were based only on reason, many Christians would, like Kenny or my colleague, find it inaccessible or implausible.

But faith goes beyond reason. Growing in faith means growing in our trust in God. As we grow in faith, we gain more and more reasons to trust.

My own faith was developed by three forces. The first was nurture. The people I trusted in and had confidence in as a child told me the story of the gospel. They nurtured me in faith and brought me up in it.

The second influence I would call "millions of particulars"—not one single dramatic episode but millions of small, seemingly inconsequential events that have affirmed my faith. Any day in which the score is fifty-one affirmations of faith to forty-nine negations of faith is one in which my faith is being built up.

The third force that has increased my faith is crisis. My faith grows when I am buffeted and tested. Spiritual death is more likely to happen when I am well-off and distracted. I kept a two-and-a-half-year vigil, including one very intense year, with my late first wife when she was dying of cancer. Seeing her pain and the apparent meaningless deprivation of her life tested and strengthened my faith. As the waves were beating the sand around our feet, we discovered we were standing on a rock.

In the midst of the pain and heartache, she and I found Romans 8 a more sensible solution than the alternatives. We found that nothing "will be able to separate us from the love of God that is in Christ Jesus our Lord" (Romans 8:39). We found strength in our midnight reading of the psalms, in our joint prayers, and in the surrounding of friends and family.

Because God is limitless, there are no limits to our faith in him. No development of mind need erode or assault faith.

♦THE DIFFERENCE TRUST MAKES
LARRY WARD

Years ago, when I was managing editor of *Christianity Today,* we had a colorful character on our staff, Charlie Claus. Charlie, whose background was in newspaper advertising, was not a Christian when he came to us. I hesitated a little before personally recommending him, but I felt working for us was what God wanted Charlie to do.

People enjoyed Charlie. When he used the telephone, he always talked at the top of his voice. One day Dr. Carl Henry stopped in astonishment outside Charlie's office, from which his very loud words could be heard. "What is that man doing?" Dr. Henry asked. Somebody answered, "He's talking to Cleveland." "Well, then," Dr. Henry said, "why doesn't he use the telephone?"

People at *Christianity Today,* realizing Charlie was not a believer, were usually careful not to ask him to pray at our morning devotions. On one or two occasions, however, someone slipped. Charlie prayed, but it was painful for him and for all of us. He used little phrases he thought were appropriate for prayer, but his words made no sense.

Eventually Charlie walked down the aisle and accepted Christ as his Savior at the first Billy Graham Crusade in Madison Square Garden. The morning after, in the joy of his newfound faith, Charlie walked into morning devotions with a big Bible under his arm. The young lady in charge said, "Mr. Claus, would you like to pray today?"

"I sure would!" he said. Closing his eyes, he began, "Lord, this is old Charlie Claus down in *Christianity Today. . . .*"

I remember responding inwardly with warmth to this childlike, trusting faith. Charlie's words were not the usual ones, but now they made perfect sense—because he had come to know God as his Father.

Growing in Faith

JOSH McDOWELL

How can I have more faith? Romans 10:17 says, "Faith comes from hearing the message, and the message is heard through the word of Christ." Faith is closely related to knowledge. A knowledge of God increases faith and belief in God.

God does not leave us without sufficient evidence to allow us to trust him. There are several ways to increase our faith-building knowledge of God.

First, the Bible shows us how God worked and still works. Increased knowledge of the Bible leads to increased faith.

Second, Jesus Christ, through his life and teachings, increases our faith in God's goodness toward us. Increased knowledge of Jesus increases faith.

Third, history points to God's work in the world. Knowledge of how he answers prayer, transforms lives, and relieves suffering builds faith.

But all this evidence will do no good unless the Holy Spirit convicts our hearts. In fact, we can know the Bible from cover to cover, study every event in the life of Christ, and look at everything Christ has done throughout history—but if the Holy Spirit does not convict us of sin and give us faith, we are not going to respond.

Matthew 6:25-34 records Jesus' words to the disciples when they were concerned about what they were going to wear and eat. Jesus didn't say to them, "Hey, look. Just believe everything's going to turn out all right. Don't worry about these things. Only believe." He didn't do that. Instead, he pointed out that his Father was in complete control of the situation and would care for them.

Look at the evidence, he said. "Look at the birds of the air; they do not sow or reap or store away in barns"—in other words, they're unemployed—"and yet your heavenly Father feeds them." Jesus used that evidence to point out to his disciples, "Are you not much more valuable than they?"

So first Jesus gave them evidence, and then the Holy Spirit convicted them of it. And he also gives us evidence of his unquestioned ability to control events and situations. One form of evidence is the historical record in Scripture. If God could deliver his people at the time of the Exodus, for example, he can surely do so again today. This is why Jewish families, during the Passover meal, recall the stories of God's deliverance from Egypt. The father does not tell these stories simply to amuse the children. He does it to give solid evidence that God has been faithful. God's faithfulness in the past gives his children a basis to believe he will continue to work in the present.

This morning I took my children out for breakfast, and we looked at the story of Abraham and Lot. I didn't relate that Bible story to my three children just to add to their cultural knowledge. My purpose was to acquaint them with the person of God, to show them how God met a need several thousand years ago. And then I related God's providence to today. I showed them that this was a God they could trust. By doing this, I was giving them evidence that God is faithful.

The more we know about God, the more faith we have in him—if we are open to the influence of the Holy Spirit, who makes God's Word come alive in our hearts.

Who Is in Charge of Your Spiritual Life?

✍ EUGENE PETERSON

Throughout the history of Christianity believers have been warned against measuring faith. When we conceive of faith as a quantity that we can increase or decrease at will, we are doing the exact opposite of what faith is: faith is response. It is directed to God who is always, always far more active toward us than we are toward him. The moment we start looking at our faith to measure it, we remove our attention from God to whom we are supposed to be responding. His activity is far more significant than ours, even when we dignify our activity with schemes to increase our faith (it is quite a different thing to ask God to increase it).

The merest hint of response, faith, on our part is adequate. The smallest crack in our cement-walled wills allows God to begin his work in us. Jesus reduced our part in the process by comparing it to a mustard seed, and he expanded our conception of what God does to the largest thing, a mountain tossed into the sea.

Faith permits God to do for us what we cannot do for ourselves, namely, integrate us into a wholeness that is salvation. Sin fragments us, throws our lives out of proportion and off balance. God wills to restore us to the harmony he intended in creation. To the extent that our lives become proportionate and balanced, our faith is confirmed.

Aware of the fragmentation of life and our inability to integrate it by working up feelings of faith and then measuring what we concoct, we find another way. First, we understand that integrating the fragments of life is something God does in us, not what we do for him. Third, we present ourselves to the Spirit who wills to work in us. We let go of the reins; we open ourselves to the Spirit.

One of the most severe impediments to an integrated life of Christian faith is moralism. Moralism is the attempt to perform one's way into maturity. Moralists think that when they learn the right thing to do and whip themselves into a better state of behavior, they actually become better. They don't. They become worse. We have no competence in integrating our lives into a spiritual whole in relation to our Redeemer. But God is good at it. Very good at it.

A central task of the Christian teacher is to get people to understand that the nature of the spiritual life is what God does in us, not what we do for him. The Christian life is a creative act. It is the kind of thing that artists do rather than carpenters. And God is the artist. I don't hammer together a spiritual life; I let

God do the creative work within me, shaping something new.

Detachment is a word that recurs throughout the teaching on the spiritual life. We are taught to detach ourselves from being in charge, and from evaluating our status. Then we accept what comes into our lives with joy, whether it is dark nights or boredom or puzzlement—things we usually think of negatively—and discover that these are the means that God employs to make us whole.

It is important to ask this question often: Who is in charge of my spiritual life? If I am in charge, I get nervous, look for signs, and measure my faith anxiously hoping that I have enough to get by. If God is in charge, I relax. But it is a relaxation that is full of energy and has nothing in common with apathy or sloth. We relax in the God who is eternally energetic in us.

♦MEASURING OUR FAITH EUGENE PETERSON

I think it's wise to completely eliminate talk about how much faith we have, or how we need more faith. All too often when we say these things we aren't talking about faith at all but a feeling we have. When we define faith as a feeling—of belief, or of piety—what we're actually measuring is not faith but an emotion. Faith is not a feeling. It is simply an act of assent, of openness, and often doesn't feel like much at all. Faith has to do with what God is doing, not with what we are feeling.

When I start measuring my faith, I'm doing it from my point of view—and I'm always looking at the wrong things. If instead I try simply to be attentive to what God is doing, I become more and more aware of what he's doing—and that's a lot. Jesus said that God gives the Spirit without measure (John 3:34). He doesn't dole it out. There's immensity here, extravagance—but I never get that picture if I'm measuring things from my side.

♦PLANTING FAITH / DAVE VEERMAN

One autumn, my daughters and I bought a few dozen bulbs for tulips and daffodils. The package displayed bright yellow, red, and purple blooms that we could expect when the flowers grew. The girls chose each bulb carefully, making sure that their favorite colors were represented.

"Now what do we do, Dad?" they asked. And I began to explain how we would plant them that day and about five months later, in the spring, they would emerge from the ground, grow, and bloom. They looked at me with unbelief filling their eyes. Then they barraged me with questions. Why did we have to wait so long for the flowers? How could we plant them now in the cold weather—when soon the freezing temperatures and the snow will come? and on and on. I tried to explain, with all the authority I could muster, that that's how bulbs work. You plant them in the fall, and they bloom in the spring. We would just have to follow the instructions and wait and see what happened.

Later I thought of how those bulbs were a parable of faith. We had to trust the instructions, let go of the bulbs, give them to the ground, and let God work. Hebrews 11:6 says that without faith it is impossible to please God, and Ephesians 2:8 states that we are saved by faith alone. Faith means doing with my life what I had to do with the bulbs—follow the instructions, give up control (let go), give it to God, and let him work.

But so often I want to dig up the bulb, to take back the control, and to make things happen *myself, now.* And God says, it doesn't work that way; it takes faith. And, by the way, faith doesn't have to be a gigantic leap, it can be a series of small steps: driving to the store, buying the bulbs, planting them, walking away, waiting. It also involves a series of choices. Putting God first, asking for his guidance, doing what you know he wants, turning over each life decision to him.

Are you living by faith, or are you trying to run your own life? Take a lesson from the flowers and plant some faith today.

What Hinders Faith?

LARRY KREIDER

Faith is something like sitting in a chair. A person doesn't think twice about throwing the weight of his body on a piece of furniture built for that purpose.

Chairs are ordinarily trustworthy. You place your faith in their reliability. That is, unless you happen to notice that a particular chair is missing a leg, which may influence you not to trust it; or unless at some time a chair collapsed beneath you, a memorable event that may make you distrust all chairs for a while.

There are things that can hinder your faith in furniture. There are also events, circumstances, and decisions that can knock a leg out from under your faith in God.

Faith is hindered by one of these things:

- contradictory evidence that appears to nullify trust
- a life experience that shatters belief
- some action or inaction that chokes the life out of faith's tender plant

These three stumbling blocks are described in the parable of the sower (Matthew 13:3-9). The seed symbolizes God's Word, the source of faith (see Romans 10:17).

The first seed is snatched up from the road before it ever has a chance to take root. There is a brief exposure to God's message—a quick whiff of its aroma, a passing glance at its beauty—but hastily it is overpowered by competing sensations.

Children or adolescents who show a budding interest in the things of God often find their faith hindered by respected adults who ridicule their newfound trust. Before their faith can take root, it is snatched up.

Adults who have caught sight of the gospel may conclude that there is not enough credible evidence to justify its claims. They too may find their faith overpowered before it is established.

Others have no problems of belief, but they discover hypocrisy or inconsistency in the person or group who brought them to faith. These people, like the others, may find their trust nullified by the contradictory evidence. "If what he says is important and true," they may ask, "then why doesn't he live by it? Perhaps it isn't true after all."

The second seed falls upon shallow soil, quickly blooms, and just as quickly wilts when exposed to heat. This plant is rootless. Along comes a desert storm, and it topples.

On August 29, 1959, as a sophomore in high school, I committed my life to Christ while attending a youth camp. Exactly one week later my nine-year-old brother, Don, was hit by a cement truck while riding his bike. He was killed instantly.

Immediately my tender plant of faith was tested. I had many questions. Why did it happen to a good kid like Don? Where was God when that cement truck was heading for Don's bike? The eyes of my soul gazed deep into the soil, searching for a root. It was there, quivering and shaken, looped onto a bigger root—Christ himself.

Not only heat can kill a rootless plant. So can lack of water and nourishment. New plants need tender, loving care either in the garden or in the greenhouse. The three essential nutrients for Christian growth are fellowship with like-minded believers, Scripture study, and regular prayer times. Growth is impossible without these ingredients.

The third seed took root, sprouted leaves, and grew into a plant. It may have even borne fruit in the beginning. But now it is barren, choked by thorns. There are many thorns waiting to destroy our faith. It can be stripped away by concerns of prestige, position, or power. Spoiled by a heart set on money and success symbols. Rotted by unquenched passions of the flesh. Made impotent by our grieving or quenching the Holy Spirit (see Ephesians 4:29-32 and 1 Thessalonians 5:19).

There are many ways in which faith can be hindered, but the good news is this: it only happens when the choice is made to allow it to be hindered. It is possible

- to use contradictory evidence as a stepping-stone to greater understanding and a clearer perception of truth
- to go through shattering experiences in the power of Christ
- to examine our actions and attitudes and root up the ones that threaten faith

Faith is not the absence of doubt, of problems, or of struggle. Rather, it is a dynamic commitment to One whose trustworthiness is proven. He invites us to test his goodness (Psalm 34:8; Malachi 3:10). Just as a chair is useless unless someone sits in it, God cannot give us his best gifts unless we trust him.

If we are willing to throw our whole weight on him, we will learn that he is able to take it. With Christ, we will break through the hindrances to faith and become like the fourth seed, the one that "produced a crop—a hundred, sixty or thirty times what was sown" (Matthew 13:8).

♦ HOW MUCH FAITH DOES IT TAKE? OSWALD HOFFMAN

People are always wondering how much faith it takes to be saved. I would say even a little faith is enough. All you need is enough faith to recognize that Christ is the forgiver and you are the forgiven.

Of course, a Christian does not stop with that germ of faith. From there we continue to grow "in the faith and in the knowledge of the Son of God" (Ephesians 4:13). As we grow, we have more and more confidence in Christ. This is not a confidence that lets us lord our faith over other people. Rather it enables us to become more understanding and more helpful than ever before.

♦ IS YOUR FAITH MATURE? / JANETTE OKE

Some Christians believe that if they have faith, God will give them whatever they ask for. This is not a mature view of faith.

When my children were little and asked for a drink, I gave it to them. I wouldn't necessarily do it for them now that they're in their twenties. I think God, like a parent, expects us to mature also. We go through a "gimme" stage in our Christian growth and expect God to be always available to us. He helps us through that stage, but he wants us to mature past it. He wants us to learn to be open and usable, able to do things for others rather than always turning in on ourselves.

Faith in faith says, "God has promised; I will ask for it; he must give it to me." Faith in God is willing to leave everything with him. Our strength increases as we continue to walk with God, because when we look back we see how God's plans were so much better than our own. Then we can be thankful he didn't limit our growth by giving us what we asked for.

Will God's Promises Really Come True?

✍ DAVID McKENNA

When we study God's promises, we discover that they are, in some ways, "too good to be true." Can we take all these promises at face value and believe that God will fulfill them?

The apostle Peter wrote, "His divine power has given us everything we need for life and godliness through our knowledge of him who called us by his own glory and goodness. Through these he has given us his very great and precious promises, so that through them you may participate in the divine nature and escape the corruption in the world caused by evil desires" (2 Peter 1:3, 4).

Peter penned those words against his background of trauma, tension, and failure in his relationship with Jesus Christ. These words are his testimony. They say, in essence, "I happen to know that God's promises are true. I can testify to that on the basis of my own experience."

Peter heard many promises from the lips of the Master. Jesus promised to make him a "fisher of men." Jesus promised that Peter, the "Rock," would be the one on whom Christ would build his Church. Years passed before these promises proved true, and Peter's words in his letter to believers are beautiful evidence of their truth.

Peter experienced his share of failure and humiliation. After he denied even knowing Jesus, he wept bitter tears of repentance. After Jesus' resurrection, the angel's first words to the women were "Tell his disciples and Peter" to meet Jesus in Galilee. Peter had been forgiven (Mark 16:7). The denial did not negate Jesus' promises to him.

We know Jesus' promises are true, because we know who he is. We see evidence for their truth in the lives of people in Scripture, and we can back them up with our own experience as well. If we look, we can see daily testimonies of God's promises coming true in our lives.

Those who lived with, talked to, and learned directly from Jesus believed in his promises and experienced their fulfillment. Because all his promises for the present have come true, we can believe they will never stop coming true. And we can trust that the promises yet to be fulfilled, though they sound too good to be true, will also happen exactly as he said.

RELATED ARTICLES
Chapter 5: **Knowing Christ**
Chapter 5: **The Quest for Obedience**
Chapter 10: **Avoid a Roller-Coaster Faith**
Chapter 18: **Faith Is Not a Trump Card**
Chapter 27: **Five Steps to Faith**

CHAPTER

8

The Value of Hope

- ✓ What is the Christian's hope for the future?
- ✓ How does hope give purpose to my life?
- ✓ Is it possible to have peace of mind in this day and age?
- ✓ What if I have lost hope?

Why Be Optimistic?

DEAN MERRILL

Would you like to be president of the United States? You may have dreamed about it as a child, but if you're past the age of fifteen, chances are you're less enamored with the idea now. You know that to lead this sprawling, diverse country and keep it from flying apart takes a special talent.

In the early stages of the 1976 presidential campaign, one columnist noted that all but one of the men willing to have a go at the presidency had grown up in medium-to-small towns: Gerald Ford in Grand Rapids, Michigan; Ronald Reagan in Dixon, Illinois; eventual winner Jimmy Carter in Plains, Georgia; and half a dozen others. The only city boy in the race was Jerry Brown from San Francisco.

The writer then ventured an explanation: Life in a small town gives you a sense that you can make a difference. Problems are not totally overwhelming; if you take them a section at a time and don't give up, you'll eventually come out on top. So these men rode their I-can-handle-it attitude all the way to national prominence.

That view is perhaps harder to cultivate in a megalopolis, where the fainthearted have plenty of reason to think, Who could make a dent in all this confusion?

Christians—whether raised in the city or the country—have a different basis for their hopefulness. They have not given up on life or progress because they have heard God say, "I can handle it." In a negative world, Christians maintain this crazy idea that human beings can be changed. A man, a woman, a teenager does not have to stay the same for life. Things don't have to go on the way they have always been.

Now obviously this is based upon belief in a God who is active. The story is told of Voltaire, the famous French skeptic who in 1778 lay dying a painful death of uremia. A Christian came to see him and spoke about how, despite all that had gone before, the philosopher could still receive forgiveness and peace on the basis of what God had done for him through the cross. Voltaire rose up in his bed, summoned what strength he had left, and flared back, "God does nothing!"

If you believe in a God who basically sits on his hands, then you have little reason to be positive about the world. We are left to our own devices for change and improvement—and how many chips should we bet on that? Precious few.

I have talked with those who spend their lives trying to help alcoholics. "Where do you begin?" I asked one man who is himself a former drunk; God had set him free nineteen years previous.

"The first step is to restore confidence," he said. "Everything else must wait until the problem drinker is led to see that he or she just might make it this time. I tell them my story; I give them God's promises; I introduce them to other ex-alcoholics who have conquered—all to make that first crucial point. Once there's hope, we're on our way."

The Bible tells an interesting story about two young men who used their hope in an active God to stay positive amid dire circumstances. In 1 Samuel 14, the Israelite army was in a desperate situation. The Philistines had five times as many chariots as the Israelites had men; the troop strength had dwindled to a mere six hundred. King Saul had clearly lost control; he couldn't make up his mind what to do. His options were severely restricted, as the Philistines had already captured all the Israelite blacksmiths, which meant no new weaponry. The cold fact was that the Israelites were all waiting to die.

But there was Jonathan, the king's son.

Did he stand and rally the army with an impassioned speech full of faith?

No. He could muster only a scrap of hope. He turned to one other person, his young armor carrier, and suggested going to check out the Philistine outpost. Why?

"Perhaps the Lord will act in our behalf. Nothing can hinder the Lord from saving, whether by many or by few" (1 Samuel 14:6).

Notice, he made no promises. No predictions. He just stated a fact: It was possible.

The two young men gingerly let themselves be seen by the swaggering enemy. "Come up to us and we'll teach you a lesson," the guards shouted.

But before the day was over, it was the other way around. Jonathan and his armor carrier had reversed the tide, and the Israelites won a stunning victory.

That's what hope can do. People in trouble often say, "I don't want to get my hopes up." Yes! Get them up! Hope is not silliness. Hope is the quiet whisper inside the Christian's heart that says, Well ... it's possible.

A speaker named Doug Wead, from whom I have learned much on this subject, occasionally teases his audiences by saying, "Do you know what my favorite verse in all of Scripture is? John 3:16? No. The Twenty-third Psalm? No. Romans 12:1, 2? No.

"My all-time favorite is Ecclesiastes 9:4." People get puzzled looks on their faces and start paging through the Old Testament. Before most of them find it, Wead quotes the verse: "Anyone who is among the living has hope—even a live dog is better off than a dead lion!"

He always draws a laugh, but his point is serious. More of us identify with dogs than with lions. We don't expect to be kings of the modern jungle. Yet even dogs can have hope.

And where there is hope, there is optimism. There is assurance that God has not run out of options yet, and neither have we.

♦ THE BASIS OF ALL HOPE / YFC EDITORS

Christians have a corner on hope. Why? Because the basis of all hope is knowing who God is. There is no hope without a God who controls the universe and promises to bring us to heaven.

Hope designates a future—that is what we hope in. Time, our period on this earth, can be seen in various ways, but only one way offers hope. Some see time as cyclical: history repeats itself and will continue to repeat itself only to get worse (and finally burn itself up). Others see time in the modern secular view that immortality exists as each generation gives birth to the next, which then gives birth to the next. But Christians see time in a straight line—God began time, has a specific purpose for each person within his divine plan, and he will bring it to an end when he returns as he promised.

Hope is *not* in most of the things our fellow humans hope in. It cannot be found in possessions, in our own strength or supposed "immortality," in people's love, in the past. Neither can it be found in human achievement, in who we are or what we have done, or in this life itself.

So where is hope? Our hope lies in our Christian growth here on earth—that we are doing what God wants for us in our particular place in time. We hope in the new heaven and new earth God has promised for us (Hebrews 13:14). We hope in Christ's second coming, in eternal life, and in resurrection (1 John 3:2, 3). We hope in the fact that this world is not all there is (Revelation 21:2, 3). And the great thing about our hope is that it is based on fact. It *will* happen because our hope is based on God, not on us.

◆ WISHING AND HOPING / EUGENE PETERSON

It is essential to distinguish between hoping and wishing. They are not the same thing.

Wishing is something all of us do. It projects what we want or think we need into the future. Just because we wish for something good or holy we think it qualifies as hope. It does not. Wishing extends our egos into the future; hope desires what God is going to do—and we don't yet know what that is.

Wishing grows out of our egos; hope grows out of our faith. Hope is oriented toward what God is doing; wishing is oriented toward what we are doing. Wishing has to do with what I want in things or people or God; hope has to do with what God wants in me and the world of things and people beyond me.

Wishing is our will projected into the future, and hope is God's will coming out of the future. Picture it in your mind: wishing is a line that comes out of me, with an arrow pointing into the future. Hoping is a line that comes out of God from the future, with an arrow pointing toward me.

Hope means being surprised, because we don't know what is best for us or how our lives are going to be completed. To cultivate hope is to suppress wishing—to refuse to fantasize about what we want, but live in anticipation of what God is going to do next.

When people say they've lost hope, what usually has happened is that they have given up wishing. Their wishes have turned out badly, they didn't get what they wished for, or they got what they wished for and it wasn't what they wanted after all. Hope, by contrast, is never disappointed (Romans 5:5).

Hope affects the Christian life by making us expectant and alive. People with minimal hope live in drudgery and boredom because they think they know what's going to happen next. They've made their assessment of God, the people around them, and themselves, and they know what's coming.

People who hope never know what's coming next. They expect it is going to be good, because God is good. Even when disasters occur, people of hope look for how God will use evil for good.

A person with hope is alive to God. Hope is powerful. It is stimulating. It keeps us on tiptoe, looking for the unexpected.

Peace of Mind in Today's World

RICHARD HALVERSON

Jesus has promised us his peace. "Peace I leave with you; my peace I give you. I do not give to you as the world gives. Do not let your hearts be troubled and do not be afraid" (John 14:27). Peace is his gift, not something we ourselves must generate. His peace does not depend upon circumstances. Rather, it is a peace that "transcends all understanding" (Philippians 4:7).

Paul said, "Do not be anxious about anything, but in everything, by prayer and petition, with thanksgiving, present your requests to God" (Philippians 4:6). This is being in his will, and this is true peace.

In Romans 8:28 Paul said that "in all things God works for the good of those who love him, who have been called according to his purpose." He defends that categorical statement by arguing from what God has already done for us.

He has foreknown us, predestined us, called us, justified us, and glorified us! Glorification is the consummation of God's redemptive work in history. Paul speaks of it as if it is already a finished work. Then of course the question is, "If God is for us, who can be against us?" (v. 31).

True peace comes only from the one who spared not his own Son, but freely gave him up on the cross. So, Paul asked, "How will he not also, along with him, graciously give us all things?" (v. 32). If nothing and no one can separate us from the love of God in Christ, as Paul asserted in verses 38 and 39, then we have every reason for peace even in this uncertain day and age.

In Hebrews 10 we read of the incarnation of Christ, so much superior to the Hebrew system of offerings and sacrifices. Our redemption was bought by a transaction between the Father and Son made in eternity, thus replacing the Old Covenant with the New. In verse 10 we read, "We have been made holy through the sacrifice of the body of Jesus Christ once for all." The author contrasts this with the old ritual in which the priest made daily sacrifices for sins and was never finished. But with Christ, our peace is accomplished forever.

In my work in Washington, D.C., I am frequently asked if, knowing intimately the situation of our government and the state of the world, I am encouraged or discouraged. I usually say yes. When people ask me what I mean, I say I am encouraged because I'm discouraged. I realize that we're reaching the limits of human efforts for peace, and now the only solution can come when man recognizes his inadequacy and turns to God for help.

Whether drug abuse or child abuse or battered wives or alcoholism or crime, the great problems of our day are simply not being solved. Rather, their incidence is rising continually. We are facing epidemics of social ills. It is my hope that we will turn to God as the only answer for our extreme need.

Dr. Louis Evans, Sr., with whom I worked in Hollywood many years ago, used to say that people were coming to Jesus Christ by the process of elimination. They would try everything else, and when nothing else worked—when they were at the end of their rope—they might look to him. As long as we think we ourselves can do something about our plight, that we can create our own peace, we're lost. But when we realize that we have exhausted our own resources and alternatives, used up our options—then perhaps we can turn to God in faith.

In that sense, our helplessness is a tremendous asset. The ego doesn't like to admit it, but the humility and helplessness we are bound to realize at some point may be our salvation.

Peace in our time? Nothing is too hard for God. In the words of Jesus, "With man this is impossible, but with God all things are possible" (Matthew 19:26).

♦ WHERE IS HOPE? / YFC EDITORS

Does anyone offer real hope? The world tries to offer security. We can buy insurance; we can put our money in various accounts to ensure financial stability; we can train for "good" careers so we'll be set for life;

we can make investments that promise good returns.

None of these is bad, and some make a lot of sense. But they do not offer real hope. Rather they seem to say, "The world is bad and it's going to get worse. Better do this in order to take care of myself."

Where is hope? The only place to find it is in the pages of the Bible. There we read that God, who controls the world and all past and future events, is bringing the world to an end in order to replace it with the world we each truly long for—one full of peace, love, joy. It cannot be found apart from God because we, left to ourselves, can *never* make such a world happen as we are basically selfish and evil. The Christian's ultimate hope is in the promises God has made. And they *will* come to pass.

How Do I Handle a Situation When It Seems Hopeless?

KEN DAVIS

Several years ago I went through a family experience that I felt was without hope. It is not easy to share information of such a personal nature with the thousands who will read this book, but if just one person can see a ray of hope from the pit of hopelessness, or if one family can be kept together as mine was, then it will be worth it.

Hopelessness is a symptom of final desperation. When one has exhausted every human effort, when every prayer has been uttered and there seem to be no more options available, hopelessness envelopes.

It was on a jet that I encountered this monster called hopelessness face to face. Over a period of years I had taken my eyes from the Lord, slowly deciding I wanted fame and fortune. With every waking moment spent trying to achieve my goals, I neglected both my family and my spiritual growth. At the end of two years I was no closer to obtaining those goals, and, in the process of trying, I had lost the love for those people and things that were closest to me. I felt I had lost all love for my wife, and I was dangerously flirting with disaster by allowing myself to become emotionally involved with someone else. There was a tremendous bitterness toward the Christians whom I felt were simply using me and anger that they would not reach out to me in my desperate need. Yet my anger was misdirected because I wouldn't allow anyone close enough to help me.

I felt I had ruined my past and closed the door on my future. There was no hope of ever loving my wife again, and I didn't care if I ever saw another Christian in my life. Although I wanted to go to heaven, beyond that I had no desire to even live the Christian life. Even the desire to get back on the right path was gone. I was in a hopeless situation.

With tears streaming down my face I said a very simple prayer. I told God that I had no desire for anything good or righteous. I told him the truth, that I didn't even want to return to loving my family or my spiritual relationship with him. I had lost all hope.

Yet way down deep in my soul I knew the truth, but I was not drawn to that truth nor did it offer any hope. But it was there. The truth was that I was headed for destruction and that my only salvation was in the Lord. The truth was that he loved me and cared about me even in the midst of this desperate situation. I was like Jonah who had run from God and found himself shut off from the world forever with virtually no hope of survival. And, like Jonah, I cried from the belly of the fish (in this case it was the belly of a DC 10). At the conclusion of my prayer I told God I had no desire to respond to his love or change the direction of my life. But the truth still remained, and, if I was to be brought from hopelessness to hope and then perhaps to the joy I had once known, he would have to do it himself. I was in his hands.

I sat back weakly, knowing that I had exhausted all other efforts of will, self-help, and psychology. I had now fulfilled my final responsibility by giving it to God. The last ray of hope died when there was no bolt of lightening or surge of emotion. No quiet glow filled the plane. But, just like Jonah's prayer, my prayer came into the temple of the Lord. Starting with that day, his Spirit began to convict me as well as heal my torn soul. He used people and events. He used his Word and the love of my family. But most of all, he simply worked a miracle in my rebellious and broken heart. He has renewed the joy of my salvation and given me a love for my family and himself that surpasses all of my greatest dreams.

I think we often perceive situations as hopeless because we place our hope in circumstances and people instead of in the Lord. The Bible says, "I can do everything through him who gives me strength" (Philippians 4:13). Why is it that we try to do all things by ourselves until the situation seems beyond hope and *then* we turn to the Lord? When I was finally flat on my back and the only direction I could see was up, then I saw that my source of salvation was in the Lord and in the simple *truth* that his love offers hope even in the face of death. There may be some who are watching hopelessly as another member of the family destroys himself and threatens to destroy the family too. You may be tempted to give up hope, but God's truth remains. God is big enough to change the heart of that person and, even more important, he can change yours.

Hopelessness is not a situation. It is an attitude toward a situation. Now is the time to realize that God is the source of our hope and give it all to him. If he can change the heart of a crusty rebel like me, no doubt he can change you and those you love.

◆ FINDING STABILITY IN A CHANGING WORLD / YFC EDITORS

The times are changing, both in the world at large and in our individual lives. No one escapes change. But how can God help provide stability?

God *never* changes. He is the same yesterday, today, and forever (Hebrews 13:8). When everything around us is changing, we can depend on and rest in our unchanging God. And he promises that nothing, not even great changes, can ever separate us from his love (Romans 8:38, 39).

Wherever we go, whatever changes occur, there is a worldwide community of believers who are all part of the body of Christ. They are there to help us keep stability because they too depend on the unchanging God.

♦ HOW TO BE A BETTER PHARISEE
EUGENE PETERSON

If we plan what we will do for the next five years in order to be better Christians—plot this all out and hang the schedule on our bulletin boards—we will simply become better Pharisees. The Christian life cannot be captured in lists and programs. We have been pulled into an enormous mystery, and that is why hope is the virtue that is indispensible to growth.

Hope keeps us alert as God slowly opens up the future to us. It keeps us alive to the unexpected. It prepares us to meet change and newness, not cowering in dread but with tiptoe anticipation, with welcoming hearts. Only God knows what we need, therefore only lively hope (not gritty determination) prepares us to receive what he is about to give us.

Good News: Jesus Is Coming
LaVONNE NEFF

Something about Christianity erases terror and gives hope—the good news that Jesus Christ, having conquered death by dying and rising again, offers his followers eternal life in a kingdom where death is unknown! Most Christians teach that this endless kingdom will be inaugurated by a cataclysmic event—the second coming of Christ.

"But really," asked a good Christian friend of mine, "what difference does it make if Jesus comes back to earth or if he just welcomes us into heaven when we die? The Second Coming doesn't seem necessary."

I have three reasons for thinking the Second Coming is both necessary and tremendously important.

First, it tells me that *God is in charge of history.* Newsmagazines contain frequent proclamations of doom. Perhaps the polar icecaps will begin to melt—only a degree or two of temperature change would start the process—and coastal cities will be flooded. Or maybe the temperature will drop slightly and turn millions of acres of farmland into wilderness. Or, if the climate stabilizes, perhaps the exploding population will eat up all food reserves within a decade or two. Or maybe the biblical trio of famine (in Africa), earthquake (in California), and war (in the Middle East) will decimate the earth's population. It doesn't make a lot of difference, according to some prognosticators, for nuclear war will most likely ravage the earth within a generation.

That kind of pessimism could make a person give up trying to make the world a better place and settle for a few years of self-gratification. But a Christian who looks for Christ's second coming knows that God is in charge of both nature and nations, and that he will not allow the world to end with either a bang or a whimper. He has a plan for this world, and he guarantees its fulfillment, no matter how many detours must first be traveled. He is in control; he will return when he is ready; and he will preserve the earth until that time. A Christian has a powerful reason to join the winning side and work to save the world, physically as well as spiritually.

I have a second reason for believing that Christ's return is tremendously important. It tells me that *God is not the author of evil.* When a beloved family member dies, the neighbors, trying to bring comfort, may say, "It must have been God's will." When a tornado rips through town and leaves dozens of families destitute, the insurance companies call it an "act of God." Is this how God behaves?

I think of Jesus on Palm Sunday, weeping at the destruction he knew was coming upon Jerusalem; standing outside Lazarus's tomb, weeping; pointing out to his disciples that not even a sparrow can fall from its nest without God's noticing. This is not a God who sends out his daily quota of hurricanes and heart attacks.

Yet if we ignore the Second Coming, we make God responsible for human sins and natural disasters alike. We imply that he must like the world just the way it is, because he is apparently going to let it go on this way forever. To be sure, he helps his friends live above their inevitable problems, and he promises a personal escape route through death. But generation will follow generation until the world eventually runs down or collides with the sun; without a Second Coming, nothing will stop evil in its tracks. If this were true, either God must like evil or else he is not powerful enough to stop it.

I protest against this unbiblical view! From Genesis to Revelation the message is this: God will not allow evil to continue indefinitely, because evil is totally foreign to his nature. When he knows the time is ripe, he will eradicate evil forever. The devil, hell, and death will all be thrown into the lake of fire (Revelation 20:10, 14). The Second Coming will be a family reunion, to be sure, but it will be more than that: it will herald the restructuring of the universe, a new heaven and a new earth, with evil eternally destroyed.

I also have an intensely personal reason for believing in the second coming of Christ. It assures me that *God has a personal interest in me.*

Right now the earth holds over 4 billion people. A few billion have lived before my day, and a few billion more may live before I die. God could have perfect control of history and never notice me at all. He could wipe out evil and me along with it. But when Jesus told his disciples he would return to earth again, he told them why: so that he and those who love him could be together (see John 14:1-3).

The biblical picture of the Second Coming is of a personal reunion between long-separated lovers. Christ is the Bridegroom; his Church, the bride. God will wipe away all tears from the eyes of the redeemed. God and his people will meet face to face; then we will know him as he now knows us. Because of

Jesus' promised Second Coming, I know I will be able to live with him forever in a world without suffering.

If there were no Second Coming, I would find Christianity much less compelling. Why should I serve a God who does not control history, who winks at evil or is powerless to prevent it, or who has no personal interest in his people?

Should I serve him because of the abundant life he offers? Paul spoke continually of thanksgiving and contentment, but Paul also said, "If only for this life we have hope in Christ, we are to be pitied more than all men" (1 Corinthians 15:19).

If there is only darkness at the end of the tunnel, I can light a candle so I can see my own feet. I can make noise and listen to it echo off the cave walls. I can reach out to keep someone else from stumbling. But the farther I walk, the nearer I come to extinction.

Why is the Second Coming important? Because it is God's announcement that the light of eternity is at the end of the tunnel. The tunnel is dark but short. Jesus' death and resurrection have made the light visible. Soon the light of his Second Coming will flood every corner of the tunnel, driving out all that is ugly and evil, releasing heavenly joy for all eternity as he welcomes his children into their everlasting home.

"He who testifies to these things says, 'Yes, I am coming soon.' Amen. Come, Lord Jesus" (Revelation 22:20).

♦ THE CHRISTIAN'S HOPE FOR THE FUTURE
ANTHONY CAMPOLO

The first aspect of the Christian's hope is what we all look for at the end of history—the second coming of Christ. Our confidence in this hope means that none of our efforts toward improving our world will be meaningless. God is going to gather up the good work he began in us and bring it to ultimate fulfillment. We can never have a sense of defeat or failure, because even if we lose, God ultimately triumphs.

This hope gives joy to our service even in the midst of troubles. We know these are only temporary. Eventually there will be victory, because the kingdom of God will be fulfilled in human history. This fact forces us to realize that everything we do with our lives is designed to build the kingdom of God. Whether I work in business, in industry, in a factory, or in a home, my responsibility is to try to be an agent to transform things so they become more and more what God wants them to be.

Second, the Christian's hope for the future is personal. I grew up believing Romans 8:28—everything in life is supposed to work together for good. It's easy to take this text superficially, to think that if I walk with Jesus and work for him, I will have wealth, prosperity, and a good time. But we can't stay on that simplistic level. When we consider the twelve apostles, we must remember that all suffered great tribulations and pain, and all but John were finally martyred. One's personal suffering, one's personal tragedy must be set in the context of what life means in terms of eternity.

If this life is all there is, then we have some real problems. But if this life is not all there is, if this life with its suffering and troubles is followed by another life in which God says to us, "Well done, good and faithful servant," then it becomes possible to tolerate the present sufferings. A better day is coming, but that better day may not be within the time-space continuum; that better day may be after time itself ceases.

Whatever happens to me is part of a larger scheme in which my sacrifices, my pain, my sufferings shall be caught up and woven into a plan of history in which God's kingdom is realized. For me, personally, all things will work together for good—if not here, then beyond this time and space. What happens to me will not be lost, because God, through my suffering and even my death, is working out his good. His good is going to be done in history, and I, as a lover of God, should be willing to endure all things for his sake and for the sake of his kingdom.

◆JESUS: THE FOUNDATION OF OUR HOPE
JOSH McDOWELL

How can I have assurance that I will be raised from the dead?

The whole issue goes back to the person of Jesus Christ. Is he who he claimed to be? Is he trustworthy? Is his character such that I can place my faith in him? If so, then I have nothing to worry about, because he said, "I am going there to prepare a place for you. And . . . I will come back and take you to be with me" (John 14:2, 3).

Study Christ's resurrection. Look at the evidence for it. Realize that if Christ could pull off the resurrection of himself, he can also pull off the resurrection of his followers. Read 1 Corinthians 15, where Paul shows that Christ's resurrection assures us that we too will be raised.

Would Jesus Christ lie to us? He said he would come back and get us. And he will.

Heaven
✍ HAROLD MYRA

We will spend a very small percentage of our lives here on this little planet called earth. Even if we live to be over a hundred, compared to eternity, that's very short. We are going to spend the vast majority of our lives in heaven.

Heaven, however, doesn't seem very prominent in people's thinking today. In the past, when perhaps half the children in each family died, people felt drawn up to heaven more than we do now. Parents thought of their lost children in heaven. Children pictured their brothers and sisters there.

Now we live for today. We expect to keep our bodies in wonderful shape and live much longer and healthier lives than our ancestors did. Because death is no longer so close at hand, we tend to feel almost immortal here on earth. For that reason, heaven does not often claim a primary role in our thinking.

My thoughts of what heaven might be like were first stimulated by C. S. Lewis in his book *Perelandra.* Other science fiction books, as well as much of Scripture—especially Isaiah and Revelation—reveal different views of heaven. Some of these descriptions are rather striking.

I've concluded, however, that it's not relevant whether the streets of heaven are really going to be made out of gold, or whether we will have pets or bear children in heaven. What is important about heaven is what we know about the character of God.

Heaven is being prepared for us by the incredible Creator. When we go to a zoo or out in the country and see what God has created, when we pick up a science magazine and look at a picture of a DNA molecule, we can't help thinking how dramatic are the things of God's creation. We can only imagine what wonders are awaiting us in heaven.

Some people picture a heavenly scenario in which we all sit around playing harps and praising God. A few like that idea, but most find it as boring as certain Sunday services. Most likely heaven has little to do with harps—but we can be sure that if harps are there, God will make the harp playing and singing more joyous than we can possibly imagine. Whatever heaven is like, it will open up new vistas of excitement and delight.

In heaven we may be in charge of the stars. We may travel from planet to planet. There may be forms of relationships that are even deeper than marriage. We can be sure there will be challenges beyond our ability now to conceive. There will be joy and creativity. The exact shape of our delight—that is what will surprise us.

Imagine people who have eaten nothing but rice all their lives. They have never left their small village. They have never seen anything beyond their narrow boundaries. Imagine saying to them, "Do you know what a smorgasbord is like?" They might respond, "From what I've heard, it sounds pretty boring. Very little rice." We cannot comprehend the realities of heaven, but what God is preparing for us will be anything but dull!

Before Christ came, certain Jews had figured out exactly and elaborately what the New Jerusalem would be like. It would be suspended above the existing city of Jerusalem. They worked out every detail precisely. But reality was totally different. When Jesus Christ came, their eschatology became irrelevant. Who would have said, "God is going to die on a cross"? No one even thought of that. Nobody reading the Scriptures could foresee exactly how the prophesies would be fulfilled, and yet everything in the Old Testament was fulfilled in Jesus.

In a sense, heaven will be like a great literary work. We read it and then say, "I never expected that!" Likewise, we will be totally dumbfounded at what heaven really is. Everybody with their charts and graphs will say, "Well, yes. It all worked out, but it sure is different from what I thought!"

Heaven is going to exceed all our expectations. It is much bigger than everything our world and consciousness can hold. In heaven we will enter the immensity of God's creativity and dynamic love. Everything in our earthly lives—our joys, hopes, sorrow, despair, and desires—will make sense in the context of heaven. There, for millions and billions and trillions of years, we will participate with God in a redeemed universe.

♦DEATH / EVELYN CHRISTENSON

I am not afraid of death, because I know it can be a blessing. It is humanism to think that the best that could ever happen to us is here on earth. That is not true.

I view death as a coronation. My death will be a victory. I want the "Hallelujah Chorus" sung at my funeral. I don't want to leave my family, but I know it is going to be fantastic on the other side. As Paul said in Philippians 1:21, "To live is Christ and to die is gain."

The keys of death are in Jesus' hands, not Satan's anymore (Revelation 1:18). When I die, I am going to get my crown. I am going to live with Jesus. I am going to be able to touch his hand. I will see my children that have died before me, my father, my husband's father. That is what death is.

There are many people whose lives seem to be prematurely snuffed out. When my seven-month-old daughter died, I came to the conclusion that the purpose for her life was fulfilled in those seven months. That experience transformed me; my view of death has come into focus because of Judy. We are not here to fulfill our own purposes, but God's.

If I am living in conformity with God's will, if I am obeying him and doing what he tells me step by step every day, then when it comes time for me to die, I know this is just the next step in his will.

RELATED ARTICLE
Chapter 9: **The Language of Heaven**

CHAPTER

9

The Meanings of Love

- ✓ How do I really love someone?
- ✓ Is love a feeling or an action?
- ✓ Is something wrong with me if I don't love someone?
- ✓ How does love for my family affect my Christian growth?
- ✓ What is the evidence of God's love for me?

What Does It Mean to Love?

✍ VERNON GROUNDS

The word *love* is used so often that it is easy to lose sight of what it actually means. First of all, love is something we do rather than something we feel. The most famous Bible passage on love, 1 Corinthians 13, does not refer to feelings or emotions. Instead, it talks about attitudes, such as patience, and actions, such as not boasting.

When I love, I am motivated to act in a certain way. For example, if I love my wife, I have a caring attitude toward her. Because I care, I desire to do everything possible to promote her well-being. If she is particularly tired some night, I volunteer to cook dinner and insist on doing the dishes. As a result, I may have to miss watching the news. But because I love her I want to do everything in my power to meet her desires and satisfy her needs, even if I have to sacrifice to do it.

Love can be expressed in three different ways. One is romantic love described, for example, in the Song of Solomon. In this kind of love, a person is passionate and possessive. The Greeks used the word *eros* to designate it. Erotic love, we must remember, is not sinful. No, God sanctions it, and it can be one of the peak experiences in human life if it is expressed with faithfulness in one exclusive relationship.

The second kind of love is reciprocal love. It may not be quite a 50-50 relationship, but both individuals in this relationship give and get in return. Most of the business of married life is transacted on this basis. It also embraces the relationship of friends like David and Jonathan. They were two equals in a very close relationship, mutually caring for each other.

The third and highest level of love is redemptive. In this relationship, we are not thinking about reciprocity or romance. We are thinking exclusively of another person's well-being, and we sacrificially do what we can to enhance that person's life. It is the attitude expressed in 1 John 3:16: "This is how we know what love is: Jesus Christ laid down his life for us." Our Lord dying on Calvary's cross is the supreme example of redemptive love. When we love at this level, we forget all about our own rights, our own interests, our own hurts. If we have this kind of love, we are willing, as Jesus was, to sacrifice anything and everything for the sake of the beloved.

Redemptive love turns upside down the notion of egocentric romance so prevalent in our society. Popular culture says that what makes us feel good is all that counts. But that concept of love contradicts the teaching of God's Word. In the Sermon on the Mount in Matthew 5:44-48 Jesus teaches that we're even to love our enemies. Most likely we do not not feel loving toward our enemies, but we are still to care for them and seek to promote their well-being.

Redemptive love is therefore volitional, not emotional. We can sacrifice for a person because we will to do so, not because we feel like doing it. While this doesn't mean redemptive love is totally devoid of emotion, it does mean the will is in control and the feeling component fades into the background.

Jesus commands us to love our neighbor. Our neighbor is not somebody we like, not somebody we are related to, not somebody we have chosen as a friend. Our neighbor is the next person we meet who is in need. That person may be our enemy or a stranger, but we are commanded to love him. You can't command emotion, but you can command an attitude that will bring constructive action. So in that sense we can love people we don't like.

Perhaps the hardest people to love are those who have deliberately wronged us; people who have, for their own motives, which we can't fathom, decided to hurt us. In loving these people we have to care enough to overcome justifiable resentment. Loving them with redemptive love is not pretending that we like them nor glossing over their wrongdoings. It is genuinely forgiving them, praying for them, and helping them if we have opportunity.

Just because we can will to care even though we do not feel any tender affection doesn't mean we are hypocrites. Even when we don't feel loving, we can be courteous, kind, helpful, and patient. This shows that by the grace of God we are willing to promote the well-being of other people. We don't have to pretend that warm emotions are motivating our actions. Love springs from obedience. If someone accuses us of being hypocrites by claiming that we can love without amorous or positive feelings, we should honestly confess that we don't have warm feelings toward everyone we love. But we can also say that as Christians we choose to care and we will to help.

As Christians we struggle to be steadfastly committed to care for people regardless of what we may feel for them. In time, affection may come. Yet the love commandment remains, feeling or no feeling.

The Kind of Love God Has for Us

JANETTE OKE

Psalm 23 is a very familiar Scripture passage that tells us much about God's great love.

The Lord is my shepherd, said the great king David. David knew all about a shepherd's love for his sheep. As a lad he had cared for his father's sheep, risking his life on more than one occasion to save a lamb from a lion or bear. He knew the agonies of the shepherd when one of the lambs was missing at day's end. He knew the tenderness with which the shepherd checked out each sheep at night for scratches or bruises. He knew all about administering the healing oil.

Jesus himself picked up the shepherd theme as he walked and taught on earth. "I am the good shepherd. The good shepherd lays down his life for the sheep" (John 10:11). Why? Because of his great love.

Let's note some of the things in Psalm 23 that the shepherd who loves his sheep does for them.

He leads me beside quiet waters. Sheep are afraid of rushing water. They will not drink from it. A sheep is not a good swimmer; the heaviness of the water-weighted wool would pull him under. So sheep seek quiet water to quench their thirst. Jesus said, "I know you—your fears and your needs. Don't worry; I'm with you. Let the quiet waters comfort and caress you. Drink thirstily, for drinking is necessary to life. Drink daily from my Word."

He restores my soul. This is my favorite verse in all the psalms, maybe because I realize that the soul is what makes us human beings special. Only to man did God give a living soul—not to sheep or cattle or the birds of the air or the fish of the deep. "And the Lord God ... breathed into his nostrils the breath of life; and man became a living soul" (Genesis 2:7).

Then man tarnished that soul. Through sin, it became twisted and weak and sinful and shameful. It was destined for destruction, for Scripture says, "The soul that sinneth, it shall die" (Ezekiel 18:20, KJV). But look what the Good Shepherd does—he restores our souls!

Have you ever seen something that has been restored? It takes a skilled craftsman to restore something to its former beauty. It also takes someone who understands what the original was like and who values its true worth. Jesus knows all that about us. He can take our soiled, spotted, crumpled souls and restore them again to be the things of beauty and fellowship that God intended when he first gave them to us. I'm glad God loves us enough to restore our souls and then daily dust and polish them to keep them from rust and corruption.

He guides me in paths of righteousness. Once our souls have been restored, it is important to keep them from becoming stained and ruined again. We need to rely on Jesus to lead us each day. Our paths need to be in righteousness instead of in those mucky, tangled trails where we had been wandering before. We need to avoid the sharp precipices of false pride and self-righteousness and the rocks of bitterness and discontent.

But sometimes the paths are steep and the way difficult even for those who follow the paths of righteousness. The psalmist said, "Even though I walk through the valley of the shadow of death. . . ." The valley of the shadow of death is not a pleasant image. It almost makes us shudder. Most of us have been there at one time or another, in that dark, deep valley where pain and despair threaten to drag us down.

Sometimes when we are in the dark valley it becomes easy to believe that we have gotten off the right path, that we are all alone, and that our Shepherd has gone on without us. But this is not so—"I will fear no evil, for you are with me; your rod and your staff, they comfort me." Yes, even in those difficult hurting times, he is with us, and he is seeking to meet our needs. Everything he has is at our disposal. Both his hands are busy caring for us. We have his full attention, because he loves us.

You prepare a table before me in the presence of my enemies. Even in the midst of enemies, he said, we can turn our backs on the flying arrows and pull up a cushiony chair to the white damask-covered tables spread with all manner of good things. We can enjoy the feast knowing that God will protect us.

When we are tempted and tested, we are not alone, because God loves us. Because he has invested so much in restoring us, because he knows our true worth, he will be there—concerned about the outcome, willing to see us victorious, encouraging and supporting us.

You anoint my head with oil; my cup overflows. In those times that the enemy darts penetrate and prick us and the ugly thorns of sin tear at our protective coat and the pain of failure cuts us to the quick, then—because he loves us—he will be there with the healing oil. He will gently seal each painful area, each draining cut, each ragged tear. He will soothe and bind our hurts, and we can take comfort and have our pain eased away if we but submit to his will.

Surely goodness and love will follow me all the days of my life. Because God loves us, he will be with us all through life. Each day that we live, he will show us his goodness in a million different ways. He will pour his mercy out on us again and again. He will never run out of goodness and mercy; there will be enough to see us all along our journey until we are safely ushered into the place that awaits us.

And I will dwell in the house of the Lord forever. You don't build and prepare a house for someone you don't love. No one wants to share a residence with someone he can't stand. We want to live with people who are special to us. A young man builds a home for the woman he loves; he wishes to share his place of abode with her forever. We live in families because we love one another.

Similarly, God loves us. He wants to live with us. He loves us so much that he is preparing a home in heaven so that we might dwell together for all eternity. Now doesn't that prove that he loves us?

♦ GOD'S LAW HELPS US LOVE
NORMAN GEISLER

Love guides our lives through law. Jesus said, "If you love me, you will obey what I command" (John 14:15). Law is just love spelled out in understandable terms. Jesus said the whole law is summarized in two commands: love the Lord your God with all your heart, and love your neighbor as yourself (Matthew 22:36-40). That is vertical and horizontal love. Loving the Lord is our vertical responsibility, and loving our neighbor is our horizontal responsibility.

God's law has two aspects to it: looking up and looking out. It spells out in detail what love means. Love isn't a gurgly feeling, but a relationship with others in which we respond to them as God would have us do. "My command is this: Love each other as I have loved you. Greater love has no one than this, that one lay down his life for his friends" (John 15:12, 13).

Love: A Responsible Attitude
✍ NORMAN GEISLER

Love starts as an attitude—willing the best for the other person. That attitude becomes an action—doing what is best for the other person. Good feelings result from the loving attitude and action. They are the by-product of love, not the impetus for it. The first step, then, is attitude, then action, then feelings. It's not the other way around.

Our attitudes need to be based on a proper understanding of who God is and who man is. God is the absolute, supreme Creator of the universe, the lover of my soul. My attitude toward him ought to be good. And man is made in the image and likeness of God and is his special creation, so I ought to care for my neighbor and treat him as though he were God. Right knowledge leads to right attitudes, and right attitudes lead to right action.

Sometimes—maybe oftentimes—we run across people we simply don't like. We just can't work up any positive feelings toward them. In these instances we need to remember that love is not a feeling. We need to will the good of the other person whether we like him or not. For example, if someone cuts you off in traffic, very often your instant reaction is "The same to you, Buddy!" You'd like to cut him off in retaliation. But if you're concerned about his well-being, even if you don't know him personally, you don't cut him off, even though you don't like what he just did. Instead you love him by treating him as you wish he had treated you (Matthew 7:12).

There are various things you can do with your negative feelings toward someone—and not all of them are biblical. You can repress them, express them, or confess them.

Repressing negative feelings is going to cause an explosion sooner or later, because you can bottle up only so much. The feelings are going to come out later on in some way.

Expressing negative feelings such as hatred or anger will avoid the harmful effects of bottling them up. That's why worldly psychologists often tell us to do that. But if you retaliate against your enemy, you're only going to add to your problem. Besides, the Bible calls hatred sin.

That leaves confessing negative feelings, and that is the biblical approach. Confess them first to God and then, if necessary, to the other person (James 5:16). The Bible says in 1 John 1:9, "If we confess our sins, he is faithful and just and will forgive us our sins and purify us from all unrighteousness." The Christian way isn't repression or expression but confession.

Love is both vertical and horizontal. The vertical dimension is our love for God, and the horizontal dimension is our love for others. Jesus commands both kinds of love.

Sometimes we will find the vertical and horizontal dimensions conflicting. For example, I became a Christian when I was seventeen. My family was non-Christian and very anti-God. My parents told me that I couldn't be a Christian, that I had to give up Christ. I had a real conflict with that. I loved my parents and wanted to honor and obey them, but I couldn't disobey God and reject him. So I had to disobey my parents in order to obey God.

Whenever there's an unavoidable conflict between the vertical responsibility and the horizontal, we must always take the vertical over the horizontal. In fact, Jesus said, "If anyone comes to me and does not hate his father and mother, his wife and children, his brothers and sisters—yes, even his own life—he cannot be my disciple" (Luke 14:26). Now this doesn't mean that we should hate our families, but that our love for God should be so great that our love for our parents looks like hate by comparison.

The fact that I couldn't obey my parents and turn away from God didn't mean I ceased loving and honoring them. I continued to love my folks by caring for them and by praying for them. Not long afterward, they realized I was sincere in dedicating and committing myself to Christ, so they asked me to pray at meals. Year later, I was able to lead my father to Christ when he was in the hospital. I shared John 3:16 with him and read his name into the verse. He responded. So we can't stop loving our parents just because we have to put Christ first. We're to continue to love and respect them.

Sometimes love demands very difficult things from us. For example, because of his love for God, Abraham was willing to offer up his son Isaac (Genesis 22). That was difficult for him to do, but Hebrews 11 says he did it by faith. Of course, God intervened and provided another sacrifice, but Abraham had no way of knowing beforehand that God would do that.

Shadrach, Meshach, and Abednego were told to worship an idol (Daniel 3). Now the Bible says we should obey human government (Titus 3:1; Romans 13:1; 1 Peter 2:13), but it also says we should obey God rather than man, if the two conflict (Acts 5:29). Daniel did that when the government commanded the people to pray to the king (Daniel 6)—he disobeyed the government and prayed to God. Shiphrah and Puah, two Hebrew midwives, were told to kill every male baby that was born (Exodus 1). But they disobeyed the government in order to obey God, and this is how the lives of many Hebrew boys—including Moses—were saved. So when our responsibilities conflict, we need to take the vertical over the horizontal.

♦ GROWING IN LOVE / NORMAN GEISLER

As I practice love, my understanding of love grows. There is a beautiful description of love in the Song of Solomon. Three successive times the singer summarizes the relationship between the lovers. The first time, it is "My lover is mine and I am his" (2:16). The next time, the relationship is reversed: "I am my lover's and my lover is mine" (6:3). Finally, "I belong to my lover, and his desire is for me" (7:10).

This shows a beautiful growth in love. In the first stage, I accept Christ, and that's wonderful. The emphasis is on what I have done. In the next stage, I realize that Christ has accepted me. Now the emphasis is on Christ, and that is a higher stage of love. And yet I'm still saying, "I also accepted him." In the third and highest stage of love, I know that Christ accepted me and desires me. I'm no longer hanging desperately on to him, but I'm resting in the fact that he is hanging on to me.

Responding in Love

OSWALD HOFFMAN

This is the good news: Faith and love were born at the foot of the cross of Christ, and they express themselves in ordinary human lives like our own.

But we're not always sure what a loving response is in a particular situation. For example, is it loving to pass over the hurtful remark a person makes? Or is it loving to bring it into the open and deal with it? Is it loving to tell a friend what others have said about him, even though you know it's going to hurt him? Or is it loving to keep silent about it and continue to care for him?

The following guidelines can help us know what to do:

1. *Use your judgment.* We have to handle these questions as they arise by using the good judgment God has given us. God does not give us a strict list of dos and don'ts to follow. He expects us to use the discretion we have.

Of course our judgment is not perfect. We will make mistakes in loving. There will be times when we have to say, "If I could do it over again, I would do it differently." But we should not let the fear of making a mistake paralyze us and keep us from acting. It is better to do what we think is loving than not to do anything at all for fear of hurting someone.

2. *Nice is not always right.* Sometimes we are accused of being unloving when really what we have done is the most loving thing under the circumstances. Acting nice does not necessarily mean being loving. Some of the roughest people I know are also the most loving. They are people of faith with whom I could trust my life, but they say things to me that really bring me up short. They don't want to be hurtful, but they are not worried about being nice. Yet they are loving.

A truly unloving response is not caring or caring only about yourself. When you care only about yourself, you're at the heart of sin.

3. *Silence can be love.* The essence of love is being able to care for someone when your natural reaction is unfavorable or even nasty. In loving, you catch yourself and remain silent. Later on you may have something to say, but right now you are quiet for the sake of love.

Insisting upon having the last word is not a loving response. The last thing said is probably the worst thing. Saying I'm sorry is the hardest thing for a person to do. But when a person says that, it's the beginning of something new. The argument ends, and the relationship begins to grow again.

"We love because [Christ] first loved us" (1 John 4:19). When we have faith in Christ, who loves and never quits loving, we can do for others what Christ has done for us.

♦WHEN YOU ARE ATTACKED
OSWALD HOFFMAN

As a radio speaker, I sometimes get bitter letters attacking something I've said. I've learned that this bitterness is not really directed at me, but at people who have deeply hurt the letter writers.

I write back to these people, accepting where they are coming from. I tell them I wish I knew what had happened in their past because I'd like to help them. About half the time they write back and say, yes, you're right; I had a bitter experience with the pastor of the congregation, or my father, or a friend, and it has stayed with me all this time.

So when people are bitter toward you, step back and see if they are reacting to a hurt they experienced a long time ago. Then treat them with love and understanding.

The Forgiving Formula

EVELYN CHRISTENSON

Several years ago my husband left the pastorate, and we moved from Rockford, Illinois, to St. Paul, Minnesota. I left behind a tremendous nest of prayer support, but I was confident I could find people in St. Paul to support my ministry in prayer. Soon after we moved, I was scheduled to speak at a prayer breakfast, and I found a few prayer chains to pray for me. When I got back, I called to thank the chairman for the prayer support. She said, "Oh, but we didn't pray." She went on to explain that someone in the church had stopped the prayer chain, because it was not their practice to pray for public speakers.

I was extremely hurt by this. The next week I went away with my husband and another couple to a mountain cabin. All week long I tried reading my Bible and praying, but I could not get through to God. I confessed my sins until I was blue in the face. Finally, Thursday morning at 5:30, I got up and went far from the cabin and threw myself on my face before God. I said, "Lord, say something. I don't care what you say, but say something."

I was beginning to panic, because I was teaching prayer seminars and yet God had not said a word to me all week. I started leafing through the Bible. When I got to 2 Corinthians 2:5, God stopped me. "If anyone has caused grief, he has not so much grieved me as he has grieved all of you."

That was my problem. I had been grieved, and amazingly God didn't disagree with me. When we are hurt by other Christians, we somehow feel that God sweeps it under the rug and says, "Don't worry about it." But he doesn't ignore it; he expects us to acknowledge that we have been grieved.

I was ready to get up from my knees and go make breakfast, thinking "Hallelujah, God agrees with me. I've been grieved." But God nudged me and said, "Don't stop—there is more in this chapter."

So I continued reading until I came to verse 7, "Now instead, you ought to forgive and comfort him so that he will not be overwhelmed by excessive sorrow."

I was supposed to forgive her. But how could I do that? She had made a fool of me. I had been the chairman of a prayer movement, prayer was my life, and when I had asked a simple prayer request, I had been slapped in the face, so to speak. It horrified me.

I waited on my knees a long time. I struggled with the Lord. Finally I said, "God, I can't do it on my own strength. You are going to have to help me."

And God did. His power, his grace, his ability to forgive came, and I forgave her. And as I forgave her, I paved the way for God to forgive me. In the Lord's Prayer, Jesus said, "Forgive us our debts as we also have forgiven our debtors" (Matthew 6:12). We are forgiven as we forgive.

But there was even more. God nudged me to read verse 8: "I urge you, therefore, to reaffirm your love for him." Since I didn't love that woman very much, I had to ask God for love. Again, I waited. The waiting was hard, but it was important. So often we ask God for something, and then we get right up and run away. So I waited until the love of God came.

I knew that not only did I have to love her in my heart, I had to show my love for her. Since I was on a mountain with no postal delivery or phone, I had to wait until we returned home and I met her in church.

The next Sunday morning the woman who had hurt me was sitting in the front of the church, and I was sitting in the back. During the service I prayed, "Lord, I do love her, and I want to affirm my love for her, but I'm not going to make a fool of myself." I kept trying to think how I could get out of it. Finally I made a bargain with the Lord that if she got to the back entry hall of the church before I got there, I would affirm my love for her. I thought I was safe, since I was a hundred feet closer to the hall.

But she got there first. People were watching us to see what I was going to do. They knew I went around teaching prayer seminars, and they wanted to know what I would do when I was hurt. I went up and put my arms around her and we settled it.

That was the hardest lesson in forgiveness I have ever learned, but forgiving that woman freed me to hear God again.

♦ FALSE CONFESSIONS / HANNAH HURNARD

Confession is very important, but we must be careful to confess only our own mistakes.

After I had talked with a dear friend of mine about the importance of confession, she said to me, "Well, I tried that, Hannah, and it only made the situation worse."

"What did you confess?" I asked.

"I went to somebody and said, 'I forgive you for being so horrible to me. I confess that I have just loathed you for the things you have done.'"

She didn't see that her confession was really a judgment of the other person.

Self-Love and Self-Centeredness

✍ LARRY KREIDER

Love is a difficult word to pin down. It means different things to different people on different occasions. I love peanuts, football, warm weather, my wife and kids, a good book, a stimulating conversation, and God.

Different levels of intensity and commitment are attached to each of these items. Though I enjoy peanuts, I'm not upset if I haven't eaten any for a while. I love football enough to make it a part of my regular Sunday afternoon TV viewing. However, I would pass on the football game if an opportunity for a memory-building event with my family came up. My love for God dictates that I won't regularly miss going to church on Sunday morning in order to go on family outings.

The term self-love also has many different connotations. As a result, there is much confusion over the role of self in the biblical understanding of personhood.

Here is the problem. Self-love and self-centeredness are usually synonymous terms in Scripture. Paul said that in the last days people would be "lovers of themselves" (1 Timothy 3:1-5). Their self-love would be made evident by their preoccupation with money, their bragging, the way they would force their own viewpoint and demand their own way, their love for damaging gossip, and their constant search for unlimited freedom and pleasure. That is a clear representation of self-centeredness.

But hold on—don't go out just yet and try to find ways to prove your self-hatred. The Bible hints at another meaning for self-love, one that is not negative.

Jesus said, for example, to "love your neighbor as yourself" (Matthew 22:39), and Paul observed that "no one ever hated his own body, but he feeds and cares for it, just as Christ does the church" (Ephesians 5:29). Both these verses refer to self-preservation—a necessary and good characteristic. Just as you deliberately take care of your physical needs, so you should seek to care for your neighbor. Just as you provide for the needs of your body, so Christ protects and preserves the Church. This kind of self-love has nothing to do with self-indulgence or preoccupation.

How, then, ought we to think about ourselves?

The starting point is God. In order to know what to think about ourselves, we need God's viewpoint. He wants us to have the right perspective, the right self-estimate. He wants us to know that he loves us and that we have infinite worth.

Martin Luther said, "It is not that you have value and therefore God loves you; God loves you, and therefore you are valuable." God chose to create you, and he has loved you from the beginning. David said, "You created my inmost being; you knit me together in my mother's womb. I praise you because I am fearfully and wonderfully made" (Psalm 139:13, 14).

But we human creatures have soiled the original garment. A proper self-estimate means that we are horrified at the way we have offended God and been untruthful to ourselves. Various biblical characters came to this awareness, and they responded in similar ways. Isaiah said, "Woe to me! . . . I am ruined!" (Isaiah 6:5). Job said, "I despise myself and repent in dust and ashes" (Job 42:6). Peter said, "Go away from me, Lord; I am a sinful man!" (Luke 5:8).

A sorrowful response to sin is entirely appropriate. The mistake some people make is to transfer their disgust and guilt over their sinfulness to their humanness.

Being human means bearing the image of God, for we are created in his image. Rejoice in your humanity. Take care of yourself mentally, emotionally, physically, and spiritually.

Then, like David, ask God to search your heart and mind for twisted attitudes, actions, or motives (Psalm 139:23, 24). Such repentance will keep the channels clear of anything that might block your relationship with God. It will also sweep away anything that might prevent a clear understanding of your worth in his eyes.

♦ LOVE IS SHOWN BY ACTIONS
JOSH McDOWELL

This morning I asked my nine-year-old son, "Do you know that I love your mother?"

"Yeah," he said.

"How do you know?" I persisted.

"You tell her all the time," he said.

"Well," I continued, "what if I lost my voice and couldn't say I loved her. Would she still know I loved her?"

"Yeah," he said. "You could write it down for her."

So I said, "OK, son, let's say I had both my arms amputated, and I can't write with my feet. Would she know I loved her?"

"Yes," he said. "I'd tell her for you."

"Wait," I said. "How would you know I loved her?"

Long pause. "By the way you treat her," he said.

It took about five minutes to get him to the point. But eventually he saw that love goes deeper than words.

The Language of Heaven
✍ HANNAH HURNARD

For many years I couldn't talk without stammering and hesitating. This was very humiliating to me. That changed when I was forty-five years old, after I had known the Lord for twenty-five years.

I had been on the mission field for nearly twenty years when the Lord told me I must now learn to talk like the people in heaven. That meant I mustn't grumble and complain anymore. I mustn't talk about other people's faults. I mustn't say things behind their backs that I wouldn't like them to say about me.

At that time I was accustomed to saying to a fellow missionary, "Let's have a little prayer together to help you change, to see if God will help you stop stumbling." The Lord Jesus said to me, "In heaven we don't talk about faults. When you pray like that, I have to get up quietly and go out of the room. That leaves you talking to the four walls."

I said, "Lord, I'm forty-five years old and my habits are fixed, but you help me alter them."

He said, "Hannah, you're an addict. You find fault and talk about other people's faults and criticize others all the time. There are plenty of other people to talk about faults—I don't need you to do so. But you're like an alcoholic. You don't dare give in to it once. If you promise not to make any exceptions, I'll help you."

"Well," I said, "only your grace could do that, Lord."

And the Lord said, "I'm going to ask for one of the heavenly beings to take a coal from off the altar and to touch your lips with it."

Jesus then told me all the things I should say—the kind, helpful, and good things they talk about in heaven. The language of heaven is called blessing. He taught me how lovely it is always to draw attention to what is good. Whenever Jesus spoke, the people "were amazed at the gracious words that came from his lips" (Luke 4:22). "For God did not send his Son into the world to condemn the world, but to save the world through him" (John 3:17).

As soon as I stopped criticizing others, I was able to talk normally without hesitating and stammering. But whenever I fell back into my old habits, my stuttering came back. I'm a person who loves to talk. If God had allowed it, I would have gotten up on platforms and showed off. I would have spoken in my own strength instead of in his. I would have gone on criticizing and talking about people, and so I had to wait until I had grown sufficiently in spirit and in grace to understand a better way.

♦ CHARACTER DISADVANTAGES
LEWIS SMEDES

We should be modest in our expectations, especially of other people. When we are disappointed in someone's character and make judgments on it, we do it without knowing what kind of temperamental or genetic disadvantages that person has.

For instance, because of cultural conditioning or psychological background, one person may find it harder than another person to be compassionate, or courageous, or committed. He may not seem to have much character. But when all is revealed at the throne of God, you may find that he has been fighting a much harder battle than yours. He may get more praise for how far he has come.

So we should be careful how we judge others.

Loving the Unloveable
✍ WILLIAM BRIGHT

Loving by faith makes for an exciting adventure. Scripture says we are to love God with all our heart, soul, and mind, and love our neighbors as ourselves. We are to love our enemies and our fellow believers. These are commands. If we are sincere in our living for Christ, we must learn how to love. Love is an act of the will that through the enabling of the Holy Spirit we claim by faith.

An outstanding lawyer came to see me one day. He had been president of the alumni association of one of the most outstanding law schools in America and was a senior partner in a very prestigious law firm. This man had a law partner who was also very well known, wealthy, and influential. Both men had big egos, and as a result they didn't like each other. They had actually put each other down for years even though they were partners. "I've disliked this man for years," the lawyer told me, "but now that I'm a Christian, I don't feel comfortable about hating him. What can I do?"

"You must go to him, ask him to forgive you for your previous attitude, and tell him that you love him," I replied.

"I don't love him," the lawyer answered. "But I don't hate him anymore either."

"Well," I said, "you're commanded to love him. If he's your neighbor, you are to love him. If he's your enemy, you are to love him. There's no way around it. You are commanded to love him."

"I'm not going to be a hypocrite," the lawyer said. "I'm not going to tell him I love him if I don't."

"It's simply a matter of the will," I explained. "You'll have to decide whether or not you're going to obey God's command. Love is not necessarily an emotion, though it can result in emotion. Jesus said, 'Whoever has my commands and obeys them, he is the one who loves me. He who loves me will be loved by my Father, and I too will love him and show myself to him' [John 14:21]. So love produces emotions, because love is an expression of the will."

I explained 1 Corinthians 13. "You are not a hypocrite if you don't have an emotional affection for someone," I said. "You love them because you are commanded to love them, and by faith you claim that love for them. The 1 Corinthians 13 kind of love is agape love, an expression of the will."

After we prayed together, he went to see his law partner. "I went into the office," he later told me, "and there was that feeling on the part of my partner of 'What do you want? What are you doing here?'"

"I've come to ask your forgiveness," the lawyer told his partner. "I love you. I've become a Christian, and I don't hate you anymore."

"When I'd picked up my partner off the floor," the lawyer continued, "he asked, 'How can I have what you have?'"

Later, they both came to share the miracle of their reconciliation.

Love is patient and kind, never jealous or boastful. It is an expression of the will. I decide as an act of the will whether or not I am going to love. Now frankly, I cannot love in the flesh. But remember how to be filled with the Spirit: act on God's command and claim God's promise. His command is to love—love God, your neighbor, your enemy. His promise is that if we ask anything according to his will, he will answer. So God says, "You love your mother-in-law, your father-in-law, your neighbor, your brother, your sister, the person who has taken advantage of you." Why do you love them? Because of God's command. How do you do it? By faith in his promise. You say, "Lord, you commanded me to love Susan. I'm going to love her. Humanly, I cannot. But on the basis of your command, I know it is your will, and I love her with the 1 Corinthians 13 kind of love. I know that if I ask anything in your name you will hear and answer. By faith, I claim love for this person."

A rancher once lost several of his prize cattle. He thought the next-door rancher had stolen them. He went to his neighbor and demanded, "Where are my cattle?"

"I didn't steal your cattle," the neighbor replied. An argument followed resulting with the threat "and if you ever come back on my property, I'll kill you."

The man whose cattle allegedly had been stolen was a Christian. He came to one of my meetings, and I challenged him, along with everybody else, to love his enemies. He felt guilty that he had been such a poor testimony to his neighbor, and he decided to ask his neighbor to forgive him. He knew he could be killed, because the man had threatened him if he ever came back.

The man drove with fear and trembling to his neighbor's house. "What do you want?" the neighbor asked angrily as he greeted him on the front porch.

"I have come to ask you to forgive me," the Christian rancher said. "I'm a Christian. I've been to a meeting where I was reminded that I'm supposed to forgive and love my enemies, and I want you to know that I've come to demonstrate my love."

The neighbor didn't know how to handle that. He wasn't a Christian. But he said, "I'm sorry for the way I acted. I want you to forgive me." Then he said, "You accused me of stealing your cattle. I didn't steal them, but they did break through the fence and come onto my property. If you hadn't accused me of stealing, I would have told you. Since you've come to ask me to forgive you, though, I want to tell you that your cattle are on my property. They have increased in number, so you have a lot more cattle than you lost. They're all yours."

The apostle Paul wrote, "For Christ's love compels us" (2 Corinthians 5:14). As he loves through me, I am able to love others—even those I never thought it was possible to love.

All You Need Is Love?

✍ JOSH McDOWELL

Is it true that all you need is love? So many people are misled here. The whole emphasis of our culture is that love makes anything right. If you're in love, it's OK. If your intentions were loving, you did the right thing.

Situational ethics teaches that there's no right or wrong before you enter into a situation. Once you're in the thick of it, whatever you do is right if your guiding factor is love. That is, in any moral situation, if you do the loving thing, then it's right.

People who believe in situational ethics quote Romans 13:8, 10: "He who loves his fellowman has fulfilled the law," and "Love is the fulfillment of the law." Look, they say, if you go into any situation and do the loving thing, then you've fulfilled the law.

But there's a problem with this viewpoint, and it becomes immediately evident when you apply it to dating. "Well," someone says, "I thought the loving thing was having sex with him. He needed me, he said please, and he wanted love. So, because I love him, it must have been right."

The problem with situational ethics, and the place where most people miss the boat, is when they say "Do the loving thing," they never define what the loving thing is. What happens is, once they're in a situation, they end up doing their own selfish thing.

It is true that the Bible says to do the loving thing (Romans 13:8), but it doesn't stop there. The Bible defines what that loving thing is. Look at Romans 13:9, the verse right after the verse on love I referred to above: "The commandments, 'Do not commit adultery,' 'Do not murder,' 'Do not steal,' 'Do not covet,' and whatever other commandment there may be, are summed up in this one rule: 'Love your neighbor as yourself.'"

The Bible is saying that in every situation, we should do the loving thing. It is then defining for us what that loving thing is. If you truly love someone, for instance, you won't murder him or steal from him. You won't even commit adultery with him.

The wonderful thing about Christianity is that it not only tells us to do the loving thing, it also tells us what that loving thing is. It is crucial, when we're working with young people, to go through the Scriptures with them and define love, showing what the loving thing is so that when they come up against a crisis, they will have something to fall back on.

The loving thing, in a given situation, may seem to be going to bed with this person. But we have to realize that as human beings, we have finite minds. We cannot know every factor about a situation. In spite of the fact that this person says, "If you love me, you'll go to bed with me," the Bible says it would not be beneficial or the real loving thing to do.

Society sucks us into doing what we think is the loving thing, and six months later we find out that what we thought was the loving thing has turned out to be one of the most detrimental things we could have done to that person. God's Word gives content to love, and if we pay attention to what it says, we will avoid later regrets.

So when somebody says, "All I need is love," I agree, but I insist that it must be the right kind of love—a love with content that describes the loving action, a knowledgeable love.

♦DO I HAVE TO FEEL LOVE?
EVELYN CHRISTENSON

Some people say love is an act, not a feeling. But feelings are part of love and forgiveness. If I don't feel love toward a person who has hurt me, I can still act loving, but I would be wearing a mask.

It is possible to step out in an act of love. But I would rather wait before God and let him give me real love. When a child hurts another child, the parent says, "Tell him you are sorry." The child says in a sulky voice, "I'm sorry." That fulfills the letter of the law, but not the spirit of the law. God wants us to have true love, not an insincere, surface love.

When people lash out at us and hurt us, they are usually threatened in some way. Forgiving others is easier when we can understand there is a reason for their lashing out at us. If we know they have a need, it's easier to reaffirm our love and comfort for them. When a person rubs me the wrong way, I pray, "Lord, give me the love you want me to have for that person right now." The Lord gives me the love, and I can feel it.

If I don't really love or forgive a person, he or she will know it by my attitude, or by the tone in my voice. Sincerity in forgiveness, not phoniness, is what we are to strive for.

Too Much Love?

✍ V. GILBERT BEERS

Is it possible to smother someone with too much love?

Smothering is certainly possible, but not with love. Smothering usually results from self-centeredness. Love is at the opposite end of the spectrum. It is a desire to do what is best for someone else.

Have you known parents who do not want to let a child grow up? They want to keep on doing the child's thinking and decision making, even when the child has finished college and married. That is smothering, not love. It is a self-centered clinging that says, "I don't want to let my baby go."

Ironically, parents who smother do not produce the effect they wish. Quite the opposite, in fact. Instead of holding onto the child, they force him or her to move away to get breathing room. An acquaintance of mine smothered his son, hoping to protect him from things that might harm him (and that would make him grow), only to learn that the son had strong feelings of resentment against him. "He never let me be my own person," the young man said.

The role of a parent is to guide a child through growing-up experiences, even those that may produce momentary hurt. We cannot protect our children from all hurt, but we can take comfort in the knowledge that the winds of life cause young plants to sink deep roots. Rather than protecting our children from problems, our role is to guide them through difficult times. We should let our children learn how to grow—either because of or in spite of their problems.

A loving parent sees the parental role as Jesus saw his role with his disciples—never to do what they could or should do themselves, but to be there with them to sustain them as they fulfill their responsibilities. That is what Jesus meant when he gave the Great Commission (Matthew 28:18-20). "I will be with you," he said; but he did not say, "I will do your work for you" or "I will keep you out of trouble or pain."

The heavenly Father did not withhold the "cup" of suffering from Jesus when Jesus prayed in Gethsemane, for suffering was the work Jesus had come to do. But we know that the Father was there at Jesus' crucifixion, for Jesus' conversation with him is recorded in the Bible (Luke 23:34, 46).

Yes, it is possible to smother a child. Not with true love, but with misguided feelings, overprotection, and a desire to keep a child from the experiences we all need in order to grow up. Smothering keeps and clings, while love gives and gives up.

It is a good idea for us to sit down now and then—perhaps with our children—to assess the way we are relating to them. What are we doing for our children that they could be doing for themselves? How much are we giving them? How much do we protect them? What is our motive for what we are doing?

Young children, of course, need our protection from forces too hurtful or challenging for them to handle. Older children need to begin facing these difficulties on their own. Parents have to strike a balance between too little and too much protection. They should let their children handle all the hurts and growing-up experiences they can deal with, given their age and maturity level, without overwhelming them with experiences that are too much for them.

We parents need the wisdom of Solomon to help us distinguish rightful protection from smothering. Solomon had the right idea when he needed wisdom. Prayer will help us find the wisdom to deal with smothering and other sticky problems too.

♦TRUE LOVE / OSWALD HOFFMAN

Love has been trivialized by so much of what has been written about it and by so many films made about it. It is often sentimentalized to the point that nobody knows what it means anymore. It is even equated with lust. But love—genuine love—is outreach, a hand extended. True love puts itself in the place of the other person.

How often I have had to tell that to people who are having marital problems. Nobody ever took the time to put himself or herself in the place of the other person. The arguments go on and on because of that.

I've known parents who have never extended such love to their children, and then children who in turn do not extend it to their parents. Parents say, "I have three sons and two daughters, and no one ever comes to visit me." Nobody is putting himself or herself in the place of anyone else.

You can't put yourself in the other person's place in one moment or in the next day or two. You have to work at it. Learning to love this way is part of the process of sanctification. But it is essential to learn to do this, because this is the way love works.

And this kind of love works miracles. It does what never could be done any other way.

The Characteristics of Mature Love

JOSH McDOWELL

The number one question people ask me, no matter what country or culture they're from, is this: How can I know I'm in love?

We're always in love. Infatuation is love—it's just a different degree, a different intensity. Puppy love is real love, but if you stick with puppy love, you're going to lead a dog's life.

The real question isn't, Am I in love? but rather, Is my love mature? Is it mature enough to produce a fulfilled, lifelong marriage relationship? Here are some characteristics of mature love.

1. Mature love is oriented to the total person, not just a certain aspect. Immature love only focuses on part of the person—sex appeal, fun quotient, religious dedication.

Lots of people base their love on the physical aspect. The amazing thing is, according to a study done at Arizona State University, a married couple spends only one-tenth of one percent of their time directly involved with their physical relationship. And yet people try to base a whole relationship on sex appeal. They need to learn that sex isn't Elmer's Glue.

Others base their love on the social aspect. "We have so much fun together," they say, "that it must be love." You can have a hilarious time with a chimpanzee, but that doesn't mean you ought to marry it.

Mature love is not even based solely on the spiritual aspect. Somebody says, "He loves Jesus, I love Jesus, we enjoy going to church and praying together—it must be love." Look, Billy Graham loves Jesus, and I love Jesus—but that doesn't mean we ought to get married.

Mature love, then, is not based on any one aspect of the individual or the relationship. It looks at the total person.

2. Mature love is shown by mutual respect and esteem. It carefully preserves the other person's integrity. It doesn't use phrases like "If you loved me, you'd . . ."

Mature love is spelled G-I-V-E. The Bible says to love your neighbor as you love yourself (Leviticus 19:18; Luke 10:27). It also says that "husbands ought to love their wives as their own bodies" (Ephesians 5:28). We are naturally concerned about our own happiness, security, and development. When the happiness, security, and development of another person becomes as important to you as your own, your love is probably mature.

3. Mature love is manifested by commitment and responsibility. Each person is committed to the relationship and responsible for it. It's not "do your own thing"; it's do our thing. This commitment needs to surface before the marriage takes place. If you don't sense it before, you won't find it afterward.

4. In mature love, there is joy in the presence of the beloved. When the two of you must be separated, you long to be together. Absence makes the heart grow fonder, and yet when you're with the person, the joy increases even more.

5. In mature love, there is dynamic growth and creativity. It cannot remain stagnant. Either it grows, or it starts to dissipate. As your love matures, you look for ways to express it to the other person. Even if you weren't particularly creative before, you become creative as you express your love. My wife, for example, makes unbelievable valentines.

6. Mature love is realistic. Immature love is blind; it thinks the beloved is perfect. Nobody's perfect, and mature love knows that. When you love in a mature way, you know the shortcomings of the other person, and yet you totally accept him or her in spite of those faults.

7. Mature lovers are able to be trusting, vulnerable, and transparent in their relationship. They can trust each other with the deepest secrets of their hearts.

Mature love takes time to develop. No couple should get married until they have given their love enough time to mature.

♦ INFATUATION OR LOVE? / YFC EDITORS

Infatuation focuses on self: What can I get out of it? Love focuses on the other person: What can I give?

Infatuation focuses on feelings. Love focuses on actions.

Infatuation idealizes the other person so that faults can't be seen. Love is realistic, sees the faults, and is willing to accept the person anyway.

Infatuation must be gratified *now*. Love is patient.

Infatuation is jealous. Love does not envy.

Infatuation is easily angered. Love easily forgives.

Infatuation is sensitive. Love keeps no record of wrongs.

Infatuation is suspicious. Love trusts.

Infatuation is inconsistent. Love never fails.

Infatuation leaves under pressure. Love sticks it out and lasts forever.

Communicating God's Love to Our Children

✍ JANETTE OKE

One of the most important things in the world to Christian parents—men and women who love God with all their hearts, souls, and minds—is to communicate that love to their children. And yet we all know that godly parents do not necessarily produce God-fearing children. What are some of the best ways to teach children about God's love, so that they will be attracted to him themselves?

First, a word of caution. It's very easy, when we are trying to teach our children about God's love, to paint him as a friend to the exclusion of all his other characteristics. If we take that too far, we can make God too human. We can change him from an awe-inspiring deity into a fairy godfather. We can show so much of his personal love for the individual (which, of course, is true) that we take away from the worshipful spirit we wish our children to have.

We must have a proper balance in the picture we paint of God. He is not a friend who loves us so much—and so foolishly—that he's going to give us everything we want. He does not exist in order to fulfill our personal desires. On the other hand, neither is he the bogeyman out to get us. Some children get frightened when they think of God's all-seeing eye constantly upon them, and while we don't want our children to think of God as a celestial vending machine, we don't want them to be terrified of him either.

We must be careful to keep a balance in our presentation of God. That's not too hard to do if we go to Scripture and teach our children the whole Word of God. Then they won't be afraid of God, because they will know he is the same as Jesus, the friend of little children. And they won't think of him as Santa Claus either, because they will also see him as the Creator and Judge, the Ancient of Days.

In teaching about God's love, the model we give is more important than the words we say. When I was very young, my dad—who at the time was not a believer—was my best example of a loving, yet demanding heavenly Father. He made it easy for me to understand about God.

I never for a moment doubted that my father loved me, but I never questioned his commands either. When he asked us to do something, we knew he expected us to carry it out completely. Even though he never spanked us, we didn't question his authority. At the same time, the love was always there, underlying everything he did. Never did I feel I couldn't crawl up on my daddy's knee and be loved and welcomed there.

Similarly, our example means more than our lectures. I need to show my children that God is an important part of my daily life. If I teach one thing and my life doesn't bear it out, then certainly my lessons will be ineffective. God must be important in my own life before I can show my children that there is good reason for him to be important in their lives too.

Do I have daily devotions? Does my daily walk show that I try to do what God says in his Word? Do I try to stay away from evil? Do I joyfully give God worship on his day? Do I give him his tithe? Do I consult God when I am making a decision or in times of need? Do I praise him for his goodness? Do I talk about him with adoration and excitement?

We must teach our children that love and obedience go together. We cannot say we love God and then disobey his Word. Once we have given our children a good biblical grounding so they know what God expects of them, we should expect them to obey.

I don't think we can convincingly teach our children to love God if we allow them to disobey us. Parents do not necessarily need to be strict and demanding, but they need to be in charge. Children must know what their limits are and adhere to them. And obedience must be consistent.

One of the most harmful things we can do to our children is to be inconsistent, to say, "These are the rules," and then enforce them on some occasions and let them slip by on others. This confuses a child. When we set up rules, we must see that they are obeyed.

It is cruel to let children grow up without discipline. I cringe every time I see parents allowing their children to boss the home—to be demanding and spoiled and rude. I wonder how such children are ever going to learn to let God have charge of their lives, when no one else has ever put any kind of discipline on them at all.

We must recognize that faith is personal. It isn't enough to be raised in a house where Mom and Dad believe in God. Each child must make a personal commitment to the Lord Jesus Christ. I think children really learn to love God only after they have made this decision.

We can't give our children their own personal faith. It comes to us from God himself, who puts his Spirit within us and makes us aware that we are his children (Romans 8:15-17; Galatians 4:6). Through his Holy Spirit he draws us close to himself, and then our love for him blossoms and grows. We must be careful not to be satisfied with secondhand faith in our children. We need to make sure that each one comes to the place of making a personal decision.

Still, we should not push for that decision before the child is ready. To be genuine, it must be a desire on the child's part rather than a decision imposed or strongly influenced by Mom and Dad. We must often hold back, giving opportunities but not pushing for this commitment until the individual is ready. Sometimes this will mean more praying time in our closets than direct dealings with the child.

Children need an excellent grounding in Scripture. They need to be familiar with the stories of both the Old and New Testaments. They need to see God as a judge and as a friend. Most of all, they need to see that God, in all his different relationships with mankind, loves them. When he judges the earth, it is as much a part of his love as when he answers prayer requests, because only through judgment can the earth be restored to the original goodness he put here for his people.

Charles Galloway sums it up well: "The need to love and be loved is the simplest of all human wants. Man needs love like he needs the sun and the rain. He perishes without it. His basic longing is to be the object of love and to be able to give love. No other need is quite so significant to his nature" (Lloyd Cory, comp., *Quote Unquote* [Wheaton, Ill.: Victor Books, 1977]).

A child certainly needs love—we all know that. Even a newborn baby will not flourish and grow without love. The medical world is discovering more and more how much the feeling of being loved and accepted has to do with our physical well-being. If a child really feels that God loves him, he is likely then to respond to God, because it is so special to be loved and accepted for oneself.

♦FORGIVING AT HOME / DAVID McKENNA

Forgiveness is costly. We must always keep in mind the fact that our forgiveness was made possible by Christ's cross. We would have no forgiveness without his pain and suffering. In the same way, forgiveness of others isn't always easy. It may be very costly indeed.

Forgiveness doesn't come naturally; it is taught. And the place for it to be taught is in the home. Forgiveness becomes real when it is practiced between husband and wife, father and daughter, mother and son, all the members of the family.

Forgiveness must begin in the home. If you cannot confess and forgive at home, you cancel out all the testimonies of forgiveness you make in public. The home is where the rubber meets the road. There is no more crucial place for teaching and learning forgiveness than in the family.

♦WORKING TOWARD UNITY IN THE BODY OF CHRIST / TOM SANDERS

How many games would a football team win if each team member did his own thing on the field? How effective would parents be in raising their children if they couldn't agree on discipline?

Working together brings victory on the field and helps us to parent more effectively. Sometimes the body of Christ fails to work together, and this is a major hindrance to answered prayer.

In Matthew 18:20, Jesus told us that when two or more of us gather in his name, he's with us. Jesus promises his presence as believers get together among themselves in unified relationships. The verse is a summary statement of what will happen in our lives *together* when Christ is Lord of our lives *individually*. We will get along because we will agree on essential things and can therefore pray with confidence (Matthew 18:19).

True unity takes work, so we need to talk together, serve, and sacrificially care for one another.

In order to experience Christ's presence when we get together, our gathering should be in his name, for his purpose. We have been created for his purpose for him to use any way he sees fit. As we put him first, our lives take on new meaning as we learn the beauty of his ways. As the people of God, we learn to enjoy one another as we corporately achieve his purpose on earth.

The Christians in Acts mightily impacted their world because *together* they acted on the word of God. They didn't major on minors; they worked to agree. Their faith was based not on their own ideas and preferences, but on the word of God. They acted on faith. Together, they touched their world in a powerful way.

This same kind of dynamism can affect our gatherings. God has promised us his presence and power when we get together for his purposes. Do we help or hinder this? Ask yourself the following questions:

1. Do I look for ways to agree with other Christians?
2. Do I learn from other Christians who may differ from me in age, financial status, interests, or even doctrinal background?
3. Do I act on what I know from Scripture and expect God to use me?
4. Is my personal prayer life hindered by broken relationships with other believers?

God promises to "show up" when we are of one mind and heart. Our unity or lack of it either helps or hinders the advance of the kingdom of God.

RELATED ARTICLES

Chapter 3: **You Have to Really Love Them**
Chapter 5: **Jesus Loves Me**
Chapter 10: **The Problem of Low Self-Esteem**
Chapter 11: **How to Show Love Even When It Hurts**
Chapter 22: **Six Tests of Love**
Chapter 26: **Reaching Out to the Lonely**

CHAPTER

10

Dealing with Difficult Emotions

- ✓ What can I do when my feelings get the better of me?
- ✓ Does God really love me the way I am?
- ✓ How can God help me when I'm depressed?
- ✓ How can I avoid a "roller-coaster" type of life?
- ✓ How can I win over worry?
- ✓ How can I control my thought life?

How to Manage Your Emotions

GARY COLLINS

We need to recognize that emotions are all right; in fact, they can be very helpful. Sometimes, especially if we get mad or really frustrated, we think emotions are bad. A Christian shouldn't be unhappy, we think. But God created emotions. They're part of being human. Emotions motivate us to action.

Emotions can cause problems, however, when we don't have them in control. Out-of-control emotions can lead to high blood pressure, muscle tension, ulcers, a variety of illnesses, or blow-ups with our kids and spouse. These negative results aren't caused so much by the emotions themselves as by our inability to control them and to use them constructively.

It's important to recognize that emotions are tied to both thinking and actions.

Emotions are related to thinking. In Philippians 4:4-7, Paul was writing from jail. He had every reason to be discouraged, but he said, "Rejoice in the Lord always. I will say it again: Rejoice! . . . Do not be anxious about anything, but in everything, by prayer and petition, with thanksgiving, present your requests to God. And the peace of God, which transcends all understanding, will guard your hearts and your minds in Christ Jesus." Paul's thinking was obviously in control of his emotions.

That may sound good, but it's difficult to tell ourselves, "Stop being anxious," or "Stop being angry," or "Stop worrying." In most cases that won't work. If I'm depressed and somebody says, "You shouldn't be depressed," I don't begin to feel happy no matter how hard I try. We may stand up in church and sing, "You should never be discouraged, take it to the Lord in prayer," but we go home still discouraged. And that's where actions come in.

Emotions are related to actions. We need to realize that thinking and actions go together. When Paul told the Philippians to rejoice and not be anxious, he told them what to do. "Let your gentleness be evident to all" (v. 5). Pray. Give thanks. Then the peace will come along.

There are times when love is more an action than an emotion. Sometimes the feeling of love goes away—and to get it back you have to do loving acts. I know one mother who became completely disgusted with her son. She was always complaining to him, always mad at him, always blowing up at him. One day the mother backed up and said, "Lord, help me to see what is good about that kid. Help me to say what is good instead of griping all the time." The mother didn't immediately feel any different about her boy, but she changed her actions. And when she began saying positive things to him, he began responding more positively. Then there was less need for the mother to explode, because the child's behavior was changing. The mother's loving action led to loving emotions on both sides.

Another action that will help manage emotions is to talk problems over with somebody who can help us keep things in perspective. We can also talk to the Lord, dealing with our emotions by prayer. We can ask the Lord to help us, or—and this is even more effective—we can look for something good in the midst of the situation and give thanks for it.

Humor is also highly beneficial—look for the funny side of your circumstances. Try not to be cynical. Studies have shown that cynicism can be fatal. A constant emphasis on the negative can disturb you physically and can even cause heart attacks and other ailments. But "a cheerful heart is good medicine" (Proverbs 17:22).

The most effective key to managing our emotions is both a thought and an action. It is the realization of how greatly we are blessed, joined with the action of giving thanks for our blessings. Thankfulness is the attitude we should have both toward God and toward others. It can change our perspective on any situation. When we are thankful, we stop looking solely at our problems and start looking at the blessings God has given us. When we are thankful, all our emotions are in control.

♦FEAR / HANNAH HURNARD

The Lord told me that whenever I was afraid of something, I should lay down that fear in his hands.

I said, "I can't stop being afraid."

"I'll teach you, Hannah," he said.

Once, as I was looking out the train window during a train trip, I saw a field covered with lovely fruit trees. In the middle was a huge scarecrow, and on the scarecrow's arms, five birds were perched.

The Lord said to me, "Hannah, there are foolish birds and wise birds. The foolish birds are frightened by scarecrows, and they fly away. But the wise birds know that all the best strawberries and cherries and raspberries grow close to a scarecrow. When they see one, they chuckle with joy and fly straight there to find the best fruit.

"Your fears are like a scarecrow. If you put your hand in mine and go up to every scarecrow, you'll always find lovely blessings."

Handling Our Feelings

✍ROBERT SCHULLER

The way to handle our feelings so they don't detract from our Christian growth is to decide to live under the discipline of resisting negative thoughts. We have to establish control sensors in our minds and hearts.

To begin, we have to sift through and sort out our feelings, discarding the negative and holding on to the positive.

All feelings are either positive or negative. I don't believe God comes through negative feelings but through positive feelings. An effective Christian is someone who is living her life under the Holy Spirit; and "the fruit of the Spirit is love, joy, peace, patience, kindness, goodness, faithfulness, gentleness and self-control" (Galatians 5:22, 23). When we open ourselves to positive thoughts we cultivate a sensitivity to a higher consciousness.

To handle our feelings, we have to learn to control our thinking. Paul said in Philippians 2:5, "Let this mind be in you, which was also in Christ Jesus" (KJV). In Romans 12:2 he urges us to "be transformed by the renewing of your mind." When writing to Timothy, Paul said, "Do your best to present yourself to God as one approved, a workman who does not need to be ashamed and who correctly handles the word of truth" (2 Timothy 2:15). In these passages Paul is talking about developing a systematic, rational perspective or philosophy of life that will help us deal with negative experiences by turning them into positive experiences.

There are five steps to cultivating the mind of Christ:

1. *Analyze your thinking.* Be aware of your thoughts. Analyze whether they're positive or negative, if they're lifting you up or dragging you down.

2. *Sterilize your thinking.* I picture a kind of metal detector in my mind—just like the ones they have in airports, only this one detects negative thoughts. If a negative thought begins to come through this detector into my mind, a buzzer goes off and I realize I shouldn't let it through.

3. *Organize your thinking around the phrase "It's possible."* I came up with the term *possibility thinking* when I read the New Testament in a red-letter edition and was struck by how often Jesus used the word *possible.* This is just another way of calling us to faith. When we become believers in God, we also become believers in the possibilities that converge in our lives.

Just as music is organized around middle C and urban construction is organized around sea level, the Christian philosophy of life is organized around these two words: *It's possible.* It's possible if ... It's possible after ... It's possible when ... It's possible with ... It's possible but ... Everything has to be organized around those words. They help us with the ups and downs of life. If we organize our thinking around them, we will establish a taproot that will bring nourishment to our souls and help us deal with negative thoughts.

4. *Conceptualize.* When I have the mind of Christ, I think big thoughts. Oftentimes the secret of solving almost any problem that produces depression or fear of failure is to think bigger than I've ever thought before. In the process of thinking bigger, I suddenly see a longer and more fruitful path ahead. Thinking big thoughts enlarges my path.

Success, by the way, is something we should welcome, not resist. Once our goals are established in the will of God, let's hope to God that we don't fail. He wants us to succeed.

5. *Actualize.* In other words, believe responsibly. Belief isn't responsible until it turns into action. As James said, "Faith by itself, if it is not accompanied by action, is dead" (2:17). Our thoughts must find expression in our deeds, or else what good are they?

By following these five steps toward developing the mind of Christ, we will deal a deathblow to negative feelings. In addition, as we cultivate the mind of Christ we will become more and more Christlike in our actions. Possibility thinking will result in positive actions, and our Christian life will bear fruit for others.

♦ AVOID A ROLLER-COASTER FAITH
ROBERT SCHULLER

In order to avoid a roller-coaster Christian life we need to have some real things to hang onto in our times of emotional instability—things such as God's promises ("Surely I will be with you always, to the very end of the age"—Matthew 28:20) and his warnings ("No one who puts his hand to the plow and looks back is fit for service in the kingdom of God"—Luke 9:62).

It is also important to have a philosophy that keeps us from ups and downs. I call my philosophy reality thinking. I know some days are going to be cloudy and some days are going to be sunny, so I won't be depressed when things aren't as good as they were yesterday.

We need to realize that just as there are hills and valleys in the geography of the land, there are good days and days that aren't so good in our lives. If you're experiencing depression, ask yourself if you're holding onto some expectation that isn't being fulfilled. If so, go back and check whether or not your expectation is realistic.

Mild depressions are normal. They're part of the ebb and flow of life. Sometimes we feel depressed simply because we're tired and we need to rest. One thing I tell myself when I'm feeling a little down is that I've never seen a roller coaster that only went down and never came up again.

How to Win over Worry

HUDSON T. ARMERDING

Most of us face two kinds of worry: doubts about God's ability to help us, and concerns about our own carelessness or thoughtlessness. We need to distinguish clearly between the two.

If we are troubled by the first kind of worry, we need to recognize that God is able and does care. That kind of worry is not appropriate for a believer. On the other hand, it is legitimate to be concerned about whether we will do things appropriately.

In 1 Corinthians 9:27 Paul said: "I beat my body and make it my slave so that after I have preached to others, I myself will not be disqualified for the prize." Paul had a legitmate worry that his own natural human and sinful tendencies might—if not properly checked—cause God's glory to be diminished in his life. This is a legitimate concern.

On the other hand, Paul's testimony in Philippians 4:11 said that he had "learned to be content whatever the circumstances." In this section he addressed the other aspect of worry—whether God has forgotten us and whether he is able to deliver us. The apostle suggested that he could be content because he knew that God knew, God cared, and God could work all things together for good (Romans 8:28). Therefore, he could accept all circumstances without worrying over whether they were good for him or not.

Here are some truths that will help us win over worry:

1. *God knows our circumstances.* Look at Psalm 139:8-10: "If I go up to the heavens, you are there; if I make my bed in the depths, you are there. If I rise on the wings of the dawn, if I settle on the far side of the sea, even there your hand will guide me, your right hand will hold me fast."

2. *We can't change our circumstances by worry.* On occasion in an airplane during a storm, I've worried about whether the plane would make it through. My worrying didn't do one bit of good to help the pilot or stop the storm. If we recognize that our worrying can't change our circumstances, we may even be able to laugh at ourselves when we feel like worrying.

3. *The fact is rarely as bad as the anticipation.* Sometimes when I've gotten up to speak knowing that critical scholars and distinguished visitors were in

the audience, I've been deeply concerned. I later found that my worry wasn't really justified; the circumstances weren't as bad as I had thought they might be. This is usually the case. We fuss about matters, and they don't turn out to be as difficult as we had anticipated while overcome with worry.

4. *Not everything has to be pleasant.* As mature believers, we need to learn to accept what happens to us, as long as it is not the result of deliberate sin. Don't think, "Well, if only I hadn't been here," or, "If only I had had the courage to do or say such-and-such." We serve a providential God who permits things to happen to us for our good. We know this from the book of Job, and we should strive to learn to accept circumstances as Job did, not wondering whether life could have been different if only we had done something else.

5. *Worriers don't accomplish much.* Concentrate on the people of faith in the Bible who were faced with compelling circumstances that could have easily induced worry. Abraham was told to go out; he could have worried about where he was going to end up. Esther could have worried so much about whether she would be executed for going in to see the king that she never would have gone. Joseph in prison could have worried that God had forgotten him and whether the dreams he had had would ever come true. Deborah, when arguing with Barak about the outcome of a campaign, could have wondered whether her efforts to get this man to work with her would really produce the proper results. But if these people had been controlled by worry, would they have been effective leaders?

"With God all things are possible" (Matthew 19:26)—we don't need to worry about him. And while there may be some justification for worrying about ourselves, even this kind of worry is rarely productive. Far better to do what needs doing, and then leave the results in the hands of our loving Father.

◆TRUST vs. FATALISM / HUDSON T. ARMERDING

We need to differentiate between trust, which is based on a specific commitment, and fatalism, which is completely passive.

With fatalism, we don't bother to interact with God because we assume that what will be, will be. When we think this way, there's no reason to do much of anything.

By contrast, trust in God is active. Our Lord's prayer in Gethsemane is an excellent example of trust. He prayed, committing himself and his circumstances to God, and then he accepted the will of his Father. That's very different from throwing up our hands and saying, "Well, whatever happens, happens."

The Problem of Low Self-Esteem

✍ DAVID SEAMANDS

I am convinced that a major part of our fallenness, our original sin, is lack of self-esteem. This is a built-in problem we all have, regardless of the kind of parenting we received. Even people whose childhood homes were close to ideal have a feeling somewhere deep inside, "I'm not OK. Others may be OK, but I'm not."

For some people, this self-doubt never becomes a full-fledged problem. For others, it does. It is especially likely to become a problem for people who, during their growing-up years, suffered through nonaccepting, nonapproving, or nonaffectionate interpersonal relationships.

Most low self-esteem comes from the picture we get of ourselves from the significant other people in our lives—our parents, our brothers and sisters, and our peers in the neighborhood, work place, and church. As human beings, we need acceptance, affirmation, and affection. If the important people in our lives give us mostly rejection, disapproval, and a feeling of being unwanted, our basic needs are not met. The result is invariably low self-esteem. We look at our reflection in these people's eyes, and we say to ourselves, "I am not valuable."

Another source of low self-esteem is poor theology—bad teaching in the church and in our homes. Too many of us have made a virtue out of a vice. We seem to believe that a self-deprecating attitude is pleasing to God, that this is part of Christian humility, even that it is necessary to sanctification and holiness. In thinking this way, we have mixed up self-worth, which is good, and carnal egotism, which is bad. The two are not the same.

The truth of the matter is that in Scripture self-belittling is not true Christian humility. It actually runs counter to some of the basic teachings of the Christian faith. For example, Jesus told us to love our neighbors as ourselves (Luke 10:27, quoting Leviticus 19:18). In saying this, he was saying we should have a proper self-esteem. We should be conscious of our own worth as a person, and we should use that worth as a basis for a proper love for others.

Likewise, Paul made self-esteem the basis for a good marriage. He said, "Husbands ought to love their wives as their own bodies. He who loves his wife loves himself. After all, no one ever hated his own body, but he feeds and cares for it" (Ephesians 5:28, 29). The Phillips translation puts it this way: "The love a man gives his wife is the extending of his love for himself to enfold her." Paul went on to say that this is the kind of relationship Christ has with his Church. "Each one of you . . . must love his wife as he loves himself," he summarized (v. 33).

Loving others as we love ourselves is not just a commandment; it's a psychological fact. We are able to love other people to the degree that we are able to love ourselves. A person with low self-esteem invariably has a hard time getting along with other people. We cannot love others unconditionally when we need to prove our own worth, but when we are convinced that we are valuable in God's eyes, we are free to reach out in love to others.

Putting down ourselves, then, is not the same as humility or holiness or sanctification. It is not what the New Testament means by crucifying ourselves (as in, for example, Galatians 2:20). Jesus does not ask us to downgrade ourselves, and our feelings of low self-esteem are not coming from God. Rather, they are coming out of our past.

If our self-esteem is based on what others think of us, we need to find a different source of information about our worth. We must get our self-estimate from God's evaluation of us. He loves us; he honors us and puts value upon us in the plans he makes for us. Paul said, "He hath made us accepted in the beloved" (Ephesians 1:6, KJV). I interpret that to mean that when we're in Christ, God looks upon us and says of us as he said of Jesus at the baptism, "This is my beloved [child], in whom I am well pleased" (Matthew 3:17, KJV).

How can we bring our self-esteem into line with God's view of us? Here are a few suggestions:

1. *Be aware of how you rate yourself.* I have suggested to people that they ask God to check them every time they belittle themselves. They have come back a week or two later completely amazed. "You know," they say, "I didn't realize this was so deeply rooted in me. I put myself down all day and all night."

2. *Learn to take in good information as well as bad.* I tell people to practice accepting compliments with a simple smile and a "thank you." They should stop spiritualizing their successes and belittling their gifts by calling such self-deprecation humility.

3. *Stop saying "I am."* Another way to get over low self-esteem is to stop using the great "I am." Only Jesus is allowed to use "I am," because he and he alone is. You and I, by contrast, are always becoming something. When we make "I am" statements—I am stupid, I am ugly, I am unloved, I am clumsy—we limit ourselves in a most unnecessary way. If we're used to making such statements, changing will require much prayer and wrestling. We can ask the Holy Spirit to check us every time we use them. In place of an "I am" put-down, we can say "I am a child of God, and he is pleased with me."

4. *Ask for help.* If our experience of rejection has been great, it will take a lot of hard work before we can value ourselves as God values us. A lot of reprogramming and healing of memories may be necessary if we have sustained terrible blows to our selfhood. We can't find this healing by ourselves; we need the help of another human being, and we should not hesitate to ask for it.

God will heal you according to his timetable. He is pleased with every new step of growth you take. His love for you is unconditional; it does not depend in any way on your lovability, your earning it, or your achieving it. It is given to you freely. Since you can't turn it on by something you do, you can't turn it off by something you do either. There's no way you can make God stop loving you. You can resist it. You can shut it off. You can fail to receive it. You can wall yourself off from it and even go to hell rather than accept it, if that's what you choose. But God will continue to love you, no matter what. And if he values you that much, what gives you the right to say you are worthless?

♦ THE FEAR OF REJECTION / YFC EDITORS

Rejection is scary. No one wants to be cast out or thrown aside for any reason. But such feelings can paralyze a person's Christian growth.

In each situation where this fear arises, you need to discern *from whom* you are trying to gain acceptance. Are you trying to please God or people (see John 5:44)? If the only thing that matters is pleasing God, then acceptance or rejection by others is really worthless by comparison.

Sometimes this fear arises because the situation is blown out of proportion. Ask yourself, What is the worst thing that could happen? and decide if rejection by this person or group is really so bad in comparison to holding onto your values and your acceptance by Christ.

Finally, admit to the fact that being accepted is important to you and make it a matter of prayer. You can learn to make this a positive trait that can work *for* you instead of letting it work against you in fear of rejection.

♦ THE COMPARISON GAME / YFC EDITORS

In Romans 12:3, Paul gave sound advice for building personal identity. He said, "For by the grace given me I say to every one of you: Do not think of yourself more highly than you ought, but rather think of yourself with sober judgment, in accordance with the measure of faith God has given you." He then went on to discuss the fact that each Christian is a valuable member of the body of Christ, with specific spiritual gifts and a special role to play.

Our self-esteem, therefore, must be based on *God* and what he has done for us and given to us, *not on comparing ourselves to others.*

No one wins the "comparison game." If you compare yourself to someone better (e.g., she knows more about the Bible; he is a better father; she is more consistent with her quiet time), you will feel inferior and think you are failing in the faith. You may even decide that you have little to offer in God's kingdom.

If, however, you compare yourself to someone worse (e.g., his marriage is falling apart; she doesn't know her Bible at all; he has a drinking problem), you will feel proud, complacent, and self-satisfied.

Instead, we should compare ourselves to Christ. After all, the goal of the Christian life is to be like him (Romans 8:29). Christ is perfect, and by keeping our eyes on him, we will see that there is *no possible way* that we can be like him on our own strength. We will feel overwhelmed by grace—although we don't deserve it, God loves us and Christ died for us. We will have an honest estimate of ourselves, and we will be forced to depend on and work with God to make the needed improvements.

Remember, God doesn't promise to make you better than anyone else. But he does promise to make you better than you would be without him.

How to Overcome Self-Pity

✍ INGRID TROBISCH

When you go through an experience of loss, it is normal and even necessary to feel pain, hurt, and sadness. This is true of Christians as well as non-Christians. If Jesus gives us the ability to love, we can expect to feel pain when our loves are taken away. Grief is the price we pay for love.

I have often said that since my husband died I have a hole in my life. Jesus has helped me to make a bridge over that hole, a place to stand and reach out to others, but I would be lying if I said the hole is not there. I recently got a letter from a Christian lady who couldn't accept that. Her idea was that if you really believe in Jesus and ask him to come in, he will fill up that hole. I am reluctant to accept that idea.

Forty years ago, about the time my father died, I discovered a relationship with my heavenly Father, and ever since then I have found that I can't even think of beginning a day without crawling up onto the lap of my heavenly Father. I don't think I could have made it through my time of grief without that very personal relationship. But Jesus has not taken away my normal human sadness at losing the man I loved for thirty years.

There is an important difference, though, between healthy sadness and unhealthy self-pity. I feel sad if one of my friends is going through an experience of loss. In the same way, I can feel sad about my own loss. It's possible to get out of myself and look at myself objectively and say, "I really do feel sorry for her," just as I feel bad about my friends when they suffer. That's healthy sadness. Unhealthy self-pity, on the other hand, is sitting on the pity pot and saying, "Poor little me—no one else has ever had as tough a time as I have."

We all fall into self-pity sometimes. I remember when I was a junior in college feeling absolutely overcome by my heavy schedule. I was taking twenty hours of classwork and working twenty hours a week. On a philosophy test, I got a very bad grade. This was not usual for me, so the dean of women called me into her office. I started telling her about all the pressures I was under. She looked at me and said, "Are you sure you're not just being sorry for yourself? Now go, and do better." For me, that was a key experience. All my life, whenever I could have told a sob story and gotten someone to feel sorry for me, I've thought, Are you sure you can't go and do better and overcome this problem?

Here are some ways to handle feelings of self-pity:

1. *Learn to distinguish self-pity from grief.* A friend who became a widow shortly after I did once said to me, "Ingrid, I feel so sore and sad." It's important to let the deep pain hurt and not to try to cover it up with an emotional bandage. When you have a fever, you have to let it take over until it's burned itself out. You can take aspirins all the time and keep right on working, but you won't get well as soon as if you lie back and rest and let your body heal itself. In fact, you might do yourself real damage. Your painful feelings are like a fever. You can cover them up, as I did when I lost my father, but it's better for you to allow yourself to feel them until they have burned themselves out and your emotions are on their way to recovery.

I believe it is natural to feel sadness for the greatest loss in my life. Feelings are neither right nor wrong; they just are. Once we've accepted that they are there, we can take them in both hands and give them to the Lord.

2. *Take care of your physical needs.* You can't pull yourself out of a depression if you don't take care of your body. You need to have adequate food, adequate fluids, adequate rest. When Elijah was sitting under the juniper tree, depressed and filled with self-pity, God didn't scold him. He sent an angel with

food and drink. Then he told Elijah to sleep. Afterward, he gave Elijah more food and drink to strengthen him for his long journey.

You also need activity. Once when I felt myself going down into the depths of self-pity, my twelve-year-old son said to me, "Mommy, don't do nothing. Do something." Just picking up a pair of socks and mending them can be helpful.

3. *Ask your friends for help.* As my husband always said, "You cannot proclaim the gospel to yourself." You can't pull yourself up by your own bootstraps. You need close friends who love you, friends you can call up who will help pull you out of your slump.

Humor is important in the healing process. You need someone who kids you a bit, who won't let you take yourself so beastly seriously, who can help you get outside yourself and laugh.

Sometimes it helps to overcome self-pity by talking with someone who is hard on you. A few months after my husband's death, my youngest daughter left home to continue her studies. She was several hundred miles away, and I was wondering how I could cope with two losses at the same time—the loss of my husband and the empty nest. A widow of more than twenty-five years, one of the most radiant, joyful persons I know, showed me my imbalance and put my thoughts back into perspective. She said, "Ingrid, I have no children." Suddenly I realized that I wasn't losing my daughter. She was just going away to school.

Coming to grips with my self-pity was the first step in opening the door to one of the most fruitful years of my life, a period that took me to four continents. When I returned home and met my youngest daughter after almost nine months of absence, I realized that our friendship was on a new level. She had become whole and independent. I had been growing, too, and we could meet in a new way.

4. *Allow God to help.* You need God's Word. Some people look up the promises they have underlined in their Bibles. Some have a treasure chest with promises they can pull out. I've been greatly helped through the years by the *Daily Texts,* a booklet prepared by the Moravian church headquarters in Bethlehem, Pennsylvania.

5. *Learn to be a hostess to yourself.* The highly self-disciplined Puritans said, "Learn to be gentle with yourself." When I plan my day, I always try to include a half hour of just celebrating. I take my nicest teacups from the shelf and make a pot of hot tea. I play a favorite record or cassette, or I read something that has nothing to do with my everyday living, or I study one of the great paintings of the world, or I sketch.

6. *Develop your self-respect.* Is your house—or your life—a mess? Then clean it up, starting with one corner, one drawer, one shelf, one problem. Each little step I take helps me reach my goal, and I replace self-pity with a feeling of self-respect.

Once when I was overwhelmed with a full basket of mending and stacks of ironing to be done, besides piles of letters to be answered, my mother-in law told me, "Just do a little every day. Don't look at what is unfinished, but congratulate yourself on what you've done." It's good to remember that nothing is 100 percent in this life. Instead of giving up hope because the journey looks so long, I take that first step.

7. *Keep on keeping on.* It's easy to think, Why have I been left out? A widow or divorcee who has lived in partnership and is now left to fend for herself naturally feels frustrated and empty. A friend of mine, forty years old and the mother of four children, was deserted by her husband. She was devastated, especially because her children blamed her for their father's desertion. She had to start her journey first of all by facing herself honestly, then by learning a new kind of self-esteem and self-love. This meant structuring her time and improving her skills. She is a much more interesting person because of it, and now people come to her for help.

We sometimes need to give ourselves a poke in the ribs, a hard nudge to push self-pity aside and to put God on the throne instead of the old martyr complex that will turn off our family and friends. We need to learn how to live out of thankfulness. The Finnish word for endurance is *sisu.* It means to keep on keeping on because there is no alternative. It means accepting even pain and grief, not giving up when the going gets hard.

♦ MY RESENTMENT BARREL / DAVID SEAMANDS

Every Christian who deals seriously with resentment needs some sort of mental imagery to help. I have what I call a "resentment barrel."

When we went out as missionaries years ago, we shipped everything in big steel drums. I picture one of these sitting under the cross. Whenever a hurt comes to me, I dump it in that barrel.

I once shared this imagery with a secretary. A week later she came back and said, "The barrel business doesn't help me, but I found something else that does. After I left your office last week, the boss told me, 'We have a lot of paper that needs shredding today.' The Lord immediately said, 'Hey, that's what you need—a resentment shredder.' " She imagines a model with several speeds. The top speed, she tells me, really chews up her resentments fast.

Whether we are putting our resentments in a barrel or a paper shredder, an incinerator or a garbage can, we all need someplace where we can dump them—permanently.

True and False Guilt

✍ HAROLD MYRA

All of us feel guilty from time to time. As Christians, we are constantly bombarded with lists of things we are supposed to do. We are challenged from the pulpit and the Christian media about how lazy we are in meeting our own spiritual needs and how cold we are toward a needy world. Because we are trying to live as we believe Christ would have us live, most of us could produce a long list of things that make us feel guilty.

Someone wryly observed that guilt is the gift that lasts forever. How terrible that so many of us suffer from never-ending guilt! When we come to Christ, we confess our sin and our guilt and are forgiven.

It is right to feel guilty when we stray from the Lord, strike out at someone, or give in to a temptation. This is true guilt, and it is designed to drive us to our knees. When we confess our sin, though, God forgives us and cleanses us. We no longer need to feel guilty about it, because it no longer exists. "As far as the east is from the west, so far has he removed our transgressions from us" (Psalm 103:12).

There is no need to feel guilty, either, for not being perfect. Many of us have impossible expectations of ourselves. We somehow think that as Christians, we should be living flawless lives. We shouldn't sin, and neither should we make embarrassing mistakes. That idea is nonsense. We are weak human beings, and we are going to fail. Such guilt is false, and it is destructive to our faith.

Satan loves to use false guilt to make us feel defeated. He wants us to be overwhelmed by a brooding sense of dejection and rejection. He would like us to think of ourselves as grubby worms with no potential for becoming like Christ. We should not allow him to ensnare us in this kind of false guilt.

If we are Christians with a balanced view of ourselves, we know we are helpless. We are aware that, although we have been made magnificently in Christ's image, we are now in a fallen human state and are helpless before him. We know that like Jesus, without the Father we can do nothing (John 5:19). But the point is, we have not been left alone. We have been forgiven, and Jesus is with us.

Rather than allowing ourselves to be trapped in false guilt, we should approach life aggressively, knowing we will make mistakes but knowing also that he has paid the price for our salvation. When we fail or give in to temptation, we should get up, confess our guilt, and then, confident of God's grace and forgiveness, move forward again.

♦CONFESSION / HANNAH HURNARD

Often we have fears and guilt feelings that we keep down inside us in our subconscious. We don't want to face up to them. We know we are uncomfortable, but we don't know why.

I've been helped by a dear lady who taught me that one of the most important things of all is to be absolutely honest, to be totally open to the light of God's presence. Take the uncomfortable feeling to God and ask him to show us its cause. Be willing to lay down any sin he shows us, to confess it, to stop it, and to put it right if possible.

Very often when I go into God's presence I think I've seen what it was I did wrong, but the uncomfortable feeling still goes on. I have to say, "Please bring this thing into the light. I haven't seen the full cause." The real cause is deep down inside me. It's something I don't want to be shown. And then when I can see it in the light of his presence, it often means costly restitution—going to somebody and making a very humiliating confession.

Only when I have done this can I be totally honest and open with God. Only when I have brought all my uncomfortable feelings to him can I have peace.

Forgiveness: The Cure for Resentment

DAVID SEAMANDS

Without any question, forgiveness is the key relational issue in the Bible. It is essential to our relationship with God, with others, and even with ourselves. Forgiveness is central to emotional and spiritual growth.

Scripture teaches us that grace and salvation are unconditional. This is absolutely true in the sense that there is no way we can earn God's grace or love; there's nothing we can do in order to achieve it; there are no conditions of merit we must meet in order to receive it. Our salvation is given to us freely as the gift of God's love. But when we read Scripture carefully, we discover that before God forgives us, he expects us to forgive others. It seems as if God has made us psychologically so that we are not able to receive his forgiveness unless we first forgive.

In Luke 6:37, Jesus states this principle: "Forgive, and you will be forgiven." Again and again he stresses this. In what we call the Lord's Prayer, he said, "Forgive us our debts, as we also have forgiven our debtors" (Matthew 6:12). A couple of verses later, he explains, "If you forgive men when they sin against you, your heavenly Father will also forgive you. But if you do not forgive men their sins, your Father will not forgive your sins" (vv. 14, 15).

In Matthew 18:23-35 Jesus tells the parable of the unforgiving servant. At the end, the man is turned over to the jailers who will keep him in debtors' prison until he pays his impossibly huge debt in full. Jesus ends with these stark words: "This is how my heavenly Father will treat each of you unless you forgive your brother from your heart" (v. 35).

In Mark 11:25, Jesus tells his disciples, "When you stand praying, if you hold anything against anyone, forgive him, so that your Father in heaven may forgive you your sins."

Again and again we get this message that Jesus expects us to be as willing to forgive others as he is to forgive us. This does not mean that divine grace is conditional, but it points to a basic biblical, emotional, psychological, and spiritual principle—if we want to receive forgiveness without giving forgiveness, we're asking God to violate his own moral nature. We're asking him to violate principles he has built into us.

If you find it hard to believe that forgiveness is a need God has built into us, look at the opposite of forgiveness—resentment. When we resent someone, we destroy our relationship with that person, of course. We also destroy our own physical health. Ask any doctor; he'll tell you about diseases and physical disorders that are closely tied to resentment. It literally eats holes in us, and that's a living metaphor of what it does to our relationships.

God's laws are a given of existence. They are built into our muscles, brains, personalities, and social interactions. His highest law, love, is what brought the world into being, and love is nourished by forgiveness. The opposite of love is hate, and hate is kept alive through resentment.

So if we're looking for emotional, spiritual, and physical well-being, forgiveness is central. Nothing we could say would exaggerate its importance.

What steps do we need to take in order to find healing and growth through forgiveness?

1. We need to face the pain and hurt done to us by the other person. Forgiveness is not whitewashing someone's behavior. It is not excusing it or avoiding the issue. It's not saying, "Well, it doesn't really hurt."

A lot of Christians are never able to forgive people because they skip this step and try to jump ahead to the second, third, or fourth steps. They tell themselves, "I ought not to feel that way" or "I ought to be spiritual enough to overlook that." They make excuses for the other person's bad behavior, or they run to counselors to find out why the other person acted that way. What they're really saying is this: "I think if I can explain it, I'll be able to explain it away—and then I won't feel this way."

But you can't forgive without first looking the hurt straight in the eye and saying, at least to yourself, "Hey, this person really hurt me."

2. We need to realize that we resent the other person. Resentment is normal. God has made us so that when we're hurt or scared, we react with anger or resentment. That is automatic. It's one of the ways we protect ourselves. But if we continue to carry resentment in our hearts, we need to forgive.

We are not always aware of the resentments we carry around. One way to see if we need to forgive is to look closely at ourselves and ask, "Do I still want to get even with this person? Do I still retain any desire, however subtle, to punish him or her?" That kind of honesty takes a lot of heart searching, and we may not be able to do it without allowing the Holy Spirit to shine his light on the depths of our heart.

We may discover what I think is the most subtle form of resentment. People say to me, "No, no, no. I don't want to get even in any way. I understand where that person is coming from, and I can accept what happened. But I do want him to know what he has done to me. Let me just once tell him all the ways he's hurt me, so he'll know how he's made me feel and the problems he's created. If I can just do that, I'll be satisfied. And then I'll forgive."

If you find yourself thinking that way, watch out. This is nothing but resentment in a thin disguise. And no matter what form your resentment takes, you have to admit it exists before you'll be able to forgive. You have to say, "Yes, I resent that. I'm angry about it. I may even be bitter about it."

Then you have to acknowledge, "But it is not my place to get even." As Paul wrote to the Romans, "Do not take revenge, my friends, but leave room for God's wrath, for it is written: 'It is mine to avenge; I will repay, says the Lord' " (Romans 12:19). I like the Phillips translation: "Never take vengeance into your own hands, my dear friends: stand back and let God punish if he will."

We need to surrender the idea that we have to let people know so we can set them straight. God has his own timing and his own way, and we have to relinquish the desire even to tell them off.

3. We need to give up blaming and learn to assume responsibility for our own behavior. I used to have an automatic reaction any time I failed at anything, from playing a game to preaching a sermon to blowing it with my

wife and family. I would say to myself, "If my mother had treated me differently, I wouldn't have messed that up." I was using my mother as a protective device.

When I really began to forgive, the Lord said, "You've got to quit playing that game. From now on, begin assuming responsibility for your own mistakes."

Unless I assumed responsibility for my present behavior, I could not forgive my mother. I needed her so I could blame somebody. When I forgave her, I had no place to hide—my behavior was my own responsibility. That's why assuming responsibility is a very large part of forgiveness.

A word of caution: This does not mean we should assume responsibility for other people's behavior. I did not say, "I must have done something terribly bad; I deserved that kind of treatment." I simply said, "She hurt me, but I can choose how to respond. Her behavior is her responsibility; my behavior is mine."

4. We need to relinquish the consequences of our forgiveness. When I had to forgive somebody, I used to say, "OK, Lord, I'm going to forgive, but I understand that your part of the deal is to change this person so that from now on everything's going to be great between us."

That is not true forgiveness. In fact, when I said that, I was hanging onto a little shred of my resentment. I didn't want to accept the person; I still wanted to change him to fit my picture of what he should be like.

True forgiveness relinquishes the consequences. Maybe there will be reconciliation; maybe there will not. Part of forgiveness is saying, "God, I forgive this person unconditionally. I relinquish the consequences to you. Whatever happens in the future, I'll let you do it."

5. We need to realize that forgiveness is a process. I have a strange theory about human emotions. I don't think humans can change their emotions simply by saying, "I will change my feelings about this matter." The best we can do is to go to God and say, "Lord, I'm unable to change my feelings, but I give you a permit to change them. I will allow you to change them. If you give me a new set of feelings toward this person, I will accept them. With your help, I will use them."

This is a continuing process. Resentment will not necessarily disappear all at once. It can return. Like grief, it can ambush you years after you think you're all over it. Again and again you may have to say, "God, I will not hold onto these feelings. I have given you my will on this matter, and now you take care of the feelings."

As memories return, Satan will try to lead us into condemnation. "See, you didn't really forgive that person," he will say. But that's a lie straight out of hell. You forgave, but human emotions tend to return. That's why it's important to realize that forgiveness is a process centered in the will. We choose not to hold onto those feelings, and we have no need to feel guilty if we have to repeat the process.

Some memories or resentments are so terribly painful that they require a counselor's help. Often we need someone to help us let the Lord heal the memories, to take the sting out of them. It is a sign of strength, not weakness, to face up to the fact that we need help and to go get it.

♦ FORGIVENESS AS MANIPULATION
DAVID SEAMANDS

A broken or difficult relationship is distressing, and it's natural to want to set it right as soon as possible. Some people think forgiveness will do this for them—it will heal the relationship and make everything wonderful again.

Maybe it will, and maybe it won't. When God orders us to forgive, he does not promise that the other person will change. If we knew that would happen, our forgiveness would be nothing better than manipulation. It would be a way to force the other person to act the way we want him to act.

True forgiveness is not manipulative. It leaves the results with God.

♦ DAMAGING FORGIVENESS
DAVID SEAMANDS

It is not always wise to rush out and confront the person we need to forgive. That person may not know he has offended us. He may be completely unaware that we resent him. If we unthinkingly spill it all out, he may learn things about our resentment that he never dreamed of.

When children do this to parents, or husbands do it to wives, or friends do it to each other, the person on the receiving end of the confrontation may be completely mystified. Worse yet, he may be deeply hurt, and a new cycle of broken relationships may occur.

When the Holy Spirit makes us aware that we need to forgive someone, it is far better to say, "God, I'm ready to forgive. I'll be obedient to your timing. When you say, 'Talk,' I'll talk. If I need to apologize, I will. But I'll wait for your direction."

Good Grief
MARTIN MARTY

Christian grief is not the same as worldly grief, because the focus is very different. Christian faith says that the occasion for grief—separation, death, failure, loss—is not the last word. God has the last word. God's will is not separation but reconciliation, not loss but restoration, not death but life. That perspective transforms worldly grief into Christian grief. But it does not erase grief.

While my first wife was dying, I experienced deep grief. It began slowly during her illness through a thousand numbing things. Coming to an empty house after visiting her at the hospital, seeing her body deteriorate, going to a necessary social function by myself, all these things brought grief.

I grieved for my wife's suffering, and I grieved for what could have happened in the next thirty years and now would never happen. I not only grieved, but I also experienced intense emotional and spiritual suffering. The pain was so great that I hope I never have to experience it again. But through the suffering, my faith in God grew. Martin Luther said that whatever he learned about theology, he learned from suffering.

My experience of grief made me vulnerable and helped me somewhat in understanding other people's grief. Before my wife died, I was a rather brisk, hurrying person (I still am, but in a different way). Good things had usually happened in my life, good things that were unbidden and unearned. As a result sometimes I was impatient with suffering people. Although close friends had experienced grief, I could not really understand what it meant to suffer. But my experience of grief left me open and porous.

In some churches, suffering is suppressed and people always smile. There are only victories and no defeats. These Christians think that God should be all-sufficient and that they should not grieve (2 Corinthians 12:9). They think they shouldn't suffer, because the inexpressible joy of Christ (1 Peter 1:8) makes everything fine. But that is not what Christianity is all about. Christianity is an affirmation in the face of suffering, but it does not make the suffering go away.

We have to be careful not to prescribe emotions when we are comforting other people. Some Christians wrote to me during my wife's illness, telling me that their prayer group was taking care of it. Their attitude was that if only she had enough faith, the cancer cells would go away. They made a moral issue of what is simply a chemical misfunction of cells in the body.

Other Christians wrote me profound letters urging me to express my anger. They would tell me to shatter something if I wanted to, or shout back at God. But I didn't feel angry at God. I felt numb and bewildered, but not angry.

I have a distant relative who lost a spouse in an accident. Several months later she boasted that she and her children had never once cried, because they knew that now he was with Jesus and all his problems were over. On one level, I thought that was fine. Christian affirmation was therapeutic and helped them get through a difficult time. But on another level I wondered if it was an authentic response. Tears are also therapeutic. Perhaps there would come a day when she would feel she missed out on the experience of grief. Still, she had to be free to find her own appropriate reaction.

Both anger and Christian affirmation are legitimate responses to grief, but they are not true responses for every Christian. A woman who has lost her spouse has good reasons to grieve, and if she does so, it is not right for another Christian to judge her as having weak faith.

A minister's wife kept a diary as she was dying. In her last entry she wrote that, although she was married to a minister and was a great expert on death and dying, all the answers were gone. On the last day she wrote, "All I want now are the tears of God."

Loneliness

✍ INGRID TROBISCH

I once copied down this quotation: "Loneliness is a hole in the soul, a prisoner tapping endlessly against the stones, waiting in vain for an answering tap." That's just how I feel when I'm lonely—isolated but not by my choice, unable to make myself heard, understood, seen, accepted, valued, or loved. Physically, loneliness is an acute attack of skin hunger. I ache to be held and stroked.

Loneliness is not the same as solitude. Solitude is a great gift. If I can have two hours all by myself in my study, it's like a tonic for my soul. That's not loneliness; it's solitude. Loneliness attacks in the dead of night. It's the bogeyman at the door. At its worst, it seems eternal—past, present, and future.

Loneliness can strike a happily married person as well as a single person. Every woman who has a productive husband, for example, knows loneliness. A girl who lived with us for two years once said, "There are two kinds of men I'll never marry—a doctor or a pastor. Their wives are so lonely." That's true of wives of men in other professions, too, of course. The more professionally successful the man is, the more lonely his wife will be.

Many people expect other people to solve their loneliness problems for them. I learned, however, that I couldn't always look to people. Friends, of course, are a great help—but they aren't always available when you think you need them.

During my thirty years overseas, I often had no peers. I certainly had Christian friends whom I could call, but as a pastor's wife I did not have close friends. People came long distances to talk with Walter, but these people were asking us for help. I had wonderful German and Austrian neighbors, but I knew they would not understand the depths of my loneliness because they were living in their homeland while I was far from mine.

Walter was aware of my loneliness, and he was very good about listening. He was lonely himself. As an East German, he had lost his home and his friends after World War II. He had been a well-known youth pastor, and he had a great circle of friends whom he couldn't reach out to either. Living in Austria, then, we were both in exile.

Once when I felt desperate I went to Salzburg to the University where a chaplain was always available and talked to him about it. He listened, and that helped. A couple of times I wrote a letter to someone I thought would understand, and just the act of writing released me from my pain. By the time I got an answer back, I had solved my problem for the time being, but it helped me just to know that someone knew and cared. Writing in my journal was also a great help.

I had to learn to fill up my alone times.

Anyone who reads never needs to stay lonely, because by reading you can get in touch with great minds and think their thoughts.

I enjoy doing handiwork in my spare moments. I have a cushion that went around the world three times before I finished it, but it helped me when I couldn't read or write.

Playing a musical instrument can help pull you out of loneliness. I play the piano—not very well—but I am often helped by singing or learning the words to a new hymn.

Loneliness is not entirely a curse. It can be a gift from God. It can be his magnet to draw us to him. He made us capable of great loneliness to assure that we won't stagnate and that we will reach beyond ourselves to him, to new experiences, and to other people—people who need us, because they are lonely too.

♦ INNER PEACE / INGRID TROBISCH

A friend once came to visit us for a month. She never went to her room except at night to sleep. The rest of the time—every waking minute—she was with one of us. Our house was very small, and after a while it began getting on my nerves. So I asked a woman who knew my friend well what the matter was. The woman told me, "She isn't at peace with herself. That's why she can't bear to spend even one hour alone in her room. She can't read a book; she can't write a letter. She has to be with other people so she won't be by herself."

The Limits of Grief

MARTIN MARTY

Grief is a natural and proper response to loss or separation. We know it is good, because God grieves. In Hosea, God grieved over Israel's waywardness (11:1-11). In the Gospels, Jesus grieved—over the city of Jerusalem (Luke 19:41), when a good friend died (John 11:33-36), and the night before he was crucified (Mark 14:32-34).

In the right proportion, grief is therapeutic. But there are limits to grief. Grief usually brings introversion and a demand on other people's time and attention. While you are grieving, you are wrapped up in being the griever, not in the person for whom you grieve. When grief is carried on too long it can lead to self-preoccupation. It can make you unaware that you are needed by other people.

When have you grieved enough? I heard a story about a woman named Anna who was married to Willy. After he died, she grieved and grieved and grieved. She wore black. She refused the attention of others and accepted no invitations. She was unwilling to be exposed to the possibility of a new life.

Finally a friend said to her, "Anna, you know what Willy would say if he could see you moping around two years after he died? He'd say, 'Get off your seat and have a good time.' "

That kind of intervention by someone who knows and loves you can help you realize you are prolonging your grief. Such a friend can help you recognize you've served your time, you've paid your dues, and now you can go on to new things.

Being aware of the cycle of grief can also help you know when you have grieved enough. The cycle begins about two days after death, when there is a ritualization of grief with a funeral. Then loneliness comes. Eventually you become happy again, although you may have periods of loneliness again. I am not an expert on the science of grief, which seems to have complex biological ties. The rhythms have sometimes been charted, but may vary from person to person.

Finally, self-examination can help you know when it is time to leave the grief behind. You can ask yourself if your grief is in proportion to your own suffering, compared to, say, the person who died after intense and prolonged physical pain. Is the deceased person's reputation enhanced by what you are doing?

When you are ready to move on, you can begin to rejoin life by an act of will. You can decide to join a club or get a job, become involved in a program or go back to school. You can decide to serve in a church group, or to date, or to adopt a child. The important thing is to have a plan of action to carry you into the future as it keeps you from dwelling on the past.

Most people resume full life—notice all the happily remarried spouses and the parents who "carry on." Yet it is natural that, unbidden, grief will come from some corner of the mind and stab intensely from time to time, and all of life will acquire a new undertone.

Giving Up

YFC EDITORS

Have you ever felt like just giving up? Everyone has faced those feelings from time to time—in an argument, at work, in marriage, during a game, and even in the Christian life. Struggles drain our energy, and eventually we wonder if it is really worth all this effort.

"Giving up" feelings can come from a variety of sources. We may just be hungry and tired, or perhaps the stress and strain from another area of life has weakened us. Whatever the reason, here are some suggestions for when you feel like giving up on the whole Christian growth experience:

1. *Check your feelings.* Have you experienced a defeat lately or been through a stressful time? Subconsciously, this may be draining your spiritual energy. Recognizing and dealing with this will give renewed energy for the Christian life.

2. *Get some rest.* Tired people find it difficult to cope with just about any task or duty. If you are exhausted, your problem is not spiritual. You just need sleep.

3. *Talk to someone.* Don't give up or try to bear this alone. Find a Christian friend and let him or her know how you feel. His or her careful listening and loving counsel will help put you back on track.

4. *Go back to the basics.* Over the months and years, you may have built the wrong idea of Christian growth, thinking that it depends on your performance. Peel back the layers of dos, don'ts, and duties and start by trusting Christ for each day. Or you may have the misconception that spiritual maturity happens overnight. In reality, God works in us slowly and surely (Philippians 2:12, 13) conforming us to the image of Christ (Romans 8:29). Look back and see what he has already accomplished in your life.

5. *Depend on God.* This sounds like a cliche, but it contains a profound truth. The fact is that your Christian growth doesn't depend on you; it depends on God. Your response must be to yield to him, allowing him to work in your

life. Simply put, if you know what God wants you to do, do it. If you don't know, ask him.

6. *Take a spiritual retreat.* Get away for a few hours or a few days and spend time alone, listening and talking to God. Allow him to refresh you spiritually and to give you a renewed desire to glorify him with your life.

Growing through Grief

INGRID TROBISCH

Death can come into anyone's life, suddenly and without warning. There was something about Walter that made me think he was going to keep going forever, but he died an almost instant death one October morning before breakfast. He came into our bedroom with our morning tea and said in a matter-of-fact voice, "Ingrid, my body is trying to tell me something, but I don't understand it." He then lay back against the bed pillows, and I gave him his cup of tea. It tipped and slipped, and I rushed to the side of the bed just as he was gasping for his last breath. When the doctor arrived five minutes later, he said, "It's too late. His heart has stopped."

Our little home was in the Austrian mountains. It was a beautiful fall day with the sun shining on the peaks. Life seemed stronger than death that morning; heavenly life seemed to come into that room a very short time after Walter died. I can't explain it, but I felt it. I knew that his new life had begun with his Lord and Master—I had no fears about that. But I was fearful for myself. I was now a widow, and I didn't know how I would go on.

For the first six months, I simply felt numb. Everything looked gray. I did what needed doing, but I seemed to be standing back and watching myself, as if I were someone else, going through the motions of living. Walter and I had often been apart—he had an extensive counseling ministry that took him all around the globe. No matter where he was, though, he would frequently telephone. I remember when it finally dawned on me that he wasn't just away on a trip, that he would never call me again.

I had to learn to absorb the terrible shock of losing my partner, and then I had to learn how to cope with day-by-day things. I couldn't have done this if I had been left alone. I needed my "circle of lovers"—friends I could reach out and touch and talk to when the going got rough. I needed them to remind me that I was still alive and that I needed to eat right, drink enough fluids, exercise, sleep. One close friend opened up her home to me, fed me, gave me innumerable cups of tea, and kept asking me kind questions. She helped me get my feelings out and talk about painful memories.

I needed my family—my mother, who had lost her husband forty years before; my five children, who were grieving along with me; my brothers and sisters. Every widow feels guilty. All of us can remember opportunities missed, unkind or thoughtless words spoken, things we wish we had done differently. I needed my pastor to assure me that God had forgiven my shortcomings.

After a few months I began to see colors again. I could feel the warm sunshine; I could enjoy children. I realized I was beginning to make peace with myself, that I was learning to live alone. But recovering from a major loss takes time, lots more time than most Americans think. The wounds don't heal in two weeks, six weeks, or even a year. In my experience, full inner healing did not come for three years, even though I was able to work and travel and speak during that time. And no woman who loved her husband will ever forget him. She doesn't want to. Just thinking back on my great storehouse of loving experiences with Walter is a great comfort to me today.

What has grief taught me? For one thing, after seeing my husband die, I had to face the fact that it could happen at any moment in my own life also. We cannot truly live until we are prepared to die. I'm not afraid of dying anymore, although I like to think I'm still needed, that the Lord still has work for me to do.

Facing the possibility of my own death has made me live with a great sense of urgency. It's as if I'm asking myself, "If this were my last day, would I have done the most important things?" This helps me set my priorities, to know the difference between big things and small things, and not to get upset about unimportant matters.

Grief has taught me a new kind of serenity. I've faced the hardest thing, that which I was most afraid of—the death of my husband. And I survived. Now there's nothing to be afraid of anymore.

Grief has strengthened my relationship with Jesus. I lost my wonderful earthly father when I was a teenager. It was about that time that I began a relationship with my heavenly Father, and I've found that all through my adult life I can't even think of beginning a day without crawling up on his lap. I could not have made it through this time of grief without that very personal relationship.

Grief has given new meaning to the Communion service. I believe that Communion is Jesus giving us his body and blood, and that in Communion we are united with him and with those who have gone before. I have felt Walter's presence very strongly during the Communion service, and I have been blessed by it.

Grief has strengthened my hope in the resurrection. Since Walter died, I have had some great Easter experiences. I know we will be reunited. That confidence grows and grows. I don't know when the resurrection will happen, but Walter and I will be there with Jesus.

The essence of the experience of grief is learning to be at peace with yourself. Only when your inner core is serene can you be at peace with the world. In spite of my wonderful friends, my precious Lord, and the joys that come to me every day, there is still an empty hole in my life. Somehow my Lord enables me to live with that hole. He hasn't filled it up yet, but he has made a bridge over it. I can live with it now, and I can stand on this bridge as I reach out to others.

◆BEATING BITTERNESS / YFC EDITORS

What causes bitterness? It happens when we create a fantasy and it doesn't come true, when our expectations turn to dust. The first act in beating bitterness is to identify its source. Are you bitter because of the acts of another person? Are you bitter at God's acts, or lack of them? If your bitterness is directed at a person, ask God to help you work through it, because in the long run you're only hurting yourself. If your bitterness is directed at God, talk to him about your feelings. Focus on his love for you and the glorious future he promises. Then repent of your attitude.

The Bible mentions some bitter people. One example was Naomi whose story is told in the book of Ruth. She was indeed bitter, and with reason. She had lost her husband and her sons and returned to her homeland saying, "Call me Mara, because the Almighty has made my life very bitter" (Ruth 1:20). But when she took her eyes off her problems and realized the great blessing God had given her in Ruth, she became not only a blessing to Ruth, but found herself blessed.

Fantasy: Aid or Danger to Spiritual Growth?

✍ JANETTE OKE

Fantasy—how many different meanings the word can have! In psychology, fantasy is wish-fulfillment in the imagination. Years ago, the word often referred to hallucinations. It can mean "wild fancies," or it can refer to a specific kind of literature.

In fiction, fantasy means stories with magical or highly fanciful elements: fairies, elves, and goblins; magic mountains and talking animals; three wishes and frogs who turn into princes. Not all fiction is, strictly speaking, fantasy. Much is realistic and true to life. Yet to read or write even realistic fiction, we must use fantasy; we still must develop our imaginations.

Many Christian classics have elements of fantasy in them. C. S. Lewis's Narnia series, as well as his space trilogy, and even parts of his heavier, philosophical works, are very fanciful, and they are now influencing their third generation of readers on behalf of Christianity. There is plenty of fantasy at work in *Pilgrim's Progress,* and this book has directed countless people to Christ since it was first published more than three hundred years ago.

Some fantasy is good, and some is bad. As a child, I remember finding Grimm's fairy tales frightening. The images they presented were so grotesque, that I think—in spite of their moral messages—they probably did me more harm than good. On the other hand, Hans Christian Andersen presented the moral values without the scare. Think of the story of the ugly duckling, for example: the little bird was considered ugly by his nest-mates but grew up to be a beautiful swan. This story reminds us that we should accept people as they are, for their lives may be quietly developing into something beautiful.

Don't lose yourself in fantasy. Some fantasy, of course, is harmful. Anything that is not true, noble, right, pure, lovely, admirable, excellent, or praiseworthy in our Christian life is not acceptable in our fantasy life either (see Philippians

4:8). Our thoughts must be kept clean and pure, so we should not fantasize things that we could not, in good conscience, partake in.

Many people today are concerned about a game called *Dungeons and Dragons.* First of all, the game itself is impure. Players assume characters and make them do things they would never consider doing in real life—murders, rapes, and so on. But the greatest concern on the part of many educators is that many of the players—often young people—get so involved in the fantasy that they can no longer separate themselves from the characters. Some young people have apparently committed suicide because of their involvement with *Dungeons and Dragons.* Any fantasy in which an individual loses his own identity to that of someone else is harmful.

When our oldest son was a preschooler, he had a great love for horses. It went further than love. Terry would say, "I wish I were a horse" or "I'd rather be a horse." When I was young, my brother and sisters and I often played we were horses, and yet never did any of us wish to be one. Terry's comments concerned me, so I spent time deliberately encouraging him to accept and appreciate the fact that he was a boy.

Children should be taught the difference between playacting and reality. They can enjoy Bert and Ernie, Cabbage Patch Kids, and little plastic soldiers, but if they appreciate their own worth, they will not lose themselves in any temporarily imagined identity.

Use fantasy constructively. In our Christian walk, we almost unconsciously fantasize a great deal. We imagine what Christ would have done in this situation. We picture how we would feel if someone did or said something to us. Would we hurt? Would we be angry? Would our day grow brighter? We use fantasy to put ourselves in someone else's shoes.

Realistic fiction can serve as a tool to see others in a different light. It can help us understand people, their hurts, and their problems. It can show us our own failures and successes realistically. It can help us grow and mature by giving us another glimpse at ourselves, as we see our own characteristics in others. Reading fiction this way is putting it to good use.

Fiction can be an effective teaching tool. Because the lessons are subtle, the reader does not feel threatened or preached at. Characters can be object lessons in the way they respond to life situations. Good behavior can bring good results: kindness brings friends, and sharing brings happiness, while selfishness brings loneliness.

One word of caution: some Christians who read novels based on biblical characters have trouble sorting out the scriptural facts from the author's added narration and slant. After reading such a book, a person should go back to the Bible and reread the scriptural account. With the biblical story firmly in mind, a person can enjoy someone else's interpretation without intertwining reality and fantasy.

Christ used stories to teach lessons, and we can do so today. Using our imaginations and fantasies in the service of our Christian walk can help us expand our horizons and grow spiritually.

RELATED ARTICLES

Chapter 2: **Recognizing the Inadequacy of Self**
Chapter 9: **Self-Love and Self-Centeredness**
Chapter 26: **How Feelings Affect the Way I Relate to Others**

CHAPTER

11

Overcoming Family Conflicts

- ✓ What does the Bible mean when it says to honor my parents?
- ✓ Dealing with divorce
- ✓ How can feelings be expressed without causing all-out war?
- ✓ How can I fight fair?
- ✓ How do I love a family member I can't stand?

Lord, Change Me

EVELYN CHRISTENSON

Two circumstances in my life in 1968 made me pray, "Lord, change me." First, my daughter turned eighteen, making her a legal adult. She announced at the dinner table one night, "Mother, I never want to hear your philosophy of life again. Do you know, Mother, that you actually change the tone of your voice when you talk about your philosophy of life?"

I ran upstairs and cried and cried. I asked the Lord, "How do I become the mother you want me to be?" His answer was, "Be quiet and don't say anything. Just let her see your reverent behavior" (see 1 Peter 3:2).

My daughter was not rebellious, but she needed to find out who she was. She went off to college, and I backed off. I went "underground" with the Lord, letting God change me to be more and more like Christ. As I did that, she saw my external behavior, but she did not hear me talk about my internal beliefs. Years later she wrote a card telling me that I had been a great influence in her life, that I modeled things for her and made it easier for her to believe God, and that I had shown her that God is faithful, the unchanging creator of the universe.

The second thing that happened was connected with the "What Happens When Women Pray" experiment in Rockford, Illinois. Our Baptist annual conference was taking place, and I gave a report on the prayer experiment. After my report, the local television station asked me to go back to the microphone and pose as if I were speaking. Unfortunately, every night on the news nothing was shown of the conference except this picture of me grinning and waving my arms at the camera.

Little by little people started heckling my husband, "How does it feel to be the husband of Evelyn Christenson?" I watched my husband shrink under this. Again, I went before the Lord and said, "I will never hurt my husband like this again. Lord, make me the wife you want me to be." I went underground for fourteen months. I kept my Sunday school class and my little neighborhood Bible study, but I gave up going to conventions and other public engagements so I could let God change me.

God does not change us overnight. He changes us bit by bit as we adjust our will to his will. This happens two ways.

1. *God changes us through his Word.* He has given us the Bible for correction, and instruction in righteousness. As I read the Word daily, I open myself up. "Lord, show me where I need to change. Show me what I need to learn." Once I know what the Bible says, I have to submit and let God change me. I must be submissive day by day to God's changing process in me. It is not enough to read that I should forgive those who hurt me, I must be willing to go to the person who has wronged me and say I have forgiven him or her.

2. *God changes us through prayer.* In prayer, I ask God to change my attitudes, my thoughts, my actions, my words. As I pray this continually throughout the day, I am allowing the Holy Spirit to work in me. Through prayer, I receive the motivation and the power to become more like Jesus Christ.

But without my desire to change, God's Word and my prayer are powerless. I need to be willing to change, even in those areas where I feel comfortable and settled. Change is not always easy. But the reward is becoming more like Christ.

♦ MUTUAL SUBMISSION / INGRID TROBISCH

Some Christians pay so much attention to Ephesians 5:22—"Wives, submit to your husbands as to the Lord"—that they completely forget the verse that introduces Paul's writing on family relationships: "Submit to one another out of reverence for Christ" (v. 21). Husbands do this by loving their wives "as Christ loved the church and gave himself up for her" (v. 25). Wives do this by responding.

♦ A HUSBAND'S NEED / INGRID TROBISCH

The greatest hurt a wife can do to her husband is not to respond—not to understand how much and how desperately he needs to be listened to, to be honored, and to be respected.

Fighting Fair

JILL AND STUART BRISCOE

Jill and I learned about fighting fair from a story about a boxer. The boxer said to his manager, "Get me the champion." The manager replied, "You're not ready." The boxer said, "Sure I am. I'm going to fight him." But the manager wisely answered, "I know you want to fight him, but I have the responsibility of getting you ready, and you're not ready. Every boxer only has so many fights in him. And it's my job to pick the right ones."

In a sense, a human being has only so many fights in him. Therefore, we have to make sure we're not constantly going into battle. Some things just aren't worth fighting over—and we have to learn to reserve our strength for the big issues.

Assume, however, that a big issue has come up and it needs to be handled. That's good; big issues usually come up when there is intelligent and heartfelt disagreement. Disagreement shows that there is a relationship, that neither person is totally dominant, that both are thinking. Ruth Graham once said, "If Billy and I agree on everything, then one of us is no longer necessary."

So disagreement is not necessarily bad. The problem, however, is that disagreement can quickly degenerate into real anger that will do lasting damage, producing bitterness and resentment. The rule of thumb at this point is in Ephesians 4:26, 27: "Do not let the sun go down while you are still angry, and do not give the devil a foothold."

To avoid doing damage with our anger, we have laid down a few "fair fighting" rules: (1) no shouting, (2) no name calling, (3) no physical violence, and (4) no verbal abuse. It takes self-control to remember the rules in the heat of the moment. We have tried to memorize those four, because the results of those actions cannot be easily mended. Once harsh words have gone, you can never recall them, and the damage can take a lifetime to put right.

To the above rules, we have added a few other ground rules to keep our fighting fair. For instance, we agree that only one person will speak at a time. There will be no interruptions. While that person is speaking, the other person commits himself or herself to listening. If necessary, the listener takes notes.

At the conclusion of what one person has to say—and probably it would be advisable to put a time limit on it—the other person has the right to ask questions for clarification. Then there is time for rebuttal. In other words, the listener is allowed to state what he or she feels is inaccurate or unfair about what has been said.

A second suggestion for fighting fair is to set a specific time for addressing the issue. It may be that the heat of the moment is not the best time to handle it. So decide, for example, that you'll discuss it after dinner, and let dinner be as pleasant as possible. This also gives time for people to cool off a bit.

It is unfortunate to use the word *fight,* because a fight usually has a winner, and you only produce winners by manufacturing losers. Therefore we feel that in any fair fight, the point is not to win or to make a loser, but to find common ground on which the relationship can function. That requires flexibility and compromise. Unless each person is willing to give a little, there's little likelihood of any lasting good coming out of the fight.

After every fight, healing inevitably needs to take place. In spite of the agreement that's been reached, somebody's going to feel a little bit sore. It might be advisable to conclude with prayer or a commitment to pray for each other in this area. Then you need to drop the subject for a period of time so healing can take place.

A fight can have positive side effects. As we listen to the other person, we're being introduced to thoughts we haven't had before and perspectives that are new to us. If the fight helps us clarify misunderstandings or identify some of our attitudes, then only good can come out of it. Thus conflict and disagreement, properly handled, can only prove beneficial.

◆ THE AFTERMATH / JILL BRISCOE

Some people have a hard time letting a fight die. They harbor hurt feelings and even dredge them up as ammunition to start a new fight. This is not fair. It is important, once an issue is resolved, to leave it alone and not bring it up again.

I spoke to a woman not long ago who told me a terrible story of verbal and physical abuse. She gave it to me in such detail that I was horrified, but as I looked at her, I didn't see one mark on her face, which was where she supposedly was hit. I thought, either this lady is not telling me the truth, or there's something wrong. So when she had finished I said to her, "I don't want to doubt your story, but I don't see any marks on your face."

She looked at me in amazement and said, "Oh, this happened twenty years ago."

And I said, "No it didn't; it happened today. And it just happened again, because you've kept it alive."

By refusing to let the fight die, this woman suffered twenty years longer than necessary.

How to Show Love Even When It Hurts

JOAN H. YOUNG

Let's face it. Sometimes there are people we must live with whom we just can't stand. It may be your great-aunt whom you only see on Thanksgiving, but who manages to ruin that holiday for you year after year. It may be a member of your immediate family, and this daily creates a source of friction and frustration. As human beings, we want to love and be loved. As Christians, we are commanded to show love to others. But loving someone who is a constant source of irritation is not an easy task. It cannot be successfully accomplished apart from God's love.

Without that one overriding principle, that God loves *me,* we cannot hope to truly love someone else, particularly if that person is difficult. We must realize that God loves and accepts us, just as imperfect as we are, and that we are special to him. Most of us, to varying degrees, work at getting along with other people in proportion to the response they give to us. We are willing to love someone if that person loves us in return. We often feel good about ourselves mostly because other people accept us. This may be the usual approach to love, but it is not God's approach. God says that because he loves us, that makes us 100 percent acceptable all the time. Therefore we can love other people, all others, not just the ones who make us feel good.

There is nothing like living with someone who is unresponsive to our love, or disagreeable, to give us a chance to test ourselves on how well we have put God's approach into action! The order of events in Philippians 4:4-7 is significant. First, find your joy in the Lord. Then be unselfish and considerate. If you are anxious about anything (in this case a relationship), pray about it. Then, last, you will feel peace. And this peace from God is something that the human mind can't understand. This is just the kind of peace that is needed when we are called on to live with someone who tests our limits continually. Following are some practical ideas that can help us to deal with an unpleasant person with whom we must live. However, none of these will work for long if we have not first believed that God loves us enough to make up for the lack of human love that we may feel.

First, remember that love is something we *do,* not something we *feel.* First Corinthians 13:4-7 is filled with action verbs, not feelings. When living with someone we do not like, this becomes increasingly obvious as we try to love that person. We will learn to practice patience and kindness, with prayer, moment by moment, whether we feel like it or not. Verse 7 says that if we love someone we will be loyal no matter what the cost (God was loyal to us, even though it cost him his Son).

Second, it helps to keep in mind that the other person may be handicapped in some way. We do not expect people with no legs to run a marathon, but we often expect people to act as emotional adults when they may never have even "learned to crawl." Sometimes we go overboard in the other direction. On the physical level, for example, we speak loudly to someone who is blind—forgetting that they are not deaf as well! Sometimes a person who has one or two emotional "hot-spots" will annoy us so much that we write him off as incapable of any healthy relational attitudes. The point is that constantly aggravating a person's trouble areas will never improve relations or help him to overcome those problems. Ephesians 4:2 says "Be patient with each other, making allowance for each other's faults because of your love" (TLB). This includes emotional faults.

Third, always be aware that the other person is not the enemy! Satan is the enemy who wants to destroy relationships, promote bad feelings, and create selfishness and enmity. When we act in unlovely ways, Satan is the winner, and we are all the losers.

When a specific situation comes up that threatens to send us off into a high-tension orbit, the best thing we can do is to consciously slow down our reactions and separate them into sections. We can pray and work at this process. The first thing that will happen is we will feel certain emotions. We may be angry, hurt, or jealous. These are natural human reactions. But we are called to live a supernatural life in Christ. Without denying these feelings we can choose to feel them internally and turn them over to God without reacting based on our feelings.

The second section of our reaction will also be internal. We can think about our feelings and choose a course of action based on God's love, rather than on those feelings, no matter how overwhelming they seem. We need to ask ourselves questions at this point: How can I be kind right now? If I say what I am thinking, will it ease the situation or cause it to deteriorate? Am I willing to let God love this person through me, even though I don't feel at all loving?

The last step will be the external one: what we actually do. And by these actions we will demonstrate whether we live by feelings or by love.

♦COPING WITH IN-LAWS / YFC EDITORS

What can you do when your in-laws treat you in such a way that you want to be anything but Christian toward them? Instead of refusing to ever see them again, you can work at making your relationship civil in several ways.

Give it time. For some reason they are not accepting you, but you need not return a like attitude.

Focus on what you have in common, not your differences. Do you agree on politics, food, cars? Capitalize on what you both agree on.

Allow them space, both physical and emotional. This is especially important if you also happen to live with them.

Respect their personhood as well as their possessions.

Treat your spouse (their son or daughter) with love and respect. That will be the best bridge to strengthening your relationship with them.

Pray for both your attitude and theirs.

◆WHAT MATTERS MOST? / JILL BRISCOE

When our daughter was a teenager, it appeared to me that she got up every morning looking for a fight. And I took her on, in everything and anything.

I used to think in the middle of those fights, What are we fighting about? Usually it was nothing. It had started over cornflakes or jeans and ended up in a knock-down, drag-out fight.

Finally Stuart said to me, "Let's keep the fights for the moral issues, for the things that really matter. Otherwise you won't have any energy when the time comes."

So I had to learn to make an immediate assessment: Is this worth fighting about? If it wasn't, then I tried to let it go. I needed my energy for the important issues.

When the Feelings Fade Away

JOHN B. PEARRELL

Recently a young man came to me and stated that he was considering a divorce. His reason: "I just don't feel the same way about my wife that I once did. The feelings are gone. I don't love her."

I am also reminded of a young Christian couple who just shared the joy of the birth of a new son. They seemed so happy. They professed a deep love for Jesus and lived what we felt were exemplary Christian lives. A few months after the birth of their son, the father left his wife to live with another woman. His reason: he was repulsed by his wife's shape as the baby grew within her.

More and more in my ministry I am hearing people say, "But I don't love my spouse anymore," or "Can't you understand? The feelings I once had are gone. I believe that I married the wrong person." What should we do when the feelings of love are gone?

Let me begin by saying that if you have had feelings like this, you are normal. Sometimes when we realize that our feelings in a marriage relationship (or any other relationship for that matter) are changing, we have a tendency to panic. You need not panic; you need not feel dirty or sinful. You need to realize that as a living, growing human being your feelings will (and should) change. The feelings I have for my wife today are not the same feelings I had when we first met and then courted. My feelings have changed; they have matured and deepened. I do not always have the same feelings of romantic love that I once had (especially when it comes time to take out the garbage), but the love we now share makes that first love pale in comparison.

The problem that we have in our modern world is that we have only one word for love. Because of this, love has become a nebulous concept. Very often when we think of love we think of warm, fuzzy, emotional feelings: I love my wife, I love my dog, I love peanut-butter-and-jelly sandwiches. Does this mean that I put my wife in the same category as peanut-butter-and-jelly sandwiches? Of course not! But we have no word in the English language to differentiate between those kinds of love.

Love has also become the common word used to refer to the physical act of intercourse, "making love." The great tragedy of our day is that we love things and use people, rather than loving people and using things. Likewise, we have traded emotional closeness and love for physical closeness and lust.

In order to understand the problem that we are addressing, we need to understand the concept of love.

The Greeks have a number of different words for love. One is *eros.* Eros is the word from which we get the English word *erotic.* Eros is an egotistical love. It is romantic love. It is probably the choice word that best approximates how we view love today. It is a legitimate form of love in the right context. Eros love says basically, "I see something very attractive about you and I desire to possess it."

The first time I met my wife, I was stunned by her sheer beauty. My heart rate increased, my mouth became dry, and my palms began to sweat. I was "in love." I could not sleep or eat. In short, my emotions had a field day. Those warm feelings are *romantic love.* But romantic love, eros, is egotistical; it is self-centered. It is legitimate, but it offers no lasting base upon which to build a marriage. Any marriage built upon romantic love alone is a mirage. It will not last. Beauty fades. Feelings dissipate. And if my only concept of love comes from those feelings, what happens when the feelings are gone?

The second word the Greeks use is *phileo.* Phileo is a mutualistic, family love. It says, "I see something in you that I like and you see something in me that you like. Let's get together on this." So phileo is more of a sharing love. It is that strange type of love that allows me to be very angry with a member of my family, but still protect and stand up for him to an outsider.

As in eros, phileo is a legitimate form of love. However, as in eros, phileo is not a love on which to build a lasting relationship. Why? Because we change. And what happens when the mutualistic benefit we obtain from one another wears thin? What happens when one party seems to be doing all the giving and the other all the taking? If the only love you know is phileo, the family splits.

The third type of love is *agape.* Agape is the type of love that God has for us. It is the love that caused him to give his Son to a world that he knew did not want him, and would reject and abuse him. It is a love that had to triumph over extreme dislike (God loathes our sin). In short, agape is a "working love." It is a love that keeps on giving regardless of the response that it gets. It is the love of 1 Corinthians 13. The middle verses of that chapter give us a tremendous definition of love, "Love is patient, love is kind. It does not envy, it does not boast, it is not proud. It is not rude, it is not self-seeking, it is not easily angered, it keeps no record of wrongs. Love does not delight in evil but rejoices with the truth. It always protects, always trusts, always hopes, always perseveres. *Love never fails*" (1 Corinthians 13:4-8).

In that definition of love are "warm feelings" or self-fulfillment mentioned? The answer is no. This is not a passive love, but an active one. It is a love that lasts if for no other reason than it is committed to the other person's well being. It is the love God has for us, and it is the type of love that we ultimately need to be committed to in our relationships if our marriages are to work.

With an understanding of love, you may still be faced with the question, What can I do—the feelings are gone? Let me offer eleven helpful hints:

1. Realize that marriage is based on commitment, not feelings. Your *feelings* are gone, but the commitment remains.

2. Learn to recognize and identify your feelings or the lack of them. What is behind them? What is causing the problem?

3. Learn to verbalize your negative feelings in an open, honest but non-threatening way (i.e., not "You jerk! You really make me angry," but, "I really feel angry when you . . ."). Remember that you are two imperfect people committed for life.

4. Keep communication lines open.

5. Recognize that you are married to a person of the opposite sex, and learn all you can about that sex through books, observation, and talking with others.

6. Deal with problems as they come up, *but* recognize that now might not be the time. In this case, make a contract to deal with the problem within a set time frame. (One counselor recommends that you begin, "Honey, do you have the time and energy to deal with this right now?" If the answer is no, then set a time within a forty-eight-hour period when you will deal with it.)

7. Don't try to change the other person—work on your reactions to him or her.

8. Spend time alone together. Don't stop the courting process at the altar.

9. Learn to listen. What is the other person trying to say? Ask for clarification.

10. Seek outside, professional help if you are having trouble in your marriage.

11. Most important: Allow Jesus Christ to be Lord of your life each day.

In any marriage, there is a need for all three of the loves mentioned above. Not all are present at the same time; they come and go depending upon the situation. But the foundation must be the selfless, *agape* love. And there is only one way to have this type of love, and that is to let the love of Jesus so grasp our lives that his love flows through us.

♦ NO MORE NEED TO TALK
INGRID TROBISCH

Louis Evely, a French priest, once said, "Some women become widows on their wedding day." In other words, once they are married their husbands feel no more need to talk with them on a deep level. For a Christian woman who thinks and feels deeply, this is a tragic loss—both for her personally and for the marriage relationship. By contrast, men who spend time really communicating with their wives are making a good investment that will be repaid as their relationship deepens and as their children blossom.

Did I Marry the Wrong Person?

DAVE VEERMAN

Marriage breakups have become epidemic, and an oft-used excuse is "I just don't love her [him] anymore." It matters little that a few short years earlier in front of a church full of witnesses the couple pledged to live together as husband and wife "for better for worse, ... 'til death us do part." It is only important that now the loving feelings have fled, replaced by doubts and dislike.

Christians are not immune to this "disease"; many of our marriages are also disintegrating. Tragically, these divorces are often rationalized in spiritual terms. A common excuse is that the couple was "not meant for each other," that each partner "married the wrong person," that the marriage itself was apparently "out of God's will."

Before tackling this issue, it is important to state that the question of marrying the wrong person is not limited to those who are seeking a divorce. Many sincere Christians harbor doubts about finding God's perfect will for their lives.

We must realize that the question "Did I marry the wrong person?" has probably crossed the mind of every person who has ever been married. The idealism of dating and engagement sooner or later crashes in the reality of marriage. No matter how hard we try to be ourselves during courtship, we still play games, wear masks, and hide our real selves. Then, after the honeymoon when the day-to-day work of living together begins, the pretenses fall and we begin to see each other for real. It's scary, and we wonder, "Did I make a mistake?"

Unfortunately, unrealistic idealism about marriage is often heightened within Christian circles that emphasize "discovering God's perfect will" and "finding the one person he has chosen for you." If a relationship has been made in heaven, then surely the marriage will be conflict- and trouble-free. People who believe this are shocked when the normal arguments and daily irritations of living together set in. Knowing that God never makes mistakes, they begin to fear that they have married the wrong person.

There are two problems with this way of thinking:

1. *It limits God.* He doesn't make mistakes, but neither does he spend his time catering to our selfish needs and whims. Analyze this statement: She's the right person for me. Doesn't it sound self-centered? It sounds as if I expect God and everyone else to meet my needs. It turns love into a noun—something I fall in and out of, something I receive from others and possess. Real love, however, is primarily a verb. It involves action and conscious choices to meet the other person's needs. Yes, God wants the very best for us, but on his terms, not ours.

2. *It ignores the clear teachings of Scripture.* According to the Bible, and verified continually by our experience, human beings sin and make mistakes

constantly. Because God is loving, he allows us to experience the results of our mistakes. Whenever we turn back to him in repentance and faith, he offers us the best possible life for us at that moment. In other words, even if you made a mistake and married the "wrong" person, God could and would turn it into good for you as you trusted him.

The Bible emphasizes in unequivocal terms the sanctity of marriage. The principle is clear from Genesis (2:24) to Jesus (Matthew 19:4-6) and Paul (Ephesians 5:31). The marriage commitment is a covenant that must not be broken while both members live, even if they think they may have made a mistake.

The concept of "God's will" is widely misunderstood. With the popular "blueprint" picture, I get the idea that he has a specific plan for me that is individualized, set in stone, and often hard to discover. In reality, God is sovereign over all of life, not just over me. His plans are dynamic, not static. They are clearly presented in Scripture, not hidden from view. Instead of searching for God's will for me, I should be asking, "How does my life line up with God's will for the world?"

The bottom line for successful marriage is commitment. I believe that any two people, committed to God and to each other, can be happy together. But conversely, any two people, no matter how compatible and well-suited to each other they may be, can be miserable together. Commitment makes the difference.

Don't fall for the lie that the grass is greener elsewhere. Don't let yourself think that your present marriage is a big mistake, and that somewhere else there is someone who is perfect for you. God has a great plan for you and your spouse, but he must be at the center of it. Commit yourselves to him and to each other.

♦ THE UNBELIEVING SPOUSE / YFC EDITORS

Being married to one who does not accept the saving message of Christ can be very difficult. Not only is it emotionally draining, but sometimes your own spiritual life can suffer.

You want, beyond all else, for your spouse to come to Christ. The best way to help him or her is to be a good spouse (1 Corinthians 7). Instead of nagging or harping, be a positive influence as you live Christ in all areas of your life. Let your spouse see what a difference Christ can make. Granted, this is difficult because all your "bad spots" are seen by your spouse. But living the life of Christ as you yourself continue to grow and mature, and loving your spouse as you are called to love, will be the best witnessing tactic you have.

Helping Children Cope with Divorce

KATHY CALLAHAN-HOWELL

When I was in grade school I remember a friend's parents divorced. I thought it was sad to have happen so young, but felt certain my parents would never divorce.

Unfortunately, at age thirteen, I was proven wrong. My parents did divorce and, despite my older age, it affected me intensely and has continued to affect me even as an adult.

We tend to think of divorce only as the parents' problem. If we consider the children, we usually worry only about the years of living with one parent. I thought when I finally moved out on my own the conflicts would end; but in each new moment in my life—graduation, marriage, ordination—I have to deal with my broken family.

Divorce is a permanent change in relationships (unless the parents remarry each other). Although the initial adjustment passes, new incidents require dealing constantly with the reality of the broken home.

The impact on children. Never forget, your children have lost from their home one of the two most important persons in their lives. Regardless of the release of tension that may occur, children will still feel the loss of the absent parent. Even though contact remains, the new time together feels vastly different than the spontaneous interactions while living together.

Before my parents' divorce, my father avoided our home, rarely appearing until late at night. He assumed his moving out would not be much different since we would still spend time together, perhaps even more often. Yet I greatly missed the brief moments of conversation with him each morning before I started my day.

Your children probably have similar feelings about the vacating parent. No matter how much time will be spent together, not living in the same home requires adjustment.

Many studies have shown the effects of the absence of one parent, which is usually the father. These effects especially intensify as children reach adolescence, a time we may consider them old enough to be adjusted. Boys need fathers to become appropriate men; girls need fathers to learn how to relate to males. Both need male and female approval as they sprout into adulthood.

Because of these needs, children should spend a great deal of time with both parents, either in joint custody or by frequent visitation. Of course, situations such as abuse or abandonment negate the possibility, but under normal circumstances contact with the absent parent looms essential.

Realize your children will exhibit some changes in behavior, attitudes, and temperament. I remember times of deep depression. Other children may display anger, regression, aggression, or laziness. Some children appear overly happy. You know your children's normal reactions—look for any signs of change whether they seem "better" or "worse." Anything out of the ordinary can represent a call for help.

If you have divorced, your children will experience turmoil. How you deal with them will make a difference in their survival. Despite your own pain, as a parent you must assist your children's adjustment.

Coping. If at all possible after you divorce, keep the rest of your life stable. You may feel a need to pull up your roots and make a complete life change. Although this may benefit you and may sometimes be necessary, your children will be devastated. They need their support systems already intact, and in reality, you probably do as well.

Your children need close proximity to their other parent. The adjustment to living without the parent in the home is difficult enough, without changing states. The trauma of losing a live-in parent, added to changing homes, church, and friends can totally overwhelm a child.

Children almost always feel some guilt for their parents' divorce. Remember they have suffered a loss and, just like a loss through death, guilt is a normal reaction. Parents need to be sensitive to this feeling and reassure children of their innocence.

Persons involved with the family can also unknowingly inflict guilt on the children. When my parents were seeking a divorce, one of my family members gave me this advice: "If you would just go to your father, and put your arms around him and ask him to come back, he would." I felt as if the whole burden was placed on my shoulders. After learning my dad's side of the story, I realized the situation was too complicated to be solved by such a request.

Parents need to refrain from statements such as "if you hadn't come along when you did," or "if we hadn't spent so much time with you children," or "if you hadn't caused us such problems." Even in your frustration, never suggest that the children have any part in your divorce. Although they may have caused an increase in stress by their presence, remember they did not decide to be born!

Besides not inflicting guilt, watch for signs of self-inflicted guilt. Ask your children how they are feeling. Notice if they suddenly become super-good. They may believe if they act good enough you will rejoin your spouse. Make sure they understand their actions did not cause your separation, nor will they remedy it.

Some divorces end in a civil relationship while others remain quite hostile. Despite how you feel toward your spouse as a marriage partner, your children benefit from your maintaining a workable relationship. Remember that your ex-spouse is still your children's parent, and they need both of you.

Avoid forcing your children to choose between you and your ex-spouse. One of my friends considered eloping because neither of her parents would attend her wedding if she invited the other one. She felt more comfortable not having a wedding than choosing between her parents. Encourage your children to relate to their other parent.

This courtesy needs to extend to the larger family as well. Even if you felt your spouse's parents contributed to your divorce, remember they are still your children's grandparents. Consider your ex-spouse's family through the eyes of your children. You may no longer feel related, but they always will be!

Not only do you need to allow your children to spend time with their other parent, you need to guard what you say to them about your ex-spouse. Even if your children hear your anger toward the other person as a mate, separate this from his or her parenting.

Kim's parents got divorced, and she and her sister moved with their mother to Florida, leaving Dad in Kentucky. Mom made it clear that Dad was a terrible person and parent. Yet Kim and her sister were shipped to Kentucky to spend the summer with their father. After she spent some time with him, Kim realized she had a really neat Dad! She was angry with her mother for brainwashing her to hate her father, and glad she had found out the truth for herself.

Although my parents failed as a married couple, they were excellent parents. Both of them were crucial to my development. Sometimes they expressed their frustrations with each other, but they didn't berate the other's parenting role. Most of the time they placed my brother and me first and endured each other's company when they had to make a public appearance as parents.

Besides not putting down the other parent, don't use your child as a "spy." Often parents ask the children if the other parent is dating, being a good parent, fulfilling certain roles. Whatever you need to know about your ex-spouse should be asked directly. Your child will feel guilty about answering questions. Children often feel they have to lie in these situations. Leave your children out of the spy business.

Your new life. Your children's adjustment depends somewhat on your desire to meet their needs. If you remain sensitive to their trauma and attempt to assist them, their adjustment will move more smoothly. Obviously your own pain interferes, but your willingness to try to help them reigns important.

Remember, your children know you are hurting. They don't expect you to be flawless and never to display your struggles. But they do need you to be considerate of them.

Be certain you receive the assistance *you* require to adjust. The healthier your transition progresses, the smoother your children's will be. Rely on your friends, pastor, even a professional counselor to assist in your emotional healing so as not to distress your children.

You may feel like a juggler balancing your needs with your children's needs. Make certain other people are meeting your needs so all the burden doesn't fall on you.

Others can minister to your children as well. They benefit from time spent with other families to learn how spouses relate to each other. Whatever caused your divorce, your children need to know marriages can work. They require working models to demonstrate how couples relate.

The key is this: Simply remember your children are hurting, too, and love them as you never have before.

♦ WHEN YOUR CHILD REJECTS CHRIST
YFC EDITORS

One of the most difficult situations for parents is when a child does not accept the Christian message. Instead of letting this become a source of despair, you can continue to grow personally and still witness to your child. First of all, you can pray for him. Pray that God will bring other believers into his life; sometimes he just needs to hear the message from someone else. Continue to live the Christian life in front of him. Let him see what knowing Christ has done for your attitude toward problems, setbacks, and pressure. Granted, the family is probably the most difficult place to witness because everyone knows you and your weaknesses so well.

You'll need to avoid the temptation to use pressure tactics and, above all, you don't want to reject him. Instead, look for subtle opportunities to witness, such as family activities that are Christian related but that you know would interest your child.

You are planting the seeds of faith, and that's where your child's faith needs to start. Then you must trust God.

Responding to Enemies
✍ HAROLD MYRA

All of us have enemies. We may not call them enemies. They may not consider themselves our enemies. But if we're alive, we have people with whom we argue, people who criticize us sharply, people who seem to go out of their way to make us miserable.

We have many reactions to our enemies. Anger. Hurt. Sorrow. Defensiveness. All these reactions are understandable. However, Jesus commanded us to love our enemies (Matthew 5:43-48). I have found that sometimes I just can't love them, but if I pray for them, God may help me come to that point. It helps me to write a difficult person's name in the book I use in my personal prayers, then to pray specifically for that individual.

Sometimes I pray for the astringent grace of God for my enemies—the grace that disciplines and sets people straight—but then I am careful to say I need the same astringent grace for myself.

Praying for my enemies, I sometimes clearly see why they are behaving as they are. Perhaps there are anxieties or lack of self-esteem or problems at home. To bring these people before the Throne and to pray for God's grace on them is very releasing.

When we pray for our enemies, we are faced with the question, Are we really willing to forgive? If we are unable to forgive, we will destroy ourselves.

Self-pity sometimes becomes a tragic emotional crutch for a person who will not forgive. In a perverse way, that person enjoys feeling sorry for himself. I'm reminded of the individual in *The Great Divorce* by C. S. Lewis who would not let go of a creature that represented lust. Self-pity is a lot like that creature.

For example, in the context of a divorce situation, if one mate will not let go of the injuries he has suffered, he cannot forgive the other. The mate who will not let go of this creature called self-pity grasps poison to his breast. Nursing such an ugly creature puts him totally out of fellowship with Christ and eventually does him more harm than his unforgiving spirit could ever do to his spouse.

We are not free until we are willing to give up our grudges and forgive the one who has wronged us. The Christian life involves accepting the flow of God's dynamic love working in ourselves and also in others—even in those who have treated us wrongly.

Jesus tells us to love our enemies, and love means wanting the very best for them. The very best obviously is God's working within them. If we can come to the point of praying for those people, in a spirit of love, that God will work mightily within them, then we can help them and ourselves also through intercessory prayer.

Mid-Life Passages for Men

LARRY KREIDER

Those who are able to successfully navigate life have one common characteristic: they anticipate and plan.

Anticipation and planning both involve a realistic understanding of time. As childhood cycles into adolescence and early adulthood, most people have worked hard at anticipation. They have planned for college, decided on a career, looked for a spouse, lived within a budget, and established inner values.

As they are cruising through their late twenties and early thirties, they believe the anticipation process is over. Their course is set, their sails are raised, and all life needs is an occasional adjustment of the rudder.

But then between the ages of thirty-five and fifty something happens. Midlife takes them by surprise. The reason so few people are prepared for the pressures of mid-life is because it is a relatively new phenomenon. Only within the last twenty-five years have we seen research and books on the subject.

The research shows that when a man reaches his mid-point, he has climbed an imaginary mountain and is ready to survey his past and evaluate his future. Most American males evaluate their performance at around age forty-five and determine whether they have made it or can make it. And the mid-life man asks, Do I feel fulfilled?

His self-assessment is strongly affected by the nature of our American society. Gordon MacDonald, in his book *Ordering Your Private World,* identifies one of the major problems in our society as "drivenness." We are a hard-driving people and feel success is measured by accomplishment, symbols of accomplishment, continued expansion, competitiveness, and abnormal busyness. Each of us has invested his ego or identity into what he thought would bring ultimate fulfillment and satisfy his longings. Unfortunately, many men at age forty-five realize that their investment has *not* brought fulfillment.

Americans also have a tendency to be so future oriented that they cannot experience the now. There's a difference between anticipating the future and living in it. The philosopher Pascal said, "We prefer the hunt to the capture." His words are applicable to many middle-aged men who are not sure how to enjoy what they've worked for because they've grown accustomed to living with the prospect of happiness, not happiness itself.

Being a media-oriented society, we are taught that the truly happy and important people of the earth are young. Life is for the Pepsi generation. We find that after working hard for the symbols of affluence—advertised by people younger than ourselves—we are considered too old to be happy and important.

Middle-aged adults, especially men, also feel they are owed some pleasurable rewards. They have been working hard all their lives trying to be good fathers and husbands, playing by the rules, looking forward to a time when they can coast with a little ease. Yet they are rudely awakened to the fact that pressures aren't subsiding, they are increasing.

In other words, American society does little to make the mid-life transition smooth and simple. Essentially it increases a man's frustrations by making happiness and fulfillment seem impossible for anyone over thirty-five. And men aged thirty-five or older have other frustrations to deal with.

Our mid-life man may feel as if he is trapped—trapped in a vise between three converging forces and four ballooning pressures. The three converging forces are the following:

1. *Biological changes.* He is losing his youthful vigor and stamina, his muscle tone, and sometimes his hair. There's a weight shift to the midriff, and his body produces less testosterone, so he's less sexually stimulated.

2. *Psychological changes.* The biological changes can effect his self-image. All of a sudden the world does not appear to offer unlimited opportunities but seems more like a closed-in, stale rerun of boring and predictable events.

3. *Social changes.* While he is dealing with the natural biological transitions and psychological changes, he is often hit with major shifts either in the work place, where he knows he would have trouble getting a job after age fifty, or in relationship to his wife, children, or friends.

This is one side of the vise. The other is a collection of pressures that he knew would probably arrive, but he underestimated their impact. These are things such as:

1. *Family pressures.* The children are now at ages where their lives and activities scream for priority attention. The house is no longer a man's private castle, but Grand Central Station. He has to check two or three other schedules before he can use his own car; he has to take a number before he can enter the bathroom; and his wife spends her days between sewing uniforms, playing taxi driver, and trying to figure out how many bodies will show up at the dinner table.

2. *Financial pressures.* In 1900, a teenager was worth five thousand dollars a year in income to the average American farm worker. Today, a teenager costs his parents eighty-two thousand dollars by age eighteen. A man finds that his

teeth not only need more attention, but his kids now need braces and wisdom teeth removed. Junior finally gets his driver's license, and it shoots the family's car insurance costs to the moon.

3. *Work pressures.* Oftentimes a man feels overlooked for a promotion, or worse yet he gets laid off due to a major downturn in the economy. Since only one percent of American workers make it to upper management positions, there's a good chance he will feel frustrated and angered for having his goals blocked, or he will be disappointed in the lack of fulfillment in the new position.

4. *Emotional isolation.* The American male is also lonely. He has learned since childhood that he has to maintain a macho image in order to be respected. According to the media, real men are aggressive, tough and cool, and act like Clint Eastwood. Such calculated coolness results in shallow relationships, especially with other men. He has to suppress any emotions that might be misunderstood as weakness, and he doesn't know who to turn to. As life edges on, he keeps pursuing bottom-line accomplishments at the expense of relationships, and with age he becomes unable to express or respond to affection, tenderness, or warmth.

Understanding the life cycle. Dr. Daniel Levinson and his researchers from Yale University studied cycles of growth in men and recorded their findings in *Seasons of a Man's Life.*

They studied forty men aged thirty-five to forty-five. These men came from four occupational groups: business executives, white-and blue-collar workers in industry, academic biologists, and novelists.

Levinson and his colleagues called the period from thirty-nine to forty-two Mid-Life Transition. This period, more than any other, bristles with threats as well as promises. A man will determine whether he will go through the pains of personal introspection and growth or move numbly and mechanically through the rest of his life.

Many men who cannot cope with the findings of introspection or the prospect of growth try to anesthetize their pain with excesses: excessive liquor, work efforts, or adventuresome sex. Such men are often seen trying frantically to get into shape, investing in a new wardrobe, and exchanging standard family cars for sports cars, motorcycles, or boats. Some try to solve the trauma of their lost youth through mid-life affairs. But such measures are only emotional novocaine. They are not constructive steps in coming to terms with mid-life.

Steps toward a solution. As the Chinese say, a journey of a thousand miles begins with a single step. Journeys take time, persistence, and the willingness to take one step at a time. The same is true in trying to find solutions to life's greatest challenges. There are no single leaps that will carry you through life's transitions, but those who are committed to working through the process every inch of the way will find a fulfilling resolution.

First of all, there is a need to *mourn the loss of youth.* At mid-life a man experiences the loss of youthful dreams, the loss of illusions of immortality, the loss of physical energy, or the loss of familiar support systems. There is a need to rather sadly bid farewell to the first half of life but then to set his focus on the second half.

The second step is to *understand that, other than childhood, no period has a greater opportunity for fulfillment.* Those who do successfully weather a mid-life passage have certain characteristics in common. There is generally an increase in personal productivity, a decrease in competitiveness, a greater desire to help people, an ability to enjoy leisure, an ability to be alone and to unleash the power of imagination, and a desire to build a more satisfying marriage relationship.

Such people, not bound by the performance pressures typical of early adulthood, often become high achievers in this more relaxed environment. They are not afraid to try new ventures after age forty because they are not afraid to fail. Their egos are no longer tied to the win/lose evaluation of the observers. They have concluded that personal well-being is somehow tied to an increasing willingness to risk change.

The third step is to *understand the basic needs of all humans not related to physical preservation.* There are three such needs. The first is a sense of self-worth. Rudolf Dreikurs said, "Underneath we are all frightened people, not sure of ourselves, of our worth, or of our place. It is this doubt of oneself, expressed in a feeling of inadequacy and inferiority, which is at the root of all maladjustment and psychopathology."

The second need of all humans is for personal intimacy, not referring just to sex, but to a deep, satisfying relationship of understanding and acceptance. Psychiatrist Paul Meier insists that "every man needs one intimate friend of the opposite sex (preferably his wife) and two friends of the same sex with whom he can share his feelings."

The third need is for a sense of purpose and meaning. Everyone who feels life is worth examining must determine the purpose of his life both in an ultimate sense and a functional sense.

Functionally, we try to determine what talents, gifts, opportunities, desires, and longings define us in our roles in life. Ultimately, we try to determine whether our lives have made the world a better place and have been focused on the noblest of values. Sometimes we travel through the years without seriously asking ourselves if we are accomplishing the real purposes of our lives. It can become very helpful and possibly threatening to sit down and write out a one-sentence statement beginning, "The purpose of my life is . . ."

We cannot leave the concept of self-worth, human intimacy, and the meaning of life dangling without addressing spiritual issues. So step four is *the willingness to not run from answering spiritual questions.* Even Carl Jung admitted that the root of mental illness among his patients over the age of thirty-five was a loss of spiritual moorings.

Many people develop a knee-jerk reaction against anything religious and develop a worldview completely void of the spiritual due to accepted misconceptions. If one was to seriously investigate spiritual reality, he could not avoid the Scriptures. What he would find on even a semithorough search is that God is seeking to find the prodigals of this world who have been scarred by the harsh realities of their self-sufficiency. He would find the arms of God open wide and uncondemning to those who place their trust in Christ as the provider of both spiritual security and significance.

Though the story of the Prodigal Son ends at the welcome-home feast, it's not hard to imagine that life would have to go on for him just as it does for every other human. He would have to find an occupation, marry, raise a family, and deal with normal times of frustration and an occasional sense of barrenness. Because he is now a family member in good standing does not make him exempt from human pain and dilemmas.

The Scriptures are full of stories of those who, though in right relationship to their Father, felt trapped, dry, weak, forgotten, unloved, unfruitful, or uncreative. Yet they all had one other thing in common—they knew how to pray. Out of despair and anguish they prayed. Alone and frightened they prayed. Hannah, Job, David, Jeremiah, Moses, and Paul left us a legacy of these cries and chronicles of prayers answered.

After studying the lives of these sojourners, you begin to pick up a pattern of how God met their deepest longings. At some point in their spiritual pilgrimage they faced a crisis. Though tempted to give up in their anguish, they persistently pursued God. At first they primarily wanted relief—relief from their excruciating circumstances. Eventually they came to realize that their sufficiency and well-being was not tied to their circumstances but to the security and significance of a wholehearted commitment to the sovereign will of God.

The fifth step on the road to a solution is *the need to deal with our own death.* No matter how health conscious a man is, he is not immortal. If we have a relationship with Christ, we can be intellectually assured that no longer is there horror in death. But the emotional acceptance depends upon our goals. Some Christians who are on the downhill side of life are frantically digging in their heels, trying to slow down the aging process because of unfulfilled desires or because they have never resolved whether self-abandonment to Christ and his will is really the core concern of their lives.

A sixth step is to *solve the clash between fantasies and reality.* Many unmet goals are a result of having a wrong opinion about what fulfills us, about our temperaments, and our gifts and abilities. From childhood, each person forms a set of values and then dreams about ways of implementing those values throughout life. Sometimes a middle-aged person needs a mid-course correction. It's amazing how people tolerate the constant pain of being career misfits but have never taken the time to analyze what makes them tick.

The seventh step is to *expand mental horizons.* Jesus was extremely hard on the Pharisees and condemned them for their hardness of heart. This religious sect thought they had everything figured out. Since they were experts in the law and had insatiable appetites for following the minutest details, they surmised there was no need to grow.

Those who have become intellectually calcified and are not "renewing their mind" (Romans 12:2) have hardened their hearts. An Englishman once said in reference to those who are mentally stale, "They've gotten off the bus." That is true, and it's because they've chosen to get off the bus. They can also decide to get back on. We know that Socrates was one of the greatest scholars of all time, but few know that he was so committed to continued growth that he learned to play the lyre in prison while awaiting his execution.

The eighth step is to *focus on relationships.* A man needs to reintroduce himself to his wife and kids and then seek ways to build friendships with other men. Few people attend funerals of those whose legacy is hard work and a large bank account. You pay your last respects to people who have left an impact, an emotional legacy.

The relationship with the wife is probably of primary importance. At mid-life a phenomenon called sexual role reversal takes place. There is a tendency for men to move toward passivity, sensuality, and tenderness. However, the wife, having been cooped up with the kids for years, is weary of the tenderness role. She is ready to become more autonomous, aggressive, and cerebral. This crisscrossing of roles can be hazardous unless each tries to help the other find fulfillment.

After the children have left home, marital happiness is potentially stronger than in previous years if each person concentrates on communicating with one another, if both are allowed to grow in the areas of their felt needs, if the husband is happy with his career, and if both understand that feelings of love come and go with various cycles of circumstances.

It is frightening when you realize how few years you have to spend quality time with your children. By the time they are old enough to carry on an adult conversation, they also have a personal schedule as crowded as yours. About the only way time will be reserved is to deliberately put it on your calendar or your to-do list.

Fortunately, my wife and I saw the clock ticking and were able to schedule family events into the hectic junior high and senior high years. We deliberately invested time and money into memorable events such as special vacations and weekend trips. There were also the nonexpensive occasions to enjoy dinner conversations, play games, watch a favorite TV program together, or rent a video movie. During these times we were looking for ways to transfer more and more authority to them and to begin to relate as adults.

Relationships with male friends need to be given high priority also. A man is very rich if he has some other male that he can confide in. To be able to work together on a project, to go hunting, fishing, or skiing, to have someone to call on at a moment's notice for lunch, cannot be measured monetarily. There is no substitute.

Anyone who addresses mid-life problems sooner or later talks about *getting into physical shape,* so reluctantly I'll make that the ninth step to a solution. I get weary of all the sermons by physical fitness freaks, but enough studies show that middle-aged men who exercise become more emotionally stable and self-confident. Successful passage through life does require emotional stability. It also benefits the mind.

The tenth step is simple and unprofound: *Change the scenery once in a while.* Variety does add spice to life. Whether it's going on a trip or joining a new organization, newness is freshness. (Just don't misinterpret this to mean you will trade your wife in on a newer model. In today's world, commitment to the same partner, for better or worse, is a new and fresh idea. Not to change the scenery is to change the scenery for many folks!)

Similar to step ten is step eleven: *Find a hobby and enjoy your leisure.* I have always admired Jay Kesler, the former president of Youth for Christ/USA and now president of Taylor University. What most people don't know is that he has a consuming hobby. He is a gifted woodworker. His home is full of furniture and furnishings that he has personally designed and built. Jay never has a chance to get bored or stale. If he isn't sharpening his vocational skills, he is sharpening the blades on his carpenter's tools. He will never run out of a challenge.

The twelfth and final step is to *find a place to contribute.* I'm not just talking about your money, but your time and energies. Do you really want to leave the world a better place than you found it? It won't happen without giving yourself away to a cause that is bigger than you and your dreams. You can start with your local church. It is a voluntary organization that cannot function without people like you. The needs of the church cover the range of skill available in the secular market.

Of course, there is a problem when a type A business executive tries to get involved in a volunteer people-oriented organization. Usually it is difficult for him to find fulfillment because it is hard to measure progress, there's not enough noticeable action, the bottom line is fuzzy, and the old hire/fire controls don't work with volunteers. Yet for all its frustrations, there is the pure joy of knowing you are about eternal matters. All of us take periodic measurement of our lives to see if we are doing anything of significance. That is why our senses were jolted in the first place as we entered mid-life.

The sad part of mid-life is that we have used up half of our potential. The positive side is that we still have half of our days to invest wisely. Corrie ten Boom said, "The measure of life, after all, is not its duration but its donation." Those who anticipate what will really matter at the end of life will die—and live—with few regrets.

RELATED ARTICLES
Chapter 22: **Long-term Marriage**
Chapter 22: **Guidance in Marriage**

CHAPTER

12

Mastering the Spiritual Disciplines

- ✓ How do spiritual disciplines help me grow?
- ✓ How do I set priorities in my life?
- ✓ What about quiet time, prayer, stewardship, fasting?
- ✓ What's the difference between discipline and spontaneity?

An Introduction to Spiritual Disciplines

RICHARD FOSTER

The very first thing we must stress about the spiritual disciplines is that they do not make us righteous. They don't give us brownie points with God, and they don't somehow instantly put us onto some superspiritual plane. What they do is provide what Jonathan Edwards called "a means of God's grace."

What are spiritual disciplines? They are activities, both individual and corporate, that we engage in as a way of placing ourselves before God so that he can begin to do his work within us. The classical spiritual disciplines include such experiences as meditation, prayer, fasting, study, simplicity, solitude, service, submission, confession, guidance, and celebration. In one form or another, these disciplines are mentioned all through Scripture, and they have been developed by the great devotional masters in the Christian world through the centuries.

The disciplined person is the person who can do what needs to be done when it needs to be done. Discipline does not make a person less spontaneous. In fact, discipline is the only way to allow spontaneity to function so as to be a real blessing. Without discipline, a person is not free. For example, I'm not free to play the piano because I have not disciplined myself to practice. Music is not a part of my ingrained habit structure. Concert pianists, though, have disciplined their lives and so are free to enjoy the piano.

Discipline works within us an ingrained habit structure of righteousness, peace, and joy in the Holy Spirit so that we are free to respond to the situation of the moment in whatever way is appropriate. We can do that because we have within us the power of God, the life of God, and our experience with God. For example, think of people who have given themselves in a healthy way to the study of Scripture. When a particular issue comes up or a particular decision needs to be made, these people have within them a whole backlog of the biblical worldview and understanding out of which they can act and speak. If they had not disciplined themselves to study Scripture, they would not have had the freedom to act spontaneously in difficult situations.

Spiritual discipline should not be forced. It can sometimes be hard work, but it is not unnatural. Three hundred years ago a wonderful Christian, Jean-Pierre de Caussade, said, "The soul—light as a feather, fluid as water, innocent as a child—responds to every moment of grace like a floating balloon." That's a perfect description of spiritual discipline.

The devotional masters, as they tried to learn to walk with God, created some of the spiritual disciplines by interpreting scriptural principles for their own time and place. A few of these disciplines seem quite strange in late-twentieth-century culture, and for this reason some Christians automatically reject them without really knowing what they are. The fact that a spiritual discipline is unfamiliar, however, does not mean that it is in opposition to the way God has taught us in the Scriptures.

We must always allow the Scripture to be our touchstone, of course. At the same time, we must remember that God has also spoken through history. He has worked with his children in the past, and we can learn by seeing what he has done. We need to look at the spiritual disciplines from a posture of humility.

We ask the Holy Spirit to teach us, to guide us, to open his truth to us, and he does this in each generation. That is why every culture has its own ways of expressing the spiritual disciplines. For example, in every generation many new books come out on prayer. These books interpret for a particular culture, a unique context, how to go about the work of prayer. I remember years ago when Rosalind Rinker's book *Prayer: Conversing with God* came on the scene. Many people were greatly helped to look at prayer in a new light. Yet her way of looking at prayer, though new, was every bit as scriptural as older ways had been.

Some cultures have needs that previous cultures never imagined. Today there are a lot of Christian books about mothers with young children. In a society where most women work, when many people live far from family and even friends, and when couples tend to have only one or two children, mothers of young children are in a situation quite different from that of their own mothers and grandmothers. Scripture does not speak directly to their situation, but wise writers can interpret scriptural principles in ways that will help them.

Through the years, symbols change. In the first century Jesus taught a lot about service by washing his disciples' feet. In our highly urban culture where we wear closed shoes and socks and drive in automobiles, washing feet is not an especially effective way to express service. We read about what Jesus did; we get the basic insight that it is important to serve others; and then we try to interpret that in our own culture. Maybe we read to an older person or mow somebody's lawn. For me, "washing feet" might be to prepare coffee for my wife each morning.

In all of these cases—prayer, parenting, service—it is helpful when wise Christians interpret Scripture for us as it applies to our situation. And this is what the devotional masters, past and present, have done in developing the spiritual disciplines. Their insights neither replace nor contradict Scripture. They are not a new revelation. They are a new illumination on how to apply scriptural insights.

God leads all those who hunger after him into ways of responding to him. He does not lead all people the same way, however. Some disciplines of the spiritual life are obligatory upon all people at all times. Prayer is one of these. All believers should want to find ways to commune with God. Still, not all believers will pray the same way. Study is another discipline that all Christians should adopt. But although all Christians should want to grow in their knowledge of God, study will take different forms according to the culture's literacy.

Other spiritual disciplines are for some people at some times. God might lead me into certain experiences that he would not lead everyone else into. In the area of prayer, for example, God will lead some people to some experiences that will not be for people in general. Some Christians benefit from fasting; others, for health reasons, should not go without food.

When we recommend spiritual disciplines, then, we must do so with a great deal of flexibility. We must not pigeonhole people. John Hyde, a missionary to India, was called "Praying Hyde" because he gave so much of his life and energies to prayer. That is a wonderful and good thing, and it should encourage me in the work of prayer. It doesn't mean, though, that I should do just as John Hyde did.

Neither must we say that a discipline must always be done in a particular way. When I was first learning about these things, I read about how some of the great people of the past would rise at four in the morning to pray. I tried that, and it was a disaster. I was so tired I could fall asleep standing up. Finally I had to realize that I had to get in touch with how my own body functions and come into some kind of rhythm in my life.

While some personality types are drawn to certain disciplines, I want to give a warning about that. It is important for us to do more than just what is natural to us. We need to be aware that we must stretch ourselves or allow God to stretch us in ways that may seem a little foreign at first.

Say I am a quiet, introverted, private person who loves solitude. That does not mean that I should never attempt to share my faith with my neighbors. Of course I should. My way of witnessing will not be just like the approach of a sociable, outgoing, life-of-the-party person. I will witness according to my own personality and character. But I should not use my preferences as an excuse for not stretching and growing. I should not select only those spiritual disciplines that seem natural to me.

If we recognize a need for discipline in our lives, where do we start? We begin by asking God what we need to do; what is the growing edge of our lives that needs developing? And then we listen for his response. And asking and listening is not something we do just once in a lifetime. For example, I function best in cycles. Recently I've had a pretty intense cycle of writing. Now I need a cycle of praying for people. How do I know that? I didn't hear any booming voice ordering me to pray, but over a process of time, as I've seen where I've been and where I need to be going, and as I've prayed and asked God for guidance, I've had a growing sense that I need to give attention to being with people.

Spiritually disciplined people don't just drift along. God will guide us. He speaks to us through the Scripture. He speaks to us through the counsel of the Christian community. We can know what we need to be about. And once we know what we are called to do at a particular time, there comes a sense of peace.

♦DOING IT GOD'S WAY / RICHARD FOSTER

When I first started practicing the spiritual disciplines I read the works of great leaders—St. Augustine, Martin Luther, John Wesley, Francis Asbury, St. Teresa—and I tried to imitate them. It was a miserable failure until I learned that God wants to work with me as an individual. Now I can read these spiritual giants and be helped by them, but I must not try to do everything the way they did.

♦MAKE THE SPIRITUAL DISCIPLINES A PART OF LIFE / HOWARD SNYDER

I'd like to suggest five ways to make spiritual disciplines a part of life:

1. *Have a daily devotional time.*

2. *Consider having some kind of personal retreat at regular intervals.* Take a day or a part of a day, howev-

er it works best, away from your usual work. For the past year I've been taking one day a month from nine in the morning until five in the afternoon. I get away to a retreat place and spend time praying, meditating, reflecting, and making entries in my journal.

I've found this gives me perspective in two directions. I look back at the past month, going over my journal entries during that time; I also look ahead at the month to come, doing some planning, some scheduling, and maybe some preparation for what's ahead. The main point, however, is not to plan but to take a time of intentional, intense prayer and self-examination. Taking stock is part of the rhythm of life.

3. *Get involved in some kind of cell group.* Meeting weekly for a couple of hours with brothers and sisters in Christ is a significant discipline in itself. It is also a useful way to make the other spiritual disciplines a part of our lives. In a small group we can check up on one another with regard to our progress in prayer and Bible study, for example. I'm involved in a group that is working on the area of personal daily devotions. Not everybody in the group was doing that, and our meeting together has allowed us to talk about the difficulties, to provide encouragement and resources, and to hold each other accountable.

4. *Use family time to develop spiritual disciplines.* The way you do this will obviously depend on your situation, but as long as you are living with somebody—children, parents, other relatives, friends—a regular household time of prayer, reflection, and Bible study can be a part of your life. If children are part of your family, your approach has to take them into account, of course. We have told Bible stories and then talked about them, sung and played the guitar or piano, shared prayer needs and prayed together.

5. *Join with other church members in regular corporate worship.*

The Purpose of the Spiritual Disciplines

RICHARD FOSTER

We must never think of the spiritual disciplines as something great in themselves. They exist for the purpose of realizing a greater good—learning to walk with God, to be in fellowship with Christ, to be transformed by the power of God.

All Christians must learn to walk with God. All believers want to become Jesus' friend. Jesus said, "You are my friends if you do what I command" (John 15:14). We all want to come into communion, into that life of hearing and obeying. We want the fruit of the Spirit—love, joy, peace, and so on—to take over our lives, and whatever helps that process is what we want to do.

It is not a good idea to keep a scorecard of our progress in the spiritual disciplines: "I've done these three things, and now I ought to turn to number four." We must try not to tie these things down too tightly. To turn the disciplines into legalism is to cut the heart and soul out of walking with God.

Neither should we ask, "How can I get the disciplines to work for me? How can I get results?" If I'm trying to figure out how to make them work, then I'm coming at spiritual discipline from the wrong direction. My part is to learn to be open and obedient to God. It's God's business, not mine, to make them work. I am to be faithful, and then God takes over. That's the work of grace.

The purpose of the disciplines is to help us enjoy God. They are not some grim duty. We are not supposed to grit our teeth and try to follow God. It's a joy to be his friend, to be in his company. He wants us to enjoy the spiritual life. The disciplines help to make the spiritual life possible. They also make it great fun. Once you experience great blessing in the presence of God, you're willing to go through all kinds of things to repeat that experience. It's glory. It's heaven.

On the other hand, following the disciplines is no guarantee of continual glory. If I had to have some kind of super experience every time I prayed or read the Bible, I'd be in trouble. I'm prepared for barren day after barren day because I just want to learn God's ways and be in his presence. I continue the disciplines even though I can't see the fruit at all times. It comes along. This is true of anything in life. People who want to play the piano have to go through all kinds of drudgery, but they know the end result will be joy. That's why they do it, and that's why we keep coming before God. We know that joy will come as a result of the whole process.

Discipline involves hard work, of course, but it needs to be enlivened by the joy of the Lord. Remember Nehemiah's words: "The joy of the Lord is your strength" (8:10). Joy makes us strong. Feelings must be disciplined, but once they are under control we need to let them have their proper place. Feelings should energize us and give a sense of lightness to our work.

For example, we don't serve people just on the basis of how we feel toward them, because then the only people we would serve would be those who are like us. Jesus taught us to love our enemies. Discipline helps us go forward and serve even those who are not like us. But as we do that, joy comes along. Our feelings may not get us started on a discipline, but they can make it pleasant once we are doing it.

The aim of discipline is to create habit structures within us. As the disciplines are more and more worked into our lives, many actions become almost second nature to us. They become habits and no longer require heroic effort on our part. In a sense, the left hand doesn't know what the right hand is doing (Matthew 6:3).

We want the disciplines to be so worked into our internal habit structures that the spontaneous thing is normal, good, and right. The hard thing to do is the evil thing, the wrong thing. Righteousness, peace, and joy in the Holy Spirit become reflex actions. We're not trying to make points with our disciplined behavior; we just see needs and we fill them. It's like breathing without trying. Almost without thinking, we do what is appropriate. Light as a feather, fluid as water, we respond to the initiatives of divine grace.

Once again, I want to encourage people to enjoy God. Augustine said, "A Christian should be a hallelujah from head to foot." The disciplines teach us how to become God's friend; how to have, as Thomas à Kempis put it, "a familiar friendship with Jesus." That's the whole point of the spiritual disciplines. There isn't any other.

♦ GOALS FOR THE DISCIPLINES
YFC EDITORS

When we decide to work on a Christian discipline, it is tempting to be either too hard or too easy on ourselves. When we decide to pray, we might think, "I'm going to get up at 5:00 A.M. and pray for an hour." Or we might say, "Well, I'm going to try to start praying."

Neither approach will get you very far in practicing the spiritual disciplines. You need a goal. But the keys to setting your goals are the following:

1. Make it attainable.
2. Make it a challenge to reach.
3. Make it measurable.

If you decide to begin to pray daily, plan to pray for five minutes instead of an hour. Also, break your goal into smaller steps, because the simpler the steps, the more likely you'll succeed.

Fasting
✍ RICHARD FOSTER

In our secular culture, people tend to fast for two reasons—to dramatize a cause and to lose weight. I am not saying that either kind of fast is necessarily bad, but neither is a spiritual discipline. The purpose of the one is manipulation and of the other is vanity.

Fasting as a spiritual discipline, by contrast, centers on God. It must be God-initiated and God-ordained. John Wesley wrote, "Let it be done unto the Lord with our eye singly fixed on Him. Let our intention herein be this, and this alone, to glorify our Father which is in heaven" (*Sermons on Several Occasions* [Epworth Press, 1971], 301).

Once we understand the central intention of fasting—to glorify God—it is safe for us to look at its secondary benefits. Fasting reveals the things that control us. Pride, anger, bitterness, jealousy, fear—if they are within us, they will surface during fasting. This is a great help if we long to be transformed into the image of Jesus Christ. We can rejoice as our weaknesses are revealed, because we know that Christ can put these false masters in their place.

There are other secondary values of fasting. It helps us keep our human cravings and desires under control. It increases our concentration and our effectiveness in intercessory prayer. It can contribute to our physical well-being and aid us as we pray for guidance. In fasting, as in everything else, we can expect God to reward "those who earnestly seek him" (Hebrews 11:6).

Fasting does not have to be a solitary experience. If you have a group of people who are sufficiently disciplined and taught, there is great value in fasting together. As a community of faith you can support one another. This doesn't always have to involve the whole church. That is a wonderful thing, but I would encourage many people to start in more humble ways.

One of my first experiences of group fasting was when about five of us were concerned to prepare for some special meetings in our church. We fasted once a week for a couple of months, and we gathered in the evening of our fast day to pray for the meetings. All of us knew what the others were going through, and so we could share our difficulties and breakthroughs together. Some had never tried fasting before, and this group experience gave them the courage and support to continue.

At other times much larger groups—churches, denominations, or even an entire country—can fast for specific reasons. If you can get Christians to unite that way, it can be wonderful. Churches who have serious problems could be substantially healed through unified group prayer and fasting. John Wesley recorded in his journal that in 1756 all the Christians in England united to fast and pray for deliverance from a threatened invasion by the French. "Humility was turned into national rejoicing," he wrote, "for the threatened invasion . . . was averted."

We usually think of fasting as abstaining from food. (There are, of course, some people who should not fast from food. They may have a medical problem, or perhaps they are pregnant or nursing.) But fasting has ramifications that go far beyond food. Properly understood, fasting is a discipline for all Christians.

Fasting is the voluntary denial of a normal function for the sake of intense spiritual activity. In our culture, we need times to fast from the media. We need to fast from gluttonous consumerism and to spend time among Christ's favorites—the broken, the bruised, and the dispossessed—not to preach to them but to learn from them. We need times to fast from the telephone, which can be an absolute taskmaster. Some people need to fast from work at some points in order to learn balance in their lives. Some need to fast from people, and some need to fast from talking so much. If we ask God where we need balance, he will teach us. It's amazing how his guidance can come through if we are open to it.

Scripture says much about fasting. Biblical characters who fasted include Moses, David, Elijah, Esther, Daniel, Paul, and Jesus Christ. In the Sermon on the Mount, Jesus taught about giving, praying, and fasting almost in the same breath. He assumed that people would fast and instructed them on how to do it properly (see Matthew 6:1-18). Many great Christians have fasted; the list includes Luther, Calvin, Knox, and Wesley, among others.

Fasting can bring spiritual breakthroughs that could never come in any other way. It is a means of God's grace and blessing that should not be neglected.

♦STEWARDSHIP: WHAT IS IT? / YFC EDITORS

The problem many Christians run into regarding *stewardship* is that they confuse it with *ownership*. These are two very different terms.

We *own* absolutely nothing. All that we have has been given to us by God. Thus, as Christians, we are concerned to be good *stewards* of what he has given us. *Steward* means "manager." *Stewardship* means managing well the resources God has given us.

What are the resources each of us have?

- time
- talent (or ability)
- treasure (or material possessions)

In order to be good stewards of these resources, we must realize that we are responsible to the owner for what we do with them. As good stewards of time, we want to use it wisely in order to make it prosper. As good stewards of our talents, we want to invest our abilities in God's kingdom, to use them in line with his purpose, which is to help his kingdom grow. As good stewards of our treasure, we want to use our material possessions to help meet the needs of others and, again, to help the kingdom grow.

♦THE PURPOSE OF STEWARDSHIP
OSWALD HOFFMAN

Unlike the words *evangelism* and *prayer*, the word *stewardship* is not found in the Bible. The concept has been developed by the church over the years, and it can mean different things to different people. Often church officials act as if the only purpose of stewardship is to collect money. But stewardship is a way of life, an attitude, a motivation for everything that we do. As Jesus said, "A man's life does not consist in the abundance of his possessions" (Luke 12:15).

Stewardship means that everything we have—our talents, our time, our possessions—belongs to God. All we possess belongs to him to be used in his service for the benefit of others. It isn't what we keep that counts, it's what we give. It's not what we hide away that counts, it's what we use.

Stewardship is not just giving money away; it's using our money and talents for the benefit of other people. Good stewardship expresses our love for God. Martin Luther said, "You can't express love unless you start with your neighbor." The apostle John said the same thing: "If anyone says, 'I love God,' yet hates his brother, he is a liar" (1 John 4:20).

I've found that people don't resent the demand of stewardship if the love of Christ is in their hearts. In fact, they are glad for opportunities to go outside themselves. And that's the real purpose of stewardship—to help us leave behind the little, dark, sacred precincts we build up for ourselves, and to teach us to depend on the One who rose from the dead and who is Lord of heaven and earth.

Simplicity
✍ RICHARD FOSTER

The spiritual discipline of simplicity means singleness of purpose toward God. Kierkegaard said, "Purity of heart is to will one thing," and by that he meant it is to will the good, which is God. Simplicity is not first a life-style. It is an inward spiritual reality that results in an outward life-style.

A simple life-style is the result of what Jesus called "the single eye": "If therefore thine eye be single, thy whole body shall be full of light" (Matthew 6:22, KJV). The single eye is an ability to focus on God, to be centered on God, to allow every priority in life to be arranged around God. God becomes the divine center of our lives.

To arrive at this kind of simplicity, we have to first believe that it is important. Through our own experience, through being with God and with his people, and through Scripture we come to believe that Christian simplicity is desirable, true, and possible. And then we begin saying, "Lord Jesus, I want you to be the center and focus of my life. I want every decision to come out of our inner fellowship. I'm willing to do whatever it takes to make that happen."

When we put ourselves in that position of commitment, God leads us in the direction he wants us to go. For example, the first time I ever saw that simplicity was necessary, I was in a Washington, D.C., airport waiting for a plane. I had brought along a little book, *A Testament of Devotion* by Thomas Kelly, to read in spare moments. I was reading a section called "On the Ability to Say Yes and No," and I began crying.

That's what I want, I thought. I want to be able to say yes to people, I want to be able to say no to people, from the divine center. I don't want my answer to be based on what people think of me, on how I can impress others, or on what kind of reputation it will build for me. I want it to be based on the call of God upon me.

When I got home I made one little commitment in response to what I had learned in the airport. I decided to give Friday nights to my family. So I did that, and then a fellow from denominational headquarters phoned me and asked me to speak on a Friday night. I had to say no. He said, "Are you busy?" At that time I didn't know I could say, "Yes, I'm very busy." I simply said, "No." I'm sure he thought I was shirking my responsibilities. But when I hung up, I felt a *Hallelujah!* inside. I don't have to be controlled by the opinions of others! I really can respond out of the divine center!

It can be a great disappointment to say no. Sometimes we really want to do something, and others want us to do it. But if we know that the call of God for us is to say no, we say it. And then we're free. That's simplicity of life, and it spills over into many other areas, including material things and overcommitted scheduling. As we learn to walk with God, we learn focus.

Simplicity, then, is getting in touch with the divine center and doing those things that flow out of it. It is also refusing to do things that do not fit with the divine center, no matter how good and attractive they may seem. To do them apart from Christ would be disobedience.

Once I began to move in the direction of Christian simplicity, I found certain things becoming far more important to me. The first was time with my wife. It seemed as if every time I asked the Lord, "What is it you want?" there seemed to come the response, "Time—with your wife in particular and your family in general." And I'd argue, "But God, that would mean saying no to all these wonderful opportunities," and God kept answering, "Do you want to be centered? Do you want to obey?"

Our time, then, is greatly affected when we begin to practice the discipline of simplicity. So is our money. Money is one of the greatest idols of our time, and people will do incredible things for it. Money is a spiritual power animated by the principalities and powers. If we do not learn to conquer the god Money in the name of Christ, we will become enslaved to it.

This is not to say that a Christian should have no money. It is possible to conquer money and then manage it for the sake of the kingdom of God. The key is to learn how to use money without serving money. This is is not an easy process, because money is not a neutral medium of exchange. It is a spiritual power. But if we are truly free from the dominion of money—not manipulated by it and not using it to manipulate others—then we can use it for the sake of the kingdom of God.

Simplicity is thus related to true poverty—not the absence of money but the absence of possessiveness. I have everything but own nothing; everything is available to me, but I control none of it. The words *my* and *mine* are removed from my vocabulary. I become like Abraham when God told him to sacrifice his son. I'm sure that by the time Abraham came down from the mountain, the words *my* and *mine* had completely changed meaning for him. He knew that his son was no longer his possession. Isaac belonged to God. And that's the attitude we are to have with money. We learn to be able to let go of it as freely as we receive it, because it doesn't belong to us. The earth is the Lord's.

Simplicity is a discipline for all Christians at all times. Exactly how it works may be different in the lives of different people. In terms of possessions, for example, some people need more than others. I don't need much by way of a house. There are four of us, and we don't need something big. But somebody with a large family, or who does large-scale entertaining, or who has a steady stream of overnight guests may need much more than I do. It isn't my business to try to straighten others out on those matters.

We must learn an inner spirit of detachment. Remember that Paul said, "I have learned the secret of being content in any and every situation, whether well fed or hungry, whether living in plenty or in want" (Philippians 4:12). The point is that we need divine grace whether or not we have money. We need grace to live in want, and we also need grace to live in plenty.

♦ PRIVILEGES / RICHARD FOSTER

Our Western first-world culture is probably the most affluent culture in all of history. Because we have so much more wealth than we possibly need, we must find ways to redirect it and use it for the blessing of the world instead of cutting off our little piece of the consumer pie and going off into a corner and eating it.

Our privileges go beyond money. For example, I've been given the incredible privilege of gaining a good education. That couldn't happen in a subsistence culture. It's a product of affluence to be able to go on for a doctorate. So I want to take the resources that have come to me as a result of this gracious gift and use them for the advancement of the kingdom of God. I don't want to use my education just to advance my own career or to improve my financial position. I want to use it to bless people.

Prayer

HOWARD SNYDER

Prayer is basic to our getting to know God—who he is, what he wants, what it means to be his child and part of his people. It includes private prayer, prayer in small groups, and participating in the prayers of the people in public worship. We need to participate in prayer for many reasons:

1. We need to be daily in touch with God to receive forgiveness and strength. As we present to the Lord our own shortcomings, he gives us strength.

2. We need guidance in day-to-day decisions we are not wise enough to make by ourselves. James told us, "If any of you lacks wisdom, he should ask God, who gives generously to all without finding fault, and it will be given to him" (1:5). A basic function of prayer is to orient our lives.

3. We need to see things from God's perspective. Prayer is not just talking to God; it's also listening to him. As we pray, we go beyond our own needs and become sensitive to the way God sees things. God speaks to us either directly or in more subtle ways, and our perspective begins to change. For example, I may bring a particular problem I'm facing to God. As I pray about it, I begin to see it in a new perspective, one that helps me function more effectively before God.

4. We are called to accomplish God's work in the world. It's not a matter of praying first and then doing God's work. Prayer is the work of the Church and thus the work of the Christian. Prayer should not be the last thing we do, but the first and the last. It should permeate all we're involved in.

Prayer is the basic way to make things happen for God. As we pray, we put ourselves in a position where God can use us. We also place God in a situation where he is able to respond. Even though God is sovereign and is able to move how and when he wishes, there is a sense in which prayer moves his hand. This does not mean that we can manipulate God through prayer, but rather that he has chosen prayer as his means of carrying out the work of the church in the world.

5. We need Christian community. We live in a very individualistic, self-centered age, often valuing our privacy more than any sense of community. In the biblical understanding of prayer, however, prayer is not just an individualistic act. It is a work of the people of God. Even when we pray by ourselves, we are a part of the praying church; but when we pray together, prayer builds relationships not only with God but with one another. Jesus said, "Where two or three come together in my name, there am I with them" (Matthew 18:20). When we come together in the name of Jesus to pray and to worship, Jesus is there in a way that often affects us more directly than when we are by ourselves. Some of the most significant prayer times I have had have been not when I was praying by myself but when I was praying with others. The fellowship of prayer helps us grow. It helps the Church become the community of God's people that God intends.

6. We need to respond to who God is. Even though prayer helps us in many

ways, it is not primarily for the purpose of meeting our own needs. We worship God, praise him, and give him our adoration because of who he is. Since God has made us to do just that, prayer does meet our needs. But we pray because God is worthy of all our praise and adoration.

♦ WANDERING THOUGHTS
DIETRICH BONHOEFFER

It is one of the particular difficulties of meditation that our thoughts are likely to wander and go their own way, toward other persons or to some events in our life. Much as this may distress and shame us again and again, we must not lose heart and become anxious, or even conclude that meditation is really not something for us. When this happens it is often a help not to snatch back our thoughts convulsively, but quite calmly to incorporate into our prayer the people and the events to which our thoughts keep straying and thus in all patience return to the starting point of the meditation.

(Dietrich Bonhoeffer, *Life Together* [New York: Harper and Row, 1954], 85.)

Solitude
✍ RICHARD FOSTER

Sometimes we need to be very active, but at other times we need to be quiet. The apostle Paul withdrew for thirteen years from the time of his conversion until he began his ministry at Antioch. He probably spent three years in the desert and then approximately ten years in his hometown of Tarsus. During that time he no doubt experienced a lot of solitude. This was followed by a period of very intense activity as Paul carried out his mission to the Gentiles. Paul needed both solitude and activity, and so do we.

Solitude as a spiritual discipline is often misunderstood. Solitude does not mean loneliness. It means finding the silence we need in order to focus upon God. Solitude is not an attempt to refresh ourselves so we can plunge back into the rat race. It is learning to ignore the rat race altogether.

In solitude, I learn that God can set me free from my bondage to the opinions of others and to my own inner compulsions. If I practice the discipline of solitude I have to disregard what other people think of me, because most people don't understand or value solitude. I also have to disregard my own grasping, grabbing attempts to somehow make it in the world. Solitude sets me free from others and from myself.

Sometimes solitude requires me to be solitary—that is, without people. If I spend time away from people, though, it is always in order to come back and to immerse myself in their lives and to be a blessing to them.

Jesus practiced solitude in order to commune with God and to give himself more fully to others. He inaugurated his ministry by spending forty days alone in the desert (Matthew 4:1-11). Before he chose the Twelve he spent the entire night alone in the desert hills (Luke 6:12). After the miraculous feeding of the five thousand Jesus "went up into the hills by himself" (Matthew 14:23). When the Twelve had returned from a preaching and healing mission, Jesus instructed them, "Come with me by yourselves to a quiet place" (Mark 6:31). As he prepared for his most holy work, Jesus sought the solitude of the Garden of Gethsemane (Matthew 26:36-46). There are many other scriptural accounts of Jesus' seeking solitude, but perhaps these are sufficient to show that solitude was a regular practice for him. So it should be for us.

It is helpful to learn to cultivate solitude in the context of daily life, whenever possible. An airplane is one of the greatest places in the world for solitude. There is no telephone; people don't know us and usually they want to be left alone. A car can be another good place to find solitude. We can find solitude when we take walks, or by stepping outside just before going to bed at night. Moments of prayer, of openness to God, can be little experiences of solitude.

We must realize, however, that given the culture in which we live, most of us need to schedule experiences into our lives that will allow for solitude and that will enable us to concentrate upon God. That's one reason that Christian camps can be helpful to many people. The key factor is that we get away from our regular routines long enough to listen to God. We spend time in Bible study, in prayer, and alone, and God works in our lives.

All of us need to structure times in which we can learn how to be alone with God. Remember that God describes himself as the still, small voice—"a gentle whisper"—that wants to speak to us if we're willing to learn to listen (1 Kings 19:12).

Many of us can't stand being alone. We need to ask ourselves why this is so. Why don't I like quiet? Why must I always have noise? Why must I always have a television or radio on? As we begin to explore our aversion to being alone, we will begin to understand the need for solitude. Many of us use other people and the media as ways of distracting us so we don't have to think. We're afraid of thinking, afraid of discovering ourselves. So we put radios over our ears like mufflers so we will never have to find ourselves without noise. That is slavery.

Others of us like being alone, but in an unhealthy way. There's danger in staying apart from others too long. We must not be isolated from hurting, bleeding humanity. We must remember that the purpose of solitude is to orient us in such a way that we can be a real blessing to people. It does not mean being antisocial.

Christ will lead us as we practice solitude. He is our present Teacher, and he will tell us if we are going off track. We can know that our practice of solitude is well balanced if our experiences produce the fruit of the Spirit in our lives and if they bring blessing to other people.

♦ SNATCHES OF TIME / RICHARD FOSTER

What are some steps into solitude? The first thing we can do is to take advantage of the "little solitudes" that fill our day. Consider the solitude of those early morning moments in bed before the family awakens. Think of the solitude of a morning cup of coffee before beginning the work of the day. There is the solitude of bumper-to-bumper traffic during the freeway rush hour. There can be little moments of rest and refreshment when we turn a corner and see a flower or a tree. Instead of vocal prayer before a meal, consider inviting everyone to join in a few moments of gathered silence. Once while driving a carload of chattering children and adults, I exclaimed, "Let's play a game and see if we can all be absolutely quiet until we reach the airport" (about five minutes away). It worked, blessedly so. Find new joy and meaning in the little walk from the subway to your home. Slip outside just before bed and taste the silent night.

These tiny snatches of time are often lost to us. What a pity! They can and should be redeemed. They are times for inner quiet, for reorienting our lives like a compass needle. They are little moments that help us to be genuinely present where we are.

(Richard Foster, *Celebration of Discipline* [San Francisco: Harper and Row, 1978], 93.)

♦ SOLITUDE AND COMMUNITY DIETRICH BONHOEFFER

Let him who cannot be alone beware of community. He will only do harm to himself and to the community. Alone you stood before God when he called you; alone you had to answer that call; alone you had to struggle and pray; and alone you will die and give an account to God. You cannot escape from yourself; for God has singled you out. If you refuse to be alone you are rejecting Christ's call to you, and you can have no part in the community of those who are called. . . .

But the reverse is also true: Let him who is not in community beware of being alone. Into the community you were called, the call was not meant for you alone; in the community of the called you bear your cross, you struggle, you pray. You are not alone, even in death, and on the Last Day you will be only one member of the great congregation of Jesus Christ. If you scorn the fellowship of the brethren, you reject the call of Jesus Christ, and thus your solitude can be only hurtful to you. . . .

We recognize, then, that only as we are within the fellowship can we be alone, and only he that is alone can live in the fellowship.

(Dietrich Bonhoeffer, *Life Together* [New York: Harper and Row, 1954], 77.)

Mutual Discipling

✍ HOWARD SNYDER

Every renewal that has happened in the history of the church has had some kind of mutual discipling. The Wesleys, for example, held "class meetings"; the seventeenth-century German Pietists had Bible study groups; and today's renewal movements also have small-group meetings. By mutual discipling I simply mean that believers gather together, either one-on-one or in a small-group relationship with other believers, so that they may be accountable to one another, build one another up, and encourage one another.

Accountability is often lacking in churches today. We live in an undisciplined age whose unwritten mottoes are "Do your own thing," "Have it your way," and "If it feels right, do it." That is not the perspective we find in Scripture. The Bible teaches that "we who are many form one body, and each member belongs to all the others" (Romans 12:5). We are charged with responsibility, not only to God, but also to one another because of our relationship to God. We need to be involved in accountable relationships that don't just depend on how we feel from day to day.

Building up and encouraging one another are other basic aspects of mutual discipling. The writer to the Hebrews helps us see how they help us grow: "Encourage one another daily, as long as it is called Today, so that none of you may be hardened by sin's deceitfulness" (3:13). This suggests that if we are not in the process of encouraging and building up one another, we will in fact be deceived by sin.

The same writer also said: "Let us consider how we may spur one another on toward love and good deeds. Let us not give up meeting together, as some are in the habit of doing, but let us encourage one another" (10:24, 25). There is a fundamental biblical and spiritual principle involved here. God has made us so that we need spiritual discipline—not just by ourselves, but with one another. God works by the power of his Spirit when we are together.

Discipline and Spontaneity

EUGENE PETERSON

The human being at birth is the most undeveloped creature on the face of the earth. We are absolutely helpless. Animals are born with well-developed instincts, so they can survive the loss of a parent at birth. We can't do that; we learn how to be human.

As infants we are born with an instinct to feed at our mother's breast; that instinct gets us started, but it doesn't carry us very far. As we grow older, we have to learn how to eat with a knife, spoon, and fork, and to drink from a cup. As every parent knows, it is a long and messy process. So a parent is prepared with patience to teach his child what he needs to know to get along in life.

It is the same in the new life in Christ. The impetus of birth is marvelous but doesn't carry us very far. So God places us in an environment with parents, brothers, and sisters in the faith who give us instruction in growing up in Christ. This instruction involves disciplines. Practicing the disciplines is learning how to eat and drink without making too big a mess, how to walk without bruising ourselves on the furniture or careening into our neighbors.

Some believers fear that discipline will crush their spontaneity. But a person who can't use a fork isn't spontaneous; he's undeveloped. Athletes and musicians engage in years of repetitive, often boring activity, but at the moment of performance they are spontaneous—their muscles and emotions and minds fully alive to the moment. The disciplines of faith prepare us for similar spontaneities—at the moment of temptation, of obedience, of praise, of witness, we are "all there," body and spirit, alive in Christ.

Discipline itself is not spontaneous but is the precondition for spontaneity. Christians practice disciplines such as prayer, Scripture reading, worship, fasting, and almsgiving not out of whim but because of decision. People who reject the disciplines are not spontaneous, but merely unbuttoned. The Christian who values spontaneity practices the disciplines for a lifetime. The disciplines give him the skills that he needs to live spontaneously.

It is possible, of course, for these practiced behaviors to lose touch with faith and become artificial. We can be like a gymnast who does push-ups all day but never gets on the rings and soars because he is so comfortably good at calisthenics. In the practice of a discipline it is possible to forget the dangerous thrill of letting our bodies sail freely in space. This is why the practice of discipline is not a private but a community affair; we need friends around who can look at us and say, "Why don't I ever see you up on the rings anymore?"

The basic test of the organic connection between discipline and spontaneity is our activity in love. The apostle John, our best instructor in these parts of the spiritual life, set this test: Do we love? Do the people around us experience this love? Love is the most spontaneous act in the world—unprogrammable and unrepeatable. But anyone who engages in acts of love for very long knows that not much comes of it apart from doggedly practiced disciplines. Good intentions don't get us much beyond buying candy on Valentine's Day.

We need to note a radical difference between habit and discipline. A habit results from laziness. It takes no thought, little effort, and involves no encounter with God or neighbor. We are always reluctant to leave a habit because even though life in the ruts is minimal, it is also painless. A discipline can look superficially the same as a habit, but the great difference is apparent when the door opens and there is a God to praise or any enemy to love. The discipline person rushes out the door; the habit person heads for a warm bed. Christians who engage in disciplined rituals of Scripture, prayer, and worship know that they have hardened into habits when they find themselves unwilling to leave them in order to enter into unscheduled acts of obedience.

The underground enemy of the spiritual life is self-interest—taking care of ourselves, making ourselves our own gods. Habits keep us attentive to ourselves; rituals break self-preoccupation, the self-enclosed routine. By breaking in on our lazy habits, the set rituals of discipline draw us into a larger world where God is the chief actor and speaker. We are shocked into attentiveness to what is beyond ourselves.

So Christian communities insist on rituals of discipline. At an appointed time each Sunday we are called out of our individual concerns into the world of worship. At appointed times through the year we are called out of the routines of calendar time that measure our histories into celebrating those events that make us aware of God's history among us. Wise Christians develop a daily ritual that provides time and space for putting self in its place and God in his place. These quiet and obscure rituals are the springs of spontaneity.

♦ WHEN DISCIPLINE FEELS DULL AND DEAD
EUGENE PETERSON

Believers must be aware that most of the time discipline feels dull and dead. We're impatient if we have to wait a long time for something, especially in America. If we don't find instant zest in a discipline, we make a negative snap judgment about it. But often what we describe as deadness, dullness, or boredom is simply our own slow waking up. We just have to live through that. Simple desire for more in our Christian lives is sufficient evidence that the life is there. Be patient and wait. It's the Spirit's work. We simply put ourselves in the way of the Spirit so he can work in us.

The Benefits of Keeping a Journal
LUCI SHAW

All my life long I've thought I should keep a journal. Madeleine L'Engle and Ginny Hearn and other friends who keep journals were pushing me to do so. But I never did until a few years ago, when the discovery that my husband, Harold, had cancer suddenly plunged us into the middle of an intense learning experience, facing things we'd never faced before. Confronted with agonizing decisions, we would cry out to the Lord, "Where are you in the middle of this?" It suddenly occurred to me that unless I made a record of what was going on, I would forget. The events, details, and people of those painful days could easily become a blur. So I started to write it all down.

I date each day's entry so I can keep track, and then I include what has happened that day. "Harold is recovering from lung surgery. He's on a respirator, and Dr. Parker came to see him and told me they're going to start a new medication. So-and-so visited." I write down the facts so that I can remember, for example, the people who say, "We promise to pray for you." Being able to go back and see their names in my journal and remember what they said is much more comforting to me than saying, "Oh, I know a lot of people are praying for me." It helps to have specifics and details down in black and white.

I put all kinds of things in my journal—not only factual, but reflective as well. My prayers go into my journal. I write down what I am asking the Lord and what I am thinking. When the doctor said this or suggested such-and-such, maybe it was what the Lord was telling us to do. Putting it down helps me keep track; my journal is a record of what has been happening in my thinking, how I interpret my life events.

If I am very discouraged or depressed, I write that down along with whatever my prayer is at that point. And when there seems to be an answer to prayer, a new direction or insight—perhaps from something someone said or a concept in a sermon or book—I write that down too. It helps me see that my life is not just random. I can see purpose and plan and direction and progression.

Of course in my journal I write down ideas I have for articles and poems, or phrases, or connections that I begin to see. My poems spring out of real life, every one of them, and if I don't write an idea down the moment I receive it, I may lose it. Even if I have a dozen ideas in a day, I can't do anything about them unless I remember them. When I write them down in my journal, I can do something with them when I have time. And because I do a lot of public speaking, I keep a section in my journal for ideas related to the topics I'm planning to speak on.

I also record other people's comments and portions of letters. During Harold's illness, we received all kinds of letters with God-given insights about our situation. I kept the letters, and I also wrote down their key points in my journal and my reactions to them.

It's practical to have a journal you can carry around, although not so small that it's difficult to write in. Some people like using big looseleaf binders, because they can take pages out or carry paper with them and add it to the journal later. I don't want anything that big, though—I would find it cumbersome. My journal is a six-by-ten-inch notebook divided into three or four different sections specified for various purposes. It will fit into most of my purses.

I've found that writing in my journal is great therapy and release for me. If I'm facing a crisis by myself, very tense and upset by a new turn of events, putting my feelings into words takes the tension out of me and puts it on the page. Or, if I'm excited about something, I want to express that too. It's not enough to have the happiness inside me; I want to put it down on paper, to capture and remember it.

Keeping a journal has turned out to be a learning experience in itself. As I write things down, I discover what I never knew before, what I never even knew I was thinking. The process of taking a free-floating idea and subjecting it to the discipline of words often clarifies one's thinking. And sometimes I even surprise myself. I write down something and then I step back in wonder, Where did that come from? An idea, like clay, becomes a new reality when it's forced into the mold of words.

Sometimes I use my journal to sharpen my writer's skills. I make it a practice to describe things to myself as I see them. I'm learning to be precise, to capture the scene or event in a few perfectly chosen words, like a prose haiku. I try to describe the color of the impatiens by my back door. Are the flowers coral, or flame? Maybe they're watermelon. But to describe the sheen on the petals, I photograph them. The color is so brilliant it's almost vulgar. It's bright and brash, yet still delicate and silky.

Keeping a journal helps me be observant of my surroundings. For example, I got very excited this spring as I noticed for the first time the different kinds of grass that grow along the roads. Looking at the blue-flowered chicory, the yellow daisies, and the Queen Anne's Lace is like watching a painting by Seurat, the French impressionist who put little dots of different colors together to make a scene. The blue flowers, I noticed, are always closer to the road, on the dry and rocky ground. Somehow the chicory survives there, but the

Queen Anne's Lace seems to need deeper, richer soil, so it's always a little further back. They look like two bands of color lining the road. As I saw this I recorded it in my journal. Very often noticing such things has real meaning for me. It can translate into something significant. Right now I'm living in rocky ground. Other times in my life I've lived in rich soil. Am I flowering the way God wants me to in the soil I'm growing in?

Describing something in my journal gives me almost total recall. It captures the moment exactly, so I can come back to what I've written and experience it all over again. It isn't necessary to fill in all the detail, because the imagination also carries it. But with reminders in my journal I can bring back a whole scene or event.

Keeping a journal helps me have a sense of control. Dealing with terminal illness meant being in a state of unknowing much of the time. There was so much unpredictability; every day was different. I couldn't plan our lives the way I'd always done it. But even if I couldn't structure the days ahead of me, I could have a grasp on what was happening to us at the moment, because I was thinking it through and putting it down on paper. It was not all out of control, random, coming at me without a pattern. By writing in my journal, I brought order out of chaos, I was making some sense of the situation.

Of course, most people aren't facing this particular kind of stress. Still, sooner or later everybody faces crises. Everyone is in touch with suffering, trouble, or struggle. Everyone has to make decisions. In nearly every stage of life we face difficulty of one kind or another. And this is one way to deal with it, with a journal.

Journaling helps develop creativity. Prose writers often discipline themselves to sit down and write for at least three or four hours every day. Flannery O'Connor wrote for three hours every morning whether she had anything to write or not. Her attitude was, if you want to be a writer, write. Don't write letters, don't read, don't do anything else. So keeping a journal is teaching me the discipline of writing every day. It's been helpful for me as a writer to learn that I can do this.

These are just some ways I've found journaling to be beneficial. There are no set rules for what a journal has to be. It can be anything you want it to be, whatever suits your mood or fits your needs. Every person has to find the way that works best for him or her. That's part of the adventure of keeping a journal.

One very important rule about journaling is that you don't write for anybody else—just yourself. That way you can be absolutely honest. You don't have to worry that what you're writing is going to shock somebody or throw them off balance. You don't have to worry that your doubts and fears are going to be "a bad witness." You write what's really in you. That's why it's accepted around my house that no one reads my journal. I don't have a lock on it, but they know that this is one of the ground rules. I extend the same right of privacy to them.

I write in my journal almost every day. It may take me fifteen or twenty minutes at one sitting, or I may write in it three or four times a day if things are happening thick and fast. On the other hand, if life is pretty routine and nothing tremendous is happening, I may go several days without writing.

The trick to journaling is to keep it current. It's a lot easier that way. It's like correspondence. If you let six months go by without writing to a good friend, you have so much stored up that the thought of writing it all down is intimidating. You don't even want to attempt it! But if you send off a note every few days your thoughts are within boundaries and the task isn't overwhelming.

Journaling is a discipline. You have to ask yourself, is this worthwhile, is this worth scheduling time to do? If it's valuable enough to you, you'll make time for it. Like Bible study or prayer, it's a matter of priorities. There are times when you neglect it; when you get back to it you ask yourself, Why was I away so long?

◆LEARN TO BE QUIET / LUCI SHAW

It is difficult to learn to be quiet, to reach a place where thoughts are not flying back and forth. It won't happen unless we deliberately work at it. We need to see the value of quietness. We have to want it enough to make it happen.

Madeleine L'Engle talks a lot about the need for being time—time to stop doing and making and rushing, time to just be. One of the most refreshing things I can do when I'm tired or "peopled-out" is to walk in the woods or to walk up a hill to where I can see a larger view.

God gives us his own marvelous created world, but we cut it down, build it over, and make parking lots where fields used to be. We don't allow the messages of God's general revelation—his word through nature—to come to us. As Christians we're very faithful to God's special revelation, the Bible, but we have this huge area of existence—the natural universe—that we ignore and very often despise.

I think Christians need to become aware of ecological issues. We of all people should be the conservationists. We didn't arrive here by accident; we've been given this world for a reason. It's full of design, beauty, wonder, and miracle!

I'm not a pantheist. I don't believe that God is in every flower and every leaf on every tree, but rather that these things are there to point us to him. They say, "Look at me. Notice my design. See the chloroplasts that receive sunlight and turn it into energy. Think of who designed me."

The created world speaks of God. If we will learn to be quiet and listen, we will be able to hear what it has to say to us.

Five Ways to Keep a Spiritual Journal

✍ HOWARD SNYDER

A spiritual journal is simply a written account of one's relationship with God. In journaling we note the people and events in our lives and reflect on how we see God working in them.

There are many ways to keep a journal. Right now I'm finding it useful to keep one with two main elements. First, I record my use of time. For more than a year now I have been been using a code I devised to keep track of my days in half-hour segments. This is a matter of accountability for me. I want to know where my time is going, just as I know where my money is going.

Second, I reflect on my life and growth. Some days this may result in no written comments at all. Some days I write only a little. At other times I write more in depth, reflecting on something I've learned about myself or a problem that has come up.

For example, as I was reflecting on the events of one day, I realized that it is very hard for me to ask people to do things. I know that ability to delegate is important for anyone in leadership, so in my journal I reflected about my own difficulty in this area. Why is delegation hard for me to do? When should I be doing it? How can I do it more effectively? How can I get over my dislike of it?

Such reflections often move me into prayer, which I may include in my journal as well. In fact, prayer and Bible study are very much a part of my journaling. I write in my journal as part of my daily Bible study time, and I often conclude my journal entry with a brief written prayer.

Here are five ways that keeping a journal can help a Christian grow:

1. Because a journal is a record, it becomes a point of reference for review. As the months and years go by, we ask ourselves, Have I grown spiritually? Our answer may depend more on how we feel at the time than on what the case really is. A journal is useful because you can go back and see where you were a year ago. You can compare your situation then with where you are now. You can say, "Oh, yes, I was dealing with that problem back there, and that's no longer a problem. I see how God has helped me in that." Or perhaps, "Yes, that is still a problem, an area where I haven't grown." Or maybe, "Here's something I've forgotten. I need to go back and work on it." Even though a journal is a subjective account, it provides an objective point of reference for the spiritual journey.

2. Writing out one's thoughts helps many people to think, meditate, and reflect. I find that as I write things down, I think them through more clearly, more carefully, and with more discipline than if I just keep them in my head. The discipline of putting words down on paper in a logical sequence clarifies one's thinking.

3. Keeping a journal often helps us to be more creative. It involves our bodies, not just our minds, helping us get in touch with areas of ourselves that we wouldn't otherwise discover. As we write, one thing will remind us of something else. We may think of symbolic ways of putting things, or we may want to write poetry. Sometimes this puts us in touch with feelings about events from our past, or with things in our subconscious mind that really help us grow.

4. Keeping a journal can be a form of conversation with God. More than just putting words down on paper, it becomes a dialogue with God. I write down my side of the conversation and meditate on it, and then listen for God to tell me something. As God responds, I record this before writing down something else of mine.

5. Keeping a journal can enrich our devotional reading. We may read something in Scripture that provides the basis for comments in our journal. Or we

may read a devotional classic. Whether we agree or disagree with it, it can provide the basis for dialogue in the journal. Such a dialogue will clarify our thoughts and make the things we read more useful to us.

How, then, does one keep a journal? This depends a lot on the person. People have different styles of writing, so a journal takes on the personality of its author. Personally, I find writing is a good way to clarify my thoughts. I don't just record events; I also analyze them. Others may prefer a straightforward prose account with less analysis. Still others are more poetic in their approach. Each person should find the form that fits best, rather than trying to fit into someone else's pattern. That may take some experimentation.

Begin by getting a loose-leaf notebook. It should be small enough to carry around easily, preferably no larger than your Bible so you can keep the two books together. In this notebook you can write your thoughts day by day. Just put down the date and then write whatever you want to include. Some people will do this daily; others less often. This is as individualistic as one's personality.

I have a friend whose journal entering is very sporadic. He may write in his journal for two or three days in a row and not open it again for some weeks. He journals as he has need. By contrast, I find it is more effective to make journal keeping a discipline and write at least something every day, even if it's very brief. Otherwise I'm prone to get out of the habit.

The important thing is not the exact method you use, but rather to begin in whatever way seems useful to you and then let your own method develop.

♦ THE TYRANNY OF THE URGENT
YFC EDITORS

If we don't get ourselves organized, it is easy for us to face what has been termed the "tyranny of the urgent." This means you spend your time dashing about doing what is most urgent rather than planning ahead so your life doesn't come to that breaking point.

Getting organized need not be difficult. It means taking note of what you need to do and prioritizing: doing the most important things first and in order, followed by things of lower priority. You need the courage to say no to some activities and to cut back on others. Finally, it is important to pray each day over what you need to do. Ask God, first thing in the morning, to help you keep your priorities straight and accomplish his will through it all during your day.

You will find that defining what is important, setting priorities, and getting organized will not be overstructured; in reality it will be liberating. You will have more time because you will have structured your time in order to make the best possible use of it.

RELATED ARTICLES
Chapter 2: **The Meaning of Surrender**
Chapter 2: **The Importance of Spiritual Exercise**
Chapter 7: **Who Is in Charge of Your Spiritual Life?**
Chapter 17: **Prayer: The Key to Spiritual Growth**

CHAPTER

13

Suffering and the Christian

- ✓ How can I grow spiritually when my body is giving me problems?
- ✓ How can I use my stress to help me grow, not break me?
- ✓ Dealing with overweight, mid-life crisis, old age, pain
- ✓ Why is there so much suffering?

Do Christians Have to Suffer?

AJITH FERNANDO

We often hear people say that since they started following Christ, their troubles have vanished. But when we look at the lives of God's chosen servants in the Bible, we see that trouble seems to have followed them wherever they went.

This is not surprising, for suffering is an essential ingredient of following Jesus. This is why there are few principles of discipleship repeated in the Gospels as often as the principle that life comes through death, that we find our souls only if we are willing to lose them. This principle can be restated this way: If we are to experience the full life Christ promised to give us, we must first experience suffering.

I want to give six reasons why suffering is important for Christian discipleship.

The first three are given in the book of Job. When Job was afflicted in numerous ways, three friends of his came and said that his suffering was a punishment for his sin (Job 4–25). The Bible presents this as a reason for the suffering that some people encounter (1 Corinthians 11:28-30). But this was not the reason for Job's suffering.

A younger person, Elihu, met Job and told him he was suffering so that he would be refined, so that the impurities in his life would be burned up (Job 32–37). The Bible also gives this as a reason for the suffering of some people (Romans 5:3, 4; James 1:2-4). But this was not the primary reason for Job's suffering either.

The first two chapters of Job tell us that his suffering was part of the battle between the forces of darkness and the forces of light. God allowed Satan to strike Job to demonstrate that Job would be faithful to God even if all his earthly blessings were taken away. Job's loyalty was proof to Satan and to the world that a person's relationship to God is deeper than the harshest earthly suffering. So a third reason God allows suffering is to demonstrate the validity of commitment to him. Suffering is often supposed to be an argument against Christianity. God can turn it into an argument for Christianity.

Suffering is woven into the fabric of life in this fallen world. People can try to avoid it, but they cannot; and so they live in fear of it and are disillusioned when they encounter it. God may call us to show the world that there is something deeper than suffering, something that gives us the strength to face suffering without fear. That something is our relationship with our unchanging, eternal God.

A fourth reason for suffering is given in Colossians 1:24, where Paul said, "Now I rejoice in what was suffered for you, and I fill up in my flesh what is still lacking in regard to Christ's afflictions." He means here that a certain amount of suffering is necessary so that the gospel can truly bear fruit in the world. Paul said he wanted to bear that suffering. In a similar vein, in 2 Corinthians 4:10 he said, "We always carry around in our body the death of Jesus, so that the life of Jesus may also be revealed in our body." Our suffering opens the door for the gospel to go out.

In a Hindu village in India, one family turned to Christ. Shortly after their conversion their child got very ill. The Hindu neighbors said the gods had cursed the family for changing religions. Though the Christians prayed hard for the child's healing, he died. But his funeral was such a triumphant event that through it the eyes of many of the villagers were opened. Their resistance to the gospel vanished, and they turned to Christ. The pain of the death of a beloved child was needed before the gospel took root in that village.

A fifth reason for suffering is the hatred of the forces of darkness for the way of light. This hatred often results in persecution. Paul said, "Everyone who wants to live a godly life in Christ Jesus will be persecuted" (2 Timothy 3:12).

Our persecutors can cause us much harm. Jesus said Satan can even kill our bodies. But Jesus also said he cannot kill the soul (Matthew 10:28).

In fact, if we are faithful, God will turn the evil planned against us into a source of blessing, to accomplish something good. This was what Joseph found out many years after his brothers had treated him cruelly and caused him much suffering (Genesis 50:20). This is why the early church regarded persecution as something glorious. Paul wrote to the Ephesians from a dreary Roman prison: "I ask you, therefore, not to be discouraged because of my sufferings for you, which are your glory" (3:13).

A sixth reason for suffering is perhaps the most beautiful of all, but it is the least spoken of. Our sufferings are a uniquely deep way of uniting us with our Lord Jesus. Paul said he wanted to know the fellowship of sharing in Christ's suffering (Philippians 3:10). Jesus "was despised and rejected by men, a man of sorrows, and familiar with suffering" (Isaiah 53:3). If we are to identify with him fully, then we must suffer with him.

But that is not all. The Bible teaches that when we suffer, Christ suffers with us. He asked the persecutor Saul, "Why do you persecute me?" (Acts 9:4). Saul was actually persecuting the Christians, but his blows were striking Christ! In shared suffering is a depth of fellowship that no other experience could produce. One of the biggest problems in the church today is the lack of depth in our Christian experience. Could this be because we have not experienced the depth of unity with Christ in and through suffering?

A Christian does not need to go in search of suffering. It will come sooner or later. When it comes, we must not be surprised or disappointed. Many who do not expect suffering get disillusioned when it comes, or they go along paths of disobedience in attempting to avoid it. James said that when we face trials of many kinds, we should consider them pure joy, because we know that good will surely come out of them (James 1:2-4).

While we are going through trials, we may think they are too intense. But Paul said these very troubles are achieving for us "an eternal glory that far outweighs them all," and that in comparison to this glory these troubles are light and momentary (2 Corinthians 4:17).

♦ A LONELY WALK / LARRY KREIDER

Cruel winds often blow through the life of a young Christian. I was fifteen when I decided to follow Christ. One of my good friends made it very clear that my decision had forced us onto opposite paths. The scene is fresh in my mind, though it happened twenty-six years ago. We were walking home from school and came to a cemetery. Now that my decision was made, he suggested that I go one direction around the cemetery and on into my own world; he would go the other direction into his.

That was a lonely walk. I was glad Christ was there to walk it with me.

Where Is God When I'm Hurting?

JOHN B. PEARRELL

The problem of pain and suffering in the Christian's life has plagued man through the centuries. Long ago Job cried out, "If only I knew where to find him; if only I could go to his dwelling!" (Job 23:3). And in the midst of pain and suffering, many echo that cry in many forms: If God is so loving, why did he let this happen? If he cares, why doesn't he do something? Where is God when it hurts? Why did he desert me? But the problem is best illustrated in the anguished cry of a young woman, who, after praying for months for her pastor to be healed of cancer, said these words after his death: "In light of the fact that God did not heal that young man after all those prayers [the whole church had been praying for him], I'm never going to bother him with another request again. Why should I? I'll only be disappointed."

Have you ever felt that way? You prayed for something, you thought you knew what God was going to do, and yet he didn't do as you asked? How should we respond when we pray and God does not answer?

Unfortunately, there are no answers this side of eternity, and there are times that we hold on by sheer grit and determination to what we know as truth, even though the circumstances may be totally against us.

What I offer here is not an exhaustive answer on the subject, but practical insights that have helped me as I wrestle with the problem of grief, suffering, and pain.

Principle number one is that *God is sovereign.* He is in control; nothing takes him by surprise. We are not sovereign; we are capable of being surprised. When something takes me by surprise, I automatically feel that this has obviously taken God by surprise as well. I think he panics just like me! That's ridiculous! Yet, we live as if God has lost control; as if he has moved off into space and has decided to let nature run it's course. Or we act as if he is our great benefactor in the sky, and when we say, "Jump," we expect him to respond, "How high?" It's no wonder we so often become disillusioned and disappointed with God. We have a wrong concept of him! God is sovereign, not us.

God is in control. And he answers prayer. He is there to do the unexpected. Sometimes when we pray, he intervenes in a pragmatic way that defies logical explanation. But that intervention is based on his sovereign choice and on his grace and goodness to us, not upon our convenience or our whims. He is free to choose how he deals with us.

In the story of John the Baptist, John was the man of whom Jesus said, "I tell you, among those born of women there is no one greater than John" (Luke 7:28). But notice this: John was in prison, and things looked pretty bleak. He sent his disciples to Jesus to ask, "Are you the one who was to come, or should we expect someone else?" (Luke 7:19). Jesus replied, "Go back and report to John what you have seen and heard: The blind receive sight, the lame walk. . . . Blessed is the man who does not fall away on account of me" (Luke 7:22, 23).

John was beginning to doubt that Jesus was the Messiah because Jesus was not doing what John thought the Messiah should do.

Sometimes we have to pray realizing that God may not work the way we think he should work. But that's OK. He's sovereign, not us. And when those times of suffering and grief come, we have but two options: dwell in bitterness over our situation; or climb the mountain of gratitude and realize that all of life is a gracious gift of a sovereign Lord and marvel that it is given in the first place.

This brings us to principle number two: *Faith is not merely receiving from God what we want,* it sometimes involves accepting what he gives without doubting him.

Because of faulty theology, we have come to believe that God wants us all healthy and wealthy. Not so. The Bible never promises us that as Christians we are exempt from trials and suffering by Christ's death. As a matter of fact there are times when Scripture promises us just the opposite! Jesus said, "In this world you will have trouble" (John 16:33). And Paul wrote: "I want to know Christ and the power of his resurrection," but the rest of the verse says, "and the fellowship of sharing in his sufferings, becoming like him in his death" (Philippians 3:10).

The promise of Christ is not to keep us from problems, it is to take care of us in them. If we are to become like Christ, then ultimately we have to welcome anything that comes our way to help that process continue. We must do that, realizing that God is sovereign and his work in us is for his glory.

The hardest prayer to pray is not "Oh God, be my good luck charm and keep me from all harm," or "Oh God, give me this or that or do this or that." The hardest prayer to pray is that of Christ in Gethsemane, "My Father, if it is possible, may this cup be taken from me. Yet not as I will, but as you will" (Matthew 26:39).

Why is that prayer so difficult? We are too busy seeking our own good to care much about seeking God's good. When that happens, our vision is clouded and we can't recognize those things that come into our lives to help conform us to his image. Instead of trusting God to work in us, we become angry and bitter.

The third and final principle is this: *Faith always leads to ultimate victory.* As Christians, we are on the winning side. If you had seen Christ on the cross, in pain and great agony, at a time when the skies were darkened and even God himself turned his back upon him, it would hardly have seemed like a victory. And yet it was precisely this act that won our redemption and God's victory over Satan in this world. And the time is coming when God's rule will be established on earth, and the problem of pain and suffering will finally be brought to an end. But until that time, we live in a sinful and fallen world. In Christ, we have freedom from sin, but we still live with the consequences of sin all around us. We suffer, but we need never suffer alone. Nor do we suffer and mourn without hope. "He who did not spare his own Son, but gave him up for us all—how will he not also, along with him, graciously give us all things?" (Romans 8:32).

May I suggest that the question should not be, Where is God when it hurts? but rather, Where am I when I hurt? You see, the mark of maturity in a Christian is not freedom from pain; it is total trust during pain. It is not easy, but it is real, and it is this attitude and this alone that will allow us to continue to grow in grace and truth. It is this maturity that strengthens us for ministry.

"Therefore we do not lose heart. Though outwardly we are wasting away, yet inwardly we are being renewed day by day. For our light and momentary troubles are achieving for us an eternal glory that far outweighs them all. So we fix our eyes not on what is seen, but on what is unseen. For what is seen is temporary, but what is unseen is eternal" (2 Corinthians 4:16-18).

♦ BODY AND SOUL TOGETHER
HAROLD MYRA

No amount of spirituality is going to cancel our normal psychological and physical dynamics. If I'm in an airplane and the pilot says we're going to crash in thirty seconds, I may feel prepared for heaven, but my body will go crazy sending out wild signals of fear and anxiety. My body, acting through natural processes, is trying to prepare me for an emergency.

In a similar way, when we feel hostile toward someone, biological and psychological changes take place within us.

I remember a time when a person was putting a great deal of pressure on me. I thought to myself, I can handle this. I'm praying about it, and it's not bothering me. But after about a year of this unrelenting pressure, I discovered I had some real stomach problems. My body was reacting to the stress even though I was bravely saying, I'm too tough to let this get to me.

Our bodies and our emotions work together. When one suffers, the other joins in. It is wise to seek help when we are under a great deal of emotional stress before the body breaks down and makes the problem even greater.

Can a Christian Be Overweight?
✍ JOHN R. THROOP

When I became a Christian, I understood early that spiritual growth did not regularly and easily appear in the Christian life. I knew that Jesus Christ had given me a starting point in my life, a place for growth to begin. I realized that spiritual growth was a process that would take discipline and perseverance. It would entail prayer and Bible study, fellowship and witness.

But I had one small problem. Or rather, I should say, one large problem. It was this growth around my middle. I was overweight—sixty-five pounds over West Point's recommendation for my age and height. Not that I was the only person in my church like that—even my pastor weighed too much! Somehow, no one I knew had made any connection between spiritual discipline and physical discipline.

I have since learned, however, that spiritual and physical fitness go together. God wants us to praise him with our minds and hearts, but he also wants us to reflect our love for him by caring for the physical frame he has given us. If we are spiritually in shape, then we must also seek to be in shape physically in order to glorify God.

Paul said, "Do you not know that your body is a temple of the Holy Spirit, who is in you, whom you have received from God? You are not your own; you were bought at a price. Therefore honor God with your body" (1 Corinthians 6:19, 20). Specifically, Paul was telling the Corinthians to flee from sexual immorality. But the wider principle, stewardship of our bodies, makes these verses apply to other sins against the body also. How we use our bodies, what we put into them, what they look like—these are all important to God.

Our bodies are not our own. They are on loan to us. Therefore we need to keep them as finely tuned as we can, to be the best physically we can be. If we misuse our bodies, all areas of our lives are affected. If we are terribly out of shape physically, our mental processes suffer. By putting the wrong kinds of food into our bodies, we can distort our reasoning ability, our spiritual lives, and our dispositions. I've never met a truly happy overweight person. Such a person is burdened spiritually and emotionally as well as physically.

The misconception that the spirit is more important than the body can be traced to Greek thinking, especially that of the Stoics and the Epicureans. These non-Christian schools of thought held that the development of the intellectual and spiritual capacities was by far the most important thing in life. The body was just a hindrance to the pursuit of the spiritual and the intellectual. This way of thinking rubbed off on the early Christian church.

The Hebrew mind knew nothing of this Greek split between the physical and the spiritual. For the Hebrew thinker, body, mind, and spirit were all joined together. What you do with your body—sexually, with food, with drink—affects your spirit. God created the whole person, and so the whole person is accountable to him. This way of thinking is authentic biblical thought in both Old and New Testaments.

Paul, a Hebrew thinker and dedicated Christian apostle, understood that physical choices are also moral and spiritual choices. "Everything is permissible for me," he said, quoting a proverb of his day, "but not everything is beneficial. 'Everything is permissible for me'—but I will not be mastered by anything" (1 Corinthians 6:12). That's as true for food as it is for sex.

Discipline is the way out of enslavement. The overweight person seems at times to be enslaved to food. Now there are people who, because of specific medical problems such as a thyroid condition, are destined to be overweight to some extent. But the large majority of overweight people are that way because they eat too much and exercise too little. In a word, they are undisciplined.

It is important, then, to bring the human activity of eating under control of the Holy Spirit, just as we bring other temptations to the Holy Spirit to be defeated. This kind of discipline is a part of what is called sanctification, or the increasing holiness of the believer.

As I grew in the Lord, I discovered that my self-concept was improving. I could now accept and love myself as the Lord desired for me. I answered a call from God to serve him in the ministry. But my physical appearance did not reflect my inner change. It told a very different story to the world. I weighed 225 pounds, and my size said, I don't really care about myself. I don't love myself.

One morning I looked in the mirror and realized that I was not being true to myself and to God. Somehow I had to bring my habits of eating too much and exercising not at all under the Spirit's control. I had to discipline myself to work at losing weight and shaping up. Now that my inside—my interior life—was in good shape, I had to let discipline reshape my body.

I wasn't sure where to start, so I went to see my family physician. He would need to examine me to be sure I was fit enough to begin to exercise. I hoped he would advise me about nutrition. Instead, he replayed what he'd been telling me for years.

"John," he said, "you've got to lose weight."

"How can I do that?" I answered.

"Eat right and get some exercise."

That's like telling a man dying of thirst in the desert that he needs water. He knows what he needs; he just doesn't know how to get it. Ideally a physician will outline specific and definable ways to accomplish what he says you must do. But if you can't find such a doctor, you can do what I did next.

I began to educate myself. I sought out people who were in shape, as far as I could tell, and I observed their eating and exercise patterns. I looked for books on overweight, nutrition, and fitness. I began to learn how food works, what calories really are, and how exercise benefits the human body.

I decided to join a health club. I wanted a place I had to go to at regular times. I knew that writing an appointment on my calendar would help me stick to my exercise program. So every Monday, Wednesday, and Friday I exercised at the club from noon to 1:30.

It was not easy. My first days in the club were pure torture. Fortunately, I was supported in prayer and educated by a Christian instructor who worked there. He encouraged me and showed me how the various machines worked to get me into shape and help me lose weight. Slowly the experience of exercising on a circuit of twelve machines became easier for me to handle. In five months, I lost eighteen pounds, in spite of the fact that I had continued to eat normally—which for me meant improperly.

After the Christmas season was over, I knew I also had to attack my eating habits. Only then could I really lose weight and get into shape. I had read carefully about dieting and knew its risks and its rewards. The main risks are two: First, many dieters do not eat a balanced diet, and their bodies do not get the nourishment they need. A good diet will include grains, vegetables and fruits, meats, and dairy products. It will be based on a set of meal plans that are easy to follow and to prepare. Second, more than 80 percent of those who go on diets regain all the weight they lose, and often a few pounds more.

As I dieted, I prayed for spiritual strength to overcome very basic temptations. Christians are great at labeling sinful things like fornication, covetousness, pornography, drunkenness, and smoking. But Christians sure do eat! Potluck suppers are paradise to an overweight person.

I had to think of ways to control my appetite for food, especially for sweets. Food had been a source of warm feeling for me. It stood for love and satisfaction. It is a way human beings get together in warm and caring ways. Jesus himself broke bread with his disciples. He didn't leave them a diet.

For a time I limited my dinner engagements and always packed a lunch. I began seeing people at times of day other than mealtimes. Some individuals were very considerate and invited me to their homes, assuring me that they would prepare whatever I needed for my diet. In fact, a number of people in my church were praying for me, and some went on diets themselves. By the time the entire exercise was finished, we as a church body had lost more than seven hundred pounds!

I began to see results from dieting and exercise put together. I added running to my schedule on the days I did not go to the health club. Slowly and gradually, I built up my distance and my speed. I did not expect immediate results. It had taken years to get out of shape, and I knew I would not get into shape right away.

For me, the key element in achieving fitness was to set goals I truly believed I could achieve. Although I needed to lose sixty-five pounds, I decided first to lose thirty pounds in six months. Then I would think about the remainder. Likewise, when I decided to take up running, I knew I was no marathoner. But I could engage in strenuous exercise for one-half hour three times a week. By working on manageable goals over a period of time, I gradually achieved a weight and a level of fitness that at first seemed out of reach.

By the time I finished my six months of diet and exercise, I had attained my first goal. I had come to enjoy my visits to the club and my runs through the community, however, so I continued my exercise program. I had never felt better in my life.

I also began to eat more normally, but not in the way I had once eaten. No longer did I feel I had to finish my plate, and I certainly did not feel I had to fill it to the brim. I actually enjoyed meals without bread and butter and salt. I enjoyed fruit more than cake and cookies and ice cream. I preferred diet soft drinks to their high-calorie, high-sugar equivalents.

By eating sensibly and exercising regularly, I continued to lose weight. I bottomed out at 158 pounds simply by continuing my new, normal, physically disciplined life. I found I was more effective on the job because I had more energy to devote to it than before. My prayer time was more fruitful because I had the power to concentrate. I used my time more effectively.

In short, my entire life became more focused and disciplined because I devoted attention to developing good exercise and eating habits. Because the body, mind, and spirit all interact, discipline in one area can lead to increased discipline and enjoyment in another area.

One exciting result of my physical discipline was entering my first road race, a ten-kilometer run in my community. I was not competing against anyone else, only against myself and my past desire to lie down whenever I got the urge to exercise. For me, victory would be to complete the race, to give it my best for the Lord.

Day in and day out I ran, slowly increasing my endurance and speed. I traced the course and became familiar with the landmarks. I envisioned crowds alongside the road chanting, "Go for it, Throop! You can do it!" The day of the race came, and I ran with nearly two thousand other men and women in varying degrees of fitness. I managed to finish in the top half of the contenders, with a time of forty-four minutes. That's an average of a seven-minute mile—not bad for someone whose only contest, before that date, was in ice cream consumption timed trials. I knew that my victory—finishing the race—was the fruit of my disciplined life.

I now compete in road races to better what I have done. I also continue the disciplines of my spiritual life in the Lord Jesus Christ as I come to maturity in him. I have grown fit and strong in my physical life as well as in my spiritual life. In fact, I generally do not distinguish between the two; they are so closely interrelated.

God designed the human body to be fit. Our spiritual discipline is incomplete unless we bring our physical frame into accord with the Master Architect's design. With the power of God through the Holy Spirit, we can pursue a discipline that leads to fitness. And with God's grace, we can stay fit as long as we live.

Learning in the Valley

EVELYN CHRISTENSON

On the one hand, our physical health is not connected to our spiritual health. Healthy people and handicapped people alike are glowing, radiant Christians.

But on the other hand, I do my best learning in the valley, not on the mountaintop. I had two miscarriages and one stillborn baby, and I could not understand why God had allowed it to happen. My husband and I were attending a Christian college. We were doing everything we were supposed to do, yet I was losing baby after baby after baby. I was heartbroken.

But God led me to Romans 8:28, which has become my philosophy: "We know that in all things God works for the good of those who love him." From God's perspective, the physical problems in my life were not meaningless. God worked out my suffering, my pain, and my losses for my good. Through the hard times, I was drawn closer to God.

For Paul, there were both negative and positive reasons why God allowed him physical suffering. The negative reason was that Paul was proud. His ministry would have been jeopardized if God had not counterbalanced his pride with pain. God used pain to keep Paul. The positive reason was that through his suffering, Paul could know God's grace and Christ's power. He could know these things in spite of having a thorn in the flesh, and God chose never to remove it (2 Corinthians 12:7-10).

Suffering can be redemptive, and so God allows us to have physical problems. When we are sick, we have time to spend with God. When we are in sorrow, we turn to God. For example, Jesus allowed sorrow in Martha's life (John 11:17-27). He didn't have Martha's undivided attention when she was cooking for him. But he did at the death of her brother. God uses infirmities and other kinds of suffering to draw us to himself. It gives us time to listen to him.

Should we then ask for pain because good things come from it? No, but we should let God work out the little problems in our lives so we can learn how he works and how he fulfills needs. When pain comes, as it inevitably will, we will be prepared. We will be able to handle the suffering with God.

When I visited Japan, a missionary introduced me to a young Christian woman with cerebral palsy. She sat on the steps of her house and turned the pages of a book with her toes. That is all she could do, but she was content in Christ.

Then the missionary took me to see the man who had led this woman to Christ. I was not prepared for what I saw.

When we arrived at his house, his mother answered the door with a lump of a man in her arms. He was forty-five years old, and every day since he had been born, she had spent six hours a day dropping food from an eye dropper into his mouth. He could communicate only by grunting and pointing one clawlike hand at a signing board with Japanese characters on it. By pointing to those characters, he indicated what he wanted to say, and his mother wrote it down.

In spite of his massive handicaps, this man was doing God's work. He published a newspaper for handicapped people in Japan, and God used that man to bring many people to Christ. Although people repeatedly prayed for him to be healed, God didn't heal him. But God used him.

Pain and suffering will come to all of us sooner or later. We are not exempt from them because we love God. But in our pain and suffering, God still uses us and draws us closer to him.

◆ GOLD IN THE MAKING / JOHN B. PEARRELL

In his book *Gold in the Making,* Ron Lee Davis tells the story of Don. One day Don noticed that he had a growth on his left ear. It turned out to be cancer. Don was very concerned over this and started to study his Bible, particularly Romans 8:28. As he studied this passage he came to realize that if he made himself available to God, God would accomplish his good, regardless of whether it felt good or not. Dr. Davis goes on to say: "Then Don knelt and prayed, 'Lord Jesus, I know you are the Great Physician, and I know you can heal me of this tumor.' Most of us would stop there, but Don went on praying, 'But, Lord, if you can get more good out of my life—more of your good—by allowing me to have cancer, then I would like to keep the cancer.'" Don kept the cancer, but during his hospital stay he won his roommate to Christ. Today that roommate is a missionary in South America. He led a nurse's aide to Christ. Today she ministers not only to people's physical needs, but their spiritual needs as well. He also led a man who is one of America's most influential businessmen to Christ. And all because Don was willing to let God work through him, no matter what the cost to [Don] might be. Dr. Davis concludes: "Everything in life can be used for God's good, *if*—if we are available, if we are willing to demonstrate a kind of maturity and character that the world does not understand, if we are willing to be conformed to the image of Christ."

Why Pain?

✍ DAVE VEERMAN

When I awoke at 3:00 A.M., my lower back was throbbing. I didn't know what was happening, but something was wrong. And the pain wouldn't subside. Regardless of body position or contortion, it continued unabated. A kidney stone—a tiny mineral deposit moving slowly through my system—had rendered me helpless.

It may be personal pain or pain observed—Grandpa's heart attack, a seven-year-old struggling against cancer, earthquake victims in a foreign country—that makes us ask why. People suffer, and questions assail our private and public thoughts: How can God allow such suffering? Is God really good?

These are valid concerns, far too important to be answered in depth in a short article. There are, however, some principles to keep in mind when we are beginning to think through and formulate a biblical response to the question of pain.

First, we must understand that pain can be good. Do you remember how your muscles felt two days after the touch football game in the park, or after your first session of working out? They hurt, but you felt good about getting in shape. The pain, even when you could hardly lift your legs, was a positive sign of muscle development. Maybe that's why locker rooms display the cliche "No pain, no gain!"

God has given us pain as a warning system. When we eat poorly, our stomachs tell us. When we twist an ankle, we stop quickly and avoid additional damage to tendons and ligaments because we feel the problem. Even my intense pain from the kidney stone was a message that something was not right inside me and that I should do something about it. I hasten to add, pain is very effective in getting our attention. Most of us want to avoid pain, and so we quickly adjust our behavior. A life without any pain would lead to disaster as we unknowingly destroyed our bodies through everyday wear and tear.

Our second principle is that pain is a part of our mortality. The fact is, no one lives forever. As finite human beings, we have built-in obsolescence—we are falling apart. Most of us live (and drive) as though pain and suffering were unusual. In reality, "one out of every one" of us dies. Pain is part of the mortality package; it is when good things happen to us that we should say, Why me? This, of course, does not trivialize suffering and death. Human persons are special creations of God, and we should work to alleviate suffering worldwide.

The third principle to remember is that pain can teach us valuable lessons. In other words, God may be allowing you to experience suffering to tell you something about him or about yourself or to cause you to change your behavior. Romans 8:28 promises that God can and will weave together for good everything that happens to us, but this doesn't mean life will be pain free. Often God will use pain to bring the good.

And remember, Jesus promised his disciples that their lives would be filled with persecutions, trials, and sorrows (John 16:31-33). Soon after he told them this, he was crucified. In the midst of suffering, therefore, we should be asking, What can I learn from this? See James 1:2-4 and Philippians 4:11-13 about the importance of our attitude toward suffering.

A warning is in order: Never tell others what God must be teaching them through their problems. See the book of Job for an example of well-meaning but very wrong and unhelpful friends who did just that.

The final principle is this: Our lives on earth are not the whole story. Eternity is infinitely longer than the longest life here, and how we spend it is infinitely more important than the quality of our lives on earth. God promises us that the mortal will be clothed with immortality (1 Corinthians 15:53-57), that our sufferings are for "a little while" (1 Peter 5:8-11), and that he has "overcome the world" (John 16:33). Eventually all suffering will end, death will be destroyed, evil and sin will be punished, and God's perfect love and justice will reign. This is the Christian's hope!

Yes, pain is difficult to endure or to observe. We often wonder how God could allow such suffering. It is good to ask such questions, but we will never know the complete answer until we can ask him face to face in heaven. In the meantime we must continue to pray that he will turn sorrow to joy, and to depend on his goodness and perfect plan for our lives.

♦ REST IN THE JOY OF THE LORD
JOHN B. PEARRELL

Alan Redpath once wrote, "There is nothing—no circumstance, no trouble, no testing—that can touch me until first of all it has gone past Christ, right through to me. If it has come that far, it has come with a great purpose, which I may not understand at the moment. But as I refuse to become panicky, as I lift up my eyes to him and accept it as coming from the throne of God for some great purpose of blessing to my own heart, no sorrow will ever disturb me, no trial will ever disarm me, no circumstance will cause me to fret, for I shall rest in the joy of what my Lord is."

RELATED ARTICLES

Chapter 2: **Discouragement: The Pain of Growth**
Chapter 3: **Finding God at Death's Door**

CHAPTER

14

Life in the Church

- ✓ Do Christians really have to go to church?
- ✓ How do I choose the right church?
- ✓ What if church is boring?
- ✓ What should church really be like?
- ✓ Dealing with hypocrites in the church
- ✓ What if a church doesn't meet my needs?

The Church's Role in Spiritual Growth

✍ RICHARD LOVELACE

Many people come to Christ through evangelism task forces or special outreach groups. But once they become Christians, they need a local congregation to nurture them. The outreach groups are like small boats that can get close enough to impale a whale with a harpoon. But the boats can't process the whales; it takes a large ship with the proper equipment to do that. Just as the small boats must always return to the larger ship, so evangelism taskforces must always come back to the church and its spiritual resources.

Individuals who lead others to Christ also need a home base to shelter and nurture them. Although we come to Christ as individuals, we grow as members of one body. Without a nest of nurture, we are vulnerable to attack by the enemy. We saw this during the Jesus Movement in the seventies. We could reach hippies through street ministry, but once they became Christians they had to be integrated into congregations to remain in their new faith.

The church plays four specific roles in a Christian's spiritual growth:

1. *Worship.* We are designed by God to grow in fellowship with other believers. God draws us together like living stones to form a house in which he delights to dwell (1 Peter 2:5). In Ephesians, Paul said we are members of God's household and become a holy temple. As we are joined together, we make a dwelling "in which God lives by his Spirit" (Ephesians 2:19-22). When we gather with other Christians for worship, our horizons are broadened and we are strengthened.

2. *Nurture.* A congregation supplies spiritual nutrients and vitamins that can only be present in a larger group. The church is the Grand Central Station where gifts are shared, comfort is exchanged, exhortation is given. We are not spiritual deep-sea divers, each with his or her own oxygen line up to God. God has designed us to share with and mutually encourage other Christians. The Bible can rescue a discouraged Christian only if he reads it, but another Christian can seek him out no matter where he is.

The church's task is to find the spiritual gifts of each church member so that every individual knows the grace he has to give to others. Unfortunately, many clergy and laity operate as if spiritual gifts are only found in full-time Christian workers. Each congregation must seek the full release and development of every member's spiritual gifts to receive God's blessings.

3. *Instruction.* When we are by ourselves it is easy to go off on a tangent. In a larger group we can hold one another accountable and share our wisdom. "As iron sharpens iron, so one man sharpens another," we read in Proverbs 27:17.

We are like pieces of coal that lose energy when taken out of the fire. To keep burning, we need other Christians. Meeting this need does not come naturally to us; our culture fosters an unhealthy individualism. But abiding in Christ means staying in touch with other parts of his body. When we fellowship with other Christians, we draw strength from them, and our lives are enriched by their spiritual gifts.

4. *Service.* In a congregation, we can pool our resources and talents to reach others for Christ. We can link up with other Christians who share a similar ministry whether it is to international students, teenagers, homeless people, or world missions. For example, caring for twenty international students would be an impossible task for one person, but a group of people from one church can easily work together to plan and carry out activities.

Spiritual growth does not occur without these elements. We are not nurtured simply by aiming at growth in a self-centered way. We become spiritually strengthened as much by our contribution to the body of Christ as we do in deliberately feeding upon spiritual nutrients.

Why Go to Church?

HOWARD SNYDER

Going to church isn't just going to a service in a building. We're really talking about what it means to be the people of God, the body of Christ, the community of God's people.

If I'm a Christian, the most important reality in my life is my relationship to Jesus Christ. The Bible teaches that if I'm joined to the head, Jesus Christ, then I'm also joined to his body, the Church. I need to view church attendance in the light of what it means to be a member of Christ's body. It's not just a matter of participating on Sunday morning; it's a matter of being a certain kind of person.

With that in mind, I suggest seven reasons we should be involved in the life of the Christian community:

1. *God has made us, through Jesus Christ, part of a people.* In saving us, he has made us a part of a new social reality—the Church on earth. As Chrisitans we are members of one another (Romans 12:5). That means we need to be with one another, with our brothers and sisters in Christ. Worship is one way we build the unity of God's new people.

2. *Worship sets us on the right path.* It sets our compass. As we worship with our brothers and sisters in Christ, we catch a view of reality from God's perspective. As we go through the week the world tends to cloud our senses, to close in around us like heavy curtains. We are tempted to see things from only a physical, human, space-time perspective. In worship the curtains are thrown back and we see the real picture. We see things from God's perspective, and our lives are redirected. We say, "Oh, yes, this is what is important. These are the priorities that must guide my life."

3. *Participation in the body of Christ is a means of growth and a means of ministry.* We are not going to be vital, growing believers unless we are in close contact with our brothers and sisters in Christ. Neither will we have an effective ministry, because God uses our involvement with other Christians to teach us how to minister. The New Testament describes the church as a community where a whole range of spiritual gifts is exercised to the praise of God and for the good of all (see Romans 12:4-8; 1 Corinthians 12–14). Worship is a place for using our various spiritual gifts, thus learning to both give and receive. People are attracted to worship when they see evidence of the Spirit's working in the whole body of believers.

4. *God has commanded us to be part of the Christian community.* I think of the various Old Testament festivals and commemorations and special covenant occasions, whether daily or weekly or at certain times during the year.

God said, in effect, "You are my people, and you are to come before me and present yourself and worship me" (see Leviticus 23). We live all our lives under God's authority, and we obey him because of who he is and who we are. We know that in obeying him we will find fullness of life.

5. *Worship is our offering to God and to one another.* Someone may say, "I think I'll stop going to church because I'm not getting much out of it." These words already betray a problem. If we are growing Christians, we participate in worship not just for what we can get but also for what we can give. Many Christians need a radical reorientation in their thinking at this point.

We should worship first of all to offer praise to God, a sacrifice of thanksgiving (Leviticus 7:12). The most important offering we give to God is the sacrifice of our lives in praise, worship, and adoration. We should participate in worship with the attitude of giving ourselves—our gifts and our lives—to God. It is precisely when we go with an attitude of giving that God speaks to us and we receive and are fed. As St. Francis said, "It is in giving that we receive." So when a person says, "I didn't get anything out of it," he may be saying, "I didn't put anything into it."

Our giving in worship is directed not only to God but also to one another. Speaking of the generosity of the Macedonian churches, Paul said, "They gave themselves first to the Lord and then to us in keeping with God's will" (2 Corinthians 8:5). Part of our worship is to "carry each other's burdens" (Galatians 6:2), to "encourage one another" (Hebrews 3:13; 10:25), to "honor one another" (Romans 12:10), to "submit to one another" (Ephesians 5:21). A whole significant stratum of biblical truth clusters around the "one another" passages in the New Testament. God calls us to give ourselves to one another.

6. *Being involved with the life of the church counteracts our self-centered individualism.* In this individualistic age, everything centers around "I" and "me." This attitude is often more pervasive in the church than we realize. It is very easy for me to interpret the whole Christian faith in terms of myself—my own needs, my own growth, and so on. Vital, authentic worship counteracts our tendency to see things only in terms of how they affect our own lives.

That's why it doesn't make sense for a person to say, "I don't like being with all those people; I can worship God just as well by myself, out under the trees." As a matter of fact, that's not true. We can't worship God just as well by ourselves as we can with one another. It's not an either/or situation; obviously private and public worship enrich each other. Spiritual disciplines by ourselves will enrich our shared life, and vice versa. We need both forms of worship. But only in being together will we really come to understand the practical meaning of the biblical passages that talk about submitting to one another and being accountable to one another.

It's one thing to affirm shared life in theory, to have this ideal and say we believe in honoring and submitting to and encouraging one another. This doesn't become real, however, until we are actually spending time with one another. Participating in community means taking up the cross and becoming like Jesus Christ. It means learning how to confront and be confronted.

7. *In our involvement with the life of the Christian community we participate in the three main functions of worship: celebration, instruction, and repentance.* We celebrate together with our brothers and sisters in the worshiping community. We are instructed as God speaks to us through his Word. We recognize our needs and we repent.

Worship is celebration. God has acted in history—down through the centuries of biblical history, during the ages of the church, and in our own believing community. In worship we celebrate who God is and how he brought redemption to earth through Jesus Christ. We celebrate the work of the Spirit in making us his people on earth.

In worship, God speaks to us through his Word. He instructs us in the way we should go. We hear God's Word read, preached, and presented in song, testimony, and perhaps drama. The Spirit speaks through the Word. In worship, we hear God's Word and respond according to what God says to us. Often this response is praise and celebration. But at other times, the appropriate response is repentance. Like Isaiah, who saw the Lord (Isaiah 6), we see our own uncleanness and repent, offering ourselves to God for his cleansing and commissioning. Worship thus involves for us the elements of celebration, instruction, and repentance.

One of the most profound truths in Scripture is that Christians really do belong to one another. What happens to one affects all. What is God doing through the church? He is making us into a believing, witnessing, reconciling community so that through the Church, Christ's body on earth, he may continue the work begun by Jesus Christ.

As this happens, said Paul, we will "all reach unity in the faith and in the knowledge of the Son of God and become mature, attaining to the whole measure of the fullness of Christ" (Ephesians 4:13). Worship is one of the most important ways we grow in Jesus Christ.

♦ GIVING THANKS FOR FELLOWSHIP
DIETRICH BONHOEFFER

If we do not give thanks daily for the Christian fellowship in which we have been placed, even where there is no great experience, no discoverable riches, but much weakness, small faith, and difficulty; if on the contrary, we only keep complaining to God that everything is so paltry and petty, so far from what we expected, then we hinder God from letting our fellowship grow according to the measure and riches which are there for us all in Jesus Christ.

(Dietrich Bonhoeffer, *Life Together* [New York: Harper and Row, 1954], 29.)

How Do I Choose the Right Church?

JILL AND STUART BRISCOE

As soon as I think of choosing the right church, I'm reminded of one simple truth: Because churches are made up exclusively of sinners, there is no such thing as the perfect church. Now I could find the right church for me to be in, and that is what I should look for. But I have to be very careful not to confuse the right church with the perfect church, because if I do so, I'm only going to get disappointed sooner or later.

Churches differ widely and, assuming you have the luxury of choice, you need to choose carefully. But as you decide, you must answer this question: Am I looking for a church that will meet my needs, or am I looking for a church in which I could have a ministry? Ideally, it ought to be both. It ought to be a church in which you're going to be ministered to, but in which you will have the opportunity to minister as well.

As you look at different churches, you need to recognize the reasons various denominations exist. Here are some areas of difference from one church to another:

1. *Churches differ in their view of church government.* The names of the churches give you a clue to this: Episcopal churches, for instance, have a strong emphasis on the episcopate, or the office of bishop. These churches have a central, hierarchical form of government. Catholic, Orthodox, Episcopal, and Methodist churches are all episcopal in this sense. Presbyterians are strongly committed to the presbytery, or government by a group of elders who meet in synods to discuss issues of importance to the whole church body. Presbyterians and Reformed churches follow this pattern. Congregational churches believe each congregation should be self-governing. Many Baptist and Bible churches, as well as the United Church of Christ, are congregational. If you have strong feelings about a right or wrong ecclesiastical structure (form of church government), that would become a factor in your choice.

2. *Churches also differ in their understanding of the sacraments—baptism and Communion.* Different denominations explain the meaning of the sacraments differently. They also administer the sacraments differently. For example, some churches have Communion every week, and some have it four times a year. In some churches, worshipers come forward to receive Communion; in others, the bread and wine are passed down the rows. Some churches baptize infants; others baptize older children or adults. Some churches baptize by immersion; others by pouring or sprinkling. If you have specific views on baptism and Communion, you will need to identify with a church where you will be in agreement.

3. *Churches differ in their attitude toward Scripture.* Some churches have a very high view of Scripture: They believe it is divinely inspired and is the final authority in matters of faith and practice. Other churches have a less literal approach to Scripture and may refer to the Bible less often. If you have a high view of Scripture, if you feel you need a steady diet of good scriptural teaching,

then clearly you're going to look for a church where this is available—both in the pulpit ministry and in the educational ministries of the church.

4. *Churches vary in worship styles.* Some churches are formal and liturgical. They concentrate on the sense of awe and reverence in coming into God's presence, and they have a keen sense of the aesthetics of worship. At the other end of the spectrum are the very relaxed places of worship where the music is more contemporary and the whole congregation is invited to participate in a very free way. Tastes in worship styles vary, and that is an important factor to consider.

5. *Churches vary in their attitudes toward ministry.* Some people feel very strongly that there are two groups of people in the church—the laity and the clergy—and that the clergy are invested with special privileges and abilities to minister, while the lay people are not. Other churches feel just as strongly that believers have an equal share in ministry, and they seek to encourage believers to engage in all kinds of ministry. Still other churches feel that the clergy has one type of ministry and the laity has another type—but both are vital. You need to decide which way you're going to go.

Another factor you may want to consider is the church's position about women. Some churches hold a doctrinal position that requires women to take a very low profile. If you're looking for a church with more activities for women, or if you, as a woman, have a spiritual gift that you would really like to exercise in the context of the church, that would be a factor in your choice.

In addition to these denominational differences, different churches emphasize different things on the congregational level as well. Clearly there are many activities that go into church life. For instance, some churches are strong in teaching, some are strong in personal discipleship, some are strong in music, some are strong in evangelism, some are strong in social concerns. If you have any leanings or interests in any of these areas, then you will want to identify with a church that is involved in that area.

It is also important to recognize that some churches will meet specific needs better than others. If you have young children, you might be concerned that there be a vital children's ministry; if you have teenagers, you'll be looking for a church where they really know how to handle that age level. For that matter, if someone in your family is handicapped, you may look for a church with ramps or a ministry to the handicapped.

If possible, attend a church close to your home. If you want to have any kind of evangelistic impact on your neighbors, it helps to have a nearby church to integrate them into.

Whatever else you do, give up looking for the perfect church. Look for a church that, in addition to meeting your needs, will give you an opportunity to serve and will help equip you to do it.

♦ CHURCH SHOPPING / STUART BRISCOE

Jill and I come from England where, if you find a church that's half-way decent, you get so excited that it never occurs to you to shop around. In the United States, you have far more options, so you can afford to be a little more choosy.

Church shopping seems inevitable in the United States, because this is a consumer-oriented society. But there is a real problem with this attitude. We have the mentality that we, the customers, are always right, and we really expect to find exactly what we want. If we don't, we are dissatisfied; instead of staying and making our church better, we leave on a quest for a church that will meet our needs. Churches begin competing for their share in the market, and some churchgoers never settle down.

Still, church shopping is not all bad. In many ways having a variety of churches available is certainly better than having nothing to choose from. But as you "shop," grow past thinking only of having your own needs met. It is perfectly legitimate to want to be ministered to and to be nurtured, but to be purely concerned about your own needs is immature. Babies need constant attention; adults know how to minister to other people's needs.

As you search for a church, look for one where you can minister as well as be ministered to, one where you can be trained to meet others' needs.

What Should Church Be Like?

✍ HOWARD SNYDER

When we talk about church, we're not talking just about our cultural understanding of the word—a building and a program. There is a wide gap between the popular Christian understanding of what the church is and the biblical understanding of the word. The New Testament word for church, *ecclesia,* means "to be called out" or "to call together" a certain kind of people to be a fellowship. In the New Testament, church is not associated with a building or with a lot of organizational structure. It's associated with people.

To determine what a church should be like, it is good to look for principles and patterns in the New Testament. There we find that the life of the Christian church was organized around three basic functions: worship, community, and witness. There are many things we do in the life of the church—prayer, Bible study, education—but all these activities fit together under the three basic functions.

These three functions are organized around the vital center of the glory of God. "So whether you eat or drink or whatever you do, do it all for the glory of God" (1 Corinthians 10:31). We are to be the people of God who live "to the praise of his glorious grace" (Ephesians 1:6). We do that through worship, community, and witness.

Having this kind of involvement in the life of the church should do three things for us. It should help us to "worship in spirit and in truth" (John 4:23, 24). It should help build us up into a responsible community where we really care for and equip one another. It should provide ministry opportunities, equipping and guiding others.

If our involvement in the church does not stimulate these things, if it does not "spur one another on toward love and good deeds" (Hebrews 10:24), if being involved in a Christian community is just a matter of our receiving but does not equip us to minister in an area that is uniquely ours, related to our own particular gifts and personalities, then the church has not really become the church in the biblical sense that God intends. Now all of us fall short in this area to some degree, but we should be striving for the kind of vital Christian community where we are worshiping, where we are being built up in the community, and where we are equipping one another for the ministry of all believers.

The Bible says we are all priests before God (Revelation 1:6; 5:10). It doesn't distinguish between those who are ministers and those who are not. The church should be a community that is in the process, by the ministry of the Holy Spirit, of equipping every believer to be in the ministry of the gospel of Jesus Christ, so that all things are done "to prepare God's people for works of service, so that the body of Christ may be built up" (Ephesians 4:12).

♦ BEFORE YOU JOIN THAT IMPERFECT CHURCH / BETSY ROSSEN ELLIOT

1. Make sure that the church offers ways to grow, to be fed, and to worship. Are there small-group Bible studies or prayer groups? Are there signs that the Lord has been using these kinds of groups—or other activities—to encourage individual response to him?

2. Meet with the pastors. What is their attitude toward Scripture, their view of lay ministry? Can you support their work, allowing for a range of opinions on questions of doctrine or practice? Can you admit that you have not uncovered all the mysteries of God, that you have areas in which to grow and things to learn?

3. Examine the denominational statements—creeds and confessions—for the historical perspective you'll need to decide for or against joining. Read up on the history of the denomination and the local church.

4. Look at your motives. Do you want to become one of the pilgrims in this church, or do you want to make a little foray in order to pass judgment? The Son of God became one of us; he didn't drop in for an occasional visit and complain about how much he missed the pearly gates.

When Church Is Boring

✍ DAVE VEERMAN

It's Sunday—time to get up, get organized, and trek to church. With half-mast eyelids and yawning mouths, the family circles the table for breakfast. Then the youngest one says, with just a touch of whine in her voice, "Do we have to go to church? It's so bo-o-o-ring."

Mom and Dad explain that church is necessary, that there will be no debate, and that everyone should hurry. Secretly, however, they agree with their youngest: "It's so bo-o-o-ring."

Can you identify with the scenario? You know you ought to be in church, but what can you do when church is boring and you aren't getting anything out of it?

Before we analyze church, it's important to take a close look at us. Unfortunately, our attitudes often reflect those of our culture, and our society says that life is supposed to be filled with fun, excitement, and entertainment. We ask our children after almost any activity, "Did you have a good time?" I remember visiting a church and hearing my daughter, who was then three, offer her evaluation of Sunday school. "I had fun, Daddy," she said, knowing that "fun" was my measure of quality.

We often approach worship with the same attitude, giving the cultural, self-centered message, "Entertain me. Give me a good show. Above all else, don't bore me!" But where in the Bible does it say that worship is supposed to be entertaining? We should check it out. Perhaps our problem with boredom is cultural.

Often our evaluations of church services betray another misconception. We say, "I don't get anything out of it." That sounds like a valid indictment, until we realize that Scripture never tells us to get anything out of it. Instead, we are supposed to put something into it. Worship should be the time for us to give praise and prayers to God. It is a time for sharing our Christian experience and insight with fellow believers. Again, our criticism is self-centered, as though the church service were supposed to revolve around us.

Then there is the question of how we approach the service itself. Do we prepare for worship? Many of us rush into the service, out of breath, brushing our windblown hair, squeezing past those who were on time. Then we anxiously watch the clock, worried about burning dinner in the oven or missing the opening kickoff. If we have that kind of attitude, it's hard for anyone to get through to us with God's message.

For a change, take time to carefully prepare for worship. Get up early and spend time as a family—or individually—committing the day to God and confessing all known sin. Then arrive at church early and sit quietly in the pew, asking God to speak to and through you that day. These few extra moments of reflection, confession, and communion can make all the difference.

You can take other steps as well. I remember sitting in the back and critiquing the service, especially the choir. Then a thought hit me: I can sing. Why don't I join the choir and be part of the solution! When you take an active role, whether as a member of the choir or as an usher or greeter, you will find your attitude changing. Instead of being an observer, you are a participant.

Another way to get involved is to outline the sermon. Later, compare your outline with someone else's (your spouse's, for example). When the pastor makes a point, get into the habit of asking, "What does that mean for me? How can I apply it to my life?"

Discipline yourself to pray during the service. Instead of letting your mind wander during the pastoral prayer, listen to what the pastor is saying and add your own silent petitions.

It can also be helpful to find a small group within the church with whom you can learn, share your feelings, and gain support. Church is more than one hour once a week. It includes many other teaching and fellowship opportunities, and you need to be involved with some of these. You will find that your involvement with the full life of the church will take some of the pressure off that one Sunday-morning service.

I am not saying that there never comes a time when a person should change churches, but the decision should be based primarily on doctrine, not on style. No church is perfect, and if you leave for the wrong reasons—especially if you leave because your needs are not being met—you will soon be dissatisfied at the new church too.

Church should be the joyous reunion of the family of God, a celebration of what Christ has done in our lives, a place where people love each other, and an opportunity to learn from God's Word. Take church seriously, and avoid those "It's-time-to-go-to-boring-church" blues.

Being an Evangelical in a Not-So-Evangelical Church

BETSY ROSSEN ELLIOT

Maybe God forgot to wind his watch.

His timing seemed a little off, according to my plans for my church. When were we going to get serious about evangelism? When would the sermons be more than nice thoughts? When could I stop feeling guilty for not working at the Christmas bazaar?

Such were my ponderings a few years ago when I started attending a mainline, not particularly evangelical church. I went to St. Thomas's with a thirst to worship, and it was quenched. But with me were people with other thirsts—some of which I shared, some of which I didn't. I often felt uncomfortable. I did not like the cavalier attitude some church members showed toward the Bible and personal spiritual experience. At the same time, they did not always appreciate my efforts to reform them.

My years at St. Thomas's included pain and rejection as well as growth in understanding and fellowship. Through my experiences in this church that included only a few evangelicals among its members, I became convinced that the church is more than any one individual, clergy member, special interest group, or philosophy. I saw that God works in mainline churches as well as in the more conservative churches I had known before. And I learned some important principles. Perhaps the most important thing I learned was that I had a lot to learn. Here are some things that I—and others in mainline churches—have found helpful:

- Pray for your church and all its leaders, clergy and laypeople, at the local and national levels. Do this regularly with others.
- Offer genuine encouragement to your clergy and leaders. For example, a friend of mine made a point of writing a brief thank-you note to her pastor after sermons that she found especially helpful or challenging.
- Make sure you are getting enough support and spiritual feeding, within or outside your church. You may wish to get in touch with renewal groups in your denomination.
- Emphasize the touchstones of your faith with fellow churchgoers—the Bible, hymns you have in common, documents that belong to the whole Christian church.
- Use existing church programs to share and serve—small groups, adult classes, women's groups, the church library, Marriage Encounter—as well as introducing new ideas.
- Treat all church members as if they know the Lord. Keeping a spiritual tally of "us" versus "them" presumes more than you can know, and can only be divisive.
- Start a Bible study group or adult class if none exists already.
- Invite your clergyman or clergywoman to hear an evangelical speaker or to an evangelical conference. Lend him or her books you have found helpful.
- Go through the proper channels with suggestions or ideas.
- If you inadvertently become part of a disagreement, play the role of peacemaker. Do what you can to put disagreeing parties in touch with each other.

Here are also a few things to avoid:

- Be aware of evangelical buzz words that may be misunderstood (evangelism, testimony, born again, Spirit-filled) and phrases that may seem judgmental.
- Don't be shocked when the evangelical superstars aren't even known, much less revered, when you drop their names at coffee hour.
- Don't disdain "hand work"—pulling weeds, working at the rummage sale, cleaning up after a potluck supper. You don't want to communicate that you're above such tasks or unwilling to pitch in.
- Don't pursue up-front, high-visibility roles too quickly. It's easy to be misunderstood.
- Avoid renewal programs that sidestep the clergy and thereby encourage an underground effort for change in your church.
- Above all, don't let a critical spirit get a toehold in your life. If you're not in a church to worship and serve, and if you're not more open to being changed than to change others, then leave.

There is a tremendous variety of spirituality in the mainline denominations. Without question, you will find practices and teachings with which you disagree. But you may also find richness in worship, warmth in fellowship, and fulfillment in service.

In Jesus' practice I find an example. He was obedient to the Jewish traditions, vowing that he did not come to destroy them. But he also did the unexpected—teaching the elders when he was only twelve years old and healing on the Sabbath. He called for new wineskins and instilled new meaning into old ways.

We need his holy boldness. We also need patience to follow his timing and the means that he uses. God's watch has not stopped; he will build his Church.

Dealing with Hypocrites in the Church

TOM MINNERY

The oddest part was that I could sense it coming without thinking about it. I would begin to feel grumpy, but it always took a moment before I remembered why. Deb and I found that if we spoke about it late at night, neither of us would sleep. Finally we made a decision: we didn't discuss it after 9:00 P.M. But try as we might to push it away, Sunday morning always came, and with it—The Problem.

I was lay leader of a congregation, once close and loving, now cracking apart. Sunday mornings were the hardest part of it. That lady over there, who looks so sweet? That folded paper in her Bible is a petition to get the pastor fired. She spent all last week circulating it, and she brought it along this morning to catch anybody she missed. That man shaking hands near the door? If truth were told, he would rather be throwing punches, he's so doubled over with spite.

Ah, yes. Sunday morning with a church full of Christians. The hatred was heavier than the study Bibles we carried. Here we were in the house of the Lord, a group of Christians who had been inflicting misery on one another all week, smothering it over just long enough to pray and sing together at one more eleven o'clock service. I suppose there's never been hypocrisy in purer form.

The poisons in that spiritual body festered and flared. The petition finally failed, and the pastor, though deeply wounded, stayed on; but the congregation split and then split again. The lasting tragedy is that several couples with newly blooming faith haven't been back to a church—any church—since.

Deb and I lasted as long as we could, until the turmoil began eating at our own spiritual vitals. Finally, turning away from our heavy involvements and our friends, we left that church. Since we made that hard decision I have done a lot of reflecting about hypocrisy in the church, and I've come to two conclusions about it.

First, hypocrisy, like beauty, is in the eye of the beholder. It is not a quality like redheadedness or measles, things easily seen and identified. It is, rather, a judgment call, and the judgment varies greatly with an individual's point of view. After all, no one sets out to achieve hypocrisy, and no one identifies it in himself even when others think he has clearly attained it.

Take, for example, the lady dressed in her best Sunday smile with that devastating petition in her Bible. Someone might justifiably point out to her that it is hypocritical to worship under the pastor's direction, pray under his leading, and sit under his teaching—while trying to get him removed from the ministry.

But I know this lady very well, and she doesn't think she's any more a hypocrite for trying to remove the pastor than I think I'm a hypocrite for trying to defend him. She sees only the hurt and confusion on the faces of those in the congregation—some of whom are her dearest friends—who have not been able to adjust to this pastor's new ways, and the only solution she can fathom is to return to the old ways.

Worst of all, in her eyes, are the real hypocrites in the church—the ones who know how her group has been alienated but who continue to stand stubbornly with the pastor while so many continue to bleed.

Well, granted, you might say. When people cannot get along with each other, one person's hypocrite is another's white knight. But what about those cases in which there clearly are not two sides? What about the deacon with the shady business practices? How about the pastor who runs off with the church secretary? What of the people who are so friendly in church on Sunday morning but never invite me to a meal? You can't argue that there are two sides in those cases. Each of these people is doing what the Bible clearly says should not be done. These people are hypocrites.

Yes, indeed they are, and they lead me to a second conclusion: There will always be hypocrites in the church. In fact, it would be practically impossible to imagine a church without hypocrites.

When a person becomes a Christian, many exciting things happen to him. The wondrous benefit of Christ's death and resurrection join him everlastingly to God's kingdom. He is empowered by the Holy Spirit to embark on a life of deep joy and contentment if he chooses it, and he is given the promise that prayers, rightly prayed, will be rightly answered.

But at the same time the Christian never becomes a pious robot. God's love does not make him God's slave. As long as he is on earth he will have the freedom to reject that love and to walk whatever path he chooses. As long as he lives he will still be bound by his human nature, which remains ever susceptible to the triple snare of the world, the flesh, and the devil.

All Christians are tempted to sin, from the new believer to the revered saint. Very often it is just that person who has accomplished the most who is the most heavily tempted by Satan. We should be saddened by Christians who succumb to sin, even serious sin, but we should not be shocked. We should realize that whenever we tread among snares, some will be caught.

Those casualties are demoralizing, but they are no reason for quitting. In this age of materialism and sensuality, the snares on the Christian's path are enormous, but they will remain until the Lord comes to claim his own and establish his kingdom fully.

Many times Christians cannot bear to admit to themselves that they are falling short, and so they do not admit it. They hide from themselves by rationalizing what they are doing. This is what we hear: "I am not gossiping, I am circulating the details so people will know how to pray specifically for the Joneses." Or, "Since God has already forgiven my sins, I don't see why I can't go all the way when I take her out Saturday night." Or yet, "I have always prayed that I will be in the Lord's will. I am very fond of the pastor, who is so much more of a Christian man than my husband. Somehow the Lord must be in it." It is this process that turns people into well-meaning hypocrites, and the damage they do to their reputations and their witness is enormous.

It is defeating, isn't it, to think that all Christians are capable of losing their way like this. And yet everything that has ever been accomplished for the faith has been accomplished by people who have strayed from the path occasionally.

It was not long after Christ gave to Peter the keys to the kingdom of heaven that Peter denied even knowing him. In his later ministry (Acts 10), Peter received a miraculous vision that confirmed for him that God's salvation was for Gentiles even though they did not follow the ceremonial cleanliness customs of the Jews. Peter embraced this revelation with great exuberance and testified about it at the council in Jerusalem (Acts 15). Yet soon afterward he slipped back into his old ways, refusing to associate with Gentiles. This angered Paul so much that he confronted Peter with his hypocrisy.

From before the foundations of the world Christ knew that Peter would stumble like this, but Christ nonetheless chose to establish his Church through Peter and the other apostles. What encouragement there is for us in this simple fact!

Consider the apostle Paul. He wrestled with personal sin far into his ministry: "What I want to do I do not do, but what I hate I do," he wrote in anguish (Romans 7:15), and he identified himself elsewhere as the very worst of sinners (1 Timothy 1:15). Paul wrote most of his second Corinthian letter in order to quell horrendous problems in that local church. There were lawsuits among members, idolatry, disorderly worship services, and even a case of incest. There was more hypocrisy in that single church than in most congregations today, yet Paul's letter is part of the inspired canon. This is a sign to us that there will always be hypocrisy in churches, although thankfully not often to this extent.

Hypocrisy will exist as long as Christians struggle with sin, and they will be doing that until the Lord returns. There was hypocrisy not only in the New Testament church but among the very apostles chosen by Christ to establish the church. Yet in the New Testament, Christ is the only individual who ever directly called anyone a hypocrite, and he leveled that charge only at learned Jews who knew the Scriptures but still rejected salvation. Never once did Christ direct that harsh word toward any of his own flock, even when they faltered.

If we are to learn to be like Christ, then here, surely, is one piece of the pattern. We should be gentle and encouraging with each other, never willing to give up on one of our own. Rather, like Christ, we should concentrate on the mighty potential that can be released when a fallen one picks himself up and begins walking once again on the path of righteousness.

♦ WHY MUST I WORSHIP WITH OTHERS?
YFC EDITORS

When we became Christians, we became part of a body of believers that makes up the body of Christ on earth. All of us together, as part of this body, use our gifts and talents to help the body continue to grow until Christ returns. Part of our "togetherness" is worship.

When we worship, we come together to glorify God—to celebrate who he is, what he has done for us all, and to learn more about him. There is great strength in the community of believers. God gave us that community as a source of strength and encouragement when individuals are feeling weak. Worshiping together revitalizes the body and renews it for the tasks and struggles ahead. God calls us to worship together: "Let us not give up meeting together, as some are in the habit of doing, but let us encourage one another—and all the more as you see the Day approaching" (Hebrews 10:25).

What Are Your Needs?
JOSH McDOWELL

If you came to me complaining that your church was not meeting your needs, the first thing I'd do is ask you what your needs are. Are you realistic in thinking that your church—or any church—can meet them?

Take a sheet of paper and list your needs. Before you pray about them, ask yourself how these needs can realistically be met. Who can meet them best—the church? a small group? an individual? Could you meet some of them yourself just by getting into Scripture?

Often as people write out and analyze their needs, all of a sudden they see that the church is not at fault. For example, you may have a need for a close friendship with someone. You go to church expecting the church as a whole to become your close friend. This is unlikely. There may be people within the church who could meet your need, but you have an important part to play as well. You need to be able to initiate friendship as well as to respond to others. Too often people say, "The church ought to meet my need for friendship," when they haven't played their own part.

Doing this exercise will help you see if it is the church or someone else who should be helping you meet your needs.

Second, I'd ask if you are personally spending time in the Word of God. The first place God will meet your needs is on a one-to-one level between you and him, in the Scriptures. Too often we don't get into the Scriptures ourselves; we don't let God meet us on a personal, intimate basis. Then we go to church and feel bad because the church is unable to meet our needs. I have found that the more a person is into the Scriptures himself, the better the church is able to meet his needs.

Third, I'd ask if you are praying for your church and your pastor by name. I have found that when people pray specifically and individually for someone or something, they become more realistic in their expectations.

Fourth, I'd suggest that you seek counsel from your pastor and others. Go to your pastor and share your needs and frustrations. He may be able to give you some tremendous insight into the situation. Go to other church leaders as well—an elder, perhaps, or a Sunday school teacher. The Bible says, "For lack of guidance a nation falls, but many advisers make victory sure" (Proverbs 11:14). This is true of an individual also. Seek those advisers and get help.

As a last resort, look for another church. God may be leading you to worship elsewhere. Maybe you're at a church with a formal worship style and you need more charisma. Or maybe the informality of your church bothers you and you need more structure.

The problem may lie in the social life rather than the worship style of the church. Perhaps you're single and your church concentrates on the family, or maybe you're seventy years old and your church is full of university students and singles. Looking for a church that will give you comfortable companionship is legitimate.

Church should be an important part of our lives, and if we are uncomfortable at church, we should not rest until we find out why and take whatever steps are necessary to make the situation better—change ourselves, change the church, or change churches.

♦ ORTHODOX DOCTRINE
RICHARD LOVELACE

Most existing denominations are very orthodox in their basic documents. They hold to the fundamental Christian truths, even though the language they use to express them may differ from church to church. As individual denominations have shared the core of their traditions, they have realized they have biblical, orthodox doctrines in common.

If you think your church teaches untrue doctrine, it has probably deviated from its original foundation. You have strong leverage to help the church regain its original position simply by using the existing charter of the denomination. Read the theological documents that have historically led the church, and use these to call the church back to its heritage, to get back in line with its own documents and creeds.

All historic denominations now have movements of spiritual renewal and theological reformation operating within them. These movements produce periodicals and newsletters that provide information and resources. If you are concerned about renewal in your denomination, get in touch with those in it who share your concerns, and find out what resources they can provide for a study group in your local congregation. Use these materials also as a basis for prayer for revival in your church. And you might offer to teach an adult education class in denominational history.

When a Church Does Not Meet Your Needs

RICHARD LOVELACE

When John and Mary became Christians through the witness of old friends who lived in another state, they decided to stay at the church they had been attending. They felt nurtured by the preaching and enjoyed the excellent music. John became a trustee and Mary served as a deacon. But soon they became upset by what they saw happening in the church.

At a deacon's meeting, Mary was frustrated to listen to the other deacons debate whether or not a poor woman should be given sixty dollars for heat when the church had a million-dollar trust fund. At the trustee meetings John saw infighting between the majority who wanted to save money and the few who wanted to utilize the church's resources for ministry.

They both began to wonder where the Spirit of God was in the church and what the church's true priorities were. The sermons began to be less satisfying, and they found themselves having less fellowship with the other members. When a new church was started in town, they began to attend, and soon they transferred their membership. Should they have stayed? Were they right to leave?

Knowing when to stay and when to leave a church is a question that has different answers for different people. The saying "Bloom where you are planted" may be good advice for a family in one church situation. But another family's needs may not be met in that fellowship.

For example, I received a letter from an English teacher who had become a Christian in a Pentecostal denomination. He wanted to integrate his understanding of literature and Christianity in his teaching. But the pastor told him to listen to another tape and go to another prayer meeting rather than participate in such worldly activities. In that context, he was stifled, and his growth was thwarted. He needed to move. And yet for another person, that same situation could produce much spiritual growth.

If possible, strong Christians should remain in their denominational backgrounds in order to minister as missionaries. When Christians leave ailing churches for healthy ones, it is like pouring water from a full glass into a full pitcher. A person who is full of truth is trying to add to a body that is already full of truth. If a person can stay in a church that needs to be renewed, he may be used by God to bring the Spirit back into the church.

1. *Band together with other members for fellowship.* Small groups for prayer and Bible study during the week may be able to meet your needs so you are strong enough to minister on Sunday. If the youth program is weak, join with other families to improve it. Work with an attitude of love and forgiveness rather than a critical spirit.

2. *Pray regularly, daily for revival.* Find at least one other person with whom to pray for the church and community. Historically, revival has come through prayer. Social reform, church renewal, and evangelistic outreach can come out of prayer meetings that are centered on the concerns of Christ's kingdom instead of our private concerns.

3. *Listen and obey God.* Along with being guided by the wisdom of a fellowship of Christians, we should be guided by the Holy Spirit speaking through God's Word. He is the only one who knows what we need and who can lead us to the right place. If we sense that the Lord is telling us to move on, we should check this out with other people. We need to be careful not to become church hoppers. If we continually move from one congregation to another, there may be something wrong with our guidance receptor. Praying with other Christians can help us determine the difference between our desire and God's will.

Whether God leads us to go or to stay, one thing is certain: God wants us to worship him with other Christians on a regular basis.

◆ THEOLOGY / RICHARD LOVELACE

Theology plays an important role in the church. It helps define what is central and timeless, and it provides a necessary guard against secular ideologies.

Nevertheless, theological systems can be dangerous. Doctrine is one step removed from biblical revelation, and it can be used to shield us from dealing directly with Scripture. It can also become so solidified over time that it fails to address the current needs of the church. Another danger comes from individual leaders who search the Scriptures for the perfect theology, force out people who do not agree with them, and then insist that all truc Christians follow them into a new church of true orthodoxy.

But these dangers are not sufficient for us to eschew theological systems and say, "No creeds but the Bible." This would lead to the even greater danger of closed minds and lack of growth. We need to entrust our minds and wills to the Holy Spirit and spend time studying theology as well as the Scriptures so the Holy Spirit can renew our minds.

When Do I Decide to Leave a Church?

TRENT BUSHNELL

There are three familiar reasons to leave a church:

I'm just not getting anything out of it is perhaps the number one reason given, and probably the most dangerous to use. I hate to break the news to you, but "getting" *from* church is an unhealthy concept *we* have created. Many Christians have simply become church shoppers, looking for the hottest program in town. We measure our churches by pastor prestige, annual budget, and the number of kids in the handbell choir. If we are looking only for maximum personal gain, we will never find that ultimate local fellowship that will please all of our "needs." Are we expecting to only receive from our church and never give of ourselves?

I will never get along with Mr. Smith (or whoever our antagonist is) is another common excuse for leaving a church. The problem here is that the grass is not greener on the other side. Each church has people in it, and the funniest thing about people is that they are human. We are anxious to change others, but have we tried to change ourselves?

The new pastor isn't as good as old Pastor Jones reflects another common but weak reason for leaving a church. As the church has become increasingly pastor centered, we find ourselves quoting the pastor instead of the Bible. This excessive pastor-worship has made us far too intolerable of small deficiencies in new pastors. Although the pastor is a vital key to a local church's success, it takes many other keys to make a church function effectively.

However, we do have to recognize that certain situations may seem to indicate a change in churches is needed. The decision is never easy. Lifelong relationships or denominational familiarity are often at stake. Personal investment in a church college or camping program are just some of the positives that tug at our hearts asking us to stay and make the best of it. But when do we leave?

But to each one of us grace has been given as Christ apportioned it . . . to prepare God's people for works of service, so that the body of Christ may be built up. From him the whole body, joined and held together by every supporting ligament, grows and builds itself up in love, as each part does its work. Ephesians 4:7, 12, 16

We see that the real heart of the issue lies in our service in the body of Christ. If we see our reasons to drive up to a church building on Sunday morning purely from an "entertain me" perspective, leaving a church will not seem difficult, and we will probably change often. If, however, we grasp the responsibility we have to hold up our end of the deal and do our part, unlimited potential will suddenly be staring us in the face. We will truly "get" only when we give ourselves away. Many dead or very ill churches need only a couple of stagnant Christians to get fired up and the entire church will begin to feel and function differently. Have we really *given* our church a chance?

There are situations when leaving may seem necessary:

When you move across town yourself. I realize most growing churches have members driving many miles in all directions to worship there. And I would remind you that much would be lost if you change churches only because of a move farther away. Ask the question, Will I become less involved as I tire of driving the distance to the old church? If so, do yourself a favor and move to a church closer to home where you can willingly serve wholeheartedly. Often a transfer to a church of the same denomination lessens the shock and keeps you in touch with friends from the previous church.

When family needs dictate it. Our primary responsibility is to our family. Because so many individual needs can be represented within a family, we will probably always wonder if our church is right for our family. Our children can become alienated from Christianity due to a negative church experience. All the idealism (they need to learn to enjoy it) doesn't lessen our responsibility to introduce them to Jesus Christ in a positive and relevant way. Even as adults who try hard to serve, we can feel trapped and unable to contribute any longer.

If this situation does exist, the family should together list the type of church to which they can contribute best, make a clean break from the old church, and immediately visit churches to find their new church home. Advance research may help select churches that most likely will fit the bill and make the searching process shorter. It is very important to immediately become active, regular members.

But be warned: A degree of guilt will almost unavoidably accompany your change in churches. Did you run away from a little bit of tension that "better" Christians could have handled? Did you leave close friends who still need you? Our common reactions to guilt are to *avoid* the source of guilt and to *devalue* the source of guilt. Indeed, we often see Christians avoid old friends and criticize their previous church. Ask God to erase the natural guilt feelings. Keep in close contact with some friends from the previous church. Pray for their ministry, rejoice in their successes, and never say anything negative about *your* old church.

RELATED ARTICLES

Chapter 6: **Why Does a Church Need Spiritual Gifts?**
Chapter 15: **One-Dimensional Churches**
Chapter 15: **Bridging the Gap Between Artists and the Church**
Chapter 15: **How Artists Can Serve the Church**
Chapter 25: **Serving the Church**
Chapter 27: **The Hidden Mission Field in Our Churches**

CHAPTER

15

Worship: Our Response to God

- ✓ How does worship help my spiritual growth?
- ✓ What should I do when I worship?
- ✓ Can worship be practical?
- ✓ Integrating worship and church programs
- ✓ How the family can become involved in worship

Responding to God in Worship

R. C. SPROUL

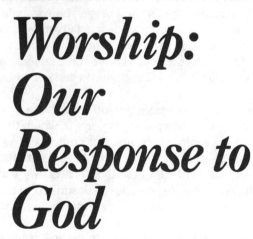

The principle purpose of worship is to glorify God. We go before him in humility, in order that we may communicate our adoration.

When we worship, we recognize who we are and who God is. Our hearts and souls are being lifted in praise and honor and glory to God. It is a recognition of the majesty of God.

There are two main reasons why we worship God. First, he commands us to, as a duty that the Creator imposes on his creation. Second, God is intrinsically worthy of worship. The vision of heaven that the apostle John records expresses this well: "Then I looked and heard the voice of many angels, numbering thousands upon thousands, and ten thousand times ten thousand. They encircled the throne and the living creatures and the elders. In a loud voice they sang: 'Worthy is the Lamb, who was slain, to receive power and wealth and wisdom and strength and honor and glory and praise!'" (Revelation 5:11, 12).

As in this passage, to say that God is worthy of worship is to say that he deserves to be worshiped. It is just. It is right. It is proper for a person to give God the honor that is God's due; we owe him that honor. On another level, worship is also for our benefit. The reason? We are created in such a manner that our own humanity is fulfilled through this highest expression of love and devotion of which human beings are capable, namely, love and devotion toward God.

Now that we realize why we worship, we can turn to the matter of how we worship. Certain elements are indispensable—praise and prayer, for example. Other elements are seen in the Old and New Testaments, especially music, as special ways that the human soul expresses adoration. The very fact that human beings are capable not only of speaking but also of communicating through song is a marvelous dimension of life and of what it means to be human.

Therefore, when we worship, we bring the whole person into this act of devotion to and communication with God. There are many ways in which this can be done. The human being is not a simple creature, but complex. If we carefully study what is in the Scriptures—that we are to worship God with the whole mind and with the whole body and with all of the five senses—we will have a new perspective on worship. For example, worship as described in the Old Testament involved visual, auditory, and even olfactory dimensions, as in the use of incense.

Sight, sound, taste, touch, smell—everything is involved in the experience of a human being. We are sensory-oriented as well as mentally oriented. Our minds, our bodies, our souls, our hearts—our whole person is to be involved in worship. I believe that if we dispense with one aspect of our humanness, we have impoverished our worship.

Another way we impoverish our worship is to have an improper attitude. The key to the proper attitude of worship is to come to a deeper understanding of the character of God, for we cannot properly worship one we do not know very deeply. If our knowledge of God is superficial, our worship will be superficial.

The strongest motivation for the majority of people who come to church on Sunday morning is for the experience of human fellowship. We come to be with other people. There is nothing wrong with wanting this; fellowship is a very important part of the life of the church. But it is not worship. What happens is that we know people, we understand people, and we relate to people, so we like to be with people. We find worship somewhat strange and somewhat difficult. It is foreign and mysterious because we have not searched the Scriptures to come to a deep understanding of the character of God. The more we know God, the more we are aware of his greatness and majesty. The more we see his worthiness to be praised and adored, the more we will want to worship. I know of no shortcuts to enhancing worship.

Finally, we are built in such a way that the more we find out who God is, the more we find out who we are. The more we discover, the more we are drawn into an intimate relationship with the God we are worshiping.

♦ ONE-DIMENSIONAL CHURCHES
R. C. SPROUL

Throughout history, there has been a tendency for churches to become one dimensional. Some churches are all intellectual—there is no visual aspect, so the churches are like civic meeting houses. There is nothing to stimulate the eye aesthetically.

On the other extreme, some people dwell too much on visualizations, and worship degenerates into a cold, deadened liturgy. This is what happened in ancient Israel, to the point of idolatry.

The same thing can happen with music. Some churches will not allow instrumentation; others encourage various styles. These decisions all affect the nature of worship.

Most worship experiences take one or two of the elements of worship and emphasize them to the exclusion of the rest. We must seek to express all that we are in worship.

What Is Worship?
✍ ROBERT WEBBER

Worship is rooted in an event—the living, dying, and rising again of Jesus Christ in history. In worship we tell and act out this event. We make the event, which happened two thousand years ago, present in our contemporary situation. All the saving and healing power of the Christ event is communicated to us as we celebrate it. That is why worship edifies us, why it builds up the church and causes us to grow.

Every celebration is rooted in an event. Each time we celebrate our birthday, for example, we're making the joy and happiness of that original event—our birth—present in the group of people gathered to celebrate it. We use symbols at birthday celebrations. We use a cake and candles, each candle representing a year. We give gifts to show our love. We sing, we play games, we are jolly, we eat potato chips, we drink Coke, and we have a lot of fun, because we are re-creating the wonder of birth and the great joy that attends anybody who is born into this life.

Worship is like a birthday party. It celebrates an event—the Christ event, which includes his birth, life, death, burial, resurrection, and ascension, as well as our anticipation of his coming again. In celebrating that event, we recreate it. We experience the joy felt by the original participants in that event. To show our joy and make the re-creation more complete, we use symbols.

All aspects of Christ's life are celebrated in every single service of worship. During certain seasons of the year, however, we accent certain parts of it. For example, during Advent and Christmas we focus on the joy of our Lord's birth. During much of the year we accent his teaching. During Easter we emphasize his death and resurrection, and at Pentecost we give attention to the coming of the Holy Spirit. Worship, then, is a way that Christ is handed down in the church from generation to generation, from century to century.

Of course we have the written record of the Christ event, and that is also an important way that he is handed down in the church. But in our very nature, we humans are given to acting things out. We like to dramatize things.

Let's say something happens to you in school and you want to share it with your family. You're sitting around the table in the evening, and you say, "Guess what happened to me in chemistry today. I was working on this experiment, and suddenly somebody came up and started talking to me. I turned around and my elbow bumped this glass container and knocked it onto the floor and all the liquid spilled out. Just then somebody came walking by and slipped on it and fell under somebody's chair. This knocked the chair over onto somebody else, and pretty soon there were six people on the floor."

My guess is that in describing that event you wouldn't just quietly sit at the table and talk about it. Much less would you write it down and read it solemnly to your family. Instead, you'd act it out. You'd stand up and show how your elbow bumped the container, how somebody came along and slipped, how the chair got knocked over. You would tell the story and act it out at the same time.

We humans are given to speech, but also to actions that portray the thing we're trying to communicate. Therefore in worship we both tell and act out an event. This event is the most important event in human history. It shapes our point of view. Out of it our whole life as Christian people proceeds.

Essentially there's a single story that underlies worship. It's the story of the universe. It's the story of the creation and the fall; Christ's incarnation, death, resurrection, and ascension; his promised coming again for the consummation of the world. It's our story too—our whole life proceeds from it. Therefore the purpose of worship is to tell it and to act it out, so as to give meaning to our lives.

If, then, worship is telling and acting out the Christ event, how do I respond to it? If I join with people to celebrate a friend's birthday, but I just sit there uninvolved and uninterested, my friend is going to be incredibly insulted. If, while the Christ event is being told and acted out, I sit there bored and passive, I am insulting God. I wouldn't do that to my friends when they celebrate their birthdays. Neither should I do it to God, whose gift to the world—Jesus Christ—is celebrated in worship.

Often people look upon worship as intellectual, dry, something we have to do. If we recognize that what we're doing is celebrating Christ, telling and acting out stories about him, that can make a big difference in our attitude toward worship.

I always insist that worship is a verb. It is not something done to us or for us; it is something done by us. We need to keep in mind that God is the audience. We often think that the preacher or the singer or the reader is the performer and that we are the audience. This is the wrong notion about worship. God is the audience, the leaders are the prompters, and the people are the actors.

About a year ago, in a church I was visiting, a woman sitting right behind me kept responding to everything going on in the service. She did this quietly, and probably not many people could hear her, but she kept saying, "Oh, yes, oh, yes, that's so true, yes, yes." At first it disturbed me a little bit, but as I realized that she was just intensely involved in what was going on, I allowed myself to be caught up in what she was doing. Her participation actually assisted me to listen more attentively to what was happening and also to respond with my inner person to it.

We need to say amen to what is happening in worship, to listen closely to the Scripture, to be involved in the hymns, songs, and choruses, to attend to what the words and the sounds that accompany the words are saying, to listen intently to the preaching and respond to it. Some people will respond out loud, saying amen and "Thanks be to God." Some will respond in their hearts. In some services there are places for public response, corporate or individual. Whatever the form, we need to involve ourselves with what is going on so that we do respond.

Worship, then, has both a divine and a human element. When Christ's presence is met with our willing response, the church is edified and we grow spiritually.

♦ LEVEL GROUND / ROBERT WEBBER

An old adage says that at the foot of the cross the ground is level. In worship we are at the foot of the cross, and everybody—the president, senators, teachers, and friends—stands on the same plane. We are all united by our common bond with Jesus Christ and our common worship of him. No one is greater than any other. No distinction is made between male and female, Jew and Greek. We are all one.

Elements of Worship

MARTIN MARTY

I have a friend who helped start a program in which people talked about theology and then witnessed to their faith in a summer resort. When I asked him what motivated him to be involved in the program he said, "Oh, I just like to lift up the presence of God in a secular place." In a sense, that is what worship does. It "lifts up" God among humans who might ignore the message.

Worship is not the act of an individual. It is a common activity with a diverse group of people. If you don't create a space and a time for worship, it can disappear. That's why we recognize God's presence, say, at ten o'clock on Sunday morning and seven o'clock on Wednesday night and three times a day at meals. That's why in times of great joy and sorrow, and at the major passages of life, we take pains to recognize God through worship. Anyone on Thanksgiving Day can be thankful for bread, but the worshiping believer is thankful to the One whose hand gives it.

The cornerstone of worship is *praise.* Praise makes the Christian church different from any other group or organization. Christians are not the only people who can bring some justice into the world. They are not the only people who can add to the world's art or philosophy. They are not the only people who put out newsletters and go to committee meetings and play in bowling leagues. But they are the only ones who praise Jesus Christ.

Also integral to worship is *preaching.* You can have a vespers service with just prayer and Scripture reading, but normally worship includes someone opening God's Word and explaining what it means to the congregation.

Another important dimension is *the common meal,* whether you call it the Lord's Supper, Holy Communion, the Eucharist, or the Mass. At this meal, God is present in a special way and we respond to him. It is an exchange between us and Christ, a ratification of the covenant.

A great German theologian with an Italian name, Romano Guardini, once said that worship is "pointless but significant." In that sense, worship is the spiritual counterpart to eating a well-prepared meal. We could survive by taking one red and two yellow vitamin pills instead of eating three meals a day. But God has given us the taste of salmon and corn and chocolate. Eating good-tasting food is pointless but significant.

We can enhance our relationship with God by worshiping him "in the beauty of holiness," just as we enhance eating by preparing good-tasting food and setting an attractive table. God can speak to me as I'm walking on the golf course or riding my bike; I can tuck God into the practical dimension of my life. But worship is a way of saying God is greater than functional activity.

In worship, the photocopy machines get turned off and the compulsive fund drive is stopped. Worship is the place where people say there are pointless but significant things in the universe and that human relations are not simply to be measured by their practical effect.

In the act of worship we suspend our normal way of doing things. We locate ourselves in places where other people have had struggles and triumphs. We suspend the practical way of looking at the world and focus on our sacred and holy God. We engage in an activity that may appear pointless for the day-to-day realities of our lives but that is eternally significant for the ultimate realities.

◆ THE CHANGING FACE OF WORSHIP / MARTIN MARTY

In worship we set up a boundary between the sacred and the secular. There we cross the threshold from the profane world and enter the sacred world. This can take place in a great cathedral, a simple church, somebody's living room, or around a campfire. Wherever and however we encounter the sacred, we carry the experience back into the world for six more days.

In worship, people always focus on the divine object. Whether it's the worship of Moravian Indians in Nicaragua or Anglicans in Africa or fundamentalists in America, the invisible God is the focus of worship.

Over the years, as worship has changed, so has the nature of that focus. From the second century until the sixteenth century, worship was characterized by sacrament, hierarchy, mystery, and sacrifice. Worship was usually centered intensely on a physical object and on a set of gestures performed in isolation in a semi-darkened place.

In the last few centuries, worship has become democratized. Churches are in the round with people facing each other. Lay people have a bigger part. Worship isn't seen as an exclusive domain of the clergy; rather, in it the congregation deals with each other and the problems around them. In medieval worship, the reserved Communion host or bread was the focus of imagination; the tall buildings beckoned the spirit to soar. Now there is more readiness to see the mystery of Christ's presence in the "two or three" into whose midst he comes.

The Purposes of Worship

✍ ROBERT WEBBER

Worship can occur in any context—in the woods, at the river, on the golf course, or during a walk to the train station. You can worship God anywhere, but I will be talking about public worship, when the body of Christ comes together to acknowledge and extol God. That kind of worship occurs only within the context of the Christian community. The writer of Hebrews tells us, "Let us not give up meeting together, as some are in the habit of doing, but let us encourage one another" (Hebrews 10:25).

Worship has many purposes, just as a diamond has many facets. We cannot appreciate the beauty of a diamond by looking at it from only one angle. It's necessary to look at it from the front, the sides, the back, the top, and even underneath. We also need to see worship from many different angles in order to fully appreciate the meaning and mystery of what it means to worship.

I am going to state several purposes of worship; these few will not at all exhaust the possibilities.

First, worship brings glory to God. We are told in Scripture that God created the world for his own glory. Not only people but also trees and rivers, rocks and clouds, the sun, the moon, and the stars, crocodiles, elephants, and even ants are made to God's glory, because the entire created order is an expression of God's creativity.

In worship we acknowledge God as the One who created everything, who gave us life, who sustains us in our day-by-day existence. We acknowledge him as the One who is so creative and so marvelous in his thoughts that he is able to bring together this entire creation with all its beauty and color. So in worship we acknowledge God for what he has done and continues to do in his creation.

We also acknowledge him in the beauty of his own person—not only for what he has done, but also for his being, the essence from which his actions flow. We acknowledge him for being holy and transcendent, righteous and merciful and just, loving and caring. These basic characteristics of God are all expressed one way or another within the context of worship.

The first purpose of worship, then, is to bring glory to God. The second purpose is one we frequently forget. Worship is to minister to God. In a prayer written by St. John Chrysostom in the fourth century is this statement: "Vouchsafe, O Lord, to receive this ministry of praise which we offer to thee." That is a wonderful insight about the purpose of worship. We, as God's creation, literally minister to him as we praise him, because he loves to be worshiped, extolled, acknowledged, and congratulated.

Some time ago I was speaking in a church about how God loves to be worshiped. In a question-and-answer session after the service, a girl sitting on the front row raised her hand and said, "You know, I'm not sure I like this description of a God who loves to be worshiped. It sounds to me as if God is egocentric."

I wasn't sure how to respond to her comment, but there was a person in the back row who was attuned to what I was saying and who also knew this girl. He was able to answer more forcefully than I could have. This is what he said: "Carol, suppose I came up to you and said, 'You are the most perfect person in all the world. I acknowledge you. I extol you. In you resides the personification of compassion, love, caring, and friendship. There isn't anybody like you in the whole world. You are the most wonderful person I know.' Carol, what would you do? Well, you would hang your head and blush. Why? Because it isn't true.

"Now, Carol, suppose we say to God, 'You're holy, you're marvelous, and in you abides all goodness and truth and beauty. You're high and holy and lifted up. We bless you, we praise your holy name, we fall before you, we worship you, we acknowledge you as the ultimate one.' What do you think God is going to do? Do you think he will hang his head, shuffle his feet in celestial dust, and say, 'Aw, shucks'? No? Why not? Because it's true!"

So when we worship God in spirit and in truth, we speak to God the truth about him. In truth he is holy, high, and lifted up. He is above everything else and everyone else. He is to be acknowledged and blessed and praised and magnified.

These two purposes of worship, then—to bring glory to God and to minister to God—are related to God. Now I want to look at two purposes of worship that are related to humans.

First, worship is the means by which Christ is handed down in the church. We need to recognize that worship is perhaps the most central thing the church does. A number of years ago I was responsible for a search committee to find a new pastor for my church. We decided that before we called a pastor we would take several months to go through the Scriptures and church history trying to determine what the church is supposed to be and do.

After an intensive period of study and brainstorming and discussion, we came to the conclusion that the church has six functions. First, the church is a worshiping community. Second, the church is a teaching community—reading, studying, learning, inwardly digesting the Word of God. Third, the church is a fellowship community, a group of people who care about each other, are committed to each other, and are willing to put themselves out for each other. Fourth, the church is a servant community. It serves the needs of the immediate community in which it finds itself and also the needs of the world. Fifth, the church is healing a community. It offers counseling, help for inner turmoil, and mending for broken lives. Sixth, the church is an evangelistic or mission community. It preaches and proclaims the gospel as it fulfills Christ's mandate to witness to the whole world, the Great Commission.

Having stated these six functions of the church, we asked ourselves, "What is the primary thing that the church must be doing?" Our study led us to the conclusion that the primary activity of the church must be worship. Worship is the central context in which our encounter with the living Christ takes place. Therefore it is the summit toward which all other church activities move.

Worship is also the source from which all other activity derives. The teaching, the fellowship, the service, the healing, and the mission of the church are all ultimately rooted in the worship of the church. We concluded that if we don't have a good worshiping community, then all the other aspects of the church are going to be affected. Our life in the world proceeds from our contact with Christ through worship.

There is a second aspect of worship as it relates to humans. Worship is the building up of the body of Christ. First Corinthians 12–14, a central New Testament passage about worship, speaks about the unity we have in Christ's body, the Church. Each of us brings to the body our gifts. Not everyone has the same gift. Whatever our gifts may be—singing, drama, liturgical dance, prayer —they're our gifts to give to the church. The gifts God has given us belong to the church, and as we give them to the life of the church, we contribute to the functioning of the body.

Public worship, then, has two purposes relating to God: It brings glory to him, and it ministers to him. It also has two purposes relating to humans: It is the means by which Christ is handed down in the church, and it builds up the body of Christ. These things happen through worship because worship has both a divine and a human element. In public worship, the gathered human community meets with the living Christ, the Son of God.

◆ THE PRACTICAL IMPLICATIONS OF WORSHIP / ROBERT WEBBER

Worship is not a selfish spiritual exercise for the well fed. It has radical social implications.

Look at preaching, for example. The preaching of the prophets—Amos, Isaiah, Micah, and others—is not pie in the sky. It has to do with the real issues of life. It touches on human suffering and pain. It relates to the way rich people misuse poor people. Through the prophets, God calls us to be on the side of the poor, the oppressed, and the suffering.

Second, look at prayer. Prayer reaches out and touches all the issues of life. Scripture instructs us to pray for kings, emperors, nations, governments, and world situations. People should read the newspaper and bring the news into the context of Christian worship. Headlines should give direction to our prayers when we pray for the needs of the world.

Third, look at baptism. Part of the baptismal vow is the renunciation of evil. Not only does this have a personal sense—I renounce the power of evil in my own life; it also has incredible social implications. It means that the church as a corporate body renounces corporate evil, the evil expressed in society.

Fourth, look at the Lord's Supper. Think of what it means to be fed at the Lord's table. At the Messianic banquet at the end of history, all peoples will be invited to sit down at the table of the Lord together. The poor, the oppressed, all the people who are unwelcome in the world will be welcome at Christ's banquet. The Eucharist points the church toward caring for these people now, in the name of Christ. Just as Christ is compassionate toward us, we need to be compassionate toward the world.

Worship, then, is exceedingly practical. Its implications touch every aspect of life.

Developing an Attitude of Worship

✍ RICHARD LOVELACE

Worship is a function of the spiritual health of a congregation. A church may have a beautiful choir singing uplifting songs with theologically correct words, a tremendous organ, and a beautiful sanctuary. But if the people's hearts are far from God and there is no foundation of prayer, worship does not take place. It is an empty experience. A healthy spiritual life results from a church's individual and corporate prayer life, the presenting of the gospel in both word and action, the presence of community, and theological soundness.

Our experience of God in worship depends on our commitment and attitude toward God. Developing an attitude of worship is not a matter of aesthetics or strategy, but an awareness of the presence of God's Spirit. A service that fosters this attitude includes no parts simply as aesthetic decoration. Every part helps concentrate people's attention on their union with Christ. In fact, the beauty of a service often has little to do with how conducive it is to worship. In many simple forms of worship, aesthetic elements are missing, but worship takes place because God is pleased to be there.

Our personal receptivity also affects our worship experience. We can go into a service one morning and get nothing out of it, not because the service is mediocre but because we are not open to receiving God's Spirit. If we are not ready to listen and worship, it doesn't matter how wonderful the service is.

Our individual backgrounds also influence our experience. We can get tired of one style of worship. If I were shut up in a room and listened to nothing but the nine Beethoven symphonies for three years, I would become utterly immune to them. People who attended unstructured church services as children may go to a liturgical service and discover a tremendous freedom in that style of worship. Other people who have been hardened by a liturgical pattern will come alive in a free-style situation.

Peter Jenkins, who wrote *A Walk across America,* had never been reached in his Episcopal background. But he found Christ in a southern black church. That church touched him in places where his spiritual callouses had not been built up. On the other hand I have a friend who was spiritually put to sleep by a solid evangelical church, but was awakened to the meaning of the gospel by reading Emil Brunner, an author who is not thoroughly orthodox and yet who has a freshness in responding to certain scriptural elements.

We need to find the style of worship that scratches where we itch, and we should not be afraid of changing worship styles if we find ourselves in a rut. The psalmist said, "Sing to the Lord a new song" (Psalm 149:1). God is a fountain of endless novelty. He is a source of constant freshness, like a symphony that uses the same themes but constantly unfolds new meanings, new ways of combining things.

Some people say they find God in nature. That is true; we do find God in the general revelation of nature. But the place where the presence of God demands the transformation of our lives is in his Word. That is his special revelation. It fences us in and puts demands on our lives. A lot of people who want to worship God on the golf course want to opt out of the demanding venture of building the kingdom of Christ. They are more interested in building their own private kingdom. We may come to Christ in an unstructured, nonchurch context, but we can't grow in Christlikeness unless we are rooted in a structured ministry.

In developing an attitude of worship we need the following:

1. *Humility and repentance.* To come before God with a true attitude of worship we need to be aware of the gap between God and us. Otherwise, in our attempts to be spiritual we may become like the Pharisees: "They are zealous for God, but their zeal is not based on knowledge. Since they did not know the righteousness that comes from God and sought to establish their own, they did not submit to God's righteousness" (Romans 10:2, 3). Our righteousness is not based on our confidence in ourselves as morally upright people.

2. *Faith.* We need a faith that frees us from the power and darkness of sin. The central sin within our personalities is unbelief. Eve demonstrated this unbelief when she gave in to temptation. Through the illumination of faith, our central darkness is healed and our spiritual blindness is removed. We receive light to see. The goal of this faith is not spiritual achievement but fellowship with God.

3. *The Holy Spirit.* He is the energy force that enables us to move forward spiritually. Through the Holy Spirit, we are made holy. He wages war against

sin (Galatians 5:16). The Holy Spirit works in us to conform us to Jesus and leads us in truth. He reveals to us the glory of God. "The Counselor, the Holy Spirit, whom the Father will send in my name, will teach you all things and will remind you of everything I have said to you" (John 14:26). By the presence of the Holy Spirit in our lives, we can worship God, who is Spirit.

♦ THE PLACE OF CREEDS IN WORSHIP / RICHARD LOVELACE

Some people recite creeds without believing them; others believe them without reciting them. We need to guard against both errors.

Creeds are vital to worship because they embody the basic truths of Christianity. The people of God need to unite in a grand affirmation of who God the Father is, who Christ is and what he has done, and who the Holy Spirit is. Reciting the Nicene or Apostles' Creed can strengthen our faith.

Creeds are also found in our hymns, in congregational prayers, and in certain passages of Scripture. As we sing them, say them, or listen to them, we are affirming our faith. So even churches that do not recite the formal creeds use the creeds in one way or another.

But often we say the creeds by rote, and then they become an empty act of worship. To enrich our understanding and use of the creeds we can do two things.

1. *Learn the creed's history.* Read a book on the creeds or the history of the Christian church. Knowing why a creed was written can deepen your understanding of it, since each creed was written to address the particular struggles the church was facing at that time. It's also important to remember that each creed has its own emphasis and none is complete in itself.

2. *Memorize to meditate.* When you know something by heart, it is easier to concentrate on the words' meaning. Think about the words as you say them, letting them sink into your consciousness. During your daily devotions, meditate on the creed to soak in its truths.

THE APOSTLES' CREED

I believe in God the Father almighty,
maker of heaven and earth;
and in Jesus Christ
his only Son our Lord,
who was conceived by the Holy Ghost,
born of the Virgin Mary,
suffered under Pontius Pilate,
was crucified, dead, and buried:
he descended into hell;
the third day he arose again from the dead;
he ascended into heaven,
and sitteth on the right hand of God the Father almighty;
from thence he shall come to judge the quick and the dead.
I believe in the Holy Ghost;
the holy catholic church;
the communion of saints;
the forgiveness of sins;
the resurrection of the body,
and the life everlasting.
Amen.

THE LORD'S PRAYER

Our Father in heaven,
hallowed be your name,
your kingdom come,
your will be done
on earth as it is in heaven.
Give us today our daily bread.
Forgive us our debts,
as we also have forgiven our debtors.
And lead us not into temptation,
but deliver us from the evil one.
For yours is the kingdom
and the power
and the glory forever.
Amen.
Matthew 6:9-13

THE TEN COMMANDMENTS

1. You shall have no other gods before me.
2. You shall not make for yourself an idol.
3. You shall not misuse the name of the Lord your God.
4. Remember the Sabbath day by keeping it holy.
5. Honor your father and your mother.
6. You shall not murder.
7. You shall not commit adultery.
8. You shall not steal.
9. You shall not give false testimony against your neighbor.
10. You shall not covet anything that belongs to your neighbor.

Exodus 20:3-17

Worship and the Lord's Supper

ROBERT WEBBER

To understand the meaning of the Lord's table, we need to look at four New Testament terms used to describe this event. Each term gives us a different insight.

First, in Acts 2:42 the Lord's table is referred to as *the breaking of bread.* In interpreting this passage, scholars understand the breaking of bread to relate to Jesus' three post-Resurrection appearances. Each time Jesus appeared to his disciples, he ate with them.

One of these experiences is described in Luke 24:13-32. Jesus was walking with two disciples on the road to Emmaus, and the night came. The disciples said to him, "Come in and stay with us." At suppertime "he took bread, gave thanks, broke it and began to give it to them" (v. 30). As these two disciples later told the other believers, this was when they recognized Jesus (v. 35). Through the breaking of the bread he became uniquely present to them. Thus the term *breaking bread* focuses on the living Christ's presence with the believers.

A second term, and perhaps the one most commonly used among Protestants, is *the Lord's Supper.* Used in 1 Corinthians 11:17-34, it emphasizes Christ's death on the cross. In Matthew 26:17-30 when Jesus and his disciples gather for that last meal together, Jesus emphasizes his coming death. So when we refer to the Lord's Supper, we focus on Christ's death. Unlike the concept of breaking bread, which produces joy as Christ's presence is recognized and his resurrection is affirmed, the concept of the Lord's Supper produces sobriety at the thought of his death.

The third term, found in 1 Corinthians 10:16 and also commonly used in Protestant churches, is *Communion.* The word is sometimes translated "participation." It refers to the mystery that when we eat the bread and drink the wine we are somehow participating in the body of Christ. Communion is more than an intellectual thing. By eating the bread and drinking the wine, we symbolize that Jesus is internalized in our lives, that we truly participate in him, and that we find our life's meaning in him.

The fourth term, used in 1 Corinthians 14:16, is the Greek word *Eucharist,* or "thanksgiving." It simply means that when we gather together around the table of the Lord, we give thanks—just as we do at the dinner table when we thank God for food. The Eucharist, the thanks given at the Lord's table, has been known historically as "the great thanksgiving." It includes our thankfulness for creation and even more for redemption.

So when we think of the meaning of the Lord's table, we need to think of these four things: Christ's presence, which brings joy; his death, which produces sobriety; participation in the mystery of our oneness with Christ; and our own personal offering of thanks over the bread and wine.

Another New Testament word that gives insight into the meaning of the Lord's table is *remembrance.* When the minister says, "Do this in remembrance of me," he is quoting from Jesus' own words recorded in Luke 22:19 and 1 Corinthians 11:24.

This word translated "remembrance" has been misunderstood. We think remembrance is something we do, as in "I remember what happened two weeks ago" or "I remember some significant event." For example, if I were to say to you, "I want you to remember your high school graduation," you would try to conjure up images of all your friends, the speaker, the joy you had in completing that part of life, the parties. But the Greek word translated "remembrance" doesn't mean that. If you were remembering your graduation in the Greek sense, you and your friends would have to come back together and re-member the event—that is, you would have to make it happen again.

When Jesus said, "Do this in remembrance of me," he was referring more to a divine action than to a human action. When we come together at the Lord's table, Christ becomes present to his body, the worshiping community, in a mysterious and unique way. His body is re-membered; it is put together again. That is to say, the body of Christ is membered together with its head, Christ himself. Christ, in union with the united body that is worshiping him, ministers to that gathered community. Christ, then, is doing the work of re-membering, and we are responding to what is happening.

The practical implication of this understanding of remembrance is this: The Lord's Supper, Communion, the breaking of bread, the Eucharist—whatever you call it—is an extremely important part of our Christian life. We need to be present at the celebration of the Lord's table as frequently as possible, because it is there in particular that divine action is taking place. Through the Lord's Supper, divine healing and comfort and sustenance occur.

I've always found that when I'm personally needy, when I'm going through a time of trouble or despair or sadness, I desperately need to let Christ minister to me at that table. When students come to me and say they are having a difficult time in their lives, I always say, "Flee to the table. Go to Communion and let Christ minister to you." Invariably these students will come back and say, "It happened. Christ really was present. He really ministered to me at the table of the Lord."

Worship and Baptism

ROBERT WEBBER

Baptism is one of the two sacraments observed by all Christians. As the rite of initiation into the body of Christ, it brings people into the worship community. Communion, the other major Christian sacrament, is the table, the food, the nourishment, that sustains Christ's family. Both baptism and Communion are necessary elements in our life of faith.

Baptism needs to be understood as a rite of passage, a movement from one state of being to another. High school graduation is a good example of a rite of passage. It represents a turning point, the end of mandatory schooling. Whatever education you take from that point on is done through choice, not compulsion. We celebrate this rite of passage, and everyone takes great joy in the accomplishment.

Baptism is a rite of passage, because it marks the transition from one way of life to another. In fact, it is a symbol of dying to the old life and rising to the new.

In the New Testament there are a lot of before-and-after pictures of the old way of life and the new. For example, in Galatians 5 Paul lists characteristics of the old life, which he calls the "sinful nature"—"sexual immorality, impurity and debauchery; idolatry and witchcraft; hatred, discord, jealousy, fits of rage, selfish ambition, dissensions, factions and envy; drunkenness, orgies, and the like" (vv. 19-21).

When we are baptized these things no longer rule our lives. We have undergone a rite of passage, and so we now "keep in step with the Spirit" (v. 25).

This is the context in which Paul lists the fruit of the Spirit: "love, joy, peace, patience, kindness, goodness, faithfulness, gentleness and self-control" (vv. 22, 23). At baptism we give our passions over to this new style of life. These characteristics are to abide in us. They are to rule us, to become our models. Baptism, then, is a movement from keeping step with the sinful nature to keeping step with the Spirit.

Paul gives another picture of this transformation in Colossians 3:5-14, where he talks about taking off the old self and putting on the new. When you take off the old self, you take off "whatever belongs to your earthly nature: sexual immorality, impurity, lust, evil desires and greed, which is idolatry, . . . anger, rage, malice, slander, and filthy language." These are all characteristics of a fallen person. When you put on the new self, you put on the characteristics of Christ: compassion, kindness, humility, gentleness, patience, willingness to forgive, and love.

In the early church, a baptismal candidate took off all his clothes and was baptized naked. Then when he came up out of the water, he received a new white robe. This underlined the imagery of taking off the old self and putting on the new self.

There are two parts to baptism: the divine action and the human response. A monk in the early church named Macarius called baptism "the hidden presence of God's grace awaiting the soul's desire." He was specifically speaking about infant baptism, but his words can also be applied to adult baptism. They emphasize the fact that two things happen in baptism: God's action, or "the hidden presence of God's grace," and the person's response, or "the soul's desire."

God's action in baptism is to create a new person with a new heart. Water plays an important part in baptism, because in the Scriptures, water is often associated with creation or re-creation. For example, in the Genesis creation account the earth is formed out of the waters. In the story of Noah, the ark floats on water to safety. When Joshua leads Israel across the river Jordan into the Promised Land, going through water is the rite of passage. These biblical images help us see the divine side, God's creative activity, that is related to the symbol of water.

Our human response to God's action is that we willingly enter into new life. We choose it. We elect to go through the washing of baptism.

Martin Luther once wrote to his people, "Live in your baptism." That's an interesting image. When I was baptized at age thirteen in the Baptist church, the minister, who was my father, said to me, "Robert, do you renounce the devil and all his works?" I said, "I do," and then he baptized me in the name of the Father and the Son and the Holy Spirit. If I follow Luther's admonition, I will be aware of my baptism daily, understanding that my baptism into Christ calls me to renounce evil. Living in my baptism—in constant commitment to doing what I promised in my baptismal vow—has some similarity to living in my marriage.

A third-century theologian, Tertullian, observed about a group of heretics, "They full well know how to destroy the little fishes"—the fish, you remember, was a symbol of the Christian church—"by taking them away from their water." He meant that if people stray from their baptismal vow, their commitment to renounce evil and to follow after Christ, if they "gratify the desires of the sinful nature" or "put on the old person" again, it is the same as renouncing their baptism.

Baptism, then, is not a shadowy event that happened to us years ago. It has practical implications for our day-by-day growth in Christ.

Growing a Christian Imagination

LUCI SHAW

Imagination is an area that has not been viewed as integral to the Christian experience. Yet it seems to me that having an imagination that can see things the way God wants them is essential if we are going to be the Christians God wants us to be.

We should develop our imaginations, because God has programmed them into us. Humans consist of body, mind, and spirit, and our minds have much potential that's not being realized. The mind is not just the intellectual, left-brain analyst that judges critically and rationally and whose thought patterns are linear. It also includes right-brain intuition and imagination, which see patterns and make connections. The right side of the brain is more impulsive and less disciplined than the left side; it can fly off in a number of different directions at once.

We need to unite left-brain thinking with right-brain thinking. We need structure and freedom working together. We need the left brains and the right brains to work together within the Church. It's all a part of being the body of Christ. The human body has a skeletal structure; that's like the left brain. But it also has beautiful hair, flawless skin, and brilliant eyes, and that's like the right brain. We need both, working together, to be whole persons.

George Herbert, a seventeenth-century metaphysical poet, wrote: "A man may look on glass, / On it may stay his eye. / Or if he pleases, through it pass, / And then the heavens espy." That's an old-fashioned way of saying that perhaps we're taken up with the surfaces of life, like window glass with fingerprints, smudges, dust, reflections, and distortions. If we would just lengthen our focus we could see through the dirty glass to the three-dimensional world beyond full of colors, textures, seasons, and movements waiting to be perceived. Many of us feel cut off by the "window glass" of dailyness, the mundane life we live, the details that tie us down and get in the way of true seeing. But here imagination helps us to adjust the focus of the inner eye so that we're really seeing what God has planned for us.

To be true see-ers, truly imaginative people, we need to take time alone to hear what God is speaking to us and to hear what our own minds are saying. Time is such a precious commodity in our culture. We're all so busy, so taken up with things that ten years from now will have little value. The urgent takes priority in our lives instead of the important. We may have to get up a little earlier or stay up later in order to schedule into our lives time to be alone.

Aloneness is something we've lost in our society; we're scared to be alone. Even when when we're by ourselves we have to have the radio or TV going.

But although we are not comfortable with silence, it's absolutely essential for imagination. Our imagination needs silence just as a flower needs water, warmth, and light.

Our imagination needs times of aloneness—not passivity (although we may need some times to just relax and let ourselves be)—but times for our minds to actively pursue certain thoughts. We often have fleeting insights, but because we're too busy we never really investigate them or let them develop. But if we take the time, our minds will carry us to places we haven't been before.

Reading is a good way to develop imagination. It's one of my primary means, because whenever I read a good novel or poem, my mind is filled with pictures that extend my horizons. Literature is a good foundation, a fruitful place to start.

We have so many resources available to us it's almost bewildering. The public library has tapes, records, and even works of art we can rent and have in our homes. Museums and art galleries are also good resources that are too often ignored.

Being part of a creative small group is another way to develop imagination. I've been part of such a group for over two years now. We meet every two weeks, usually on a Friday or Saturday, and do a variety of things together. For example, one weekend we went to Stratford, Ontario, and saw five Shakespeare plays.

Each time we meet, we do something different. One week we'll play a dictionary game. Sometimes we'll have dinner, sometimes a picnic, other times just coffee and dessert. Sometimes we'll listen to a sermon on tape and then discuss it, or all read the same book ahead of time and review it. Sometimes we just get together and talk or listen to music. We're very laid back, and we vary what we do every time. One member of our group has led us in exercises in imaginative prayer. For example, imagine your favorite place in the world, wherever that may be. Then imagine Jesus is there with you, and you are alone with him. You're in conversation together, and then Jesus tells you the thing you most want to hear, the thing you've always wanted somebody to say to you. For instance, he might say he loves you in the way you've always wanted to be loved. And you just take it from there—each person fills in the details.

Here's another imaginative exercise. Imagine you're standing on a riverbank. There's a treasure chest on the bottom of the river. You dive down, bring the chest to the surface, and open it up. And inside the treasure chest is your heart's desire. We all think about that for a while and then share what we find when we open the chest.

If these exercises are done in a spirit of prayer, and we're asking the Holy Spirit to direct our thinking and our imagination, it's amazing what insights we can come up with about ourselves, what we're really all about, what God is saying to us.

Exercises like these can help our imaginations grow. Imagination is like a muscle; if it's never used it just shrinks away and becomes passive, thin, and weak. And that's what most of our imaginations are like, unfortunately.

But developing the imagination is such an individual thing that it's impossible to dictate what each person should do. Imaginative exercises, reading widely, spending time in quiet and meditation can help, but each of us has to think about it on our own. We each have to reflect and pray and ask God to show us in what direction we should move.

♦ WHAT IS IMAGINATION? / LUCI SHAW

Imagination is seeing at a level different from the purely physical pictures of things not present with you right now. When I say the word *mother,* you see a mental picture of your mother, even if she's not in the room with you, even if she's a thousand miles away. Imagination brings things into your awareness by means of memory and by making connections.

Imagination is not sentimentality. It's not getting all mushy; it's not just emotion, although emotion is involved. Imagination is triggered by the senses. Hearing, sight, smell, touch, and taste are all involved in the imagination.

Imagination makes analogies possible. If someone talks about the growth of plants, in your mind you see a seed being planted and the green unfolding. You can then make the connection between plant growth and the growth of a human being. Your imagination links the two concepts.

God wants us to exercise our imaginations. Jesus said we should have ears to hear and eyes to see. What he wants us to hear and see are spiritual realities, not physical ones; and spiritual realities and the imagination are very closely connected. The Bible is crammed full of pictures. If God were just a propositional God, he would have presented truth to us in a totally different form. We can't open a page in the Bible without finding imagery, pictures, metaphor, simile, and other figures of speech being used creatively by God.

♦ SPONTANEITY vs. PLANNING
LARRY CHRISTENSON

Many people assume that to be led by the Spirit in worship is to be completely spontaneous. They think that nothing should be written down or planned ahead of time.

In one situation, that may be true; but in another, the Holy Spirit may direct the worshiper to lay everything out ahead of time. He may even move the worshiper to write out some prayers he is going to give.

If the Spirit inspires a person four weeks beforehand, the person has a month to practice what he has written. This sort of preparation can make for a detailed, yet smooth, service of worship.

What is important is not whether an act of worship is spontaneous or planned, but whether the Holy Spirit called for that particular approach at that time.

Integrating Worship and Church Programs

DAVID McKENNA

Churches tend to make worship a self-contained experience that happens for one hour on Sunday morning. But to be totally effective, worship must be integrated into the total life of the church, the home, and the individuals that make up that church. When worship is thus integrated, the church and its people have a sense of moving together all the time, not just during the Sunday morning service.

The most effective method for personal growth among church members is an integrated and reinforcing program in which worship relates to education, and education relates to the other programs of the church. It is wonderful that many churches use an integrated Sunday school curriculum that provides for all the classes—no matter what age level—to be studying the same topic and passage of Scripture in a lesson related to their abilities. It would be even better if the Sunday school topic related to the pastor's topic in the worship service. Thus, the total life of the church would be in focused harmony.

I commend the pastors who have the children with their parents during the first part of worship, then allow the children to go to separate classes. But, when the children go to their classes, how does the lesson there relate to the pastor's message to the adults? Does it relate at all? Most likely not. We tend to isolate worship, yet it is one of the most critical dimensions of Christian growth.

Not only should worship be integrated into the church context, but it also needs to be integrated into the home. In Acts 2, when Luke described the New Testament church after Pentecost, we cannot miss the fact that the total life of believers was tied together in the worship context. Every day they met together in corporate worship; then they broke bread in their homes and ate together with glad and sincere hearts praising God.

There is a direct connection between worship at church and worship at home. Unless one reinforces the other, it is hard for individuals to grow spiritually. In my view, however, most families are absolutely frustrated because they want to worship together and teach their children, but they don't know how. Church leaders and concerned members need to confront this as both a desperate need and a serious problem.

Whenever the primary function of the home in fostering personal growth is forfeited to any professional agency, even one as good as the church, we end up with more problems than we solve. Today's children are learning about sex and drugs from the secular school system, not from their parents. Similarly, they are learning about worship from the church, not at home. Worship should be as alive, vital, and significant in individual homes during the week as it is Sunday morning at church.

I know of a church in Harlem that has a terrific integrated program. The subject of the Sunday morning worship becomes the subject of the Sunday evening service. The pastor gives families "assignments" to do at home to get them thinking and talking about the subject at hand. When people come to church on Wednesday night, another angle of the topic is addressed. Such continuity integrates the church and the home, and personal spiritual growth is reinforced.

It is helpful when the pastor announces the text for his message of the following week and gives tips on how to use it in family worship so that families can prepare for the next Sunday. Parents can then read the text for family devotions, talk about its historical or cultural aspects, talk about life applications, discuss questions among family members, and so on, all at different family worship times during the week.

Imagine the lively dynamics of mind and spirit that would take place when the pastor then preaches on Sunday! Great excitement can happen in a church when its members are so involved in the worship that their minds are on it all week long!

Worship need not be a self-contained experience. It can come alive in all programs of the church, in the families of the church, and in the lives of each individual member.

♦FAMILY WORSHIP / DAVID McKENNA

Here are some practical suggestions for integrating the worship of the church into your family's daily activities:

1. Open the conversation at the Sunday dinner table with a question, affirmation, or conflict related to the pastor's sermon of the morning.
2. Search for supporting Scriptures to read in daily devotions with the introduction, "I have been thinking about the pastor's message or our Sunday school lesson. . . ."
3. Give a personal testimony to the family on how the sermon, songs, or Scripture of the worship service came back in a time of decision, crisis, or trial.
4. Relate the truth of worship to a current event or moral crisis while watching TV or reading the newspaper.
5. Put up a tent card on the family dining table on which might be written the Scripture of the sermon or the Sunday school lesson to be quoted together as a prelude to table grace, or sing together a verse of a hymn that was used in the worship service.
6. Suggest to the family, "In every worship service, I find something to help me, even though it seems the service is boring and everyone is down. Today, for instance, I got help from . . ."

Bridging the Gap between Artists and the Church

LUCI SHAW

Pastors are always looking for ways to make church life interesting, practical, and valuable. Opening the church to artists and incorporating the arts—such as dance, drama, music, poetry reading, stained glass or banners—into the church service will expose believers to innovative ways of worship and modes of seeing, and may ultimately inject new life into the church. It will also be a big step in the direction of closing the gap between artists and the church.

Many church leaders harbor a fear and suspicion of the arts in general. Conservative churches used to be totally opposed to theater, drama, dance, fiction, and fantasy. Perhaps they thought that the arts were false, frivolous, and vain; or they mistakenly believed that the arts had nothing to do with real life or practical Christianity. Even nowadays it seems that many churches are blind to beauty. Too many churches have substituted efficiency for aesthetic values.

The suspicion extends to the artists themselves, and with good reason. Many artists, particularly secular artists, lead irresponsible lives. They're impulsive, rebellious, and live on the fringes of society. They tend to be protesters who rock the boat, and pastors and Bible teachers find that threatening. They're intimidated by it.

But these very qualities exhibited by artists—the creative ability to see things in a new way, even if that leads to protest or change—can be turned to good use within the church. Too often, however, artists are just as suspicious of the church as the church is of them. "The church is rigid and legalistic," they say. "We never hear any fresh language; the Good News is always couched in the same old phrases and in the same tones of voice. We want something that will excite us and spark our imaginations."

The fact that this gap between artists and the church exists is ironic, because Jesus himself was as iconoclastic as any artist. He broke with tradition at every point and introduced new ways of acting and reacting. For example, he gave shocking examples to bring the truth alive. He'd say, "If your eye does something wrong, gouge it out." Or, "If your hand is at fault, cut it off." He didn't mean those things literally. He was using hyperbole to make a point. So often when we get stuck in a rut, artists are the people who can help us see old truths in new ways. And very often art shocks. But we need that shock, that sting. Art exaggerates to help us see life more clearly.

Artists can be catalysts. Just as a good preacher opens our eyes to spiritual truths, so can a good artist. An artist's work can promote discussion. There probably will be pros and cons—people who support the work and others who oppose it—but disagreement can clarify issues and sharpen perceptions.

If the stalemate between artists and the church is to be overcome, somehow artists must take the initiative. Church leaders are not likely to reach out to artists on a grand scale, because the power is in their hands and they generally support the status quo. Thus artists are going to have to come to a pastor and say, "Look, here's a body of Christians with many gifts, but they're not exercising the gifts I can contribute. May I be a part of this church, and be a servant? I want to put myself under your leadership and start taking responsibility. I want to feed my gifts into the mainstream of church life."

It's very difficult for artists to submit themselves to something they view as legalistic or stereotyped, and yet they need to make that beginning. If church leaders see artists making themselves accountable, being responsible, working hard, and even being willing to do mundane tasks that other people avoid, then they'll begin to build a trust relationship that will be very fruitful for both sides.

An artist who wants to make a difference in his or her church needs to realize that there will be much work to do, both in identifying the artistic potential that's already in the church and in encouraging creativity in adults and children. I suspect that within every congregation lies much buried artistic potential. It's there, but it's been stifled. Very often women have artistic gifts, but in many churches they're commanded to be quiet and passive, and that becomes everyone's loss. The church needs the enrichment of the arts, but too often it denies itself the resources it already has. Artists can look for those unseen seeds of creativity and nurture them until they bear fruit for the church and the Lord.

Believers need to be reeducated, to learn that the arts can enrich their lives and open new worlds to them. The most effective education begins in the home, with parents who are willing to expose their children to various kinds of art. For example, in the home I grew up in, we were voracious readers. We children read constantly, and our parents read aloud to us. Nowadays, with all the technological advances, we can bring our children art in other forms as well: on video cassettes, tapes, or records.

Families can be taught to work with their children when they see they have gifts. I've known of families in Japan who, discovering that one of their children had a musical gift, have encouraged, backed, and aided that child in every possible way. These families produced some outstanding people, because they set the goal of helping their children be the very best artists possible.

It may be easier for children to learn to be open to the arts because it's their nature to do things spontaneously, but adults can learn too. The church can aid the learning process. For example, it can sponsor a good film series on Sunday evenings, or it can host a writers' conference and invite church members to participate.

The arts may incite suspicion because they have to do with change, and change is risky. Art is risky. But living life as a Christian under the Holy Spirit is risky too. (This is why some people have been afraid of the charismatic renewal; they fear anything that takes their lives out of their own exclusive control.) Moving out into the unknown is scary, and it's particularly difficult for people if they're insecure and don't have confidence in their own identity. But if we have a strong identity as God's children, we can afford to be more open and confident about taking chances. And then we'll be more open to hearing from the Spirit in nontraditional ways—dance, drama, literature, and art.

◆ AWE AND MYSTERY / ROBERT WEBBER

We need to recognize that we can never totally comprehend God. He is mysterious, and we need to worship him in his mystery and his "beyondness." This is why awe and reverence are part of expressing the glory of God.

How Artists Can Serve the Church

LUCI SHAW

When Jesus told us to have eyes to see and ears to hear, he didn't just mean seeing and hearing ordinary things. He wanted us to look through the ordinary to something beyond, to things that defy expression in everyday language. This is what art does—it sees, and shows, what lies beyond the rational.

The arts can be used in the church in various ways. I've seen drama, for example, used effectively in church services and evangelistic rallies. David Watson, one of England's best-known evangelists, had a dramatic troupe who traveled with him. When he was speaking in an evangelistic meeting, he'd make a point, and then the troupe would dramatize it. All the way through his talk, they'd act out what he was saying.

He prepared his sermons with the troupe in mind, using incidents or stories that could be represented on stage. What the audience would take away with them was not just somebody's voice in their head, but a visual image. Watson knew they would remember the people on stage—what they were doing, their colors, their movements, the sounds of their voices, and the plot they were working out. It was like a story, and a story is more easily remembered than a sermon outline because it is not abstract. It seems to have a life of its own. So drama can attract and hold an audience that a mere sermon might not reach.

Increasingly, dance is being used liturgically. This art form is difficult for some people to accept because of its association with carnality and the lusts of the flesh. But King David danced in worship. Some Christians have never been exposed to dance that glorifies God. When they think of dancing, they think of something strange to them like break dancing or disco dancing. If these people could see some really dynamic dancing that speaks of God and of his grace and his beauty, maybe their eyes would be opened. Body movement can express emotions that we simply can't express rationally.

Poetry is another art form that can be used in the church. I am a poet, and churches I have been part of have often included a time in the worship service where I can read a poem that illustrates a specific theme. In the church I currently attend, the rector bases his sermons on the Scripture readings planned for that day by the Episcopal church. If he sends me the texts in advance, I'll find maybe two or three poems that fit into that theme. In place of one of the anthems, I'll read a poem. It's been very well received. People remember things that give them a slightly different view, that approach life from another angle.

I'd like to see artists on the worship planning committees of churches. It would inject a fresh and original way of glorifying God. That doesn't mean the artists would promote their particular art form. Artists just have a way of seeing experience differently. They're innovative. They're not tied to precedent quite as strongly as the more staid traditionalists.

It might be interesting to take a theme, such as growth, and ask various kinds of artists to focus on it and contribute something on a Sunday. Have all the members of the congregation bring something that speaks to them of growth or share something that was involved in their own personal growth. Someone could write a play or a skit, and other people could act in it. Some could make banners, and musicians could perform or write songs about growth. All kinds of artistic endeavors could reinforce the same theme, looking at it from various angles.

Vacation Bible School is an area that could effectively use creative and fresh ideas to enlarge children's appreciation of the Bible and of Christian doctrine. The arts can make Vacation Bible School lively and interesting without being gimmicky.

In James Brabazon's biography of Dorothy Sayers, he tells how, as a good friend of novelist Charles Williams, she said of herself: "Whereas Williams was a practicing mystic, I'm a complete moron, being almost completely without intuition of any kind." (It's hard for me to believe that, but that's the way she perceived herself.) She went on, "I can only apprehend intellectually what the mystics grasp directly. But when I enter into Charles' type of mind, by imagination, and look through its windows as it were, I see places where I cannot myself go."

Likewise, in our churches we need to be open enough to say, "OK, my gifts lie in this direction, but I'm a moron as far as such-and-such goes. Let's bring somebody into the church who is gifted in those areas and ask him or her to explain these things or give us examples of how they can enrich us." Our churches don't need fear, suspicion, pulling back, and protectiveness. They need an attitude of openness that will welcome the fresh air from God that the arts can let in.

Worship and the Arts

ROBERT WEBBER

Some years ago I began to feel that the context in which I was worshiping was too intellectual. Everything was a matter of the head. It was cerebral. It was not engaging my whole person.

In this sermon-oriented approach to worship, I heard one brain communicating with another brain. But my worship wasn't coming from the heart. It did not engage my senses. I didn't worship with my sight or with my smelling or with my taste or with my hearing. I felt that this approach to worship was bankrupt, and as a result I began to seek ways to worship with my whole being—my body and my senses as well as my brain.

To recognize the necessity of involving the senses in worship, we have to accept God's revelation in both the Old Testament and the New. Sense-oriented worship is mostly depicted in the Old Testament. There is a New Testament passage, however, that describes it also. Revelation 4 and 5 evoke all the beauty and splendor and appeal to the senses that are part of heavenly worship. Because the early Christian church attempted to reproduce the kind of worship described in this passage, its worship services eventually came to resemble the sense-oriented worship of the Old Testament.

Early Christian worship involved the body. The worshipers dressed the presider in their finest clothes, for example. A lot of the people were poor, so this became their one artistic expression of the importance of what they were doing. Their worship also involved bodily actions such as walking, stretching out the hands to receive the bread and the wine, perhaps lifting the hands during prayer. There was a lot more physical involvement in early Christian worship than we experience in most of our Protestant churches today.

As the church developed, the use of aesthetic signs—the arts—to evoke worship became more elaborate. Every Christian community has at least two symbols: the pulpit, which is the symbol of the Word, and the table, which is the symbol of the Lord's Supper. These symbols can be put up in a field or a garage or a basement—any place where people gather to worship. They do not have to be beautiful or artistically designed.

But once the church began putting up church buildings, Christian artists began making these symbols beautiful. This was their gift to the community of believers, a gift intended to enhance worship. The church building became a place in which members of the body of Christ gathered together among rich symbols of their faith.

While use of the arts is not absolutely necessary for worship, it is a way of setting creation free and bringing it into worship. Liturgical dance, for example, sets movement free. A stained glass window sets color and light free. The dance and the window participate in the worship of God. This is not inappropriate to say, because the purpose of the whole creation is to bring glory to God.

Any time a symbol becomes something that we worship—if we worship the stained glass or the dance, the light or the movement—then obviously the symbol has become an idol. We need to break away from that. As Protestants, however, we need to recognize that lack of art can also become an idol. It is possible that we idolize our freedom from the creation. Right now I think the cutting edge of worship renewal is rediscovering the place of the arts in the life of worship.

◆ POETRY: A SOURCE OF BEAUTY AND JOY / LUCI SHAW

I have people say to me, "What's the point of a poem? Why can't you say what you want to say in plain prose?" I often make the analogy that poetry is to prose as singing is to speech, or dancing, jumping, and skipping are to walking.

Poetry says something that simply cannot be said in any other way.

There's value in art simply for the sake of its beauty and the joy it brings. It doesn't have to make a doctrinal statement. You don't have to include the four spiritual laws in every piece of art. There can be wonderful Christian symbolism in art, but there is also art that simply reflects life truly, and that also has value.

A lot of my poetry doesn't speak specifically or directly about God or biblical truth. It may reflect what I'm thinking or feeling that day; it may just talk about slices of my daily life, but presents them in a way that has integrity.

I've also had people say to me, "I've never read poetry. I could never understand what it was about. But when I heard you read a poem aloud, it came alive for me." This has happened again and again. People listen to poetry and suddenly hear or see something they have never noticed before.

There are possibilities here. Reading poetry aloud is something new we can do in the church. It opens people's minds and eyes and helps them see God's creation in a new light.

Worship: A Way Station on the Christian Journey

✍ ROBERT WEBBER

Many of you have been involved in walks for particular causes. I've done this several times myself—finding people who would contribute a nickel or a quarter or a dollar a mile while I walked maybe twenty-five miles. That's a long way to walk in a day. Fortunately on those journeys we would pass way stations where we could stop and be refreshed, drink and eat and be strengthened to continue our journey.

I like to think of public worship as a way station on the Christian journey. From the Christian point of view, life is a journey culminating in the new heavens and the new earth. Everything we do—washing dishes, talking to a friend, playing football, cheerleading, eating in the school cafeteria—is in the context of that journey. Public worship is the way the Christian family and community strengthens us and nurtures us so that we can keep going.

Let me try to describe what I mean by nurture. Let's say that when my first child was born I brought him home, put him in the driveway, and said, "John, this is our home. Most of us reside inside that door over there. If you need anything, just holler." You know good and well that John would not grow and develop and mature out there on the driveway, because a child needs the community of the family. He needs to be loved, given food, changed, touched, cared for. That's nurturing, and that's what we need for our spiritual journey.

We would never think of allowing somebody to journey through life with no human contact, with no nurturing, without any fellowship. No one goes from infancy to adolescence to young adulthood to full adulthood and maturity without continual contact and interaction with other people. There's always somebody there to help us, to instruct us, to guide us, to assist us when we fall down, to help us through difficult times. Often our helpers come from our families.

When we are born into a family, we bear its name. We are connected to a mother, a father, perhaps brothers and sister, grandparents, and other relatives. There's no way we can escape it. Even if we try to deny it, we still belong to it. As we journey through life, our family members are nearby to assist us. We are not always aware of their help, but if it were all taken away from us, we would immediately know how dependent we are on these relationships.

The church is also our family. As Christians, we bear the name of the head of our family. The members of our Christian family help and nurture us in many ways. One way is by joining with us in worship. When we come together in public worship, we have family time.

In families, it is important to come together to eat. The ritual of sitting down and taking a meal together gives us security. It establishes relationships and gives us a context in which we can express both our joys and our frustrations. Worship is like a family meal. It's a time in which God meets his community, relationships are strengthened and sustained, and nourishment is provided.

Often our values are formed at the dinner table. In our home, at least, that is where crucial discussions take place. That is where we talk about the meaning of life and the attitudes we should take toward other people. Likewise, we form values when we meet together in worship. Through preaching, singing, and fellowship, we learn the moral expectations of the Christian faith. We learn what attitudes we are called to take toward other people. In the context of worship we are called to become a forgiving people, a loving people. If we are attuned to what is happening, our values are shaped by our presence in worship.

Worship, then, nurtures us so that we are able to continue our journey to the Promised Land. It establishes relationships with other people on that journey—people who can help us and be helped by us as needs arise. It shapes values so that we know where we are going and how to get there. Public worship may not take up much of our time, but it is still an important way station. It enables us to "run with perseverance the race marked out for us" (Hebrews 12:1).

RELATED ARTICLES

Chapter 14: **Why Go to Church?**
Chapter 14: **What Should Church Be Like?**
Chapter 14: **Why Must I Worship with Others?**

CHAPTER

16

The Bible: God's Word to His People

- ✓ Why should I study the Bible? Can it really help me?
- ✓ How should I study the Bible?
- ✓ How do I apply the Bible to my life?
- ✓ How do we know the Bible is true and right?
- ✓ What if I don't get anything out of the Bible?

Does God Speak through the Bible?

AJITH FERNANDO

Perhaps the simplest way to describe the Christian life is as a relationship with God. In a human relationship there must be conversation, and this is so in the Christian life too. We speak to God through prayer, and God speaks to us in numerous ways. The most common way he speaks to us is through the Scriptures.

The prayer of Psalm 119:18 should always be in our hearts when we approach the Scriptures: "Open my eyes that I may see wonderful things in your law." This prayer says that God shows us wonderful things, but we are not totally passive in the process. We must look into the law (the Bible). God has spoken to us in the Bible, and we must read his words carefully to understand what they mean. If we don't do this, we may get a message he did not intend.

How does God speak to us from the Bible? Let me suggest three ways. The first is through direct guidelines for a situation we face. Here God is like a guide giving us instructions on what we should do. For example, if we are facing trouble from a person who opposes us, we may read that Christians must love their enemies (Matthew 5:43-46). Here are some questions that will help us discover the guidelines God desires to give us from a passage:

- Is there a promise for me to claim?
- Is there a command for me to obey?
- Is there a sin for me to avoid?
- Is there an example for me to follow?

We need to be asking questions such as these whenever we read the Bible.

Many are content with general applications of what they read and so do not get clear guidelines from God. We must endeavor to be specific in our applications. An example of a general application is "Christians must love their enemies." A more specific application of this same verse is "I must love Bob, even though he has hurt me by spreading slanderous stories about me." A still more specific application is "Bob's child is sick, and his car is out of order. Bob has hurt me by spreading slanderous stories about me. I am very busy today. But I will offer to take him and his child to see the doctor."

A second way God speaks to us is by giving us biblical principles. These are truths about topics such as what God is like and how he acts, or the nature of man, the world, heaven, hell, or the Christian life. Here God is like a teacher who presents important facts in a classroom. These facts may not have an immediate application to our lives, but we still need to take them and hide them in our hearts (Psalm 119:11). In this way we fill up a reservoir of truth in our hearts that can be tapped when the need arises.

On a bright day when we are faced with no problems, we read in Genesis 50:20 that even though Joseph's brothers intended to harm him, God used their evil to do something good. We may find no immediate application in our lives from that truth. But an important principle goes into our "reservoir." This principle states that because God is sovereign, if we are faithful to him he will use even the evil that people plan against us to do something marvelous.

Quite some time later someone hurts us very badly. As a result, we are faced with what looks like a bleak future. Our first reaction is to panic or to be disillusioned. Then, from the reservoir, the truth of Genesis 50:20 emerges. God is sovereign. He will work things out for good. We must concentrate on being obedient to him. Our perspective changes and, despite the pain, we have peace in our hearts.

How important it is for us to fill up this reservoir of truth! This is what makes a person spiritually strong, for it gives him inner resources to adequately face the challenges he encounters. So we must not be discouraged if no clear application for a specific situation comes to us each time we read the Bible. The Bible is God's Word, so whenever we read it God can teach us something very important to be used immediately or later on.

A third way God speaks to us is through what we may call special messages. God always desires to speak to us, but often we are so out of tune with him that we cannot hear his voice. When we read the Bible we often automatically get into a listening mood, so God can break through what we are reading with a message for us.

A Christian businessman has to make a decision as to whether to launch out on a bold new venture. He has studied the feasibility of this venture. There is risk involved, but he could succeed. He has looked at the way it relates to his Christian commitment—the most important factor in his life—and he has found that there is no apparent conflict there. Of course he has fears about whether it will succeed, yet these should not stop an enterprising businessman. But he wants to know whether this venture is God's will for him. If he has doubts about this, however attractive the project is, he will not launch out on it.

Yet Scripture cannot give him specific guidance about this decision. It can only give him guidelines to help him make the decision. Often at a time like this, God leaves it to the individual to take the initiative and make the decision. Sometimes, however, he sends him a special message that helps him decide.

One day, during his regular time for Bible reading, our businessman reads Joshua 1:1-9. Here God urges Joshua to move forward, trusting in him, without being afraid of the dangers ahead. God assures him of triumph. The passage seems relevant to his situation. He discerns that God arranged for him to read it on this day so that he might get a clear message about the decision he is to make. He launches out on his new venture, believing God directed him to do so.

The sovereign God can arrange things so as to have us read a specific passage on the very day we most need to hear its message. So the fact that we read that passage on that day may not be simply a coincidence. It may well be an instance of direct divine guidance.

God's special messages do not come only in the area of guidance. He may also send messages of comfort, of encouragement, of warning, and of rebuke.

Of course with such messages we can never be 100 percent sure that what we heard was God's voice. These messages do not carry the authority of Scripture. The clear guidelines of Scripture are without error. We cannot speak with such certainty about these personal messages.

We know, for example, that we can twist the Scriptures to say what we want them to say. Similarly, we can imagine that God has given us a certain message when actually God had nothing to do with it. So we must be careful about the use of these special messages. We can be sure that God will not ask us to do something that contradicts the clear guidelines of Scripture. So we can say without hesitation that a message that contradicts a scriptural principle cannot be from God.

A good rule to adopt here is not to go in search of these special messages. God will speak to us if he wishes to. If we go in search of messages, it is easy to mistake our imagination for the voice of God.

God speaks to us through the Bible, then, in three ways: he gives us direct guidelines for a situation we face; he teaches us biblical principles that may help us now or later; and he speaks to us directly in special messages. God wants to communicate with us. It is up to us to spend time with the Scriptures to give him a chance to speak.

How Can We Know the Bible Is Reliable?

NORMAN GEISLER

First, we can know the Bible is reliable because Jesus said it is reliable. He said, "Until heaven and earth disappear, not the smallest letter, not the least stroke of a pen, will by any means disappear from the Law until everything is accomplished" (Matthew 5:18). Jesus called the Bible the "word of God" and said "the Scripture cannot be broken" (John 10:34, 35). Since Jesus is the Son of God, we can trust what he said about the Word of God.

Second, many prophecies show the Bible had a supernatural origin. The Bible made numerous predictions, sometimes hundreds of years in advance, that were literally and accurately fulfilled. For example, it predicted the ancestral line from which Jesus would come (Genesis 15; 2 Samuel 7). It also foretold the very city of Bethlehem in which Jesus would be born (Micah 5:2). Further, the Scriptures prophesied how Jesus would be born (of a virgin) in Isaiah 7:14.

Third, archeology has confirmed the Bible. There are literally thousands of archeological discoveries that confirm the truth of what is presented in the Bible. And not one single find has refuted anything taught in the Bible.

Fourth, historical documents have confirmed the biblical record. There are more early Greek manuscripts for the New Testament than for any book from the ancient world. Many classics survive on only a handful of manuscripts, some even have only two. Yet the New Testament has 5,366 Greek manuscripts dating all the way back to just after the end of the first century when the books were originally written. The discovery of the Dead Sea scrolls confirmed the accuracy of the Old Testament manuscripts. And the recent discovery of thousands of tablets at Ebla support the historical nature of the early chapters of Genesis.

Fifth, the Bible is the most influential book in the world. The Bible has been translated into more languages, published in more copies, and influenced more lives than any other book in the world. It has converted millions of people, transformed whole countries, and changed the course of civilization. As Hebrews 4:12 declares, "The word of God is living and active. Sharper than any double-edged sword, it penetrates even to dividing soul and spirit."

Sixth, the Bible has an amazing unity amid great diversity that is best explained as a work of Deity. Unlike most books, the Bible has about thirty-five authors. It was written in two major languages (Hebrew and Greek) over a period of about sixteen hundred years (c. 1500 B.C.–A.D. 100). It covers hundreds of different topics by authors from widely diverse backgrounds (kings, shepherds, doctor, tax collector, fishermen). Yet in spite of all of this, the Bible is one book with one message: people are sinners, but God loves us and Christ died and rose for us so that we can be forgiven (John 3:16; Romans 5:8; 10:9, 10).

Seventh, the Bible is a book written by prophets of God who were confirmed by acts of God (miracles). There were tests for a true prophet (Deuteronomy 13). Whenever necessary, God confirmed his spokesmen by miracles as he did Moses (Exodus 4). God provided the sign to confirm their sermons, a miracle to support their message. Thus the prophets who wrote the Bible were moved by the Spirit of God (2 Peter 1:20, 21) and confirmed by acts of God (2 Corinthians 12:12), to record the inspired Word of God (2 Timothy 3:16, 17).

There need be no doubt concerning the reliability of the Bible. It's message is the same today and it promises to have a profound impact on the lives of those who read and believe.

Why I Trust the Bible

✍ CHARLES COLSON

At its simplest level, if God is God and cannot err, and if the Scriptures are God's Word, then it has to be infallible. An infallible God cannot err. Scripture, which comes from God, by definition has to be infallible. How could it be God's Word and at the same time be fallible? People who don't deal with this question are engaging in sophistry—they're really saying that they don't believe that Scripture is God's Word. That's the first threshold issue: Is the Bible truly the Word of God? That's where I began my own study, because if the answer is yes, then the Bible must be without error.

A journalist some years ago went back to the archeological evidence in order to debunk the Bible. He came away converted. The Bible, he discovered, was the most extraordinary document he had ever studied. It projected the truth of history in periods when there was no other historical account. Archeological evidence is demonstrating that it is absolutely correct, even in the most meticulous details. I think it is impossible to look at the totality of Scripture and attribute it to anything other than the work of the Holy Spirit.

Through three and a half millenia, these documents have survived, not only as holy writ, but as historical records, basically unchallenged. Over the ages the Bible has withstood every single challenge or test.

After studying the debates at the canonical council where it was determined which books were worthy of being called Scripture, I am convinced that the process truly sought the mind of God. The probative tests that were applied to determine whether or not a writing was Scripture were tougher than anything in the scientific method.

Many critics in the last two hundred years have looked for holes in the Bible. They asserted, for example, that there was no evidence that the psalms were written at the time of David, more than a thousand years before Christ, because they contain information not known in those days. The psalms were written in the Maccabean era, the critics said. Then came the discovery of the Dead Sea scrolls. Today no reputable scholar would argue that the psalms all came from the time of the Maccabees. In Psalm 22 we see a precise description of the crucifixion, which wasn't even invented until a hundred years before Christ. One has to conclude that the psalms were inspired by God.

The discovery of the Hittite Empire is another verification of the accuracy of the Bible. Critics claimed that the Bible erred in speaking of such a kingdom of which there was no other historical record. Yet within the last fifty years, archeologists have discovered that there was indeed a Hittite Empire, just as the Bible said, with a finely defined language.

One by one, scholarly attacks upon the Scriptures have been discredited by archeological discoveries and other evidence. What is bound together in a book called the Bible is historically accurate, was correctly compiled, and is extraordinary because no book has a history like it. It prophesied events long before they occurred. Those prophecies are fulfilled in the facts of history. To say that the Bible, which stands up to all tests and attacks, is nonetheless just a book of human origin, is simply an unenlightened position. That is not the view of a scholar—it's the position of someone who has an atheistic presupposition and therefore has to say that in order to discredit the Bible.

When I say that the Bible is God's Word, I mean in its original autographs. In the process of translating and copying through the years, the original autographs could have been mistakenly changed in some places. But in its original autographs the Bible has to be without error.

To my way of thinking, the resurrection of Christ is one of the most powerful attestations to the accuracy of Scripture. The evidence of the resurrection of Christ is more powerful than anything I ever argued in a court of law. Eleven eyewitnesses wrote independently, corroborating one another. For forty years they were persecuted for their statements that Christ had risen from the dead, and yet they never denied him. I, for one, was in a cover-up, and I saw how fallible man is, how easily and quickly we renounce people to save our own hides. No one could ever convince me that the most powerless of the apostles of Christ could have maintained a lie for forty years. Their story had to be true. They had to have seen Jesus resurrected from the dead.

God's Word is infallible; God's people are not. We are fallible, and therefore we sometimes interpret things in a different way than God intended. Two people can read the same verse of Scripture and come to different conclusions. That's the result of free will, and I would not be so arrogant as to say that my interpretation is correct as opposed to someone else's. But out of that process of trying to interpret God's Word, truth emerges, though at times some of us may be off base in one way or another. This is the tension of the Christian life. If it were otherwise, we would be nothing but robots. Part of that tension is healthy and the consequence of God having made us in his image with minds of our own.

The most remarkable thing, though, is the difference the Scripture makes in the lives of those who sincerely follow it. I've never found anyone who said, "I've studied the Bible; I've lived it for years—and it doesn't work for me." The people I've talked to say that the more they truly absorb Scripture and seek to live by its precepts, they find that God is able to accomplish amazing things for his purposes through their lives.

♦ DON'T PUT YOUR FAITH IN THE BIBLE
JOSH McDOWELL

The foundation of our faith is not the Bible. That's where many people make a mistake. It's not the Bible, it's Jesus Christ.

In John 5:39, 40 Jesus said, "You diligently study the Scriptures because you think that by them you possess eternal life. These are the Scriptures that testify about me, yet you refuse to come to me to have life." In other words, these unbelieving, though religious, people thought the Bible was their foundation. But the Bible is not to be the foundation of our faith—Jesus is. The Bible is to direct us to Christ.

If you base your faith on the Scriptures, you have rules without a relationship. And rules without relationship lead to rebellion. If you base your faith on the Christ of the Scriptures, you have rules within a relationship—and that leads to response.

The Inspiration of Scripture
ISABEL ANDERS THROOP

One of the first things we need to recognize about the inspiration of Scripture is that it is partly a mystery to us. This is a point not stressed often enough: the fact that we do not totally understand and cannot completely explain how the great God chose to communicate his truth to humankind. Rather, we accept the divine inspiration of Scripture by faith.

God has spoken—what a miracle! The Lord himself has communicated with his creatures in a way they can understand and act on—how astounding! How can human language contain ultimate truth? Christians believe the language of the Bible brings truth to us as God's Spirit breathes in and through it. The Spirit makes the divine Word alive and enlightens us, giving us eyes to see and ears to hear.

Jesus described the divine communication process for his disciples. "Why do you speak in parables?" they had asked. He assured them that those with spiritual ears would be able to hear and understand. The stumbling block to receiving the word, he said, is having a calloused heart. (See Matthew 13:9-16.)

The words themselves—even Christ's words—are not magical. They do not work mechanically every time a Bible verse is read, spoken, or repeated. Even when Jesus himself spoke the words to a live audience, his presence and authority did not guarantee success. This is because the divine communication is a conversation between two people—a speaker and a listener. The listener can choose whether to receive the words of Christ or to reject them.

When we talk about inspiration, it is very important that we steer clear of two equal and opposite heresies. We must take a middle course between superstition on the one hand and lack of faith on the other. God did not magically zap the Bible writers into trances, out of which they wrote Scripture. They fully cooperated with the writing process, though they could not have understood (nor can we) the depth of all they wrote.

But neither did God go off to another part of the universe while a few wise men on earth put together their observations on religion as best they could. If the Bible were only a human book, it could easily be discarded when it doesn't seem to fit modern-day situations. Such a book would not inspire faith. In fact, one would tend to approach it with the "calloused heart" that prevents understanding.

No, God worked with and through the Bible writers, using their human abilities, interests, and purposes to accomplish his own aims. In Scripture, the human and the divine come together in miraculous unity—and this is a great mystery. It would be almost impossible to imagine if we did not also acknowledge just such a mystery in Jesus Christ.

Jesus was both completely God and completely man. We are told that "the Word became flesh and dwelt among us, full of grace and truth" (John 1:14, RSV). In this passage Jesus is called God's saying, speech, or Word. Just as Jesus broke the barrier between God and man by being both God and man himself, so the Bible bridges the vast communication gap by being both earthly and heavenly. This is a mystery we accept by faith in order to receive the Word into our lives.

When "men moved by the Holy Spirit spoke from God" (2 Peter 1:21, RSV), they were filled with power to accomplish a heavenly task. The authors and their earthly purposes were drawn into God's purpose; their talents and obedience were all used by God for his eternal purpose. They became part of God's eternal plan. They were so filled with the Spirit that their words became sanctified for God's use, and God's perspective was able to shine through their writing.

Yet it is clear from reading the Bible that the prophets and poets and historians who authored the books remained themselves—normal human beings. In writing their books and letters, they used ordinary skills of recollection, compilation, research, selection of detail, inclusion and exclusion of certain facts. Luke, for example, opens his Gospel by referring to the research he has done:

Many have undertaken to draw up an account of the things that have been fulfilled among us, just as they were handed down to us by those who from the first were eyewitnesses and servants of the word. Therefore, since I myself have carefully investigated everything from the beginning, it seemed good also to me to write an orderly account for you, most excellent Theophilus, so that you may know the certainty of the things you have been taught. Luke 1:1-4

In John 14:26 we find a reference to the human attribute of memory, so necessary to the biblical writers: "The Holy Spirit, whom the Father will send in my name, ... will remind you of everything I have said to you."

God chose to use human effort and inclination, and earthly disciplines of writing and recording, as he chooses to use all worthy human work. He took the biblical authors' skills, sanctified them, and used them for his glory in the transmission of his Word to future generations, including us.

What part of Scripture is human, and what part divine?

It is a seamless garment. There is a unity to the Word that makes it impossible to draw such lines. Again we must consider the mystery of the incarnation, the fact that Christ himself was both completely human and totally divine. Likewise the Bible, even as it uses human language and modes of communication, somehow is God's eternal Word.

To say that we understand this would be folly. But to believe it and to live in the truth of inspiration is the beginning of wisdom. "I delight in your decrees; I will not neglect your word" (Psalm 119:16). Just as we exercise faith to believe in our redemption through Jesus Christ, so we approach the Bible in faith.

As Peter said to our Lord, "To whom shall we go? You have the words of eternal life" (John 6:68).

Windows in Scripture

LUCI SHAW

I remember hearing Stuart Briscoe tell of a young man who was scared to read the Bible for fear he wouldn't understand it. The Bible is a pretty massive book. It can intimidate someone who hasn't been brought up in a Christian home and exposed to it in gradual stages. How does such a person approach it? Or get into it?

Briscoe said this young man thought of the Bible as an old house—a complicated Victorian house with all kinds of windows and levels, dusty passages, closets, and secret rooms. For him, it was also like a haunted house, and he was afraid to go into it until he realized that the whole house was full of light. The light came through beveled, stained-glass windows, and those windows turned it into rainbow colors within that dusty, dark old building. That thought took away all the young man's fear and introduced him to joy.

I think the windows that let the light into that old house are the Bible's word pictures. Those images aren't random; they were planned in God's providence as he inspired human writers whose imaginations were exercised as they wrote and who included pictures of God in the form of poetry, descriptions, images, and stories.

The first chapters of Genesis, for example, are pure poetry. They contain poetic rhythms, idea sequences, and repetitions.

In Deuteronomy we find rich descriptions connected with the story of the building of the tabernacle. The writer listed all the materials and art needed to produce this beautiiful place to worship God. Yahweh, interested in design and beauty, specified that the priests' robes should have bells and pomegranates around the hems. That's two kinds of beauty—the musical beauty of the tinkling of the bells and the visual beauty of the shape and color of pomegranates. If God wasn't interested in beauty, why would he bother to give such detailed instructions?

The books of Ezekiel and Daniel are full of the most bizarre images. We don't know what to make of the strange creatures we read about in these inspired books. And in Revelation, we find animals with seven heads and a woman with the moon under her feet. This is imagery. It's not the sort of rational, practical, three-point sermon we often associate with God speaking to us.

The Bible does not always confront us with the strange and bizarre. It is full of natural images too. Very often it points to the simple and the familiar. For his parables, Jesus took very ordinary things: the sower and the seed, the mustard seed that grew into a tree, the wheat and the tares, sheep, grapevines. He used agricultural images the people knew very well.

Many of Jesus' parables are more than images; they are also stories. In only two cases does Jesus explain a parable. When his followers ask him, he explains the parable of the sower, and he explains the parable of the wheat and tares. But you don't have to have a rational explanation for a parable; you have to feel it, you have to enter completely into the experience in the story. Then you know intuitively what Jesus is saying. When he's talking about finding the lost sheep, you understand that he is the shepherd and you are the sheep. You imagine what it must feel like to be out all night, lost, torn with brambles, soaking wet, shivering with cold, and in danger of falling over a cliff. And then the shepherd comes and holds you in his arms, and you feel the warmth of his body, the security of his strength. If you can enter into the parable, it's something you can feel. The emotions and all the senses are involved in that understanding.

The Bible is not always easy to understand. God himself is a mysterious being. But he has given us word pictures to let his light into our understanding—pictures that point beyond themselves to him.

Believing and Interpreting the Bible

R. C. SPROUL

Many people wonder, Do I have to believe everything in the Bible to be a Christian?

No, the Bible does not say that one has to believe everything in it to be saved. But as to the question, Do I have to believe everything in the Bible to be a totally sanctified Christian? I would say yes. I believe that we are required to believe, to trust, and to obey every word that comes from the mouth of God. If the Bible comes from the mouth of God, it imposes this obligation on us to believe everything in it.

Still, not everyone who is a Christian is persuaded that the Bible is in fact the inerrant Word of God. It is an issue that divides believers, for there are true believers who are not persuaded that the Bible is the Word of God. Because modern criticism of the Scriptures has so complicated matters, many Christians have lost confidence in some parts of the Bible.

This leads us to a related issue: What does it mean "to believe in"? It is one thing to believe that something is true; it is another matter to believe in a person. I believe that George Washington was a historical person, but I do not trust in him for my salvation. Similarly, believing in Christ is a kind of faith that is multidimensional and goes beyond simple intellectual assent. When we "believe in the Bible," we mean that it is more than just intellectually true. We proclaim that its truth has life-changing implications.

Then we may ask, "Must I believe everything in the Bible literally?" The only way to believe anything in the Scriptures is to believe it literally because the word *literal* means "as it is written." Just as during the Protestant Reformation, this means we interpret historical events as historical events, symbols as symbols, parables as parables, and so forth.

Today, some believe that literal interpretation means that we interpret everything in the Bible as if it were historical narrative. Instead, literal interpretation involves a careful and complicated process of identifying what it is that the Bible is saying. It would be wrong to interpret a poem by a standard of interpretation foreign to poetry. To take a newspaper report and turn it into a poem would violate the original intention of the reporter. To take a poem and turn it into a newspaper article would violate the intent of the poet. Therefore, to interpret the Bible correctly, we must understand the form and the style in which various parts of it are written and then interpret it accordingly.

To interpret correctly, we use principles of interpretation that apply to all written material. The fact that the Bible is the Word of God does not give us license to turn it into magic. For instance, some people believe they can get all kinds of bizarre revelations from it when they interpret the Scriptures in ways they were never intended to be interpreted. "Lucky dipping" is one of these approaches: we have a question, so we open up the Bible anywhere, as if it was a Ouija board, and dip our finger in to get the answer. That is distortion, not interpretation.

The Bible must be interpreted as it was written. Divine inspiration does not change verbs into nouns and nouns into verbs. This, however, is not to say that it is just another book—it is the written Word of God. We must be careful.

A key principle is to interpret an individual piece of Scripture in the light of the whole, that is, according to context. There is an immediate context, but there is also an overall context to which we must be alert. I urge a responsible attempt to understand the literary structure of Scripture and interpret by grammatical/historical exegesis.

This means that we interpret according to the way in which a scriptural passage was originally written and what it was intended to mean. Such an approach calls for a lot of homework—to understand the words of Scripture, the historical situation in which it was written, the background and customs of the people, the original language, and so forth.

Does this mean that only scholars should study the Bible? No, anyone can benefit eternally from the reading of the Scriptures. The message that determines our destiny is so clear and simple that a child can understand it. But if a person wants to grasp the whole counsel of God—the deeper knowledge of the Scriptures—he or she needs to work with the technical tools of biblical interpretation. That is why Christ established teachers in the church who would devote themselves to careful, minute studies of difficult portions of the Bible. Not everybody is called to do this. But God has called some to this task because we all want to be instructed from the depth of the Scriptures, beyond the bare, essential message of salvation.

♦ LETTING THE BIBLE READ US
RICHARD OWEN ROBERTS

Reading the Bible is an essential part of our Christian walk, but we must take care not to stop there. I must not keep coming to the Bible only for information about God and truth. I must also come so that the Bible might analyze me and tell me where I'm wrong and what changes are needed in my life. In fact, I would say that the essential difference between the Bible and every other book is that the other books are meant to be read, whereas the Bible is truly meant to read us.

How to Tell If the Bible Is Being Misused
HUDSON T. ARMERDING

If you suspect that the person you are talking with is misusing the Bible, the first thing you need to ask is whether this person is placing some other authority on the same level as Scripture. This may be a book, such as the *Book of Mormon,* or a personality, such as a particular leader or preacher.

It is a typical cultic approach to suggest that there is another authority parallel to Scripture. Generally the person will say that the Bible is true, but the proper interpretation of what it says is located in this other document or in this other personality.

If this is what the person is saying to you, find out who would be the final authority in the event of a conflict. In my conversation with Mormons, they have eventually said that the *Pearl of Great Price* or the *Book of Mormon* really are the final authorities and that Scripture must be understood in light of these later and more definitive revelations. Some people say they put Scripture first, but they only accept a favorite interpreter's view of what it means.

Second, ask whether this person's interpretation of Scripture is some new or exotic doctrine that has not been emphasized by God's people in the past two thousand years. Occasionally I meet people today who are saying that the correct view of homosexuality has been obscured from the church for two thousand years, and that only now is it being understood properly. Similarly, Jehovah's Witnesses insist that the way the church looked at Scripture was incorrect until they came along less than a hundred years ago.

We need to have a reasonable skepticism. It would seem that God in his providence would have disclosed a proper interpretation down the centuries and wouldn't have reserved something vital for the present. This kind of view should be a major warning that the Bible is being misused.

Third, we need to be sure that a particular point is consistent with all of Scripture. Some people—such as those who believe in the gospel of health and wealth—take a few passages out of context and seek to make them normative. However, in reality, they're inconsistent with the rest of Scripture. We must check to see whether a particular proposition is consistent with all of what Scripture teaches.

For example, some people claim there is no law but love. If we love someone and it's a meaningful relationship, then any action is appropriate. But in John 14:15 Jesus said, "If you love me, you will obey what I command." We must realize that there's a prescriptive or definitive element to biblical love. It's necessary to take the concept of love and relate it to the total teaching of Scripture to get the balance.

Fourth, we should be highly cautious if the person's primary emphasis is on experience, because experiences are so variable. If the proposition is rooted in experience alone, then it's subject to change.

I remember talking to a youth leader from a liberal church. He told me that if he had a meaningful experience with communism tomorrow, he would become a communist rather than a Christian because experience is the only criterion for belief. It's important for people to realize that experience alone, apart from the context of Scripture, is a major area to be questioned.

In summary, believers should be slow to accept even a plausible proposition. Just as if you were buying a product, you should take time to back off and reflect before signing the contract. This is especially important if the approach seems to differ from what the church has understood down through the years.

Spend time in prayer, in reflective consideration of Scripture, and in consultation with others who are rooted in the Word. Don't be convinced of an unusual doctrine because of an evening's conversation with a winsome personality. We are called to be as harmless as doves—but as wise as serpents.

♦ INTERPRETING SCRIPTURE PROPERLY
HUDSON T. ARMERDING

A basic question for properly interpreting Scripture is this: What is the clearest grammatical statement of the passage? To find this, you may need to compare two or three translations to be sure you understand what the passage is saying.

Next, try to locate the passage in both its historical and biblical contexts. Know the setting. What historical events were happening at about that time? What was the prevailing worldview? How did people live?

Then try to see whether the same major concept is mentioned in other places in the Bible. If it is, see if your interpretation of it is consistent with the emphases found elsewhere.

I've found this threefold approach to interpreting Scripture very helpful. When I examine the grammatical, historical, and biblical contexts of a passage, I am able to avoid *eisegesis*, reading something into the text that isn't there.

The Importance of Bible Study
CLARK H. PINNOCK

What if I don't get anything out of the Bible? It is often boring and difficult to understand. Do I have to keep on reading it?

You are in serious trouble if this is your problem. You need to be engaged regularly in meaningful Bible study if you are to grow as a Christian and be effective in the ministry God has given you. After all, the Bible was given to us by the Lord to perform many valuable functions in our lives.

The Bible is the yardstick of truth, especially in the areas of theology and ethics. It gives us a portrait of God and leads us to worship him intelligently. It sheds light upon the daily path, and it is a spur to obedience. We could say that the Bible is our most important sacrament, our daily ration of spiritual food, the chief means of both growth and equipment.

Read Psalm 119 to get a feeling for the value the inspired writer placed on the Scriptures. They are the road to intimacy with God, for they tell you how to enter into his presence and abide in his will. So if lack of interest in the Bible is your problem, please take it very seriously and determine to solve it. Not to do so is to give Satan his golden opportunity to nullify your effectiveness as a believer.

It might help to recall three important truths about the Bible. First, it is a fact that God himself gave it to us. It is God's written Word, and it deserves an attentive and believing response.

Second, it is also a fact that real human beings wrote the Bible from within authentic historical settings and with genuine purposes of their own. So it is necessary to try to determine what the text meant when it was first written down. This is the point at which some people have a problem. They are not willing to expend the effort to study the Bible carefully, and therefore it remains for them a largely closed book. Remember, the Bible will not always yield its treasures to a hasty reading.

Third, the Spirit of God uses the Bible as a means of grace in the lives of believers, so we should approach the text prayerfully and with a sense of expectancy. As we know, God hides his truth from the proud and reveals it to the humble and the childlike. As we read the Bible, we should ask not only what this text meant when it was first penned, but also what it means now to us. What is its significance in our lives? Do not forget that our motive for Bible reading ought always to be obedience, learning how we can follow the Lord more faithfully.

There are two sides to Bible reading. First, there is the objective, textual side. Second, there is the subjective, Holy Spirit side. As far as the text is concerned, the Bible was written to be understood by anyone. In large part, it can be. The key to effective understanding is to be discerning in your reading. Listen to the text. Let it speak. Observe its context and ultimately its place within the whole Bible. Notice the changeover from Old to New Testament, and take account of the type of literature you are reading.

You are a fortunate person if you can sit under wise Bible expositors. You can find them in books, if not in your local pulpit. Donald Grey Barnhouse was a tremendous help to me in my early years, as John R. W. Stott is now. This is because there are snags in understanding the Bible at certain points, and it helps to have a trusted expert at your elbow for consultation. Fortunately the church possesses many such people with gifts of sober judgment and spiritual discernment.

On the subjective, Holy Spirit side of Bible study, it is important to hide God's Word in our hearts. Remember how Mary kept all that Jesus told her and pondered it in her heart (Luke 2:51). We need to meditate on the Scriptures and open ourselves to God to be changed by him through them. I underline verses as I read to call attention to the places from which God speaks to me. Often I find that the next time through I see important truths not underlined and marvel at the inexhaustible treasure the Bible really is. Think of it as a great painting or symphony, and expect to be moved by it.

Remember that we come to the Bible with a lot of baggage. We have a lot of opinions and biases that might prevent us from hearing God's Word. In order to counteract the negative effects of personal bias, it is important to listen to what other Bible readers see in the text as a way of releasing fresh truth we might never have grasped on our own. This is the value of small-group Bible study.

Let me make some practical suggestions. You need to have some plan of action in place to carry you through the times when Bible reading feels like more of a duty than a pleasure. First, get yourself a good Bible translation. Today's English Version (TEV), sometimes called *The Good News Bible*, is a good starter, because it is spirited and readable and really carries you along. (It also has cute line drawings!) Another very readable version is *The Living*

Bible (TLB). The New International Version (NIV) is likely to become the standard Bible for evangelicals and is probably the best solid study Bible.

Second, here are some suggestions for procedure. The American Bible Society will give you a leaflet to help you read through the entire Bible in one year. My family also finds the Scripture Union notes on the text to be very helpful, and there are other similar study aids. They keep you on a steady path and offer you a little pointed comment each day to take you beyond yourself and your resources.

I have four ribbon markers in my Bible. At this moment one is in Deuteronomy, one in Psalms, one in John, and one in Romans. I dip into Scripture at four points on a regular basis, and it gives me a feeling of the whole.

At times I take a book such as Mark and study it specially. I read it through quickly and then start to analyze it. Sometimes I will use a commentary in this exercise. It gets me deeper than usual into the text, and this pays dividends. You are fortunate if your church library stocks resources that aid solid Bible study. If not, make it a request to the church leaders.

Perhaps the main thing I ought to say is this: Get serious about reading your Bible effectively. If you do not, you are likely to starve yourself spiritually and nullify your Christian testimony. By being serious, I mean setting aside the time for it. How is it that you can read a newspaper every day and a pile of magazines every week and watch a few hours of TV and yet not have the time for this indispensable activity?

You had better take seriously what the psalmist wrote about the true believer: "His delight is in the law of the Lord, and on his law he meditates day and night. He is like a tree planted by streams of water, which yields its fruit in season and whose leaf does not wither. Whatever he does prospers" (Psalm 1:2, 3).

♦ APPLYING THE BIBLE TO DAILY LIFE
HOWARD HENDRICKS

1. *Know.* To apply a Bible passage, you have to know what it says. If you don't know what it says, you may apply it incorrectly. Good application is always built on good interpretation. If the interpretation is wrong, so is the application.

2. *Relate.* Relate the passage to your life. Does the passage show a sin to avoid, a promise to claim, a prayer to recite, a command to obey, a condition to meet, a verse to memorize, an error to identify, a challenge to face?

3. *Meditate.* Think of specific ways to apply the passage to your life. If studying the passage has made you realize you need to appreciate a family member or a coworker, spend time thinking about what the person does that you appreciate. Then come up with a concrete way to express your gratitude.

4. *Practice.* Having an idea of what I want to do is not application. I have to translate it into actual experience. When the passage has resulted in changed action or attitude, then I have applied it.

Get to Know Your Bible

JAMES BOICE

Worship, fellowship, prayer, and serving God are all important for a Christian. But no element of the Christian life is more important than Bible study. The other elements influence Christian growth, but they cannot replace actually studying and getting to know the written Word of God.

We can do many things to help us know the Bible:

1. *Study the Bible daily.* Of course we can turn to the Bible more than once a day. And some days the press of business or the disruption of our schedules will cause us to miss our study time. But we should discipline our lives to include a daily period of Bible study just as we discipline ourselves to sleep eight hours, brush our teeth, and eat three good meals every day.

How much time should we spend studying? That varies with the individual. Some people who are mature in the faith and who have the time study for an hour or two a day.

On the other hand, new Christians may find it difficult to concentrate on the Bible for a long period of time. Some Christians may have tight schedules. They may spend only ten or fifteen minutes a day.

Of course, longer is better than shorter, as long as the time is productive and other responsibilities are not neglected. But the length of time is not as crucial as studying the Bible regularly.

Studying the Bible at the same time every day helps us get into the habit. What time should that be? In the morning? At night? Again, it depends upon the individual. Choose a time when you are alert. Some people are night people. But for most of us, the best time is in the morning. At night, we're tired after a long, hard day, and we can't concentrate.

2. *Study the Bible comprehensively.* Become acquainted with the entire Bible, not just one book or one section. You can easily read through the Bible in a year by reading a little more than three chapters a day. That's an easy program to follow, and it will expose you to everything. Some of what you read may not seem to relate to your life, but remember 2 Timothy 3:16: "All Scripture is God-breathed and is useful for teaching, rebuking, correcting and training in righteousness."

3. *Study the Bible systematically.* Reading the Bible at random by flipping here and there is not the best way. Reading whatever strikes our fancy leads to a lack of proportion and depth. When we do this, we end up reading the things we want to read. We choose the areas that interest or entertain us, and we ignore other passages that are necessary for our Christian growth. Pick a section and study it thoroughly. Read for application as well as for content.

4. *Study the Bible prayerfully.* This will keep you from studying the Bible for its own sake. At the time of Christ, experts in the law could tell how many pages a book had and how many letters there were on each page. Because of them we have accurate copies of the Bible today. But Jesus told them that for

all their study of Scripture they missed the whole point. They didn't believe in him. (See John 5:39, 40.)

Even modern-day Christians can fall into this trap. A person can be able to name all twelve apostles or all the tribes of Israel, all the kings, all the periods of biblical history as well as all the other biblical facts, and yet not profit from that knowledge spiritually.

The way to get out of that trap is by prayer. The author of Psalm 119 indicated a proper attitude: "Do good to your servant, and I will live; I will obey your word. Open my eyes that I may see wonderful things in your law" (vv. 17, 18).

If I pray like this as I begin to study Scripture, I won't approach it in a merely intellectual way. Instead, I will have the attitude that God is now going to speak to me. What is God going to say? What must I do as a result?

5. *Study the Bible obediently.* You need to ask personal questions as you study. How does this apply to me? Does this tell me something I should do? Or something I shouldn't do? What does it tell me about the will of God for my life? What does it tell me about how to please God? Am I pleasing him?

James 1:22 talks about the importance of obedience. "Do not merely listen to the word, and so deceive yourselves. Do what it says." We need to cultivate prompt, exact, unquestioning, joyous obedience. When we do that, God makes himself real to us through Scripture.

♦ STUDY FOR STRENGTH / JAMES BOICE

Regular meals are necessary for us to be healthy and alert. On occasion we may miss a meal, but we can't do that too often. In the same way we must regularly study God's Word if we are to become spiritually strong. If we neglect Bible reading, we grow indifferent to God. Then we grow lax in spiritual things, and we make ourselves vulnerable to temptation and sin.

Five Keys to Studying the Bible

✍ JAMES BOICE

If you are unfamiliar with the Bible, one of the Gospels is a good place to start. The life of Christ is basic to everything else in Christianity, and the Gospels open up his life to us. The Gospels of John or Mark are especially good.

After having studied one of the Gospels, you could go on to Acts. Acts tells of the early history of the church, the expansion of the gospel in Jerusalem and throughout the Roman Empire.

At that point you could also read one or more of the Epistles. Paul's letters reflect on and explain the meaning of Christ's death and the filling of the Holy Spirit. In the Epistles we also find counsels on Christian living with illustrations of both good and bad conduct. Ephesians is a good place to begin; so is Romans, the greatest doctrinal book in the New Testament.

In your exploration of the Bible, don't neglect the Old Testament. Genesis is an excellent place to start. The psalms are always valuable as part of one's devotions, too.

There are five parts to studying systematically:

1. *Read the book through carefully.* Do this as many as four or five times to get the general scope of the book in mind, perhaps reading aloud once. Every time you read it, something new will strike you.

2. *Divide the book into major sections.* The sections will not necessarily be the same as the chapters in the Bible. Then divide each section into subsections and paragraphs. At this stage the goal should be to see which verses belong together, what subjects are covered, and what is the sequence of subjects.

3. *Relate the sections to each other.* You could ask these questions: Which are the main sections or subjects? Which are the introductions? Which are digressions? Where are the applications? What do the applications relate to?

After you have analyzed the book in this way, you should be able to answer questions such as these: What is this book all about? Why was it written? What does the author hope to see happen as a result of the writing of the book? Study little words like *but, and, because, therefore,* and *since* because they are clues to the flow of the text.

4. *Make a summary.* The summary can cover what is said in each section, why it is said, to whom it is written, and what changes are supposed to come in our lives because of it. If you are studying Romans, for example, you should be able to say, This book was written to the church of Rome and also applies to other churches in other places. It's a general statement of Christian doctrine. It says the human race is lost in sin. The answer to that predicament is the righteousness of God through Jesus Christ. Romans explains the gospel, and it applies doctrines to show how Christians are supposed to live.

5. *Study key words.* Don't get bogged down in this. The general flow of the thought is more important than dissecting every word. But thought flows from words, and you can't really understand what is being said without understanding key terms. For example, in Romans the word *righteousness* is used thirty-five times. All the references are important and throw light on one another. You can't understand the book of Romans without understanding what that word *righteousness* is all about.

♦ TIPS FOR BIBLE STUDY
HOWARD HENDRICKS

In many ways, studying the Bible is similar to studying history, literature, language, or science. We apply the same mental discipline. But in one important way, studying the Bible is completely different. We can study math, for example, without having it particularly change our lives. But when we study the Bible, we confront moral questions. Our lives can be changed through Bible study, and that makes it unique.

We need five basic tools to study the Bible: (1) a good study Bible that is an accurate translation and has paragraphic divisions; (2) a complete

concordance, like Strong's or Young's; (3) a Bible dictionary to look up background material; (4) a Bible atlas to learn where the events take place; and (5) a one-volume commentary such as the *Wycliffe Bible Commentary* to check what someone else has said about the passage.

I ask three basic questions when I study the Bible:

1. *Observation.* What do I see? What is happening in the passage? Is it a miracle, a parable? Where is this taking place? When is it taking place? Who are the people?

2. *Interpretation.* What does it mean? Why is this passage in the Bible? What is its place in the broad overview of biblical teaching?

3. *Application.* How does it work in my life? What difference does this passage make to me? How can I apply it in my home, in my office, at school?

What Will the Bible Do for Me?

JOHN PERKINS

The Bible contains the words from God. It is the revelation we know of God. All Scripture was given to its writers by the inspiration of God (2 Timothy 3:16), so the Bible is an inspired book that comes from God. Therefore, before we come to the Bible and ask what it can do for us, we must have a correct understanding of God.

God is the God of the universe. God is the God of creation. God is the God of all power. God is the God for all humanity. He is more than a Baptist, more than a Presbyterian. He is not a middle-class suburban God. Once we realize the Bible is holy because it contains the words of the one and only God, then our attitude toward his words will be reverence and a sincere desire to obey.

The Bible is given by God for encouragement and for rebuke to help us grow to maturity. The Bible is the source of that daily voice, that daily inspiration that comes from God. The Holy Spirit has a vital role in our Bible reading. The Spirit makes the Word of God real and witnesses that what we're hearing from God are in fact God's words to us.

Since the Bible was divinely given and inspired by God, then it is inspired to us when we receive it through the Holy Spirit. When the Holy Spirit is alive and well in us, and we are reading the Bible with a sense of obedience, that's when the Bible helps us grow and develop.

We should not read the Bible thinking that the more we know, the better we will be. It's not more information we need, not even about the Bible. We need to be ready to obey the Word of God. It is not those who hear the Word of God who will be blessed, but those who obey the Word of God (James 1:22). We need to read the Scripture with the desire to apply it to our lives, and adjust our lives based upon this instruction that has been divinely given.

The Bible can educate our ethics and tell us what God expects. God put his plans for our lives in this book, and he wants us to use what we know. We have a God who loves the world. And we have a God who responds to those who come into a relationship with him. Therefore, God desires to use us to reach outside ourselves, to participate with him to reach the world's people. The powerful voice of Scripture is our response to the poor. If we don't have a positive attitude toward the poor, I wonder whether we understand the God of Scripture.

We need to come to Scripture without our prejudices. The Bible says he that hungers and thirsts after righteousness shall be filled (Matthew 5:6). So you've got to come with a simple hunger and thirst, you've got to come with a sense of need. There has to be a desire and a brokenness, a realization that you're not sufficient on your own.

Too often today, people, because they are rich materially, don't come to God in the realization that they are needy. They come to God for a little lift on Sunday morning. They don't come to the Word of God expecting it to be reproduced and lived out in their lives.

So there's not that great hunger. The Lord wants me to come with a sense of hunger. In my own life, what has kept me searching after God has a lot to do with the fact that I only went to the third grade in school. Everything I go out after, I have to go out after hard. When I read the Scripture, I have to ask, What is God saying here? Then I have to try to understand the application. I come to God as an ignorant person, and he gives me some understanding. Then when I have gained understanding, I want to share.

Most of us read the Scripture in order to teach others, to evangelize. That's not the first motivation for learning the Bible. The first motivation is to answer these questions: What is God saying in his Word to me? And how am I going to obey what he's saying? That's what it's about.

♦ HOW CAN THE BIBLE CHANGE MY LIFE?
YFC EDITORS

When you read the Bible, you must do more than learn facts. You need to take what is said and *apply* it to your daily life. The bridge between such application and a truly changed life includes the following:

1. *Action steps.* What must I do in order to make what God says in this verse a part of my life?

2. *Schedule.* What will I do each day to make this more and more natural to me?

3. *Accountability.* Who can I ask to check up on me and make sure I'm doing what I said I would do?

Why Read the Old Testament?
JOHN PERKINS

The Bible is the unfolding of God's plan. It is God's witness of himself and his character. Sometimes Christians want to rush to the New Testament without spending time in the Old, but they should not do so.

The Old Testament tells about creation, the evidence of the Creator. When we see the sun, the moon, the stars, we see God's handiwork. Without a sound creation theology, your theology gets weak. In the New Testament, creation plays a very important part. In the beginning, God created the heavens and the earth (Genesis 1:1); in the Gospels, all things are made by him (John 1:3); in the Epistles, by faith we understand that the world was framed by the word of God (Hebrews 11:3). Creation plays a major part in our understanding of God. We see the power of God in creation.

The Old Testament also tells about justice. Justice was needed as prideful people abused God's creation. It is impossible to understand the importance of justice without listening to the Old Testament prophets calling Israel back to a proper use of creation and a loving relationship to each other. We see the love of God in justice.

The Old Testament stories show man God's love. He showed his love for humanity at the Flood. He showed it when he called Abraham and created of him a nation-state. He showed it when he pulled his people out of slavery in Egypt. He showed it in selecting Israel, in nurturing and caring for that nation, even in their rebellion. The Old Testament helps us see how God loves each one of us. He cares for us even in our rebellion.

The Old Testament is important for its examples of real people who dealt with real temptation and sin, because if we learn from the examples we can avoid their mistakes. It offers clear pictures of human frailty. It also spotlights the character of individuals and doesn't conceal their sins. It shows us that David was a man after God's own heart, but it also shows that David committed sexual sin and murder. We can see the bad effects of all the temptations, and we can use those as warnings for our lives. The Old Testament teaches how God worked with people in the past so that we can have a clue as to how he is working now.

The Old Testament sets the stage for the activities of the New Testament. Paul talks about God working through the law so that the seed, Jesus Christ, the One promised, could come (Galatians 3:19). When Jesus came, he was the perfect revelation of God, and the Cross was God's greatest act. But Jesus' life and death would not make sense without the backdrop of the Old Testament history and prophecies.

The Old Testament foreshadows the glory of Jesus' first coming, but it looks on to a greater glory. The lamb and the lion shall lie down together (Isaiah 11:6; 65:25). God will set up a kingdom that will never end (Daniel 2:44). The Old Testament foreshadows a fantastic glory yet to be revealed.

◆NOT JUST ANOTHER BOOK / YFC EDITORS

The Bible is not just another book. You can't just read the story, put it down, and be glad you read it. The Bible is God's Word—living and vital. The Holy Spirit makes it new every day in your life. You need to read it every day because different principles will speak to you at different times in life. You need to constantly study and restudy so you can apply it to situations you face. James said, "Anyone who listens to the word but does not do what it says is like a man who looks at his face in a mirror and, after looking at himself, goes away and immediately forgets what he looks like. But the man who looks intently into the perfect law that gives freedom, and continues to do this, not forgetting what he has heard, but doing it—he will be blessed in what he does" (1:23-25).

Learn to Listen to the Word

EUGENE PETERSON

When we talk about applying the Word to life we inadvertently cause much mischief. The Bible is not a medicine chest out of which we take things and swallow or apply them to improve ourselves before God. To use the word *apply* leads us to suppose that our job is to pick and choose from God's Word, that we are in charge of what happens with it. But in actuality, we are being spoken to; we are being shaped, created, and redeemed by the Word.

We are mistaken when we look at the Bible as a spiritual toolbox. We can't take things out of the Bible and make them work for us. The whole process of the spiritual life is to come before the God who is alive, who becomes present to us in his Word, and who by means of that Word creates and redeems. We don't use Scripture; God uses Scripture to work his will in us.

The Bible is God's Word, the Word he is speaking to us, not putting in our possession. That is why we come to the Bible with reverence, submission, and attentiveness. Instead of looking at Scripture, we need to turn our eyes into ears and listen to Scripture.

It is a great blessing to have God's Word written so that we can read it at any time, but that the Word is written also involves us in difficulties not attended to often enough. These difficulties are at the very center of the spiritual life. The difficulties radiate out of a position of ownership—supposing that we own the Word, rather than letting the Word possess us. The simple act of buying a Bible has subtle side effects we need to counter. It is easy to suppose that since we bought it, we own it, and therefore can use it the way we wish.

This danger was not as acute when most Christians were illiterate, for they never read Scripture; they heard it. The words of the Bible were first spoken and listened to. Most of it was in oral form before it was written down. Even the Epistles, which originated as writings, were read aloud and listened to in the churches to which they were written.

Hearing a word is different from reading a word. When we hear, we are poised for response; something is happening. A listener doesn't take a word or a phrase, then walk off and analyze it—that would be to miss the message. A speaking person presents a whole message to us, and we respond as whole persons. But the moment the message is written down, we can stop listening if we are so minded.

Our whole educational system trains us to read Scripture in the wrong way. It teaches us to read it for information, to get a doctrine out of it, to make an argument from it. All the time the Spirit is speaking to us, drawing us into a relationship of love and faith. But we are busy grabbing verses and running off into our studies to try to figure them out. That is rude. We wouldn't tolerate this behavior with our children, but we positively encourage it in our churches. We need to do much less studying of Scripture and more praying before Scripture. Rather than analyzing the Word, we need to let it speak to us.

One of the great tasks of the Christian life is to open our ears before Scripture. The central way is through worship. Worship is fundamentally an act of listening and answering to the Word of God. The sanctuary, the basic gathering place for Christians, is not a study hall or a lecture room.

Another way believers can develop listening ears is by noticing that the Bible comes to us as a story. It does not come to us systematized into doctrine, or arranged as moral instruction. It is a story; and the story form is as important as the truth the story tells. This narrative style is intended to shape the way we read, for our spiritual life will not prosper if we are not drawn into the action of God through history, a story that has a beginning, an end, and a plot. Listening to Scripture in the form of story we learn that we are also in the story, traveling toward God, being drawn toward him. We develop a sense of journeying and discipleship. If we fail to develop this "story sense" we inevitably start "applying" the Bible—taking charge of a verse or doctrine or moral with which we intend to fix some fragment of ourselves. This is an excellent recipe for creating good Pharisees (who were great readers of Scripture, but notoriously poor listeners to God).

It is also important to listen to Scripture in its double context: the context out of which it was spoken and listened to in Israel and Christ, and the context of our listening lives. God uses the same sentence to speak different things to different people. This is because we are at different stages of growth. We know how this works in families: a father tells a story and the two-year-old hears one dimension, the fifteen-year-old another, the wife still another. They all hear the same story; they all listen accurately; they all respond differently, but also appropriately. Since our contexts change daily, we keep listening to Scripture daily.

Our ancestors did this better than we do. They came before Scripture in a listening/responding way rather than in an academic/manipulative way. Becoming familiar with their reverent listening stance before Scripture helps us see the poverty of our students-getting-ready-for-an-exam approach. We are never exempt from the temptation to "use" and "apply" Scripture rather than submit to it and let God call forth things in us we didn't know were there. We have to be continually on guard. Our approach must be reading/listening to Scripture, letting the Word use us rather than using the Word for our well-intentioned but still self-defined purposes.

♦GOOD CHRISTIANS OR PIOUS SINNERS?
EUGENE PETERSON

Why don't some people listen to the Bible? Perhaps they don't want God to speak to them. Instead, they want to tell God what to do, and they use the Bible for their own purposes.

That willfulness is very deep in us,

but we may not recognize it because we disguise it with religious motives. We think we're being good Christians when we're just being pious sinners.

Bible Study and Devotional Reading

ISABEL ANDERS THROOP

What is the difference between studying the Bible and reading it devotionally?

The difference is highlighted by the biblical example of Mary and Martha. Martha busied herself serving, doing, ministering in tangible ways. Mary, her sister, who was a lover of Jesus' presence, sat at his feet and was nourished by his words.

There is nothing wrong with active, methodical service—the process of accumulating Bible facts, memorizing and storing them in order to "use" the Word. In fact, we must have a knowledge of the Word before we can fall in love with the Bible and begin to enter into its life in a devotional way, integrating it into our own spirits. Being occupied in Bible study is being a worker, but reading the Word devotionally is being a lover.

We are all called to be both workers and lovers, to embrace the active life and to learn to sit quietly at Jesus' feet through meditative prayer and Bible reading. The church fathers called the latter practice *lectio divina,* or divine reading. They assumed that God's holy Word would bring a devotional response, that it would affect not only the mind of a person, but also the spirit. In other words, the whole person would become engaged in communion and grow in relationship with the Author of Scripture, God himself.

Should we concentrate on learning first and let the devotional response just happen?

First, we need to decide what our purpose is in coming to the Scriptures on a given day. Not that our purposes can't overlap. But if we are looking for answers to specific questions, doing an inductive book study, preparing to interpret a passage, then we are doing the active work of Bible study. In the process of feeding our minds the information, however, it would be difficult not to be personally moved by the beauty and love of God as evidenced in his Word.

Yet clearly our purpose in Bible study is primarily to collect data, compare facts, and put them together in some form either in our minds, on paper, or for a sermon or talk to be delivered. In this process we become coworkers with the line of biblical prophets, teachers, and writers who offered themselves to be carriers of God's truth. This is a high calling, but a humbling one as well, for we are always earthen vessels subject to misunderstanding, wrong emphasis, wordiness, obscurity, or imbalance. Yet in spite of our inability and limitations (all humans have them) the Word will somehow shine through. We are assured in Isaiah 55:11 that God's Word will accomplish whatever God purposes for it.

We are to be the best students we can be, more diligent than we would be at school, for we are handling divine truths, words of life that can change people's whole direction and transform their actions if they heed them. So prayer beforehand, though a devotional practice, is appropriate as part of Bible study. Then all our skills of observation, checking, cross-referencing, compiling, and researching will make up our Bible study work.

There are a number of reasons to undertake Bible study: (1) to become better acquainted with the Scriptures for our own assurance and to be able to answer anyone who asks about the hope that is in us; (2) to answer specific questions that arise in daily living or decision making; (3) to study a book of the Bible or a particular theme in Scripture for Christian nurture and edification; and (4) to prepare to speak, write, or otherwise share our findings with others.

While some scholars might approach the biblical text simply for information or research, it is hard to imagine anyone who is a committed Christian not also entering into the written Word for reasons of faith and belief. In other words, even in active Bible study, we are still lovers of God's Word.

Then what characterizes devotional reading of Scripture?

1. The purpose of reading Scripture as a lover is to commune with God himself, to hear the promises, comfort, and admonition that he wants to direct to our hearts in a personal way, not just as cold print on paper. One characteristic of a lover is expectancy—waiting excitedly for what the time with the loved one will yield, as Mary waited for the words Christ would utter as she sat at his feet. We can practice expectancy by praying for a quietness, a centering on God and his presence as we open his Word. It is hard to make the transition from the busy working world to a quiet, solitary spot where we commune only with God. Yet it is worth seeking to achieve. Only as we purpose in our hearts to make time for this will it occur. And only as we choose to make it a priority and a consistent practice will we see its fruit in our lives.

2. In devotional reading of Scripture, we are seeking not primarily content or answers, but growth, a heart change, a moving toward Christ in our attitude and spirit. That is not so easily measured as answers to a Bible study lesson, but we may still be aware that a devotional time has been productive and enriching. This assurance comes as a feeling of peace, of resolve, of conviction to go back to our everyday lives stronger and more attuned to God's will for our lives. We may not feel something every time, but the general direction and pattern of our lives will be affected by genuine communing with God in devotional prayer and Scripture reading. We will miss it if we are away from it for a time. We will find our hearts turning to God in devotional, prayerful thoughts at other times of the day, even when we are not in our quiet, set-aside time. Thus gradually we learn what it is to be in an attitude of prayer, to "pray without ceasing" through the day.

3. We also will find the words of Scripture—phrases of promise and joy, notes of praise—coming into our minds because of this time spent at Jesus' feet listening to his Word. We will see that the events of our own lives start to get woven in with the truths of Scripture. God begins to illuminate our under-

standing of his Word so that we find ourselves practicing biblical standards without consciously thinking about them first. That is, we will graduate from doing what the Bible says by rote—applying an answer to a question like filling in a blank—to walking in the way of Christ naturally, making choices in accord with what he has taught us in that time of listening and waiting on him.

While Bible study and devotional reading will overlap, it is good to be aware that we need both emphases. We may find, during a time of Bible study begun simply to seek answers or to do our duty, our hearts being spontaneously awakened in prayer as we react to God's truth before us. We should allow our eyes to rest on those phrases and verses that especially speak to our hearts at that moment. God uses our response to these words to help us learn and grow.

When we must go away from our retreat we will actually find our tasks lighter and our work smoother because of the joy of fellowship that has come from meeting the Author as well as reading his words.

It is appropriate to pray whenever we approach Scripture that the Lord will quicken his lively Word in our hearts, teaching us whatever it is he desires for us to gain from the time spent in deliberate study or meditation. This prayer he will surely answer. Then we need not worry overmuch about mixing study and devotional reading, because if our desire is for the Lord himself, it will not matter. God's Word will be accomplishing his purpose in us, and we will come away changed.

If you have felt like Martha, overburdened with too much study and too little time to sit at Jesus' feet and listen to his words, consider sitting down for a short time each day and praying for communion. Not a garnering of facts, but eyes to see and ears to hear God's words to you. Take time to be Mary, too!

♦ MEANINGFUL DEVOTIONS
HOWARD HENDRICKS

Many of us were taught that the morning is the best time for devotions. But we may need to be creative. Perhaps our lunch break or after supper is the best time for us. Night people would do better to stay in bed the half hour in the morning so they can be civil during the day and have their devotions in the evening.

We need to be realistic in deciding how long our devotions should be. Regularity is more important than the amount of time we spend. For most people, two hours of Bible study is unrealistic. Looking at how much time we have available, we should begin small and expand as we can. If we have time for only fifteen minutes a day, then we can start with that.

Most people get wiped out because they start big and get carried away with idealism. They start with an hour a day for devotions, and although it goes well for a while, they eventually get off the track and feel guilty. Soon they aren't spending any time at all. Regularity is more important than the amount of time spent.

The point is this: Where is your heart? What do you want to do? If you want to meet with the Lord, you will find time for that. When you get off track, for whatever reason, you will get back on as soon as possible.

Our devotional times are most meaningful if we see them not as a legalistic duty but as an opportunity to worship God. We can also bring meaning to our devotional times by making them application-oriented. When we pray, "Lord, what message do you have for me that I can use in my life today?" he will give us what we need.

Living Out Bible Metaphors

✍ LUCI SHAW

The metaphors in the Bible can relate to our own lives, to where we are on our spiritual journey. They can give images to our passages.

I began to be intrigued by this concept while I was reading the story of the prophet Ezekiel. Ezekiel was told to give his message to the people of God not just in words, but in actions, in various scenes that he acted out.

For example, God told him to take a clay tablet and draw a map of Jerusalem on it. Then he was to build models of battering rams and camps around it, so that it would represent a city under siege. God then told him,

Lie on your left side and put the sin of the house of Israel upon yourself. You are to bear their sin for the number of days you lie on your side. I have assigned you the same number of days as the years of their sin. So for 390 days you will bear the sin of the house of Israel.

After you have finished this, lie down again, this time on your right side, and bear the sin of the house of Judah. I have assigned you 40 days, a day for each year. Turn your face toward the siege of Jerusalem and with bared arm prophesy against her. I will tie you up with ropes so that you cannot turn from one side to the other until you have finished the days of your siege. Ezekiel 4:4-8

Can you imagine that? Ezekiel was allowed to have food and water within reach, but he had to stay in that one position. All the people could see him, and quite a sight he must have been! Ezekiel had become a living metaphor. He was acting out God's message to the people.

Then he had to take a sword, shave his beard and his head, weigh the hair, and divide it in thirds. God told him to shake one third of it around Israel, to burn one third, and to throw the rest to the wind. These actions all symbolized what God was going to do to the children of Israel. In effect God said, "This is Jerusalem, and this is you. You're a living metaphor, a picture of what I'm going to do to these people. Nothing else has worked. I've been sending messages to them and rebuking them and calling them to myself. I just don't take no's, but maybe they'll understand through you, Ezekiel."

The prophet Jeremiah was also a living metaphor. God told him, in our vernacular, to bury his linen shorts in the riverbank where it was wet and muddy. Then the people would see that they were like God's garment that was becoming all wet and muddy with sin. It's a vivid image of what was about to happen. Jeremiah also had to carry a basket of good and bad fruit on his head. The good figs symbolized people who obeyed God and were blessed, and the bad figs stood for the people who hadn't responded to the Lord and who thus had gone rotten with sin.

The story of Hosea is perhaps the best-known living metaphor in the Bible. Hosea was told by God to marry a prostitute. He loved her and was faithful to her, even though she flaunted her own unfaithfulness. Every time she ran off he pursued her and brought her back to him. This is beautiful symbolism for how God was pursuing Israel and would bring her back into covenant relationship with himself, how he would make the relationship right.

John Stott said that in the thirteenth chapter of John, where Jesus washed the disciples' feet, Jesus himself was a living metaphor. Stott wrote:

Jesus' actions were a deliberate parable of his mission. John seems clearly to have understood this for he introduces the incident with these words. "Jesus, knowing . . . that he had come from God and was going to God, rose from supper . . . " (vv. 3, 4). That is, knowing these things, he dramatized them in action. . . . Thus Jesus "rose from supper," as he had risen from his heavenly throne. He "laid aside his garments," as he had laid aside his glory and emptied himself of it. He then "girded himself with a towel" (the badge of servitude), as in the Incarnation he had taken the form of a servant. Next, he began "to wash the disciples' feet, and to wipe them with the towel," as he went to the cross to secure our cleansing from sin. After this he put his garments back on "and resumed his place," as he returned to his heavenly glory and sat down at the Father's right hand. By these actions he was dramatizing his whole earthly career. He was teaching them about himself, who he was, where he had come from and where he was going. (God's Book for God's People [InterVarsity Press, 1982], 77, 78)

It's possible for us to tap into some of the biblical metaphors. Now I'm not saying we're going to undergo the trials of Ezekiel or Hosea, although God may call us to do some very difficult things. Perhaps we will be more like Job, who was a sign to all the people around him. God allowed him to be an object lesson of suffering. He allowed Satan to do awful things to him to prove it's possible to be faithful to God under stress and difficulty. And Job fulfilled that metaphor. He obeyed God and lived through it all.

Jonah was a metaphor too. He showed how God persists, even with somebody who's rebellious and unwilling to do what he's told. Incredibly, Jesus compared himself with that reluctant prophet. He said, "As Jonah was three days and three nights in the belly of a huge fish, so the Son of Man will be three days and three nights in the heart of the earth" (Matthew 12:40).

We have to learn how to live out the Bible metaphors. My father was an example of how that is possible. He was a doctor, an explorer, and a missionary in the Solomon Islands around the turn of the century. In those days the Solomon Islanders were cannibals, and several of his colleagues were killed and eaten by them. But when my father found out that these primitive people responded to humor, he would jump up and down, make faces, hop around on one foot, and generally make them laugh at his antics. The natives were completely disarmed. They would collapse on the beach with laughter. There was no way they could be afraid of or antagonistic toward this comical man.

My father thought of himself as a bridge from one nation and culture to another. He was a very learned, cultured, dignified Britisher, and yet he was able to bridge the gap between the modern Western world and the Solomon Islands so that ultimately people were brought into the kingdom of God.

Some metaphors that I'm living out are green, growth, and water. (In fact, my first book of poetry was called *Listen to the Green,* and my second was *The Secret Trees,* so you can see how that metaphor comes into play in my life.) Several years ago my husband and I were in Israel. We went on a trip to the Jordan Valley and the Dead Sea, which is the driest, most arid, inhospitable place I can think of on the face of the earth. There isn't a vestige of green to be seen anywhere; everything is baked to death. The soil is so acidic and salty that very little will grow in it. The day we drove there the temperature was about 115 degrees, and that was at ten in the morning. The air was so dry we had to rub our skin with lotion every few minutes or our faces felt as if they would crack open.

As we went down into the valley, which is several hundred feet below sea level, we noticed in the distance a beautiful oasis of green—Jericho. It stood out like an emerald in the middle of all the dry, sterile, arid desert.

Later, when we drove into Jericho, we saw a little fruit stand where we bought honey, loquats, oranges, and other fruit. On this side of the street were beautiful flowering vines, palm trees, and groves of green, growing things. But on the other side of the street, which marked the city limits, there was just desert—not one green thing—and this barrenness stretched all the way to the Dead Sea.

When we stood perfectly still and quiet, we discerned what made the difference: we could hear the gurgle of water in the irrigation ditches that crisscross Jericho. They're not pipes, but open, stone-lined conduits that pump water up from underground springs. The people dip into the water as they need it, and they channel it into their fields. It's the water that makes the difference between orchards and desert.

The Scriptures are full of the image of water as the element that makes life possible. Jeremiah 17:5-8 reads:

This is what the Lord says: "Cursed is the one who trusts in man, who depends on flesh for his strength and whose heart turns away from the Lord. He will be like a bush in the wastelands; he will not see prosperity when it comes. He will dwell in the parched places of the desert, in a salt land where no one lives. But blessed is the man who trusts in the Lord, whose confidence is in him. He will be like a tree planted by the water that sends out its roots by the stream. It does not fear when heat comes; its leaves are always green. It has no worries in a year of drought and never fails to bear fruit."

That water is the Holy Spirit.

Isaiah 44:3, 4 says: "I will pour water on the thirsty land, and streams on the dry ground; I will pour out my Spirit on your offspring, and my blessing on your descendants. They will spring up like grass in a meadow, like poplar trees by flowing streams." The water of God is a necessity in my life. If I cut myself off from its source, if I ignore the Scriptures, if I refuse to let my imagination be replenished by God's images and his messages to me, then I'm going to go dry, shrivel up, and blow away. Water is a very important biblical metaphor that's stayed with me all my life.

As we read the Scriptures, we need to keep alert for its pictures. Then we need to discover where our own gifts and interests fit in with the biblical metaphors. We won't have just one metaphor for our entire life; the metaphors will change as the seasons of our lives change.

Through these metaphors we can learn much about the Lord and about ourselves, about how we should relate to Christ and to other people, about what our actions and attitudes should be, about what fruits of the Spirit we need to be developing. And all this learning and growth can come through paying attention to the pictures and metaphors in the Bible.

RELATED ARTICLES

Chapter 4: **God Speaks to Us through Scripture**
Chapter 22: **The Bible: The Final Authority in Decision Making**
Chapter 27: **Using the Bible in Witnessing**

CHAPTER

17

The Importance of Prayer

- ✓ Does prayer really make a difference?
- ✓ What is prayer?
- ✓ How do we pray?
- ✓ Why should I pray if God knows everything already?
- ✓ Does God really answer prayer?

Responding to God in Prayer

JAMES BOICE

We need two things in order to grow in our Christian lives. One is Bible study—God's way of talking to us. The other is prayer—our way of talking to God. As we study the Bible, we're led to respond to God in prayer. And as we pray, if we really are allowing the Holy Spirit to have his way with us, we inevitably will be directed back to Scripture.

Reuben A. Torrey, in his book *How to Pray* (New York: Revell, 1900), lists eleven reasons why prayer is important:

- because there is a devil, and prayer is a God-appointed means of resisting him (Ephesians 6:12, 13)
- because prayer is God's way for us to obtain what we need from him (James 4:2)

- because God gave us a pattern in the apostles, who considered prayer one of the most important businesses of their lives (Acts 6:1-4)
- because prayer occupied a very prominent place in our Lord's life (Mark 1:35; Luke 6:12)
- because prayer is the present ministry of our Lord, who is now interceding for us (Romans 8:34; Hebrews 7:25)
- because prayer is the means God has appointed for our receiving mercy from him and for finding "grace to help us in our time of need" (Hebrews 4:16)
- because prayer is the means of obtaining the fullness of God's joy
- because prayer with thanksgiving is the means of obtaining freedom from anxiety and, in anxiety's place, "the peace of God, which transcends all understanding" (Philippians 4:6, 7)
- because prayer is the method appointed for obtaining the fullness of God's Holy Spirit (Luke 11:13)
- because prayer is the means by which we are to keep watchful and alert as Christ's return approaches (Luke 21:24-36)
- because prayer is used by God to promote our spiritual growth, bring power into our work, lead others to faith in Christ, and bring all other blessings to Christ's church (Psalm 139:23, 24; Matthew 7:7, 8)

Just because we recognize the importance of prayer, however, doesn't mean we understand everything about prayer. One of my favorite stories about prayer concerns two of the greatest evangelists the English-speaking world has ever seen.

George Whitefield, a Calvinist, believed in predestination. John Wesley, an Arminian, believed in free will. The two men worked together many times. One day they started early in the morning preaching in the field, and then they visited people all day. At night they preached together again. Then they returned to where they were staying and, utterly exhausted, got ready for bed.

They both knelt down beside the bed. Whitefield prayed something like this: "Lord, we thank you for everything that has happened this day. All of this is in your hands, and we trust you to work it all out according to your perfect will again." Having prayed thus, he got up and climbed into bed.

Wesley had hardly gotten past the invocation in his prayer in this length of time. He looked up and said, "Mr. Whitefield, is this where your Calvinism leads you?" Then he bowed his head again and went on praying.

Whitefield pulled up the covers and went to sleep. About two hours later, he woke up and saw that Wesley was still on his knees beside the bed. He couldn't believe it. He got out of bed, went around to where Wesley was kneeling, and touched him. Wesley was fast asleep. Whitefield said, "Mr. Wesley, is this where your Arminianism leads you?"

If Wesley and Whitefield didn't have all the answers about prayer, we should not be surprised if we don't understand everything about it either. But like Wesley and Whitefield, we continue to pray in obedience to our Lord, and he gives us strength to do his will.

Prayer will always be a mystery to us. We're told on the one hand that prayer is very effective. James 5:16 says, "The prayer of a righteous man is powerful and effective." Earlier in the same letter, James said, "You do not have, because you do not ask God" (4:2). Jesus said several times, especially in John, "Ask and you will receive, and your joy will be complete" (16:24). Will our praying change God's mind? That's difficult to answer, but let me answer like this. God has a plan of action for the history of this world. God's plan is perfect, for God's will is perfect. Suppose we began to pray, desiring to change God's perfect will. What would happen if we succeeded? We would bring something less than perfection into the world. Our prayers would be dangerous. If that's what we mean by changing God's mind, I hope prayer doesn't do that. I don't want anything to interfere with God's will.

On the other hand, if we pray, will things happen that would not happen if we did not pray? The answer is certainly yes. But how does that work? If God has a perfect, sovereign will, how can our prayers have any effect whatsoever? The answer is this: God never accomplishes his purposes without means.

Prayer is one of the means God has appointed by which to accomplish his will. God says, "I'm going to do this, and the means by which I'm going to do it is prayer. I'm going to do it in response to the prayers of my people."

This not only means that God knows what we are going to pray. It also means, in some way our finite minds cannot possibly comprehend, that if we do not pray, the thing will not happen. If we pray according to God's will, which is what we should do, it will happen. If God has determined something to happen and we don't pray, are we keeping God's will from being accomplished? No, it doesn't work that way, because God's will embraces all the variables in ways we cannot fully understand.

We have a great responsibility in prayer. Prayer is not an empty exercise. It is vital. We have to take those verses at face value; if we don't receive, it's because we don't ask. If we ask according to God's will in the name of Christ, we will receive.

Christians often say, and rightly so, "if it be your will." If we mean by that what we should mean—that we certainly don't want to ask for anything contrary to God's will, and that we want God to override our prayers if we are asking for the wrong things—then it's proper to use that phrase in our prayers.

But often when we say "if it be your will" we are really giving God an escape clause. What we're saying is this: "I don't think it is really going to happen. I don't really trust God to do it. I'm going to say 'if it be your will' so that, when it doesn't happen, I can say, 'Obviously it wasn't God's will.' " That's not right.

We can learn from Martin Luther what it means to be bold in prayer. In 1540, when Luther was an old man, his friend and assistant Myconius became sick. Expecting to die in a very short time, he sent Luther a farewell letter. When Luther got the letter, he sent back a reply that went like this: "I command you in the name of God to live, because I still have need of you in the work of reforming the church. The Lord will never let me hear that you are dead, but will permit you to survive me. For this I am praying. This is my will, and may my will be done, because I seek only to glorify the name of God."

When we read something like that, we are shocked. It seems wrong for Luther, or ourselves following his footsteps, to say "my will be done." But Luther added, "because I seek only to glorify the name of God." He was praying boldly—and properly.

Although Myconius had lost the ability to speak by the time Luther's letter came, in a short time he revived and soon recovered completely. He lived six more years, outliving Luther by two months.

We should be careful, of course, not to be presumptuous in prayer. We should not presume automatically that our hearts are always right with God. But on the other hand, we can never be too bold in prayer.

We can look into God's face and say, "Father, I don't pray this for myself, and I don't want my selfish will to be done. I want your will to be done. Because I want your will to be done, this is what I ask for, and I ask for it boldly. I ask you to do it now, and do it in such a way that everybody will give glory to you." If more Christians prayed like that, we would see profound changes in our lives and in our world.

♦ WHAT PRAYER IS / RICHARD FOSTER

Prayer is not simply trying to find an answer or asking for help to overcome this or that. Prayer is mainly creating an open, empty space where God can come in and be our friend. Jesus said, "You are my friends if you do what I command" (John 15:14). We are trying to enter into an intimate friendship with God so that we will have a greater and greater sense of what pleases him. And that's what we work on when we pray: we look for a life of intimacy with God, not for specific answers to requests. As we come into this intimacy, the other things begin to fall into place.

Prayer: The Key to Spiritual Growth

✍ WILLIAM BRIGHT

Through the centuries, men and women of God have always prayed, and wherever people know how to pray, God blesses. One of the great examples of that today is the church in Korea. It is the most praying church in modern times, and the most rapidly growing. I spoke for a week of meetings there for Explo '74 when the crowds averaged from five hundred thousand to 1.5 million. When I returned there in 1980, the crowds were from 2 million to almost 3 million every night. One evening more than a million people indicated that they had received Christ. The church has grown from 3 million in 1974 to 11 million in 1985, growth unprecedented in all of history. The Korean people know how to pray like no other people since the first century.

We pray because we are commanded to. We pray because our Lord modeled it. Christ not only spent much of his time while on earth in prayer, but even now, as he sits at the right hand of the Father, he is dedicating his time to praying on our behalf. We pray, also, because it is one of God's ways of providing what we need. Scripture says, "You do not have, because you do not ask God" (James 4:2).

Many people pray and nothing happens because there is sin in their lives. Scripture says that the Spirit makes intercession for us with groanings that cannot be uttered. Only when people are filled with the Holy Spirit can they really pray.

What are the results of prayer? We are drawn closer to Christ. We become more like him. And we reap spiritual dividends. We live a more holy life, a more exciting, more fruitful life, a life that brings greater honor and glory to God. Jesus instructed his disciples, "Ask the Lord of the harvest, therefore, to send out workers into his harvest field" (Matthew 9:38). One of the ways I believe God has sent sixteen thousand full-time and associate staff to Campus Crusade is through prayer. We pray, and God sends them. It's amazing.

We have seen many dramatic answers to prayer. One day our board of directors met to discuss a special urgent need for $1 million. There had never been a time in the history of the ministry when we needed so much money. This was in 1973, following Explo '72, the most important event in the history of our ministry until that time. Misplaced confidence in others resulted in this unexpected deficit. We felt strongly led to pray that God would work a miracle. "Lord," we prayed, "we need a million dollars to meet our obligations." The following Tuesday one of my associates came running to me with good news. "So and so is on the phone and he wants to give us $1.1 million!" I had never heard of him, but my associate said, "He says he knows you and loves you and that God used you to change his life." When I got on the telephone, the man said, "I have sold some property and God has told me to send you this money, and I've been instructed that you will know what to do with it."

One of the most dramatic answers to prayer I've ever seen was my father's conversion. My mother was a saintly woman who dedicated me to the Lord before I was even born and prayed for me every day of her life. But my father, although he was a good, moral man and a wonderful person I loved dearly, was not a Christian. I assumed that women were supposed to be spiritual and men were supposed to be the ones who "got things done."

In the course of events, through my mother's prayers and through the ministry of the church, I became a Christian. I was so excited that I immediately thought of my father. My mother didn't need my prayers. She was already a giant of a woman. But my father needed Christ. Within six months, God had worked in miraculous ways, even arranging an evangelistic campaign in a cold little Methodist church in our community. My mother had gone there for years, but my father was not a member. The very week the meetings were to start, I was able to stop home on my way from California. That week my father went with mother and me to the meetings. I introduced him to Christ who made a dramatic change in his life and in our family.

To me, prayer is talking to God. As I pray through the Scripture, as I worship and praise and adore the Lord, I ask him, "Lord, is there someone you want me to talk to? Who is it you want me to pray for?" Certain people and circumstances come to mind. Often I ask about the spiritual welfare of family and associates. I ask, "Is there something I need to know? Is there anything I can do for them?" and the Lord tells me what to do. The God who controls the laws of the universe, who works in the affairs of men and nations, tells me what he wants me to do. I know there are people who don't believe that God speaks to men today as he did during Bible times, but I do and have for forty years. As a result, the Christian life has been a great joy and a tremendous adventure with our Lord. This, I believe, is the great privilege of every believer.

I invite God to speak to me as I read the Scriptures, which I believe were divinely inspired of God through the Holy Spirit, who anointed holy men of old to record holy truth. I ask the Holy Spirit to show me what he wants me to know and to understand how he wants me to respond to what I read from his Word. As I read, I pray.

In Psalm 1, we read that the man who does certain things "is like a tree planted by streams of water, which yields its fruit in season and whose leaf does not wither. Whatever he does prospers" (Psalm 1:3). Now what are the things that guarantee a joyful, fruitful, prosperous life? First of all, he meditates on the Lord, on the Word of God day and night. He delights in doing everything God wants him to do. And he is always seeking ways to follow God more closely.

I pray, "Lord, I want to be that kind of person who loves you, who delights in your Word daily, who takes joy in doing everything you want him to do. And I want to follow you more closely, not for selfish reasons, but because I love you and I want to please you." The end result is a rich, exciting, adventuresome life. As the Bible says, "Delight yourself in the Lord and he will give you the desires of your heart" (Psalm 37:4).

The Spirit's Prayer for His People

LARRY CHRISTENSON

Jesus said, "God is spirit, and his worshipers must worship in spirit and in truth" (John 4:24). The Holy Spirit's role in worship is to bring us into the presence of the Father, wrapped in the righteousness of Christ.

The Spirit presents us much as the priests presented the Old Testament sacrifices. The Israelites themselves did not prepare the offering for the altar; instead the priests slaughtered the animals and laid them upon the altar before God. In the same way, the Holy Spirit presents us as living sacrifices before the Father. It is not through our own action or desire or initiative that we are presented—the Spirit himself becomes the agent and the executor of our prayers.

Paul said in Romans 8:26, 27: "The Spirit helps us in our weakness. We do not know what we ought to pray, but the Spirit himself intercedes for us with groans that words cannot express. And he who searches our hearts knows the mind of the Spirit, because the Spirit intercedes for the saints in accordance with God's will."

Though the Holy Spirit intercedes for us in several ways, I believe this passage focuses specifically on the prayer that goes beyond conscious understanding. I call this the "above-and-beyond prayer." It may be, as some New Testament scholars maintain, that Paul is referring here to speaking in tongues.

The Scriptures clearly indicate the unique power of the spoken word. In fact, its power transcends the limits of our finite understanding. The gift of tongues allows a wider frame of reference for the release of God's power. One blessing this gift brings is an increased ability to release my concerns to God. When I don't know how to pray, I can speak in tongues and trust that the Spirit will articulate my concerns in an appropriate way.

I don't just pray, "God, you take care of this situation. You understand it better than I do." Instead I pray, "Lord, I'm going to pray beyond the limits of my understanding. I'm going to trust the Spirit to articulate this prayer."

The Scriptures indicate that the Spirit accomplishes this prayer "in accordance with God's will." We are moved in this prayer toward the will and purpose of God. This is not a static or predictable movement. The Spirit is flexible; his work can't be nailed down to a specific methodology.

I discovered this when I first got involved with a healing ministry in a California congregation. We experienced a dramatic healing of cancer. We thought we had discovered a right method of prayer. The Holy Spirit disabused us of this notion quickly—the next time we tried the method, it didn't work. It was the Spirit we had to take hold of, not a method.

Every situation is different. We are continually driven to seek God anew. We must constantly ask the Father, What do I do now?

That's the difference between walking in the Spirit and walking in the flesh. In the flesh we can learn certain practices and become skillful in them. In the Spirit, however, our only skill is our ability to hear the Spirit and to follow his leadings.

If we do not cultivate this humble, listening attitude, the Spirit will force it upon us. He will not let us manipulate him. We must be brutally honest with ourselves. If something does not work out as we had hoped, we must ask ourselves if we have truly received the Lord's word in that situation. We must go daily in prayer before the Lord, seeking anew his will and his direction. That is what is meant by praying "in spirit and in truth."

♦ TO WHOM SHOULD WE PRAY?
LARRY CHRISTENSON

There is ample evidence in Scripture that we can address our prayers to any one of the persons of the Trinity. Jesus and the Father both receive worship in the New Testament, and Jesus spoke about the coming Counselor in terms that associate the Father and the Son with the Holy Spirit (see John 14:15–16:16). God has revealed himself in three persons, so according to where we are and what kind of things we're praying about, we might address our prayer to the Father, the Son, or the Holy Spirit. No matter which one we pray to, of course, the whole Trinity is involved in our prayer.

Not only can we address God as different persons; we can also address him by different names. God is called many names in Scripture. Each name is like a window that opens up the horizon in our understanding of and relationship with God. We can use a whole spectrum of biblical names as do the psalms—and they are a guide for prayer. If I call him my Good Shepherd, my focus is somewhat different than if I call him my High Priest. The Great I Am is a different focus from Our Father. Each is true, but each concentrates on a different aspect of who God is.

God's revelation of himself in three persons, and through many names, provides us with a variety of avenues for approaching him, answering to the variety of our needs and callings.

How to Pray

VERNON GROUNDS

When we consider how to pray, we need to beware of overanalyzing what is a natural, spontaneous activity. We can easily become like the centipede who was doing just fine until someone asked him how he knew which foot to put forward first. When he stopped to think about it, he became so befuddled he couldn't get started again. In the same way, we should not become so concerned about how to pray that we end up unable to carry on simple conversations with our heavenly Father. Still, we can improve our prayer lives by considering the Bible's guidelines regarding prayer:

1. *We should pray regularly.* This is especially important for anyone who is beginning to pray. Some structure is essential, some discipline. Even people who have been praying a long time need to bear in mind the importance of habit and the danger of letting habit degenerate into legalism.

Years ago, I came across a saying that was very helpful to me: "The rut of routine can become the groove of grace." The discipline of prayer can indeed degenerate into a rut of routine. But it's only when I'm willing to persist in moving along in those ruts that I can experience at least occasionally the blessing of shifting into a groove of grace.

So I pray regularly, whether or not it's an earthshaking experience. I pray whether or not heaven comes down and glory fills my soul. I pray because I believe God is faithful and the Spirit is at work regardless of how I feel. Developing the habit of prayer does more for my spiritual life in the long run than waiting for sporadic impulses to motivate me to pray.

The Bible admonishes us to pray constantly. Luke 18:1 reads, "They should always pray and not give up," and 1 Thessalonians 5:17, "Pray continually." We read these verses and may wonder how that can be done. These texts imply that moment by moment we depend on God for his guidance. They also mean we recognize that every fleeting breath we take is a gift from God. Praying continually does not necessarily imply a conscious communication between ourselves and the Lord. Instead, it implies that prayer is a discipline and a habit, something we have made the rule and practice of our lives.

2. *We should pray honestly.* We come to a heavenly Father who loves us and isn't going to be alienated by our candor as we talk to him. There's nothing we shouldn't say to God. There isn't a thought in our minds that he doesn't already know. So we might as well share it with him, whether we put it into words or express it nonverbally. We are free in him to express whatever we're thinking. As Psalm 139:23, 24 says, "Search me, O God, and know my heart; test me and know my anxious thoughts. See if there is any offensive way in me, and lead me in the way everlasting."

3. *We should pray with confidence.* Hebrews 4:16 is more of an entreaty than a directive, "Let us then approach the throne of grace with confidence, so that we may receive mercy and find grace to help us in our time of need." In some translations, the word *boldly* is used in place of *with confidence.* In Greek the word means "complete openness of speech." It means telling God exactly how we feel about ourselves and about life's circumstances. We should pray with an attitude of openness, freedom, and confidence.

In my own prayer routine, I try to pray every day. Of course there are days when that routine gets interrupted. But almost every day without fail I find some time to talk with the Lord. When I'm at home in Colorado I go to my study in the evening and usually turn on the classical music station to the point where I can barely hear it. For me a soft musical background creates an environment conducive to prayer.

I usually walk back and forth or simply sit and look at the Rocky Mountains through a window as I spend at least a half hour talking with the Lord. During this time, I tell him honestly what is on my heart, what I'm feeling and thinking. Then I ask for those things that concern me. I pray not only for myself, but for my family, for government leaders, for the church, for the seminary where I work, for missions.

Prayer is not just one-way communication. It involves listening as well as talking. We believe that through his Word God speaks to us. We read Scripture and seek to listen as God speaks through it. We read and then pray, and then read again and pray some more. There are people who pray and then meditate, seeking to focus their attention on God. While they do not testify to an audible message, they testify that they gain clarified insights into the nature and the will of God. God speaks to us through other avenues as well—a book, a testimony, a sermon, a hymn. We need to guard against talking too much and listening too little.

Prayer is not always verbal. We can lift up our souls or pour out our hearts to God without speaking any words, just thinking them. There are times when we can't consciously formulate in language what is surging within our souls. At those times we fall back on Romans 8:26, "We do not know what we ought to pray for, but the Spirit himself intercedes for us with groans that words cannot express."

Sometimes written prayers may be helpful. There are marvelous collections, such as John Baillie's *Diary of Private Prayer,* which can often express better than I can the feelings and desires deepest in my heart. I can read some of these silently. Or I can read them out loud, adding my own amen. I am reading exactly what I wish I could say but don't have the capacity to verbalize. I'm grateful for brothers or sisters who had the words to voice what is in my heart.

But regardless of what discipline we follow, what methods we use, the most important thing is to pray—regularly, honestly, and confidently.

♦ PRAYING IN JESUS' NAME
LARRY CHRISTENSON

Jesus has promised to supply us with everything we need in order to do what he has sent us to do. We can confidently pray in his name when we know that our request is in agreement with his purpose.

When a manager needs to order a million dollars' worth of equipment for his department, he places the order in his company's name. He knows the supplier will recognize the order, because it comes from a solid, reputable company. He also knows the company will provide the money, because it was the company that asked him to get the equipment in the first place. It is needed to get the job done.

When we pray in Jesus' name, we come into God's presence in the authority of Jesus—clothed in his righteousness and with his call upon our life. We tell the Father what we need in order to do what Jesus calls us to do in a particular situation. We draw upon heaven's resources, which Jesus has made available to us, to carry out our calling. We trust that whatever we truly need, God will supply.

Talking to a Holy God
DAVE VEERMAN

On Wednesday nights my family piled into the car and drove dutifully to church for prayer meeting. Even in grade school, I would sit among the adults, listening quietly, sometimes even praying. Prayer was formal. In those heads-bowed-eyes-closed moments I heard a basketful of *thees, thous,* and *shouldests,* and I concluded that prayers were said with a certain language. (We certainly didn't talk that way at home.)

Another misconception of prayer, but related to the first, is that it only takes place in church or some other "holy" spot. I knew this wasn't totally true because we prayed a lot at home, but for many people this is a real issue.

The Bible provides two "bookend" concepts of prayer. On one end we read that prayer is communication with a holy God, an infinite, eternal Being, the Sovereign of the universe (Colossians 1:15-18) against whom we have sinned. Our response, therefore, should be reverence (2 Corinthians 7:1), honoring and praising God for who he is and what he does.

At the other end is the truth that because of what Christ has done, we may come boldly into God's presence (Hebrews 4:16), asking him for anything in Christ's name (John 14:13, 14).

In the middle of these two biblical truths lies the practical reality. Because God is sovereign and holy, we must come to him with reverence and respect, rejecting casualness and flippancy. He is *not* our "big buddy in the sky." At the same time, however, we need not fear him if we are his children through faith in Jesus Christ. We can indeed talk to God about anything, at any time, in any place. And, because we have an intimate relationship with him, we can discuss matters as with our closest friend, using our own words.

There is another application from this tension between "holiness" and "familiarity." We should build into our lives times of deep communication and worship. This is a necessary part of being Christ's disciple, and a church building or other "holy" place may set the atmosphere where this can take place. Sometimes it just means sitting there, listening and meditating on God's goodness and love.

The Bible also tells us, however, to "pray continually" (1 Thessalonians 5:17). This implies a constant chattering, talking to him about everything, all day long. God wants us to be totally honest with him, telling him about our deepest needs and committing every decision to his control. These prayers can be aloud or silent, with head bowed or with eyes wide open, at home or at work.

The fact is that we need to understand both ends to live in the middle. God wants us to know that he is holy and in control; but he also wants us to be confident in our love relationship with him.

Don't reserve your prayers for church. Prayer must be central in our lives—it is our lifeline, our vital communication link with God.

♦WHEN SHOULD I PRAY? / DAVE VEERMAN

"Pray continually," Paul urged the Thessalonians (1 Thessalonians 5:17). They must have wondered, as we do, just exactly what he meant. After all, how can we pray all the time? There are so many other tasks that must be done at home, at work, and even at church. And many of these, God commands us to do! So how can we afford to spend every waking (or sleeping!) moment praying?

Paul, of course, did not mean that we should abandon everything and devote ourselves solely to prayer. His own life included preaching, witnessing, socializing, writing, and even tent making. He is telling us, however, that our lives must be saturated with prayer. In other words, our communication with God should be so close and natural that it is like breathing; something we do unconsciously, but without which we cannot live.

Praying continually means talking to God throughout the day, about everything, just as we would a loved one accompanying us on a trip. It is sort of a constant chattering, letting him know how we feel, asking for his advice and direction, and sharing our thoughts and feelings.

Praying continually also involves listening—being sensitive to what God is telling us through his Word, circumstances, our thoughts, and other people. It means having our "antennaes" out, sensing and following his signals to us.

This continual praying, however, does not cover all the times of prayer. There are also those special hours that must be spent struggling through a problem with him, pouring out our deepest feelings to him, praising and thanking him for who he is, or just meditating and listening to him.

And there are public and group prayers in church, at Bible studies, and before meals. These are valid and proper times to pray.

The point is that prayer is the very lifeblood of our relationship with God and must be a vital part of our lives—not just a ritual, a way to begin and end meetings, or an emergency kit. We can and should pray continually about *everything*.

How Sin Affects Prayer

✍ EVELYN CHRISTENSON

Jesus promised in John 15:7, "If you remain in me and my words remain in you, ask whatever you wish, and it will be given you." But he mentions two conditions: if we are not abiding and if we are not obeying, we will not have that power.

Sin prevents us from having power in prayer. "The eyes of the Lord are on the righteous and his ears are attentive to their prayer, but the face of the Lord is against those who do evil" (1 Peter 3:12). There are two kinds of sin. The first is global sin. It is referred to in the singular—sin, not sins. Since Adam and Eve, everyone born on this planet is born in a state of sin.

In John 16:5-11 Jesus tells the disciples he will not stay with them, but he will send the Holy Spirit who will convict the world of sin. And earlier he said, "Whoever does not believe stands condemned already because he has not believed in the name of God's one and only Son" (John 3:18). That is global sin, and we are all born into it. We leave that state of sin the moment we accept Jesus Christ. Then we are justified and we become new creations in Jesus Christ. God sees us as if we had never sinned (1 John 1:9), and we are not condemned (Romans 8:1).

The second class of sin has to do with specific offenses. It is referred to in the plural—sins—and is mentioned in the Lord's Prayer: "Forgive us our debts [or sins], as we also have forgiven our debtors [those who sin against us]" (Matthew 6:12). These are the sins we commit after we become Christians.

In our prayer seminars, I spend the first hour telling the participants about the power of prayer and the answers to prayer that are possible. Then I read a list of twenty-three Bible verses about sin. This opens our minds to our sin—not our shortcomings or our personality traits, but our sin. After that, we meet in groups of four and everyone confesses out loud a sin or sins. This is the first time the participants are asked to pray aloud, and it is a powerful time.

After this I say, "I want to give you a chance to pray one more prayer. If by some chance you are not absolutely sure you know Jesus Christ as Savior and Lord, I want you, having now confessed your sin, to pray."

I quote Mark 1:15, "Repent and believe the good news!" It isn't believe and repent, it's repent and believe. They have already repented and confessed their sin; now all that is left is to believe and to ask Jesus Christ to become Savior and Lord.

Once we have asked forgiveness for our sin and our sins, we are ready to experience God's power in prayer.

♦ PRAYER SNOBBERY / EVELYN CHRISTENSON

I recently attended an international prayer assembly. One of our goals was to publish an international call to prayer. As we discussed whom we were going to invite to pray with us around the world, we ran into difficulties.

A delegate would say, "Oh, we can't include him." Another delegate would object—"Yes, he would be OK." A third delegate would say, "If I went back home and said we are going to pray with those people, no one would join in."

As secretary of the group, I had been writing all these comments down. Finally I said, "I don't know how to word this. Shall I say that we will pray with everyone with whom we will spend eternity, or shall I say—" Before I finished, everyone started to laugh. They realized how ridiculous it was to decide who had a right to pray.

We need the Lord to forgive our spiritual superiority that leads us to think some people's prayers are worth more than others.

How Do I Get to Know God through Prayer?

TRENT BUSHNELL

If we aren't as close to God today as we were yesterday, who moved? A cute question, but also a practical one. The key word is *moved.* We cannot shift into neutral in our relationship with Christ and coast through life. Each decision we make moves us closer to or farther from God and his perfect will for our lives. How can prayer move us forward?

We don't get to know a person without spending time with him or her, sharing in conversation, activities, even conflict or difficulties. God desires the same attention we give to other important relationships in our lives. Prayer is an opportunity to express ourselves to the Creator, with whom we are building a personal relationship.

Periodically I have the front wheels on my cars aligned. With good tires, the car would actually do fine without the extra expense. But with the alignment, my car handles better and the tires last longer.

I like to think of prayer as a daily alignment. Without it we can roll through life and try hard to be Christian examples. We can try to overcome difficult situations and feel good about our relationship with God. But in the process we often feel slightly misdirected and maybe chewed up around the edges.

The answer to this tough question, then, is *do it!* The expected and simple answer, yet we often neglect regular personal prayer. We miss the opportunity to tune in to God and get on the right track. We start the day without renewing our burden for others and offering our availability to God so that he can count on us if an opportunity to use us arises.

The Bible encourages us to pray about everything: "Do not be anxious about anything, but in everything, by prayer and petition, with thanksgiving, present your requests to God. And the peace of God, which transcends all understanding, will guard your hearts and your minds in Christ Jesus" (Philippians 4:6, 7).

Prayer reduces anxiety in our Christian walk. We can see God work through us instead of feeling like the lone Christian taking on the universe.

The question of knowing God implies *knowledge* about him, but also *feeling as if* he is really there. Philippians 4:7 is a tremendous reminder to us that spending time with God regularly, specifically including prayer, will bring God's peace. Note the snowball effect: those close to God get continually closer through an active prayer life. "Come near to God and he will come near to you" (James 4:8).

According to Philippians, his peace "will guard" our hearts and minds. As we go about our daily business, our feelings and thoughts will be aligned with Christ's so we are able to please him.

Relying only on feelings is sure to cause us to be misaligned and sent on the wrong track. Regular prayer can "guard" our feelings by keeping them in balance with our minds, or what we know about God.

Need a prayer alignment? Commit yourself to a daily prayer life with specific requests and goals for your relationship with Christ. Write down special people and needs and pray faithfully for them. Sound good? *Do it!*

Constant Prayer: A Natural Response to God

DAVE BASTEDO

They say death and taxes are the only things you can count on. Not so! All around me things happen again and again that are constant and unceasing. One of the qualities of something unceasing is that it usually goes unnoticed. My senses and brain adapt to any constant stimulation by lessening its impact. I am not normally aware of the clothes on my body, the average light in my eyes, or the sound of traffic. This unconscious quality of unceasing activities is, I believe, also true for prayer. Praying without ceasing would seem to indicate that I'm praying constantly, as naturally as I'm breathing.

Breathing is a good model for constant prayer. Breathing brings life and health to my body, likewise prayer to my spiritual life. Something is very wrong if I'm finding it difficult to breathe. My spiritual state will also be more labored and depressed without regular prayer. So for prayer to be unceasing, it's going to be a very natural, regular occurrence that I seldom notice. Like breathing, it will be something so habitual that it rarely calls my attention, except perhaps in the extremes of sorrow or joy.

If I am going to put constant prayer into practice, I will need to understand two things. I need a right understanding of what prayer is and I need to see it as a growth process, not an instantaneous gift.

God is a person, not a process. He deals with me personally. Prayer is the communicative expression of my relationship with God. It is intimate conversation and communion with my personal God that takes place, not at special times such as at meals, bedtime, or in church, but on a continual basis. The constant give and take results in my becoming more and more like him.

Jesus told us to pray that God's will be done here on earth and that we are the instruments by which he will carry out his will. We are his body, the body of Christ. Our goal is to imitate him (Ephesians 5:1), to become more and more deeply involved in his wants, purposes, and desires for this world. As we tune our lives to his wavelength, we become channels of his love. In that living, active, and loving state, our whole life becomes an unceasing prayer to God.

One doesn't *try* to pray without ceasing. As we encourage our relationship with God, prayer follows as the light of day follows the sun; as breath follows the new life. As breath draws oxygen, our moment-by-moment need from our environment, so prayer draws our very life from God. Breathing doesn't cause a lot of excitement; neither does prayer, our quiet intimate exchange with God. As we begin to pray it usually takes much willpower and effort. As our relationship with God becomes more natural, prayer becomes a regular give and take that fills our life with love, joy, and peace, but of which we're rarely aware.

Jesus stresses the intimacy of prayer and condemns its showy observance. There are times to draw away in lonely, intense communion but there should also be an everyday, continual communion with God to be healthy in our spiritual lives. Family counselors will tell us that the most critical element in a healthy relationship is good communication. That communication should take place in a continual interchange. We can come to God all day long with our joys, sorrows, worries, pleasures, and pains. We can ask in brief moments for guidance, help, strength, and intercession for others. I commune with God driving in my car, in a checkout line at the supermarket, visiting a friend.

Our relationship with God and the communicating prayerful part of our lives is cyclical. Our continual, everyday communication with God builds and channels his life with us, which encourages us to pray. We must desire to commune with him. Likewise, anything that separates our natural communion (e.g., our sin or false guilt) often quenches our desire to pray.

We pray unceasingly, as we breathe unceasingly, unconsciously as a natural result of a healthy life. Unceasing prayer is the by-product of a growing, deepening relationship with the personal God of our universe. It is mostly unconscious, a natural response to our daily activities and needs. It is found in the small everyday events of life. It results from God's life in us and our desire for him, not in our efforts to pray without ceasing. We pray with our lives wherever we are. We become more and more like him in the give and take of unceasing prayer.

What Does It Mean to Listen to God?

BECKY TIRABASSI

What does it mean to listen? The dictionary's definition of listening is threefold: (1) make a conscious effort to hear, (2) give heed, and (3) take advice.

The concepts are the same when listening to God. To listen to God would include being a receptive, attentive listener, and willing to take advice—or obey what is heard.

Most people hear, but few listen. Active listening takes a *conscious effort.* Have you ever tried to talk on the phone with one person, while another person is prodding you with questions and additional thoughts? Not only is this confusing, but you usually don't grasp what either person is saying. Life is full of interruptions, noise, and people to converse with. That won't change. One of the first priorities in making an effort to listen to God is to find a quiet place, relatively free of interruption, where you can hear him. This might be a room with a comfortable chair or desk and no telephone. It may even be an out-of-the-way restaurant early in the morning. Wherever it is, it should be a place that will allow you to "listen" to God with concentration and attentiveness.

Another issue involved in consciously listening to God is *time.* In any relationship that is mutual and growing, a time commitment is a priority. So it is with God. Personally, I set aside a specific amount of time each morning that I consider my personal "appointment" with God. In fact, I schedule it into my date book the night before, planning for it in my coming day, assuring myself that I have reserved the time for my appointment with God as I would for someone else with whom I meet regularly.

During this time, I write my thoughts and prayer concerns in detail and read through four or five chapters of Psalms. I include in my writing the verses that give me comfort or conviction in reference to what I've been sharing with the Lord. In this way, I feel he is responding to me and I am listening to his counsel.

Familiarizing yourself with the Word of God through regular study, meditation, and memorization are all part of making a conscious effort to listen to God.

The second part of the definition, to give heed, involves giving thought to what you have heard and mulling it over.

For the Christian, the Word allows God to get our attention by sparking a thought as we read, or gives specific direction and conviction regarding our life-style or actions. It is at this point we must decide if and when we will respond to what we have heard.

One morning, I got up at 5:00 A.M. in order to have my time with God before meeting friends to attend a women's seminar. The very last section of my quiet time is called "listening." I found myself writing the words, "Watch your driving." I thought that was odd, and not particularly spiritual or profound. But with plenty of time to spare, I drove to the meeting, doubting that I would be faced with the temptation to speed. Nonetheless, by the time I was to meet my friends, I was still fifteen minutes away and I knew that the "test" had begun. I seemed to be stopped by every red light and with each minute, I grew more impatient. With one mile to go, I headed down a long descending hill and let down my defenses. Two flashing red lights appeared behind me and an officer motioned me over! Besides the sixty-dollar ticket and making myself even more late, I was *most* distressed that I *had not* listened to God as he seemed to have warned me in advance. When I tearfully pulled into the restaurant parking lot, my friends had not even arrived! Oh, what I learned about listening attentively that day!

Each of us must come to know his voice, recognizing it as we know the voice of a close friend. By reading, memorizing, and meditating on the Word of God you will begin to "hear" his voice speaking directly to you. In addition, you will grow to discern his Holy Spirit interacting in your daily thoughts, convicting and teaching you about God's truths (John 16:13). You will sense that God regularly uses others, such as your family members, pastor, close Christian friends, and even children to draw your attention toward his principles through their words. Often Christian literature and autobiographies will also give encouragement and direction as you listen for God's voice.

Finally, listening to God includes a teachable attitude, a willingness to take the advice given. Once you have heard from God, are you willing to obey? Perhaps you are even afraid to hear what he has to say, so you find yourself avoiding his voice.

If you are not sure if God is speaking to you or if you have heard him, ask yourself a few questions and answer them honestly:

1. Do I know his voice? Jesus said the sheep know the Shepherd's voice and follow (John 10:2-5). A personal relationship with the Shepherd is the first step in listening.

2. Are my ears clear from any blockage to hearing? Is there sin in my life that I have not confessed or admitted to God? Is there someone I have not forgiven?

3. Am I willing to obey him when he does speak to me?

In order to listen to God, make yourself available by setting aside a regular time each day in a quiet place; be attentive when you are there, as well as throughout the day; and take an "attitude check" regularly.

To look into the Word of God is the best place to find the answers to the question, Is he really listening? Both the Old and New Testaments reveal God's listening characteristics.

In the Old Testament, Isaiah wrote of God, "Before they call I will answer; while they are still speaking I will hear" (Isaiah 65:24). The book of Psalms is filled with verses of continuous pleas and requests by the writer for God to listen to him. Throughout the chapters, the psalmist logged repeatedly God's responses as proof that God is listening (Psalm 10:17; 18:6; 23; 86).

In the New Testament, Jesus told us in Matthew 7 to *ask, seek,* and *knock* and he would respond. James told us to ask of God and he would give us wisdom (James 1:5). In 1 John 1:9, we are exhorted to come to God with our sins, confessing them, and he will forgive us and cleanse us of them. Numerous Scriptures in the New Testament beckon us to "draw near to God with a sincere heart in full assurance of faith" because of Christ's sacrifice for our sins (Hebrews 10:22).

Men throughout the centuries have asked of God and been heard as they have recorded and documented many miracles. It is my conviction that these men are role models for us, not necessarily special and chosen above other men. God is not approachable by only a few, but desires to commune with us. In Revelation 3:20 he says, "Here I am! I stand at the door and knock. If anyone hears my voice and opens the door, I will go in and eat with him, and he with me."

Discover for yourself the dialogue involved in speaking to God of your needs and desires, and actively listening to him speak to you through his Word, his Spirit, and others. Set aside time, be willing and teachable, and wait to hear his response!

Are Some Prayers Insignificant?

✍ LARRY WARD

We have to remind ourselves continually that God has a perfect plan for us. Every action we take and every choice we make becomes a part of that plan—no matter how small and insignificant it seems to us.

Years ago one of my colleagues made a scoffing reference to people who pray for a parking spot. "God answers our prayers, of course, but he doesn't want us to bother him with trivial things like that," the person said.

I responded, "Hey, wait a minute. Let the scoffers scoff! I'm going to keep on trusting for a parking place and remembering that if God is God at all, he is God of all!"

It's true that where I park my car is usually unimportant. And yet in some circumstances, parking spaces can be very important. If I park in a no-parking zone, for instance, parking can even become a moral question!

I remember the time a missionary who was escorting me in a foreign country came late to pick me up. I kept looking at my watch, realizing that a number of high government officials were waiting for me and that the success of my presentation depended a great deal on my being there to give it. As it turned out, the missionary had been driving around the block over and over again because he hadn't wanted to put a nickel in the parking meter. That parking problem almost cost my organization some valuable contacts in a needy country.

I pray every day of my life, asking God to guide every inch of my movement and every second of my time. That means big things, and it also means little things. It includes moral choices, and it includes choices that do not have moral implications. As I look back over the years, I think the most significant way God has led in my life has been through the synchronization of his purposes. Miracles of timing have repeatedly occurred, and little things that would not otherwise have significance suddenly became important.

For example, I once missed a flight leaving Africa. This "misfortune" led to a chance meeting with an ambassador from another African country whom I had missed when I was in his country. En route to Paris, I had no idea how I could track this man down. But because I missed my flight, I ended up on the bus with the very ambassador I needed to see. Out of that meeting came a program of help that took hundreds of thousands of pounds of desperately needed food into his country. God had watched over that day and timed things for his own purposes.

Another time, I explained to the non-Christian friend with whom I was traveling that he was going to witness God's timing. He would see God put things together. At our first stop, with a four-hour wait between planes, we decided to go to the U.S. embassy so my friend could have some needed adjustments made to his passport.

At the embassy we learned that U.S. officials and the Belgian air force had joined forces to put together a food airdrop. The ambassador, however, had never before performed an airdrop and was not sure how to proceed. I had just spent a year in Bangladesh engineering similar airdrops, so I passed on information about things we had done right and things we had done wrong.

Even though we were there for only four hours, I could fly on that important first airdrop effort and coach the inexperienced crew.

We had trusted God with our whole day, right down to the tiniest details, and therefore the day's activities became a mosaic where every part fit together beautifully. God put it all together and enabled us to make a significant contribution.

We can trust God to superintend every aspect of life because he is God of all. We can pray about everything that in any way affects us, because he is willing to gather up the details and make them part of his plan.

I have a prayer I often say. I ask God to guide me through each new day, because I have never lived it before and will never live it again. I ask for his grace and direction in everything, because I know his greatness extends to every aspect of life—every choice, every decision, every move. I depend on him for every breath and every step, and each breath and each step is part of his perfect plan for me.

♦ LEARNING TO PRAY WITH OTHERS
VERNON GROUNDS

We all need corporate worship and prayer. If we never pray with others, our intercession is likely to become egocentric.

Not everyone feels comfortable praying in groups, however. If spontaneous prayer in a group makes you uncomfortable, stick to a more struc-

tured liturgical practice. I think it is possible to learn to pray comfortably in a group. Here are some ideas to try:

1. Talk to God as familiarly as you would to a friend. Forget thees and thous and speak naturally about things that concern you.

2. Experiment. Use a verse of Scripture or phrase from the Lord's prayer to express your thoughts.

3. If you don't feel able to pray out loud in a group, then remain silent and pray subvocally. Think the words instead of saying them. Eventually you will gain the courage to start with a short expression of praise or a brief petition.

Does God Answer Prayers?

LARRY WARD

"Ask and it will be given to you; seek and you will find; knock and the door will be opened to you. . . . Which of you, if his son asks for bread, will give him a stone? . . . If you, then, though you are evil, know how to give good gifts to your children, how much more will your Father in heaven give good gifts to those who ask him!" (Matthew 7:7-11).

When we pray, we get answers. If God is omniscient—all knowing—he obviously knows what we have prayed about. If he is all loving, he's going to give us the answer that is best for us.

We have to realize that God's answer may not be exactly what we want. It may not even be what we recognize or accept as an answer. But if we have asked in faith, confident that we are not seeking anything contrary to Scripture, then whatever comes to us we should regard as his answer and as what is best for us.

The word *answer* implies two-way communication. One person is requesting, and another—in the case of prayer, God himself—is responding. We are finite and limited, and sometimes we ask for the wrong things at the wrong time. Fortunately, at the other end of the communication is the infinite God who knows all things and answers our prayers according to his wisdom.

One answer God sometimes give is "wait awhile." My beloved friend Dr. V. Raymond Edman, former president of Wheaton College, wrote, "God's delays are not God's denials. Never doubt in the darkness what God has told you in the light."

So often I've seen the truth of that statement in my own experience. I may have an idea, for example, that seems perfectly sound to me. Everything in my experience and training suggests that my idea is worth implementing. But two or three years have to go by while I'm churning that idea over in my head, waiting for God's perfect timing. Then, at last, the necessary circumstances are arranged, and the idea becomes a reality.

Honesty compels me to say that, at times, God has not revealed his whole answer to me. I will cite one experience. Some years ago my colleagues and I were concerned about the thousands of refugees pouring into Thailand from other Indo-Chinese countries. Among them were the Hmong—intelligent, beautiful people who seemed to have stepped out of a time machine. They were brought out of the obscure reaches of their jungles into modern civilization, and we knew they would not easily fit into urban life.

One remarkable young tribesman said to me, "Sir, I know you want to help our people. Please do not take us to a developed country where we will not fit in. Somewhere there must be a developing country with people like us where we can go and develop with them and contribute to the country's development."

In time I was led to Bolivia, which seemed to be the answer to the tribesman's hopes. With only nine people per square mile, Bolivia desperately needed to develop its agricultural economy. When I outlined our plan for resettling the Hmong in Bolivia, a state official slapped his desk and said, "This is the hope of Bolivia!"

But the plan that looked so beautiful did not work out. Bolivia changed governments, and the Hmong were not allowed to enter. I don't know why God blocked that solution to the Hmong's problem. I do know, however, that in his providence the situation turned to good.

Because we had been so sure the plan would work, we had moved staff into Bolivia. Shortly thereafter, Bolivia began to suffer from famine. Our organization had a proven track record in food distribution, and soon we found ourselves distributing food every day to hundreds of thousands of people.

Our original plan did not work out, even though we had done our best, at every point checking our motives and putting our trust in God. But God set in motion another plan. When we don't understand what God's overall plan is, we must be prepared to accept his answer whatever it may be. When we come to God in trusting faith, asking for answers to our prayers, we are assured that, even though we do not fully comprehend his responses to our requests, our best interests and our well-being are totally safe in his hands.

The Importance of Praying for Others

JOAN H. YOUNG

Praying for ourselves and about our own problems often takes up the greatest bulk of our prayer time. Those who are closest to us—our children, spouses, parents, good friends in trouble—are probably next in line. It is certainly acceptable and right that we should pray for these people. But should we stop there in our petitions? There are lots of other people in the world; how will we ever get anything done if we take so much time to pray for a bunch of them? Is it really that important? God seems to think it is.

First Peter 2:5 says we are God's holy priests. What does a priest do? Hebrews 5:1 states it most clearly, though "merely a man like anyone else, . . . he is chosen to speak for all other men in their dealings with God" (TLB). One of our main roles as Christians is to ask God to work in the lives of people on earth. Ephesians 6:18 specifically says "keep praying earnestly for all Christians everywhere" (TLB).

We often give prayer the "brushoff" and use it as a last resort—if nothing else works, then we try praying. This is just the opposite of its real intent: to be our most powerful weapon against the adversities of this world. When we pray, we enable God to put his omnipotent abilities to work on this planet. He tells us this over and over, but we somehow miss the message. Paul explained to the Corinthians that he was an "ordinary, weak human being," but that he used "God's mighty weapons" rather than "human plans and methods to win [his] battles" (2 Corinthians 10:3, 4,TLB). Where is there great power to do things for God? James said it is in the "earnest prayer of a righteous man"! He goes on to add that there will be "wonderful results" (5:16, TLB). Jesus himself, in John 15:16, told his disciples to bear fruit. His very next sentence instructed them to ask the Father for things—to pray.

We have the privilege of walking right into God's presence and requesting him to help people. Andrew Murray put it this way, "As God's . . . representative on earth, redeemed man has the power to determine the history of this earth through his prayers." The wonder is that we don't do it more!

The Joy of Intercessory Prayer

✍ HAROLD MYRA

Intercessory prayer is a phrase that turns off a lot of people. For one thing, they don't know what it means; for another, they don't know how to do it. Yet intercessory prayer is neither hard to understand nor complicated to practice. It simply means to bring the needs of other people before God.

Intercessory prayer can be a beautiful, enriching part of our Christian lives. Paul tells us in Romans 8:26 that "the Spirit himself intercedes for us with groans that words cannot express." In Hebrews 7:25 we read that Jesus "always lives to intercede for [those who come to God through him]." Ever since I was a child, that thought has fascinated me—the Spirit himself is praying for me with such anguished love that the groans cannot be uttered.

Our popular view of God is that he is active in the American vein of getting things done. We don't think of God sitting around praying. Intercessory prayer seems to be a proper endeavor for little old ladies, but not for us.

As a child I remember hearing about "prayer warriors" who sat praying with their knitting in their laps. Because they were frail, the only thing they could do was pray. We young, physically able people, by contrast, went out and evangelized or witnessed or did what we thought were important things. But that shows a distorted view of what is important—for the Holy Spirit himself even spends time praying for us.

Most Christians carry an enormous load of guilt. We feel we are not doing what we ought. We feel enormous pressures to get involved in many activities, from political action to church involvement to being great family people, and in the rush we give prayer only a small space in our lives. Yet, realistically, it is totally impossible for any human being to do everything he or she feels required to do. Paradoxically, I've found that when I give prayer more time—especially when I intercede for others—other parts of my life become unblocked, and I see progress in many areas of my daily routines.

I think the busiest among us would see tremendous changes if we would take the time to intercede for each other. Men and women who have the Spirit of Christ gain a sense of peace, love, and joy by becoming involved in intercessory prayer.

Intercessory prayer is a joyous expression of our faith and a beautiful opportunity to commit fellow human beings to God's care. It's an opportunity to think about a person, perhaps a spouse or a child, and ask for God's blessing or healing to come to him or her.

One form of intercessory prayer is to think of someone and then picture clear water or the light of Christ pouring over that person. Another form is to ask God verbally to bless or bring peace to that person. The satisfaction that comes from doing this for someone is incredible.

Intercessory prayer gives us a deep sense of joy. We feel solidarity with other Christians. After praying for other people, we think, "I have brought them before the throne of God. My time has been well spent. They are now in the hands of our loving, healing Lord." As Christians, what better blessing can we offer our fellow human beings?

Can My Prayers Influence World Leaders?

VERNON GROUNDS

When we pray for our political and government leaders we are faced with an insoluble paradox. This is the age-old dilemma of how God's sovereignty works together with human freedom. If God, who is all-knowing and all-powerful, purposes everything that comes to pass, what is the point of prayer? Does prayer make any difference when events unfold with a predestined inexorability?

Regardless of how we try to solve this problem theoretically, we need to realize that the Bible views prayer as making a difference. An old cliche puts it, "Prayer is either a force or a farce." In the Bible prayer is not viewed as a farce. It is viewed, rather, as a powerful force and an indispensable factor by which righteousness prevails and the will of God is accomplished.

Prayer can have an influence on world leaders. Pray and there will be outcomes that, apart from prayer, would never happen. It's not that our prayers change what is going to happen but that, in God's prevision of history, he includes our prayers as factors that have a bearing on the outworking of events. Perhaps we can draw a parallel between the mind of God and an inconceivably complex computer. According to Scripture, God knows from all eternity what is going to happen. He knows when we will pray and when we won't. In his omniscient programming of events in time and space God has taken this information into account. He has planned the sequence of events in keeping with our ministry of intercession.

So we need to recognize our obligation to pray. In 1 Timothy 2:1, 2, one of the most important passages in the Scriptures regarding intercession, the apostle Paul engaged in a fervent exhortation: "I urge, then, first of all, that requests, prayers, intercession and thanksgiving be made for everyone—for kings and all those in authority, that we may live peaceful and quiet lives in all godliness and holiness." So we need to pray for our leaders because they are unconscious instruments in his hand. King Nebuchadnezzar in the book of Daniel exemplifies this fact. Chapter 4 describes how Nebuchadnezzar was smitten with a psychic disorder and, through this divine intervention, brought to an amazing confession of faith and a change of imperial policy.

Caesar Augustus was another leader who served unwittingly as God's instrument. He issued a decree for his vast domain to be taxed (Luke 2). That decree set in motion the ponderous machinery of the Roman Empire so the Messiah could be born in Bethlehem. These and other examples of God's sovereign working permit us to assume that behind the scenes people were praying just as we pray now for rulers and kings and those in authority everywhere. And God answered those prayers.

Not only do we pray for leaders because they are the unconscious instruments of God's purposes, we also pray for them because it benefits us. As Paul mentions in 1 Timothy, one reason for such praying is that we may lead quiet and peaceful lives. In Jeremiah 29 the prophet sends a letter to the exiles in Babylon. He instructs them to pray for the peace and prosperity of that pagan nation because in its welfare their own welfare will be safeguarded. "Seek the peace and prosperity of the city to which I have carried you into exile. Pray to the Lord for it, because if it prospers, you too will prosper" (Jeremiah 29:7).

As we pray for our leaders and for various political issues, we will realize no doubt that other Christians are asking that God will grant the antithesis of our own plan. He sorts out these contradictory prayers in keeping with his will. Our responsibility is to pray with the utmost discernment, honesty, and humility. We should not dictate to God, but tell him honestly how we perceive an issue and then ask him to answer in keeping with his wisdom and love.

This means operating on the Gethsemane principle. We add as the controlling postscript to any prayer, "Not as I will, but as you will" (Matthew 26:39). In the Garden of Gethsemane the night before he was crucified, Jesus longed that the cup might pass from him. But in the end, he trustfully put himself in his Father's hand. This final act of faith is to trust God's wisdom and love and goodness above our own discernment or even in contradiction to our own desires.

In pleading with God, I may be mistaken even though I use my intelligence as fully as possible. People on the other side of an issue may have a keener insight into God's will. So I pray, "I trust you, Father. Even if what you bring to pass is contrary to what I'm asking, I still have the confidence that this is as it ought to be. Your will be done, not mine."

Paul touched on this issue in Romans 14. God had not spoken clearly regarding the eating of meat or the keeping of the Sabbath in the gospel age, and these became controversial issues among the Christians in first-century Rome. Paul taught that on nonrevealed matters, each person should be fully persuaded in his own mind. But he likewise taught that we should treat Christians of a conviction different from ours with love, respect, courtesy, and, above all, humility. We should know where we stand on an issue and pray accordingly; yet we should also be gentle with those who disagree with us.

Finally, we should remember Proverbs 21:1, "The king's heart is in the hand of the Lord; he directs it like a watercourse wherever he pleases." We don't know how God does that in response to our prayers, but we know we're commanded to pray. Let God work out the theoretical puzzles. It is enough for us to know that our prayers make a difference.

♦ THE UNITED STATES'S PLACE IN THE WORLD / VERNON GROUNDS

God cares what happens to the United States, but he does not have a preferential concern for our country. He cares for other countries as well. Our country plays its significant role in world affairs, but other countries also play theirs. God wants our country to be righteous, an influence for good, a source of missionary activity. But the United States does not have a unique messianic function to fulfill in history.

Why Should I Pray If God Knows Everything?

✍ JOAN H. YOUNG

Omnipresent, omnipotent, omniscient—three words that certainly sound awesome enough to apply to a god. And they *are* true of our wonderful God! The fact that he is omnipresent—everywhere at once—gives us security or reminds us that our sins cannot be hidden. His omnipotence—the fact that he has all power—assures us that there is nothing too hard for God. Sometimes we wonder why he does not to use that power to immediately right some of the injustices of this world, but we are usually able to believe (if not fully understand) that he has chosen to limit his power on earth for this era of time.

But even those of us who love the Lord sometimes have trouble with the idea that a God who is omniscient—who knows everything—needs to be *asked* for things in prayer. Especially with our business-minded American efficiency, it seems like some immense waste of time to bother God with every little thing that he already knows. But strange as it seems, God has also chosen to limit this feature of his ability, so that it becomes necessary, in most cases, for people to ask for blessings and help in order for them to receive it.

Probably the best reason for us to pray, even though God knows what we need, is because Jesus did it. He is always our supreme example (Hebrews

12:2). While here on earth, Jesus prayed for himself, the most outstanding example of which is his night in the Garden of Gethsemane. In John 17:1-5, Jesus prayed that God the Father would be glorified through his life. The rest of John 17 records Jesus' prayers for his disciples, and then on through time to include a prayer for us!

When Jesus prayed for Lazarus to be raised from the dead, he made an interesting statement. "Jesus looked up and said, 'Father, I thank you that you have heard me. I knew that you always hear me, but I said this for the benefit of the people standing here, that they may believe that you sent me'" (John 11:41, 42). Notice what Jesus *did not* say. He did not say, "Father I know you know this already, but I'm asking you just for these people to hear it." There did not seem to be any question in his mind about the idea that he needed to ask. Rather, he made the prayer an example in order to prove that the Father had heard his request. The Father always hears us, but we are responsible for the asking. Jesus himself followed this rule.

Jesus still lives in heaven to pray for us. Hebrews 7:25 says he "always lives to intercede." Prayer is somehow an integral part of the very being of God: God the Son asks things of God the Father, and they are done! Hebrews 4:13-16 addresses the very question we are asking: "[God] knows about everyone, everywhere. Everything about us is bare and wide open to [him]. . . . Jesus the Son . . . has gone to heaven itself to help us. . . . So let us come boldly to the very throne of God . . . to receive his mercy and to find grace to help us in our times of need" (TLB).

In a very real way, this is a continuation of the idea that God chooses to work through us. Mankind was created in God's image, and was given dominion over the earth. Men and women were given the power to control the destiny of this world. God's original and continuing purpose for earth was that people would fulfill his will. Adam and Eve talked with God in the garden. Because this seems so remote, and sinless creation so different from what we now know, we don't seem to think of this as prayer. But it was. God and Adam communicated about the destiny of this world. God himself brought the animals to Adam to be named.

When we turned over the authority of this planet to Satan (by sin), we made it much more difficult for God to fulfill his will. Of course we know that he sent his Son to redeem us. But as we pray, we can still discover and enable God to work his will on this earth and in our lives. The "model prayer" points this out, as we are taught to pray "your will be done on earth as it is in heaven." Of course we will add specific requests to this outline for prayer, as given us by Jesus.

Actually, as complex as this sounds, the best advice on the topic that I've ever read comes from a flying horse named Fledge. In *The Magician's Nephew* by C. S. Lewis, two children are sent by Aslan on a mission that will influence the destiny of Narnia for many years. They ride on Fledge's back for a whole day, and when they come down to rest for the night, Fledge begins a dinner of fresh green grass. The children realize that they have nothing to eat (much to the surprise of the horse, who didn't know they couldn't eat grass). Tempers begin to flare and the boy, Digory, says, "Well, I *do* think someone might have arranged about our meals."

"I'm sure Aslan would have, if you'd asked him," said Fledge.

"Wouldn't he know without being asked?" said Polly.

"I've no doubt he would," said the Horse (still with his mouth full). "But I've a sort of idea he likes to be asked."

RELATED ARTICLES

Chapter 4: God Speaks to Us Today
Chapter 4: God Speaks through Thoughts
Chapter 12: Prayer
Chapter 15: The Lord's Prayer

CHAPTER

18

When God Seems Far Away

✓ What should I do when it feels like God has abandoned me?

✓ I don't feel close to God. Did I lose him?

✓ Where is God when I need him most?

✓ What do I do with my doubts?

✓ Why doesn't God make himself more visible to me?

Where Is God When Things Go Wrong?

✍ JAY KESLER

"God must not love me, or that terrible thing would not have happened." If you've ever said or thought those words, you need to clear away a big misunderstanding. It is a misunderstanding to think that God is directly connected to everything that happens in his creation. You know, of course, that everything was made by God and that nothing in the world was made without him (John 1:3). You need, however, to keep this truth in mind:

1. *Much of the daily operation of the world is governed by the laws God set in motion—and not by God's direct intervention.*

The laws of physics, for instance, govern what happens to moving bodies. They are not suspended when Christians run afoul of them. A Christian driving a car on the ice at eighty miles per hour will find that his automobile reacts in precisely the same manner as a non-Christian's car in the same situation. When that car loses control and hits another car head-on, the Christian cannot expect God to intervene and suspend the laws of physics. The Christian's car will be no less smashed up than a non-Christian's would be, and the innocent driver of the second car will be no less dead if he is hit by a Christian than if he is hit by a non-Christian.

Just as God rarely intervenes to prevent the physical consequences of our actions, neither does he intervene to cause bad things to happen. God does not pick up one car and slam it into another on the freeway. When this happens, it is the result of independent actions taken by individual persons, actions that then ran into the law of physics that says two objects cannot occupy the same space at the same time. When they attempt to, you have a collision and often a catastrophe.

When disaster strikes a Christian—whether he has violated God's principles or whether he has been the innocent victim of someone else who has violated them—this does not indicate that God does not love the person. Instead, it demonstrates how the world has been created to operate. Once we understand this fact, we are usually less likely to be angry at God when disaster strikes—especially if we also understand two additional truths.

2. *What looks like disaster now may be beneficial to us in the long run.* God has revealed himself to us in terms of the parent-child relationship. If we think of God as a Father, we may better understand his ways.

As our Father, God has information we don't possess. That is, he sees the larger picture. When he allows trials to come our way, it may be because he is looking at the situation from a wider angle. This often happens in our dealings with our children. If a small child says, "Please, I would like to have that beautiful, nice, shiny, long butcher knife," and the parent responds, "No, you can't play with that," he is not being unfair to the child but rather is protecting the child from danger. Perhaps when we can see things from God's point of view, we will understand why many of our desires and requests have not been met.

One of the deepest and best-developed stories on this subject, in my opinion, is in Sheldon Vanauken's book *A Severe Mercy.* The author's wife has died, and C. S. Lewis offers an explanation. It is possible, Lewis suggests, that their love was so very self-centered, the two of them so wrapped up in each other, that God allowed her to be taken from him—incidentally to heaven to be with him—rather than to remain where their mutual selfishness was causing them to be of little use to the world around them. Lewis called this "a severe mercy"—and it is indeed severe. But if we could see from God's point of view, perhaps it wouldn't seem so severe after all.

A great many of our struggles, particularly when we feel we have been mistreated, probably would be understandable if we could see the whole picture. With distance and hindsight, we may begin to get glimpses of why God treated us as he did. Interestingly, I have rarely heard people give testimonies where they thank God for some mountaintop experience. Almost always, people thank him for some valley, some deep difficulty that, at the time, was absolutely mind bending. When they were going through it, they may have thought it would destroy them, but in retrospect they see how God used it to his glory and made them better persons because of it. This recognition has inspired much of the world's great literature and philosophy.

3. *By stepping back and letting nature take its course, God may be teaching us valuable lessons.* This truth is also closely related to the parent-child relationship God wants to have with us. Just as we allow certain things to happen to our children without interfering, so God does with us. If parents build too many safety nets around their children, the children will become unable to function on their own. A son or daughter, for instance, will become financially irresponsible by constantly being bailed out by parents. Sometimes parents have to stand by and watch their children struggle with their financial needs and work their way out of difficulty in order to help the children develop the ability to live independently.

During such an experience, the children may feel their parents are being unfair, arbitrary, or even cruel. They wish their parents would simply step in and bail them out. But in fact the parents are wiser to stand back and let their children experience the natural consequences of their actions. This kind of restraint on the part of the parents is beneficial to children in the long run. Parents do not step back in order to torture their children, but to help them grow.

Understanding these three truths—that the laws of nature operate for Christian and non-Christian alike, that our perspective is limited, and that natural consequences can help us grow—helps us relate God's love to the troubling experiences of daily life. Since God has revealed himself to us as a parent, I reject all ideas that make him anything less than a good parent. God, our heavenly Father, is infinitely better than any parent on earth—so much better that the very finest parent-child relationship ever known on earth only barely scratches the surface of the kind of relationship we can have with God. I may not always understand why I have to go through certain trials, but I can trust my heavenly Father to do what is best for me in the long run.

When God Seems Far Away

MARTIN MARTY

During the "death of God" movement, I was on a television program with Rabbi Abraham Joshua Heschel. Somebody made a remark about the absence of God. The rabbi jumped up in irritation, knocking over a glass of water. "I'm not sure of your presence or my presence, but I am sure of God's presence," he said.

He was not just saying that for effect; he really meant it. Like Brother Lawrence, who practiced the presence of God amidst the pots and pans of the kitchen, the rabbi was bathed in the presence of God. But people like Rabbi Heschel are an exception. The gift of knowing God's presence in all times and in all places is very rare and is usually given to a simple person like a peasant woman or a child.

Sometimes I go about my daily business pushing God to the back of my mind where he gets fainter and fainter. When I sense God is absent, I do not need to panic. There are several things I can do:

1. *I can pay attention to the feeling of absence.* I can remember that the dark night of the soul, when God seems unreachable, is not unique to me. Many Christians, from New Testament times until the present, have experienced something similar. It is nothing new.

2. *I can put myself in places where I am likely to experience God.* I should keep on attending church and reading the Bible even if there are boring stretches where nothing happens. J. B. Phillips once said that you can't sit at the breakfast table complaining that the train never goes by if your house isn't near the tracks. If I pursue a frantic 168-hour week without setting aside a day and an hour to meet with God, if I am never with people to whom the presence of God is vivid, if I allow no space for silence, if I never let God's Word reach me, no doubt I will find each week I am a little drier than the week before. I need some kind of spiritual stimuli such as reading the right book, hearing the appropriate music, receiving God's Word from another human being to spark my awareness of God.

3. *I can learn from greatness.* In many ways, I'm a hitchhiker on the spirituality of others. I'm not a deeply religious person who receives clear signals from God. So I often reach for a classic on Christian prayer such as Baille's *A Diary of Private Prayer.* When I read these prayers, they open doors and windows in my soul. I will also read poets such as Gerard Manley Hopkins or John Donne.

I've gone on walks through the woods by myself and gotten good exercise, but little else. The next day, however, I might walk the same path with a nature lover. This person will hear a bobolink while smelling clover while sensing a two-degree drop in temperature while noticing a new shade of Indian paintbrush. Reading the great spiritual masters is like that. They have been attentive to the path of God's presence and can help point out things I may have missed.

4. *I can be patient.* I may live through long patches of life where God's presence is not vivid. But God can speak in absence. God is not known only in enthusiasms and ecstasy and solace and joy. God is also present in the midst of sorrows and doubts and anxieties. I must learn to be patient so I can be attentive to his signals.

5. *I can be responsive when those signals come.* I must be willing to suspend some disbelief. I must suspend some sense of absence to allow the Presence to break in. Every little lowercase yes can become, if I don't resist it, an upper-

case Yes. And eventually, the affirmation grows bigger and bigger.

6. *I can open myself to God through worship.* I do this best in the presence of other Christians rather than by myself. But some people go to the desert or the mountaintop or their room. However I do it, I need to have a ritual—not necessarily a formal liturgy, but a structure to build upon. Once I find what works, I can do more of it.

Personally, I haven't yet faced the agony or despair of the totally dark night. I have had the usual share of apathy, numbness, paralysis, frustration, and bewilderment. I've gone through grief and suffering. I have had a sense of agony for others, but I haven't had the prolonged sense of agony of the absence of God. That may still happen.

Instead of black nights, I have gray nights. And gray, misty nights are often more confusing than the really black night when you are forced to find a flashlight to survive.

But whether our dark nights are gray or black, we can accept the silence, learn from people for whom God is intensely present, and place ourselves where we will be able to experience him anew.

♦ TALKING TO THE CEILING / YFC EDITORS

What can I do when I feel distant from God, when my prayers seem to bounce off the ceiling?

First, recognize that your prayers *are* being heard. Second, look for the "ceiling," the barrier that is making you feel distant. Is there some unconfessed sin in your life? Is there someone you need to forgive? If you don't find a specific barrier, then recognize that there are times in life when you just have such feelings. You may be tired, depressed, lonely. Talk to God about those feelings, realizing that he hears and cares. Then get out of yourself. Go to be with other believers in worship, in prayer, or in fellowship. Do an act of kindness or service for another person. You'll find once you come out of yourself that God was never gone.

Where Is God When I Need Him Most?

✍ DAVID McKENNA

In his essay "The World's Last Night" C. S. Lewis wrote that those of us who think we are especially blessed because God answers all our prayers should not be quite so confident. If God could really trust us, he would put us out on some lonely outpost where every lesson we had ever learned would be tested and where he would not answer our prayers—as he did with his Son on the cross. According to Lewis, when you ask the question, Where is God when I need him most? you have to ask the parallel question, Where was God when Christ needed him most?

There are times when God's silence and "absence" is a compliment to our faith. In those times, God is saying, "I can trust your faith in me." This is one way God increases our trust in him.

Consider Job who cried against the heavens and a God who didn't respond. Asserting his own righteousness and innocence before God, he screamed out the question of God's absence in the face of injustice. All he wanted was for God to answer him. But God maintained silence.

During the times of anguish, however, as Job dealt with his own thoughts and the opinions of his "comforters," he had breakthroughs of insight. "If I go to the east, he is not there; if I go to the west, I do not find him. When he is at work in the north, I do not see him; when he turns to the south, I catch no glimpse of him," Job admitted. But notice his insight in the next verse: "But he knows the way that I take; when he has tested me, I will come forth as gold" (Job 23:8-10).

Out of Job's deepest despair, even in his realization that God didn't always answer when he needed him most, came a faith that held on and trusted that the results of the testing would be "gold."

After the death of his wife, C. S. Lewis dealt with the same question, Where is God when I need him most? He compiled his thoughts in his book *A Grief Observed.* Lewis observed that God is often present when we don't seem to need him, but when we desperately need him, he strangely disappears. Not only does he not answer when we call, but we can almost hear him slam the door on us and double-bolt it.

In reality, said Lewis, our question is not, Where is God when I need him most? but, Is this the way God really is—brutal, unkind, unanswering? This feeling of being deserted was all a part of the process of working through his grief, and it is likewise a part of the experience of every believer who faces such times of trial.

We do not move to a higher level of faith and trust in God without going through a time of comparative darkness. It may seem like a contradiction, but through our times of deepest need God is leading us to a greater faith. And the end result is pure gold.

♦HAS GOD ABANDONED ME? / LEWIS SMEDES

Many of us have felt as if God has abandoned us at terrible moments of our lives. We felt alone, as if we had been cheated of our heavenly Father's love.

What should we do when God seems to have left us? First, wait. And then wait some more. There are times when you are hanging by your fingernails, dangling in the winds of pain. Sometimes he seems to be on a leave of absence and you can only wait. He will come back—that was the biblical experience from beginning to end. The Israelites, the prophets, the psalmists lamented, Where is he when we need him? They had to wait; so do we.

Second, do not be too quick to accept explanations for what feels like abandonment. A woman whose child was killed by a drunk driver told me, "I think that God was trying to teach me something. I needed to grow in a certain way." That reasoning may have worked for her, but ultimately I think she will discover that God was not so interested in her growth that he would kill her child to help her grow. Do not jump to rational conclusions to satisfy yourself.

Third, wait some more. And more.

Fourth, be aware that to be human, you must be vulnerable to suffering and pain. If you want to be human and enjoy human relationships, you must be vulnerable to being rejected and unloved. Life without pain is not human; suffering is often the price we pay for the richness of life.

Fifth, wait some more. Let him finally persuade you in some mysterious way that, in spite of what appears to be abandonment, he was there. He was there suffering with you. He was in pain with you. Where was he when you needed him? He was there, hurting with you.

Finally, turn your eyes on the goodness of life that is always there, even in the midst of your immense pain. Praise God for the goodness of life. I believe that it is heresy to praise him for bad things. But start praising him for the good things, and you will have primed the pump to begin to feel the good things. As you rediscover good things, you will discover that he has not abandoned you after all.

Our Quiet Confidence in Christ

ADRIAN ROGERS

Many times when people invite Jesus into their lives they feel close to him initially. But after a while they no longer feel his presence, and they begin to wonder if they've somehow "lost" him. It's important for us to understand that once a person truly knows the Lord Jesus Christ as his or her personal Savior, he or she has become a partaker of the divine nature and can never again be a lost soul. John 10:27-29 makes that very clear: "My sheep listen to my voice; I know them, and they follow me. I give them eternal life, and they shall never perish; no one can snatch them out of my hand. My Father, who has given them to me, is greater than all; no one can snatch them out of my Father's hand."

My suggestion to a person who is having difficulty feeling the Lord's presence is to put feeling on a shelf and forget about it for a moment. Anyone who lives in the realm of feeling is going to have difficulty in the spiritual realm from time to time, because salvation is God's deepest work and our emotions are the shallowest part of our nature. God doesn't do his deepest work in the shallowest part.

People are body, soul, and spirit. The soul deals primarily with our feelings, but reality is a matter of the spirit. It is with our spirits that we truly know God. So forget about your feelings for a moment and go straight to the facts—the Word of God.

In John 8:32 Jesus said, "You will know the truth, and the truth will set you free." The truth is whatever God says, and knowing it makes us free. And strangely enough, people who truly know their relationship with Jesus Christ, who understand the doctrine of grace, and who stop living in the shallowness of feeling, will most probably have all the "feeling" they need.

I don't know I'm saved because of the way I feel; I feel happy and full of joy because I know I'm saved. My feelings grow out of my assurance rather than vice versa. Of course, unconfessed and unrepented sin could cause me to lose my joy. Joy is not emotional ecstasy. True biblical joy is a quiet confidence that I belong to God.

Joy and happiness are not synonymous. Happiness depends upon what happens, but joy is established by the presence of Jesus Christ in our lives. Sin is the only thing that can take joy away—our own sin, not what somebody else does to us.

When I don't sense Christ's presence in my life, I ask myself if I'm looking for some surface emotion, for a fleshly ecstasy. If that's true, I remind myself that ecstasy is not what God has promised I'll feel all the time. Those feelings are a "side benefit" to being a Christian; they usually aren't our common everyday experience. However, if I don't sense peace in my heart, if I don't have deep abiding joy, I ask myself if there is any unconfessed, unrepented sin in my life. Then I confess it, and by faith I claim forgiveness. At that moment, God restores his joy to my life.

Keeping Off the Spiritual Roller Coaster

GARY COLLINS

If we're not careful, our spiritual lives can become roller coasters—times of dryness interspersed with mountaintop experiences. There are ten questions you might ask about your spiritual life. These are not a cure-all for spiritual problems, but they are good questions to get us thinking and to get us back on track when we start growing dry in our spiritual lives.

1. *Am I a believer?* How can I be spiritually mature if I'm not even born again?

2. *Am I sinning?* Everyone sins at times, but we know that "if we confess our sins, he is faithful and just and will forgive us our sins and purify us from all unrighteousness" (1 John 1:9). Sometimes our spiritual lives are down because we're deliberately doing something we know isn't honoring the Lord. It's hard to be spiritual leaders when we're stumbling.

3. *Am I out of shape physically?* If we allow our bodies to be sluggish, we don't think clearly and we don't work efficiently. If we're exhausted—perhaps from being up all night with the kids—we shouldn't be surprised if we seem to be struggling spiritually. We all know it's important to read the Scriptures, but sometimes it's almost as important to get a good rest.

4. *Am I spiritually undernourished?* Am I skipping church because I'm busy? Am I neglecting Bible study and prayer? We become undernourished physically and lose our vitality if we don't eat. The same principle is equally valid when applied to the spiritual realm.

5. *Am I spiritually overfed?* Some of us are stuffed with a steady diet of Christian radio, the electronic church, conferences, and Christian books. That can make us spiritually bloated. We need to do more than take in spiritual nourishment. We also need to reach out to others.

6. *Am I legalistic and hypocritical?* It's very easy—especially if we're parents and home all day—to develop a holier-than-thou attitude. That can ruin us spiritually. I recall a Christian woman who looked down on us because our

kids were really active dynamos and not all that well behaved. This woman had one child, and he was very passive, quiet, and polite. This woman would look at my wife as if she were saying, "Why can't you control your kids? Why don't you have time for the local women's Bible study? Why are you so disorganized?" My wife felt very threatened. But then this lady had a second and then a third child. Those two kids were hellions. All of a sudden everything fell apart! Somehow her superior attitude disappeared.

7. *Am I thinking clearly?* It's easy to have wrong perspectives, especially when we get caught in the world's values. The drive for success, for example, is a worldly trap that catches many of us. We start pushing for success according to the world's values and forget that Jesus said, "Whoever wants to become great among you must be your servant" (Matthew 20:26).

8. *Is my life unbalanced?* We all face the danger of putting too much focus on one area—our work, sports, or even church activities—and then neglecting other areas that are equally important.

9. *Am I spiritually powered?* Sometimes we get program-oriented and forget that our power comes from the Lord. If we don't have that spiritual power, our programs will get pretty flat. We need to ask ourselves if the Holy Spirit is active in our lives. If we are trying to be spiritually independent—trying to grow on our own and foolishly ignoring God—we shouldn't be surprised if we aren't growing!

10. *Have I lost my perspective on what God is really like?* Sometimes we make God too small. In our thoughts and actions, we limit his power, his love, and even his intelligence. We have to keep going back to the Word, continually reminding ourselves of God's great attributes and characteristics. God expects us to fellowship with him, and as we do, he will reveal more and more of himself to us.

◆ FAITH IS NOT A TRUMP CARD / JAY KESLER

In Hebrews 11, we read about people of faith who were able to stop the mouths of lions and quench fire. We also read about others who were eaten by lions and burned alive. All of these people were heroes of faith.

So we see that faith is not a trump card that can take any hand. Instead, it is a matter of trusting God in spite of circumstances.

Dealing with Doubt

✍ JAY KESLER

We often begin a discussion of doubt by quoting James 1:6, 7: "He who doubts is like a wave of the sea, blown and tossed by the wind. That man should not think he will receive anything from the Lord; he is a double-minded man, unstable in all he does."

This verse could mislead us if we are not clear about what doubt means in this context. In the Bible, faith means obeying God and trusting in him in spite of prevailing circumstances. The great men of faith trusted in God even though circumstances around them seemed to indicate that everything had come unglued, that God had let them down. Some of the Old Testament patriarchs had to wait more than a hundred years to see their faith rewarded; others experienced the opposite of what they wanted. Still, they maintained their faith in God, even though their world came apart.

The doubt James is talking about is the opposite of this kind of faith. It is the kind of doubt that causes us to disobey God or to lose our confidence in him. This kind of doubt is sin.

On the other hand, doubt that involves asking questions is not forbidden. In fact, the Bible encourages it. We are encouraged, for instance, to "test the spirits" (1 John 4:1); that is, to doubt them, put them to the test, and then reject the ones that do not turn out to be fruitful. This is the same process we would use in testing any hypothesis, and it is based on systematic doubt.

Faith, in this sense, is based on doubt. That is, doubt is the material we feed in at one end. Then we test our doubt by obeying God and trusting his Word, and suddenly our doubt turns to confidence in God and we are filled with faith.

This process is necessary all through our lives. Day by day we obey God and do his commands in spite of what the world around us encourages us to do. As we do this, we realize that God has never failed us, and we begin to develop more and more confidence in him. I often think of David standing before Goliath—a man much larger and stronger than himself, a warrior that common sense would say to run from. But David had tested God in other situations, and he said, "The Lord who delivered me from the paw of the lion and the paw of the bear will deliver me from the hand of this Philistine" (1 Samuel 17:37). We walk with God and trust and obey him, and then when we run into difficulties, we remind ourselves that the God who has taken care of us in the past will also take care of us in the present and future.

Doubt is swallowed up by faith when faith is seen as more than simple intellectual belief, but rather as obedience to God in the midst of circumstances and difficulties that baffle human experience. As you read the book of Job, you will discover that that was the way Job saw it. Job insisted he had been consistently faithful to God, and the disasters in his life were not related to disobedience. To an outside observer—certainly to Job's friends and his wife—it looked as if God had deserted him. But Job hung onto his belief and continued to trust in God. Eventually God restored everything to him and rewarded him for not denying his faith, even though every circumstance argued against his belief in a loving God.

The best way to deal with doubt, then, is not to deny it but to live in a way that builds faith.

◆ GENUINE DOUBTS / R. C. SPROUL

When doubts arise—in ourselves or in others—we must take them seriously. God honors the fact that people have honest, genuine doubts, especially when they have difficulty harmonizing certain aspects of their experience with their concept of God.

For example, if I am taught to believe that God is all-loving, and then a tragedy comes into my life, I may wonder whether or not there is anybody home up there who really cares about me, who loves me. If I do not have a deep understanding of the character of God and how he relates to suffering and tragedy, I will have a crisis of faith.

The only solution is to expand our understanding of God, of people, and of how the two interrelate. There is no shortcut to such searching of the Scriptures. But each doubt, each person, must be handled with respect.

When Life Is Just Too Much

INGRID TROBISCH

Psychological burnout is something a high-school music teacher could have after preparing his students for a contest and putting on a Christmas concert and maybe directing the church choir besides. The poor teacher is just plain worn out. Or it could happen to a person who works ten or twelve hours a day waiting tables at a restaurant and then goes home and has family problems to face. It's the tremendous fatigue that comes when life is just too much.

Psychological burnout happened to Jesus from time to time. People crowded him constantly, and although he loved them all, sometimes he had to get away. He had to go up in the mountains or out on the lake.

Spiritual dryness is different. You know you are suffering from it when you read the Word of God and it seems dead to you. You're supposed to give a talk at a Christian meeting and you can't think of one new living thought. Spiritual dryness often happens after a spiritual high; for example, after a Christian convention where thousands and thousands of people gather to hear one good talk after another. When the meetings are over, many people go home and wonder, What's wrong with me? I seem to have lost it.

When spiritual dryness occurs—and it happens to every Christian—the first thing to treat is your body. Your body is the base from which you operate, and if it is having problems, spiritual problems seem larger. Are you getting good food? Are you overtired? Is there something you could do for your body that would also help your spirit?

Once, in Finland, we were going through a time of spiritual dryness. We had a free day so we went into the sauna and sweated it all out. Walter couldn't cry, but he could sweat wonderfully. It's also good to swim or hike, to get out in nature and do physical things until you can put your problem aside for a while.

I know a pastor who never took the time to refresh his spirit, and when he retired he decided he didn't want to have anything more to do with the church. He still attends, but he won't go to the same church twice in a row because he can't bear the thought of getting involved again. He could have avoided this total burnout—psychological and spiritual—if he had paid attention to the signs when he was younger.

If I were addressing a roomful of Christian leaders right now, I'd tell them they are sinning if they don't take time for themselves and their partners. I think couples need at least one hand-holding day a week when they can have time alone together. Everyone needs time to pursue interests not related to their jobs. People need regular exercise, regular vacations. Yet so many Christian leaders, because they are doing the Lord's work, think they are no longer human. By ignoring their natural needs, they set themselves up for spiritual dryness.

Prescription for Spiritual Dryness

WALTER TROBISCH

Joy is the most natural expression of a life lived in close fellowship with the living God. In Psalm 84:2, the psalmist sings joyfully, "My heart and my flesh cry out for the living God." However, we all know that there are days or even weeks and months when we cannot echo the psalmist. Our heart does not sing for joy, let alone our flesh. In fact, any joyful feeling seems far away, and all our efforts to bring about such a feeling fail.

The living God seems dead. We read the Bible, but its words do not speak to us. Our devotional life becomes an empty habit. We have no desire to pray. The sacraments leave us indifferent. Christian virtues strike us as dull and unattractive. Our conscience becomes insensitive and blunt.

Such periods of spiritual dryness cause a tremendous amount of suffering in the life of a Christian. If at least he could be silent during such periods! But the world around him needs and expects his love. The sick and the dying want to be comforted. Hurt and lonely people want to be understood. Nobody knows what desperation is who has never faced another human being craving help when inside he feels completely empty and dry.

In one sense it does not matter whether we feel joyful in our encounter with God. What counts is that we believe in God's Word and its promises even if we do not feel anything of his power. Nevertheless, we should not conclude that this state of faith without feeling is normal for a Christian. It is not, and we should endeavor to overcome it.

To overcome spiritual dryness, we first have to understand its causes. I would venture to give five possible reasons:

1. *Sin.* Sometimes a definite transgression of God's commandments that a person refuses to admit puts him into a state of dryness. My experience in counseling, however, has taught me that people who suffer from spiritual dryness are often very conscientious, sincere Christians who long for the nearness of the Lord and who are most careful to follow his will. Their problem is that in spite of this, they feel remote from God and cannot help themselves.

2. *Undernourishment and inertia.* It is not enough for a Christian to study the Bible only for a special purpose—in order to prepare a sermon, a Bible study, or a message for a specific occasion. The daily quiet time where he allows his heavenly Father to address him personally is as important for his

spiritual health as his daily meals are for his physical health. If he gives out continuously without taking in, he will run dry. Spiritual dryness may also result from not feeding others. Many Christians are not inactive because they ran dry; rather, they ran dry because they are inactive.

3. *Overfeeding and overstrain.* We are often afflicted with spiritual dryness after religious highlight experiences. After a retreat or Bible camp, after Christmas, Easter, Pentecost, when we have been blessed by the richness of God's Word, we may suddenly fall into utmost poverty. Or we may suffer from spiritual overstrain. After a heavy week of teaching Christianity courses, leading Bible studies, and preaching sermons, Christian leaders may feel dead in their hearts on weekends. Such spiritual overstrain can even affect a person over a longer period of time. A forced religious education in childhood—an overfeeding with joyless family devotions—may result in an adult dried-up state of indifference concerning spiritual matters.

4. *Disregard of our body.* Body and soul are a unity, and a sick mind can be the cause for a sick body. It can also work the other way around: disregard of our physical life may affect our psychological health and cause spiritual "drought." We Christians tend to overemphasize the spiritual side and underestimate the importance of biological facts—body chemistry, atmospheric pressure, weather, water and air pollution. It is true, a good pianist may be able to play on an old instrument. But even the best pianist cannot give full expression to the music he would like to play if the piano is out of tune.

5. *Loss of balance.* Our conversion to Jesus Christ does not relieve us from observing the order of the creation of which we are a part. God's creation is built upon the balance between work and rest. "And God blessed the seventh day and made it holy, because on it he rested from all the work of creating that he had done" (Genesis 2:3). In this respect, our lives are often hopelessly out of balance. We are overworked and proud of it. But if we neglect this rhythm that God has put into his creation, we lose our creative spiritual forces. Spiritual dryness results.

Help for those who suffer from spiritual dryness must relate to its cause.

1. *Forgiveness.* Confession and renewed assurance of forgiveness is the only help if a definite sin has been committed and is recognized as cause. However, the counselor should not make the mistake of Job's friends who insisted that sin must be the cause of his problems.

2. *Discipline and responsibility.* If undernourishment is the cause, new discipline in personal devotional life is indispensable. We depend too much on secondhand sermons and devotions. Learning from others is good and necessary, but we need to learn to live more by firsthand experience—to dig out our spiritual food ourselves through personal Bible study. It is good to make a decision about the best time for daily devotions. We may need a Bible reading guide and instruction in prayer. We may also need to be willing to take on a certain responsibility in God's kingdom. Fulfilling a task, even a small one, will help to heal spiritual dryness caused by inertia.

3. *Religious fasting.* When spiritual dryness is caused by overfeeding, telling

a person to pray more, study the Bible longer, and attend more church meetings would be like advising a diabetic to eat more sweets. It is probably much more helpful to prescribe for such a person a period of spiritual fasting. He should limit his devotional life to a minimum, pray only shortly, abstain from reading religious books, and step back from congregational activities for a while—until the appetite for spiritual food is aroused again.

4. *Diet and exercise.* Sleep and rest is the first answer in cases where the physical aspect has been neglected. Diet is also important. Does it include enough vitamins? More fruits and vegetables should be recommended and hiking and swimming encouraged. Clean air, good digestion, and sunshine may do more good for our spiritual health than sermons.

5. *Playful serenity.* A new balance of life may be difficult to achieve. It may demand a complete rearrangement of one's work and schedule, a change in one's life-style. Do I take time out to relax, to celebrate, to play games? Do I sometimes do something without a purpose, allow myself to be absorbed by a hobby? Such playful serenity may be a greater testimony for our Lord than pious seriousness. It may also revive in us new creative forces and open the gates to new spiritual depths.

All who have lived an intensive religious life—I think of Luther, Pascal, Kierkegaard—had to struggle through periods of spiritual dryness, sometimes to the point of desperation. The intensity of such suffering may be in direct relationship to the intensity of a person's life with God, just as deep valleys show up only in the face of high mountains. Therefore we do not need to be ashamed of dryness. We can give up our attempts to hide it by pretending to be joyful when we are not.

I have always been deeply comforted by the thought that suffering because God seems far away is only possible because at other times I have experienced his nearness. If we look at it this way, then the suffering because of spiritual dryness may be a sign that the Holy Spirit is present in us. It may contain the promise of new spiritual health. Every desert contains the promise of a new advent: "He turned the desert into pools of water and the parched ground into flowing springs; there he brought the hungry to live, and they founded a city where they could settle. They sowed fields and planted vineyards that yielded a fruitful harvest" (Psalm 107:35-37).

◆ WHAT TO DO WHEN YOU FEEL WEAK
ANTHONY CAMPOLO

When I feel weak, one of the first things I do to regain my confidence in Christ is to stop everything, go off by myself, and just think about Jesus. I get away and simply start saying over and over, "Jesus, I love you; Jesus, I love you; Jesus, I love you." After about five or ten minutes, it closes out everything in the world and I become totally focused on Jesus. Strange as it may seem, I find great strength, not in figuring out what Jesus has to say about my problem, but in shutting out everything else and thinking about Jesus and how wonderful he is.

There is an old gospel chorus: "Turn your eyes upon Jesus, look full in His wonderful face; and the things of earth will grow strangely dim in the light of His glory and grace." I find this is true. If I can go apart from everyone, get in a room alone, and just focus on Jesus, I forget myself. Being focused on Jesus gives me tremendous strength. I come out of such times of meditation with great peace and confidence.

Until a few years ago, I tended to make my Christianity into something just between Jesus and me. I've learned over the past few years that every Christian also needs a support group. A group of four of us have chosen to support one another. We get together once a week, have an early breakfast, and then talk, share, pray, and support each other. This little fellowship group strengthens and sustains me. The others sense when I'm weak; they know when I'm falling apart; they are aware when I need support. They, as brothers in Christ, help me regain my strength and confidence in Christ.

Every Christian needs a support group that can meet at least once a week. Without a support group it is very easy to lose one's equilibrium. The world keeps making us feel like failures, but a little group gives us triumph and victory and makes our faith viable. A person without a support system of some sort doesn't stand a chance of surviving in a world that weakens and discourages him or her.

I have two ways, then, of meeting times of weakness. Meditation focused on Jesus helps me gain strength and confidence. My support group revitalizes my commitments, encourages me to continue to believe the things I've always believed, and makes my beliefs all the more meaningful in the times when I'm especially weak.

When Perfectionism Makes God Seem Far Away

DAVID SEAMANDS

Perfectionism is the idea that God's love, acceptance, and approval are based on my perfect performance. Unless I perform perfectly, God will not love me. I will be worthless and unlovable, and God will be angry at me.

Perfectionism sees God like Santa Claus in the children's song. He makes his list, checks it twice, and knows if you've been naughty or nice—so you'd better be good and you'd better watch out, because he's coming to town! One of the "God is dead" theologians had this view of God. Someone asked him, "What is your definition of God?" He snorted and said, "God is the little voice within me that's always saying, 'That's not quite good enough.' "

The love of a perfectionist's God is conditional. His grace depends on human performance. Since I never meet his conditions, I can hardly expect him to help me. Not until I achieve, clean up my act, and climb up the ladder can I expect him to accept me.

This kind of scheme makes God seem very far away. There's a good reason for that. Deep down in our hearts, we can't stand a God like that. He makes us angry. We don't want him to get too close, because he makes us uncomfortable. So, even though "in him we live and move and have our being" (Acts

17:28), we keep him at a safe distance. And because he is unpleasable, he also seems unreachable.

It's a vicious circle: God seems far away, so I work very hard to reach him. I fail, however, and then I feel guilty. The guilt makes me sure that God doesn't accept me, and that makes him seem even farther away. How can a person get off this treadmill of impossible expectations and crushing guilt?

The only answer is grace.

First, I have to realize that the God I fear is not the true God at all, but rather an image I have created of him. My picture of God may be based on my parents or a teacher or a minister or a community—but if I see him as a harsh and unloving taskmaster, I am not looking at the God revealed by Jesus Christ.

It is not God who is making me feel lousy. It may feel like God or my conscience speaking to me. I may be able to pick up the Scriptures and find verses on condemnation, guilt, and judgment that reinforce my mood. Perfectionists have a marvelous talent for doing that. Somehow, however, they miss all the loving Scriptures as they rush to the harsh warnings.

The trouble is, nobody can live too long with a stern, unaccepting God. He's going to get rid of me, or I'm going to get rid of him. Either I will have a nervous breakdown, or I will break away from the faith.

Second, I have to be sure the standard I have set for myself is no higher than the standard God has set for me. When I work with perfectionists, I often find that they resist anything I try to tell them about God's gracious love. "You're lowering God," they say. "He's perfect, and you can't make him comfortable with sin."

"The problem is," I tell these people, "that you have set standards for yourself that are higher than God's standards. You have built no grace into your standards." If God is willing to forgive me, to pick me up and dust me off and set me on my feet again, I should be willing to let him do this. God asks us to relate to him as loving children. He does not ask us to lead sinless, mistake-proof lives.

Third, serious perfectionists need the help of another human being. You may wish to call this person a counselor (in my definition, a counselor is a temporary assistant to the Holy Spirit), although he can be a friend, a minister, or a psychologist.

Perfectionists tend to think they can solve their problems directly with God and through his Word—if they only pray more and read more and think the right thoughts, their concerns will melt away. That sounds good, but it can't be done.

When a perfectionist is truly troubled, reading the Word simply adds to his misery. It doesn't help him, because everything he reads passes through a negative filter that says, "I can't measure up. I'll never make it." Words that look gracious to other people look condemning to him. He is a damaged love receptor—his receiving equipment is so twisted and damaged that even though the station out there is sending beautiful pictures and playing beautiful music, by the time it gets to him it looks like snow and sounds like static.

Wrong concepts of God are rooted in wrong relationships during life's early developmental stages. These patterns of thinking and acting are programmed into us. The only way to get out of the perfectionist pattern is to learn new ways of relating—in trust and unconditional love—with another human being. And that's where the counselor comes in. Humans caused the damage in the first place, and only loving and gracious humans can undo it.

Getting over a longstanding habit of perfectionism can take a long time. By God's grace, however, it can be done. When we come to understand God's gracious and loving nature, when we are willing to accept his grace for ourselves, and when we can allow other people to become channels of that grace to us, we will be on the road back to God again.

(Condensed from *Spiritual Dryness* by Walter Trobisch, © 1970 by Walter Trobisch, and reprinted with permission of Intervarsity Press, Downers Grove, IL 60515.)

Feelings toward God

✍ LARRY KREIDER

Dietrich Bonhoeffer, the famous German theologian executed by the Third Reich for his involvement in a plot to kill Hitler, loved God. He loved God so much that he was willing to go against popular German thought, even if it meant offering his life, as the cost of his discipleship. Yet Bonhoeffer struggled with the difference between his public reputation and what he knew was his inner reality.

If Bonhoeffer struggled with his feelings and was willing to admit weariness in spiritual matters, we can take heart when our feelings are not as we wish they were. A successful spiritual journey can take place with or without constant feelings of love toward God.

Certain passages of Scripture create tension. According to Jesus, the greatest commandment is this: "Love the Lord your God with all your heart and with all your soul and with all your mind" (Matthew 22:37).

Some equate this wholehearted love with feelings—feelings of adoration, worship, and ecstasy. They seem able to draw from a spontaneous and bottomless well that allows them to feel love regularly and without effort. Others try to force a similar feeling, but the harder they try, the less they feel. They are like insomniacs who go to bed at eight o'clock and try to force sleep.

C. S. Lewis compared the beginning of the Christian life to planting a bulb and waiting for it to bloom. Those who impatiently decide to dig up the plant to see if there is any delight in it not only find no fragrance at all but also kill the flower in the process.

Scriptural teaching on love indicates that we need to plant two bulbs before our feelings will bloom. The first is active, giving love. We need to understand that love is a verb; it involves action. "For God so loved the world that he gave . . ." (John 3:16). Those who love are givers. God gives his children life, beauty, joy, and meaning. People imitate him by giving of whatever resources they possess, regardless of their feelings. They give time, talent, and treasures.

The second bulb is obedience. A common theme in the Old Testament is that God wants obedience, not sacrifice. In the New Testament, we have the supreme example of obedience—Jesus. He didn't feel like going to the cross. He even asked the Father if there was another way. But with bloody sweat pouring from his brow he said, "Yet not my will, but yours be done" (Luke 22:42).

Once the two bulbs of active love and obedience are planted, feelings will follow. How, where, and when this happens is up to God. There are, however, certain things that regulate our feelings—things we can understand and sometimes control. Knowing about these things prevents us from prematurely uprooting our bulbs. I will mention eight of them; undoubtedly there are more.

1. *Temperament differences.* Fortunately people are not all born with the same personality type. Some are action and result oriented, while others like to be around people and talk. Some want to control, count, and keep things in order, while others want to think, dream, and design. By nature, some people are more in tune with their feelings than others. You should not feel guilty over your unique personality, and you should not compare your emotional responses with someone else's.

2. *Circumstances.* It is often hard to feel magnanimous when we are plagued with little annoyances. Those of us who have experienced power outages after a hurricane in hot, humid Houston do not always feel loving when food is rotting in the refrigerator, we're bailing water from the living room, and we can't cook on the electric stove. But although we cannot control many of our circumstances, we can control our attitude toward them. Viktor Frankl, a psychiatrist who survived the concentration camp at Auschwitz and escaped the gas chambers, said the camp guards could control everything in his life except his attitude toward his suffering.

3. *Physical health.* This needs little explanation. Sickness creates emotions that compete with the warm feelings of worship.

4. *Anger.* The Spirit of God works within us to mold us into obedient givers so that we can experience his presence. However, by holding onto anger we reduce his touch in our lives. Paul says anger grieves the Spirit (Ephesians 4:29-32).

5. *Low self-image.* When a person feels bad about himself he subconsciously blames God for his condition. After all, God created him as he is. A person who feels this way should recognize that God not only has made him a particular way, he has also given him the potential to change.

6. *Uncontrolled drives.* It is impossible to love God while feeling guilty. To love God wholeheartedly, one must be obedient. A person feels free to make worship part of his life again when things have been cleared up through forgiveness and when he is living in obedience to God.

7. *People and places.* Feelings are often affected by the chemistry of relationships and the atmosphere of places. Some people draw you toward good feelings about God, while others create tension. Some locations trigger worship, while others chill worshipful thoughts.

8. *Different stages in life.* Each stage in life carries its own baggage of pressures and tensions. It also has its unique way of expressing feelings. A child may feel a wonder as new understandings about God unfold. An adolescent can feel the joy of being liberated from peer pressures. A college student, seeing how all disciplines of study shed light on God's truth, experiences intellectual satisfaction. Young adults, seeing that Scriptures on interpersonal relationships and child raising are as valid today as when they were written, rejoice to know there is a guiding light. Middle-aged adults seek for new feelings of worth, intimacy, and meaning amidst shifting physical and financial demands. The elderly lean heavily on God's provision in times of sorrow and on his promises of eternal life.

Though Bonhoeffer did not always have the feelings he wanted in his quest to serve God, he rested in the shelter of knowing that, although he didn't understand everything about himself or God, he was still God's child. He never lost that feeling of security.

"Who am I? They mock me, these lonely questions of mine.
"Whoever I am, Thou knowest, O God, I am thine!"

Joy and the Christian Life

DAVID McKENNA

Joy is a unique and genuine biblical term. Many people confuse joy with happiness, but there is a radical difference. Happiness is dependent on circumstances, while joy is independent of them. Happiness is a surface response to good things; joy is a deep-down response that endures whether what happens around people is good or bad.

The worldly view of happiness is looking out for Number One and negotiating your personal good in all you do. The greatest good is your happiness. Ironically, such an attitude rarely leads to what it promises.

The Christian view of happiness is totally the opposite. If you have Christ in you, you do not enter into human relationships in order to make yourself happy, but in order to give of yourself. This sacrificial love grows out of the Christlike spirit of agape, something people without Christ cannot do or even imagine. The good of others, not your own happiness, is the criterion by which you judge your actions. When you give yourself away, you receive the joy that Christ desired for you. Thus, happiness and joy are radically different.

In his autobiography, *Surprised by Joy,* C. S. Lewis described his pursuit of joy. He tried to find it in humanism, communism, eroticism, and other human philosophies and searches. But they only led him to the traces where joy had been. He did not find joy for himself until he realized that joy would come only as a result of putting Christ first in his life.

Joy is never an end in itself. It is only as you make Christ your overwhelming first priority that joy, almost unconsciously, comes. If you seek it you will lose it; it can't be caught.

The secularist is not seeking joy; he is seeking happiness. Joy is a quality given by Christ. Hebrews 12:2 says, "Let us fix our eyes on Jesus, the author and perfecter of our faith, who for the joy set before him endured the cross, scorning its shame, and sat down at the right hand of the throne of God." Jesus had the endurance to go through the pain and suffering because he had the end in view. He was affirming his purpose for the redemption of the world, and so he never lost sight of the joy that was set before him. Joy would come to him out of the suffering because he gave himself for the redemption of mankind.

Jesus prayed that his disciples might have his joy: "I say these things while I am still in the world, so that they [the disciples] may have the full measure of my joy within them" (John 17:13). The joy of Christ is transferred to us as we go about the task of telling the world about him.

Sometimes we just don't feel any joy. If we begin to ask ourselves if we've lost the joy of our Christian lives, we need to ask if we are confusing means and ends. If we seek joy as an end in itself, we will lose it. If we've lost the joy of the Christian life, we need to put back into perspective what God is calling us to do and consider if Christ is still truly first in our lives. Joy is not "lost," but it can be "misplaced" if our other priorities get out of line.

Joy is not something to be worked toward, not a goal to be reached, not an end in itself. It is, instead, the spontaneous result of our relationship with Christ.

RELATED ARTICLES

Chapter 5: **How to Keep Your Focus on Christ**
Chapter 10: **Avoid a Roller-Coaster Faith**

CHAPTER

19

A Christian Life-style in a Secular World

- ✓ What difference should being a Christian make?
- ✓ How are Christian values different?
- ✓ How do I maintain my values?
- ✓ How do I stand up for what is right?
- ✓ What if Christians have opposing values?

What It Means to Live a Holy Life

CHARLES COLSON

Christians tend to think of holiness as not smoking, drinking, dancing, going to movies, or hanging around with those who do. That's a very mistaken view of the subject. Holiness may involve avoiding those things, if that's how God leads us. But in this "negative" view of holiness, too often we end up worshiping rules rather than the Rule-maker. We think we've won a spiritual beauty contest if we keep all the rules; we get arrogant and self-righteous—and we destroy our witness. We miss the bigger picture when, by adhering to the letter of the law, we miss its spirit.

Rules often confine us to personal piety rather than impel us to take on the full character of God and be holy people. If we are in a church or culture where people have covenanted together to live under certain rules, because in their view that amounts to being scriptural, it is crucially important that we not think of rule-keeping as the main ingredient of Christianity. Satisfying spiritual scorecards does not fulfill our obligation to Christ.

I've been in a prison where a volunteer said, "This inmate smokes. He can't be a Christian." I know, however, that inmate has just laid his life on the line to win other people to Christ. I think he's exhibiting more holiness than someone who sits in his living room and never does anything for the kingdom, but can say, "I don't smoke, drink, or swear." That person may be very pious and may be looking toward a crown in heaven, but he isn't doing what God commanded.

In the Old Testament, God told the Jews that he would pitch his tent and dwell in their midst. That is the basic covenant between God and his people. In the New Testament, God lived among his people in the person of Jesus Christ. As John 1:14 records, "The Word became flesh and lived for a while among us." When, literally translated from the Greek, this means that God pitched a tent and lived in our midst.

If God is going to live in us, we must be a holy people in whom a holy God can abide. We must allow God to work through our lives in the full range of things that are of concern to him. These include the things that are out of order in society such as the needs of the suffering, the hungry, the poor, the homeless, and the imprisoned. He is concerned that there be just and right relationships among people, and that we love one another and have compassion for each other.

When we really understand the character of God as it is revealed in the Old and New Testaments, we begin to say, "I want to conform to the image of God." We don't just wash our faces, put on good clothes, and sit comfortably in our pews. We go out and meet the needs of hurting people around us, becoming instruments of righteousness in society. We evangelize. We are concerned with the conditions in our cities and neighborhoods. Our hearts break for those who are hurting in our midst. Holiness means being people who reflect the character of God, as his invisible kingdom is made visible through our lives.

One of the greatest examples of holiness I can see in the world today is Mother Teresa. She has demonstrated true Christianity by self-sacrifice, giving, going where no one else wanted to go, caring for the homeless and the helpless. I always thought the old adage "God helps those who help themselves" was in the Bible until I became a Christian. As I read God's Word, I found that just the opposite is true. God helps those who can't help themselves. Mother Teresa has given her life to helping people who can't help themselves, who have no other usefulness in the world's eyes other than that they are creations of God.

In my book *Loving God,* I cited examples of ordinary people who were holy.

One was a woman who spends her lunch hour every day in prison. She leaves her office, eats a sandwich behind the wheel of her car, and gives her time to lonely prisoners: visiting them, listening to them, sharing the Christ they can see in her. Another was a United States senator who spent ten days, during a very busy time in the Senate, at the bedside of a dying friend, simply because he felt that was what he had to do. A third was a retired businessman who felt compassion for people in poverty in Haiti. He took old machines and started a rug factory, helping people both to find work and to find Christ.

Mother Teresa lives a very strong devotional life. This is where holiness begins. We become holy through absorbing Scripture into our lives and then living obedient lives. Mother Teresa also never fails to talk about Christ in everything she does. Yet she goes further. She not only talks about Christianity, she lives it. A lot of people get involved in good works, but then they fail to talk about Jesus at all. Being holy is both proclaiming and demonstrating. It is, as Mother Teresa defines it, acceptance of the will of God and then allowing that acceptance to radically change our lives.

Humility: The Unwanted Virtue

AJITH FERNANDO

In the first century, the Greek word for humility was used only in a derogatory sense. Humility was regarded as a sign of weakness and low-mindedness.

The followers of Jesus, the Servant Lord, took that same Greek word and used it in the New Testament as a supreme virtue. In fact, the New Testament presents humility as the distinctive trait of a truly great person.

Today, too, most people are not very interested in humility. It seems to go against the grain of self-interest, which rules many people, and of popular attempts to overcome low self-esteem. Many people feel that assertiveness is the way to overcome low self-esteem, and they see humility as a barrier to assertiveness.

Indeed, we see today some very unattractive models of what is called humility. The behavior of some "humble" people is very abrasive. There is no brightness in their lives. They are proud of their "humility," and they use it judgmentally in their relationships with those they regard as not humble. So their humility serves only to alienate them from others.

What a contrast Jesus was! The naturalness and winsomeness of his humility softened the most hardened sinners and made them seek his company.

Some people who think they are humble are really insipid. The so-called humility of these people makes them reluctant to push themselves far enough forward to do anything significant or out of the ordinary. They think it is wrong to assert their will over anybody or any situation. They end up doing little to alleviate the pain of this hurting world.

Again, Jesus contrasts with this false view of humility. Jesus' humility was not insipid—it was shocking. Peter and the other disciples were shocked when, in humility, he washed their feet. They were equally shocked when he fearlessly drove the money-changers out of the Jerusalem temple.

These examples from Jesus' life show that humble people can also get things done. Actually, insipidity often arises from pride. What passes for humility is in reality fear of making mistakes. Because of this fear, these supposedly humble people don't want to take the initiative in anything. But this fear is a form of pride.

How can we develop biblical humility? The first thing I must say about this is that if humility is a problem for us, it may be because we have low self-esteem. An overwhelming sense of inferiority and insecurity will affect our attitude to ourselves and may cause us to use any means to restore our self-esteem. So a solution to our problem with humility must be closely connected with a solution to our problem with self-esteem.

I have been greatly helped by what a great Christian of the last century, J. C. Ryle, said about humility. Commenting on Christ's parable about the places of honor at the banquet table (Luke 14:7-11), he said that the root and spring of humility is right knowledge about God, about ourselves, and about Christ's love.

Our pride cannot long survive if we find out about God's majesty and holiness and then realize how sinful we are by comparison. Then, if we also come to understand that Christ loved us so much that he died for us, we are filled with a joyous humility. We are joyous because Christ's love has transformed our lives. We are humble because we realize that we do not deserve such love. So God's remedy for pride is the gospel, which says that God is holy, that man is sinful, and that Christ's grace is greater than man's sin.

One who has been transformed by Christ's forgiving love is full of gratitude to God for what he has done for him. Gratitude and humility are an inseparable pair. If you are truly grateful to God, you cannot be proud, for you realize that all your goodness and worth comes from God. You did not deserve it. You also realize that God has given you a place in his family, that you are a child of the King of kings and Lord of lords, a prince in the eternal kingdom whose affairs are the only things that really matter.

Here is the answer to the problem of low self-esteem: God loves us. He accepts us. He gives us a place in his kingdom. He gives us an important job to do. We are secure in him. We are important people. But because of our gratitude to God for these blessings, we cannot be proud about our importance. And because our self-esteem problem is solved, we are not going to use unhumble means to try to compensate for low self-esteem.

Gratitude also takes away the abrasiveness often associated with humility. The grace of God that has flooded into our lives makes us gracious. Having been loved with an everlasting love, we are able to regard others with loving concern (1 John 4:19). We spend our energies not pushing ourselves forward, but letting the love of Christ flow from us to others. Like our Master, we become servants. According to the Christian scale of values, there is no greater honor on earth than to be a servant.

This mixture of gratitude and humility gives us the strength to fulfill some of the obligations of humility presented in the Scriptures. Philippians 2:3 says, "In humility consider others better than yourselves." In our competitive society this procedure looks like a threat to our security. But a Christian whose life is overwhelmed with gratitude to God finds his security in God and does not need to defeat others in order to be secure. He has the inner strength to concentrate on pushing others forward.

If the answer to the problem of humility lies in knowing the great truths of the gospel, why do most of us who have accepted the gospel still struggle with pride and low self-esteem? This is because in Christianity knowledge is experiential. The gospel tells us we are important to God, but if we have not grasped what that means, it cannot influence our experience. So we continue to struggle with problems of inferiority. As we grow deeper in our experiential knowledge of God, as the thrill of being a child of God becomes more and more real to us, humility and self-esteem will emerge as by-products even without our realizing it.

Our primary focus should not be on trying to be humble. Indeed, the Bible urges us to be humble (Ephesians 4:2) and gives us models of humility that we should follow (John 13:1-17; Philippians 2:1-11). Heeding these words on humility is a necessary part of one's growth into humility. But trying to follow these models is useless unless Jesus is the focus of our lives.

Our motivation is not to become humble, but to be like Jesus. Our focus should be on him—on thanking him for his kindness, on enjoying him, on loving him, on obeying him, and on honoring him. Pride has a difficult time surviving in such an environment. Almost without our knowledge, humility will become part of us as we become more and more like the one who is the focus of our lives—Jesus, the Servant Lord.

A humble person, consumed with a passion for Christ, does not need to be afraid of launching out on bold ventures if they will bring honor to God. Sometimes such a venture may give him some prominence. If prominence helps further his God-honoring cause, he need not shun it. Yet, in following this path, he runs the risk of crossing the border of humility and becoming proud. When God sees us succumbing to this temptation, he often sends some "disciplines" to bring us back to the path of humility (Hebrews 12:4-11). These disciplines are a major means God uses to help us stay humble.

A capable young Christian student who worked hard at his studies did not do well at his final examination for some unexplainable reason. When he graduated he did not get the high honors he deserved. Because of this he forfeited much praise and esteem, and he earned much humiliation. Later he realized that God had allowed this to happen because he had become too proud about his abilities and achievements. He would have used success at his graduation in a way that would have detracted from God's glory. God sent him failure to help him become humble. God knew that humility would be of far greater value to him than the honor that success would have brought him.

God often sends failure and other humiliating experiences to check the pride that may be growing in our hearts. We can be grateful for such experiences, or we can thwart the good end God desires us to have from these "disciplines" by becoming angry or bitter. In submission to God we must let him train us. Hebrews 12:11 says, "No discipline seems pleasant at the time, but painful. Later on, however, it produces a harvest of righteousness and peace for those who have been trained by it."

Managing Time

HOWARD HENDRICKS

A mark of maturity is a person's ability to manage time. Time is one thing we all have in common. We don't all have the same IQ, the same spiritual gifts, or identical personalities, but we all have twenty-four hours a day at our disposal. What distinguishes us is not the amount of time we have, but how we use our time.

Good time management involves six principles.

1. *Have a clear goal.* We achieve what we aim for; our objective determines our outcome. The greatest time waster is having goals that are not well-defined—or having no goals at all. If we don't have a clear idea of what we want to accomplish, we often do things that don't need to be done.

2. *Have a detailed plan.* We need to understand from the outset where we want to go and exactly how we want to get there. For example, if we are going to give a dinner party for twenty people, we need to know what we are going to serve, what food we need to buy, when we will prepare the dishes, and where people will sit.

3. *Make a to-do list every day.* This works best when we write it down, because when we see it on paper we sometimes discover an activity is not as important as we originally thought. In addition, when we list everything we need to do, it is easier to refuse to do what is not on the list. A good list helps us distinguish between the urgent and the important.

Making a list does not mean rigidly adhering to it at the expense of letting the Spirit work in our lives. We need to be flexible. A schedule is not a straitjacket; it is a tool to help us accomplish our objectives. We need to be flexible enough to allow the Spirit of God to invade our lives with divinely appointed interruptions. Otherwise, the schedule becomes our master rather than a tool.

4. *Set priorities.* A businessman once told me about the 80-20 rule. He said that for any task, 80 percent of the value is contained in 20 percent of the activity. If you concentrate on the 20 percent of the job that is worth 80 percent of the value, you will accomplish more. I often ask myself, What is the most valuable use of my time right now? And I remind myself of the statement, "You never have time to do everything, but you always have time to do the important things."

5. *Handle items only once.* We can get more done if we concentrate on one

task at a time and stay with it until it is finished. Otherwise we end up shuffling papers and backtracking to complete chores.

6. *Develop a sense of priority about your task.* Procrastination is one of the biggest time killers. We need to follow the motto "Do it now."

Having God's perspective can also help us use our time effectively. In Psalm 90, Moses looked back at the end of his life and said, "Teach us to number our days aright, that we may gain a heart of wisdom" (v. 12). Life took on a new perspective for Moses when he realized he didn't have all eternity to do his work on earth. When he developed that perspective, he realized he needed wisdom to use his time profitably.

People often use the excuse "I don't have time" for not serving God. But Ephesians 2:10 says we are created in Christ Jesus to do good works. If we don't have time, we're either doing things God never intended for us to do in the first place, or we're doing them in the wrong way.

We need only to be as organized as is necessary to meet our need. Organization is not an end, but a means to the end. We may be either overorganized and compulsive, or underorganized and complacent. We need to study ourselves to learn how we organize ourselves best. People tend to get discouraged when they compare themselves to someone else. Comparison is a sin. We are unique individuals and should ask, What is best for me? How do I function best? When am I most efficient? When am I least efficient? In what time increments do I work best?

Personally, I work best in hour-and-a-half periods. After that, I am just putting in time without accomplishing anything. I used to stay at my desk longer than an hour and a half because I thought that was being dedicated. But it was inefficient. I would go talk to my secretary or make a telephone call, but I would not be working. I finally discovered I got more done when I took a break and came back to my work later.

What we need to avoid is the tyranny of the urgent. The classic illustration of this is seen in Jesus Christ. He ministered here for only three and a half years, but he was never in a hurry. He always had time to do the Father's will because he had clear-cut objectives: he knew why he came and what he came to do.

By contrast, most people do the immediate task rather than the important one. Insistent pressures call for action right now. For example, a doctor's appointment at three o'clock is urgent. Playing with our children is important. We do the demanding things that pressure us but put off the important ones—our spouse, our children, our devotions.

We lose sight of importance because we lack a focused purpose. But if we don't plan our lives, somebody else will. Most of us don't plan to fail, we fail to plan. When we lose sight of our objectives, we concentrate on doing, but this is motion without meaning.

The key to overcoming the tyranny of the urgent is learning to say no. Say no to something every day, just to get in the habit. We have to say no to many things in order to be able to say yes to the important things.

◆ KEYS TO ORGANIZING YOUR LIFE
HOWARD HENDRICKS

To help organize your life, ask yourself four basic questions:

1. *What do I want?* In thinking through your answer, consider not only right now but your entire life. Many successful people spend their whole lives achieving what they want, and when they finally reach their goal, they realize it isn't what they wanted after all. The real question is this: What do I want at the end of my life? What will give me ultimate fulfillment?

2. *What price am I willing to pay?* I would love to be a concert pianist, but I heard Van Cliburn say, "I spend eight hours a day in practice, two of them in finger exercises alone." Suddenly I realized I didn't want to play the piano that badly. Achievement comes with a high price tag.

3. *How will I get where I want to go?* Different people will choose different routes. Some people are good at organization; others are not. Some focus on each task as it comes along; others make lists and prioritize. Each type of person can arrive at his chosen destination if he takes his personality into consideration as he plans the journey.

4. *What is my power source?* We need to commit ourselves to accomplishing our objectives. We need self-control, good time management, and a willingness to work hard. Some people have tremendous ability but do not apply it. They are like Niagara Falls without a hydro-electric plant. We need discipline to harness our energy.

Basic Moral Characteristics
LEWIS SMEDES

Character is what we truly are, compared with what we seem to be. You can appear to be generous even when your heart is that of a skinflint.

Character is different from piety. By piety, I mean a personal relationship with God. By character, I mean the quality of the person. Even so, they are certainly inseparable; God is quite interested in character, and there is something wrong if a pious person does not have a good moral character.

Similarly, there is a relationship between having character and doing good things. In fact, they are so interrelated that I consider it nonsense to say, "He never does anything good, but at heart he's a good person."

The flip side is that, as I mentioned above, you can do good things for the wrong reasons. You can act like a philanthropist in order to get your name on a plaque. You can do good in order to be saved by good works. Thus, doing good things is not a sure sign of being a good person. But you also can have a good character and sometimes do bad things—a good character is not a perfect one.

A good character is a person who regularly does good things, because she has an inner disposition to do them. She does not merely luck out once in awhile and do some good thing. She has a readiness for the good; the good is drawn out of her in various situations. People come to depend on her character, just as they grow to expect lying and cheating from a bad person. As Jesus said, "By their fruit you will recognize them" (Matthew 7:20; see also 12:33-37).

When considering what makes for good moral character, the word *virtue* comes to mind. The ancient Greeks used the word to mean "excellence." I would like to consider the classic definition of virtue as part of our description of character.

In the Greek catalog, there were four cardinal virtues—four things that you should never leave home without. The first is *discernment.* Unless you are able to discern what is really going on in a situation, what people are feeling, and what is important, you will always make wrong decisions. My theory is that the greatest moral disputes of any age are differences not so much in moral theory as in the power of discernment. This virtue is the essence of Paul's advice: "Do not conform any longer to the pattern of this world, but be transformed by the renewing of your mind. Then you will be able to test and approve what God's will is—his good, pleasing and perfect will" (Romans 12:2).

The second virtue is *courage.* It is the power to do well when the air is turbulent and the going gets tough. It is having the character to do well when things are tempting, when things are painful. It is easy to be a mother when a baby is cooing and gurgling over breakfast; it takes courage to be a mother when the child suffers from a terrible and incurable handicap. Courage is the power to do well in the face of a threat—to your life, to your security, to your future, to the things you hold dear. The Old Testament is a symphony of variations on the theme of courage.

Temperance is the third virtue. It means being in charge of your own life. To manage, to control, to be able to orchestrate all the stuff that is going on inside. Of course, by control of one's life, I do not mean that a Christian gallops ahead on his own, oblivious of Christ's lordship. A temperate person gives control to God, and in turn accepts genuine responsibility as a challenge from God. The temperate person does not let circumstances, substances, or other people control him. Like other gifts of the Spirit, temperance needs to be practiced, lest we lose it.

The fourth virtue is *justice.* The person of justice determines always to be fair and does not treat one person differently from another. It is rejecting questions such as Whose wheel is squeaking the loudest? or Who will reward me the most? The prophets called out for justice, stating God's case against Israel: "He has showed you, O man, what is good. And what does the Lord require of you? To act justly and to love mercy and to walk humbly with your God" (Micah 6:8).

In addition to these four virtues, there are many other qualities that God wants to nurture in us. Let us briefly mention just two: honesty and the willingness to make and keep commitments. I call these the bread and butter of the Spirit because they are less glamorous than the fruit of the Spirit.

In the long run, God will not ask you how happy you were. He will ask, What sort of person were you?

Moral Issues vs. Matters of Propriety

LEWIS SMEDES

"It is a sin to go to a movie!"

Such prohibitions would come down from the elders of my church as they came out of their smoke-filled meeting room—just before they went home for a cold glass of beer. People of other denominations would of course find the behavior of people in our church sinful.

In their quest for holiness, some Christians attacked movies and theater; others, alcohol or tobacco, jewelry or certain styles of dress, or birth control. Is it possible for churches to pass rules that God does not pass? Yes, and we should resist unbiblical legislation of our consciences.

Most important, we must distinguish basic moral issues from peripheral issues. Not everything in morality is of equal importance; there are questions that are not central to our obedience to Christ. How can you tell when a person or a Christian community is majoring in the minors? The Scriptures tell us where the core is, what the absolutes are.

God's absolutes can be seen in the Ten Commandments and in the prophets, to name only two sources. He loves justice and mercy; that is what he requires of us, as Micah 6:8 records. Honesty in speech and actions, respect for others' property and dignity, honor for father and mother, worship of God, sexual fidelity—these and other subjects form the cores of religious behavior.

Look to the New Testament example as well. Jesus preached and lived out God's standards of love for neighbor as for self and of commitment to God. And Paul described in 1 Corinthians 13 what love in action looks like: it is patient, kind, not proud, not self-seeking, hopeful, persevering, and more.

When we move out from this core to the edges, we then deal with matters of propriety. People moralize about propriety, but whether you wear jewelry or use makeup is peripheral. What is proper can be very important, even crucial at times, but it is not central to our faith. Adultery, idolatry, selfishness—these are core.

It is easy to major in the minors because matters of propriety are most obvious. If I pollute a river because of my company's practices, that is not immediately noticeable. But if I drink wine, people notice. People can see a wedding ring on my finger or the length of a woman's skirt, and such relatively unimportant matters can be bothersome within the Christian community.

If a person believes that a church is putting a burden on him that God does not, what can he do? He may feel caught, because it can be difficult to divorce "Thus saith the Lord" from "This is the way I interpret the voice of God." There are times when it is right to try to change a church's standards. Many denominations provide for avenues of protest in which you can state your case up to the highest administrative levels.

If this is unsuccessful—or there is no allowance for dissent—and you still believe your conscience is clean before God, it may be time to change churches. Some people, however, make behavioral compromises because of other things that keep them in the church; keeping the fellowship is worth compromise on nonessentials. Still others say, "The only way I can challenge these people is to do what they prohibit and let them decide what they want to do with me." That is very calculated and should be done only in matters of great significance, such as the morality of a particular war.

Questions of propriety have been around since the early days of the church. Paul addressed the very problem in Romans 14 and 15, especially concerning eating meat that had been sacrificed to idols. Some Christians believed it was an abomination to eat it, but others felt free to do so. The apostle counseled, "The man who eats everything must not look down on him who does not, and the man who does not eat everything must not condemn the man who does, for God has accepted him. Who are you to judge someone else's servant? To his own master he stands or falls. . . . Therefore let us stop passing judgment on one another. Instead, make up your mind not to put any stumbling block or obstacle in your brother's way" (Romans 14:3, 4, 13).

One rule is crucial: Never allow anyone to obligate you to go against your conscience. Paul spoke of "weaker brothers" who are not free to behave a certain way. They should not control your conscience, even when they say, "Tsk, tsk, we're offended by what you're doing." But neither should you tempt them to go against their consciences; and there are times when, out of respect for their consciences, you "do not eat the meat."

The sin is not in the activity but in the violation of conscience—yours or the weaker brother's. To apply the meat-eating question today, let us think about moviegoing. If a fellow believer said, "I'm indignant that you went to the movie theater last week," I would say, "That's your problem; you'll have to deal with that." But if I said, "Let's go to the movies" to a young person who has been reared to believe that movies are wrong, that would be wrong. I would be seducing him or her to go against conscience. Love for the brethren is more compelling than my liberty.

When Values Collide

✍ KATHY CALLAHAN-HOWELL

As Christians, we struggle to keep ourselves free from sin and immorality. At times, especially as new converts, this means removing ourselves from friendships that influence us to sin. Yet we will never make an impact on the world if we do not befriend nonbelievers, despite their immorality.

Paul addressed this issue in dealing with the Corinthians:

I have written you in my letter not to associate with sexually immoral people—not at all meaning the people of this world who are immoral, or the greedy and swindlers, or idolaters. In that case you would have to leave this world. But now I am writing you that you must not associate with anyone who calls himself a brother but is sexually immoral or greedy, an idolater or a slanderer, a drunkard or a swindler. With such a man do not even eat.

What business is it of mine to judge those outside the church? Are you not to judge those inside? God will judge those outside. "Expel the wicked man from among you." 1 Corinthians 5:9-13

Paul drew a clear distinction between our behavior toward the immoral people inside and outside the church. We must associate with those outside the church. Christ called us to love sinners, not judge them.

Outside the church. Many years after my parents divorced, a woman moved in with my father. I continued my previous close relationship with my dad and began to befriend his new roommate. My mother complained, "Isn't visiting him just condoning the relationship?" But I explained that he knew very well I did not approve of his sin. However, I could not expect to be a good influence if I stopped loving him. If I cut off our relationship, I would have no chance to demonstrate the love of Christ.

Consider your own condition before believing in Christ. Perhaps you did not participate in any gross immoralities. Yet what if no Christian had cared for you due to your faults? How would you ever have heard about Christ?

Take for example a coworker who is homosexual. We'll call him Scott. If you project a condemning attitude toward homosexuality, Scott will never listen to your words of witness. However, if you love Scott as a person as God does, you may help him gain Christ. You may have an opportunity to share with him that you believe homosexuality to be immoral, but be sure your comments fall on a friendship, and they may be heard.

We can't expect people without Christ to live by biblical morals. Many people seem to manage, but without the Holy Spirit, biblical principles prove difficult to follow. Our concern should be that our unbelieving friends find Christ, then the morality should follow. Trying to change a person's homosexual, drug, or drinking habits, or other such drastic life changes, often requires the redeeming action of Christ. Don't expect the change to come before the conversion.

Paul reminded the Corinthians to continue to associate with the immoral people of the world. Jesus modeled this as he socialized with the disreputable people of his day, such as tax collectors and prostitutes. We must befriend those around us who do not yet know Christ.

Many people you work with, live by, or associate with may participate in activities you are strongly opposed to as a Christian. This may curtail the extent of your friendship because you must refuse to drink, gamble, or cheat with them. Certainly you should not compromise your own values for the sake of the relationship.

However, you can concentrate on activities that avoid value conflicts, such as having lunch together, playing a game of golf, or spending a day shopping. Find activities you both enjoy that contain no compromises. Build your relationship on these positive experiences. During such moments you may find opportunity to discuss your beliefs. If an issue does arise, be sure to state your views without condemning your friend. Simply state what you believe to be right according to the Bible. Allow the Bible to be the authority, not you.

Most of all, pray for opportunities to share your faith in Christ. Remember, sharing Christ benefits your friend more than sharing values. With Christ will come the values. Ask yourself, Do I have any non-Christian friends I am cultivating a relationship with? Am I open to opportunities to share my faith? Do I share my values when asked?

Inside the church. On the other hand, Paul instructed quite differently concerning those within the church. Persons claiming Christ must refrain from immorality. Paul had asked the Corinthians to expel a brother who had been warned previously concerning sinful actions. Later Paul instructed the church to readmit the repentant brother.

Christians must exhibit integrity. We must act according to our stated beliefs. As members of the church, we are accountable to one another. When a member lives in sin, the church must confront that person. Jesus taught this in Luke 17:3. "If your brother sins, rebuke him, and if he repents, forgive him." We are called to confront and to forgive.

Both confrontation and forgiveness cause us difficulty. We prefer telling someone else, complaining, and gossiping. Jesus explained in Matthew 18:15-17 that we are to confront the person alone, then with others. If we love our fellow Christians we will confront them, especially if we are directly affected.

Therefore, if a man in our church moves in with his girlfriend, we have a responsibility to remind him of the immorality of this action. If a woman cheats on her husband, we are called to speak to her. Hopefully a loving word will bring repentance.

Sadly, once the person repents, we often have even more difficulty forgiving. We can't seem to forget that someone committed adultery or stole from the church treasury. Despite what we say, our minds still hold their sin against them. A new Christian admits struggling with homosexuality, and we never trust him again. Our divorced friend wears a certain stigma due to her failure.

The essence of Christianity is mercy. God forgives, forgets, and makes all things new. Even sins committed after a conversion are forgivable, and no sin rates worse than any other. If God can forgive my selfishness, he can forgive my friend's divorce. In the midst of sin we must confront, but after repentance we must forgive and renew.

Consider how you can enter a ministry of forgiveness. Look around your church. Are there people left out due to a past divorce, homosexuality, adultery, or just because they don't measure up? Think about ways you can include these people in your life and help them feel accepted.

The seekers. Between those outside and inside the church fall a third group: those people searching for Christ. They lie somewhere between the beginning of a spiritual awakening and a full public commitment to Christ. During this process they require much patience.

Some persons have an instant conversion experience. Others evolve slowly into Christians. In both groups are people who immediately make a total life change, ceasing any immoral activity and beginning new Christian habits. Yet some people struggle with changes and revisions.

Every person's journey demonstrates different direction. We can't expect everyone to change instantly. We must be patient and ask God to guide the person to change what is necessary.

A couple in my Bible study were living together. They were committed strongly to each other; in fact, the man had quit his job to move when the woman was transferred. Both had been previously married and did not choose to remarry.

As they continued to attend the Bible study, God began to work a change in their lives. I prayed that God would lead them to get married, and before long they announced their wedding plans. God convicted them; I didn't say a word.

Often we must simply be patient and allow the Holy Spirit to lead people to change. However, sometimes people do require guidance from other Christians. One excellent opportunity arises when they choose to join the local church. Most churches have some sort of instruction and examination procedure. Such a time allows the pastor to ask about certain areas of their lives that may need correction.

If people continue in their sin after a period of time, they fall into the "inside the church" category and may need to be spoken to accordingly. However, we must remember to be patient with new believers. God knows better than we how much they can change at once. If they are open to his Spirit he will instruct them. We should pray for their openness and obedience.

The value of the value. Finally, sometimes when our values collide we must consider what the value is. The Bible makes clear statements on immorality. However, some values remain less crucial, such as personal habits of dress or entertainment. Television may be shunned by some and lauded by others. Stylish clothes may be required by some peoples' professions and avoided by others due to a desire for simplicity.

Some values are personal and not clearly dictated by Scripture. These matters may be discussed openly yet should not cause friction between persons, in or out of the church.

When our values collide with another person's, we must consider the weight of the conflict. If the matter is crucial we need to remember the other person's spiritual state. We must continue to love the other person despite all other factors. If we would pray for them instead of complaining, we might find resolution, if only within ourselves.

◆ SURVIVING IN THE SEA OF SECULARISM OSWALD HOFFMAN

Cultural attitudes seep slowly into our lives, so slowly that they are hard to fight. In the apostolic age, people were assaulted by the pagan culture in which they lived. Today we have the same paganism, even if it comes in a different form. Secularism is a sea that surrounds us all.

Even the church is affected by it. For example, we have accepted the secular virtue of size. We judge our success or failure by the number of people we have gained during the year. But things may have happened in people's lives that cannot be measured. Perhaps their spiritual lives were deepened. Since that kind of growth cannot be counted, we tend to overlook it. It does not add to our status—and we desperately want to be successful in the world's eyes.

Don't Be Afraid to Take a Stand

BECKY TIRABASSI

Are you afraid to take a stand that might offend your non-Christian friends? A good exercise in defining specific fears is to list some of the fears and decide if they are realistic and probable. List the fears on one side of a sheet of paper and on the other side of the paper detail the possible stances you might take. In addition, you might want to evaluate what the possible repercussions might be if you *do* take a stand versus keeping quiet on the issue.

Then you must pinpoint your fears. It may be that you are afraid of losing the closeness that has developed between certain friends and yourself. Your "group" of friends may have given you your identity, image, or reputation. You may be afraid to lose the security of having someone who will always be there and has known you for a long period of time. As your Christian principles begin to pop up into conversation, you may be afraid of rejection.

Essentially all Christians approach this juncture in their personal Christianity when they have to defend what they believe. Over the years, I have watched many people struggle with fears relating to their faith. Much of the success in overcoming these is in taking a good look at your own personality and how you relate to people in general. Are you normally shy and quiet, or are you opinionated and argumentative?

For any Christian, if your closest friends are non-Christians you will probably find yourself having to take a stand regularly for your differing values and morals. Perhaps you are placing too much emphasis on your fellowship with non-Christian friends. This is not to say that you cannot carry on with these relationships, but growth in Christ should be drawing you to seek Christian friends and fellowship as your closest peers and confidants. It is extremely difficult to maintain a solid Christian walk without the influence of other Christians in your life. Perhaps this will become a time of evaluation of your life-style and friends. Do your friends determine your convictions, or does the Word of God and his Holy Spirit within you (Psalm 118:6, 8)?

Part of your inability to defend your faith may be that you are unsure or unknowledgeable of what the Bible says regarding a Christian's values, morals, and conduct. If you struggle with what to say to your non-Christian friends and how to say it, then begin to study the Bible. Any number of Christian people (including your pastor, parent, Bible study leader, or older Christian friend) can direct you to workbooks and study guides that will give you confidence and assurance of your convictions as based on the Word of God. Anything is hard to defend if you are not convinced of its truth! In essence, know what you believe!

Another suggestion for overcoming these fears would be to seek advice on the types of responses that others have used in specific situations. For example, if you have already had a confrontation with a non-Christian friend, use that situation in a role play with someone who will help you with what to say. Practicing will give you experience in defending your faith, speaking the truth in love (Ephesians 4:15) and being firm, but not overbearing. Put yourself in your non-Christian friend's shoes; remind yourself of the feelings and doubts that you had as a non-Christian. Share your thoughts and beliefs without a demeaning attitude. Introduce humor at appropriate times and keep the tension from mounting by comments that would put both of you at ease. Don't defend by arguing and remember to be a good listener. Never forget, your actions speak louder than your words. "Walking your talk" will be evidence that you have taken a stand!

As you continue to grow in your convictions and beliefs, read the Bible regularly to remind and refresh yourself of God's desires for you as a Christian. In addition, maintain a mature group of strong Christian friends as your closest peer influence. It shouldn't be long before your faith will take hold and your fears will fade. You may just find your non-Christian friends following you!

Finally, use conversational prayer with God as a continual source of releasing your fears, expressing your deepest anxieties and needs, and asking for his help and guidance. Peter exhorts you in 1 Peter 3:15, 16, "But in your hearts set apart Christ as Lord. Always be prepared to give an answer to everyone who asks you to give the reason for the hope you have. But do this with gentleness and respect, keeping a clear conscience, so that those who speak maliciously against your good behavior in Christ may be ashamed of their slander."

◆ GOD'S WORK IN NON-CHRISTIANS
LEWIS SMEDES

Some Christians get embarrassed that non-Christians, so-called pagans, can do good. They feel a little gypped by it. They feel that maybe their witness has lost its point. They say, "If you can get to be that good without the Spirit, then why bother? What's the point of all my dedication?"

What we should do is thank God that he is God. The Spirit is the Spirit not only of salvation and redemption but also of creation. Any good in character—wherever it is found—comes ultimately from the Spirit. Why make a dichotomy, and why be disappointed when non-Christians have good character? Why not rejoice in it? Be thankful that people are not as bad as they could be.

Opposing Values
LEWIS SMEDES

The values held by Christians and those held by non-Christians are not necessarily opposed.

For instance, non-Christians and Christians can agree on the immorality of nuclear war. They can and do agree about the immorality of racism or pollution of the environment. And they both agree and disagree on specifics such as abortion, honesty in business and personal matters, and many other issues of morality. There is much common ground for which we should thank God. People who are not Christians have a conscience, and they have some sense of what God requires, as Paul described in Romans 2:14, 15: "Indeed, when Gentiles, who do not have the law, do by nature things required by the law, they are a law for themselves, even though they do not have the law, since they show that the requirements of the law are written on their hearts, their consciences also bearing witness and their thoughts now accusing, now even defending them."

But the word *worldly* implies an opposition to Christianity, as in the injunction to "not conform any longer to the pattern of this world" (Romans 12:2). John put it even stronger when he wrote, "Do not love the world or anything in the world. If anyone loves the world, the love of the Father is not in him" (1 John 2:15). The world is very antagonistic to Christianity. But we must not simply contrast "Christian" with "worldly" in general but with worldliness in a particular place and in a particular culture, for the values of the world change. There is a time, for instance, when worldliness in economics idolizes individualism. In another time and another place, worldliness idolizes totalitarianism.

One of the most crucial conflicts today is between the ultimate value of individual happiness versus the value of commitment. The world says that I have a supreme right to fulfill and maximize myself—my needs for pleasure, for happiness, for peace, for love. A Christian value that is more important than my right to happiness is my duty to be committed to people, to my community, to my church. The most fundamental moral antagonism is between the absolutizing of individual rights and the God-given duty to keep commitments.

How can I tell when I am following the Bible and when I am simply going along with worldly emphases? One way is to keep reading the Bible. There are issues in life, however, on which the Bible does not speak to us directly. There are issues on which ethicists can give us important guidance. The Bible does not say whether to buy South African Krugerrands, but it is a deep moral issue. The Bible does not say whether it is fair or right or good to prevent a child with AIDS from going to your children's school. The Bible has no passage indicating whether to proceed with the Strategic Defense Initiative.

Ethicists can help you make up your mind and see what sorts of decisions are most congruent with the Bible, the most consistent with difficult principles. By this I do not want to make a dichotomy between following the Scriptures and following ethicists. But sometimes it is good to hold the Bible in one hand and a good ethical exposition in the other.

I teach ethics. To carry on an ethical discussion on the conflicts and ambiguities in our lives today, we need to read the Bible to keep grounded in what God really wants. We also need to read the ethicists and the newspaper to know what the issues are so that we can discern the will of God in concrete and specific instances. Not all ethicists are worldly, and God can communicate through their wisdom.

The ultimate answer is to keep reading the Bible and keep asking questions of students of the Bible. Make yourself willing to be instructed.

♦ PERSONAL MORALITY vs. SOCIAL MORALITY / LEWIS SMEDES

Some denominations have a tendency to stress personal morality over and against social morality. You can attend some churches without being made aware that there is a morality of how to treat your environment. But sensitivity to the world that God made is a very big moral issue.

Other churches ignore the fact that there is a great moral issue involved in peace keeping. Some churchgoers never become sensitive to the horror and immorality of war.

Certainly there can be differences in emphases among denominations. But we cannot be so concerned about personal salvation and individual morality that we are oblivious to ecological, political, or social morality.

Morality Maze

✍ DAVE VEERMAN

The church of my youth emphasized worldliness—avoiding it, that is. We young people were challenged to "come out from them and be separate" (2 Corinthians 6:17), and this "separation" was defined as avoiding a prescribed list of no-nos. In the fifties, the list included drinking, smoking, dancing, going to movies, and playing cards (otherwise known as "the filthy five"). "Good" Christian teenagers, then, were expected to conform to these standards of morality. Over the last few years, the list has changed, but the situation has remained pretty much the same.

This is not a twentieth-century phenomenon. From Jesus being hassled by the Pharisees (Matthew 12:9-14) and Paul pressed by Judaizers (Acts 15:1-5), church history is replete with morality conflicts and those who expect others to conform to their particular standard of behavior.

Of course, not all of these struggles are negative. Morality is important, and Christians should hold high biblical standards. In fact, Paul told the Corinthian Christians that their moral sense had eroded to a shameful state (1 Corinthians 5:6-8).

Where then do we draw the line? How far should we go in living according to other church members' standards of morality?

In answering this question, first of all we must understand that this is an "intramural" conflict. In other words, it is not a discussion between believers and unbelievers. How we interact with our non-Christian culture is another topic. What we are discussing here is the difference of opinion among Christians—over the application of biblical principles, the "gray" areas of Scripture, or the interpretation of a specific passage.

With this understanding, let us turn to the principles that should guide us through the maze of ideas and pressures.

1. *Every person is responsible for his or her own behavior* (Romans 14:12). You cannot blame anyone else for your mistakes, *and* you should not live off the faith of others. You must make your own decisions about morality based on God's Word, the counsel of others, and the leading of the Holy Spirit.

2. *Christians are to love each other* (John 13:35). No matter what your disagreement with another believer, you must relate to him or her in love.

3. *Christians should learn from each other* (Romans 12:3-5, 10). Each believer has special, spiritual gifts to help build up the church—Christians need each other. When a brother or sister in Christ shows a biblical insight, be open to what he or she has to say, evaluating it in the light of Scripture.

4. *"Stronger" Christians have a responsibility for "weaker" Christians* (1 Corinthians 8:9). There may be certain activities that are not wrong per se (they are not prohibited by Scripture and you don't feel guilty about them), but they may cause real problems for some who are very sensitive in those areas. If you know about such a person, you should be careful how you act around him or her. In other words, don't flaunt your freedom (1 Corinthians 6:12).

5. *A local church should be exemplified by humility and unity* (Ephesians 4:1-6). Pride probably splits more churches than anything else. When faced with any conflict in the church, you should approach it carefully with humility, attempting to keep unity.

6. *There is a place for confrontation* (1 Corinthians 5:11). In extreme situations (e.g., flagrant or continued sin), Christians must be confronted with their sin—but this must also be done in love.

If you find yourself under pressure to conform to someone else's standards of morality, carefully analyze his or her point of view, humbly listening with an open mind. Compare what he says to Scripture and talk it over with other mature Christians. If, however, resolution is impossible, you may have to find another church. But if it comes to this, leave quickly, with humility and love.

♦ OBSTACLES / HOWARD HENDRICKS

Obstacles are what we see when we take our eyes off our goal.

Do Christians Do Their Work Differently Than Others?

✍ TOM BASSFORD

Is there such a thing as a Christian work ethic? Do Christians do their work any differently or any better than others? Does God give us any guidelines as to how we as Christians should do our work? There is a work ethic that all Christians are responsible to and should live up to. It is not true that this same work ethic is only attainable by Christians. Proverbs is filled with countless work principles that many non-Christians also practice because they just make plain old good sense for anybody and everybody.

When we talk about a work ethic we're talking about a value system as it relates to work. What do we consider proper, important, and right in matters and decisions concerning work? Our answer to that question uncovers our work ethic. Our work ethic affects how we view work, our employers, other employees, and customers. It also reflects our attitudes about money, responsibility, honesty, and other character qualities.

We make decisions all day long about the quantity and quality of our work. Some are easy decisions and others tempt us to compromise certain values. The things we feel are proper, important, and right will make up our work ethic, and that work ethic will in turn be the basis for the decisions we make about our work. No matter how small or seemingly insignificant the incident is, it reflects a person's attitudes about things such as honesty and consideration for others. In each decision, something rises to the top as most important to us. It will be that most important thing that will ultimately effect our decision.

The second question as to whether Christians do their work any differently than anyone else is a mute one. As Christians our comparisons should not be with others—Christian or non-Christian—but with God. So as we look at this issue of work ethic for the Christian it's important to keep two things in mind. First, remember that many non-Christians live up to this same work ethic equally as well as any Christian, and many Christians live far below it. Second, remember that our measuring stick for good work habits (and anything else for that matter) is God, not the person next to us, no matter how good he or she is.

So, what is most important or most right in a work ethic? God has given guidelines. Scripture has an abundance of examples and guidance on the subject.

It is God's intent that our relationship with him completely permeate our lives. In other words, Christianity is a life-style. It's a commitment to God's value system and priorities in all areas and at all stages of life. Therefore, when we read, "You shall not steal," we know it to be true whether we are tempted to steal candy from a store, cheat on our income taxes at home, or permanently "borrow" tools from work. Therefore, everything we have learned and know to be true about the Christian life is applicable to our work ethic. Loving our enemies, turning the other cheek, treating others as we want to be treated, sharing, caring, being hospitable, going the extra mile, not judging or talking behind someone's back are all as important in the marketplace as they are in the Sunday morning worship service.

Our first place to look for guidance in developing a good work ethic is in the general truth of Scripture and all that it has to say about relationships, values, priorities, and personal character. Scripture also shows some specific attitudes and characteristics of a good worker, outlined below:

1. *Good use of time.* No employer likes to see employees wasting time. A good worker seeks to spend time at the task for which he or she is being paid. Making the most of the time at work is one characteristic of a good worker.

2. *Diligence.* The dictionary says diligence is persistent, attentive, and energetic application to a task. A diligent worker is willing to stick with a task until it's done and done right. He doesn't abandon a job or do it halfway because it's boring. Being diligent doesn't mean he must do perfect work. It means that he is thorough and conscientious. "Diligent hands will rule, but laziness ends in slave labor" (Proverbs 12:24).

3. *Integrity.* Integrity is that part of us that believes in the principle of the matter as well as the matter itself. Integrity isn't concerned with the difference between "white lies" and "black lies"; it sees them all as lies and avoids them on the principle of lying being wrong. Integrity doesn't compromise virtue no matter how small or seemingly insignificant the situation. The person of integrity believes the means to the end are as important as the end itself.

4. *Respect for authority.* From the Garden of Eden to the present day, mankind has had more than a little difficulty being told what to do. One of the qualities of a good worker is he can handle being instructed and, at times, even told what to do. That's not to say he must always like it or even agree with it. If that happens, he has two options. He can submit and give in to the wishes of those in position above him. Or he can disagree agreeably.

When we do disagree with decisions and policies in our work we have every right to express our dissatisfaction. However, our complaints need to be aired to the right people, in the right place, at the right time, and with the right attitude. As we share our frustrations and thoughts it's just as important to listen as it is to talk—closemindedness is as much a problem for employees as it is for employers. In the end we may understand our boss's position a little better. Whatever the outcome, there is something to be said for disagreeing agreeably.

The following characteristics of a good worker are specifically for the Christian. These characteristics don't guarantee that the Christian who practices them will perform their work better than anyone else. Instead they have more effect on the individual than on the quality of their work.

1. *Awareness of God's expectations.* As children we were motivated by the fear of our parents' wrath. We knew that there was punishment if we didn't do the things they expected from us, and so, in order to avoid that punishment, we did what they wanted. God expects the proper use of our gifts and talents in

the area of work. In the parable of the talents we recognize that the important issue wasn't "how much" each person brought back to the master, but what they *did* with their talents. Everyone was treated the same in the parable except the one person who buried his talent; the rest were rewarded, he was punished (Matthew 25:14-30). Whether we like it or not, God's expectations carry both rewards and punishments. For some this is a motivating force, for others this motivation makes way for the next characteristic of a good work ethic.

2. *Desire to glorify God.* "And whatever you do, whether in word or deed, do it all in the name of the Lord Jesus, giving thanks to God the Father through him" (Colossians 3:17). In the same way that love and respect are a better basis for a relationship than fear, so this principle is a better basis for our obedience to God than the previous point. When we develop a work ethic with God's principles at the center, we please him, and this should be the Christian's primary goal. This attitude also helps us keep a perspective on our accomplishments. The important question is not, How much glory will this bring me? but rather, How will this honor and glorify God?

3. *Remember the Sabbath.* One of the Ten Commandments is, "Remember the Sabbath day by keeping it holy" (Exodus 20:8). Although Jesus stated in Mark 2:27, "The Sabbath was made for man, not man for the Sabbath," that does not release us from the commandment to keep the Sabbath day holy. God still expects us to keep the Sabbath holy. By taking time to reflect upon the state of our relationship with him and resting from our occupational work as much as possible, remember the Sabbath.

When we consider that somewhere around half of our waking hours are spent on the job, it makes sense that we should develop a healthy attitude about what we do during that time. It's important for a person to believe in what they do and then do it to the best of their ability. As Christians we must never forget that our actions and attitudes at work are a direct reflection upon the One we call Lord. "Let your light shine before men, that they may see your good deeds and praise your Father in heaven" (Matthew 5:16).

♦ THE PLACE OF LEISURE
HOWARD HENDRICKS

Leisure is the investment of time in our emotional, personal, and private lives. This investment is important. Twelve times in the Gospels, Jesus took the initiative in providing leisure for his disciples. Mark 6 is a good illustration. The disciples were too busy to eat but Jesus said, "Come with me by yourselves to a quiet place and get some rest" (Mark 6:31).

Leisure is not a luxury; it is a necessity. We need time to recoup our strength and energies. We need time to restore our perspective and experience a change of pace. Life is a lot like a violin. The strings have to be loosened occasionally, or they will break.

Leisure is not the same for everyone. One person may relax skiing down the slope at top speed. For another person getting out in the backyard and putting hands in the dirt is relaxing.

As Christians, we are in danger of denying our humanity when we deny our need for relaxation. Because the body is the temple of the Holy Spirit, we don't smoke, drink alcohol excessively, or take drugs. But instead we misuse our bodies by overeating and underexercising. Physical well-being is essential to our spiritual life.

We sing the song "Take time to be holy." We can't be holy in a hurry, but we are always in a hurry. To counter our pressure-packed society we need time alone, away from the rush. We need to be by ourselves to nourish our spirit, our emotions, and our body.

Truth-Telling

DAVE VEERMAN

Several years ago a popular television show featured three contestants at a time, each of whom would make the same dramatic claim. For example, "I climbed Mount Everest." Then through a series of questions and answers, a celebrity panel would try to determine the genuine mountain climber. The program was quite appropriately titled "To Tell the Truth."

Recently I thought of that old show as I was listening to the news. There were conflicting reports from the Middle East in the wake of the cruise liner hijacking; competing politicians in the heat of the campaign blasting each other; countercharges, rebuttals, and denials in labor-management negotiations; and accusations of false reporting by the media. Every person heard or quoted claimed *to be telling the truth.* But because of the obvious contradictions, in each case *someone* had to be lying.

Lies fill our culture and our lives, flying from lips, pencils, and keyboards as easily as dandelion seeds in the breeze. We invent excuses for unwanted callers, "reasons" for our poor performance, and convenient "emergencies" to avoid social events. Lying has become second nature to us, and we expect it from others. In fact, even when there is no opposing viewpoint presented, we wonder if the spokesperson really is telling the truth.

In contrast to this prevailing attitude and habit are the words of Jesus. He said that he is the "truth," that the Holy Spirit would guide his disciples into "all truth," and that he, the truth, would "set them free." In fact, he said, lies are from Satan, "the father of lies." The followers of Christ are to "speak the truth" and "live the truth."

Stop for a moment and take a "truth-check" of your life. Are you known as a person who tells the truth or someone who always has an excuse for everything? Are you reliable—the kind of person who actually does the assignment for which you volunteered? When you say, "I'll be there," will you? Does your life back up your claim to be a follower of Christ?

The world needs people who can be trusted, believed, and relied on. Be a person such as Paul describes in Ephesians 4:15 who "speaks the truth in love."

Try a Video Fast

JAMES C. GALVIN

Jesus, our Good Shepherd, came so that we might live life to its fullest. He said, "I have come that they may have life, and have it to the full" (John 10:10). Unfortunately, many of the sheep today are too tired, and would rather watch TV. It's not as though we are watching other people live life to the fullest on TV; they are living life the wrong way. What is pictured is empty and counterfeit. And even if we could watch others on television live life to the fullest according to biblical values, wouldn't it be more exciting to live it ourselves?

Many of us are aware of the negative impact television has on our lives. Repeated exposure to violence can make us passive. Snacking while we watch TV can make us overweight. TV heroes are often associated with smoking, drugs, and alcohol. Many of the shows promote ethnic and racial stereotyping. Thirty-minute plots suggest simple answers to life's complex problems. But this assault on our health and our values is not the worst part of television.

What's more frightening than what television does to us is what it prevents. Television prevents active exercise. The health of America's children has declined over the past two decades, in part, because of an average of twenty to twenty-five hours a week sitting in front of a television. Television prevents us from reading. Television inhibits family communication. Talking is limited because the TV is on, and meaningful encounters are difficult during commercials. Our actions, speaking louder than words, would lead others to conclude that prime-time programming is more interesting to us than our own children. Television prevents meaningful relationships, not only in our own families, but among friends from church, and neighbors. It is much easier to have the TV entertain us than it is to try to show hospitality to others.

More significantly, television prevents us from being good stewards of our lives. At worst, TV is harmful to our spiritual growth. At best, it is a waste of time. When Jesus told the parable of the talents (Matthew 25:14-30), he taught that we must be good stewards of whatever God has given us, including time, treasure, and talent. It's frightening to consider how many Christians are burying theirs in front of the tube.

Probably the most radical solution to all of this is to turn the TV off. Unfortunately, many Christians are either unable or unwilling to do so. In this respect, television parallels any type of addiction. Millions of Christians are addicted to TV and refuse to acknowledge their dependence. They find it difficult to reverse these negative trends in their lives and families, yet talk themselves into believing that television has many positive benefits. It may help them relax, and relaxing is good, but there are other ways to relax without vegetating. For anyone with an addiction, however, cutting down doesn't work. The best solution is to quit, cold turkey. But for most people, simply getting rid of the television is too difficult. As a step in the right direction, try a video fast: forty days and forty nights without TV.

I saw the effects of TV more clearly when I watched a program every once in a while after this video fast. The jokes were no longer that funny, most having sexual implications. The situational comedies were tragic. The life-styles portrayed were unrealistic. The commercials insulted my intelligence and my humanity. What I saw most clearly, however, was that the values portrayed on the shows contradict biblical values. Life-styles portrayed as natural and normal are unrealistic and empty. Most religious people are portrayed as lunatics. Just like not eating for a couple of days will awaken your taste buds to new and subtle flavors, this video fast awakened my senses to the subtle messages and non-Christian values inherent in the programming of the shows and the commercials.

Besides seeing the negatives of a TV addiction, a forty-day fast will give the average person about a hundred "extra" hours of life to live. What could be done with this time? Reading the entire Bible through from cover to cover only takes about fifty to sixty hours. That leaves about forty to fifty hours that you can spend caring for the needs of your family and friends, or in fellowship with other Christians. Before the forty days are over, you could read several classics or begin a new hobby. You could explore and discover a new shared activity for the whole family.

If you leave the TV off all year you will have added a thousand hours to your life. If you leave it off for a decade you will have gained ten thousand hours. This is enough time to have studied both Greek and Hebrew so that you can read the Bible in the original languages. You could complete a B.A. and a Master's degree in any subject area. Volunteering in church and community programs would provide rewards far richer and longer lasting than the programming on TV. In short, *you will be living life instead of watching other people live it.*

Some families have legitimate concerns about the negative influence of such a fast. A video fast will be difficult and will upset the normal routine, but the harmful effects can be counteracted in some other way. For example, some families may be afraid that boredom will cause depression and fighting among children. But the pain of boredom can push the whole family to work together to discover shared activities. There is time to take a walk, to begin a family hobby, or to do work around the house, for the church, or for a needy family together.

Some people are afraid of being isolated from the news. It's almost a cliche among journalists that television is like getting the news by machine gun—all one can really gain from the nightly news is headlines, not the news. If you want the story, too, you must read it. Reading a newspaper or a weekly newsmagazine can help you understand the issues much better than any television news broadcast.

Some people are also concerned about the good programming that would be missed. The educational stations present many fine productions, such as Sesame Street for children. Your kids will not start school at a disadvantage missing educational programs. Elementary school teachers know that the creative, expensive programming on these shows makes their job much more difficult. They write a letter or number on the blackboard and it just sits there.

It doesn't jump, dance, or sing. The child watching television twenty to twenty-five hours per week finds this rather dull. The child raised without a television will find school much more stimulating. It *is* true that many good programs will be missed. But are they really worth wading through all the trash? Why not read about it instead? For every helpful, beneficial program on television, your local library has several helpful, beneficial books.

Let no one be misled—a forty-day video fast is not easy. Habits are difficult to change. To unplug the television and replace it with staring at the walls will cause boredom, depression, isolation from the news, and regret for missing favorite programs. Therefore, regular TV time must be replaced with alternate family rituals or personal activities to fill the vacuum. For example, 7:00 to 9:00 P.M. can be declared reading time or game time. Family devotions can also become a regular routine during what used to be prime TV time.

With all of life to live, why watch others live it? With all the good influences in the world, why consistently expose ourselves to the bad? If we are serious about our own spiritual growth, why bury our opportunities in front of the television? Do we expect to be rewarded for this investment? Giving up television is difficult, and a forty-day video fast, as an experiment, is a good first step. As faithful stewards, we must use this time that has been freed up to honor God and not use it merely to win the admiration of others. Let's not forget what Jesus taught about fasting:

When you fast, do not look somber as the hypocrites do, for they disfigure their faces to show men they are fasting. I tell you the truth, they have received their reward in full. But when you fast, put oil on your head and wash your face, so that it will not be obvious to men that you are fasting, but only to your Father, who is unseen; and your Father, who sees what is done in secret, will reward you. Matthew 6:16-18

So beware of complaining or rationalizing. Unplug your television and put it in the closet. Although going without television is difficult at first, a forty-day video fast can help you be a better steward of your time and help you live your life to the fullest.

♦ TV vs. MORAL VALUES / YFC EDITORS

Does TV negatively influence our values? It can. TV is not something we should watch without discretion. Many of the values portrayed on TV are the opposite of the Christian values we are putting into our lives and attempting to teach our children. When we watch and enjoy programs where adultery, homosexuality, and immorality are portrayed as normal and acceptable, we are condoning that behavior and, perhaps very subtly, affecting our own values and the values we've taught our children.

Consider your TV viewing habits. Is the TV the center of your home and family activities? How many TVs do you have? Do TV programs control your family schedule? What do you watch? How do you react to what you watch? Use discretion with how much and what is watched. Use what is portrayed on TV as a discussion starter to talk about Christian values, and why they are different and far more fulfilling than the values and life-styles portrayed on TV.

Don't allow "the world" to negatively influence your values by letting them into your home in the form of television entertainment.

RELATED ARTICLES

Chapter 13: **Can a Christian Be Overweight?**
Chapter 20: **The Believer's Battle with Temptation**
Chapter 20: **Overcoming Temptation**
Chapter 20: **Handling Temptation**
Chapter 21: **Serious Sexual Temptation**
Chapter 21: **The Twisting: The Problem of Pornography**
Chapter 21: **Is Homosexuality Wrong?**
Chapter 24: **Politics and Bad Morals**

CHAPTER

20

Sin and the Christian

- ✓ What is sin? Can it become an opportunity for growth?
- ✓ How are sin and temptation related?
- ✓ If Jesus died for my sins, why do I keep sinning?
- ✓ How can I deal with the guilt I feel?
- ✓ Does God forgive even the "big" sins?
- ✓ Why does God allow us to be tempted?

The Believer's Battle with Temptation

ADRIAN ROGERS

All of us know what it's like to be tempted; it's an experience common to all believers. In 1 Corinthians 10:13 Paul wrote: "No temptation has seized you except what is common to man."

It isn't a sin to be tempted. Even the Lord Jesus was tempted. As Hebrews 4:15 says: "We do not have a high priest who is unable to sympathize with our weakness, but we have one who has been tempted in every way, just as we are—yet was without sin." If we were never tempted we would never know victory, and if we never knew victory, we'd never know the joy of being overcomers.

No one can avoid temptation. If someone claims that he can, then he's saying he's better than the Son of God. So it's senseless to ask how to avoid temptation. A better question is this: How can one overcome temptation?

Most people deal with temptation in one of three ways. Some people just give in to temptation. Their attitude is, Why fight it? They're like the woman who said, "I can overcome anything but temptation." They've adopted the philosophy, "If it feels good, do it." Perhaps they will put it in a more sophisticated way and say, "Whatever is natural is beautiful, and whatever is beautiful must be right." So they live on an animal plane, concerned with only three things: self-gratification, self-preservation, and self-propagation. Most Americans are living like this.

A second way people deal with temptation—one that's just as wrong and just as futile—is to try to overcome it by one's own efforts. I'm reminded of the story of the little boy sitting under a farmer's apple tree. The farmer came by and said to him, "What are you doing? Are you trying to steal an apple?" And the boy said, "No sir, I'm trying not to." So often we try not to, but we fall because in our own strength we are no match for the onslaughts of temptation.

The third way to deal with temptation is to overcome it through the Lord Jesus Christ. In 1 Corinthians 10:13, after Paul said that no temptation has seized us except what is common to man, he goes on to say, "God is faithful; he will not let you be tempted beyond what you can bear. But when you are tempted, he will also provide a way out so that you can stand up under it."

Temptation attacks in one of three areas: the body, the soul, or the spirit. The body itself is not evil or sinful, but it can become the seat of temptation. We can also sin with our souls; that is, in our thought lives, our emotions, or our attitudes. We can even sin with our spirits—the area of our life where we know God—because "God is spirit, and his worshipers must worship him in spirit and in truth" (John 4:24).

We are tempted in each of these areas by certain impulses. For example, the flesh wars primarily against the body. Sins such as drunkenness, brutality, violence, and sexual immorality are all sins of the flesh. They find their expression through the body.

The soul is tempted by the world. The world tries to conform the soul—the emotional, volitional, intellectual part of our nature—to its value system, which is contrary to God's. So the worldly Christian is a person who has been squeezed by and "conformed to this world," as Paul mentioned in Romans 12:1, 2.

The devil wars against the spirit. The devil is not really all that interested in getting us to do things such as commit adultery. He would really rather have a person live a life of honor, pleasure, and productivity and be godless than to have that person be a drunk in the gutter. A drunk in the gutter isn't a good advertisement for the devil. What the devil tries to do is drive a wedge between us and God, between our spirit and God's. He wars primarily against our spiritual relationship.

Knowing both the seat and the source of our temptation can aid us in overcoming it. When we are tempted, we should analyze what's going on. We should ask ourselves, What really is the source of my temptation? If the source is the flesh warring against the body, we are to flee. The Bible tells us to get away from those kinds of things, not to stick around and try to fight them.

The "way to escape" that God provides for us in those situations is the king's highway—two legs and a hard run. Second Timothy 2:22 says: "Flee the evil desires of youth, and pursue righteousness, faith, love and peace, along with those who call on the Lord out of a pure heart." First Corinthians 6:18 tells us, "Flee from sexual immorality." If we find ourselves in a particularly seductive or tempting situation, we're just to get away from it. When Potiphar's wife tried to seduce Joseph, he fled. We're to be first-class cowards when it comes to this kind of temptation. In college I had a little motto on my desk: "He who would not fall down ought not to walk in slippery places." Stay away from seductive people, from tempting atmospheres, from all kinds of fleshly temptations. We're never told to fight them; we're told to flee them.

On the other hand, if the temptation is the world warring against our soul, we can't flee that, because we're in this world. A worldly Christian is someone who has lost his vision of Jesus, who has not been fulfilled by him. That's because a worldly Christian is seeking fulfillment in the wrong way. The way to overcome this kind of temptation is to fall deeply in love with Jesus again. A Christian who has Jesus, who is indeed the love of the Father, doesn't need the world.

I don't have to be worldly to find fulfillment. My faith makes Jesus Christ real to me; when I've seen Jesus, and know him, and love him, I don't need to go to the world to get my jollies. There's a little chorus that says, "Turn your eyes upon Jesus, look full in His wonderful face; and the things of earth will grow strangely dim in the light of His glory and grace." If I'm feasting on Jesus and finding my satisfaction in him, then I don't have to be in the back alleys eating tin cans with the devil's billy goats.

Third, if I'm being tempted by the devil, if he's trying to drive a wedge between myself and Christ, I can't flee. The devil is going to have to flee from me. Satan often attacks in the area of my faith and my relationship with God. In order to fight this temptation, I need to take the shield of faith to "extinguish all the flaming arrows of the evil one" (Ephesians 6:16), and I need to resist the devil. In James 4:7 the apostle said, "Resist the devil, and he will flee from you."

If I resist the devil, he will flee. I can actually speak out loud to the devil. Jesus did. He said, "Out of my sight, Satan! You are a stumbling block to me; you do not have in mind the things of God, but the things of men" (Matthew 16:23). When the devil comes to attack my faith, to criticize the Lord Jesus to me, or to try to make me doubt, I can take authority over him. I can say, "Satan, in the name of Jesus I resist you. I refuse you, I rebuke you, and I deny you. You have no rights or authority in my life. My body is a temple of the Holy Spirit.

You're trespassing on my Father's property, and in the name of Jesus, be gone." If I do that, the devil will flee from me. I know this is true, because it has happened in my own life.

So don't give in to temptation, and don't try to overcome it in your own strength. Overcome it through Jesus. When you're tempted, analyze it to see what area you're being tempted in: the body, the soul, or the spirit. Look at the source of the temptation: the flesh, the world, or the devil. And then deal with the temptation accordingly.

◆FILLING LEGITIMATE DESIRES ILLEGITIMATELY / ADRIAN ROGERS

The devil is a pervert. He cannot create things himself. He can only take the things that God created and twist them. We sin when we give in to the devil's temptations and try to fulfill a legitmate God-given desire in an illegitimate way.

For example, food is a God-given necessity, but gluttony is a sin. A loving marriage is a God-given blessing, but adultery is sin. Having and enjoying material things is a God-given privilege, but pride, dishonesty, stealing, and selfishness are sins.

When we are tempted, we need to figure out what legitimate desire the devil is trying to pervert. Then we need to find God's way to fulfill that desire legitimately. If we do that, we'll have no itch the devil can scratch.

Rather than always trying not to sin, we ought to turn our focus in another direction—on finding our satisfaction in the Lord Jesus Christ.

I think parents, pastors, schoolteachers, and youth workers often make this mistake with young people. We try to keep our young people from doing wrong. If you've ever tried to take a bone away from a dog, you know that's a good way to get bit. The way to do it is to lay a piece of red meat in front of the dog. He will drop the bone in order to grab the meat. We need to show young people how they can get their needs legitimately fulfilled in the Lord Jesus Christ. Then they won't have to guard the bones.

Overcoming Temptation

✍ LUIS PALAU

Temptation is a mystery that is difficult to define or understand. There is an inclination inside each of us to do wrong because we are a fallen race.

Often knowingly, sometimes unknowingly, we are inclined to do wrong by an inner urge. The Bible calls the source of this urge the flesh, or the old nature. We are in a lifelong struggle, but God knows what we are going through. As James 1:12-15 expresses it, "Blessed is the man who perseveres under trial, because when he has stood the test, he will receive the crown of life that God has promised to those who love him."

The passage continues, "When tempted, no one should say, 'God is tempting me.' For God cannot be tempted by evil, nor does he tempt anyone; but each one is tempted when, by his own evil desire, he is dragged away and enticed. Then, after desire has conceived, it gives birth to sin; and sin, when it is full-grown, gives birth to death" (vv. 13-15).

So God does not tempt people; temptation is born in the human heart. Yet temptation itself is not a sin but rather the luring and enticement that we feel toward sin. When we give in to the evil to which we are attracted, when we follow through on its appeal, that is when it becomes sin.

Surprisingly, temptation can have a very positive effect. It can build character because it tests us. When we resist the temptation to do what God forbids, we are saying to God, "I'd sure love to do this. It's very appealing, very attractive, but you said no. Therefore, I won't do it, because I love you." God rejoices in this response; in fact, he is so excited about it that, in the words of James, he gives us "the crown of life."

I believe that the crown of life is not merely enjoying eternity in a complete way. It is something we enjoy here on earth every time we overcome temptation with the power of the indwelling Holy Spirit. It is the sense of conquest, the sense of really living, because when we succumb to temptation we enter into the sphere of death. We are in the dark, the death area. But when we overcome temptation, out of love to the Lord, we are living in the light in the fullest sense.

Because this develops our character, temptation is allowed by God, though he himself does not tempt us. When we do not resist temptation and fall for the allurement and the enticement, we experience death—not physical death or even hell, because we are believers, but losing the sense of life. We lose the sense of the smile of God, the sense of having pleased him. We lose the thrill of living, and, until we confess our sin and are cleansed on the spot, we remain under a cloud that covers the sunshine. If we do confess—that is, agree with God that we have sinned and ask for forgiveness—we can bounce back and start living again.

Psalm 32 describes what hidden sin can do to a person, for David tells what his anguish was like before he confessed his sin—apparently his adultery with Bathsheba, although the particular sin is not central to the psalm's message. David said, "When I kept silent, my bones wasted away through my groaning all day long. For day and night your hand was heavy upon me; my strength was sapped as in the heat of summer. Then I acknowledged my sin to you and did not cover up my iniquity. I said, 'I will confess my transgressions to the Lord'—and you forgave the guilt of my sin" (vv. 3-5).

With this kind of hope for us sinners, we too can rejoice: "Blessed is he whose transgressions are forgiven, whose sins are covered. Blessed is the man whose sin the Lord does not count against him and in whose spirit is no deceit" (vv. 1, 2). Having such a spirit is a worthy goal for a Christian, for it is deceit to try to fool ourselves and God about sin.

Many believers are easy prey concerning three temptations in particular. The first is self-righteousness, a form of pride. It implies that we feel somehow superior to others and, although we may not be conscious of it, even to the Lord himself. We practice it when we criticize others and when we act horrified at other people's sins.

Second, Christians are prone to rejecting the sacrificial view of life. American culture fosters this, for it urges us to assert ourselves at the cost of others. But Jesus called us to serve others, even to the point of death, by taking our crosses and following him (Mark 10:38).

Third, Christians are tempted to justify and defend moral behavior that God forbids. Too many rationalize sin by saying, "Well, none of us is perfect." It is dangerous to get so used to sin that we lose our power to discern it. Even pornography—which has become available through magazines and books sold everywhere, as well as through X-rated movies and home videos—is seen by Christians as more and more attractive, to their spiritual downfall.

How can a Christian overcome these and other temptations? Walk in the light of the Word of God, so that you remain very sensitive to any form of darkness. Stay in Scripture day by day, not just when you feel that the pressure is on—lest it be too late.

When you do succumb to temptation, even in a minor way, confess it to God immediately. Confession should be part of your daily routine, as soon as you become conscious that you have done something that has grieved the Holy Spirit. Admit it to God then and there; do not put it in your gunnysack and wait for some great day to dump the whole thing on the altar. The quicker you confess, the stronger you become against temptation the next time.

Finally, take the good advice of the apostle Paul: "Flee the evil desires of youth, and pursue righteousness, faith, love and peace, along with those who call on the Lord out of a pure heart" (2 Timothy 2:22). There are times when the only way to overcome temptation is to run from it. Get away from the situations, places, and people who make it easy for you to compromise your values. Just as a recovering alcoholic or a drug addict must stay away from his or her old haunts, running away can be the smartest and most courageous course of action.

We each have weaknesses that we will have to deal with all our lives, such as a foul temper, impure talk, a sexual sin, or lying. Past generations called these "besetting sins," as compared with other temptations that may be easier to overcome. "A man is a slave to whatever has mastered him" (2 Peter 2:19), but we do have a choice of masters. As Jesus put it, "I tell you the truth, everyone who sins is a slave to sin. Now a slave has no permanent place in the family, but a son belongs to it forever. So if the Son sets you free, you will be free indeed" (John 8:34; see also Romans 6:16, 17).

♦ CONFRONTING SIN / YFC EDITORS

Suppose you need to confront someone in the church who is sinning. What is the best way to do it?

First, check your motives. Are you doing this truly for the person's good and the good of the body, or are you acting out of revenge or because you want to embarrass the person?

Next, check your facts. Are they really facts or hearsay? Are you sure you have all your facts straight?

Go to the person individually and explain why you think the behavior is wrong and harmful both to the person and to the body.

If the person refuses to listen or to

see his behavior as wrong, then you must go to the church leadership with the situation and let them deal with it (Matthew 18:15-17). These instructions do not apply to petty quarrels or indifferences, but only to open, flagrant sin that is seriously hampering the efforts of the church or the growth of other believers.

♦HANDLING TEMPTATION / YFC EDITORS

A. GOD'S WAY	B. MY WAY	C. HOW WE CHANGE (process)
1. God provides escape. We can bear it (1 Corinthians 10:13). 2. We will be better Christians because of it (James 1:2, 3). 3. Jesus knows what we are going through (Hebrews 4:15).	1. I believe there's no way out (like it often, too). 2. No one knows my situation. 3. I *know* I'll fail.	Belief (actual belief)
1. We should be glad (James 1:2). 2. We should be joyful (1 Peter 1:6).	1. I feel guilty and defeated. 2. I don't like temptation. 3. I do like temptation.	Attitude (feeling expressed)
1. Rejoice (1 Peter 1:6). 2. Submit to God. Resist the devil (James 4:7). 3. Be aware. Be careful (1 Peter 5:8).	1. I'm grouchy to people around me. 2. I try to handle it myself. 3. I don't resist. I get into situations where I know I'll be tempted.	Action (noticeable act)
1. The devil will flee (James 4:7). 2. We will honor the Lord (1 Peter 1:7). 3. We will be able to bear it (1 Corinthians 10:13).	1. The devil keeps bugging me until I give in. 2. I don't make the Lord very happy. 3. I give in.	Accomplishment (result of the act)

♦SATAN IDENTIFIED AS . . . / YFC EDITORS

SCRIPTURE	TITLE	PURPOSE	METHOD
2 Corinthians 4:4	God of evil world	Keep people from the gospel	Blinds people
Ephesians 2:2	Mighty prince of power of the air	Against the Lord	Works in hearts, pressures conformity

SCRIPTURE	TITLE	PURPOSE	METHOD
1 Peter 5:8	Great enemy, roaring lion		Attack ruthlessly
Matthew 4:1-11	Satan	Tempt Christ	Strike in weakness, question identity, misquote Scripture, sensational appeal, appeal to pride, shortcut God's plan
2 Corinthians 11:14	Satan, angel of light	Deceive	Appear attractive
John 8:44	Devil, murderer, hater of truth, father of liars	Deceive, destroy	Lie
Genesis 3:1-13	Serpent		Question God's words, appeal of pride
1 Timothy 4:1-4		Turn people away from Christ	Inspire lying teachers who appear good
Matthew 24:24		Deceive God's chosen ones	False prophets, false Christs
Matthew 13:24-30; 13:36-43	Satan, devil, enemy	Hurt the people of Christ	Live among Christians
James 3:15, 16	Devil	Cause disorder	Inspire jealousy, selfishness
Colossians 1:13	Satan	Enslave in darkness	
Job 1:6-12; 2:4-6	Satan	Tempt Job to curse God	Take possessions, take health

The Battle with Sin

DAVID McKENNA

God gave the human race great potential. From the very beginning in the Garden of Eden, God had plans for his creation. Man would have an intimate relationship with God and the opportunity to love other human beings. But into this perfect picture came an ugly element—sin.

Sin means missing the mark, and therefore missing God's potential for our lives. When we sin, our lives—all our decisions and actions—go way off target for what God desires of us. Sin alienates us from God and leaves us unable to do his will.

Alienation from God began when Satan tempted Eve. He raised a question, "Did God really say, 'You must not eat from any tree in the garden'?" (Genesis 3:1). He subtly turned Eve's thinking, causing her to consider that perhaps God was holding something back from her. Knowing good and evil—what could be so bad about that? But in taking the fruit from the serpent, Adam and

Eve rebelled against God, elevating themselves and their desires into competition with God. And alienation from God followed until God provided a way of access back to himself.

Since that fateful day in the garden, we have all been born with sinful natures. We naturally want to elevate ourselves, compete with God, and do what we want with no restrictions. We are all guilty sinners, alienated from God.

Guilt is downplayed in our world today. I think our society, and even the church, will be judged for lessening the needed effects of guilt. Some guilt, certainly, is unhealthy. We should not carry guilt for things over which we have no control. Neither should we continue to carry guilt for forgiven sin. But guilt is often healthy because it makes us aware of our sin. We are not really in tune with God if we never feel guilt over sin, because we are sinners. Guilt makes us realize that we are naked before God with nothing left of our pride, our self-elevation. We are truly sinners before God, and nothing we do can change that.

So what do we do when we realize we've sinned, when we feel the guilt? How do we restore our relationship with God?

First of all, we should be glad for the guilt we feel. The Bible tells us that the Holy Spirit convicts us. To realize we've sinned is a confession in itself and is the first step back.

Next we look to God's promise, "If we confess our sins, he is faithful and just and will forgive us our sins and purify us from all unrighteousness" (1 John 1:9). This verse tells us what to do when we've sinned—we must confess that we have sinned and need forgiveness.

Then if we confess, God promises to forgive. He takes care of that sin once and for all. He restores our relationship with him. That isn't to say we will never sin again, but if we go on to the work of the Holy Spirit in our living: "Quick as the apple of an eye, O God, my conscience make! Awake my soul when sin is nigh, and keep it still awake."

Forgiveness needs to be reemphasized among Christians today. It has been devalued by people who don't understand the seriousness of sin. Forgiveness should never be offered thoughtlessly or flippantly. At the center of forgiveness is always the cross of Christ. Without his body on the cross, forgiveness would not even be available. Forgiveness is costly, and we need to see it from that perspective. There is no forgiveness without tears, without a price to be paid, without the sacrifice of Christ.

Because of Christ's sacrifice, sin need not defeat us; it can be an opportunity for growth. Look at Peter, for example. He obviously sinned, but even more important, he confessed, was forgiven, and lived a changed life after that. Sin can become a context for learning and growing.

If sin is just something we confess and for which we ask forgiveness, leaving it at that, we'll probably fall back into it because we haven't learned anything from it. But if we are willing to learn from our sin, the Holy Spirit will enter in and teach us. He will put our sin in the context of the larger perspective of truth, and he will give us insights into sin's implications. If we are tempted by that sin again, he pricks our conscience and helps us not to repeat it. Christians who fall into the same sin again and again are spiritually stunted. God wants us to grow in grace.

Though we cannot eliminate the temptation to sin, we are not left without redemptive resources. God is on our side, Jesus is advocating for us, and the Holy Spirit is making us aware of our weaknesses as our Teacher and Guide. But first we must admit our need willingly and, each day, renew our relationship with God. Only then can we live a truly victorious and righteous life.

♦ MY LIFE IS WORSE NOW THAN BEFORE
YFC EDITORS

What do you do when becoming a Christian only seems to make your life worse? You seem to sin more and life seems more difficult. Did you make a wrong decision?

No, your decision to accept the lordship of Christ was absolutely the best decision you'll ever make. But becoming a Christian does complicate life in several ways. First, you are suddenly more sensitive to sin. You probably aren't sinning more, you are just more aware of your sins. Second, the Bible promises that being a Christian often means suffering in this world. Before you were a Christian, Satan was pleased with the way you were living. Now that you believe in Jesus Christ, you are open to his attacks. And he does attack because he wants you to follow him, not Jesus. Finally, instead of just worrying about yourself and gratifying *your* needs, you now have to consider what God wants.

Indeed, your life may seem worse than it was before. But remember that you are now on the side of the ultimate Winner and he will not leave you without help to face your daily struggles.

What Happens When I Sin
✍ HOWARD HENDRICKS

The theological definition of sin is any lack of conformity to the will of God. Most theologians would distinguish between two kinds of sin. One is the sin of omission—the things we fail to do. The other is the sin of commission—the things we do that are wrong.

When the word *sin (hamartia)* is used in the New Testament, it means "to miss the mark." The mark it misses is God. Our sin may involve other people, but our real sin is against God. David realized this when he said, "Against you, you only, have I sinned" (Psalm 51:4). In one sense that was not true. He sinned against Bathsheba and Uriah, he sinned against the nation, he sinned against himself. But he realized that his sin was ultimately against God.

When I sin, fellowship with my heavenly Father is broken. There is a difference between fellowship being broken and a relationship being broken. If I offend my wife, I break the fellowship, but I don't break the marriage relationship. We may not talk for a day, but we are still married. In the same way sin affects my fellowship with God but not my relationship with him.

When we sin, we have only two options. We can cover it, or we can confess it. If we say we don't sin, we make God a liar (1 John 1:10). To confess our sins we need to follow the ABCs: *Admission,* admitting we have sinned; *Brokenness,* agreeing with God about our sin; and *Change,* turning away from our sin in repentance.

We have not truly confessed our sins until we stop them. If we continue to practice our sins, we are just playing games. We have to change our habit patterns.

How can we be free from the results of sin? Paul said in Romans 7:19, "What I do is not the good I want to do; no, the evil I do not want to do—this I keep on doing." But Jesus said, "If the Son sets you free, you will be free indeed" (John 8:36). Freedom from sin results from two things: walking in the light (learning what God wants of me) and obeying God's commands.

If we want freedom from sin, we have to answer the question, How badly do I want to respond to what God says? If we want to respond, that is exactly what will happen. We are free to choose, but we are not free to escape the consequences. A person on the tenth floor of a building is free to jump out the window, but once he jumps out the window, he is a slave to the law that will dash him on the concrete below.

Christian living is a matter of right choices and decisions. We must remember, however, that though the choice is ours, the power is God's. We choose to do something, but then the Lord does it through us. If this were not the case, none of us could be Christians.

We are all bound to sin, because we are all sinners. The question is not, When will we stop sinning? but, What can we learn from our failures? When we realize we can't conquer sin—only God can—then we have discovered the essence of the Christian life.

The Christian life is not difficult; it is impossible. It is a supernatural life. When I try, I fail; but when I trust, God succeeds.

♦ WHY AM I STILL SO IMMATURE?

YFC EDITORS

Human beings are complex. After we become Christians we do become new people, but that's just the beginning of a growth process. There is a tendency to think that once we get one part of our lives under control, everything else naturally follows along. But we grow in different areas at different times in our lives.

At times you may feel strong in some areas and weak and immature in other areas. That is natural. You may not have the knowledge others have in some areas, so don't compare your maturity in one part of your life to the same area in other people. Instead, realize that you are growing and, when you notice a weak area, turn it over to God and ask him to help you. As you grow in that area, others will come to light. Rejoice that God is revealing these so that you can continue to grow and mature.

How Can I Cope with Sin?

R. C. SPROUL

"Why do I do the things I don't want to do, and I don't do the things that I should?"

We have all asked ourselves and God that question. The apostle Paul described his own dilemma in Romans 7 and 8. Stated simply, the reason why we do the things we do not want to do is that we want to do them more than we do not want to do them.

In a sense, every time we do anything, we do what we want to do the most. We have desires within us that conflict. For example, why do overweight people continue to eat too much when they know that such behavior is unhealthy? If asked, they would say that they want to lose weight, but when it comes down to the moment of decision—to eat or not to eat—they decide at the moment that it is more desirable to eat than to be hungry, so they eat.

All of us always choose according to our greatest desire at any given moment. But our desire levels change. When a person has a full stomach, it is easy to go on a diet. It is when we are hungry that dieting becomes difficult because our desire for food suddenly intensifies. It overcomes our desire for dieting.

Within each of us is a conflict of desires. There still remain the wicked desires that are part of the fallen nature with which we are born. But those who are born again also have a new desire, a new inclination for the things of Christ. In many ways, life does not become complicated until we become Christians; then we really feel the conflict of desires between doing what pleases God and doing those things that tempt us.

Therefore, the whole question of Christian growth comes down to this: How can I strengthen the new nature and put to death the old nature? It is a lifelong struggle, which means that we have to feed the good desire. In similar fashion, many overweight people find success in joining groups such as Weight Watchers. They are instructed and directed with a whole new understanding of eating habits that can influence the desires to accomplish their goals and avoid the pitfalls.

So it is with spiritual growth. We need to feed the new nature constantly. That is what the Bible calls us to do—to put the old nature to death, to starve it out. We feed the new nature by filling our minds with the things of God, being faithful in church attendance, and staying deeply involved in the means of grace.

This does not mean that we expect perfection this side of heaven. There are those who teach that a person can be perfected in this world. This is a very serious error. In order for people to believe that they have reached perfection, they must either lie to themselves about their own performance or adjust downward the laws of God. Certainly there must be improvement in Christian character from the day of rebirth to the day of entering into glory—but not perfection.

While we are still on earth, we also have the devil to contend with. Many people say jokingly, "The devil made me do it!" But as far as the actual commission of sin is concerned, the blame is 100 percent human. The devil can tempt and entice, but he cannot compel the believer to sin. The only way the devil could do that would be to possess a Christian, but if this were the case, the Holy Spirit could not possibly live within the Christian. The Scriptures teach us that "the one who is in you is greater than the one who is in the world" (1 John 4:4).

With the Holy Spirit within us, the devil can tempt us from without, but he cannot possess us and force us to sin. So to say the devil made me do it is either to say I am not a Christian or to pass the buck, as Eve did. Satan may be actively trying to seduce us and persuade us, for he does tempt and accuse, but we can never pass off our human responsibility onto him.

♦GROWING IN GRACE / R. C. SPROUL

What is it about certain Christians—is there something distinctive about their walk with God? One of the marks of the great saints of the church is that they grew in grace. And the more they grew in godliness, the more aware they became of their continued need to grow.

Nevertheless, God did not reveal to them all of their sinfulness at once. If he did, they probably would have perished from the revelation. The same is true for us. There is a gentleness with God the Holy Spirit as he helps us to grow gradually.

Regret: Help or Hindrance?

DEAN MERRILL

Here is an unpopular statement: Regret isn't all bad.

In our age when people push to feel good no matter what happens, regret is viewed as a negative emotion, a hindrance to mental health, a weight to be cast off.

The trouble is that regret is the legitimate aftertaste of doing wrong. It's part of the way God made us. I look back to the last time I launched a sarcastic line in a conversation—a delicious choice of words! But they carried a sting; they hurt someone, and I regret saying them. I should have been less pungent and more kind.

It is regret that pushes me to apologize to the injured person. It is regret that moves me to confess to God. It is regret that nudges me to guard my tongue more carefully in the future.

If I refuse to deal with regret, I can go no further as a Christian.

In a book I wrote called *Another Chance: How God Overrides Our Big Mistakes,* I outlined four stages of dealing with sin:

1. First comes the return of confidence, the understanding that maybe God can do something with this mess after all.

2. Then comes the need for confrontation. What happened cannot be forgotten, hidden in a woodpile, under the rug, or anywhere else. We are responsible.

3. Next, it's time for confession—getting verbal about the misdeed. Naturally, we don't like this. We'd much rather "not talk about it." But we must. We must say the same thing God says—that what happened was a violation of his guidelines.

4. Finally, we are able to move on to new things, a restored sense of self-esteem, an open future. We smile again because we are forgiven and restored by the One whose mercy endures forever.

Regret is the compelling force that prods us into stage two. It is a necessary part of the process.

But we must not stall at stage two. Some Christians have trouble moving along the rest of the track. They rehash and rehash the sins of the past, amplifying and distorting the tape as they go along. This is hardly God's intention.

Once we complete the confession stage, "there is now no condemnation for those who are in Christ Jesus," says Romans 8:1, 2, "because . . . the law of the Spirit of life set me free." The same author, Paul, wrote to the Galatians, "It is for freedom that Christ has set us free. Stand firm, then, and do not let yourselves be burdened again by a yoke of slavery" (5:1).

He wrote those things from his personal experience with regret. Paul had a past that would have kept a psychiatrist busy for years. The apostle could close his eyes at any moment and see himself guarding a pile of coats while, a few yards away, the skull of Stephen was being smashed by flying rocks. He could remember a score or more of midnight raids on the homes of Christians—beating down doors, jerking husbands, wives, and children out of bed, hauling them off to dungeons. He had terrorized a whole region, from Jerusalem to Damascus, until not a Christian was left who did not wince at the mention of his name.

How did he overcome the guilt? The regret? The nightmares?

To the Philippian church he wrote, "Not that I . . . have already been made perfect, but I press on to take hold of that for which Christ Jesus took hold of me. Brothers, I do not consider myself yet to have taken hold of it. But one thing I do: Forgetting what is behind and straining toward what is ahead, I press on toward the goal to win the prize for which God has called me heavenward in Christ Jesus" (3:12-14).

An Akron, Ohio, counselor and former pastor, Dr. Richard Dobbins, tells about one woman in her middle forties who came to see him. Throughout two sessions, Evelyn (not her actual name) spoke in generalities about her life and difficulties, but in the third session the truth emerged. She had become pregnant as a teenager and had married the church youth group president only three months before their child was born.

Amazingly, they had stayed in the same area all those years and lived down the reproach. They even continued in the same church. But Evelyn always wondered whether her husband truly loved her or had married her only out of obligation. He said he loved her, he was a good husband, but still . . .

Now came a frightening twist. Her best friend in high school, who knew all the unseemly details, had moved away soon afterward—but was returning to town. And in Evelyn's mind, time stood still. She and this woman were teenagers again, and it was only a matter of weeks before the story would be all over town once more.

In Dr. Dobbins's office, she began to weep convulsively. Quietly he said, "Evelyn, have you asked the Lord to forgive you of this?"

"Ho!" she said through her tears. "Have I asked the Lord to forgive me? A hundred times!"

"Well, do you believe he has?"

"Oh, yes—that's not the problem. The problem is, how can I ever forgive myself?"

Dobbins again sat quietly for a moment. Then he said, "Tell me, are you holier than God is?" He paused. "Must God sacrifice another Son on another cross for the sake of your conscience?"

Another pause. Then, "If the death of Christ was good enough to merit your forgiveness in God's sight, is it not good enough for you?"

Evelyn was speechless. The truth came burrowing into her spirit. For ten minutes she could do nothing but weep. Finally she lifted her head, and there was peace on her face. They had prayer together, and then she said, "This is the first time in more than twenty years that I feel no condemnation."

Jesus died that the people of God might not hang onto guilt and regret. That is why 1 John 1:9 promises, "If we confess our sins, he is faithful and just and will forgive us our sins and purify us from all unrighteousness."

♦A SLAVE TO SIN / DEAN MERRILL

In his book *Will Daylight Come?* Richard Hoefler tells a homey story about a boy and his sister visiting their grandparents' farm. Johnny was given a slingshot and began practicing, trying to hit trees with small stones.

His skill improved, and coming into the barnyard, he spied Grandma's pet duck. On an impulse he took aim and let fly. The duck dropped dead.

The boy panicked. What now? Desperately he hid the duck in the woodpile, only to look up and see his sister watching. Sally had seen it all, but she said nothing.

After lunch that day, Grandma said, "Sally, let's wash the dishes."

But Sally said, "Johnny told me he wanted to help in the kitchen today. Didn't you, Johnny?" She leaned over to whisper in his ear, "Remember the duck!"

Johnny did the dishes.

Later, Grandpa suggested taking the children fishing. But Grandma said, "Well, I need Sally to help make supper."

Sally smiled and said, "That's all taken care of. Johnny wants to do it." Again she whispered, "Remember the duck." Johnny stayed while Sally went fishing.

After several days of doing double chores—his own and Sally's—Johnny could stand it no longer. He confessed to Grandma about the duck.

"I know," she said, giving him a hug. "I was standing at the window when it happened. Because I love you, I forgive you. I was wondering how long you'd let Sally make a slave of you."

Regret is the nagging sister that will not let our offenses rest. We finally realize we have no choice but to own up to them.

Two Kinds of Pride

JAY KESLER

There are two kinds of pride. One is the opposite of humility; it is very bad. The other is the opposite of shame; it is very good.

The kind of pride that is the opposite of humility leaves God and other circumstances out of our successes. It claims that whatever we have achieved, we have achieved by our own virtue.

The essence of this kind of pride is self-centeredness and selfishness, and it is condemned by Scripture. This does not mean, however, that the Bible is opposed to the self. The self is one of God's good creations; selfishness is worshiping the creation rather than the creator.

Bad pride is the kind of selfishness that always wants to be center stage, that takes all the credit, that leaves God out, that gives no thanks to other people, that goes it alone. It is the opposite of what God desires for us.

We read in 1 John 1:3: "We proclaim to you what we have seen and heard, so that you also may have fellowship with us. And our fellowship is with the Father and with his Son, Jesus Christ." The goal of godliness is fellowship with God and with other people. A godly person wants the participation of God and other people in all his activities. He knows that no man is an island.

By contrast, the kind of pride that is the opposite of shame has to do with a job well done, with excellence, with striving for the best, with rising above mediocrity. In a Christian, this kind of pride attempts to give of its best to the Master.

People who misunderstand the difference between the two kinds of pride may have a misimpression of the Christian faith. Christianity is not opposed to excellence. It is not opposed to putting forth your best effort, excelling, and achieving. No, it is only opposed to a person's thinking he can excel without God's help.

Selfish pride is the opposite of thankfulness and gratitude. It shows no gratitude to God for a healthy body, a healthy mind, good parents, a good national heritage, a good diet, and a thousand other blessings over which the person has no control. A person filled with selfish pride thinks he has created himself through his own efforts.

This kind of pride is shortsighted. It does not understand that if God's blessings are stripped away, the person would be nothing at all and could accomplish nothing for himself or for others. This is the kind of pride that "goes before destruction" (Proverbs 16:18), the kind God must strip from us before we can know our dependence upon him and turn to him in helplessness for his abiding strength.

The other kind of pride, the kind that is opposite to shame, doesn't crawl out from between the mattress and springs and say, "I'm a worm; step on me." It doesn't finish playing a solo and say, "It was nothing." It is not unable to accept a compliment.

The pride that is opposite to shame can say thank you and give credit where credit is due. It can thank God for his gifts and, at the same time, acknowledge good work when it is done. The person who can accept a compliment is not arrogant. He knows where his dextrous fingers come from, who gave him his mind and his sense of rhythm.

Christians should be encouraged to excellence and accomplishments for the glory of God, just as they are discouraged from independence and self-centeredness. A gifted Christian who is able to achieve great things should always be aware of how fragile his successes are. He must constantly worship God for the wonderful and unmerited favors shown him. He must desire constantly to bring glory to God through his excellent work.

When Michelangelo walked away from the Sistine Chapel, he knew he had done a beautiful work, and he was proud of it. Yet when a person looks at the ceiling of that chapel, he is always drawn toward God. He is inspired to worship God, not Michelangelo. The art is great, but because it is aimed at glorifying the heavenly Father, the observer is moved to worship.

Pride in our work is good; being puffed up with self-importance is bad. God intended us to do good works, but the purpose of those works is to bring glory to him, not us (Matthew 5:16).

♦ CHANGING A BAD REPUTATION
YFC EDITORS

"I've become a Christian, but I have such a bad reputation. How can I possibly change it?"

If you find yourself in this situation, you need to realize that although your sins have been forgiven, the consequences of your sins were not erased. Your reputation is a part of those consequences and may not be easily changed.

But there are practical ways to begin the change in other people's minds:

1. Start living your life differently. Apply your Christian faith to your actions in everyday life.

2. If you have wronged someone, go to that person, apologize, and make restitution.

3. Realize that you'll never be able to run down and correct all the gossip and opinions of others. You must let people see how you've changed so that they can form new opinions. And that will take patience.

Freedom from Guilt
✍ JAY KESLER

I used to be a confirmed legalist. I put sins into categories, and I figured that because I didn't do the eight or ten sins most often mentioned from the pulpit, I must be all right with God. I had a supermarket view of heaven: when I got to heaven, I thought, unlike other people who would have to line up, their grocery carts filled with their sins, in order to be checked in and receive the grace of God, I would simply breeze through the check-out line marked "seven items or less."

As I matured, I began to realize that this was a superficial understanding of sin, the human condition, and why Christ had to die on the cross. I began to realize that I had actually sinned—not just those conscious sins that one confesses in prayer meeting in order to be part of the group, but seriously. I was guilty, and I deserved condemnation.

It was only when I began to understand the depth of my sin to the degree that I could almost taste it that I began to realize what Jesus Christ had done for me.

It is good to feel guilty about our sins. They rob us of the joys God wants us to have. They try to find happiness where it cannot be found. They hurt people, especially the people we love most. Once we begin to understand the seriousness of our sin, we can turn our attention from the sin to the miraculous work of Jesus Christ on the cross.

I began to understand hymns such as "Amazing Grace"—I knew what it was to feel like a wretch, and I knew how amazing God's forgiveness seemed. "And can it be that I should gain an interest in the Savior's blood" began to make real sense to me. So did, "Oh, to grace how great a debtor daily I'm constrained to be."

One is entering Christian growth when he or she begins to understand the connection between guilt and grace. That is, "where sin increased, grace increased all the more" (Romans 5:20). A person who is convicted of sin and feels honest guilt over it is prepared to turn from it. He knows he is undone. He knows there is nothing he can do to save himself. He knows that only through grace—unmerited favor—can he come to God; not through works of righteousness that he has done, but through God's saving mercy.

Sin is not just an infraction of God's rules; it is a condition of the human heart. But whatever the condition of our heart, we can come to Christ, knowing he will receive us as we are. In fact, God accepts us and saves us even though he knows we will commit even more sins down the road.

Paul spoke eloquently of guilt in 2 Corinthians 7:8-11. He contrasts "worldly sorrow" that brings death with "godly sorrow" that brings repentance. We call the world's sorrow "remorse." This is the constant punishment of oneself, the attempt to pay for one's sin on a human level. Self-directed guilt eventually leads to denial and even to self-destruction. When Judas felt this sort of guilt, he committed suicide.

Godly sorrow, by contrast, is repentance. It means understanding the terribleness of sin, just as Judas understood it. But instead of turning toward oneself in self-destruction, the repentant sinner turns to God's gracious offer of forgiveness. He hears Jesus say, "Come to me, all you who are weary and burdened, and I will give you rest" (Matthew 11:28). He hears God say, "Though your sins are like scarlet, they shall be as white as snow" (Isaiah 1:18).

Simon Peter, after he had denied the Lord three times, didn't go out into the garden and hang himself as Judas did. Instead he turned toward God in repentance and became a leader of the early church.

The distinction between remorse and repentance is the essence of the difference between man-centered guilt and God-centered repentance. Sometimes we think one of our sins is going to be the straw that breaks the camel's back; we suspect God cannot handle it. This is to make God look no better than man. A human being might find it impossible to forgive an extreme sin. But God, because he is God, has offered us something far greater than any man could offer—his grace. Grace is sufficient to forgive our worst sins, even the special one that embarrasses us so deeply and brings us so much guilt. All that is required for Christ to wash it away is for us to bring it to God, seeking his forgiveness and wishing to turn from it.

We are not saved by our virtue and sincerity but by God's power and grace. Ephesians 2:8, 9 puts it this way: "It is by grace you have been saved, through faith—and this not from yourselves, it is the gift of God—not by works, so that no one can boast." There are those who would even make faith into a work; that is why God gave us this verse. It reminds us that faith itself comes from God, and that the whole work of salvation is done by Jesus Christ.

He removes our guilt by his virtue, not ours. Our sorrow and our faith alike are powerless to effect our salvation; we are saved only by Christ's atonement on the cross for our sins.

♦ WHY JESUS DIED / JAY KESLER

Years ago I went to a missionary friend in South America and confessed to him that even though I loved the Lord with all my heart and desired to serve him with complete dedication, I was still guilty of sin.

My friend turned to me and said, "If you could live without sin, God would have told you to do it. The fact that you cannot live without sin is why Jesus died on the cross. Your sin is not a blot on the work of Christ—it is the reason for it."

That was when I began to understand what Jesus Christ had done for me.

The Master of Deceit

YFC EDITORS

Before you became a Christian, you only had the power to do wrong. When you invited Christ into your life, you received a new nature, a new desire and power to do the right thing. But the old nature stayed on. They're at war over everything you think, say, and do.

But the major reason for the conflict in your life is the second most powerful person in the universe, Satan. He's real, he's powerful, and he's out to stop everything God wants to do with your life.

Before you knew Christ, you were in Satan's family, and he was pleased because you were on your way to hell. He didn't bother you at all. He didn't have to. At this point you had conflict, only you were in conflict with God himself!

When you became a Christian, Satan lost you. You were delivered from his family and born into God's family. That put you on God's side and guaranteed that you would be in conflict with God's archenemy. Satan can't have you, but he has another plan. He is dedicated to ruining your life as a Christian and embarrassing God by thwarting everything Jesus died for. That's why it's so important to become like Jesus. When you don't, you play right into Satan's hands!

But all of Satan's attacks on you have one thing in common. They're all based on a *lie* (John 8:44). Any offer he makes is an empty illusion. He can't and won't make a good offer!

Satan's strategy for bringing you down usually comes in one of five attacks:

- doubt (see 1 John 5:13)
- discouragement (see 1 Peter 5:7)
- diversion (see Matthew 6:33)
- defeat (see Philippians 3:13, 14)
- delay (see John 9:4)

Do these sound familiar? We've just never realized that Satan was behind them!

♦ CONFESSING SIN / YFC EDITORS

Sin always needs to be confessed to God, because when we sin, it is always against God.

If you have wronged another person, that sin usually needs to be confessed to the other person as well. But this must be done with consideration. If your confession would do more harm than good to that person, or would be dredging up things better left forgotten, then it is better not to tell the person and to leave your confession with God.

If you feel, after such considerations, that you need to confess your sin and apologize to another person, go to that person and ask sincerely, putting the fault on yourself (even if you think the other person wasn't exactly faultless). You must deal only with your own sin. Say, "I was wrong when I did that, and I need your forgiveness."

You need to be willing to ask for forgiveness regardless of how you think the person will respond.

♦ CONFESSION IS GOOD FOR THE SOUL YFC EDITORS

If Jesus forgave me for my sins, do I have to keep asking him to forgive me every time I sin?

Yes and no. When Jesus died for your sins, he died for all sins, past, present, and future. Sins you committed years ago, and sins you will commit in the future have already been forgiven. Your forgiveness is total, complete, and whole.

At the same time, the life of a Christian is a life of repentance. We

should continually be coming to Christ, humbly confessing our sins and acknowledging the price he paid to forgive them.

Confession does not obtain forgiveness; we already have that. Instead, it removes the barrier to communication with God that we put up when we sin.

The Great Divorce

C. S. LEWIS

I saw coming towards us a Ghost who carried something on his shoulder. What sat on his shoulder was a little red lizard, and it was twitching its tail like a whip and whispering things in his ear. As we caught sight of him he turned his head to the reptile with a snarl of impatience. "Shut up, I tell you!" he said. It wagged its tail and continued to whisper to him. He ceased snarling, and presently began to smile. Then he turned and started to limp westward, away from the mountains.

"Off so soon?" said a voice.

The speaker was more or less human in shape but larger than a man, and so bright that I could hardly look at him. His presence smote on my eyes and on my body too (for there was heat coming from him as well as light) like the morning sun at the beginning of a tyrannous summer day.

"Yes. I'm off," said the Ghost. "Thanks for all your hospitality. But it's no good, you see. I told this little chap" (here he indicated the lizard), "that he'd have to be quiet if he came—which he insisted on doing. Of course his stuff won't do here: I realize that. But he won't stop. I shall just have to go home."

"Would you like me to make him quiet?" said the flaming Spirit—an angel, as I now understood.

"Of course I would," said the Ghost.

"Then I will kill him," said the Angel, taking a step forward.

"Oh—ah—look out! You're burning me. Keep away," said the Ghost, retreating.

"Don't you want him killed?"

"You didn't say anything about killing him at first. I hardly meant to bother you with anything so drastic as that."

"It's the only way," said the Angel, whose burning hands were now very close to the lizard. "Shall I kill it?"

"Well, that's a further question. I'm quite open to consider it, but it's a new point, isn't it? I mean, for the moment I was only thinking about silencing it because up here—well, it's so embarrassing."

"May I kill it?"

"Well, there's time to discuss that later."

"There is no time. May I kill it?"

"Please, I never meant to be such a nuisance. Please—really—don't bother. Look! It's gone to sleep of its own accord. I'm sure it'll be all right now. Thanks ever so much."

"May I kill it?"

"Honestly, I don't think there's the slightest necessity for that. I'm sure I shall be able to keep it in order now. I think the gradual process would be far better than killing it."

"The gradual process is of no use at all."

"Don't you think so? Well, I'll think over what you've said very carefully. I honestly will. In fact I'd let you kill it now, but as a matter of fact I'm not feeling frightfully well today. It would be silly to do it now. I'd need to be in good health for the operation. Some other day, perhaps."

"There is no other day. All days are present now."

"Get back! You're burning me. How can I tell you to kill it? You'd kill me if you did."

"It is not so."

"Why, you're hurting me now."

"I never said it wouldn't hurt you. I said it wouldn't kill you."

"Why are you torturing me? You are jeering at me. How can I let you tear me to pieces? If you wanted to help me, why didn't you kill the damned thing without asking me—before I knew? It would be all over by now if you had."

"I cannot kill it against your will. It is impossible. Have I your permission?"

The Angel's hands were almost closed on the Lizard, but not quite. Then the Lizard began chattering to the Ghost so loud that even I could hear what it was saying.

"Be careful," it said. "He can do what he says. He can kill me. One fatal word from you and he will! Then you'll be without me for ever and ever. It's not natural. How could you live? You'd be only a sort of ghost, not a real man as you are now. He doesn't understand. He's only a cold, bloodless abstract thing. It may be natural for him, but it isn't for us. Yes, yes, I know there are no real pleasures now, only dreams. But aren't they better than nothing? And I'll be so good. I admit I've sometimes gone too far in the past, but I promise I won't do it again. I'll give you nothing but really nice dreams—all sweet and fresh and almost innocent. You might say, quite innocent. . . ."

"Have I your permission?" said the Angel to the Ghost.

"I know it will kill me."

"It won't. But supposing it did?"

"You're right. It would be better to be dead than to live with this creature."

"Then I may?"

"Damn and blast you! Go on can't you? Get it over. Do what you like," bellowed the Ghost: but ended, whimpering, "God help me. God help me."

Next moment the Ghost gave a scream of agony such as I never heard on Earth. The Burning One closed his crimson grip on the reptile: twisted it, while it bit and writhed, and then flung it, broken backed, on the turf.

"Ow! That's done for me," gasped the Ghost, reeling backwards.

For a moment I could make out nothing distinctly. Then I saw, unmistakably solid but growing every moment solider, the upper arm and the shoulder of a man. Then, brighter still and stronger, the legs and hands. The neck and golden head materialized while I watched, and if my attention had not wavered

I should have seen the actual completing of a man—an immense man, naked, not much smaller than the angel. What distracted me was the fact that at the same moment something seemed to be happening to the Lizard. At first I thought the operation had failed. So far from dying, the creature was still struggling and even growing bigger as it struggled. And as it grew it changed. Its hinder parts grew rounder. The tail, still flickering, became a tail of hair that flickered between huge and glossy buttocks. Suddenly I started back, rubbing my eyes. What stood before me was the greatest stallion I have ever seen, silvery white but with mane and tail of gold. It was smooth and shining, rippled with swells of flesh and muscle, whinnying and stamping with its hoofs. At each stamp the land shook and the trees dindled.

The new-made man turned and clapped the new horse's neck. It nosed his bright body. Horse and master breathed each into the other's nostrils. The man turned from it, flung himself at the feet of the Burning One, and embraced them. When he rose I thought his face shone with tears. In joyous haste the young man leaped upon the horse's back. Turning in his seat he waved a farewell, then nudged the stallion with his heels. They were off before I well knew what was happening. There was riding if you like! I came out as quickly as I could from among the bushes to follow them with my eyes; but already they were only like a shooting star far off on the green plain, and soon among the foothills of the mountains. Then I saw them winding up, scaling what seemed impossible steeps, and quicker every moment, till near the dim brow of the landscape, so high that I must strain my neck to see them, they vanished, bright themselves, into the rose-brightness of that everlasting morning.

"Do ye understand all this, my Son?" said the Teacher.

"I don't know about all, Sir," said I. "Am I right in thinking the Lizard really turned into the Horse?"

"Aye. But it was killed first. Ye'll not forget that part of the story?"

"I'll try not to, Sir. But does it mean that everything—everything—that is in us can go on to the Mountains?"

"Nothing, not even the best and noblest, can go on as it now is. Nothing, not even what is lowest and most bestial, will not be raised again if it submits to death. It is sown a natural body, it is raised a spiritual body. Flesh and blood cannot come to the Mountains. Not because they are too rank, but because they are too weak. What is a Lizard compared with a stallion? Lust is a poor, weak, whimpering, whispering thing compared with that richness and energy of desire which will arise when lust has been killed."

(C. S. Lewis, *The Great Divorce* [New York: Macmillan, 1946], 98-105, slightly condensed.)

RELATED ARTICLES

Chapter 10: **Confession**
Chapter 19: **What It Means to Live a Holy Life**
Chapter 21: **Sexual Sin and Christian Growth**

CHAPTER

21

Sex and the Christian

- ✓ Are sexual sins worse than other sins?
- ✓ What's wrong with homosexuality, pornography, adultery, premarital sex?
- ✓ How does sexual sin hinder spiritual growth?
- ✓ How can one control lustful thoughts?
- ✓ How do you avoid sexual temptation?

Sex Outside Marriage—Does God Care?

JOHN CROSBY

American life in the twentieth century has changed enormously in almost every facet. Nowhere is this more striking than in our social attitudes toward sex! From the prudish attitudes of the Victorian Age we have come to a point where anything goes, and we are encouraged to seek sex outside of marriage. In light of this enormous shift, how does the biblical concept of fidelity fit in?

Why should Christians reserve intercourse for marriage?

God has received the label of the Old Man who doesn't want us to have any fun, and that's often the case when referring to sex. It's difficult to see how we love God by abstaining from intercourse, just because we are told to. No one is hurt, are they?

God's concern for us is expressed in the limits he sets in the Bible. God answers that the problem isn't that we think too highly about sex, but not highly enough. Intercourse is reserved for marriage because it's so special that it can be best developed only in a protected environment. Sex outside of marriage loses the focus for which God planned it, to weld two people together on all levels, not just the physical! God says that intercourse goes far beyond physical coupling, so we degrade and damage it when we limit ourselves to "just sex."

God shows that there are practical reasons, too, for committing yourself to only one person sexually. Let me share three:

1. At its best, sex involves tremendous vulnerability and intimacy, that develops a *bond of trust* between people. Sexual experience outside marriage weakens that trust. If we find that our partner sees sex as something that can be done with others, the trust is shaken. Even when the sexual experience takes place before marriage, the seed of mistrust is planted. If this person played around before, how do we know that it won't happen again?

2. Extramarital sex brings the threat of *comparison* for both partners. Memories of past sexual experiences can make full enjoyment of the present more difficult. The faithful partner is left with the wonder of how he or she compares, or if the spouse is fully satisfied. At its best, sex gives us a boost to our self-image, but past experience can assail their confidence.

3. Finally, sex outside marriage *warps our view of sex* itself. We begin to see sex as love, instead of being an expression of love itself. When we limit sex to the purely sensual, we find ourselves unable to enjoy relationships to the full without its "charge."

God's command to confine sex within marriage is intended (as are all his commands) for our own good. As we explore the reality of God's gift of sex and compare it with the myths and lies of our culture, fidelity comes to light as a force that strengthens our deepest relationships. Sex is a wonderful expression of love, but a poor substitute for the real thing.

Sexual Sin and Christian Growth

EARL WILSON

One of the most amazing statements in the Bible relates directly to sexual sin. After warning us to "flee from sexual immorality," Paul concluded that "he who sins sexually sins against his own body" (1 Corinthians 6:18). In other words, he hurts not only others, but also himself.

I understand this to mean that inappropriate use of God's gift of sex may result in physical illnesses such as socially transmitted diseases, social problems such as unwanted pregnancy, and mental problems such as guilt and sexual obsession. These problems are very real, and it is because God loves us that he has warned us against them.

It is clear that we will not grow as Christians when we are spending most of our physical, emotional, and spiritual resources dealing with the consequences of sexual sin. If this is our situation, Satan doesn't need to worry about sidetracking us. We have sidetracked ourselves.

Let's be specific about how Christian growth is impeded by sexual sin. First and foremost, when you are giving all your attention to sex you don't have the energy or inclination to worship God. You can't worship both the God of heaven and the god of this world, sex. I asked one college-age friend when he last talked to God. He laughed nervously and said, "You don't worship much when you spend all your time cruising." And yet the highest command God has given us is to worship him. We will not grow if we do not worship.

Second, sexual sin hinders our growth by locking us to our guilt. Julie said, "I don't seem to be able to grow as a Christian, because I am always so burdened down with guilt. I go farther than God wants me to go, and then I can't stand myself. I want love, and I want to feel good about myself, but trying to find either from the sexual angle has been a disaster."

Bob reported similar feelings of guilt as the result of masturbation. His conclusion was simple: "The fleeting minutes of pleasure just don't make up for the hours of pain I put myself through afterward."

Guilt is not something to toy with. It is a major mental health problem. Avoiding sexual sin is a major way to avoid guilt. The freer of guilt we become, the readier we are to grow.

Third, sexual sin tends to reduce us to merely physical beings. Pete said, "It's pretty hard to think of myself as body, soul, and spirit when all I ever think about is my body. I'm afraid I have reduced myself to a phallic symbol."

I encouraged Pete to fight his problem. "Don't settle for less than your total person," I chided. "Who knows, some girl may be bright enough to love you for your mind!" It was a new thought to him, but as he began to grow as a Christian, he began to like it.

Fourth, preoccupation with sex hinders growth by making us believe that every high has to be sexual or erotic. We somehow come to believe that if things are not out of this world in terms of physical sensation, they can't be worthwhile. Nothing could be further from the truth. In fact, Scripture talks about the temporary nature of physical pleasures. The delights of God, by contrast, are forever (see Hebrews 11:24-28).

Betty was into having a good time, but unfortunately this usually meant looking for sexual pleasure. "It was a blast to be pursued by the hunks," she exclaimed. "But I made bad decisions when they caught me, and after that, nothing else seemed to matter. It took me several years to get back to the real things in life. I thought God couldn't compete with the thrills. Now I'm beginning to understand that the thrills take second place." Betty is free to grow again.

"I just didn't have time for fellowship," Mark explained. "It's no wonder I didn't grow. I was spending hours at parties and more hours in sex-related activities, but none of that helped me grow." It wasn't until Mark met Bonnie and was challenged by her depth as a person and as a believer that he finally got back on track.

"My friendship with Bonnie brought me closer to Christ," he observed. "When I was living for sex I didn't have contact with the kind of people who challenge you to grow."

Not only was Mark's spiritual growth adversely affected by his sexual involvement, so were his other relationships. Relationships stop growing when people reduce the content of their friendships to each other's bodies. Growth of friendship demands involvement with the other person in all his or her dimensions—intellectual and spiritual as well as physical. This is more time consuming than simple sexual involvement, but it has a much broader payoff.

Last, sexual sin hinders spiritual growth because it results in a lack of desire for God. You can't serve both God and money, because when you spend all your energies making money you have no energy or desire left for God (Matthew 6:24). Similarly, you can't serve both God and sexual sin. They work at cross purposes.

I asked Jim about his relationship with Christ. He astounded me by saying he didn't believe anymore. It took a couple of hours of talking before we got to the root of the problem. "It isn't that I've stopped believing," Jim said. "I'm involved in other stuff that takes all my time."

"What kind of stuff?" I asked.

With a red face, Jim disclosed that he had become sexually active and was spending all his time "on the make." "To be honest," he said, "I rarely think about God anymore."

I challenged Jim to be honest and admit he was pushing God aside. His problem wasn't a belief problem—it was a behavior problem. Once he got that straight, he was free to consider the possibility of growing again. Jim found that his desire for God returned slowly, but it did return.

Jim began to make right choices again. Like the other persons I have mentioned, he went through a period of stunted growth because of his sexual sins. Fortunately, he did not make the poorest choice of all—to continue to neglect his relationship with God in order to pursue his sexual sin.

Sex often results in life, but sexual sin always results in stagnation, cessation of growth, and spiritual death.

◆THE LOSS OF INNOCENCE / LUIS PALAU

In our society, there is a sad loss of innocence. Instead of the thrill of anticipation that should be a young person's approach to marriage, there is little expectation. Many feel they know all there is to know by the time they enter high school. Many have already "done it all."

Sadly, the mystery is gone for them. We need to protect our children, particularly from the contamination of pornography.

Sinners Anonymous: Are Sexual Sins Worse Than Other Sins?

DAVE VEERMAN

A number of years ago, a friend of mine explained that in our evangelical churches we accept, forgive, and even provide pulpit time for former drug addicts, bank robbers, and even murderers, but we have no place for those who have committed "sex" sins. These people we treat as though they have leprosy, shouting "unclean, unclean" by our actions. We say that Christ died for all our sins and that his forgiveness is available for anyone, but we act as though sexual transgressions are the exceptions. But are these sins worse than others? And why do churches treat people that way?

Of course there is no excuse for Christians to withhold love and forgiveness from their brothers and sisters in Christ—especially when there is true repentance. In reality, it is during this sensitive "post-sin" time that these people most need our understanding, acceptance, and fellowship. But it is also easy to understand why sexual sins are seen as worse than others. They involve a very personal part of our lives and are closely related to our personhood. One of our identifying characteristics is sex, and the sex drive is an integral part of us. Thus, when someone hurts us sexually, he or she is attacking and violating the very core of who we are.

Sex sins are also difficult to forgive because we can identify so readily with them. Our society is sex-saturated, and most of us have entertained sinful, sexual thoughts. It is human nature to condemn in others that for which we are also guilty.

In reality, all of us are sinners; we fall short of God's ideal and deserve his judgment (Romans 3:23). Unless we see ourselves as sinners saved by grace, we will find it difficult to forgive others. When confronted by the woman caught in the act of adultery, Jesus told the crowd of male accusers to stone her only if they were guiltless. He then turned to the woman, forgave her, and told her to leave her life of sin (John 8:1-11). Our response should be the same. When confronted by *anyone* who has repented of *any* sin, we should praise God and accept him or her into our fellowship.

Having said this, however, I must hasten to add that sexual sins are *very serious* and must not be ignored or minimized. When James wrote, "For whoever keeps the whole law and yet stumbles at just one point is guilty of breaking all of it" (2:10), he was emphasizing the fact that no one is guiltless before God—all have sinned. He was *not* teaching that all sins are the same. And when Jesus said in the Sermon on the Mount, "You have heard that it was said, 'Do not commit adultery.' But I tell you that anyone who looks at a woman lustfully has already committed adultery with her in his heart" (Matthew 5:27, 28), he was not teaching that the act and the thought are the same (and, as some have rationalized, you might as well "do it" since you've thought it). He was blasting the hypocritical attitude of people who justify themselves and rationalize their private sins by claiming innocence of the "major" public sins. Again, *all* of us are guilty before God.

Sexual sins are very serious because they are not only against God and ourselves, but they also involve other people. Similar to assault, stealing, and murder, sexual violence involves two or more human persons—beings created in the image of God. (Note: rape, formerly labeled as a sexual crime, is now considered a crime of violence.) There are the victims to consider—many of them are powerless or helpless women and children.

Sexual sins also display a casual or callous disregard for human life. The main purpose of sex is to create life, and sexual intercourse outside of marriage shouts, "I don't care. I only want to satisfy my needs!" Babies produced by such unions are often aborted or born and neglected. Sex should be a very special experience between husband and wife in an atmosphere of love and patience, not a hurried, passionate, self-centered act.

Sexual sins also degrade people, bringing them down to the level of objects to use or things to own. Lust, fed by pornography, is an example of this. We see a naked body and imagine all sorts of sexual fantasies with no regard for the person pictured. Or we force other people to do something to satisfy our needs, regardless of their feelings or desires. People are to be loved and nurtured, not used and discarded. Sexual sin is serious and must not be ignored or minimized.

As we scan a newspaper or hear a newscast, a litany of sex-related sins assaults our senses—child pornography, incest, date rape, adultery, prostitution, homosexuality, and others. These are terrible crimes and, most important, sins against God and his creation. But these sinners are not beyond forgiveness. Like you and me, if they sincerely turn away from their sin, confess it to God, and trust in him, they will be forgiven (1 John 1:9). As God's children, we are their brothers and sisters and should extend our forgiveness too.

Controlling Our Thoughts

EARL WILSON

Don was a new Christian, and he was very serious about growing in his new life of faith. Quite active sexually before he became a believer, he was now trying to get his thought life back in control. One day in desperation he said to me, "The summers are the worst for me. Trying to control your thoughts around girls in bun huggers, bikinis, or French-cut swimsuits is like trying to diet in a chocolate factory."

I could identify with Don's problem. Summer, winter, spring, and fall both men and women are constantly bombarded with sexual stimuli. We live in a sexually explicit society, and it has created a generation of people obsessed with the body and sex. Modern music and video technology have brought sexual stimuli right into our cars and living rooms. The only way to escape is by controlling our thoughts.

It is not easy to learn to control our thoughts, but it is not impossible either. Here are some ideas that can help.

The first step is to truly want to control your thoughts. This is a real area of conflict for most of us. On the one hand, we want to be free from the sexual obsession that comes from the sexual stimulus overload. On the other hand, we are created as sexual beings, and we are naturally drawn to all the sexual invitations around us.

The challenge for the Christian who wants to grow is not to be controlled by anything other than Jesus Christ. If we want to grow, then we have to control our thinking in those areas that compete with our love for the Lord. In other words, we need to learn to flee sexual temptation with our minds as well as our bodies.

Don said, "I realized I had to change. I was at a place where I rarely had a thought that didn't have sexual overtones."

Once you are sure of your desire to change, the next step is awareness of what you are actually thinking about. You cannot control your thoughts until you know what they are. Some people have been helped by playing "a penny for your thoughts." Put twenty-five pennies in your right pocket. Each time you are conscious of thinking sexual thoughts, transfer a penny to your left pocket. How long will it take to empty the right pocket? An hour? Half a day? Two days?

You can also use pennies to help you become more aware of the places in which you are most bombarded with sexual stimuli. How long do your pennies remain in your right pocket when you watch TV? At school? At a shopping mall? In a bookstore? The more you become aware of the sources of sexual stimulus overload, the more you can do something about it.

A large rubber band can help you take the next step—reorienting your mind. It is time to stop the sexy thoughts and start learning more wholesome thinking. Wear the rubber band loosely on your left wrist. Whenever you give in to an undesirable thought, give your wrist a good flip. It will hurt, but it won't damage your tissue. One person jokingly said, "I thought I would wear that rubber band out, but it did help."

It is helpful to learn to stop unwanted thoughts, but these techniques are not totally effective unless you also learn to substitute better thoughts. The mind is never a vacuum. If you remove one thought without replacing it with another, you will not succeed in keeping it away for long. If you aren't going to think about sex all the time, then what are you going to think about?

For a Christian, an obvious choice is to think about God. This is called worship. Thoughts of God lead to liberation from sexual obsession. Think about his goodness and his creative powers. Think about what he wants to do with your life. Give him a chance to shape your heart and mind around things that are pure, admirable, excellent, and praiseworthy (see Paul's list in Philippians 4:8 of good things to think about).

Think also about others and how you can best relate to them. Take the time you now spend pondering your sexual appetites and think of all the good you could do for them.

Julie decided to replace her sexual fantasies with more constructive thinking about her relationships with friends of both sexes. When her sexual thoughts began, she immediately turned to thinking about relating to someone in a nonsexual way. She would relive a pleasant conversation with Mark or plan a surprise for her friend Sue, who was very lonely. She came up with some good ideas, and before long she was amazed at how excited she was about the new things she was learning.

"I became a new person," she mused. "It was neat to realize that I didn't have to stay in the same old sexual rut." Don't get me wrong. This change wasn't immediate. It required Julie to bring herself back to where she wanted to be over and over again. You only succeed when you are willing to hang in there.

There is one final aid you will need in controlling your thoughts. It is simple to remember. It is called starting over. When you fail, you don't give up—you start over. Psychologist Paul Hauck warns, "Don't let slips add up." Just because you failed to control your thoughts while watching the movie doesn't mean you have to give up. Instead, use the memory of this failure to challenge yourself even more to start a new winning streak.

As human beings, we fail repeatedly. The key to success is to avoid getting bogged down in our failures. We must always work to improve our batting average.

Ted Williams was the most successful batter who ever played in the major leagues. The truth is, however, that he made an out six out of ten times when he went to bat. Imagine what would have happened if he had given up after making an out. When a hitting streak was broken with an out, he determined even more to get back on the trail of success. It worked for him, and now he is in the hall of fame.

God doesn't require us to be perfect in order to be in his hall of fame. He only requires us to be persistent. David struggled with sexual sin. He couldn't handle seeing beautiful Bathsheba bathe. He failed, but he did not remain in his failure. Instead he repented and chose the way of growth. As a result, we have a model to follow.

We know that success is possible. We honor God when we hang in there no matter how frequently the temptation comes. It only takes prayer, pennies, rubber bands, persistence, and more prayer.

Serious Sexual Temptation

KEN STEINKEN

I'm sure you've heard many times that the place to turn first with any temptation is to God. That certainly is the place to start. Prayer is important to open our hearts to the working of God's Spirit. But I would guess that if you're struggling with sexual temptations, you've already made it a matter of prayer. You're frustrated. You've taken it to God and it seems as if you've gotten nowhere with it. It may even seem to have gotten worse. So now where do you turn? The answer is you have to go beyond yourself. You have to allow God to work through others. Here's why.

How many times have you found yourself yielding to a sexual temptation? Once? Probably not. You may go for periods of time when you are able to abstain. You may even think that you've conquered it. But suddenly you find yourself in the midst of it. Perhaps you were bored, under some stress, or maybe you were feeling lonely. Something sets you off. And then a familiar chain of events takes place with the momentum of an avalanche. Even though you see it happening, you feel powerless to stop it. And then it's over. You may be overwhelmed with guilt. Maybe not. In either case you build up a new strength, a greater resolve that you will not yield to this temptation again.

What you've just experienced is referred to by counselors as a compulsive behavior pattern. It's a form of addiction like alcoholism or drug abuse. The dangerous thing is that there are elements within the behavior that can bring some satisfaction. Left to yourself, the desire for this satisfaction will at some point overpower you. And you will fall again.

Here are some steps you need to take to break out of the endless cycle:

1. Admit your behavior is compulsive and you are powerless to change it.

2. Consider the dangers: your behavior (a) is harmful to you, (b) may be harmful to others, or (c) is *not* condoned by society and may lead into trouble with the law.

3. Realize that the temptation will not disappear. You need to find a different way to deal with it. You will always struggle with it.

4. Serious problems need to be taken seriously: get help. You can't do it by yourself.

That is the bottom line. Get help. "The key step is talking to somebody," says Dr. Greg Swenson, a psychologist from Rapid City, South Dakota. "Then it's no longer 'my little secret.' When you acknowledge it to somebody you feel more accountable."

Accountability is important. One counselor told me of a Christian man who was regularly involved with "peeping." When the counselor discovered he was involved in a men's Bible study group, he suggested he share it with them. The man went back and did. That was two years ago and the man has not been "peeping" since.

"Sexual habits stick with us longer than other habits," explains Rapid City counselor Jim Gardiner. "They are self-reinforcing. The momentary feelings they produce are exciting. Though guilt may follow and bring mental pain, this is not enough of a motivator to end the behavior."

But who can you share this kind of secret with? Dr. Cliff Penner, psychologist from Pasadena, California, and author of the *Gift of Sex* says, "You need to go someplace where you feel free to talk and feel support." He offers these guidelines to help your search. It should be someone

- with whom you have an established relationship
- with whom you've shared confidential matters in the past and who has

kept your confidence, or you may know him to be trustworthy from someone else

- who has not told you confidential things about other people
- you have not felt to be judgmental in other matters that you've talked about with him

If you don't know someone who fits this description, then consider going to your pastor. Pastors are used to keeping matters confidential, and most of them won't be blown away by your secret. If they've been a pastor long, there's a good chance they have heard it before from someone else. And if they haven't, they have been around to know that it happens. If you don't feel you can go to your pastor for some reason, then you should get together with a professional counselor. In fact, if you are not satisfied with the results of talking with a friend or pastor, you may want to go to a counselor as well.

"Many times your behavior is linked to a problem that you're not dealing with," says Jim Gardiner. "Counseling can help you overcome it more thoroughly." Dr. Swenson points out, "Even if you can refrain from your behavior that is not enough. The behavior shows that something's amiss in your sexual development. Therapy can help develop a more appropriate sexuality and help you relate to others sexually as well as personally."

If you don't know a counselor to go to, Dr. Swenson suggests calling several to speak to them anonymously. Tell them what your problem is and ask them how they would handle it. Ask them what they recommend you should do. This will give you an idea who you would feel comfortable talking with in person. Pray that God will help you in your decision.

If you are reluctant to take any of these steps, then at least do this. Get a copy of the Fall 1982 issue of *Leadership* magazine and read the article titled "Anatomy of Lust." It's long, but you'll be ministered to and challenged by it. You can order a back issue for $5.00 from Back Issue Sales, Post Office Box 9020, St. Paul, Minnesota 55190.

Also, get the book by Patrick Carnes titled *Sexual Addiction.* If your local library does not have it, you can order it from Compcare Publications, 2415 Annapolis Lane, Minneapolis, Minnesota 55441, or through most bookstores.

After you've read one or both of these, I pray you'll be ready to come back to this book and do what needs to be done. Find a confidante and share your secret.

"Therefore confess your sins to each other and pray for each other so that you may be healed" (James 5:16).

Undefiled Sex in Marriage

DAVE VEERMAN

According to the "gospel of our culture," sex is the ultimate pleasure, the greatest good, and the supreme expression of one's personhood. From situation comedies to serious dramas, and in literature, films, and television, men and women chase the sexual experience. Our screens and minds are filled with every imaginable, extramarital combination.

Standing in sharp contrast, and contradiction, is the biblical standard of sex and marriage. One spouse, commitment, sexual union reserved for marriage, faithfulness—these and other scriptural commands seem quaint, out of date, and irrelevant to contemporary minds obsessed with freedom, pleasure, and "doing your own thing." It is no wonder, then, that Christians can feel pressured and confused in a world of gray morality, fuzzy values, and blurred principles. Even those intent on following God's rules and guidelines as revealed in his Word can have questions about the meaning and practice of sex. How should Christians view sex *within marriage?*

First we must realize that *sex is good.* God created male and female perfect, and before the Fall God declared that "for this reason a man will leave his father and mother and be united to his wife, and they will become one flesh" (Genesis 2:24). God, not modern pornographers, invented sex, and he made human beings sexual on purpose.

The second principle is that to be fully enjoyed and used, *sex must be practiced within the rules and guidelines given by God.* He wants us to enjoy life and each other—this can only happen as we follow his "sex manual." This, of course, is true for all of life, not just sex.

Third, we must understand that *in our culture sex has been overrated and undervalued.* Sex is not the "ultimate" in any sense of the word, but because of the continual media bombardment, we can begin to believe this myth. Many Christian young people, saving themselves for marriage, have expected far too much from sex; so marriage becomes a letdown and they harbor doubts about themselves or their spouses. Having said this, it is important to add, however, that sex is an important part of marriage. Through this physical union, a husband and wife can discover, explore, and *know* each other in the fullest sense. It is a beautiful way to express love, voluntarily submitting to your spouse and trying to meet his or her needs. And we must not forget the most basic purpose of sex: to propagate the species, to form human life, new beings bearing the image of God. When this is forgotten or ignored, with pleasure the only concern, babies becomes "fetuses" to be expelled (killed) as inconveniences to self-centered life-styles.

Sex must not be overrated, even in marriage, but it must not be undervalued. This is such an important consideration in Scripture that Paul spent two chapters chiding and instructing the Corinthians about their sexual practices (1 Corinthians 6–7). The key verse in his discussion was 6:13: " 'Food for the stomach and the stomach for food'—but God will destroy them both. The body is not meant for sexual immorality, but for the Lord, and the Lord for the body." And verses 18 and 19 state, "Flee from sexual immorality. All other sins a man commits are outside his body, but he who sins sexually sins against his own body. Do you not know that your body is a temple of the Holy Spirit, who is in you, whom you have received from God? You are not your own."

Within marriage, then, sex is to be enjoyed as pleasure, as a way to express love, and as the way to bring children into the world. With the above stated principles as our foundation, here are other biblical teachings about sex *within* marriage.

1. *"The marriage bed is undefiled"* (Hebrews 13:4). This means that sex is good within marriage; but it does not teach that "anything goes." Too often our sexual appetites are whetted by the world and we try to copy every new position and experience. Remember, sex is not an end in itself; it is the means to an end. Don't try to keep up with some imagined ideal of sexual prowess.

2. *Everything we do must be motivated by love.* In 1 Corinthians 13 we find God's description of love. "Love is patient, love is kind, . . . it is not self-seeking" (verses 4, 5). Love is not something we "make," by "making" someone else give us pleasure. Love is acting toward another person with his or her highest good in mind.

3. *Sex must not be used as a weapon.* When a person wants something, the other can withhold whatever it is he wants to punish him. This attitude of punishment or retaliation is often used with sex. Love and sex must never be used this way. Consider again 1 Corinthians 13 and all of Jesus' statements about giving and serving. At the same time, however, this does not mean we should give in and turn over our bodies to the other person, regardless of the animosity between us. It means first resolving those problems and removing those barriers that keep us from each other. According to Paul, sex must only be withheld for the purposes of prayer and fasting, and then only by mutual consent (1 Corinthians 7:5).

4. *Sex is not a "right" to demand.* You cannot be responsible for how your mate acts or reacts. You can only control yourself and your relationship with God; therefore, don't attempt to force him or her to submit to your amorous desires, physically, emotionally, or with a barrage of Bible verses. Again, love is the key. Sexual foreplay begins long before you hop into bed. How you treat each other all day will, to a great extent, determine how you treat each other at night. If your partner has a real problem in this area, pray for him or her and for yourself. Perhaps counseling is needed with a Christian therapist trained in this field.

Within marriage, sex is to be enjoyed as God intended, under his guidance. Remember these principles, and instead of thinking of excuses for "not tonight," consider how you can build a beautiful, meaningful, sexual relationship with your spouse.

Masturbation

DAVID SEAMANDS

In the church today you can find extremely varied views on masturbation, ranging from those who think it is always sinful to those who say it is a gift from God, a wise provision for young people.

One reason the views vary so widely is that there is no clear, direct word on masturbation anywhere in Scripture. A couple of generations ago, Genesis 38:8-11 and 1 Corinthians 6:9, 10 were used to condemn masturbation. The first is the story of Onan's failure to obey the ancient Hebrew law requiring a man to father children by his dead brother's widow. The second, in the King James Version, refers to "abusers of themselves," a passage correctly translated nowadays as "homosexuals." Both onanism and self-abuse were formerly used to mean masturbation, but neither of these texts is actually talking about that practice.

Some people argue from Scripture's silence that masturbation cannot be wrong. Arguments from silence can be dangerous; lots of temptations we face today are never mentioned in Scripture. Nevertheless, we know that masturbation is both ancient and universal—the earliest mention of it is in the Egyptian Book of the Dead, dated somewhere around 1500 B.C. We can observe that Scripture covers just about every other sexual activity—fornication, adultery, homosexuality, bestiality. You name it and it is there, mentioned quite explicitly. I think we have a right to ask why, since masturbation is so universal and so ancient a sexual practice, it is nowhere mentioned in the Bible if it is always a sin.

From a scientific, medical standpoint, we now know that masturbation causes no mental or physical harm. There are no moral arguments against it for health reasons, like the anti-smoking arguments based on the dangers of cancer, emphysema, and heart disease.

Since there is no direct word from Scripture, and since there are no moral arguments based on dangers to physical health, we will have to use other Christian principles to determine whether masturbation is right or wrong. I have personally concluded that masturbation in itself is neither good nor evil. To determine whether it is right or wrong, other questions have to be asked.

1. Is the thought life pure? In Matthew 5:27, 28 Jesus said, "You have heard that it was said, 'Do not commit adultery.' But I tell you that anyone who looks at a woman lustfully has already committed adultery with her in his heart." Mental fornication or adultery is wrong, and it is a definite deterrent to spiritual growth. Fantasies about actions that would be immoral to carry out in real life are wrong.

But this does not mean all fantasies are wrong. I know of married couples who, when separated, masturbate and think of each other. This is within the context of their married life and can't be classed as mental adultery.

What is more, not all masturbation is accompanied by fantasies. Studies indicate that about one-fourth of males and one-half of females do not fantasize when they masturbate. With them, masturbation is simply a physical release from sexual tension.

Obviously one cannot have a pure thought life while using pornography to stimulate erotic fantasies about illicit acts. But some people are able to masturbate without thinking impure thoughts.

2. Is the social and relational life healthy? Some people use masturbation as an escape from social life. When masturbation becomes a substitute for prop-

er interpersonal relationships, when it is used as a means of escaping the pressures of loneliness, frustration, and depression, it harms the personality and stunts spiritual growth.

Through many years of counseling I have come to distinguish between masturbation as a temporary and occasional means of relieving normal sexual build-up, and masturbation as a compulsive habit that feeds and is fed by deeper emotional hang-ups. Occasional masturbation is almost an inevitable part of normal growing up, particularly for teenage boys. Compulsive masturbation, by contrast, is fueled by serious problems: inability to relate to people, especially those of the opposite sex; depression, deep-seated resentment. In situations like these, masturbation is just a symptom of the deeper problem.

Parents, pastors, and Christian counselors must learn to discern the difference between various types of masturbation. For many Christians, masturbation is a peg on which to hang their guilt, and yet the real problem may not be masturbation at all.

If a person is concerned about masturbation, how can he deal with it?

It is usually futile to try a direct, frontal, spiritual attack on it. Instead of lessening the problem, this tends to make it worse. Nothing provokes masturbation more than creating a lot of anxiety about it. In fact, the frontal attack often creates a downward spiral: the person tries prayer and Scripture reading and promise making, only to break those promises and feel simply terrible and try the same approach all over again.

Prayer can be helpful—or it can be damaging. Damaging prayers are negative. They tell God how bad we are, and they create even more guilt and anxiety and depression. Helpful prayers offer words of assurance about God's accepting love. They point to his faithfulness even when we fail: "Thank you, Lord, for loving me, for healing me, for helping me with all my problems." Positive praying helps break the vicious circle of guilt and despair.

No one is sure whether masturbation produces guilt or whether guilt produces masturbation. Whichever the case, a direct frontal attack only makes the situation worse. Far better to help people get their minds off the guilt and anxiety by explaining that this is a gray area where rightness and wrongness depends on other factors.

How then should a person deal with masturbation? Indirectly. Pay attention to social life, to interpersonal relationships. Socialize, don't fantasize. Get out of the house and do things with real people. Make friends, particularly of the opposite sex—real flesh-and-blood people that you can enjoy as persons without fantasizing about them sexually at all.

When a person does these things, sometimes a compulsive habit can be broken in only a few weeks or months. Masturbation is reduced from being the focus of the person's existence to being only a minor, occasional means of relieving sexual tension. In fact, the person may eventually abandon it altogether.

The true joys of making friends and finding companionship through healthy dating relationships can fill the need that was formerly filled by a poor substitute. The person doesn't need to masturbate anymore. He has grown up, matured, put away childish things.

♦ THINK ABOUT IMPORTANT THINGS
DAVID SEAMANDS

Christians need to stop making masturbation or nonmasturbation a sort of spiritual barometer. A lot of them come in to me and say, "I haven't masturbated for six months. I'm doing fine. I'm getting along great with the Lord, I'm filled with the Spirit, and he's using me powerfully."

Or, sadly, "Oh, no, I've failed again. I'm not filled with the Spirit anymore. This is terrible. I'm hopeless. God can't use me."

I think that's ridiculous. Masturbation is not your chief sin, and nonmasturbation is not your chief virtue. God is interested in a lot of other things that are more important than masturbation. Do you love your enemies? Are you able to forgive those who have wronged you? Are you generous with your time and resources? Are you concerned when others are hurting?

In Paul's day, the cities were filled with nasty, dirty, pornographic things. But he didn't write, "Don't think about all these bad things." Instead he said, "Whatever is true, whatever is noble, whatever is right, whatever is pure, whatever is lovely, whatever is admirable—if anything is excellent or praiseworthy—think about such things" (Philippians 4:8).

Don't get so obsessed with masturbating—or not masturbating—that you lose sight of the important things.

The Twisting: The Problem of Pornography
DAVE VEERMAN

The sex drive is a gift from God, and sex should be seen as good, valuable, and part of what it means to be fully human, made in the image of God. In our culture, however, sex has been twisted and degraded. Lust, displacing love, motivates men and women to use and discard each other—"no deposit, no return." Pornography has become a billion-dollar business, feeding off this twisted urge with bookstands and video stores peddling flesh like so much hamburger—and customers pay and consume.

Christians are not immune to this sensual onslaught. We are "sinners saved by grace," but we are still sinners. And, if we're normal, our hormones push the sex drive into full gear in typical lust-producing situations. To be unaffected by society's sex obsession, we would have to be emasculated or isolated. Serious Christians attempting, through the Holy Spirit's power, to live "pure and holy lives" wonder how to respond. Without retreating or wearing blinders, we can take action to stem the tide of personal lust. Let me suggest that we do the following:

1. *Recognize our weaknesses.* It is foolish to pretend that we are strong enough to resist. Sexual problems are not reserved for terrible persons or

perverts. Normal people have sexual thoughts and urges. Add the sin nature and society's obsession, and the mix can be volatile. Satan will attack us where we are most vulnerable.

2. *Avoid lust-producing situations.* Just as an alcoholic should not hang around a bar to prove he can resist, we should not meet lust head-on to prove our strength. We are weak; therefore, when we see a difficult situation approaching, we should avoid it. This relates especially to our reading and viewing habits. We can be sure that R-and X-rated films will cause problems.

3. *Rely on the Holy Spirit's power.* Only God can defeat sin. When faced with temptation, therefore, we must ask him for the power to resist. Ephesians 6:18 says, "Pray in the Spirit on all occasions with all kinds of prayers and requests."

4. *Control the media.* Television and radio are almost inseparable parts of our lives, but we can control, to a great extent, what we see and hear. If, for example, the temptation to watch an X-rated movie in the privacy of your own home would be too great, don't subscribe to the movie channel on cable. And, if you know that certain programs are "dirty," turn the television off or change stations. We are not helpless pawns; we can exercise some discipline and control.

By taking these steps we will not feed the sinful desires that come into our lives, and we will reflect the principle of Philippians 4:8: "Whatever is true, whatever is noble, whatever is right, whatever is pure, whatever is lovely, whatever is admirable—if anything is excellent or praiseworthy—think about such things." It is true that we do and become what we think, so guard your thoughts!

There is a great difference, however, between responding to pornography that finds us and trying to find pornography. Even Christians can fall prey to the twisting and become obsessed with sex. If these persons really want to change, beyond taking the steps outlined above, they should seek out a trained professional. Often there is an underlying emotional reason for the behavior, and their obsession is the symptom. Through sensitive, Christ-centered counseling, these people can be helped.

Lust need not saturate our thoughts and control our actions. We can *choose* to focus on Christ, to ask for God's strength, and to take practical steps to minimize the problems. Remember, "No temptation has seized you except what is common to man. And God is faithful; he will not let you be tempted beyond what you can bear. But when you are tempted, he will also provide a way out so that you can stand up under it" (1 Corinthians 10:13).

Is Homosexuality Wrong?

EARL WILSON

Thousands of people today have identified themselves as homosexuals or "gays." Both terms are used to describe people whose sexual preference is for persons of the same sex.

Many of those thousands of people are believers in Jesus Christ—born-again or evangelical Christians. Such persons are caught in the dilemma of being inclined toward a way of life that appears to be condemned in Scripture. No wonder they ask, Is homosexuality wrong? Didn't God make me this way? If not, how did I become this way? What can I do about it?

Is homosexuality wrong?

As a compassionate believer, I have tried to read Scripture in such a way as to condone homosexuality. Frankly, it can't be done. Homosexual lust is referred to time and time again as sin, and we are told to avoid it—just as we are told to avoid heterosexual lust. Homosexual sin is neither worse nor better than heterosexual sin. Scripture condemns both alike.

Homosexuality is wrong because it involves unnatural sexual acts. The only purpose for such acts is pleasure, and the pleasure becomes an end in itself. Homosexuals do not raise families, and they very, very rarely remain faithful to each other. In fact, most homosexual sex is anonymous sex; that is, it is sex with a stranger who wants and expects to remain a stranger. Relationship possibilities for homosexuals are extremely limited.

Homosexuality is wrong, then, because Scripture says it is wrong. It is also wrong because it leads to unhealthy rather than healthy relationships. There is nothing gay about being a homosexual. Most of my friends who are homosexuals are sad and disillusioned people. They don't like their lot in life. They don't understand it, and they don't know what to do about it.

They struggle with this question: Didn't God make me this way?

Scripture is clear that God did not create anyone homosexual. He created males and he created females, and he commanded them to be one flesh. Homosexuality, like materialism or cancer, is the result of sin in the world. God has permitted homosexuality just as he has permitted greed and disease.

God never intended that greed or homosexuality be practiced or that cancer be allowed to spread unchecked. We are kidding ourselves when we blame God for homosexuality and then reason that it must be OK to practice it. God never invented the problem; man did. God never condones the practice; only man does.

If God did not make me homosexual, how did I become this way?

In my experience working with persons with same-sex preference, I have discovered that homosexuals are a very heterogeneous group. All homosexuals are not alike, and I do not believe that all persons develop same-sex preference in the same way.

I have found it helpful to distinguish between two types of persons with same-sex preference. (I have described both types in my book *Sexual Sanity*

[InterVarsity Press, 1984].) The first I call true homosexuals. These are persons who have never been attracted to persons of the opposite sex and indeed may have been biologically predisposed to same-sex preference. This type of sexual preference is very difficult to change, but fortunately it is far less common than most believe. Of all the homosexuals I have known, I believe only 10 to 20 percent are true homosexuals. Who, then, are the remaining 80 to 90 percent?

I call this larger group homosexual pleasure-seekers. These persons may be bisexual—that is, they have sex with persons of both sexes, but mostly with persons of the same sex—or they may seek sexual pleasure exclusively with persons of the same sex. I call them pleasure-seekers because they are obsessed with pleasure and take gigantic risks in order to get it. For many, the threat of AIDS seems to be no threat at all.

I believe the homosexual pleasure-seeker is capable of changing sexual preference and of leading a normal life. The key is in breaking the sexual obsession.

The Gay Rights Movement and other civil rights groups have gone out of their way to convince people with same-sex preference that they were born that way and that they cannot change. I believe this is a lie that must be confronted.

If you are a person with same-sex preference, do not swallow the lie without first exploring your situation thoroughly with a counselor who can offer you some hope. Don't automatically condemn yourself to a life of anonymous sex and self-hatred without looking for other possibilities. Even though some may be predisposed to same-sex preference, the majority have learned that preference and can therefore unlearn it. The life you save may be your own.

What can I do about my homosexuality?

I have already started to answer the question. Challenge the lie. Do not assume that the preference you have now cannot be changed. If you want more out of life, you may find it.

Dick said, "Once I came to realize that change was possible, I got an entirely new outlook on life." Relearning was hard. It took several months of meeting with me, but the change was astounding. Dick changed from a person of gloom and despair to a person with a future. He began to accept himself as a man, and he began to enjoy the beauty of women. He now looks forward to marriage and a family, to finding pleasure in the safety and acceptance of his marriage rather than in the dangerous world of sexual promiscuity. He is alive.

Once again I say, Don't buy the lie! Give God a chance to show you how you can get to the place where he wants you to be.

If you seek counseling, find a counselor who believes in change and who has had success in helping people change. It may be costly in terms of both time and money, but, after all, you are worth it.

If you and your counselor determine that change may not be possible for you, I encourage you to seek the celibate life. Sexual sin will only destroy you, and you are too valuable to God and to your fellowman to be slowly destroyed. The bottom line is that homosexuality is wrong because it leads to destruction. Choose life!

How Do I Deal with My Fears That I Am Homosexual?

DR. ROGER TIRABASSI

Homosexuality is an issue that, when mentioned in the Christian community, elicits highly emotional responses. Many react with a condemning tone. It is often a taboo subject. For the person who might question his vulnerability to such behavior, the tendency to suppress such thoughts is likely. Those who have dealt with this problem are more able to be compassionate and accepting without condoning such behavior.

Fleeting thoughts of homosexuality are common, even to Christians. Many children, while growing up, experiment both heterosexually and homosexually. There is a sense of discovery that characterizes the young child and often progresses into adolescence. Some men and women fear being homosexual because of such curiosity. It is important to realize the normality of such experiences.

There are others who have homosexual tendencies and who need to seek professional Christian help. Following are some signs that would be indicative of such need:

1. No interest in dating or in the opposite sex.
2. Spending almost all of one's time with people of the same sex.
3. Females who desire to look mannish, or males who desire to look feminine (it is however, a fallacy to believe that this can identity a homosexual).
4. When one has desires both heterosexually and homosexually.
5. Anxiety reaction when relating to homosexuals.
6. Depressive reaction when relating to homosexuality.
7. Fears of relating to the opposite sex.
8. Desire to be involved with homosexual pornographic literature.
9. Frequenting homosexual gathering-places.
10. A compulsion to be physically intimate with a person of the same sex.

Unfortunately, it is rare when a homosexual seeks a change in behavior, and many erroneously believe what he or she is doing is natural and acceptable. Because of the unconscious motivations there is little motivation to change. There is much more hope for the person who has a true Christian conversion. In such cases the person realizes his behavior is not pleasing to God, and he is much more likely to seek help in overcoming his problem. Scripture is clear on the fact that such behavior is not in God's plan (Leviticus 18:22; Romans 1:26, 27; 1 Corinthians 6:9 are a few places where the condemnation of such acts is cited).

There is a danger and a warning for the Christian helper who might be attempting to assist a homosexual. It is often erroneously assumed that such behavior is strictly symptomatic of a spiritual problem. While the spiritual area should not be ignored, it should not always be the focal point of such conflict. Many times the root is not in the spiritual at all, and by focusing on this area the individual can be forced into deeper guilt, pushing him further from God rather than drawing him closer. Again, this does not mean the helper should condone such behavior, but that he understands the dilemma the person finds himself or herself in.

There have been three conventional analyses of motivation for homosexual conduct: past power conflicts, dependency dynamics, and sexual gratification. Of the root causes, most seem to be the result of abnormal personality development. There is an exceptionally high correlation between highly dominant, cruel, and overindulgent parents. An example could be a male who lacked a warm relationship with his father. He may have failed to develop a masculine identity and therefore seeks unnatural sexual choices. Homosexuality could also be the result of an overindulgent mother or a cold, distant parent. In the case of the female homosexual, a masculine identity has been formed. Similar parent-child difficulties are most likely involved. Many times the issue of failure becomes key to the dynamics that lead to the sexual identity of the homosexual. When one grows up feeling like a failure, it can have consequences that are displayed in sexual identity. The dynamics in each case should be looked at with the help of a skilled therapist. When uncovered, the therapist can assist the homosexual by lessening the energy and drive given to such behavior. With proper help in understanding himself and then focusing on such areas as new relationships, new insights, and impulse control, the chances of success are extremely positive.

It is also important to note that rationalizations can play a detrimental role in seeking help, or in relapses. Thoughts about one's inability to relate to the opposite sex, fear of rejection, feelings of not having any friends, or of losing relationships that have become very meaningful have serious negative consequences.

Scripture is clear that homosexuality is not God's will for our lives. Those who find themselves in such relationships, or are tempted to be, should seek professional Christian counseling. Christian counselors are trained to hold such matters in utmost confidence, and will even help if lack of financial ability is an obstacle.

Help for the Homosexual

KATHY CALLAHAN-HOWELL

In today's culture homosexuality has become a hot issue. Of course it has risen to prominence in previous cultures as well. The debate rages in Christian circles with one side declaring acceptance and the other condemnation. It's no surprise most of us are simply confused.

To understand what God intended for human sexuality, we must consider its creation. When God created people, he created them male and female in his image. Although we use male pronouns for God, we must realize he is not specifically male, but he is a person. God is the essence of male and female in perfect combination. Otherwise only men would be in his image, which contradicts the creation account in Genesis.

God's intention for human sexuality centers in marriage. One woman and one man become one flesh. They are united permanently as one person, and one facet of their unity is their sexual relationship. Although sex brings pleasure, its central purpose is procreation. God expects married couples to enjoy sex, yet he also created it to reproduce our race.

Any sexual relationship other than heterosexual monogamy is contrary to God's plan. This includes premarital sex, extramarital sex, and homosexual sex. None is any "worse" in God's eyes. Only heterosexual marital sex fits his plan, partly because of the procreational aspect. Children should not be born outside of a marriage and family. Homosexual relationships cannot produce children.

In addition, sex creates intimate bonds between two people. Persons participating in a sexual relationship reach a dimension not possible in other ways as the married people become one flesh. Such bonding should not occur outside of the commitment and security of marriage. Breaking such a bond creates intense loss and trauma. God desires people who bond sexually to remain bonded and not experience the crisis of severing the relationship. Extramarital sex lacks the commitment necessary for healthy continuance.

God's plan is for one woman and one man to experience sex only with each other within marriage. Some people are called to singleness and celibacy, but any sex must exist within the context of marriage. Anything else falls short of God's plan.

Some people believe homosexuals are always wicked people choosing to be perverted and sinful. Others are convinced homosexuality is genetic and unavoidable, even God-created. Neither view represents reality.

No genetic causes have been discovered for homosexuality. However, environmental factors have been noticed, such as father absence or neglect, mother dominance, physical or sexual abuse by parents or others, and sexual immaturity. Any number of factors may contribute to an individual's sexual preference.

One fact seems clear: although causes are difficult to assess, hardly anyone *chooses* to have homosexual preferences. This attitude develops due to factors out of the person's control. Therefore the person develops a homosexual orientation without deciding to. If you are homosexual, you probably feel you did not choose to be and do not really know how or when it happened.

However, homosexual orientation and homosexual activity are not synonymous. The person doesn't choose the preference for same sex partners, but he or she does choose whether to act on it. Just like any sin, we do not choose to be tempted, but we do choose to give in or not.

It is important to remember as we consider homosexuality that God loves all people, despite any sin imaginable. God loves homosexuals, prostitutes, thieves, even gossips and complainers. He does not rank sins or categorize them, and he loves all of us despite any sin we commit.

In fact, he will love the homosexual who remains an actively practicing homosexual. However, he does not love the sin and it prevents the person from loving him completely. God has the amazing ability to separate sin from sinner, a gift we must attempt to exhibit.

God has no anger toward the preference for homosexuality, for that was not chosen. In fact he feels compassion for those who must struggle with such temptation. Yet he does desire the activity to cease.

Help is often needed for the homosexual who wants to stop this sinful activity. Some people have little struggle in changing their life-styles and others are delivered instantly at their conversion. However, most people struggle long and hard to change.

Becoming celibate is quite a burden. A person may never lose the homosexual preference and simply has to survive without a sexual relationship. Great courage is required for this decision.

Help is available, however. There are community resources; some churches have support groups, counseling, and programs for those choosing to change. An example is Spring Forth Ministry in Cincinnati led by a reformed homosexual and providing a support group and counseling. This ministry practices healing by Christ of old memories that triggered the problem.

Other simple steps can be taken. The homosexual must change the group of friends, break contact with any previous partners, and avoid places where homosexual contacts were made in the past. The cleaner the break, the more successful it will be.

The person must replace homosexual thoughts by getting involved in new activities, such as ministry opportunities, and keeping busy with exciting new options. He or she will need some people who can share the burden and will listen to the struggles.

If there are failures, the person needs to be forgiven, forgive himself, and so on. A progress report is an encouragement. God loves the repentant person immensely and is pleased with efforts to change. He must be depended on for strength, relying on prayer and time to make "old things new."

For some reason, perhaps our fear of our own weaknesses, we in the church have especially rejected homosexuals. We would rather deal with anyone else but such a person.

God sees no such distinctions. We need to reach out to the hurting homosexuals in our community. They are spiritual beings reaching out to God, only to have his earthly representatives reject them.

We should quit worrying about their sin and just love them. God will take care of this sin—we are called to reach out. They need no more guilt, they need instead a helping hand.

We must remember also not to condemn their sexual preference, which may never change. If we have the privilege of ministering to a homosexual, we should support his or her struggle to cease the activity. We need to remember the difficulty of remaining celibate, and be patient and forgiving as they make this journey.

Most of all, we must remember they are people; they need to be trusted and utilized. We could even assign them a responsibility in the church, remove from our minds all ridiculous stereotypes and love them as God does.

Interview: Dealing with the Past

DAVID SEAMANDS

When a person who has had a bad sex-related experience comes to you, how do you help her deal with it emotionally?

The first thing I tell her is that she has to face it. Many have never really looked at the hurt and the pain. "It's too much for me," they say. "I've tried to forget all those things." I don't think they'll succeed at forgetting.

I can understand why people would try to sweep a sexual trauma under the rug. Besides the personal pain of dealing with it openly, they also fear the reaction of their family or church or community if the truth comes out. So a lot of people just say, "Praise the Lord, he's handled all that," and they don't face their pain—until, in the intimacies of marriage or other serious interpersonal relationships, the whole thing blows up on them.

So my first plea is that this person should face the pain before it destroys her.

What do you mean—face the pain? What specifically should she do?

First, she needs to find somebody to talk with. I'll be almost categorical here—when a person has suffered from serious sexual trauma, she can almost never handle her pain by herself. She needs someone else to share the pain with and to assist her through her time of healing. This can be a friend, a pastor, or a professional counselor.

Once she has found a helper, she needs to find the courage to get it all out in the open in the presence of the cross. She has been living with an inner hell; now she needs to get it outside of herself and into the light.

Then she needs to work on forgiveness. She must not try to jump ahead to this step, because she has to discover the real issue before she'll know what needs forgiving. With whom is she really angry? The incestuous father, the mother who knew all about it and didn't do anything, the teacher who refused to listen?

I once counseled a woman who had been sexually abused by an uncle. She discovered she was really angriest at her mother, who refused to believe her when she tried to tell her what was going on. Recently, in a great act of courage and surrounded with a lot of prayer and counseling, she confronted her mother. She was shocked by the older woman's tearful reply, "Honey, I could never help you because I was never able to help myself: I also had this experience."

Facing the pain was extremely difficult for this woman, but once she did so, great healing came to her entire family.

How can a person forgive someone who has hurt her so badly?

This is one of the hardest areas of bad sexual experience. The pain is so great and the betrayal so deep that to forgive requires the supernatural grace of the Lord. It can happen only in prayer—very deep prayer.

The abused person also needs to receive forgiveness. It can be extremely difficult for her to forgive herself.

Why would she need to forgive herself?

She may have horrible feelings of guilt. There are women who, because they felt utterly worthless, said to themselves, "Well, I'm just a piece of garbage anyhow, so it doesn't really make any difference"—and then they allowed all sorts of things to be done to them.

Or there are those who actively initiated sexual activities that they knew were wrong, feeling they were somehow getting even with men in the process.

Or there are those who neither initiated nor accepted, but who later realize that, though they hated the person and the activity, sex being sex, they enjoyed it and wanted it. That is a terrible realization, and a counselor has to deal with it very, very gently. It's almost more than the human mind can bear.

There are even those who did not initiate, did not accept, and did not enjoy the sex—but they still feel as if the incident were somehow their fault. If they hadn't been bad, they tell themselves, it would never have happened to them.

Human assistance is very important here: The person wants to know, "Though I was a victim, where did my responsibility come in, and where have I made the wrong choices?" This is not something she can figure out on her own. A lot of forgiveness is required.

Most cases of sexual abuse require healing of the memories. That's not the answer to everything, of course, and it's not helpful for everybody. I try to be very careful not to make it a cure-all. But it is particularly helpful in cases of past sexual sin or abuse.

Why is healing of the memories important?

It seems as if people have to go back to the place in their personality development where they're stuck. We use the term *emotional hang-up,* and that's very descriptive of what happens. Something happens to a young child, and her emotional life hangs up—stops—at that point. She doesn't grow any more in that area. She grows mentally and physically, but emotionally she's still a six-or eight-year-old being raped by her stepfather. Her personality is stuck, and we have to go back there so Christ can release her to grow.

That's why you get the most wonderful men and women—bright, smart, able to relate—who are nevertheless emotionally unfit for marriage. In that one area, they are still little children. That takes inner healing. It requires visualizing, going back in time, and having Jesus heal the little girl or little boy who was violated.

How do you deal with abortion?

I usually try to go back into the woman's memory, and together we try to minister even to the unborn child that was aborted. Sometimes the woman seems to need to obtain forgiveness from the aborted child. So I ask her to visualize the child in her imagination, and I ask, "What is this baby saying to you?"

Recently I dealt with a wonderful Christian woman who had had an abortion many years ago. The pain of it had just erupted in her personality. It was as if her unborn child was able to release her from the pain by saying, "I want you to get on with your life and really serve God. I don't want you to be tied to me any longer. I free you." It was a great releasing experience. We can say it's only imaginary, but I think the Holy Spirit works through the imagination.

What effect do past sexual experiences have on present sexuality?

They can have a great effect on sexual identity and on sexual relationships. Even after the memories are healed, it usually takes time to reprogram the person sexually. It takes work together with husbands and wives. It takes patience, prayer, and therapy to free them to enjoy this God-given gift apart from the garbage that wants to ooze back into their thoughts. It takes reprogramming and counseling, and it doesn't happen overnight.

Why can't a person just pray and find healing?

Those memories are so strong, so intense, that they color everything the person does. Whatever she tries—prayer, Scripture reading, meditation—she will run it through a filter that gives her the message, "You are no good. You are hopeless." She can't find healing that way. Her memories have to be healed first.

It may take two or three sessions before she finds release, but once she is freed of her negative memories, she is ready for reprogramming. That is when she can use Scripture and prayer to change her thoughts, her assumptions, her false ideas. Because she's no longer hung up in her past, she's free to grow.

Doesn't God ever intervene and release a person immediately?

We can't limit the grace of God. I've seen those occasional mind-blowing experiences, where God just steps in and releases people. That's great. But usually sexual reprogramming is necessary.

But the person can find forgiveness directly from God. . . .

Yes and no. I don't know why this is, but almost all sex-related traumas and sins require the help of another human being. These people need absolution—an authoritative word from a human being that God has forgiven them. I can't figure that out. Not all sins require that. Many can be dealt with directly with God. But I've found that in almost every instance of sexual sin I've dealt with, human help is necessary.

I think that when it's a sexual sin, people feel so dehumanized—so used, violated, molested, hurt, guilty, and shameful—that they almost need someone to welcome them back into the human race. "You are OK, you are forgiven, you are human." It's almost as if the counselor, pastor, or friend restores their humanity to them. That's the closest I can get to an explanation.

So I think the helping person must use the authority given to the Christian church in Scripture—"Whatever you bind on earth will be bound in heaven, and whatever you loose on earth will be loosed in heaven" (Matthew 16:19). This person must be very authoritative. I become like a priest in this. I lay hands on people, I give them communion, I call them by name and say, "You are forgiven. You are cleansed. Your virtue is restored."

Do you mean a person can regain sexual innocence?

I don't care for that way of putting it. You can't undo what has been done. But you can rewrite your autobiography in a way that gives it meaning. You can interpret it in a different way. As Joseph said to his brothers, "You intended to harm me, but God intended it for good" (Genesis 50:20). Paul pointed out that "in all things God works for the good of those who love him, who have been called according to his purpose" (Romans 8:28).

That's what reprogramming is all about—rewriting a life, even those horrible experiences that were intended to harm. You can't change the fact that the experiences were evil. You can't say they were innocent. But they can be redeemed and used in ministry to other people in a marvelous way.

I mentioned a woman who discovered that her mother also had been a victim of incest. The change in her was remarkable. Before, she always wore the sloppiest kind of blue jeans, almost as if she were saying, "I'm trying to be as ugly as I can." Now her whole appearance has changed. She wears dresses, grooms herself well, looks great. For the first time she has a dating relationship with someone who's worthy of her.

Recently she has volunteered to be on an abuse and rape call-in line. She told me, "It's amazing. People start telling me stories, often about incest and abuse at an early age, and they stop in the middle and say, "I don't know why I'm telling you this. You couldn't possibly understand.'"

Right away she says, "Wait a minute. I do understand." Then she shares just in slight detail her story. And that, she says, opens up the floodgates.

Because of the tremendous pain she went through, she is now in ministry. God is using her to help other suffering people—and that's even better than regaining innocence.

RELATED ARTICLES

Chapter 20: **The Battle with Sin**
Chapter 20: **Filling Legitimate Desires Illegitimately**
Chapter 20: **Overcoming Temptation**

CHAPTER

22

Determining God's Will

- ✓ How do I find God's will for my life?
- ✓ In what ways does God communicate his will to me?
- ✓ How do God's guidance and my responsibility fit together?
- ✓ What if I'm afraid to know God's will?
- ✓ How do I know I'm marrying the right person?

Decision Making and the Sovereignty of God

✍ CLARK H. PINNOCK

On occasion I have been asked, "If God is sovereign, why should I bother to make decisions?"

It is obvious that people who ask this question are defining sovereign in a way that creates problems for their decision making. They must think that God's sovereignty causes everything to happen just the way it does, so that no other agent can do anything about it. In that case, why pretend to be a significant actor whose decisions really make a difference? Our decisions would not matter—whatever would be, would be.

It is sad that so many Christians have been so badly misinformed about the true nature of God's sovereignty as to fall into despair concerning their own significance as agents. Any belief in determinism, even when it is called sovereignty, results in resignation and robs people of initiative. If everything is going to happen as God ordained it, there is nothing any of us can do to change the outcome. Even our so-called decisions are 100 percent determined by fate or God according to this definition of his sovereignty.

The way around this problem is to see that it is not a real problem at all. What has happened is that the questioner has defined sovereign incorrectly. Sovereignty does not mean determinism. The Bible teaches that God is the Creator and Lord of the world, but that does not make him a puppet master pulling all the strings. On the contrary, it seems plain both from the Bible and from our experience that God made a world with intelligent structures in place and human agents—people with a capacity for making free choices—to inhabit it. God did not guard the privilege of making significant decisions for himself alone, but gave some of that privilege and responsibility to us. This is the only possible way to understand why he holds us morally responsible for the way we exercise that gift. If, for example, God determined events such as cruelty or theft, there would be no justice in holding us responsible if we committed these acts.

The most important thing, then, is not to define God's sovereignty wrongly. It is not to be confused, as it often is, with any kind of determinism. God created man in his image to exercise responsible dominion over the earth. He made us capable of loving and entering into a relationship with him. None of these things make any sense unless we are nondetermined agents.

Of course God took a risk in creating free creatures like ourselves. It would have been easier if he had just programmed us to do what is right all the time. But God must have considered the risk worth taking. He must have considered the possibility of making humans who functioned just like machines. But he decided not to do it. He made free creatures instead. It may have been because he wanted to establish a personal covenant with human beings, in which case freedom would be essential. You cannot have a love relationship that is forced.

I suppose the clearest evidence that sovereignty cannot mean determinism is the fact of human sin. God gave us true freedom, and we used this gift to reject God's plan for us and to turn away from him. If sovereignty meant determinism, it would follow that God wanted us to sin and thus is himself the author of sin. But that blasphemy is emphatically not the biblical view of the matter.

On the contrary, God is grieved over the sinful uses to which we have put our gift of freedom. Far from determining the sins that we do, God loathes them. Obviously God has granted a measure of true freedom to his creatures and lets them use it even in ways that displease him.

It is important not to think of God's sovereignty as a determining blueprint of everything that will ever happen, as though God froze everything in place before the world even got started. Sovereignty in a biblical sense refers to the rule of God, who is working out his goals in the sphere of history. The goals themselves are unchangeable, but the way in which God moves toward realizing them is flexible and responsive to what happens. It is not a controlled situation where only what God predestined happens. That would be a pretty simple kind of world to have to rule over. Rather it is a world with free agents in it, one that requires a flexible sovereignty to reign over it.

We are now in a position to answer the initial question. If God is sovereign, why should we bother to make decisions? Because God's sovereignty is not of the Islamic type, which controls things down to the last detail. It is the kind of flexible sovereignty that invites us to cooperate with it in realizing the future.

We see that in prayer so clearly. God invites us into partnership with himself in the running of the universe. He actually accepts our prayers as factors leading him to act in one way rather than another. We cannot say that prayer changes things unless we reject the determinist definition of sovereignty.

Our decisions matter, because God honors them in the context of his own shaping of the future. God's sovereignty is magnified, not diminished, when we recognize that he has given us real freedom. Our dignity could not be greater than when we see the importance God himself places upon what we decide. "I have set before you life and death. . . . Now choose life" (Deuteronomy 30:19)!

♦ GOD'S PERSPECTIVE AND OURS
DAVE VEERMAN

A perspective is a point of view, a way of seeing things. As finite human beings, our perspective is severely limited. Your three-year-old son, for example, may think he knows everything—but you know better. His perspective is limited by his age and experience.

Try looking at a picture about an inch away from your eyes. All you can see is a blur of colors or dots. Now move the picture away and watch the picture come into focus. Your original perspective was limited because of your closeness to the picture.

By contrast, God's perspective is unlimited. He has seen it all, and he sees it all. God sees the whole picture. He knows about events, circumstances, and people totally outside your line of vision. Proverbs 3:5, 6 promises that God will direct your paths. The secret is to trust in him "with all your heart and lean not on your own understanding."

Finding God's Will
✍ CHERYL AND DAVID ASPY

Through the years, one of the most difficult aspects of spiritual growth for me has been finding the sometimes fine and sometimes broad line between my will for my life and God's will. I tried many things: attending church, reading the Bible, talking with others. I recommend all these worthy activities, but they still left me with nagging doubts. I and other Christians I know used many approaches to discovering God's will, but none seemed adequate.

Many Christians think God reveals his will through otherwise unexplainable life-changing events. For example, if a job offer comes along unsolicited, then it must be God's will.

Some devise tests for God, bargaining that if he really wants us to do a certain thing, then he must do something for us first.

Others never seek God's will unless they come to an impasse in their lives. They seem to think God should be bothered only with the really big things. If they ask him for guidance too often, they apparently fear, they might use him up.

During the past two years, two truths have been made clear to me. These truths have freed me from my doubts. They were not revealed with bolts of lightning or high drama, but in words spoken from pulpits by two godly men: Pastor W. A. Criswell from Dallas, Texas, and Pastor Ed Jager from Amherst, Massachusetts.

The first truth answered my question about how much responsibility I should take for my Christian life. Pastor Criswell told the congregation that it is not enough to pray for a job; we should also check the want ads, call the employment agency, ask friends for leads, and even knock on a few doors. He made his point clearly: As the old proverb puts it, "God has promised every bird his due, but he doesn't always throw it into the nest." It is important to strive to achieve what God wants, believing his guidance will direct our efforts.

This is clearly the lesson of the parable of the talents. God asks us to use our talents to the fullest. Then he can give us more, because we have demonstrated that we are ready to take the next step. God asks us to exhaust our repertoire, and then to take the next step on faith. Unless we first earnestly seek God's will through prayer and then do everything we know to do, we are denying God the gift of our service.

When we pray and then strive to meet our needs, we are in no way "working" our way to heaven. Salvation is clearly a gift that cannot be bought with works. Taking steps on faith is another matter entirely. God asks us to give him everything—our requests as well as the labor of our hands. He will magnify what we give him and use it for our growth.

The second truth that has helped remove many of my doubts about knowing God's will came to me in a sermon by Pastor Jager. Paraphrasing St. Augustine, he said, "Love God, and do as you please." The teenager sitting in front of us turned to his dad with an expression of glee, as if now he would be free to do all those things he had previously been denied. His father shook his head no.

The statement does not mean, as the teenager interpreted it, "anything goes." It means that when we love, we are likely to choose behavior that will please the object of our love. I often think how easy it is to love my daughter. I don't worry about doing the minimum for her, because my love propels me to be the best parent I can be. When God is the object of our love, this truth is even more evident. If we love God, we will not try to give the minimum response. Our love encourages us to give a full, deep commitment to his teachings.

I believe it is God's will that we learn to love him more fully. Those life choices, then, that enhance that goal must also be in his will. If there seems to be no difference in how a choice affects that goal, then God will use either in his service.

Translating these truths into everyday life is simply a process of identifying their implications.

1. Ask God for the things you need, the guidance you seek.

2. Do everything you can to satisfy the need. This may mean opening yourself to new information, new people, or new experiences, for God may speak to us in many ways. We must be constant learners as we strive to find God's will for our lives.

3. Actively seek to love God more every day. This may seem like a strange assignment, but love can be increased or diminished by our mental activities. Take time to think about God's goodness and love every day. Dwell on life's positives rather than on the negatives. This might be as specific as writing down good things as part of your daily meditation. Give love a healthy climate, and it will grow. The more we love God, the more acutely we hear his harmonious messages through the cacophony of life.

4. Have faith. This last step is also the first. Faith in God should underlie all our goals and efforts.

In short, then, pray, strive, and love, taking each step in the belief that God will work all things for good (Romans 8:28). There is much security and confidence in that belief.

♦ IS GOD'S WILL INDIVIDUALISTIC?
DAVE VEERMAN

In America we are very conscious of the individual. We stress individual freedoms and rights. This strong emphasis can easily slide into self-centeredness as we "look out for number one" above everything else.

We ask, What is God's will for my life? Where in Scripture do you find mention of God's will being so individualistic? Of course God is interested in the individual (see Psalm 139, for example). But his focus of attention is much bigger than any one person's life.

Instead of focusing your attention on yourself, ask first, "What is God's will for the world?" Then you can ask, "How am I fitting into it?"

Jesus taught that the secret to living a fulfilled life is to "seek first his kingdom and his righteousness" (Matthew 6:33).

Seeking God's Will for Your Life

ANTHONY CAMPOLO

We learn from the book of Acts that as the members of the early church sought to learn God's will, they waited for consensus before they took action. As the apostles and elders wrote to the Gentile believers, "We all agreed . . . " (Acts 15:25). The early church made decisions not on the basis of a majority vote, but when everyone agreed on an issue.

I have a support group of three men that meet with me regularly. They know me, they know my talents, they know my weaknesses. Whenever I have a decision to make and I'm seeking God's will, I do not simply ponder it by myself. I bring it to my support group. Because they know me so well, I can lay out my concern before them and they will pledge themselves to work through this issue with me. We pray about the decision; we discuss it. I know I have discovered the will of God when all four of us are in perfect agreement.

I need this support group because, in making decisions, it's hard to know for sure whether one is seeking one's own will or God's will. Often we want things so much and so deeply that we are able to talk ourselves into believing that God wants what we want. For example, I was talking to a guy who was about to leave his wife to marry another woman. His wife was not a Christian; this other woman was a Christian. He had talked himself into believing that this divorce and remarriage were the will of God. I couldn't convince him otherwise. I asked him if he had talked to anyone else about his decision, and he said no. Why hadn't he? He explained, "Because I know what other people will say, and they don't know the will of God as I know it." Such egocentric thoughts can cause people to think their own will is God's will.

Sometimes people say, "The Spirit is really leading me." How do they know it's the Spirit of God and not a demonic spirit or their own ego? Good Christian friends can help you make that distinction. They correct you and make you aware that you may be following your own inclinations rather than God's Spirit. If they love you, they will be honest with you. If they love you, they will help you avoid big mistakes.

When I taught in a seminary, I became extremely depressed by the large number of students who obviously should not have been there. I asked myself how these guys, who had no gift for delivering sermons, could end up in seminaries and eventually in churches. I knew they would kill churches, so I asked them about their decision to attend seminary. I always asked the same question: "What confirmation did you get that this sense of calling was really of God?" In every case there was none. I think a support group would have helped to steer these guys in a direction where they truly had gifts and talents.

I've experienced this help in my own life. At one time I had an opportunity to take a job that would have been a significant improvement for me, a job with high prestige and much social recognition. When I ran this by my group they said, "Tony, we know it's very ego-gratifying to be asked to do this, but we know your personality, we know your temperament, we know your gifts. If you become president of that college, two things will happen: you'll ruin the college and the college will ruin you." Then we prayed and talked about it. If it had been up to me, I would have taken the job, but I submitted myself to my brothers and thus avoided a major disaster.

In discovering the will of God, each of us needs a support group. We must be willing to submit ourselves to the members of that group and not override their judgment when they tell us that what we are about to do is contrary to God's will. God often speaks through our brothers and sisters in Christ much more effectively than he speaks to us directly, because sometimes our egos get in the way of direct communication.

Support groups should be made up of persons of the same sex. The kind of intimacy generated in such a group could lead into sexual relationships if the group were mixed. Often I meet Christians whose lives have been destroyed through sexual involvement outside marriage. In almost every case, the relationship began as a spiritual one—people praying and seeking God's will together. Paul's advice to Timothy was absolutely correct—the older women should minister to the younger women and the older men to the younger men. It's safer that way. (See 1 Timothy 5:1, 2.)

Choose people who are like you so they will understand you; choose people with whom you have a natural affinity. Jesus said you should love everybody, but you need not be intimate with everybody. Some people are easier for you to love than others. From those people you can develop a small support group to pray for each other and help each other discover God's will.

The people in a support group should be of comparable social and educational backgrounds so they understand each other best. They must also be bold enough to be able to advise each other correctly. They must not be the least bit intimidated by each other. For instance, I would never invite one of my students into a support group because a student would be intimidated by me. Likewise, an employee would probably be intimidated by an employer. Family members, especially close ones, might not have the objectivity to participate in such a support group. A balance must also be sought in terms of personality types. One very laid back, passive type would be overwhelmed by several strongly assertive personalities, and conversely, one outspoken leader might take over and dominate a group of more reticent, easy-going friends. There must be a feeling of equality—of honesty and openness.

Finally, a support group must be solidly based on Scripture, committed to becoming totally surrendered to God. This isn't just a group of Christians, this is a group of Christians coming together for the purpose of growing in the Spirit.

Searching for God's will is an everyday, continuous process. Vital to this process is a small, intimate group of trusted Christians who will listen to your choices, help you think through the alternatives in light of who you are and in light of God's Word, and pray with you about it. After all that is done and when agreement is reached, you will have found God's will. Then your next decision will be to surrender to it.

◆ DETERMINING GOD'S WILL
DAVE VEERMAN

Are you facing a difficult decision that isn't specifically covered in Scripture—such as where to go to college, how to spend your money, or whether or not to put Grandma in a rest home? Follow these steps to be certain of doing God's will.

1. *Focus on God* (Matthew 6:33-34). Are you willing to do what God wants, no matter what it is? Ask yourself these questions: What is God's will for the world? Am I fitting into his plans?

2. *Obey what God has already told you* (Romans 13:8). Is there something you know God wants you to do (quit a bad habit, forgive your sister)? Obey in this known area before venturing into the unknown.

3. *Pray* (Philippians 4:6). Ask God to show you his will, working through the Word, other people, and your mind.

4. *Study the Bible* (2 Timothy 2:15; 3:16, 17). God speaks to us through his Word; we must read it to learn what he has to say. In reading the Bible, look for principles and not specific words or proof texts.

5. *Get counsel* (Proverbs 20:5, 18). Share your concerns with people who know you and who know the Bible. Ask for their advice. Non-Christians who know you well can also offer valuable insight.

6. *Think* (Romans 12:2, James 1:5). Weigh all the facts. Write down your priorities. Analyze past experiences and present goals. Using your head, not your heart, think through the pros and cons of the decision.

7. *Act in confidence* (James 1:6-8). If you have followed the six previous steps, you can make a decision and be confident of God's guidance. Certainly it will be a step of faith, but that's what the Christian life is all about—walking by faith. Remember, "without faith it is impossible to please God" (Hebrews 11:6).

Meetings for Clearness
RICHARD FOSTER

Quakers are known for their belief in personal illumination: God will reveal his will to the individual through an inner witness of the Spirit. When the Quakers got started in seventeenth-century England, there were any number of groups that shared their belief in private revelation. The other groups became increasingly eccentric and survive only in history books. What saved the Quakers from excessive individualism was their willingness to present their personal insights to the community for judgment and counsel.

In the Quaker tradition, one way of learning God's will is through a "meeting for clearness." When people are facing a major decision, they will gather a group together and share their situation with them. With the group, they can discuss ideas and pray together. The idea is that in community they are seeking clearness from the Lord.

Meetings for clearness are often held for couples who are considering marriage. I can't back this up with statistics, but I've heard it said that in the three hundred years the Quakers have held meetings for clearness, there has never been a divorce among couples who have gone through the process.

Another common reason for a meeting for clearness is to help a person make a vocational decision.

I was once present at a meeting for clearness for a fellow who was trying to decide whether he should go to seminary or not. He gathered four of us together besides himself and his wife—my wife and me and another couple. I knew what the man in the other couple believed about seminary. He didn't like it. He thought it destroyed people. And I am favorably disposed toward seminary just by inclination. Maybe that's why the young man asked us both to participate.

We had a meal together. We talked. He shared his dreams. We prayed. We laughed. We sang. We were quiet. But neither the other man nor I ever offered our opinion as to whether or not the young man should go to seminary. In fact, I was really moved by the other man's willingness to listen, even though he could hardly imagine any good thing could come out of seminary.

After we prayed together at the end of our meeting, the young man said, "You know, I just believe I ought to go." We had never said a word for or against seminary, but out of the meeting he had a sense of knowing what he should do. That's how meetings for clearness often work.

Another time, I was in a meeting for clearness for a dear Baptist brother and his wife. They had never done anything like this before, but they had an important vocational decision to make and they wanted to do the Lord's will. They were involved in Christian work that was definitely good, important, and kingdom building, but they felt that the pressures that went along with it were harming their young marriage. Would it be selfish of them to change jobs in order to devote more time to each other? Would it be irresponsible to let down their employers and the people they worked with?

Rather hesitantly they gathered a small group. In this case we offered our counsel. We told them that they were not being selfish and that they did not need to feel guilty. They needed time to develop their marriage. To seek other employment would be a responsible decision for them to make. It was good for them to hear someone say, You have permission. This is not some evil desire that you have. You need to make this move.

How can a meeting for clearness come about?

A meeting for clearness does not have to be large. It can involve as few as half a dozen people who are known for their spiritual wisdom, their maturity, their insight. People who belong to a loving church fellowship can call a group together out of its bosom. The pastor or elders or other leaders of a healthy church can gather a group. Some churches have officially designated groups that are available to help. I've had people ask me to gather a group for them, and that's been great. Others have done it on their own.

If you gather your own group, do it prayerfully. You'll have to fight the tendency to include only your friends, people who are going to agree with you. Such a group will not bring clearness. It will only reinforce what you've already decided. And that isn't the point of a meeting for clearness.

The group does not come together in order to share opinions or prejudices.

It comes to be open to God and to hear what he has to say. The idea is that if we listen to God, he will tell us what he wants us to do. If we do this within the community of faith, discerning people can evaluate how we are doing, help us understand our motives, release us from false guilt, and support us in our decision. God will give us discernment, and we will feel peace—clearness—about the path we are to take.

♦STAYING OPEN TO CHANGE / JANETTE OKE

When we are faced with difficult decisions, we must pray for God's direction, and then we must proceed logically unless God very specifically leads us some other way.

This is why it is important for us to know what Scripture teaches—we need to understand it, so we can obey it. We have to be careful not to confuse our own desires with God's divine will. So often we get our own ideas of what we think would be good for us or for someone else, and we end up pursuing something that might not be God's will at all. We need to look to God for direction and then leave ourselves open to change if he shows us that our plans are not really the best way to go.

Whenever we pray for guidance, we must be open to change. We must realize that we are, after all, human—and thus we can be in error, even though a decision looks completely logical and convincing from our viewpoint. We do not think as God thinks. We do not see things as he sees them.

He can see the future as well as the past and the present, and he can understand what is best for us. What looks like an answer right now might not be the suitable answer down the road, so God in his wisdom and love may withhold what we want in order to give us something better. I don't think God ever denies us things just to deny us. It's always with a purpose.

Only God knows what the future holds, so we should be open to letting him change our direction for us.

The Bible: The Final Authority in Decision Making

LUIS PALAU

The Bible is the final authority on right and wrong. Why? It is the revelation of God, inspired by the Holy Spirit, through which he has given his moral instruction.

The Ten Commandments, for example, are to protect us from ourselves and to protect society itself. We do not always instinctively know right from wrong, although our being made in the image and likeness of God should give us some sense of the "basics." We are a fallen race. Left to ourselves, we would be morally adrift, as the Hitlers and Idi Amins of this world prove.

Relativism is the result of ignoring God's revelation. Our choice is to get back to the Bible or go back to the jungle—a moral jungle. The decay of many European nations can be traced to people's turning their backs on the final authority of the Bible. If God had intended us to live lives of moral relativism—everyone does what feels right at the time—he would have given us Ten Suggestions instead of Ten Commandments.

But how do we know that the Bible is reliable? The first step is definitely a step of faith, but the proof is in the result that such a step produces. As we begin to put into practice what the Bible teaches, we find that God delivers on his promises. His Word is true, for it describes the world as it really is and brings the renewed life that Jesus offers.

To follow the moral imperatives of the Bible, one must first read it. That may sound obvious, but many people either attack or doubt the Bible but seldom read it. I have been reading the Scriptures regularly for more than thirty years, and I still discover new things. Second, we agree to live under the new covenant, ready to obey the commands that Jesus gives. Most issues of right and wrong in the New Testament are quite simple and clear; no matter how painful some may seem, they are not difficult to understand. In the familiar words of Mark Twain, "It's not the things that I don't understand about the Bible that bother me, it's the things I do understand."

The Bible does not, however, pretend to give instruction on every problem known to humanity, so there are times when God's will seems unclear. These are times when we apply biblical principles and sanctified common sense, guided by the indwelling Holy Spirit. We learn to walk in the Spirit and be sensitive to God by saturating ourselves with the Scriptures.

The apostle Paul said, "Let the peace of Christ rule in your hearts, since as members of one body you were called to peace. And be thankful. Let the word of Christ dwell in you richly" (Colossians 3:15, 16). The picture is of a referee ruling in our lives—we keep playing the game and enjoying ourselves, but we must be quick to listen for the referee's whistle and abide by his decisions.

There are many areas for which we lack God's instruction, but that is what makes the Christian life exciting. After so many years of marriage, I probably know about 95 percent of what my wife, Pat, likes and dislikes. This is wonderful, but that mysterious 5 percent keeps our lives interesting. Similarly, as we read God's Word, we learn his preferences, but he remains a mystery in many ways. He gives us principles, his presence, and the peace of the Holy Spirit, but we are free to choose again and again. As we become mature in Christ, we make better choices and we learn.

♦ GOD'S WILL AND THE AMERICAN DREAM
DAVE VEERMAN

Materialism is part of our culture—the American Dream includes personal ownership and accumulation of things. Some Americans believe that God wants all Christians to be always wealthy and healthy. Reread James 1, however, and see what follows the discussion of God's will. James immediately talks about facing difficulties and problems. Don't forget that Jesus was crucified and that millions have suffered and died for their faith. Jesus warned his disciples that they would have trouble in the world (John 16:33). Clearly God's will may be to take you through some pretty rough times.

Obedience and God's Will

LARRY CHRISTENSON

Faith and obedience are almost interchangeable terms. My faith is revealed as I live in obedience to God, allowing his will to become my will. Sometimes obeying means to accept a truth; at other times obeying may mean to do something God wants done. Obedience is my way of saying yes to God's sovereignty. When I obey, I say, Lord, you are sovereign, and my life is open to you for your will to take place.

There are certain general things we as believers need to obey before we find specific directions for running our lives. It's like practicing the piano: we have to do scales and finger exercises if we hope to play concertos. Everybody is called to obey God's moral laws, to have fellowship with other Christians, and to study the Word. As we obey God in these general areas, we are saying, Lord, I want you to take over my life. I'm going to obey in the areas that are binding on all Christians. As I do, I expect you to become more specific in directing my life.

Obeying God's will is related to obeying his written Word. When we obey God's Word, we are obeying his will. But where the Bible is general, his will for our lives is specific. The Bible lays down general principles; for example, that we should serve God with our life and in our vocation, whatever it is. But the question of which job we should take is specific. If all the jobs we are considering can fit into God's general principles, then we will need to know which particular job is God's will for us.

God speaks to us in a variety of ways. I sometimes think of it as a radio with several channels. Here are some ways he might speak: through *Scripture,* which on some issues will be quite specific; through *circumstances;* through *the counsel of other Christians*—people who know us, our situation, and God's Word; through *an inner witness of the Holy Spirit*; through *spiritual gifts* such as a word of prophecy, of knowledge, or of wisdom; through *one's station in life* (for example, as a father I don't have to wonder if it is God's will for me to get up and go to work; taking care of my family is a requirement of my station in life).

Once I have made a decision, how can I know if I've chosen the right thing? One way God confirms decisions is by bringing unity to those who are seeking his will. In a family, for instance, God may confirm his will by bringing the husband and wife to unity. In a church, the Lord's will may be confirmed by unity among the believers.

On the other hand, how do I know when I am not in God's will? Does he tell me? In order to "hear" God, I need to cultivate the art of listening, being willing to let God speak in the ways he chooses. He may use another person to tell me I'm on the wrong track, as he used Nathan with David (2 Samuel 12). Or he may use any of his other ways of communicating with me. I have to be alert and willing to listen, though, or I may miss his message.

Often God will speak through a channel or a situation that is difficult to take. It is never easy to accept a word of rebuke, no matter who says it. It causes a certain humiliation that should force me not into denial, but into repentance. Then my humiliation can become humility, a positive quality.

Faith and obedience go hand in hand as we walk through life. Our faith expresses itself in obedience; we receive direction for obedience by our faith in God's guidance.

♦ EMOTIONS / DAVE VEERMAN

Emotions can be very persuasive. When you feel good about a decision, you tend to assume it's God's choice as well as your own. But emotions are volatile and unreliable.

How often a girl has been told by more than one guy that it was God's will for her to marry him . . . and him . . . and him! Obviously some of her suitors misread their feelings.

The Bible does not tell us to rely on feelings. Instead, it says to renew our minds. "Then you will be able to test and approve what God's will is—his good, pleasing and perfect will" (Romans 12:2).

Applying God's Will to Our Lives

LARRY CHRISTENSON

Whenever we obey God's Word, we are obeying his will. But his will must become specific. The general principles of the Bible must be turned into specific applications.

For example, the Bible says to go into all the world and preach the gospel. That's a general principle for the church. The specific application of this to my life, however, is found in the answer to such questions as these: What do I do here in my town? Whom would God have me contact? Do I have a ministry in a wider circle? How would he have me live out my part in his Great Commission?

Scripture will communicate God's will to us—sometimes naturally (we read and know what to do), sometimes supernaturally (God speaks in an inner witness of the Holy Spirit to a need in our lives). God may also communicate his will through circumstances, through mature Christian counsel, or even through a conversation with a person where we receive a piece of advice that we recognize as God speaking to us.

God can communicate his will through other people. In families, we will live in greater harmony if we recognize that we are all seeking God's will and that God can choose to speak through anyone. God may speak to parents through their children. I try to listen to my children with real courtesy, not only because of our relationship but because each one is a child of God who may, on occasion, speak God's word to me. Children are limited in their experience, but I can remember specific instances when God spoke to our family through one of the children.

In seeking God's guidance, it is important to remember that everything has to be tuned to Scripture. God's will is never out of tune with his Word.

For instance, one should never seek guidance from a wrong source. A Christian should never use anything having to do with the occult to seek God's will—horoscopes, Ouija boards, spirit mediums. Scripture warns against these.

You can also go off track if you try to make a method out of God's leading. For example, if you prayed for fifteen minutes after reading Psalm 23 and got your answer last time, don't expect God to answer the same way next time. As soon as you make a method out of finding God's will, you are back under the law and are not walking with the living Lord. God might use familiar things to communicate with you, but you have to be sensitive to the vast difference between God's giving to you and your trying to manipulate God.

Can feelings communicate God's will to us? Feelings in tune with the Holy Spirit, free of our own inner desires or motives, can help us find and follow God's will. For instance, we may be seeking God's will for a new job, and he may seem to say no. That could be the Spirit saying, "This is not for you—look elsewhere." But it could also be the Spirit saying, "I want you to persevere in faith."

There is Scripture to support both possibilities. The Spirit has to tell us whether this situation calls for accepting the no answer or going back and trying to get the job anyway. There is no rule of thumb, no method. The Spirit has to sort it out for us, and we have to determine to follow what we understand to be his leading.

All believers are bound by God's Word, but God's specific will for each of us will be different. We must each seek his will individually and follow as he leads. Christianity comes alive when the general becomes specific. People can be lulled into an apathetic state by telling them over and over, "You're saved, God loves you, God forgives you," without ever applying those truths to their individual lives.

Once when my sister was a little girl, she plugged her ears during the sermon and said to our mother in a loud whisper, "Tell me when he's through." After church Mother asked why she did that. She explained, "He kept saying, 'God forgives you, God forgives you, God forgives you,' and I heard him the first time."

Many Christians hear the basic message the first time. What they need then is to hear God's specific and individual application for their own lives. That's what makes the Christian life exciting.

Each of us has a job to do, a calling to fulfill, a partnership with Christ that is highly personal according to the gifts he has given us. Following God's will is truly exciting as we live out the life we have received from him.

Qualified by Need

✍ RICHARD HALVERSON

Having received Jesus as Savior in 1936 in Los Angeles, California, I have walked with Christ for nearly fifty years. As I look back over my life, at every step of the way I can say that God has done things through my weakness rather than because of my strength.

For example, in my last year of seminary when I thought I was going to a chaplaincy in New York, suddenly the job fell through. I was devastated. But thirty minutes later I got a call asking me to go to southern California to be managing director of Forest Home conference grounds for the summer. And that is where I met my wife. Six months later we were married. But I had no idea where we would go from there.

The man who had led me to Christ wanted me to go to Kansas City to assist him in his church. I did. But I had wanted all along to become a military chaplain, so as I worked with him I was also trying to get in at Fort Leavenworth. Everything seemed to be up in the air for a year and a half, and finally, to be fair to my friend, I decided to resign from his church and wait on God about the army chaplaincy.

My friend agreed. Then a week after my resignation was final, I got word that I couldn't be accepted for the chaplaincy because of physical reasons. So my wife and I went back to California and worked at Forest Home for another summer, all the while doing everything I could to link up with the Naval district as a chaplain. But again it didn't work.

Meanwhile I was called to pastor a church, and I knew God was leading me into another kind of ministry. After a year and a half I resigned and joined Louis Evans at Hollywood Presbyterian Church. I declined his invitation four times, and finally he persuaded me to come by telling me I could still pursue what I felt God was leading me toward—the chaplaincy. I stayed at that church for nine years.

One morning Abraham Brady, founder of the Prayer Breakfast movement, dropped in and invited me to become his associate. Then two and a half years later Fourth Presbyterian Church wanted me to become their pastor, and I declined. But they urged me to come and continue my other areas of ministry—and I was there for more than twenty-two years. Then I was called to be Chaplain of the Senate, where I am today.

Not one of those transitions did I initiate myself. Each move came out of my not knowing what I should do. So it is clear to me that whatever God has done with me throughout my life, he has had to work through my weakness. Thus I've learned that weakness is the greatest asset we can offer him. Our need itself is our prime qualification for our pilgrimage with Christ. And his strength is always made perfect in our weakness (2 Corinthians 12:9).

The Glory of the Second Choice

LARRY WARD

I ache for people who think they have made the wrong choices in their lives. "God wanted me to be a missionary," I sometimes hear, "but I turned my back on him." People who say that often imply that one bad choice or decision has damaged their entire lives.

And yet such people need to remember that even if they had said yes, they would not necessarily have been productive missionaries. To be effective, they would have had to keep on saying yes. They would have had to yield their lives, and then keep on yielding them.

They also have to remember that maybe God didn't really want them to go to the mission field at all; maybe he just wanted them to be willing to go.

In any case, once the moment is past, no one is helped by continually looking back at it. Now all these people can do is to take God's gifts of time and choice and choose to do God's will as they currently understand it.

For example, a person who is concerned about world hunger does not necessarily have to fly a light plane across parched deserts in order to do something about it. Right from his suburban home he can write about it, solicit funds, teach Sunday school, or advocate various relief programs. In his own way, he can be a voice that points others to God.

About forty years ago there was an article by Herbert Lockyer in *Christian Digest* about the "glory of the second choice." Addressing himself specifically to people who feel they have missed God's first choice for their lives, he drew attention to the fact that God can still bless them in a significant second choice.

What a mistake it is for people to live in an attitude of negativism because they think they have missed the one great opportunity God offered. With such an oppressive feeling of guilt, these people cannot be responsive to God. They cannot trust and obey him step by step, because they do not think they are on the right path.

Obviously it is best to feel secure in God's first choice for us. He will make his will plain to us if we are really determined to do it; we can be sure of that. I can think back to times when God has practically written with letters of fire in the sky to underline his will for me: Yes! This is the right choice; this is my will. Yes! This is the way you should walk.

But if we think we have missed his first choice for us, we have only one question to ask: Lord, what is your first choice for me now?

We need to remember the character of God. He's not a vengeful God who is trying to find things to hold against us. He's always ready to listen and help when we call on him.

Maybe I missed a step or made a wrong decision for whatever reason yesterday or twenty years ago or five minutes ago. But if I come to God now, he's ready to help. He's always ready to guide me when I seek to know his will so that I can act on it.

♦ HOW GOD CAN USE MY LIFE
ROBERT SCHULLER

God wants to be wherever there are people. As God puts you in places where your life touches others, he's giving you fabulous opportunities to reflect the joy, gladness, and love of Jesus. Whether you're a gas-station attendant, a waitress, a clerk in a store, or a receptionist, you're in a powerful position to be used by God to spread some joy and encouragement and love around.

God can use those in the healing professions, authors, teachers, judges, those involved in social welfare or anthropological activity. If you're in research or scientific development God can surely use you, because he's saving some of his biggest surprises for the next generation; incredible secrets are still locked within our universe waiting to be discovered by mathematicians and research scientists.

There is no area of life where God can't use you. We need to realize continually that no person is too small for God's love and that no project is unimportant in his whole scheme of things. We also need to think big, because God will give us a task in proportion to our view of our own capacity. If we see ourselves as large buckets, God will pour in big challenges, big expectations.

Long-Term Marriage
✍ MADELEINE L'ENGLE

Marriage, like friendship, must be worked at; it requires patience and forbearance and understanding and coming to terms with the person you actually married—rather than the person you might have liked to marry.

My husband, Hugh, and I were married for over forty years until his death. We were well aware that any long-term marriage does not come easily or freely; it has to be constantly worked at, even after many years.

It was very important to me that we be married in a church, and that we say our vows "for richer, for poorer, in sickness and in health, for better or worse, 'til death us do part." I said those promises in front of God, and many times that fact has been what has held me.

All marriages are like a baby. They go through painful periods of growth and change; and it isn't until you arrive at that next stage, each time, that you discover it was worth all those growing pains.

When I became engaged to Hugh, a cousin of mine (now pushing ninety), of whom I'm very fond, said to me, "Now, sex is only a third of the marriage; and it's a very important third. But the other two-thirds are also very important, and sometimes what you do with them can make it or break it."

Much of the other two-thirds is sharing. The most important time in our family was the evening meal. It was a tradition in our marriage that we took time to sit down together for dinner. Sometimes it was at five o'clock and sometimes not until nine, but we ate together with our best china and silver and candlelight. Breaking bread together is sacred, a time to honor each other.

But marriage is not just for ourselves; it is also for others. We cannot grow and nurture our marriages only in isolation, because, especially as Christians, we are aware that we are part of a much greater whole. This is one of the things my husband taught me, because I was an only child and not used to a lot of people. But as a couple we kept our doors open. We had a sizable apartment in New York, and we opened our rooms to friends of our children who came to the city and couldn't afford a hotel. We didn't close our doors on the rest of the world, because part of our marriage was ministry.

Now I see the rest of the two-thirds as compatibility: Do you like the same people? Do you like the same music, the same authors (more or less)? What is your idea of fun? If you agree on these things, then you don't have to worry about others' expectations of you.

Once when Hugh was out mowing the lawn, a woman, knowing we spent part of our year in New York City, stopped and told him she was thinking of moving there. "Tell me all about the hot night spots," she insisted. He just laughed. That was not within our frame of reference. I wouldn't have made it with a man who wanted to rush around to be entertained all the time.

It's important in marriage to be able to have fun together, to have the same basic sense of humor, and also to be able to laugh—gently—at each other. We need to accept our own foibles and fumbles, because we all have them. And mutual laughter is sometimes the best way to cope when things go awry.

I'm not sure how well I would have done with a man who was my political opposite. I'm not an extremist in either direction, but I cherish the beliefs we had in common. I would have great difficulty being married to an extremist. I could not be married to an atheist. Even though Hugh's expression of faith and mine were different, it was the same faith. I was born and raised in the Episcopal church, and it is very important to me now. Although I left the church after all my early years in Anglican boarding schools, I returned; and my way of expressing my faith is symbolic and sacramental. Hugh came out of a staunch Southern Baptist background and moved to the United Church of Christ. So when we were in New York in the winter, we were Episcopalians; and in Connecticut in the summer we were Congregationalists. The two ways of approaching God are different, yet the God we adore is the same one, so it was not a strain on us.

But couples cannot expect to arrive at large compromises without work and sometimes counseling. I suggest premarital instruction as well as counseling during the engagement period, perhaps by a couple who has been married a long time, has gone through problems, and has come our further committed to the union. I think also that some ongoing marriage counseling, dialogue with an expert on recurring issues, can be very valuable.

I knew a Church of England minister who not only counseled couples before marriage for a number of sessions, but every year on their wedding anniversary sent them a letter—he kept up with them all. And very few of the couples that he married got divorced, I'm sure partly due to his follow-through.

The extent of our own marriage counseling was hilarious. We were both actors, working a Philip Barry play, *The Joyous Season,* which was having a long run in Chicago. We had planned to be married in New York but decided not to wait. So one Sunday we set out looking for a church, and we walked into St. Chrysostom's downtown churchyard. When we talked to the minister he asked us, "Have you ever been married before?" and we said no. That was the extent of our marriage counseling. We managed somehow anyway, but things might have been a little easier if we had had a little more help beforehand to let us know what to expect.

Marriage counseling can be especially helpful if the people come from broken homes, as more and more people do. I think young people need to be given a realistic vision of the way marriage is, not an image of peachy perfection. One naive young woman asked, "You mean you quarrel after you're married?" Of course you do, but there are different ways of quarreling: one way is to be nasty and unfair, and the other is to allow disagreements into the open so that they can be dealt with in a healthy way. Coming to each other with differing points of view allows a meeting place for ideas and decisions to be born. If there is no such meeting place in your premarital squabbles, that should serve as a warning.

I have a theory that many of the young couples who live together before marriage today are not rebelling against the morality of their parents' generation, but against the immorality of that generation. So many of them come from homes in which the parents have been married in church and made lofty promises, and then they got divorced and remarried, or were unfaithful but stayed in the relationship. I think the young people don't want that hypocrisy. When they make the promises, they want to be sure they mean them. Some, of course, do not take marriage seriously, but I think it is because they have had their hopes killed of a truly creative and lasting love with someone over the long haul. They haven't seen enough successful models of such marriages.

On the reverse side, I see the church becoming more important to some couples, more involved in their marriages and ongoing family life. The church offers programs such as Marriage Encounter, for instance, and most groups are much more ecumenical than they used to be. People are not shut out when they come for help just because they come from a different tradition; intermarriage between denominations doesn't seem as unusual, and some couples make compromises as did Hugh and I.

I believe that marriage at its best is an icon of the Godhead, of the Trinity. It provides an earthly way for us to understand what the Creator God is like. Thus it is a sacrament, a visible reflection of things invisible. I believe that when two people are joined in this sacrament they become more than the sum of their individual selves. As an icon, a good marriage serves to reveal to the world the possibility of spiritual union. It is a sign of hope, and it is desperately needed in our times.

There always must be the incarnational side—two people, flesh and blood, somehow, imperfectly, pointing to these holy things. If our marriage has been graced by a long duration, it's not due to us. It has been and always will be God's grace. We never accomplish anything just on our own merit. Unless the Spirit is working, nothing is going to happen.

I remember once, around our thirty-fifth wedding anniversary, it was snow-ing and I was going somewhere in a taxi. I mentioned to the taxi driver that my husband and I had been married thirty-five years, and that for a writer and an actor, that was really quite a record. He took his hands off the wheel, turned around, and said, "Lady, that's not a record—that's a miracle!" And he was absolutely right.

◆ BEFORE YOU DECIDE TO MARRY
JANETTE OKE

Our dreadful divorce statistics should force us to take a closer look at our premarriage decisions.

I believe the husband has been given the position of head of the home. If the husband and wife cannot resolve a difference of opinion, it is the wife who is supposed to submit. Sometimes, however, this relationship deteriorates, and the husband becomes a tyrant. This is not what God intended at all.

Because submission is difficult in good marriages and dangerous in bad ones, it is very important that a woman look carefully at the man she is in love with before she marries him. She should ask herself some hard questions: Will I be willing to submit to him? Where will it lead me? Will he love me as God intended? If she discovers she is unwilling to submit to this man, then she should look for another partner. Only if she can see him as he is and still love him enough to submit to him joyfully does she stand a good chance of creating a good marriage with him.

Guidance in Marriage
✍ INGRID TROBISCH

When I was a small girl, my father explained to me in a very natural way where babies come from. Then he said, "You are not too young to pray for the boy who will someday become your husband." I took that advice seriously. When I had dates as a high school and college student, I would have a little dialogue with the Lord. "Is he the one?" I'd ask, and he'd say, "No, not yet. Wait."

After a while the waiting didn't seem to make any sense. I thought surely by the time I left for my first mission appointment in Africa I would have a husband. But I didn't. And then one evening in a small town in Germany, Walter got up to speak, and it was as if the Lord said, "This is the one you've been praying for."

The Lord may not always point out mates that specifically, but I would like to think he guides us to the mate he has in mind for us. My old boyfriends may be very nice men with fine families, but I have a hard time imagining walking those twenty-seven years with any man besides Walter and still being in the center of God's will.

Now and then you hear of a case where a man says to a woman—or a woman says to a man—"The Lord has told me that we should marry each other." I believe that it has to be a mutual telling. If the Lord tells one person, he will tell the other. I didn't know it at the time, but more than a year before the Lord pointed Walter out to me, he had pointed me out to Walter. If someone said the Lord had told him I should marry him, and the Lord had not given me the same message, I'd just say, "Well, he hasn't told me."

It's possible, of course, that God would pick out someone who might not get the message. Gladys Aylward, for example, prayed and had the deep assurance that when she went to China God would send her the one he had chosen for her. But he simply didn't come. He must have been disobedient to God's call.

If you're in doubt about marrying a particular person, don't do it. Wait until you feel certain. There are many things worse than not being married. One of them is being married to the wrong man. Another is getting married too young. I think it was a great plus for me that I was twenty-six and Walter was twenty-eight when we got married. Both of us had already had full careers. I had taught for two years in Cameroon, and he had been pastor of a large church. It's helpful to be established before getting married. Otherwise you have to grow up together. That can be great too, but beginning a marriage while either of you is still in school may mean you will have more struggles.

On the other hand, it is certainly better to get married and be legal about it than to live together in a trial marriage. Sometimes Walter would talk with a couple who would say, "We can't get married because we don't have our furniture yet." If they were otherwise ready for marriage, he'd say, "Forget it—you can live with camp cots if you have to."

Although most of us tend to rush ahead of God, some people seem unable to come to decisions. They wait endlessly, because they are not absolutely certain about God's will. But you have to go one way or the other, and sometimes you just have to take that first step. As long as you are not disobeying God, he will continue to guide you. If he wants you to go in the other direction, he'll turn you around.

If you're going to get married, you have to get engaged. Why not go ahead and get engaged, and let the engagement be a trial period? Not of sleeping together, but of checking out how this marriage would fit into God's plans for both of you. Walter did this. He was engaged to a young woman who, like him, was serious about obeying God's will. Neither one could come to any peace about the proposed marriage. It was a happy day for both of them when they broke the engagement a year later. And the day the engagement was officially broken, he received the invitation to come to the States to study. That's where we met.

Here are some ideas that will help you recognize the person God wants you to marry:

1. *Don't think about getting married until you're grown up.* It's good for the young woman to be at least twenty-three or twenty-four—old enough to know who she is and to have learned how to live alone. Sometimes it takes a young man longer than that.

2. *Marry someone you love.* It is not in God's will to unite you forever with someone you don't enjoy being with. The two of you should be able to talk for hours on end without getting bored.

3. *Marry someone whose sense of time is compatible with your own.* Some people, when they say they'll be home at 6:00, really mean 5:45. Others mean midnight. You and your partner do not need to have identical approaches to the clock, but if you can't accept each other's attitudes, your marriage will be a catastrophe.

4. *Look carefully at your future spouse's parents.* Child abusers create child abusers. A young woman should observe how her young man's father treats his mother. Wife abuse also is handed down from father to son. Of course, God can heal people from simply dreadful homes. How long has your beloved been a Christian? What kind of walk has he or she had? What kind of grandparents does he or she have? I'm convinced that sometimes children are saved because of good grandparents.

5. *Get to know your future spouse in normal settings.* Do everyday things together: wash clothes, go shopping, clean house for an older person, hang wallpaper. You really find out who the other person is when you do a project together.

6. *Get some kind of third-party counseling.* Talk to your pastor or a trusted teacher, or attend a retreat for engaged couples. Take a personality inventory to see if you understand each other. We've had young people break their engagement because they discovered they didn't really know each other. They were just projecting their own image onto the other person, and this person wasn't that way at all.

7. *Don't let your engagement last forever.* If you're together most of the time, six months is long enough for you to know for sure if you're meant for each other. If you're apart and can't see each other often, you might want to wait a year. If you still have doubts at the end of this time, this may not be the marriage partner God has in mind for you.

♦ LEARNING TO LIVE ALONE
INGRID TROBISCH

Marriage will not cure problems of deep loneliness. There is only one thing harder than living by yourself, and that is living with another person. It is important to learn how to live alone before trying to live as a couple. Either way, you have to be at peace with yourself or you will be unhappy.

♦ SIX TESTS OF LOVE / WALTER TROBISCH

1. *The sharing test:* Are we able to share together? Do I want to become happy or make happy?
2. *The strength test:* Does our love give us new strength and fill us with creative energy, or does it take away our strength and energy?
3. *The respect test:* Do we respect each other? Am I proud of my partner? Would I want him (or her) to be the father (or mother) of my children?
4. *The habit test:* Do we only love each other or do we also·

like each other? Am I willing to accept the other person—habits, shortcomings, and all?
5. *The quarrel test:* Are we able to forgive each other and to give in to each other?
6. *The time test:* Has our love summered and wintered? Have we known each other long enough?
(Adapted from Walter Trobisch, *I Married You* [New York: Harper and Row, 1971], 75-77.)

RELATED ARTICLES
Chapter 4: **God's Will**
Chapter 5: **The Quest for Obedience**
Chapter 11: **Did I Marry the Wrong Person?**

CHAPTER

23

Christians in the Work Force

- ✓ How can I know which career God wants me to follow?
- ✓ How do I keep my daily routine from dragging me down spiritually?
- ✓ Does money—or lack of it—hinder Christian growth?
- ✓ What is the Christian view of money?

Christians and Stress

JOHN R. THROOP

Is it normal for Christians to feel stress? Or is stress somehow a denial of the power of God in our lives and of our trust in him?

The Bible seems to indicate that stress is evidence of a life that is not in conformity to God's will. Jesus clearly expects his followers to have a high level of trust. He said, "Do not worry about your life, what you will eat or drink;

or about your body, what you will wear. Is not life more important than food, and the body more important than clothes? Look at the birds of the air; they do not sow or reap or store away in barns, and yet your heavenly Father feeds them. . . . So do not worry, saying, 'What shall we eat?' or 'What shall we drink?' or 'What shall we wear?' For the pagans run after all these things, and your heavenly Father knows that you need them. But seek first his kingdom and his righteousness, and all these things will be given to you as well. Therefore do not worry about tomorrow, for tomorrow will worry about itself. Each day has enough trouble of its own" (Matthew 6:25, 26, 31-34).

Jesus calls his followers not to worry about their lives. Paul also advised those who would be Christians to follow his own example: "Do not be anxious about anything, but in everything, by prayer and petition, with thanksgiving, present your requests to God. And the peace of God, which transcends all understanding, will guard your hearts and minds in Christ Jesus" (Philippians 4:6, 7). To live a life of anxiety or stress would seem to be living a life contrary to what God expects of us.

Yet we all experience anxiety or stress at many points in our lives. Sometimes stress happens when times are hard—when a loved one has died, or when we have lost a job. Other times stress is related to a good event, but one that still brings on anxiety—graduating from college or getting married or beginning the first job in our career. Day in and day out there are times of stress and anxiety for even the most mature Christian.

To be faced with anxiety or stress seems to be part of the human condition, a part of our fallenness. Not all things in life are certain, and we often desire to have a larger measure of control than we actually do. So perhaps, Is it normal for Christians to feel stress? is the wrong question. The more important question is this: In a world filled with stress, what should the Christian's attitude be?

Stress is a part of living. It is the tension of being alive; our human response to the world that surrounds us, the creation that God has given us. Yet stress can build up to unacceptable levels, and ultimately stress can kill. Stress as a part of human life must be accepted, but how we cope with stress will determine what part it plays in our lives.

Stress is both a physiological and a psychological response. A situation presents itself, and stress is our preparation for response. Stress mobilizes all the body's resources to come to a point of decision.

Ancient human beings faced stress when they encountered a wild animal. In a split second, as soon as they saw the animal (the stresser), their adrenal glands were activated and they decided whether to fight or flee. Their bodies and minds were prepared for either course of action.

Today we do not face wild animals, but we have stresses that evoke in us the same "fight or flight" reaction. The difference between us and those ancient hunters is that we cannot be as spontaneous in our response. Let's say the boss comes into your office late Friday afternoon and says, "Jones, I want these financial reports in final form by Monday at 8:30 in the morning." You have a wonderful weekend planned with your family and important church business to attend to on Sunday morning. The workload is really too much for you, yet you want to please your boss because you are hoping for a raise.

Faced with dangerous or difficult situations, all humans have the "fight or flight" response. Only you and I react more guardedly than the ancient hunters did. Our instinct may be to fight the boss, even to the point of a punch in the nose. But more often we choose to flee instead, because we fear the risks involved with fighting. Jones may have begun to perspire. His face may be flushed, his fists clenched, his jaw tight, his back stiff. But Jones mutters, "No problem" to the boss's demands.

Jones goes home, having internalized the stress. By now his stomach is churning as his anger mounts. He opens the door, hoping to unload his troubles on his understanding and caring wife, but she greets him by saying, "Guess what Tracy did today?" In his first three minutes home, Jones learns that Tracy fell off her bike and needed ten stitches. Drew, his son, got into a fight with a neighbor kid whose father is sure to phone soon for a talk.

As Jones goes to change into more comfortable clothes, the phone rings. It is the pastor asking him whether he can make a special and very important meeting tomorrow morning at the church. Jones, feeling obligated to go, says yes although that will mean time away from both his family and his work assignment. You can imagine how Jones is feeling now. His life is out of control, and he feels absolutely wrung out.

Jones is suffering from a negative form of stress: distress. This stress is ruining his health. It results in far more than migraine headaches, stomach ulcers, and similar maladies associated with stress. Bad stress has been linked to six of the biggest killers in America: heart disease, cancer, lung disease, cirrhosis of the liver, suicide, and stroke. It aggravates chronic diseases such as diabetes and multiple sclerosis. It accelerates the aging process and suppresses the body's immune system. Thus persons under severe stress tend to become ill much more frequently, and their illnesses last far longer than do those of people under more normal loads of stress.

There are levels of stress that are comfortable to live with as well as levels that are uncomfortable. Researchers assign points to life events, both good and bad, to help us determine what level of stress we face. If our level is high, even if we manage well, we still find ourselves tired—even exhausted—as our bodies seek a balance from being "up" all the time.

For example, in a single calendar year I moved three times, got married, carried a heavy workload as an assistant pastor in an active church, was invited to take my first full-time church assignment where I would be on my own, and learned I was going to become a father for the first time. In addition, my wife and I had to make some major financial decisions connected with our marriage and our moving.

We have always joked that we chose to get the majority of our stresses out of the way in one year so that we could lead a quiet and normal life afterward. Of course, that is not the case. Nor would we want it to be. But we both experienced a deep sense of tiredness after that eventful year that took nearly one more year to overcome, with the additional stress of living each day. Check out your stress level—it may explain why you feel the way you do.

Not all stress is distress. Some stress, such as that caused by getting married, wanting and conceiving children, and getting a new job, is good stress—but we react physically and psychologically nonetheless. The distinguished stress researcher Hans Selye coined the term *eustress,* or good stress, to describe those stimuli that produce anxiety for good.

Human beings cannot live without stimulation. Even some distress may be good for us, for by that distress we determine the seriousness of a situation and thereby gauge our response. But how is it possible to cope with stress in a Christian manner? How can one be faithful in stressful situations? How can one find that peace "which transcends all understanding"?

First, we must understand that much of life is beyond our control. Much of our distress and worry arises from our illusion that somehow we are much more in control of our destinies than we really are. We act as though we were God, even when we clearly recognize his sovereignty in our lives. We forget that we live our lives under God, subject to his will.

Yes, we have responsibilities to the commitments we make, but we must always keep in clear focus that we are under God and thus do not control our lives. We must listen carefully to him and realize that what is happening around us and through us is not just our own lives being lived out; it is part of a greater work that God is doing. We must be careful in stressful moments to focus not on what we do or on what the other persons in the situation are doing, but to be open to what God could be doing at this time.

It's a great relief not to be as God, but to be under him, to be led by him. When we give up trying so hard to control what happens to us, and when we accept our limitations—we cannot do everything or be everything—then the accumulation of stress in our lives begins to disappear. The result is the peace that passes understanding, what Alcoholics Anonymous calls serenity. In fact, they use the Serenity Prayer, which sums up how a Christian can deal effectively with stress: "God grant me the serenity to accept the things I cannot change, the courage to change the things I can, and the wisdom to know the difference."

Stress—whether distress or eustress—can either help us grow and develop, or it can break us. It can help our Christian growth by reminding us of our human limitations and of the need always to be seeking God's will. Christian faith helps us recognize that what is happening in this world is far larger than what we can see or feel or touch or smell or taste, far larger than the events that seem so large and potent in our lives. Our faith shows us God at work in the events that affect us. It helps us trust fully and completely in him as the provider of all good, to recognize with Paul that "in all things God works for the good of those who love him, who have been called according to his purpose" (Romans 8:28).

Too much stress reminds us of our human finitude and creatureliness. It also reminds us that a balanced life is the life God desires for us, a life of health and joy—spiritual, mental, and physical. God has given us our bodies on loan. We are to care for them and to glorify him in them. He wants stress to affect us positively, energizing us for the work he has given us to do—not to debilitate us.

The first step in coping with stress, then, is to understand that we cannot control everything. The second step is to plan a sensible life-style that gives us some measure of relief from the pressures we will inevitably face.

We can take measures to ensure that stress does not become a debilitating force in our lives. In order to live a balanced life, we must recognize that God is to be worshiped above all. Thus an essential element in managing stress is to take quiet time. Set aside a period of time every day, at least half an hour (split into morning and evening shifts, if need be) for study and meditation on Scripture and for quiet prayer. Don't think of it as another task to be accomplished and checked off in a busy day, but rather as the preface and conclusion for the business. Prayer and meditation help to put the business of life into proper perspective, which is a large part of winning the battle against stress.

It is also important to take care of yourself. Take time every day to exercise. Physical activity is a wonderful counteractive measure against stress build-up. It is a physical release of pent-up energy. I run every day, and I schedule my running time on my calendar to be sure that other events do not crowd it out. You may have other methods of making sure you exercise—but you need to take that time to keep your life in balance.

It is a good idea to cultivate a hobby or outside interest that is noncompetitive and that does not involve responsibility to work or to family. Some paint, others fish, others garden or build model ships or airplanes. I lose myself in crossword puzzles. I don't feel I have to complete them; just playing with the words gives me satisfaction.

Friendships are vital, too, to maintaining a balanced life. Deep friendships allow true sharing and intimacy about what really is important in life. They provide perspective, vitally important for seeing God at work. Friendships need time for cultivation, so you need to set regular time aside to lay aside your work and spend time with your friends. Time with your spouse is essential. That is one friendship you can keep up on a regular basis, but it is by no means the only friendship you should have.

Stress, then, is an ever-present factor in human life. The Christian is not immune to stress simply because he has faith in Jesus Christ. All human beings experience distress and eustress. How we cope with stress is what makes the difference.

For Christians, the proper response to stress is to realize that Jesus Christ is all-sufficient for what really matters. Then we need to understand that God desires a balanced and wholesome life for each of his people. These two insights free us to live out the principles of our faith. Since God is capable and in charge, we do not have to control every aspect of our lives. Trusting our loving God, we can take the time to do what needs to be done to make our lives balanced, harmonious, and healthy.

A Christian Look at Vocation

HUDSON T. ARMERDING

In Scripture there are two aspects to calling. The first, illustrated in Romans 8, deals with God's effectual call unto salvation and justification. The second, mentioned in 1 Corinthians 7, is the calling to a particular vocation or way of life. So Scripture speaks of calling into the family of God, and then calling to activity as part of the family of God.

Within the category of calling to activity within the family of God, there are two areas of focus. The first is within the church. In 1 Corinthians 12:4-6 Paul said, "There are different kinds of gifts, but the same Spirit. There are different kinds of service, but the same Lord. There are different kinds of working, but the same God works all of them in all men." In other words, God equips each of us and assigns us a place within the body where we have unique functioning. This is a calling within the body of Christ for ministry to the body of Christ.

Then there is a calling within society. First of all, we have the creation mandate found in Genesis 1: We are to subdue the earth, control it, and have oversight over it. Second, in the New Testament Jesus makes it plain that we are called to be salt and light in our society.

Many people ask, How do I know what I'm called to do in particular? We need first of all to make a commitment to the Lord that we will do whatever God wants us to do. It's not a matter of just responding to what looks attractive or what is going to pay the best salary or have the best retirement benefits. It's a matter of deliberately subjecting ourselves to the Lord, saying, "I am under your sovereignty and want to do what you want me to do."

After doing that, we need to analyze our capabilities. We can screen out areas where God obviously wouldn't call us to work. For example, a person with excellent mechanical skills but who is poor in abstract thinking would not be called to become a professor of philosophy. The reverse is also true: the professor of philosophy wouldn't be called to be an automobile mechanic if he didn't have those natural capabilities.

If after this analysis God orders our circumstances so that an attractive opportunity comes up, we should, by faith, accept it.

We need to realize that God does not always call us immediately to what will be our ultimate calling in life. There are temporary, short-term calls that can flow together in preparation for God's major calling for us. A study of the characters in Scripture makes this plain.

Look at Moses, who had a splendid preparation in Egypt, but then needed forty years in the desert to temper his impulsiveness until he was balanced enough—at age eighty—to lead God's people.

Or look at Joseph, who had to spend an apprenticeship as a slave and as a prisoner before being called to assist Pharaoh in governing Egypt.

Moses' and Joseph's experiences indicate that God not only calls us, he also prepares us through sometimes difficult circumstances until our calling and our abilities coincide. If we try to accelerate things or press too hard, we may upset the exquisite supernatural timing that takes place in the providence of God. It is better to accept a temporary calling without believing it is the final place of service, trusting God that future opportunities will build on this preparation.

♦ KINDS OF VOCATIONS
HUDSON T. ARMERDING

Every activity that is not explicitly forbidden in Scripture is legitimately open as a vocation to a believer.

God dignifies all work, so it's not appropriate for a person to feel that what he or she is doing is insignificant compared to what Billy Graham or Mother Teresa are doing. In God's sight, the important thing is to follow his call, whether to an obscure or a prominent position. Being a seller of purple, a centurion, a servant, or a carpenter can all be callings from God.

In 1 Corinthians 12, Paul talked about how the "weaker" parts are needful for the functioning of the whole body. That should assure us—especially if we haven't been called to something glamorous—that our work is significant in God's sight and necessary for the full functioning of God's whole enterprise in the world.

A Christian View of Daily Work
✍ ADRIAN ROGERS

All daily work can be sacred. The Bible says in Proverbs 14:23, "All hard work brings a profit." Our work should be a blessing, not a source of boredom; dignity, not drudgery; meaningful, not monotonous.

We've artificially divided work up into the secular and the sacred, but the Bible doesn't do that. Our job ought to be our place of ministry, our place of service to the Lord Jesus. Where we work is to be our temple of devotion and our lamp stand for witness.

When Paul wrote to the Ephesians about work, he said, "Slaves, obey your earthly masters with respect and fear, and with sincerity of heart, just as you would obey Christ" (Ephesians 6:5). That means that every Christian should regard his or her work as sacred. We need to realize that when we go to the job, we're working not only for our employer but also for Jesus.

As a pastor I've seen many people who want to quit their jobs so they can go into "full-time Christian service." In their minds this means being a minister or missionary or on the staff of a Christian organization. God calls people to these types of jobs, and this is great; but it does not somehow make these jobs more sacred than others.

In the New Testament every day is a holy day, every place is sacred, and every deed is spiritual service when a person is living and walking in the Spirit. If we don't understand that, we're going to be miserable on our jobs, wanting to leave them so we can "serve Jesus." We won't realize that the Lord wants us to serve him right where we are.

Our jobs are the best places of all to witness for Jesus and to serve him. Here are some guidelines on how to do that:

1. *Do not brag.* In Matthew 5:16 Jesus said, "Let your light shine before men, that they may see your good deeds and praise your Father in heaven." The job is a tremendous lamp stand, but our light is to glow, not to glare. Others are to see the light and not the candle. Self-righteous people are obnoxious everywhere, but especially at work.

2. *Do not nag.* Don't always be talking down to the unsaved people around you—they will hate to see you coming. Colossians 4:5, 6 tells us, "Be wise in the way you act toward outsiders; make the most of every opportunity. Let your conversation be always full of grace, seasoned with salt, so that you may know how to answer everyone." The Christian who comes to work preaching to people needs to understand that the pulpit is the place for preaching. No one has ever been nagged to Jesus.

3. *Do not lag.* Christians on the job ought to carry even more than their part of the workload. It's an absolute sin for believers to do less than their best. Ephesians 6:6 says, "Obey them [your bosses] not only to win their favor when their eye is on you, but like slaves of Christ, doing the will of God from your heart." In other words, we're not to be clock-watchers, but Christ's servants doing God's will from the heart. We should have such a reputation for good work that when an employer goes to an employment agency to get workers, she should say, "If you have any Christians, please send them over." Colossians 3:23 tells us, "Whatever you do, work at it with all your heart, as working for the Lord, not for men."

4. *Do not sag.* Never let down in your Christian life, never compromise. Keep full of joy, because God's joy is your strength. You need to store up on that joy in the morning before you go to work. You need to live victoriously on that job, because people who don't know the Lord are watching you. I have observed that most people in the work place aren't all that interested in heaven or hell—what they really want to know is how to hack it on Monday. When they see victory in your life, they're going to want to know why.

In 1 Peter 3:15 the apostle wrote, "Always be prepared to give an answer to everyone who asks you to give the reason for the hope that you have." And we're to do it in meekness and fear. When others see us living in victory on the job, then we're going to have a very effective opportunity to witness.

As Christians we need to see that our daily job has eternal significance, because we're serving Jesus while we work.

♦ ARE SOME JOBS MORE CHRISTIAN THAN OTHERS? / DAVID McKENNA

It is biblical to say that every Christian must be in ministry, but to say that one job is more Christian than another is false. A Christian can have a ministry in any number of jobs.

We should not imagine a ladder with the most Christian job at the top and the least Christian job at the bottom. That isn't biblical. The ladder has to be laid flat, so that almost every vocation becomes a potential ministry for the Christian. I use the word *vocation* instead of job, because vocation carries the sense of calling.

One day at Seattle Pacific University, I walked out to my car and saw a girl pulling weeds in the garden. When I said hello to her, I recognized her as one of the previous year's graduates. I asked why she was pulling weeds. She replied, "I'm waiting for a teaching career in English to open up. And I'm learning so much here—for right now, this is my ministry." What a positive view she brought to the idea of ministry. No one could tell her that teaching would be more spiritual than landscaping.

We make a job "Christian" by the quality of the work we do, our honesty and integrity. When a tire store in our town discovered six employees stealing their inventory, they fired the culprits and called our seminary to see if six students would be interested in working. Why? "Your students know how to work, and they are honest."

That's a Christian testimony. It is not that some jobs are more Christian than others, but that a Christian can make any job a ministry and a means of witness.

The Three *R*s of Choosing a Career

DAVID McKENNA

In my years of counseling college young people who are at the point of choosing careers, I find that among Christian students the most important question is, How can I find God's will for my life? Certainly part of that is the question of career.

This question is not restricted to college students. I also hear it from older people ready to move into a second or third career. For people who are growing and changing, it's a question that must be faced all through life.

As I've faced career changes in my life, I've worked up a simple, Bible-based formula for helping me make specific decisions about career options. I call it "The Three *R*s for Finding the Will of God." The three *R*s are *Reason, Righteousness,* and *Revelation.*

I must preface these steps by saying that too often, when we seek God's will in a certain career choice, we want to short-circuit the process. We want the revelation without having gone through the process of reason and righteousness. But to make a solid decision, we have to be willing to take the steps in turn.

1. *Reason.* I am a firm believer that God has given us intelligence and his Word to help us discern his will. It is amazing how many people make erroneous decisions when Scripture makes some things perfectly clear.

Where Scripture does not give specific directives, Christians need to use common sense with reference to career choices. We can ask ourselves basic questions about our gifts and our interests. Do we want to work with people? Or do we prefer working with things or numbers or ideas? Reason can tell us certain basic things about ourselves and help us place that information against the known facts about the decision at hand. I don't think God will mismatch our career calling and our gifts. So we use our reason to do all the research we can and to study his Word in order to make discriminating choices.

I have developed three specific, personal questions relating to my own gifts and interests. I believe these questions are Spirit-given and reason-guided, and they help me make intelligent decisions about opportunities presented to me. In any job I have I need to be able to minister. If I cannot minister, I cannot be in that career. I have the gift of leadership, so I need to be able to lead. I also have a desire to be creative, so I need work that leaves room for some kind of developmental and innovative thinking.

When I consider a job offer, these are my criteria: (1) How can I serve? (2) How can I lead? (3) How can I create? If I cannot answer these questions satisfactorily, I know the job is not for me. For example, I once turned down a position because, though I could serve, I was supposed to be a manager in a maintenance function rather than a leader in a creative function.

These are the questions I ask; your questions will be different if your gifts and interests are different. It is not wise to copy someone else's questions, but it is very important to have questions of your own.

Reason, when it is enlightened by the Holy Spirit, is vital to discovering God's will in a job choice. But reason has to be complemented by righteousness.

2. *Righteousness.* This step involves asking, Is my heart right with God? It is a false assumption that God will lead me through my reason if my heart isn't right with him. How can God get through to me if I'm not listening? My mind must be ready, but so must my heart. It is best not to ask this question only when a crisis arises and a decision needs to be made. Instead, ask it every day and stay in tune with God.

If I am using my God-given reason and living according to God's will, then I need to wait for the third *R.*

3. *Revelation.* If you have had a thorough reason and righteousness checkup, you may need to say to the Lord, "I need some evidence of the right way, some leading from you"—in other words, revelation. And when you come to that critical turning point, some evidence will come. The Lord will reveal himself. But he won't do it with a premature sign in the sky; he won't do it until you've had reason and righteousness as starting points.

God's will for your career is not some tangled mystery that he is trying to keep you from discovering. God wants to tell you his will as much as you want to know it. You need have no doubts that you're doing what God wants. You and he, working together, will come up with the answer, but remember, it's one step at a time.

◆ WHAT IF I CAN'T FIGURE OUT MY CALLING? / HUDSON T. ARMERDING

God will not punish us if we can't figure out what our calling is, as long as we're asking God for his wisdom (James 1:5) and eagerly desiring the best gifts (1 Corinthians 12:31). Proverbs 3:5, 6 tells us: "Trust in the Lord

with all your heart and lean not on your own understanding; in all your ways acknowledge him, and he will make your paths straight."

Punishment would be the result of refusing to pay attention or deliberately disobeying. If we have a clear call but respond, "I'm sorry, but that's not glamorous enough," or "It doesn't have enough benefits," then I think God will reprimand us.

If we can't figure out what our calling is, though, we are not disobeying. We ought to be content to trust God and wait, to "be still before the Lord and wait patiently for him" (Psalm 37:7).

Are Quality and Excellence Christian Traits?

✍ YFC EDITORS

Murphy's Law states that if anything can go wrong, it will. While no one is quite sure who this Mr. Murphy is or was, we are all too familiar with the truth of his insightful dictum. And over the years, a number of corollaries have been added. It has been said, for example, that the appliance will break right after the warranty expires. Too many consumers can identify with that statement having purchased the toaster or television and watched it fall apart a few months later. Whatever happened to quality? they wonder.

Whether it is a product or a service, poor workmanship seems to be epidemic in our society. The operative seems to be to do whatever makes a buck and to do as little as possible to get by.

As Christians, however, we are called to a higher standard: excellence. Writing to first-century slaves, Paul said, "Whatever you do, work at it with all your heart, as working for the Lord, not for men, since you know that you will receive an inheritance from the Lord as a reward. It is the Lord Christ you are serving" (Colossians 3:23, 24). Whatever our "role" or job, therefore, we must do our best for our employer: God.

Christians should be committed to quality and excellence also because *all* that we do must be done for God's glory (1 Corinthians 10:31). "All" means everything; this command is not limited to worship and praise in church or to "Christian work."

In addition, Christians should work hard and well as a part of their stewardship of God's resources. We have been given time, talent, and treasure, which we are to invest for the kingdom of God. As responsible stewards, we must not squander or hoard these resources (Matthew 25:14-30).

Finally, work done by Christians should be marked by quality because it reflects on our moral standards. If we don't give a full day's work for which we accept pay, we are stealing from our employer and being dishonest. As followers of Jesus Christ, we are to called to stand out from the crowd as "light," "salt," and good moral examples. We must not dishonor his name by stooping to the accepted level of behavior and workmanship.

Christians must be committed to excellence in all they do, not according to the world's standards or to make more money, but because our faith in Christ demands it. He is our "boss," we live to glorify him, we are good stewards of his resources, and we have a high moral standard. "Each one should test his own actions. Then he can take pride in himself, without comparing himself to somebody else" (Galatians 6:4).

Work, Work, Work!

DAVE VEERMAN

Lightly holding the microphone in her left hand, and with a serious smile and carefully outlined eyes sparkling, she turns to the camera and begins to speak softly. "I used to perform for my own glory, trying to achieve fame and fortune." She pauses for a moment and lifts her right hand heavenward as she continues, "But now I sing for Jesus! And at every performance, at Vegas or in church, I give all the glory to him."

Behold, the "Christian" entertainer—and there are Christian wrestlers, dancers, golfers, doctors, waiters, artists, and on and on—all claiming to do their special type of work for the glory of God. It seems as if every occupation is open to the designation "Christian," from entomologists to entrepreneurs and homemakers to hammock makers. A few years ago I even read the "testimony" of a "Christian" stripper! Is this possible? Or are there some jobs that are off limits to Christians?

It is true that *everything* we do should be done for God's glory (Colossians 3:17), but this does *not* mean that we can do everything. There are very clear, biblical principles that should govern how we live, including what we do for a living. Let us consider these.

1. *We must obey God's commands* (1 Samuel 15:22; Acts 5:29). Throughout Scripture, there is a strong call to obedience—doing what God has told us in every situation. This principle has several applications for our occupations.

God does not contradict himself and will not tell us to do something that violates his previous commands. God will not "call" us to sin. It would be impossible, therefore, to be a "Christian" prostitute, a "Christian" gangster, or a "Christian" drug dealer.

The end does not justify the means. In other words, it is never right to sin for "good" reasons or to achieve a "righteous" goal. Therefore, a person who steals money to give it to poor people is misled. "Christian" bank robber is a contradiction of terms.

We must be careful that our "small" part doesn't contribute to a larger sin. It is easy to rationalize a particular job with, "I was only following orders" (that's how Hitler's cohorts defended themselves) or "I'm just doing my job" (this excuse could be used by a crime syndicate "bag man"). If the job is part of a larger disobedience, it is wrong.

2. *We must consider God's priorities.* In Matthew 6:33 Jesus told us to seek *first* God's kingdom and righteousness. Elsewhere we read of the importance of family relationships—parents, children, and spouses (1 Timothy 5:8).

When evaluating an occupation, then, we should consider whether it moves us toward God and how it affects our families. Does this job provide an adequate living wage? Does this promotion pull me away from the family? Will this position help me become the kind of person God wants me to be?

3. *We must be good stewards* (Matthew 25:14-30). As Christians, we have the responsibility to use well what God has entrusted to us. It is not enough to put in our time on a job, for money or any kind of remuneration. Life is too short and too valuable to waste in meaningless work. When choosing a career or occupation, we must ask if it is a good investment of our lives. Will the world be a better place because of what we do? Perhaps the best question to ask is, What if there were no ____, would the world be better or worse? Garbage collecting or ditch digging, therefore, could be very meaningful work. Playing professional football or working in a large corporation that makes products of very little value, however, would seem to be difficult to justify.

A "Christian" job, therefore, is one that does not violate God's Word, is consistent with God's priorities, and provides a valuable and needed service to society. But choosing work is just the beginning. It is also important to do the work itself in a Christian way. A doctor, for example, performs a very necessary and Christ-honoring service; but there are M.D.s who are only seeking their own glory and wealth. To them, "healing" is not nearly as important as its wages.

Colossians 3:23 teaches us to work hard at our jobs as though we were working for God and not just for men. The *way* we do our work, then, must be honoring to God.

It is also important to exhibit the highest standard of morality on the job. Stealing of time and materials by employees is common today. But, Christians are called to be different—to put in an honest day's work for a day's wages.

Finally, the Christian worker is to honor God through the quality of his or her relationships. God is love (1 John 4:8), and we are to reflect his love in all our relationships. At work, this includes employers, superiors, fellow employees, and customers.

A college student once told me how he continually shared the gospel with his fellow workers. He thought this was the way to make the job "Christian." He got fired, and I wasn't surprised. Undoubtedly his employer (who may have been a Christian) felt that my friend should have spent more time working and less time talking. Yes, as Christians we should share our faith with others. But *being* a Christian on the job and *doing* God's work involves

- the type of work—meaningful and God honoring
- the way we work—full energy and honestly
- the way we relate—reflecting Christ's love.

Now, get to work!

◆DEALING WITH AN UNETHICAL EMPLOYER / YFC EDITORS

Working for an unethical employer is a touchy situation. Several things must be considered.

First of all, you need to realize that you will probably, at one time or another, disagree with your employer's policies or methods for handling certain situations. You may feel that what he or she is doing is wrong. But you need to distinguish between a difference of opinion and a truly unethical act. If your employer asks you personally to do something you know is wrong (for instance, he wants you to lie for him) you need to honestly explain your convictions, and depending on your relationship with your employer, you may need to confront him or her with what you perceive. Before doing so, be sure you have all the facts. Avoid making accusations that are not based on facts. Perhaps he doesn't realize the consequences of his policies. Perhaps he does, but would change his policies if someone presented him with a better, more ethical option. Or, you may discover that the structure is corrupt. At that point, you may have to make the hard choice to be the whistle-blower. Before doing that, make sure you have wise counsel from other Christians. Be willing to accept the consequences, which may mean you'll soon be job-hunting.

Acting Like a Christian While Being the Boss

✍ STUART BRISCOE

It is tough to fire an employee or to tell him he's not doing his job properly. The rule of thumb for a Christian in this difficult area is, I believe, to speak the truth in love (see Ephesians 4:15).

For instance, if I'm in a position of authority and someone in my department is not performing up to standard, then I'm going to have to tell him the truth about it, even if the truth is very painful indeed. The truth may be that my employee is incompetent and lazy. He may not be earning his salary. He may be a luxury the business can no longer afford.

Furthermore, if the employee is a Christian, I may need to tell him that his irresponsibility reflects not only on himself, but also on all others who profess the name of Christ. I may need to advise him to get his life straight before God before he does more damage.

All of that is truth. But how am I going to express it? I could be overbearing. I could cut the employee down. I could refuse to listen. But that would be wrong. Even though I would be telling the truth, it would not be the truth in love.

To speak the truth in love, we need to keep the employee's well-being in mind. Here are some pointers for communicating difficult truth in a business situation.

1. *Explain what the problem is.* Bear in mind what Paul said to Timothy about Scripture—that it is profitable for teaching, correcting, and training as

well as for rebuke. That means we not only show the person what is wrong, we also show him what is right.

2. *Be sure the employee knows what you expect of him.* Sometimes people do things wrong because we leaders have not told them what we want. If leaders are prepared to show workers what is unacceptable, they also need to show what is expected. If that is not being done, then the leader is at fault as much as the employee.

3. *Help the employee do his job better.* That may mean taking some pressures off him or breaking the job into more manageable pieces.

4. *Give him time for improvement.* Let him know that when the time is up, you will evaluate him again. If he is doing well, you will both be satisfied. If he is not, he will be terminated.

5. *If you eventually have to terminate an employee, err on the side of kindness.* Explain why you're doing this, so the employee can learn a lesson from it. Give him healthy severance pay to tide him over while he looks for a new job. Do what you can to help him get another position.

6. *Nevertheless, don't sweep things under the rug.* You are not helping an employee by hiding the truth from him about his job performance, and neither are you helping him by giving an untruthful recommendation because you don't want to hurt his chances. If you have explained to him the reason for his termination, he should not be surprised if you mention this problem on a recommendation. And in the long run, having to face up to his problem could be the best thing that ever happened to him.

♦ MAKING TOUGH DECISIONS
JILL AND STUART BRISCOE

What part does God play in helping us make tough decisions?

God is on our side, and he wants us to do what is best. So when we ask his guidance, he's not going to keep the answer from us.

He may not always guide in specific ways, but he gives general principles to help us. We can apply those principles to the decision we have to make by asking ourselves pointed questions: Is the decision I am about to make in accordance with biblical truth? Do the people who know me best think my plan is a very good idea? If I do this, will it adversely affect the people close to me?

As church leaders, sometimes we have to decide on something that is not going to meet with general approval. What has been most helpful to us is the realization that we are required to be committed to what is good, right, and true.

Our natural inclinations are to go for what is popular, comfortable, and profitable. There's no reason why what is good, right, and true should not also be popular, comfortable, and profitable, but when our preferences conflict with God's, we have some decisions to make.

For instance, I might have to decide between what is right and what is profitable. If I've made solid Christian commitments, I know I have to go with what is right, whether or not it's profitable. The hard part of that decision is not deciding, but doing. It can be tough to choose to walk away from a deal or even a job.

But if I'm committed to biblical principles, I know what I must do. I must go with what is good and right and true, no matter what popular opinion says to the contrary. And then I must live with the inevitable fallout.

Competition: When Does It Go Too Far?

YFC EDITORS

"We're number one! We're number one! We're number one!" The chant fills the stadium during the closing seconds of the big game. And across the nation, the chant is repeated by countless sports fans as they bask in imminent victory. We are obsessed with victory, winning, being rated the best. People will do almost anything to gain that top ranking—cheat, berate the referee, fight the opposition—and some sink to levels of despair when they lose. All for the sake of being "Number One"—for a year or a week or a moment.

Competition has become our way of life; it is woven into the fabric of our culture. We compete in our economics (free enterprise), our physical attractiveness (beauty contests), our education (valedictorian, honors), and even our neighborhoods ("best lawn award"). We seem to have a contest for just about everything imaginable.

Ideally, competition should push and motivate us to do well, to do our very best. And that can be true *if* we compete against a "standard" (e.g., the clock) or ourselves (the last performance).

But competition can be unhealthy and even destructive. If, for example, competition simply means winning, then you only have to do what it takes to win, not necessarily what is your best or what is good. "Winning" just means doing better than the competition, and this could involve putting him or her down or cheating.

Competition can also lead to continual comparisons of ourselves with others. Then, if we compare ourselves to someone better, we can become discouraged—or with someone worse, we can become proud. This even bleeds over into religious life. The Pharisees were tremendous "spiritual competitors," but in God's eyes, they were losers (Matthew 23:25-28).

Christians, however, have a higher standard. We are called to be "like Christ" (Romans 8:29), and all that we do must be judged by God's standards. In addition, God's values are the opposite of the world's. Listen to what Jesus said in Matthew 19:30: "But many who are first will be last, and many who are last will be first." With every winner there is a loser, and Jesus had much to say in support of the "losers" in society.

As one committed to Jesus Christ, don't fall for the world's standards of self-esteem and success. Build your identity on who you are in Christ and do your very best at everything, to glorify him.

A Christian View of Money

HUDSON T. ARMERDING

The Christian view of money differs radically from the world's view. The world's view is that money is something we obtain by our own efforts, by good fortune, or by luck. It's for our gratification and use, and very often is an end in itself. Many people enjoy the challenge of making money just as much as the joy of spending it.

The world sees my money as the product of my own effort. It's mine. Some economic theorists even say that taxation is robbery because the money really belongs to the individual.

The Christian view of money is that it comes to us so that we can use it in ways that will bring glory to God. It is not something over which we have final jurisdiction; we are only stewards of God's wealth. A good illustration of this principle is found in the parable of the talents, which shows that even the money we gain from work is ours because God provides opportunities for us.

As believers, we are always held accountable for the way we use our money. The account of Ananias and Sapphira in Acts 5 is very compelling. Peter said to Ananias: "Didn't it [the land] belong to you before it was sold? And after it was sold, wasn't the money at your disposal?" In other words, Ananias was accountable for the way in which he used the money. He was judged because he misrepresented and misused his resources.

We can enjoy God's good gifts if we use them responsibly and if we don't cling to them with the attitude that if they're taken away from us, we'll be desolated. I differ with those who believe that having any possessions is wrong. I feel that God gives us good gifts richly to enjoy, and the wealthy people in Scripture are a good illustration of that principle. I also feel strongly, though, that those who have riches need to view clearly the world's demands and needs, seeking to respond to them.

We need to be on our guard against what Thorstein Veblen called conspicuous consumption—having too many things that we cannot possibly justify. For example, instead of adequate transportation, we may want several luxurious vehicles; or instead of comfortable shelter, we may insist upon a palatial mansion. Conspicuous consumption indicates that we haven't necessarily addressed the world's needs, for which we as Christians are responsible.

In Ephesians 4:28 Paul wrote: "He who has been stealing must steal no longer, but must work, doing something useful with his own hands, that he may have something to share with those in need." The enjoyment of God's good gifts must be tempered by the necessity of meeting needs, primarily of those that are in the household of faith.

Chapters 12, 16, and 18 of the Gospel of Luke all give warnings about money. In the twelfth chapter, in the story of the rich fool, we see that money should never be a Christian's security. In the sixteenth chapter, in the story of the rich man and Lazarus, we see that even the people of God can get so preoccupied with money that they ignore Scripture. In the eighteenth chapter, in the account of Jesus' conversation with the rich young ruler, we see how money can temper the complete dedication we should have to the Lord.

Christians need to ask themselves this question: If the Lord took away all my financial resources, would I still love him and want to trust him, or would I curse him for having withdrawn my blessings? Are my financial resources so important that if the Lord took them away, I'd no longer trust him or be willing to serve him?

Job is a wonderful illustration of a believer who did not let money—or lack of it—stand in the way of his love for God. His wife said, "Curse God and die," but Job replied, "You are talking like a foolish woman. Shall we accept good from God, and not trouble?" (Job 2:9, 10). "Naked I came from my mother's womb, and naked I will depart. The Lord gave and the Lord has taken away; may the name of the Lord be praised" (Job 1:21).

Christians should be aware that some important and earnest people today are suggesting that if we are obedient and have enough faith, God will make us all wealthy. This is not taught or illustrated in the Holy Scriptures.

For instance, the faithful Christians listed in Hebrews 11 obviously lost all their possessions, yet one could never appropriately argue that they were lacking in faith or were unimportant in God's sight. It would certainly be a travesty to suggest that they didn't merit God's favor because they lost everything and were persecuted. And when you think of earnest people in totalitarian areas today, or people of the past who lost everything for the Lord's sake, it would be unconscionable even to suggest that they weren't people of faith or hadn't trusted God enough for his blessing.

I cannot accept the thesis that God will make us wealthy and healthy if we simply have enough faith and trust him. Rather, he will furnish some of us with material resources as we exercise appropriate stewardship and are willing to use what we have in accordance with the Holy Scriptures.

Very often preachers will encourage people to give, claiming that God will give them back ten times the amount they give. They base this on Malachi 3:10: "'Bring the whole tithe into the storehouse, that there may be food in my house. Test me in this,' says the Lord Almighty, 'and see if I will not throw open the floodgates of heaven and pour out so much blessing that you will not have room enough for it.'"

I firmly believe that God will make provision for our needs as we are faithful in stewardship. We had this happen once again the other day. We made a contribution, and the next day, very unexpectedly, the money came back from a different source. But we've also had times where we've made a contribution, and the money hasn't come back. It isn't a strict cause and effect relationship. God in his providence may want to defer things or formulate the blessing in a different dimension. Instead of dollars, he may give us a sense of spiritual blessing.

The Christians in Macedonia gave out of "their extreme poverty" (2 Corinthians 8:2). There is no suggestion that they got back what they gave in a material sense, but God nevertheless blessed them for their faithfulness. Money can be a blessing, but for the Christian it is far from the ultimate blessing.

♦ PRACTICAL GUIDELINES TO MONEY MANAGEMENT / HUDSON T. ARMERDING

1. *Recognize that any money you have has been given to you in trust.* You are accountable to God for the way in which you use it.
2. *Give a tithe and additional offerings toward the support of God's work.* We have a Christian duty not only to support the preaching of the Word but also to care for the people who don't have enough: widows, orphans, and others who are in need.
3. *Recognize the trap and enticement of conspicuous consumption.* Prayerfully look at what you buy, and ask the Lord for wisdom in regard to your purchases.
4. *Live within your means.* I'm not suggesting that people should never go into debt; but if they do, they should know they will be able to manage their debt and work themselves out of it within a reasonable amount of time. Indebtedness for a house—if it takes no more than 25 or 30 percent of your income—is often manageable. Taking out a loan for schooling is also legitimate. It is not exercising good stewardship, however, to pay the 18 to 21 percent interest charged to credit-card holders who do not pay their bill in full each month.
5. *Examine your spending decisions.* Defer gratification by seriously asking, Do I need a new vehicle if the present one is working fine? Is it really good stewardship to buy a new car just because the one we have now is two or three years old and isn't the latest style? I wouldn't criticize someone just because he bought something I wouldn't buy, but I would criticize him if he did so without asking the Lord about it or sitting down to decide whether or not he really needed it and could afford it.
6. *Get into a program of saving.* This includes having a budget, putting money into savings accounts, and properly investing your money. It is necessary to put some money aside with each paycheck—even if your income isn't very high—to save for emergencies. You may want to increase the amount you save as your income grows.
7. *Be on guard against emotional or impulsive buying.* Don't try to keep up with a certain social status. Realize that you are accountable to God for how you use your money and resources.

Money and Spiritual Growth

✍ YFC EDITORS

How can money—or the lack of it—hinder spiritual growth?

Strangely enough, having too much money or too little money results in basically the same problems, and both can hinder spiritual growth. As Agur, a writer in Proverbs, so aptly put it, "Give me neither poverty nor riches, but give me only my daily bread. Otherwise, I may have too much and disown you and say, 'Who is the Lord?' Or I may become poor and steal, and so dishonor the name of my God" (Proverbs 30:8, 9). Whether you have money to blow or barely enough to live on, both can result in the following:

1. *Money becomes the center and focus of your life.* It can become an idol. When you have much, you realize its power in our world. When you have little, your concern or worry over it can become paramount over faith in God himself.

2. *Money is seen idealistically.* With lots of money, you feel yourself with extreme power—though that power rests on a very shaky foundation. With very little money, you tend to think that a few bucks will solve all your problems.

3. *Money becomes an obsession.* Those who have much constantly want more. Those who don't have enough, constantly want more too.

4. *Money causes worry.* When you're wealthy, you worry about losing your wealth, being used for it, or being robbed or cheated out of it. When you have no money, you worry about how to get and pay for all that you need and want.

5. *Money changes your attitudes.* Wealth causes many to become suspicious, stingy, and Scrooge-like. On the other hand, lack of money can cause jealousy and resentment of the wealthy, and an overly stingy attitude out of habit.

6. *Money changes your priorities.* When money gets the better of you, whether rich or poor, it can make you love things and use people, just the opposite of what God intended. It can make you focus on your earthly treasure, which is temporary, while forgetting your real goal: treasure in heaven.

But money, or the lack of it, need not hinder spiritual growth. The secret is to learn contentment. Paul said, "I have learned the secret of being content in any and every situation, whether well fed or hungry, whether living in plenty or in want" (Philippians 4:12). When we learn to be thankful for our *daily* bread (not worrying about what we'll eat tomorrow), when we learn that this world and its riches or problems are temporary, then we have learned the secret of contentment whether we are rich or struggling.

Money is not bad in itself, it is the *love* of money that causes all the trouble. When you discover that you are thinking more about money than about your family, your own peacefulness, or God, then money has begun to control you and will hinder your spiritual growth. It has become your real god. When you love God and trust him to care for you every day whether your treasure is great or small, then you have money in the right perspective and you will continue to grow. And as you grow, you will learn how to use the large or small amount God has given to you in order to glorify him.

Your treasure will not be where your heart is; the Bible says that your heart will be where your treasure is.

♦ GETTING FREE OF MONEY'S POWER
RICHARD FOSTER

We once owned a big swing set. It was not the kind of tinny thing you buy in stores; it was made of sturdy iron pipes. Our kids were getting beyond the age of swing sets, so we decided to sell it at a garage sale. I went out to try to decide what price to put on it.

As I was looking it over I thought, This is really a good piece of equipment. I ought to get a pretty good price. And then I thought, If I just touched up the paint on it some, and if I fixed the seat on this little glider, I could up the ante.

As I was standing in the backyard looking over the swing set, I began to recognize a spirit of greed I thought I had dealt with long ago. This is spiritually threatening, I thought. This is really dangerous.

So I went inside and said to Carolynn, after telling her about what had been going on with me, "Honey, would you mind if we just gave that swing set away?"

She said, "No, not at all."

And I thought, Rats!

But we found another couple who really could make good use of it. They didn't have the money to buy that kind of thing. So we gave it to them. I didn't even have to paint it.

The spirit of greed does not go away meekly. It keeps coming back. You have to deal with it, or it will win you.

RELATED ARTICLES
Chapter 12: **The Tyranny of the Urgent**
Chapter 18: **When Perfectionism Makes God Seem Far Away**
Chapter 19: **Do Christians Do Their Work Differently Than Others?**

CHAPTER 24

Politics and Christianity

- ✓ I'm just one person—what can I do about world problems?
- ✓ Has God lost control of the world?
- ✓ How can I promote justice?
- ✓ Christians and politics
- ✓ When Christians agree to disagree

Should Christians Be Politically Involved?

MARK HATFIELD

From its beginning, our nation has been influenced by the Christian faith. At the Constitutional Convention in 1787, prayer was offered by the leaders for wisdom and guidance in setting up the republic. They did not intend to separate the values of Christianity from our system of government, but to assure individual liberty they established in the constitution a strong separation of the institutional church from the government. Thus, the government could not set up a preference for one religion by special privileges. As a result of the separation of church and state, we find great religious diversity in our country.

Because of that constitutional separation, Christianity in the form of the institutional, organized church is constrained from formal integration with our government. But Christianity in the form of an individual's theological identification with the body of Christ can and should play a part in the political process.

Working as individuals within the political system is not contrary to our Christian faith. We believe in the redemption of humanity, a redemption that takes place on an individual basis, not on an institutional basis. Likewise, our political influence comes from the involvement of individuals, not institutions. In fact, any free and democratic society must be based on the strong participation of individual citizens. Without this, it devolves into an elitism or anarchy. The vision, abilities, character, and skills of individuals are a positive and necessary force in a democracy.

Jesus admonished his followers to become the light, the salt, and the yeast in society (Matthew 5:13-16; 13:33). Wherever these elements are added, they transform the environment. In the same way, we penetrate and permeate political institutions with Christian values and beliefs.

It would be wise for all of us to carefully examine the warning provided by de Tocqueville. He said: "Once religion is mixed with the bitter passions of the world it cannot avoid losing influence: The Church cannot share the temporal power of the state without being the object of a portion of that animosity which the latter excites."

Of course, we have a constitutional privilege and right to create a political party based on Christian principles. But there is danger in such an approach. Some Christians would begin to view the party as the only way to express biblical thinking. Then, instead of dynamic diversity working among Christians, conformity would become the rule.

A Christian political group could create a political philosophy that would, for all practical purposes, take precedence over the biblical gospel. The group, feeling intensely about a particular political issue, would tend to judge a person's relationship to Christ by what the person thinks about that issue, not by what the person thinks about Jesus Christ. God tells us that the only way we can affirm our Christian commitment is by the fruits of the Spirit (Galatians 5:24). Love, joy, and peace are evidence of the Holy Spirit within us, not our stand on school prayer, abortion, or capital punishment.

We can have far more impact by working within a secular political organization to help our laws reflect Christian values than by separating ourselves and banding together with other believers as a "Christian Political Movement."

Some Christians believe that being salt and yeast means being separate from the political process. But the common denominator of every political issue is a spiritual problem. For instance, when we deal with environmental problems, we are not only concerned with the environment for the sake of the environment; we are also concerned with the spiritual issue of stewardship. When we talk about an unfair tax system rife with loopholes, we are talking about the spiritual issues of fairness and justice. When we consider the problem of corruption in politics, again we are talking about spiritual questions—honesty and integrity. We need to maintain a spiritual perspective on these secular issues.

Even if we are not involved by our actions or by public identification with a political party, we still have important political roles to play. We have a responsibility to vote. Even more important, we are instructed to pray for those in political office (1 Timothy 2:1, 2). We need to pray for the issues confronting our society and for the hurting individuals within our society. And we have a responsibility to reach out to minister to the poor.

Whether we choose to work directly in politics or to support it with our votes and prayers, the political process in a democratic country gives us a vital opportunity to demonstrate our love for Christ.

♦ FAITHFULNESS, NOT SUCCESS
MARK HATFIELD

A number of years ago I visited Mother Teresa in Calcutta, India, and spent a day going with her from mission to mission, seeing the misery and the devastating poverty and the hellishness. At the end of the day, I turned to her and asked if she grew weary when she saw how little she was able to accomplish in light of the magnitude of the task. With a smile on her face, she quickly responded, "Oh, no, for you see, the Lord has not called me to be successful; he has called me to be faithful."

We too are called to be faithful, not successful. The world does not understand this; even the church sometimes urges us to achieve in the way the world measures success. To keep on the track of faithfulness rather than successfulness, we need to be surrounded by people who will keep us humble—perhaps a covenant group relationship with other Christians who meet together to pray and to be accountable to each other. We also need to study the Word and pray daily.

Being faithful may mean joining a political party, writing our congressman, or organizing a protest. All of these manifestations of concern are legitimate. But unless our actions are grounded in a relationship to Christ, we will be overwhelmed by discouragement, because many of our actions will seem to fail. That is when we should keep Mother Teresa's words in mind—the Lord has called us to be faithful, not successful.

Christians and Politics
NORMAN GEISLER

As Christian believers, we are called to be light in a dark place, salt penetrating a rotten world. James 4:17 says, "Anyone, then, who knows the good he ought to do and doesn't do it, sins." As Edmund Burke remarked, "All that is necessary for evil to prevail is for good men to do nothing."

We Christians have a moral obligation to be involved in our world. Our platform ought to be 1 Timothy 2:1-3: "I urge, then, first of all, that requests, prayers, intercession and thanksgiving be made for everyone—for kings and all those in authority, that we may live peaceful and quiet lives in all godliness and holiness. This is good, and pleases God our Savior." The ability to ensure justice, peace, and an open door for the gospel is what we should look for as we decide what type of government to support.

In Paul's day, the form of government was empire. Although citizens could not elect Caesar, they could pray for him. It's hypocritical to pray for something for which you're not willing to work. If we're obligated to pray for a government in accordance with 1 Timothy 2, then we're also morally obligated to work for it.

No one party has the corner on truth. Republicans aren't always right, and neither are Democrats. So Christians need to be careful about tying themselves too closely to one political party. Many issues have important moral implications, and Christians ought to support godly principles wherever they are found. We should vote principle, not just party.

What principles are worth upholding and fighting for? Godliness, justice, goodness, righteousness, life, defending the innocent, helping the poor—in other words, issues that are clearly spelled out in the Bible. Whichever candidate best supports these values ought to have our support, regardless of his political affiliation.

Principles translate into issues. For example, defending innocent lives is a principle, and abortion on demand is an issue. Because of their principles, Christians will know how to react on the issues of the day.

A Christian who bases his moral beliefs on Scripture will oppose abortion on demand. Psalm 139 makes it plain that the unborn child is a human being loved and cared for by God. Throughout the Bible, God shows compassion on the weak and the helpless—and who is more helpless than an unwanted fetus? Thus Christians should try to get politicians out of office if they favor abortion on demand.

When there is a clear-cut moral issue, Christians are obligated to become involved. On some issues, however, Christians hold the same principles but disagree over the means to put them into action. War is one of those issues. Activists say a Christian should always go to war when the government commands it. Pacifists say we should never go to war, even if the government commands it. And selectivists say we should sometimes go to war; it depends on whether or not it is a just war. You'll find Christians on all sides of this issue. I think they all agree with the same principle—that justice and peace should be preserved—but they disagree as to the best way to arrive there.

In spite of the fact that we won't always agree with each other, we Christians need to get involved in politics. If good people don't get involved in running the government, then evil people will. It's not going to do us any good to curse the darkness; we have to light a few candles.

Joining Faith and Politics

MARTIN MARTY

Christians often try to discern what the one true Christian position is for a political issue. Frequently the position they reach is not based solely on what is found in the Bible. That's because the Bible does not give a decisive answer on most political issues. As a result, Christians can be found on both sides of almost any political issue.

Politically, the Bible is more like a library than a single book. It is difficult to come up with a black-and-white answer that fits every diverse situation. For example, some people try to apply Jesus' words about nonresistance (Luke 6:27-31) to every act of injustice. But in practice, I don't know anyone who always turns the other cheek. On the other hand, Christians should not ignore those verses. Even though the verses might not apply to every situation, the One who spoke them remains decisive, and Christians need to consider what he says.

If it is difficult to know what a Christian political position is, how can Christians know what their political involvement should be? There are several guidelines a Christian can follow.

1. *Not to be involved is to be involved.* Not to take a stand is to take a stand. When we look back at history, we see that those who weren't for the abolition of slavery were contributing to its existence. Those Catholics and Lutherans in Germany who didn't speak up against Hitler were, in a sense, supporting him. They weren't taking a stand when a stand was needed.

Sometimes Christians will say they don't want to be involved politically, but they are really saying they don't care about the current political issues. Some Christians who today make fighting abortion their main cause once said it was sinful for Christians to be in politics. Once they thought there was no cause worthy of the risk of being tainted by politics; now they have found an issue.

2. *Politics should not be the prime activity of the church.* Politics does not preach the kingdom of God. Politics does not fulfill the will of God. It does not save souls. It is simply a modest act that works against selfishness and violence.

In preaching God's kingdom, Christians try to create a space for the presence of God in the world. In political involvement, Christians try hold God's plumb line to the world (Amos 7:7-9). We do this even though in holding the plumb line, our hands are shaky and our perspective is distorted. God has called us to be salt and light in the world, and this is our duty.

3. *Love God and act reasonably.* In deciding what stand to take, Christians should let their love for God be their filter. Beyond that they should act reasonably. They won't choose the right stand all the time, but that is a risk they have to take.

For example, in supporting world hunger, I might support people who use a pesticide overseas. Crops grow, and thousands of hungry people are fed. I feel good about my support. But suppose that some years later, the discovery is made that that pesticide contributes to cancer. Of course I would profoundly, profoundly regret that. But does that mean I should not have tried to help feed anybody? No, that would have been immoral. Being wrong is a risk I take when I try to do right. I have to act, but I can act repentantly.

Politics seeks to minimize violence. It works to assure that no one person or organization has a disproportionate amount of control. But working together for good can never be done without compromise. To compel attention and gather votes, Christians must make coalitions. To make coalitions, Christians must make compromises. When it comes to politics, no Christian is pure.

Christians need to be involved in politics, but we must remember not to confuse politics with bringing in the kingdom. The proclamation of the kingdom influences political action, but political action is not the center of the kingdom.

Individual Involvement in Politics

MARK HATFIELD

When we talk about a Christian's political involvment, we should realize that not all involvement is physical. In New York City in a building facing Times Square, a group of Catholic nuns meets every day to pray for the street people. From the world's perspective they are skirting the real task, withdrawing from the misery on the street. But praying for street ministries is both biblical and a vibrant spiritual involvement. The nuns are as much involved as those who are physically ministering to the needy people. A retiree who is not physically capable of being out on the action front and yet organizes a prayer group in a retirement center is still very much involved. The power of prayer is immeasurable and vital.

Each individual has to seek his or her calling from God. Christ calls people to different ministries. We cannot assume that everyone must have our calling, nor can we prescribe a calling for another individual. Another person's role within the body of Christ will be different from ours.

Some of us are called to reform politics from within the structure. Others of us are called to be a part of a citizen endeavor. Some of us are called to serve on a local school board or city council. Others may be involved in a citizen group to fight pornography or child abuse.

As Christians called to involvement in politics in whatever form, our real mission is to affirm our love and obedience to Christ. Our long-term commitment and our immediate commitment are one and the same—to serve as ambassadors of Jesus Christ; to be the voice, the healing, and the reconciling and liberating force of Jesus. We have Christ in us, the hope of glory (Colossians 1:27). We are witnesses of redemption, of the Good News. As Christians, that mission must undergird our role in politics, just as it is evidenced in our family lives and our role in the marketplace.

Sin manifests itself in evil, in oppression, in injustice, in jealousy, in rivalry, in hate, in poverty. The basic Christian values are the exact opposite—healing, reconciling, encouraging, feeding the poor, visiting the sick and the prisoners. We have the message of the Good News that indeed God has dealt with the forces of injustice and evil. We have the armor of the Word of God and the energizing of the Holy Spirit. We must be involved in both ministry and politics—in the unique way God has called each of us to serve.

♦ROOTED IN CHRIST / MARK HATFIELD

To make an effective contribution in our ministry, whether it be politics or social service or whatever, we need to start with our personal relationship to Christ. We can't give out more than we have within. Only through Christ living in us will we have the energy, the wisdom, the compassion, the vision, and the patience we need. We have to start with the relationship and grow in that relationship. Christ will lead, he will direct, he will present opportunities to reach out.

Political Diversity and Moral Unity

✍ TOM MINNERY

Can two Christians have opposite political views, yet both be morally correct? Certainly they can.

As Christians, we are called to season the society in which we live with the salt of moral wisdom, justice, and compassion. Our laws, our traditions, our entire culture should be improved by virtue of the Christians who inhabit it and press their godly imprint upon it.

Whenever American Christians seek to affect society for good, they find themselves in the realm of politics; for in a democracy such as ours, the political arena is where these public issues are debated and settled. And in the practice of politics, there are many routes to the same goal. It should not be surprising, then, when Christians—who strive for the same moral goals—differ on the proper political strategies to reach them.

Let's take an example. All Christians agree that humans, made in the image of God, are of priceless value and should be spared the horror of nuclear war. After all, what could be a greater rebuff to God's creation than to obliterate it? Thus many Christians have become greatly concerned about the proliferation of nuclear weapons in our own country and around the world.

But what is the best way to prevent nuclear war? Should our government follow its present policy of deterrence by seeking to maintain so large a nuclear arsenal that any nation would be foolish to attack? Or should it take the risk of disarming first, hoping that other nations will follow suit?

There are many Christians on both sides of that question. Proponents of each side proclaim that peace and preservation of human life is their goal, but which one will succeed? The biblical mandate for peace is clear, but the method to achieve it is not so clear.

A difficulty can arise when Christians enter opposite sides of the political arena. Sometimes they claim that theirs is the only proper moral position, when actually they are not debating the moral principle at all but rather the political strategy to reach it.

Senator Edward Kennedy once said that the sharper his political difference with an opponent, the more respect he accords his opponent's motives, unless it is proven to him that those motives are not praiseworthy. This is an excellent guideline for limiting the rancor of political debate. Christians have been arguing the nuclear issue for a long time without reaching consensus. They should realize that they are debating political strategy, not morality, and they should honor the motives of the Christians who oppose them politically.

There is another issue on which Christians agree in moral principle but divide politically—the elimination of poverty. Nearly everyone agrees that the sensible way to reduce the poverty level is to create more jobs, but here the agreement ends.

Political conservatives contend that the best way to produce meaningful work is for the government to cut regulations and lower taxes, thereby allowing businesses to prosper and create new jobs.

Critics of this thinking, who are by and large political liberals, say this won't work because many people who are unemployed are not trained for most industrial jobs. Even if they were, these critics say, companies would not expand their businesses in the large northern cities that have the largest pools of unemployed.

Political liberals would like the government to establish massive make-work job programs so people could be employed immediately where they live, at jobs they are able to handle. Conservatives respond by saying that when these programs end, people are once again out of work. Besides that, they contend, the administrative overhead is costly and the programs are inefficient.

The issue of how to help poor people climb the economic ladder, then, frequently and legitimately divides Christians, who are to be found among the ranks of the politically conservative as well as the politically liberal. Here again, the two sides are debating not the moral principle of helping the unemployed and the poverty stricken, but the proper political strategy to accomplish this goal.

Biblical Christians who enter the political arena often have no greater knowledge of proper political courses than do others. What they should have, however, is a proper notion of moral principle grounded in God's Word. If they do, they may still sharply disagree on political strategies. As long as the debate is over matters of politics and not the underlying moral principles, it is perfectly proper for Christians to disagree.

♦ THE DYNAMICS OF DIVERSITY
MARK HATFIELD

We are responsible to bring the message of Christ into every facet of life. We can join a political party, write our congressman, picket, march, hold a vigil. But while we do these things, we have to be careful that our

political agendas do not become a divisive force within the body of Christ.

I am anti-abortion, but I know some fine Christians who see it in a different light. I am opposed to capital punishment, but there are some fine Christians who are in favor of it. I am opposed to the nuclear arms race, but there are some fine Christians who feel that all these arms are necessary for the defense of the country.

There is great danger when someone says, "This is the Christian position on a certain political issue." That implies that any other viewpoint is not Christian. Political stands do not determine our salvation; our relationship to the person of Jesus Christ does. I think that relationship alone determines our right to be called a Christian.

What can we do when we disagree with other Christians politically? We can retain our political convictions and still be united with other Christians. To experience that, a basis of love is required. My wife and I have cast opposing votes in a number of elections. She has strong political views that are often totally opposite to mine. But it has done nothing to rupture our marriage, because we are united in our love for each other and in our common love for Jesus Christ. We discuss the issues we disagree on, but we realize that they are secondary to our love for each other and our love for Christ.

Why Christians Disagree Politically

TOM MINNERY

Christian take opposite sides on political issues for many reasons. Some differences grow out of the way they read Scripture. Others can be traced to their interpretation of the Constitution.

Looking first at Scripture, we find a double emphasis in the New Testament that can produce differences in political judgment among Christians. First of all, they are to hold certain beliefs. Second, they are to act on those beliefs. Oftentimes, however, Christians believe without acting or act without fully believing.

We come to faith, first and foremost, by simply believing in Christ. As Jesus told Nicodemus, "For God so loved the world that he gave his one and only Son, that whoever believes in him shall not perish but have eternal life" (John 3:16). Many Christians, then, think the church's primary emphasis should be calling the unsaved to belief in Christ. They are, of course, correct.

James, however, asks this further question: "What good is it, my brothers, if a man claims to have faith but has no deeds? Can such faith save him?" (James 2:14). James proceeds to argue that believers should perform good deeds, thereby proving their faith. James, of course, is also correct. Vital Christianity manifests itself in good works, which are the natural outgrowth of faith in Christ.

What does this have to do with politics? Early in the twentieth century, Christians tended to divide into two camps. Fundamentalists emphasized correctness of belief. Liberals emphasized doing good works.

Fundamentalists—who continued to emphasize the historic tenets of the faith—accused liberal Christians of weak belief. To a large extent, the critics were correct. The liberal wing of the church had, in fact, embraced theories of the Bible that tended to empty it of its divine inspiration. Many liberals no longer believed in the inerrancy of the Bible, the Virgin Birth, the literal resurrection, and the second coming of Christ. They believed in the importance of good works, but by and large they had lost the vital faith that must precede them.

Fundamentalists accused liberal Christians of reducing Christianity to little more than a society for social work. They were deeply suspicious of the "social gospel," as liberalism's human-centered emphasis was often called. In reaction, fundamentalists tended to oppose the government's social programs, beloved by liberals.

Today, Christian conservatives and liberals still eye each other with deep suspicion. Conservatives still place their emphasis on belief, although to their credit, their social concern has been rising in recent years. Politically, conservatives tend to stand for a strong defense and the spread of American-style capitalist democracy to other countries, because our system of government has, historically, been so closely associated with the spread of the Christian faith.

More liberal Christians are less likely to emphasize the importance of belief, more likely to look for immediate solutions to social ills. Less ready to export capitalism, they are more likely to emphasize the greed that that economic system produces. Liberals tend to be attracted to socialistic economic systems, which promise (but have yet to produce) a classless society in which all are treated equitably, particularly in the realm of monetary income.

Thus different ways of looking at Scripture have caused many significant political differences between conservatives and liberals in matters of national defense and foreign policy. Another potential source of disagreement lies in the way Christians read the Constitution, especially the Bill of Rights.

All Christians agree on the moral principle behind the First Amendment to the Constitution as it applies to religious freedom—all wish to be free to practice their own religion. Christians may radically disagree, however, on how to interpret that amendment in actual practice. Sincere Christians frequently find themselves on opposing sides of pitched political battles on this topic.

The First Amendment says that "Congress shall make no law respecting an establishment of religion, or prohibiting the free exercise thereof." Two general principles can be derived from this statement.

First, religion is to be free of any entangling alliance with government. Many American revolutionists feared the dominance of the Anglican church, the state-established church of England that had been corrupted by government-sanctioned power and status. The American revolutionaries wanted to be sure that in their new nation, no particular church would be the official church.

Second, religion must be free to influence government with its high moral principles. But to what extent can religion influence government without making government an instrument of Christian evangelism, or making Christianity captive to politicians who mouth Christian platitudes in order to manipulate it politically? Christians differ in their evaluation.

Some Christians battle against every alliance between government and religion. Others applaud every government leader who expresses religious beliefs and sympathies, for they believe that leaders who uphold Christian values, or at least say they do, are likely to take moral actions.

The first group fears that government will edge its way into the life of the church and will attempt to control matters that are better left between the individual and God. It also points out that civil religion is always a watered-down version of true Christianity and may do more harm than good to the church.

The second group, by contrast, sees danger in keeping Christian values completely separated from government, because then only non-Christian influences will be brought to bear on our laws and public policies. It points out that in a democracy, Christians have as much right to be heard as anyone else.

In the matter of relations between church and state, as in the matter of political conservatism and liberalism, sincere Christians are found in both camps. There are godly people on both sides attempting to be faithful to Scripture and to the Constitution. There are strengths in both sides—and tremendous dangers. Rather than calling our Christian opponents names, we would do better to look for the elements in their position that would help to balance our own position. We need to learn from each other, even if we never totally agree with one another.

♦ WHEN CHRISTIANS AGREE TO DISAGREE / MARTIN MARTY

After the Vietnam War, congregations had to decide whether they would support their own young men who had taken refuge in Canada or Sweden and who now wanted to return with amnesty to the United States. Although the decision would not affect the entire country and no lives were at stake, it was an important issue for the families involved. But the church did not have a single clear position.

One church I know discussed the issue and realized it contained two competing values. One side said, "Unless we're pacifists, we have to allow that the nation must defend itself and citizens must support that need. If we give amnesty to everybody who runs across the line when a war comes, how will we ever find soldiers the next time?" That position has some legitimacy, and there are biblical arguments for it.

But the other side said, "Wait a minute. Aren't we in the reconciliation business? Here's a chance for us to restore a member of our own congregation. His only mistake was being right too early. Now the whole country says he's right. We could rebuild his family by accepting this man, and we do value families." That is another legitimate position, also with biblical support.

So how can Christians agree to disagree on issues like this?

1. *Listen to one another.* Too often we jump to conclusions about the opposite side of an issue without listening to what the people on it have to say.

2. *Make the Bible your anchor.* We must hold one another to the biblical

context and theological norms. We must remember the church's tradition of moral reflection.

3. *Dig into discussion.* We need to present the different options and urge all sides to discuss the issues. That's how our consciences are formed.

4. *Love, don't leave.* There will be times when, after we have discussed all sides of an issue, we will not be able to agree with other Christians. Then we accept them, remembering not what divides us, but what binds us together—Christ's love.

Politics and Bad Morals

✍ TOM MINNERY

It is possible for sincere Christians to agree on moral principles and yet differ on the political means necessary to accomplish their purposes. But sometimes Christians allow their personal circumstances, not God's Word, to shape their moral views. When this happens, Christians pop up on unexpected sides of political issues. In such cases, it is no longer possible for Christians to differ politically yet agree morally, for the moral principles have been bent out of shape by one side.

A good example of this occurred more than a century ago during a time of grave crisis in our nation's history. A group of Presbyterians from eleven states adopted a resolution that said, in part, "We stand upon the foundation of the prophets and apostles, Jesus Christ himself being the chief cornerstone. . . . We utterly refuse to break our communion with Abraham, Isaac and Jacob, with Moses, David and Isaiah, with the apostles, prophets and martyrs, with all the noble army of confessors who have gone to glory."

What Christian today would not applaud the deep conviction behind those words? The trouble is that these Christians were affirming, in 1861, the right of Americans to own slaves.

Many southern religious leaders, including Baptists, Methodists, and Roman Catholics, agreed wholeheartedly with these southern-state Presbyterians. They were basing their belief chiefly on the fact that in its many references to slavery, the Bible does not specifically condemn it. This, of course, is a grossly narrow view of the biblical concepts of love and justice.

The fact is that hundreds of pastors who defended the institution of slavery were slave owners themselves. Had they opposed slavery, they would have placed themselves under personal economic hardship. They would also have put themselves at odds with many in their congregations who also were slaveholders. The principle here is that it is always dangerous to try to interpret what the Bible says about a controversial topic when the one making the interpretation is predisposed to see only one side of the controversy.

This kind of Scripture twisting happens today as well. Some Christians who practice homosexuality put the Bible through excruciating contortions in their efforts to produce an interpretation that condones their life-style. Some of these people then go on to work politically for the passage of communal living laws that justify homosexual relationships and that tear down the sacred notion of the nuclear family, a very strong biblical concept.

Another example is that of Christians who live comfortable suburban lifestyles and find it easy to ignore Bible passages requiring God's people to stand for fair play and justice for the poor and less fortunate. Suburban living tends to insulate people from the needs of those in different economic circumstances. Thus it becomes easy for some suburban congregations to adopt political viewpoints that appear uncompassionate when compared with the political views that their urban brethren tend to uphold.

Christians will often disagree on political matters. But they should not disagree on the underlying moral principles, and they most definitely should not interpret moral principles from the vantage point of their own self-interest. When this happens, they discredit themselves and the wonderful gospel for which they claim to stand.

◆ CHRISTIANS AND POLITICAL CONFLICT
MARTIN MARTY

When I was a minister in Washington, D.C., I had to deal with two Christians who all but slugged each other on the floor of the House of Representatives and then bought each other and their families lunch two days later. They weren't the best of friends, but they knew they had to keep the process going.

If they could do that, it seems to me that in our congregations we should decide *a priori* that we will not break the fellowship, no matter how intense the disagreements.

We can't expect to live in a perfect world in which Christians always act charitably toward those who disagree with them. Even if you keep politics entirely out of the life of a congregation, there will still be conflict. That's in the nature of intimate social groups. If there is freedom, there is going to be conflict.

The great denominations of America—the Baptists, the Methodists, and the Presbyterians—split over the Civil War. They had identical gospels, and yet they divided. One got together in 1939, one got together in 1984, and one still hasn't gotten back together. I don't know how you can prevent splits if one party wants to put the other out, or if one wants to take its bat and ball and go home, but I think it is misunderstanding the nature of Christian community to act that way.

Certainly communion is not based upon people's agreeing on every detail about the earthly pilgrimage. We don't know enough about the future to know who's right, although people always think they are. Historical outcomes are often just the opposite of what's intended. In fact, my own folly may help to bring about that opposite outcome. Remembering that fact may help give us the humility to stay in community in spite of political disagreements.

What Can One Person Do?

CALVIN MILLER

The world's problems look so big that sometimes I am tempted to say, What can one insignificant person do to help solve them? This is really a self-centered thing to say. It is not rooted in good theology. Actually there are no insignificant persons. Even though there are billions of people living right now and billions of others who have gone before, I still matter to God. If I were the only person who needed Jesus, he still would have died on the cross. I am redeemed by a personal Savior who does not think I am insignificant.

The first thing I must do in contemplating the world's problems is to understand that I am significant. I must not allow myself to be intimidated by sheer numbers; yes, there are 5 billion people out there, but God has endowed me with gifts that equip me to serve. Still, I wonder—where am I going to begin?

A friend of mine went with a medical team to Bangladesh to help clean up after an awful storm some years ago. These dedicated scientists had only a limited amount of medicine, and many people were dying. What seemed an immense plain was covered with silent or groaning forms. It was an awful feeling, my friend said, to have to play God, to look out over a sea of bodies—some dead, some not quite dead, and some who might live—and decide who would get the scarce medicine. He began to go person by person, looking into each individual set of eyes. As he saw these people one at a time, he was enabled to minister to them.

I've discovered, in my walk with Jesus Christ, that although I must teach the gospel to every creature, I must do it one person at a time. It doesn't matter how many people are there; each is an individual, and I win them just one at a time.

Jesus taught thousands of people at times, but at other times he had wonderful dialogues with individuals—the woman at the well, Nicodemus, the man born blind, the thief on the cross, and many others. He didn't just talk with them one at a time, he saw them one at a time too. We also have to do this if we're going to be significant in his service.

There are so many problems in this world that it can be hard to decide which ones to tackle. Here are my criteria. First I consider *proximity*. Which problems are closest to me geographically? Which do I have to walk around every day? It is possible to go to a missions seminar and become deeply concerned about people halfway around the world. Then we may leave the church and drive through a needy neighborhood in our own city, still thinking about those people on the other side of the globe. I resent such hypocrisy. I think God calls us to minister wherever we are.

I have a good friend who is an evangelist. Recently he served a church in England. This church, he said, had compassion. They were always witnessing to people in a London slum district. One day after the service, my friend walked out into the street in front of this elegant church and began to share

Christ with people right there. After all, they were close to the church. It was their neighborhood. And even though the people didn't look like they needed the Lord, they turned out to be as needy as anyone. We should begin to serve right where we are.

Another criterion for deciding which problem to tackle is *relationship.* If we have a relative or a very close friend who has a problem, that's the place to start helping. As Paul wrote, "If anyone does not provide for his relatives, and especially for his immediate family, he has denied the faith and is worse than an unbeliever" (1 Timothy 5:8).

Moving out just a little, another criterion is *identity.* We can help people best if we can identify with them—people who talk our language, who live in our neighborhood, who have jobs like ours, who like to talk about the things that interest us. We can tackle problems better with people who understand us. Once sociological barriers come between us and others, it gets harder to minister to them.

And finally, we can most effectively minister to people who *esteem* us. If they respect us, they will listen and they will open up to Christ's words. If they don't already respect us, we will have to earn their esteem before we can effectively minister to them. So if we see problems among people who already hold us in high esteem, we can confidently and more immediately offer our help.

What I'm saying is that we do not need to look halfway around the world to find people to help. We don't need to seek out strange and exotic people. If we look in our own neighborhoods, in our own families, among people very much like we are, who already like and respect us, we can find plenty of opportunity to help. So proximity, relationship, identity, and esteem are good criteria for helping us decide how and where to start changing our world. If God wants us to serve in some more distant place, he will make this very clear to us, but only after we have had compassion for those ills near at hand.

♦ LONE WOLVES AND GROUPIES
CALVIN MILLER

Some people serve God better in groups; others do their best work alone. Those who prefer fellowship are no more nor less spiritual than those who prefer solitude. Both can serve effectively. What is important for me is to find out my own style, because I will not serve effectively in someone else's shoes.

I admire people like David Livingstone, for example, who are willing to follow God in absolute loneliness. Many of God's great mystics and visionaries were loners. Artists are often loners by nature. I think one reason they see things that almost nobody else sees is that they've used their solitude to train their perception.

On the other hand, some kinds of ministry cannot be accomplished by individuals. We Christians can reach a long way if we reach together. If we band together, we can feed a lot of people and we can work with God to redeem the world.

God uses people who work best alone, and he uses people who work best in groups. It is important, though, that we use neither solitude nor fellowship as a way of excluding people who are different from us. We Christians must show the world that God has turned us into lovers. It doesn't matter that one of us speaks in tongues and another does not, that one of us has been sprinkled and one immersed. We can have our own opinions in these areas and still band together, pool our resources, and let the world see us loving each other and caring for the world Jesus died to save.

God Is in Control

✍ CALVIN MILLER

Nowadays, much of the time, life seems to have gone out of control. Several nations have the nuclear bomb, and several more will be developing it soon. History seems senseless. Men kill and order others to kill. Armies destroy and hurt. World leaders seem to do Satan's will, and Christians may wonder if God has lost control of his world.

He has not!

Although Satan is the prince of this world (John 12:31), he has been judged and condemned (John 16:11). God is sovereign over all men and nations, and all must make a final account with him. At the time of the final reckoning, every problem—personal and national—will be set right. But as of now, evil is a terrible thing, and, until it is destroyed, life will sometimes appear out of control.

The trouble is that evil has burrowed into the human personality. It is in all of us. We don't always act in the best interest of others. Feeling coerced by the political system, or by what others will think of us, or by the values of those around us, we surrender our Christian freedom and choose to do what we know is wrong. At the end of World War II, the world was horrified to discover that brilliant men with PhDs could build gas chambers. Their level of intelligence had nothing to do with their ability to choose to do right. One military leader after another at the Nuremberg trials said, "I was only taking orders."

How can I say God is in control when all around me I see evil? Consider the ending of the book of Habakkuk. The prophet is living in a time of natural and military calamities. "Destruction and violence are before me; there is strife, and conflict abounds. Therefore the law is paralyzed, and justice never prevails. The wicked hem in the righteous, so that justice is perverted" (1:3, 4).

But Habakkuk has faith that, in the end, the Lord will save his people. He describes the future day of judgment when "you came out to deliver your people" (3:13), and he proclaims his faith that God is in control in spite of appearances: "Though the fig tree does not bud and there are no grapes on the vines, though the olive crop fails and the fields produce no food, though there are no sheep in the pen and no cattle in the stalls, yet I will rejoice in the Lord, I will be joyful in God my Savior. The Sovereign Lord is my strength" (3:17-19). No matter how things look, we can have faith that God will never abandon this world. He is always sovereign in this universe.

There are no limits to God's ultimate control, but his temporary control can be thwarted by human self-will. In his great love for us, he gives us the right to shake our fists in his face and to tell him to get lost. But his great hope is that we will turn in hunger to him. When we do this, our discipleship means something to him, because we have chosen to love him.

The amount of freedom God gives us is truly amazing. If I were God, I would probably have rubbed out Adolf Hitler. A group of German theologians including Dietrich Bonhoeffer wanted to do just that—that's why Bonhoeffer was executed. God seems to allow us the freedom to go to almost any length we wish.

Still, biblical accounts of the judgment keep us aware that at some point there will be a reckoning. We will all stand before the judgment seat of Christ (see Revelation 20; 2 Corinthians 5:10). We often wish this day of reckoning would come a bit more quickly, but Peter explains why it does not: "With the Lord a day is like a thousand years, and a thousand years are like a day. The Lord is not slow in keeping his promise, as some understand slowness. He is patient with you, not wanting anyone to perish, but everyone to come to repentance" (2 Peter 3:8, 9).

God's sovereignty is something like a parent's. The time comes for most of us parents when the best thing we can do for our children is to let them do something foolish. We hate to let them do it because of the hurt it will bring them, but if they won't listen to us we often have no other recourse. So we stand by and pray while they go wrong. Then we must often bail them out of something we knew was wrong. Yes, they often get hurt in the process. But that is loving sovereignty.

I think that God, like a parent, often stands by and watches us. He hurts to see his children disobey, but he never coerces us. Instead he calls to us and woos us back until we want to seek his pleasure. When we turn from our evil ways and come back to him, his joy is marvelous.

♦ WORKING WITH SECULAR AGENCIES
CALVIN MILLER

Christians should be willing to work with anyone who is proclaiming the Good News. A Christian who works in a secular group can bring to that group a dynamic that the rest of them don't have—the God dynamic. If a great humanitarian work is being done by humanitarian people without any reference to God, the moment a Christ-man or a Christ-woman joins the group, something new comes in. The Christian is not just passing out cups of cold water in the name of strong human feeling. He or she is passing them out in the name of Jesus. The difference will be noticed. Christians working with non-Christians can open the world up to see the Christ that their souls adore.

Why Should I Care about a Just Society?

JOHN PERKINS

God created man to live in a perfect environment, the Garden of Eden. He was told to work in that environment, to take care of it. Once he was outside the garden, he was told to work to make his environment better. God made him responsible for the earth, and he gave him the creativity he would need to do the job.

Our environment is the society we live in. The quality of our society tells us whether we have obeyed or disobeyed God's command to be responsible for our earth. Jesus said that we're to be salt and light in the world (Matthew 5:13-16). The society in which we live is the place we must make better.

In the last twenty-five or thirty years we have created a new suburban community, but we have ignored our responsibilities to the ghetto. The prisons are being filled, and the welfare rolls are long. Crime has its roots in these ghetto areas, because they are neglected. Education is poor; the better things our culture provides are not available; and we are paying for it.

A lot of what has happened to us in terms of crime, divorce, drug abuse, and many other social problems is a result of people's indifference. Even abortion has become typical because we've lost our view of the importance of life.

Until recent years, the evangelical church has not seen the importance of taking responsibility for society. We have thought that the most important thing was to get people saved. We thought that if we changed people, we'd change society. I think we have to do both. We have to change people, and then we have to engage those people in changing society. This is the only way society will be saved.

It's crucial that we have a creative, biblical concept of justice; otherwise we'll go off to picketing or other such activities to try to obtain justice. And sometimes we think that those activities are justice within themselves. Believers need a good concept of justice and of what makes a just society. We need to know what we're working toward. The Bible tells us what we need to know.

When God got ready for Moses to build the tabernacle, he told him to do it after the pattern in heaven (Hebrews 8:5). As God tells us how to make society, he shows us the heavenly pattern. In heaven there's no death, there's no crime. In a just society, there is no death or crime either. Justice is always an economic issue. It's understanding who owns what; it's understanding how we manage God's resources. The Bible teaches that the earth is the Lord's with all its resources (Psalm 50:12). Injustice then, is depriving people from using those resources in a proper way.

The concept of justice comes from the idea of rest. It comes from the Sabbath, a time of rest for former slaves (see Deuteronomy 5:12-15). We work for justice when we help those who have not enjoyed God or enjoyed the fruit of creation. We work to help them get jobs, to get skills, to learn, to worship. And to me, those are the roots of justice.

The way to work for justice, as far as I'm concerned, is to help people come to know this great God of provision. You then help them learn to work with their own hands, to become workers together with God. When they have done this, you make sure they can enjoy the fruit of their labor.

Justice occurs when dignity is affirmed, when people are able to recognize that they are loved by God and that they have skills and talents that need to be developed. Justice is helping people reach their full potential in God.

Taking a Christian Stand on Human Rights

VERNON GROUNDS

Throughout Scripture, there is an emphasis on protecting and promoting the rights of other people, particularly marginal groups such as widows, orphans, and aliens who are unable to safeguard their own rights. Like everyone else, they are entitled to the basic necessities of life.

In Luke 13, a woman who had been physically disabled for years came to Jesus. He asked, "Should not this woman, a daughter of Abraham, whom Satan has kept bound for eighteen long years, be set free on the Sabbath day from what bound her?" (Luke 13:16). His critics felt no obligation to minister to her. But she had a need, and to Jesus that need constituted a sort of claim.

As a Christian, I am under obligation to seek for other people the rights, privileges, and opportunities that I desire for myself. This is the principle of the golden rule in Matthew 7:12, "In everything, do to others what you would have them do to you, for this sums up the Law and the Prophets." If I think my children have a right to good food, then certainly other children also have a right to good food. If I feel my kids have a right to a decent education, then I should be concerned that other children also have a decent education. It's my obligation under God to love my neighbor as I love myself. Hence I should do whatever I can, within the orbit of my opportunities and resources, to enhance the decency and dignity of human life. I should do what I can to affect positively the destiny of other human beings.

The average Christian suburbanite is insulated from needy people, but there are still many things we can do for them. Individually, I can't do much, but when I add my effort to the efforts of others, things can be accomplished.

First, *we ought to read.* This means staying informed on the pertinent issues of our day. We should know what is going on. We can do this by reading the newspapers and a weekly newsmagazine.

Certainly we should pray. We should pray for the rulers and those in authority as well as for the needy themselves. I've often wondered what would happen if we could get the 40 million Americans who claim to be born again to devote five minutes of focused prayer every day to public issues and to needs all around the world. If we could get a great volume of daily intercession for crucial issues as they arise, I wonder what the results would be. Prayer can be a powerful factor.

We need to talk. We need to discuss issues with other Christians by telling them what we think and why we think it and then listening to their opinions. As we express our opinions and listen to other people, we learn by that interaction.

We need to vote. And in order to vote intelligently, we need to read and talk so we can understand for whom and what we should vote. We should know why we support certain candidates and oppose others, why we favor some proposals and not others.

We ought to write. We should write to our newspapers, our local officials, and members of Congress.

We should join. We can unite with other Christians and sometimes non-Christians in organizations that are working for civic righteousness. My own involvement includes being on the board of Evangelicals for Social Action, an organization that promotes civic righteousness and spiritual renewal as well as justice, freedom, and peace. I also actively support some other national organizations.

Each of these efforts taken alone is insignificant, but when their impact is multiplied, they make a tremendous difference.

♦ DISAGREEING ABOUT POLITICS
VERNON GROUNDS

You can probably find a Christian holding almost any position on any political issue. Because there is so much disagreement, some Christians don't want to be politically involved at all. But disagreement is not foreign to Christians. We have long disagreed about certain doctrinal issues, yet Christians continue to worship and work together.

There are issues that are undebatable, I think. For example, the Word of God is so clear-cut with regard to abortion that we don't have to engage in argument about it. But on many issues the Word of God doesn't speak with clarity. It lays down principles, but then we have to do our best to apply those principles to specific situations.

Christians need to study, think, discuss, and pray—and then reach their own conclusions. God holds them accountable for the use they make of their intelligence and their opportunities to explore various issues, whether philosophical or political. I would urge people to talk and read and pray and have the courage to follow the guidance of the Holy Spirit, even though they may arrive at an unpopular conclusion.

What Is Our Responsibility to the Poor?
AJITH FERNANDO

The Bible describes God as having a special concern for the poor and needy. Deuteronomy 10:18 says, "He defends the cause of the fatherless and the widow, and loves the alien, giving him food and clothing." The next verse is a charge to God's servants to reflect this same attitude: "You are to love those who are aliens." Often the Bible presents concern for the poor as an accurate measure of an individual's faithfulness (Luke 3:11; James 2:14-19).

As Christians we should always be thinking about how we can fulfill our responsibility to the poor and needy. They are our neighbors, and we are to love our neighbors as ourselves (see Luke 10:27-37). This becomes all the more urgent when we realize that one-fifth of the world's population lives in absolute poverty while another fifth consumes four-fifths of the world's income. A large percentage of this second category identify themselves as Christian. When Jesus saw the hungry crowds, he fed them (Mark 8:1-10). As his followers, we too should do something to feed the starving millions in the world today.

There are many who say that if only the poor would work hard, they could improve their lot in life. The Bible recognizes that some people are to blame for their poverty. There are lazy people (Proverbs 6:6-11; 10:4), drunkards, and gluttons (Proverbs 23:20, 21). Yet many of the world's poor are placed in surroundings that are not conducive to self-advancement. They lack the basic requirements for keeping healthy. Even if they want to do well, they cannot. In such environments, most people lack the ambition to succeed because they think it is not possible for them to escape from the rut they are in. They struggle with feelings of inferiority, and this keeps them from developing a healthy ambition to achieve. An exceptional person may succeed in freeing himself from the shackles of poverty, but such a person is rare. We cannot expect all to be like him.

This is why the Bible, in both Old and New Testaments, gives elaborate guidelines about assistance to the poor and needy. One of our greatest responsibilities is to help change the environment in which these people live. This often involves the introduction of policies and programs aimed at eliminating the unjust causes of poverty. The Bible says over and over again that the poor, because they are powerless, fall victim to exploitation (see, for example, Isaiah 10:1-4).

So we Christians need to support programs aimed to improve the health, education, housing, and legal rights of the poor. Indeed, such programs are often abused. This is inevitable, for we are working with fallen individuals. We need to ensure that safeguards are included to minimize abuses, but the abuses should not dissuade us from this work.

How can Christians support such schemes? Some may serve as volunteers or full-time workers in organizations that help the poor. Some may help raise the awareness of the general public of the needs of the poor. There is a great need for preachers and Christian journalists who will highlight these needs. Some may use their professions as springboards to help the poor. I am thinking of lawyers, bankers, teachers, and technical specialists such as agriculturalists who all have expertise that could be directed against poverty.

Those not directly involved with helping the poor can give financially to those who are. Proverbs 19:17 says, "He who is kind to the poor lends to the Lord, and he will reward him for what he has done." Voting to bring in programs that will help the poor also becomes a Christian responsibility. Sometimes such programs cause the comfortable and the wealthy to sacrifice some of their own privileges. Christians gladly sacrifice for the underprivileged, because sacrifice is an important aspect of the Christian life-style.

Yet we know that however much we help the poor and change their social and economic conditions, this does not deal with the worst form of poverty—spiritual poverty. The most serious poverty of all comes from the separation from God in this world that results in eternal punishment in the next. So our primary responsibility toward the poor is to preach the gospel to them.

Sadly, however, in many countries the gospel has had very little impact on the poor. The poor have not been interested in following our Lord Jesus Christ. Sometimes this is because they feel we are not interested in their problems. Until we show them that we are concerned about their needs, we will not earn the right to be heard by them.

Another reason the poor are not interested in our gospel is our life-style. Often our life-style is so distant from theirs that the contact we have with them is on a very superficial level. This has made our witness ineffective.

If we are to be effective witnesses among the poor, we must be able to identify with them. But if we present an image of affluence we cannot identify effectively with them. The only ones who will be attracted to us will be the selfish "rice Christians" who will come to us to grab whatever material benefits they can get. If our life-style is markedly different from that of the poor, they will not believe we can understand them. They may even resent our help because they view it as crumbs from our tables given out of our excess—not out of genuine concern, but from a reluctant sense of duty.

God may be calling us to reduce our catalogue of what we regard as essentials, because the poor regard them as unnecessary luxuries. By reducing our catalogue of essentials, we will spend less and so will have more money to give to the poor. More important, our life-style will be less offensive to the poor. This will keep the door open to them and will give us a greater chance to share the gospel of Christ.

Obedience to Christ may result in inconvenience and even suffering. We may feel humiliated when we compare our life-style with the prosperity of our friends. But this should not surprise us. Suffering has always been inseparably linked to Christian discipleship (Luke 9:23-26). What should surprise us is to find a disciple of Christ who is not experiencing suffering for his Lord's sake.

♦ HOW OUR LIFE-STYLE AFFECTS OUR MINISTRY / AJITH FERNANDO

Some Christians defend their affluent life-style by saying it opens doors that enable them to witness to other affluent people. These Christians should note that when Jesus lived on earth, he did not have the trappings of affluence. Yet he was able to identify with wealthy people such as Zacchaeus, Nicodemus, and Joseph of Arimathea. He did this not by becoming rich but by showing genuine concern for these people and by presenting a message that was clearly relevant to their lives.

We do not need to be rich in order to minister to the rich. By contrast, it may be necessary to become poor in order to minister to the poor. An affluent life-style is unlikely to help our ministry to the rich, and it will almost certainly hinder or even cancel our witness to the poor. The poor resent affluence. So we would do well to heed Paul's call to follow the example of Christ, who, "though he was rich, yet for your sakes he became poor, so that you through his poverty might become rich" (2 Corinthians 8:9).

♦ WHAT SHOULD WE DO WITH OUR POSSESSIONS? / AJITH FERNANDO

The Bible does not command poverty as a norm for all Christians. It commands us to be rich in our generosity (1 Timothy 6:18). In fact, in Ephesians 4:28 Paul said that giving to the needy is a primary reason for working hard and earning money.

Yet the Bible warns us that riches can lead us astray (1 Timothy 6:9, 10) and tells us not to trust in them (Proverbs 11:28). The true disciple surrenders everything he has to Christ (Luke 14:33). If—with an attitude of surrender to Christ and concern for the needy and the work of the kingdom—we are sensitive to God's voice, then he will show us what to do with what we possess. When he shows us this, we must obey without hesitating.

Civil Disobedience and the Christian

✍ ANTHONY CAMPOLO

How can one obey God and not the government? It is obvious from Romans 13 that every Christian is subject to the higher authorities. We are always subject to the government, but at times we may not be able to obey the government. The early Christians very often had to disobey the government when it required them to act in a manner contrary to the known will of God. They had to obey God and not the government. (See, for example, the story of Peter and John in Acts 4:1-22.)

The government always gives you two choices: obey or be punished. When Christians find they must oppose the government on biblical grounds, they must present themselves for arrest.

During the Vietnam War, I counseled many Christian young men who were students at the university where I taught. They believed the war was immoral, and many felt they ought to go to Canada so they wouldn't be drafted. I argued, "You have no right to run to Canada." They responded, "Is it right for us to be drafted into the army and forced to kill people when we believe this war is contrary to the will of God?" My answer was this: "You do not have to be drafted; you do not have to serve in this war. But if you choose to go against the government, you have to face the consequences. Pick up your draft notice, say that although you are not a conscientious objector you refuse to serve in this war, and turn yourself in for arrest."

As a Christian I must not take the government lightly. I must respect the government and be willing to subject myself to it, because the Bible tells me to do so. I cannot always obey the government, however. If it asks me to do something contrary to the will of God, I cannot obey. I disobey the government and surrender to the second option: I submit myself to the punishment the government exercises on the disobedient. This was Dietrich Bonhoeffer's belief; this is why he—although he could easily have escaped the Auschwitz concentration camp and death—deliberately went back to Germany, stood up to Hitler, went to jail, and died.

It is part of the Christian's testimony to submit to the government's punishment and simultaneously refuse to do what is immoral. This approach gives the Christian an opportunity to tell God's message to evil governments. Many governments have been more changed by martyrs than by the armies that have opposed them on the battlefield.

We should resist the government when it does something immoral, and we should be willing to go to jail and die at the hands of the government when it calls upon us to act against the known will of God. But one does not destroy the government, because, as Romans 13:1 says, it is established by God.

RELATED ARTICLES
Chapter 17: **Can My Prayer Influence World Leaders?**
Chapter 19: **Personal Morality vs. Social Morality**

CHAPTER

25

The Meaning of Service

- ✓ How does serving others help me grow spiritually?
- ✓ How can I serve others?
- ✓ What does it mean to be a servant to others?
- ✓ What is the Christian's responsibility to the poor and needy?
- ✓ How can I serve my church?
- ✓ Isn't submission a sign of weakness?

Service and Spiritual Growth

V. GILBERT BEERS

One snowy night last winter I gathered some firewood for our fireplace. The night was cold, but as soon as I put the logs on the fire, the room filled with warmth. The wood itself was gnarled and gray, weathered from lying outside for several seasons. There was nothing beautiful or warm about it. But when expended, it cheered our home and family, and we delighted in its glow for quite some time.

When we serve others, we become like the burning firewood. Unattractive in ourselves, we release God's glory when we are expended for him.

In the autumn, my wife and I planted some tulip and daffodil bulbs. If you have planted any of these, you remember how unattractive each bulb is. But in the spring, these ugly lumps release their beauty, and people marvel at the colorful sight.

When we serve others, we become like those flower bulbs. Unattractive in ourselves, we release Jesus' beauty when we are expended for him.

These two illustrations show how warmth and beauty are released when ordinary things are expended. But the illustrations are incomplete. The serving Christian is more fortunate than the firewood or the bulbs. Wood and bulbs, when expending themselves to bring warmth and beauty, do not themselves become more attractive. The Christian does.

Christian service brings Christ—his beauty and his warmth—to the ones who are served. It also brings Christ's gifts to the one who is serving. Serving God and others is like attending a banquet. In the delights of the feast, we find our strength and sustenance.

Our children have all served as counselors or staff members at Christian camps. Through the years, I have observed them and their friends grow through serving. I believe that the counselors and staff members receive far more from the camping experience than the campers do, although the campers are abundantly helped also. Growth comes from service, not from being served. Just as bodily strength increases with exercise, faith grows as we use it.

Our motive for serving God and others, however, should never be what we will get out of it. If that becomes our motive, we are not giving with a clean heart, and God will not reward us with his full blessing. But if we serve because we want to give, we will get back much more than we give. We will grow in Christ and in our capacity to serve even more effectively.

The parable of the talents tells us much about the rewards for effective service (Matthew 25:14-30). The faithless servant was given no reward. His unused talent was taken from him, and he was sent away from the presence of the master. But the faithful servants were rewarded, not with great riches to keep for themselves, but with greater opportunities to serve.

A person with a serving heart appreciates this kind of reward. He or she realizes that serving our Lord and Master, Jesus Christ, is best rewarded with greater opportunities to serve. That is because through service we grow spiritually and become larger vessels to carry his word of life to those who need it.

If we serve for reward, our reward will not be greater service, for we will have served with a poor motive. But if we serve Christ because we want to please him, he will give us the greatest of rewards—the opportunity to serve him even more effectively. In the course of serving him, we ourselves will grow spiritually. We will become more effective servants, prepared for the greater service he will give us. Spiritual growth is not a greater amount of piety, but a greater capacity to serve Jesus. As we serve, we become more like him, better equipped to carry out his Great Commission.

Something beautiful happens when we become more effective vessels to carry the Lord's blessings to others. Created in his image, we grow to resemble him more closely as we do his work. A spiritually mature person is winsome and attractive, bearing the marks of Christ. There is no greater reward than this.

Serving the Church

HOWARD HENDRICKS

The church has a hard time getting people to serve because it has never distinguished between church work and the work of the church. There are two churches—the church gathered and the church scattered. Church work happens at the church building with 10 to 20 percent of the church members involved. The work of the church goes on during the week, wherever a church member may be.

When someone asks us where our church is, we say that at eleven o'clock on Sunday morning it is at Fourth and Main. But at eleven o'clock on Monday morning it is all over the community in offices, schools, homes, and factories. The work of the church is for 100 percent of the believers, 100 percent of the time. People think serving God has to take place in a church building. But we can serve God just as well in our homes and at our jobs.

In recruiting people to volunteer at church, we need to declare a moratorium on three things.

First, we need to stop public announcements that beg people to become involved. "Won't you please come next Tuesday; we're going visiting. Last Tuesday nobody showed up, so won't you please help us out?" If we do that, the next Tuesday nobody will show up except the two people we should never send visiting. The impression given when we beg publicly is that God is hard up.

Second, we should ban last-minute appointments. The Sunday school superintendent sneaks into the adult department, taps someone on the shoulder sitting at the end of the row, and gives him a life sentence in the junior department. What people learn is not to sit on the end of a row in the adult department if they don't want to become a Sunday school teacher.

Third, we should do away with arm-twisting techniques. We tell a person, "We have been all over this church, and we can't get anyone to take this high-school class. We've lost seven teachers in the last eight months, and we are desperate. We have finally gotten to your name. Won't you take it?" The person says, "Well, I'm busy," and we say, "It won't take a lot of your time, and it sure would help us a lot."

How we enlist a person determines how he or she will serve. We need placement committees whose main job is to match a person with a job.

The placement committee makes an appointment to talk with the person and tell him or her exactly what the task involves and what the church will provide in terms of training and resources. The committee then asks the person to pray about it. Asking the person to pray is not just a spiritual gimmick. A person should not say yes to the church before saying yes to God. But neither should he or she say no to the church before saying no to God.

Our church has a motto: We expect a lot of you, and you can expect a lot of us. In other words, there are certain standards for teachers, for people who go visiting, for deacons. We never ask a person to help without giving him or her proper training. As a result, our helpers do a good job, and they are happy to volunteer their time and talents to the church.

♦ REGAINING AN AUDIENCE FOR THE GOSPEL / HOWARD HENDRICKS

The gospel has not lost its power in the late twentieth century, but in too many churches it has lost its audience. One reason for this is our building-centered and program-centered approach to evangelism. We say, "Here we are, you lucky sinners. Come to church. Welcome." There is no verse in Scripture that tells a lost person to go to church. But there are plenty of verses that tell the believer to go to the lost world.

We ought to focus on life-style evangelism where we build relationships with lost people in our network of contacts, in our community, in our office, in our tennis club, in our school. By getting to know the people we see frequently, we earn the right to be heard. We share social events, athletics, concerts, and the office water cooler, and we use this common ground as a basis of leading them to Christ.

Churches should have programs to meet the needs of every age group, from the youngest child to the oldest senior citizen. Are we focusing on the single-parent family, on the blended family of stepparents and stepchildren, on unmarried adults? Address the concerns of the aging, the fastest growing segment in the American population. Minister to a secular culture through business and professional people, to the disabled, to prisoners.

In short, the church must become community sensitive. It has to have its antennas up to find out what is going on in the community, who the hurting people are, and what it can do to meet those needs.

What? Me, a Servant?

SHAWN ROBINSON

You have taken your first step of faith by coming forward and saying, "Yes Jesus, I want you to be Lord and Savior of my life." You turn toward the new life with renewed hope and high expectations.

Now it's time to take the second step and reality suddenly sinks in—What does a Christian do? What type of life-style am I to exemplify as I attempt to live out my commitment to Christ on a daily basis?

The role models are few and far between because, as a whole, our society looks up to the tough guys, the people with money and power, as the epitome of human success. In the Broadway musical "Annie," the character of Daddy Warbucks best personifies today's "typical" leader when he says, "It doesn't matter who you step on on your way up, as long as you don't come back down."

Yet in this sea of super-sophistication, Jesus says the Christian is to be one who contradicts the social standards of today's society. But what made Jesus radically different? "For even the Son of Man did not come to be served, but to serve, and to give his life as a ransom for many" (Mark 10:45). To *serve* and to *give* is radical, and we're called to do the same.

"And we know that in all things God works for the good of those who love him, who have been called according to his purpose. For those God foreknew he also predestined *to be conformed to the likeness of his Son"* (Romans 8:28, 29). And, as Philippians 2:5 says, "Your attitude should be the same as that of Christ Jesus."

What? Me, a servant? How could I possibly make a difference in someone else's life?

Like Moses, we may feel incapable of the work Jesus gives us. But what sets us apart from the rest of the world as Christians is not just what we say, but what we do—how we live our lives on a daily basis.

One of the most godly people I know has never written a book or preached a sermon, but, oh, how she listens! So often we take for granted such seemingly small gifts, and yet it is the small things that show others that the God who is in us is real. One of my close friends came to Christ not because of a great sermon he had heard, but because a Christian was faithful in visiting him every day for a month after he had been in an accident for drunk driving.

None of us is insignificant. We can all make an impact! We may not be a Billy Graham, but God will put us into positions where we can serve and glorify him. All we have to do is ask.

One of the great heroes of the New Testament is Stephen. He ministered to people by waiting on tables! The early church was growing by leaps and bounds (more than three thousand people became Christians on the day of Pentecost alone). A dispute arose over the food distributed among the believers. The apostles knew they had to keep preaching and needed some help in handling the administrative details. So seven men (including Stephen) were *carefully* chosen for the task. The disciples knew that these men would make a great impact on the lives of those about them.

So what happened? The Word of God kept on spreading, not just because of great preachers like Peter and John, but because of others like Stephen who "full of God's grace and power, did great wonders and miraculous signs among the people" (Acts 6:8). And Stephen was just a table server!

Stephen wasn't any less important than the others because of his position. He merely allowed God to use him as he lived out a life of obedience. The ordinary became the extraordinary, the mundane became the exciting, all because Stephen was willing to serve and to give everything in order to glorify his Lord.

How are you serving God right now? Have you looked for ways that you can minister to others at work, home, or school?

Yes, you, a servant! It is only in service that you can find true joy and fulfillment in expressing the hope that is in you. Jesus got involved in the lives of people and he told his disciples to do the same:

Then the righteous will answer him, "Lord, when did we see you hungry and feed you, or thirsty and give you something to drink? When did we see you a stranger and invite you in, or needing clothes and clothe you? When did we see you sick or in prison and go to visit you?"

The King will reply, "I tell you the truth, whatever you did for one of the least of these brothers of mine, you did for me." Matthew 25:37-40

♦ WHOM DO I SERVE? / YFC EDITORS

Service is too often misrepresented as menial, downgrading, and undesirable. But the Bible's view of service is far different—it is one of the highest callings of mankind. Service is raised to such a high place because it is an attitude that meets people's needs. When you see a need, are you willing to respond? And when you help meet a need (when you serve) your acts are really acts of praise to God.

Whom do you serve? You are called to serve both God and others. And the Bible doesn't distinguish between service to other Christians and nonbelievers. You are called to meet the needs you see.

How do you serve? The way to get the proper attitude toward service is to focus on Jesus Christ. He is the ultimate example of a servant. You are to follow his example.

Redeem the Time!

DAVE VEERMAN

"Redeeming the time because the days are evil," he read, and then the preacher closed the well-worn King James Bible and proceeded to exhort us to use every available moment to spread the gospel. "There's so little time," he said.

It's true, of course—there *is* very little time. Life is short, no matter how long we live, and Jesus is coming soon! As responsible Christians, therefore, we should make every moment count for him. But herein lies the problem. What does it mean "to redeem the time," "to make every moment count"? Does this mean that Christians should never relax, play, celebrate, read, or fellowship?

This time tension is very real and cannot be easily dismissed. Here are some biblical principles to consider.

1. *Urgency.* Our lives are like "mist that appears for a little while and then vanishes" (James 4:15); we really do not have a lot of time to live for Christ.

And life is short for those who do not know Christ. There is an urgency to our task as messengers of God's Good News: people who die without Christ go to hell. They will not hear unless we tell them (Romans 10:14). We must take every God-given opportunity to tell people about Christ.

2. *Love.* Christians' lives are to be marked by love. Paul said it is the greatest gift (1 Corinthians 13:13), and John told us to love each other (1 John 3:11). Love is the evidence of Christ in our lives (John 13:35), it is the motivation for selfless service to others (Matthew 25:34-40), and it is the bridge for effective communication of the gospel (James 2:14-18). Whatever we do, including evangelism, must be bathed in love.

3. *Stewardship.* A steward is a person charged with taking care of something that belongs to someone else. Christians are called stewards because they have the responsibility to care for all that God has given to them (Matthew 25:14-30). This includes talents, abilities, gifts, possessions, relationships, money, and time. *Everything* that we do as Christians should glorify God (Colossians 3:17). Stewardship also involves our bodies. We should take care of these "temples" (1 Corinthians 6:19) so that we can serve him. Certainly we cannot spread the gospel very well if we are sick or otherwise physically immobilized because of the neglect or abuse of our bodies. Sleep, rest, exercise, food, relaxation, and laughter are all positive ingredients in good body care.

4. *Priorities.* Scripture makes it very clear that the main focus of our lives should be God's "kingdom and his righteousness" (Matthew 6:33). Everything that we do, therefore, should fall into place after this number one priority. And the Bible makes it clear that we are *whole* people, not just "spirits" or "physical beings." Our faith must be applied to *every* aspect of our lives: physical, social, mental, and spiritual. This includes our minds (Romans 12:1, 2), our relationships (Philippians 2:4; 1 Thessalonians 4:9), and our bodies (1 Corinthians 6:19). Jesus provides the perfect example: he "grew in wisdom and stature, and in favor with God and men" (Luke 2:52).

Widen your perspective and think about your life as a whole (not just a moment or a year). Now digest and internalize these biblical principles. Are you wasting precious time? Your task is urgent. Are you compartmentalizing your faith? God wants *all* of you. Are you misusing or abusing what God has entrusted to you? Develop your mind, your body, and your relationships. Are you engulfed by anxiety and stress? Relax, unwind, play.

In its fuller context, our "redeeming the time" verse states, "So be careful how you act; these are difficult days. Don't be fools; be wise: make the most of every opportunity you have for doing good. Don't act thoughtlessly, but try to find out and do whatever the Lord wants you to" (Ephesians 5:15-17, TLB).

Amen.

Submission and Strength

JANETTE OKE

Submission—what a dreadful word, and not at all popular in our present society! One dictionary says submission is "to yield to the authority of another, surrender, resign, refer to judgment or discretion, comply with, be subject, yield." Jesus, quoting Moses, said it much better: "Love your neighbor as yourself" (Leviticus 19:18; Luke 10:27).

Who is our neighbor? Everyone we come in contact with. Does that mean we are to submit to everyone? Is that what Scripture is saying?

We must be careful to distinguish between submitting to other people as individuals and submitting to their beliefs, notions, or idiosyncrasies. There is no question about it: we are to take a decided stand against untruths, false doctrines, corruption, and so on.

And yet as we oppose wrong ideas, we are to submit to individuals who hold them. It is possible to be submissive and still "fight the good fight of the faith" (1 Timothy 6:12), "stand your ground" (Ephesians 6:13), "declare it fearlessly" (Ephesians 6:20), and "contend for the faith that was once for all entrusted to the saints" (Jude 3).

Scripture tells us to "honor one another above [ourselves]" (Romans 12:10). We should begin by submitting ourselves to God. We can do so in confidence that the God who created us and redeemed us knows what is best for us.

Submitting our will to someone else—even God—is probably the most difficult thing we are ever asked to do. As I look at the New Testament stories about Christ, I am amazed that the very King of glory could totally hand over his own will—"Not my will, but yours be done" (Luke 22:42). God wants us to do the same. He wants everything we have and everything we are.

There is always some little area we want to hang onto for ourselves. We are often unconscious of that area until we suddenly bump into it. Then we realize that once again we have to go to the cross in submission. We have to be submissive before we can really be useful to God, before he can bless us and use us as a tool of ministry.

After submitting to God, we are to submit to one another. Scripture tells us to love our neighbors as ourselves, which means I will put my neighbor's needs at least equal with my own. We are even told to love our enemies. Most of us don't have many out-and-out enemies, but there are always those who put us down, ridicule us, and harm us in small ways. We need to submit to these people in the Lord, learning to respond in love.

If we see each person around us as someone worthy of God's love, then we will find it easier to submit to that person. Each person living on our planet earth was created by God. Adam and Eve were made in his image, and even though we have marred that creation through sin, there is still some of God's image in our friends, our neighbors, and the strangers that walk among us, from the noblest to the most degraded person we meet.

How do we submit to others? Scripture talks of turning the other cheek

(Matthew 5:39). This is not the macho thing to do. It does not sound right in a society where everything is focused on me—doing my own thing, taking care of number one. It is not natural to turn the other cheek, to honor others above ourselves. It might be easy if everyone else were doing it; the only problem is, we may find ourselves submitting all by ourselves.

There are those—even among Christians—who have not learned to submit or who have given up because it is so difficult. When we put these people above ourselves, they may not extend us the same honor in return. We must be prepared for that. Submission should not be a one-way street (Ephesians 5:21 says, "Submit to one another out of reverence for Christ"), but sometimes it has to be—and we still must be willing to submit.

Submission is difficult because we were created with free wills, the ability to choose. To give over that free will is against our nature. Of course, after sin entered the world submission became even more difficult. Our flesh rebels against submission. We want to be our own person, do our own thing, be the captain of our own ship, steer our own course. We want to be in control.

Satan does not want us to submit. If we continually refuse to submit and struggle along in our own way in our relationship with God or with other people, we will live in constant agitation and disunity. Satan encourages us to hold out, because he knows it will result in our destruction.

Submission goes beyond actions to attitude. If a store clerk barks at you because she has had a bad day and you submit in silence without retaliating, you're going to walk away with a good feeling. If a car pushes in front of you on a busy freeway and you manage somehow to give the driver a nod and a smile, you make your own day and give the other driver something to think about as well. Submission is good for you physically. It does not start the adrenalin flowing.

Still, submission does not mean allowing ourselves to be trampled all over. It does not mean giving up our own opinions. I don't think God asks us to be wishy-washy. In fact, we Christians should have the most authenticity and individuality and integrity of anyone in the world. Everyone around us should be able to see what we stand for. But there again we are looking at how we relate to ideas, not how we relate to other people. We take our stand on the Christian faith, but we do not fight people in order to do so. We submit to others by showing a deep caring and concern for them, not by allowing them to dictate our beliefs or life-style.

We submit to others in order to win them to the Lord or build them up in the faith. If we are going to help others grow toward God, we need to be strong ourselves so we can reach out without losing our balance. We must be sure of where we stand; we must have sorted out the world's philosophies against what Scripture has to say; and we must know why we believe as we do. The stronger we are within ourselves, the better able we are to submit to others in true love.

An immature Christian finds submission very difficult. It is natural for man to want his own way. There is danger, too, in submitting to man's "ideas" when you are unsure of God's commands. But once you are grounded in the Word and know where you stand, you can stand firm and still "honor one another above yourselves."

Corrie ten Boom was a strong Christian woman who, because of her experiences during World War II, hated Nazi prison camps with every fiber of her being. One day after she had given a talk, she came face to face with a man who, as one of her guards when she was imprisoned, had mistreated her. Now he was a Christian.

It was not easy for Miss ten Boom to adopt a submissive attitude toward this man. But God helped her separate his actions from his person. She knew his role in the prison camp flew in the face of God's teachings on how Christians are to treat other human beings, and yet God gave her the strength to love him as an individual. Because her faith was strong, she was able to reach out and shake his hand. That is submission.

♦EMPTY NEST / INGRID TROBISCH

Children leave their parents, but parents must also leave their children. If someone asks me, "What shall I do about my empty nest?" I answer, "Fill it up real quick. Let your children go, and then reach out to others who need you." You won't lose your children that way. In fact, you will get them back as adult friends. You will also gain new relationships as you follow new ways of helping others.

RELATED ARTICLES
Chapter 1: Lip Service or Life Service?
Chapter 3: Called to Be a Servant
Chapter 3: A Great Man with a Servant's Heart
Chapter 15: How Artists Can Serve the Church

CHAPTER

26

How to Be a True Friend

- ✓ How do I find good friends?
- ✓ Should I make or keep non-Christian friends?
- ✓ How do I break down communication barriers?
- ✓ What are the qualities of a good friend?
- ✓ How do my feelings affect my relationships?

Vulnerability: A Key to Friendship

JAY KESLER

There are Christians who are willing to have you confess your sins to them so they can offer you forgiveness, brushing crumbs from the Christian table so you can grovel and pick them up. This is a power game. After all, who doesn't want to offer gifts to others? Receiving is much more difficult: when we are willing to receive, we show our weakness. But it is only possible to develop friendship when both parties are willing to be vulnerable, to expose their weakness to each other.

Vulnerability is at the heart of the incarnation. God obviously could have spoken to the world through skywriting. He could have made an announcement in a huge voice from the top of some mountain. But instead he chose to become a human being and live among us, experiencing all that we experience.

Isaiah 53:3 describes what he experienced here: "He was despised and rejected by men, a man of sorrows, and familiar with suffering. Like one from whom men hide their faces he was despised, and we esteemed him not."

Philippians 2:6, 7 makes his experience graphic: "Though he was God, [he] did not demand and cling to his rights as God, but laid aside his mighty power and glory, taking the disguise of a slave and becoming like men" (TLB).

If the Lord of the universe was willing to become vulnerable to the human beings he had created, it is no wonder that Paul tells us, "Your attitude should be the same as that of Christ Jesus" (Philippians 2:5).

Vulnerability requires us to relate to other people without hiding behind masks, without taking a position of superiority, without protecting ourselves. A vulnerable person dares to walk naked, as it were, among his fellow men without any fear of embarrassment. Only vulnerable people can relate to one another in trust and love; this is why people who have once tasted open, transparent relationships never want to go back to role playing.

There are dangers in vulnerability, of course. A vulnerable person can be betrayed. People may tell his secrets. People may laugh at him. But the rewards of being vulnerable far outweigh the risks. If he must pay for vulnerability with misunderstanding and criticism, he can be sure that Jesus experienced the same kind of rejection when he identified with human weakness—when he became vulnerable to and for mankind.

After all, he didn't have to expose himself to us. As the gospel song says, "he could have called ten thousand angels" to rescue him from people's misunderstanding, hurts, and rejections. Instead, he remained faithful to his incarnational role; he continued to be one of us.

It takes a great deal of strength to be vulnerable, and here indeed "we who are strong ought to bear with the failings of the weak" (Romans 15:1). In this case the weak are those who are afraid to trust others. This weakness brings about isolation of the soul. Eventually it robs them of all human help as they live lives of quiet desperation. By using our strength to become weak like Jesus Christ, we help them escape the bondage of their loneliness and estrangement. We invite them to join the human race. We teach them to confess their faults to one another (James 5:16) rather than keeping them bottled up inside, to bear one another's burdens (Galatians 6:2) rather than trying to go it alone.

When we help others become vulnerable, when we become vulnerable ourselves, we begin to experience what God intended in the Christian community.

♦ FINDING FRIENDS / STUART BRISCOE

You don't need a shopping list as you look for friends. Friendships happen; they are not the result of careful, calculated survey. And it's natural that you'll like some people better than others.

Good friendships start with acquaintances with whom we have something in common. There's a mutual attraction; you enjoy being together. You find the other person invigorating, challenging, and fun. You find that he or she gives you the right kind of ear, the right kind of support. And friendship grows.

I think of some of the close friendships I developed when I was a Marine commando. Not one of my closest friends was a believer, and I would not have been particularly drawn to any of them in normal circumstances. But when I took the time to get to know these men, I discovered their admirable qualities and began to enjoy them immensely. As long as our lives depended on each other, we were close friends and enjoyed a special camaraderie.

I think sometimes we miss out on friendships because we're too busy looking when we should be discovering.

On Friendship: An Interview with Madeleine L'Engle

✍ ISABEL ANDERS THROOP

What is friendship?

Friendship can be a mirror in which I am able to see myself and realize, by focusing on my friend, what I need to do to become more fully human. To me friendship is what makes the world go round. I treasure my friends; I know they are going to accept me as I am with all my faults and flaws and enthusiasms—but I too will have that kind of loving acceptance of them. I do not mean a permissive acceptance in which I never point out something I think is wrong or less than it could be. There is a definite sense of responsibility in friendship as in other relationships. For instance, there is the responsibility of my editor to point out what I need to do to change my writing to make a book better. That is how friends are mirrors—or should be.

Two things seem to be especially important in friendship: one is simply *auld lang syne*—the fact that you've known someone a long time, watched him or her grow and develop, and as long as your paths haven't taken you radically apart, you share that sense of a past history. You don't have to have everything in common. I have some friends I've known since adolescence, and in many ways our lives are quite different, but we have known each other's families and have grown up sharing a great deal of life in common. The second basis for friendship is compatibility: laughing at the same things, crying at the same things, caring to ask the great questions together—the cosmic questions. I have one very good friend of only a few years' duration. She is also a writer, and we can't get together without talking about God. Now that's a very good basis for friendship, a concern about our Creator.

How does one's relationship to God affect friendship?

If there is a radical difference in two people's conception of God, I don't think a deep and comfortable friendship will grow—because our understanding of God's nature affects how we think of ourselves and everything else in the world as well. If someone views God primarily as an angry, vengeful judge, that person is not likely to want to be close friends with me. I see the God of Scripture as a loving, forgiving God. There are different emphases among Christians, and I do have friends whose approach to God is different from mine. Yet I can hear them and they listen to me; we're not closing doors on each other.

How do friends enrich us?

Most of my friends are really creative people in one way or another. My oldest and closest friend—since adolescence—is a brilliant physician. Although I write fiction and she is in science, we have the exact same response to walking across a beautiful landscape and suddenly seeing a fringed gentian, which is a rare treasure. We respond in very similar ways to the loveliness of the Creator reflected in his works. I can think of a contrasting example with another friend who goes all the way back to my boarding school days. I remember the two of us screaming at each other over the interpretation of a Shakespeare play or a Browning poem, and people would say, "That's the end of that friendship." And then half an hour later we would be walking down the hall, arm in arm, not only still friends, but in perfect harmony. Yet we always had sense enough not to be roommates.

What about destructive friendships? What if we sense it is best to break off a relationship?

If our friendship is not helping at all, or if we sense that the other person is trying to remake us into someone we're not, then perhaps we have to withdraw temporarily. I don't think we should ever slam a door forever on a friendship. When I was first out of college and working in the theater in New York, I got involved with a very talented group of young actors and actresses, and I very slowly began to realize that they were living a rather promiscuous life-style. They led a kind of life I did not consider appropriate for me, as someone who was trying to serve God. So I withdrew in a way that I hoped would make a statement, as graciously as possible. I realized that my staying involved with that group and possibly even getting drawn into their lives further would have been very destructive for me.

How do friendships begin?

Real friendships seem to begin in adolescence; that is when we are able consciously to build relationships. At that point young people begin to understand the principle of friendship and are able to make choices. I remember I would go out with a boy and know that friendship was possible if we could talk about God and discuss ideas. I could usually tell very quickly on meeting a person if there was a basis for friendship. If the conversation remained on a totally frivolous level, I knew I wasn't going to make a permanent friend.

Besides shallowness, what else should we beware of in friendships?

It's hard to be friends with people who think they always know best—because that is a form of manipulation. Sometimes it is not malicious, but it is nevertheless destructive. Manipulation is, at its root, pride—*hubris*—thinking you are equal to God, you know everything, and you have the right to control other people. Manipulation is not the basis for either friendship or any true understanding of human nature. We are all children of God, bearing within us (sometimes very much hidden) the image of God, which is a sign of ongoing creation. I just don't agree with the idea that God created everything and said, "Oh, good, it's finished." He didn't say it was finished until he was on the cross. When God created everything he said, "It's good. It's very good." When I saw my newborn grandson this past spring, I held a gorgeous little baby, complete, perfect—but anything but finished! In the same way I believe we are called as human beings to create along with our Creator—to help each other forward toward the coming of the kingdom. That is just the opposite of manipulation.

What are some attributes of friends that stand out in your memory?

There is a French word, *disponible,* that means being available at any time, no matter how inconvenient it is. I have friends who are interesting, amusing, and enjoyable. But I know that if I were in a real bind I would not call them at two in the morning. Then there are other friends whom I know I could call any time—never trivially—but if there were a real reason, they would be *disponible.* I try to live by this standard as well.

Should friendship be between people who are equals?

Certainly there should be a high degree of mutuality in friendship. We are never exact equals with our friends. But there is a certain interdependence you create, in which you each give different gifts. If you are overly dependent in a relationship, you tend to idolize the other person, and then you are asking of that person something that should be asked only of God. There are times in every friendship when one person's need is greater than the other's, but then the scene shifts and the other needs more. That is mutuality, and it is what really makes friendship work. Mutuality can exist among people of widely differing ages and characteristics. All through my life I have had an enormously wide chronological age span among my friends. When I was young, many of my friends were a great deal older; and now that I'm getting older I have many friends quite a bit younger—and many my own age. But despite age differences, there is often a coming together of ideas and a likemindedness on many issues.

What do we know about the process through which friends are made and formed?

Well, for one thing, it takes time. You may meet a person and have instant rapport. But before it can grow into real friendship you have to get to know each other over a period of time. Some people I meet cause me to think, This is a seed that might flower into a beautiful friendship. And often that expectation is fulfilled, but occasionally it's not. As in anything worth growing, there is the necessity of faithfulness to that original seed, the watering, the gestation, the flowering in time. Friendship involves discipline as well as beauty. It takes time to get together on a regular basis; it is an effort to sit down and write letters, because we all live very busy lives, and it would be so easy to let these things go. But as in marriage—in any strong relationship—we work at it in order to enjoy the freedom of our love.

Friendship shouldn't depend entirely on feeling. Feeling is important, but being cross or disappointed in someone shouldn't destroy the relationship. We shouldn't give up on it or turn it off because it isn't all rosy. Sometimes we as friends have to wait until the other person can give again. The friendship is asked to lie dormant until it can flower and flourish again.

Levels of Friendship

✍ JILL AND STUART BRISCOE

Jill: Friends are a necessity. I don't think we can function fully as normal human beings without friendship.

When we were involved in missions, I was encouraged not to have any close friends. I was told, quite reasonably, that having friends would cause trouble, jealousy, and conflict in a close-knit Christian community. And there is no question about it, it can cause trouble. But because my husband—my best friend—was on the road for months at a time, I needed close friends.

Stuart: Scripture has a lot to say about friendship. God regarded Abraham and Moses as his friends and had a very special relationship with them. There were other intense friendships: woman to woman as with Ruth and Naomi; man to man as with David and Jonathan; older and younger as with Barnabas and John Mark.

Everybody has a longing for belonging—a desire for someone to express caring in a significant way, a desire for cooperative experiences, a desire to share thoughts and experiences. People are looking for acceptance; they want to be part of something bigger than themselves. There's a lot in a person that looks for friendship.

Jill: I turned to the Scriptures and found that Jesus made no apology for having friends. He had one best friend, John, three very good friends, twelve good friends, and seventy pretty good friends. I like to draw concentric circles and see how Jesus Christ enjoyed and encouraged friendship. His closest friends are in the center, and the others are in the larger surrounding circles.

It's been a great help for me to put my own groups of friends into those circles. My closest friend is my husband. Who are my three very good friends? Who are the twelve good friends I can invest a little more time and energy and build friendships with? And who are the seventy, my good friends here and there?

It has helped me to see that I don't need to feel guilty for not taking the same amount of time with the seventy that I need to spend with the twelve and the three.

Stuart: I think we can give names to your concentric circles. The outside circle holds your acquaintances. You can have many acquaintances. Then working toward the middle are the more tentative friendships, people that are closer than acquaintances but not quite close enough to share your heart. On the inside are the bosom buddies, the people with whom you have a real closeness. To maintain that closeness, three things are imperative.

First is loyalty. This doesn't mean "my friend, right or wrong." It means, however, that I am going to stick with this person so thoroughly that when she's right, she'll have my support, and when she's wrong, she'll have my criticism. As the book of Proverbs says, "Faithful are the wounds of a friend" (27:6).

Second comes reciprocity. Friends have to be willing to share in a very real sense with each other. Each needs to be willing to be vulnerable, to open his or her heart. Without reciprocity, friendship will never go much beyond the acquaintance level.

Third, honesty is vital. There is much superficiality in relationships. We are concerned to project the right image, to convey a positive impression whatever the true condition might be. When asked, "How are you today?" we answer, "Fine!" when it is often not true. A real friend wants to know how we really are and a genuine friendship will allow me and encourage me to share genuine feelings and receive necessary help and encouragement. Real friends don't play games—they work at helping.

Loyalty, reciprocity, and honesty—those are the three key words of friendship.

♦ MAKING FRIENDS / STUART BRISCOE

There's no reason why your colleagues in Christian warfare shouldn't become your best friends. Age need not be a barrier either—our children and our parents and grandparents are among our very best friends.

When you get into establishing friendships, recognize that not everybody will want to be your friend. People have the freedom to make that choice. If you try to force friendship, it will cause problems. Friendships must be freely offered.

The strongest and best friendships are made as you serve alongside somebody, doing something for the kingdom's sake. The enjoyment of working together for the Lord can bring the most delightful friendships into your life.

The key to having friends is being friendly, and Christians should be the friendliest people around. They should be taking initiatives to reach out to people. Encouragement is a great ministry, and it can be going on all the time.

Breaking Down Communication Barriers

✍ DAVID AND CHERYL ASPY

When you decide to try to start a relationship with another person, it is sometimes necessary to take the full responsibility for the success of the venture. This means that at the beginning you may have to do all the reaching out.

This is difficult, of course, so before beginning this kind of effort, be sure you are prepared to persevere even if you receive no help from the other person. In fact, you may receive only hostility and rejection. Thus the preliminary step in establishing a new relationship is to be certain you are prepared to carry the full burden of establishing communication.

Once you have decided to take this responsibility, you can increase your chances of success by following these four steps:

1. *Present yourself well.* Using body language effectively is a skill well worth developing. Posture yourself so the other person perceives that you really want to talk. Your whole body should say, "I want to communicate with you. I want to hear what you have to say."

To communicate a desire to hear another person, lean toward her slightly. For example, when you really want to hear a little child, you position yourself at the child's level so that you can communicate. Next, look the other person in the eye if possible. Your eyes should be friendly and inviting, not hostile and demanding. Hold your hands in an open position, as you would if you were trying to catch an egg. Square your shoulders with those of the other person so that your right shoulder is opposite her left shoulder and your left is opposite her right. Place your feet squarely on the floor so as to say, "I am here, and I am not going to run away."

2. *See the other person.* Having positioned yourself to tell the other person, "I want to communicate with you," observe her carefully. Your eyes will give you information about the context in which you are meeting as well as about the person's reaction to it. For instance, if you are a doctor meeting patients in your office, you may notice that many of them seem nervous and fearful. If you respond by saying, "It's a little scary to come to a doctor's office," you will communicate that you have some understanding of your patients' experience.

3. *Hear the other person.* As you are learning to use body language effectively, begin to develop another important communicating skill: hear the other person's words. To fully comprehend the message she is trying to send you, it is necessary to listen to the words she uses. You may feel overwhelmed by the torrent of words coming at you. When this happens, try to get the big picture

those words are painting. For example, when a person says many bad things about herself, the big picture is that her whole life is very difficult at this time.

The tone of a person's voice tells us a great deal about what is happening inside her. It gives us clues about her real feelings. There are many ways to say *Mother,* for example, and the tone used communicates just as much as the word itself.

4. *Respond to the other person.* If you have presented yourself well and done a good job of listening and seeing, you are ready for the next step—responding to the other person.

It is important to each of us that our words be valued. By responding to others, we communicate that we care enough to listen to them and to involve ourselves with their concerns. Our responses should show the other person that we respect her. Demonstrate that respect by using words that let her know she has been heard.

When people tell us life is painful for them, and when we see their pain reflected in their posture, their clothing, and their tone of voice, we should respond to them by saying something such as "You feel really down because life is very hurtful." This tells them that they have been heard and understood and that someone cares enough to listen to their pain.

Our responses can build bridges to the other person and may overcome some of the communication barriers. Carl Rogers said that life is like being in a barrel. We tap on the side of the barrel, hoping someone will hear our sounds and tap back to us. Then, and only then, do we know that someone has really heard us. In that moment we are affirmed.

How do we overcome communication barriers? After accepting the responsibility of reaching out, we follow these four steps: (1) we use body language to communicate our undivided attention; (2) we use our eyes to see other people and their context; (3) we use our ears to hear their words and tone of voice; and (4) we say words that will let them know we understand their feelings and the reason for them.

Of course there is no guarantee that we can overcome communication barriers. But if we follow these steps, we can be sure we have tried honestly to do so. As we seek to communicate with others, we need God's help. Thus the most formidable barriers give the greatest opportunities to grow in our reliance upon God. He will give us the love to "hang in there" until he removes the stumbling blocks.

Reaching Out to the Lonely

✍ PAMELA BARDEN

"Do not forget to entertain strangers, for by so doing some people have entertained angels without knowing it" (Hebrews 13:2).

Does that familiar verse give you the idea that hospitality to strangers is a Christian duty? Ouch!

For most of us, busy and comfortable in our busy-ness, that's an idea whose time has not yet come. An occasional cake for a new neighbor or a hurried greeting in church seems to fulfill our obligation.

Sometimes we argue that people are lonely because they choose to be lonely. They have voluntarily built up walls that isolate them from other people. But few people build airtight walls with no small cracks or cloudy windows left just in case someone might want to look in.

Some people are lonely through no fault of their own. They just moved cross-country or cross-town; her husband and companion of thirty-five years has just died; he's away from home for the first time at college; they just immigrated to America, leaving behind family, language, and customs.

Whatever the reason for a person's loneliness, our reaching out can be a meaningful experience for everyone involved—or it can be a slap in the face. We all know people who say, "Good morning, how's it going?" but are long gone before you can begin to reply. It's no fun to be used to fill someone's quota of "good mornings."

To be truly meaningful and appreciated, your efforts must be consistent, sincere, and long-term. Alleviating loneliness isn't a shot in the dark; it's an effort that's repeated over and over. It's a series of steps, and it's hard work. That is why you can probably concentrate on no more than a few lonely people at one time.

First of all, identify "your" lonely people. New neighbors are a logical choice because they are close by. Their license plates will tell you if they're from across town or across the country.

When college students arrive in town, don't gravitate toward the tan, blond, homecoming-king type. He won't be lonely for long! It's often the quiet, awkward student who most needs an adult to help him or her through the adjustment.

Widows, widowers, and shut-ins often receive abundant attention right after the funeral or during the days just following the accident or illness. Two or three months later, the plants have withered, the cards have stopped coming, they're off the church prayer list, and they're lonely. But who cares?

Once you commit yourself to a lonely person, write his or her name on a piece of paper and post it on the refrigerator door where you'll see it often. Find out what he or she likes to be called. Often a widow longs to be called by her first name instead of Mrs. Jones. Make an effort to find out. Then use the preferred name every time you speak to the person.

Arrange contacts. These may be sporadic greeting cards chosen especially for that person. Don't rely only on the telephone; some elderly people and foreigners are uncomfortable with telephones. Offer to give the newcomer or student a tour of the area. The important thing is to keep in touch and to take time to visit every time you see that person.

In many cases, a small, appropriate gift is in order. It doesn't need to be expensive; the gift should never be used to create an obligation. New neighbors always appreciate plants, especially if they just moved a distance and were not able to bring theirs along. Vegetables from your overflowing garden are a readily available and welcome gift. A small craft item, a book, a cutting from a special plant, a loaf of homemade bread—these are simple gifts that say, "I thought about you."

Invite your lonely person to go places with you. This doesn't stop with church, either. Take a new neighbor to the grocery store. Invite a college student along on a ride to the farm stand or apple orchard. Take an elderly friend to the public library. Help a recent immigrant find ethnic food stores. Taking a lonely person along while you buy shoes for your three-year-old could be the highlight of that person's day.

Be flexible. A trip to the bank could be expanded to include a stop at the post office. A friendly hello could lead to a physician's reference. Don't force the person to conform to your agenda. Remember, you're committed to that person and his or her needs.

For many people, a listener is the best cure for loneliness. Mrs. Jones may want to show you photos of her family. The new neighbor may spend hours telling you how much better the school system was back in Brownsville. The student may discuss—in depth—the dissection of a frog. Listening is a dying art; try to revive it with a lonely person.

If you live in a growing community, you might help organize a neighborhood Bible study. A men's fellowship allows friendships to grow as yard tools are exchanged. The new person in the office may enjoy joining you for a lunchtime shopping trip or a salad.

Reaching out to lonely people is not expensive, but it is time consuming. You can't rid a garden of weeds in one cursory weed-pulling session. Loneliness, like a weed, is deep-rooted. Time, effort, creative solutions, and persistence are keys to attacking it at its roots.

Reaching out to a lonely person is rewarding—to you as well as to that person. You may "travel" as you hear the new neighbor talk about her old hometown. You'll feel younger as the college student tells you about the attractive girls on campus. You'll experience the joy of deep love as the widow shares about her marriage. You'll be grateful for your own health as you visit with the shut-in.

As you reach out to the lonely, you'll develop new friends from varying backgrounds. As you fulfill the command of Hebrews 13:2 to show hospitality to strangers, you'll reflect Christ's love for all of us. And who knows, you may meet an angel, too!

◆ NEEDED: A COMPASSIONATE PERSON
PAMELA BARDEN

It's amazing, even in our "liberated" society, how many women in their fifties and up, left without a mate or with an invalid husband, are truly helpless. They can't drive, they've never paid the bills, they don't know anything about the family finances, and their children are too far away to be much help. These women desperately need a compassionate person to teach them basic survival skills. They don't need platitudes and cards; they need driving lessons!

The Qualities of a Good Friend

ADRIAN ROGERS

The person who has a good friend and is a good friend is a very rich and fulfilled person indeed. A good friendship should display these characteristics:

1. *Good friendship is selfless.* Proverbs 17:17 tells us that "a friend loves at all times." True friendship therefore is not based on changing conditions. There are people who say, "I'll be your friend if, or when, or until, or because." These are all conditions, and conditions may change. But a real friend loves at all times. A friend who says, "I love you if" or "I love you when" is not a Bible kind of friend. A true friend says, "I love you, period. I love you at all times. My love is selfless and unconditional."

2. *Genuine friendship is steadfast.* Again, Proverbs 17:17 says that "a friend loves at all times." An English publication offered a prize for the best definition of friendship. One definition that won honorable mention was this: "A friend is one who multiplies our joys and divides our grief." Another one said: "A friend is one who understands our silence." But the definition that won the prize was this: "A friend is one who comes in when the world has gone out." How true that is! If you want to really know how many friends you have and who they are, make a mistake and see what happens. Get into difficulty and see how many supposed friends stick with you. True friendship is steadfast.

3. *True friendship is sacrificial.* Proverbs 18:24 says, "A man of many companions may come to ruin, but there is a friend who sticks closer than a brother." True friendship is costly, but it's worth it. The Indian word for friend comes from a compound word meaning "one who carries my sorrows upon his back." So if I would be a friend, I have to live sacrificially toward the one who is receiving my friendship.

4. *True friendship is sanctifying.* Proverbs 27:17 tells us, "As iron sharpens iron, so one man sharpens another." A real friend will make you a better person. True friendship is going to put the edge on your life; it's going to sharpen you. It will make you more keen. You'll be a better and more useful person because of that friendship.

True friendship will not blunt your influence or dull your spirituality. A real friend is one who cares enough to confront you when you are wrong. The Bible says in Proverbs 27:6, "The kisses of an enemy may be profuse, but faithful are the wounds of a friend." Flattery is not friendship. A flatterer is the flip side of a hypocrite: A hypocrite says behind your back what he will not say to your face, but a flatterer says to your face what he will not say behind your back. A true friend, by contrast, is honest with you and with others.

Influencing the Spiritual Growth of My Friends

TERRY PRISK

In our society today, most Christians do not experience the abundant Christian life. The reason is they are not sharing the Good News of Jesus Christ, the reality of his love, with others. It does not mean that all people need to be evangelists or pastors or teachers, but the Scriptures are clear that we are all to be part of evangelism, whether by praying, giving evangelistic ministries, or sharing principles of Scripture with those close to us. The Scriptures say, "Always be prepared to give an answer to everyone who asks you to give the reason for the hope that you have" (1 Peter 3:15). Once we have begun sharing, we realize that the spiritual growth of those who believe is extremely important. But how can we be involved in the spiritual growth of our friends?

One way to see our Christian friends grow and get excited about their faith is to let them see our excitement at the insights the Lord teaches us in his Word. For them to see the assurance that God answers prayer, we can share with them examples of how God has answered prayer in our lives. Perhaps the biggest way we can help our friends is to let them see the excitement we have when we share our faith and people respond to the Good News of Jesus Christ.

I influence the spiritual growth of my friends by being an example of growth and enthusiasm. As I care for my spiritual growth through Bible reading and prayer, I influence my friends by keeping them spiritually accountable and by providing opportunities for them to grow, whether it is taking them to a concert, a Bible study, or literally pulling from everyday life examples of God's reality.

Scripture says, "Pray continually" (1 Thessalonians 5:17). If we believe in the power, reality, and significance of prayer, we will actively pray for those individuals who are not where they should be spiritually.

There are many stories of individuals who have committed their lives to Jesus Christ, of families who are Christ-centered, who believed because someone took the time to care about their spiritual needs. Another word for concern and continued care about spiritual growth is discipleship.

Discipleship is not passing along ten lesson plans on how to live the Christian life. It is being an example in all situations of Christ's love. That doesn't mean we won't blow it sometimes, but how we handle it when we do is significant. In fact, influencing the spiritual growth of our peers, our friends, our family can also be done by saying, "I'm sorry, I was wrong."

I know of a young man who came up to one of his peers and said, "Christianity is what your life is all about. I want to be a part of it."

You can influence the spiritual growth of your friends through your attitude, your behavior, and your conversation. Those are the *ABC*s of your influence: *attitude, behavior, conversation.* How are you doing on your *ABC*s?

How Knowing Jesus Will Help You Be a Friend

✍ ADRIAN ROGERS

Meeting and knowing Jesus Christ will help us be better friends with others. These three easy steps show us how to be a friend:

1. *I must recognize that God loves me and accepts me.* In Ephesians 1:6 Paul said that we are "accepted in the beloved" (KJV). The beloved is Christ, and we are accepted in him.

Everybody needs and wants acceptance. In all of us there is a built-in yearning and longing to be accepted. Madison Avenue knows this—that's why companies are able to sell toothpaste, automobiles, clothes, and everything else the way they do. We get conned into believing that if we use certain products, people will accept us.

Here's the secret of acceptance: God has accepted me. He doesn't accept me because there's anything good in me, but because he loves me. Romans 5:8 says, "God demonstrates his own love for us in this: While we were still sinners, Christ died for us." God just accepts us. The Bible calls this grace. We don't deserve it, but we are valuable because of it.

2. *I must accept God's acceptance of me.* That's faith. I simply say, "Lord Jesus, I receive that. I don't deserve it, but I receive it by faith." When Jesus accepts me, and I accept that he accepts me, then for the first time I can accept myself.

There's nothing wrong with loving yourself. Now I don't mean we're to stand in front of a mirror and sing, "How Great Thou Art." A person who does that is sick. But I am to have a healthy acceptance of myself. I know that God loves me, and if God loves me, I can love what God loves.

3. *I must accept others.* Once I accept myself, I don't have to put you down in order to feel important. I don't have to be "leeching" you in a possessive relationship, which really isn't a friendship at all. I don't have to be manipulating you, using you, abusing you, or being threatened by you, because I'm at peace with myself. Because I have accepted myself, I can accept you.

And now for the first time you can really accept me, because when I accept you, you're drawn to me. We can become true friends.

So, to sum it all up, God accepts me—that's grace. I accept that he accepts me—that's faith. I accept myself—that's peace. I accept others—that's love. In return, others accept me—that's friendship and fellowship. The foundation of the whole process is Jesus loving me. Because of his acceptance of me, and because of the friendship I have with him, I can become a true friend to others.

◆STEPS TO BEING A FRIEND
ADRIAN ROGERS

Having friends is less important than being a friend. I believe there are three steps to being a friend:

1. *Know the best friend, Jesus.* Proverbs 18:24 says, "There is a friend who sticks closer than a brother." No better description of Jesus can be given. Jesus calls us his own friends. In John 15:15 Jesus said, "I no longer call you servants, because a servant does not know his master's business. Instead, I have called you friends, for everything that I learned from my Father I have made known to you." Even his enemies had to admit that Jesus was a friend of sinners. He wants to be your friend, no matter who you are or what you've done (see Matthew 11:19).

2. *If we want friends, we need to take the initiative.* We need to stop waiting to be loved and start loving somebody, stop waiting for somebody to give to us and start giving to others. Galatians 6:7 says, "Do not be deceived: God cannot be mocked. A man reaps what he sows." If we want friendship, then we must sow for friendship. That's what Jesus did. He loved us first. His love was selfless, steadfast, sacrificial, and sanctifying. We ought to have the same kind of love that Jesus had.

3. *Create opportunities for friendship.* A church is an excellent place to meet friends, because there you will most likely meet people who share your outlook on life. Take the first step and introduce yourself. You have to be willing to risk a little embarrassment or even rejection, but you can do this if you're at peace with yourself. Be yourself, but be your best self. Be reasonable—don't try to high-pressure people to be your friend.

Don't expect too much too soon. Friendships develop slowly, like a beautiful flower. But do expect results if you follow these principles. I think it was Dale Carnegie who said, "You can make more friends in two months by becoming really interested in other people than you can in two years by trying to get other people interested in you."

How Can I Reach Out to Others?
TERRY PRISK

A common question for Christians who desire to live the life of Christ is, How can I reach others through friendship? John 11:1-44 talks about a very special friendship: Jesus' friendship with and love for Martha, Mary, and Lazarus.

This particular passage very clearly shows that love takes action—a willingness to risk, a willingness to follow through. First of all, the question that is asked is, What is love? Love is, simply stated, the moment I do something for God or someone else and it costs me something. Love is not sloppy agape, it does not lose its flavor like bubble gum. Love is continual.

What does it mean that love takes action? In the story in John's Gospel of the death of Lazarus, Jesus loved enough to wait, and then he loved enough to go to Mary and Martha in order to perform a great miracle and bring Lazarus back to life.

We will not be able to show our love by bringing people back to life, but we must put action behind our thoughts and our lip service. This is important in all the small things of life. If we tell a person that we are going to get back to them, then we must call or visit. That is reaching out through friendship. If we tell an individual who has gone through a tough experience that we will write them or call them, then we must do so.

Love is willing to risk, willing to get beyond our own comfort zones to reach out and minister to the needs of other people. Love is willing to say, "At times I will risk not doing what my friends want to do but do what the Lord is calling me to do."

I remember a story I once heard about a young girl who was in a fancy restaurant complete with waiters, waitresses, and maitre d's. A young man was carrying a large tray of glasses and, as he approached, the young lady could see that he was mentally handicapped. One insensitive man decided to keep his feet in the aisle, and the young man fell and glasses went everywhere. Because of his handicap, people began to laugh, and the man who had caused the mishap enjoyed the attention he'd gained. But the young girl stood up, walked past the waiters, got down on her hands and knees, and began to pick up the glasses with the young man. The restaurant became silent. That young lady was willing to risk. Love is willing to risk.

I reach out in friendship to others when I make a commitment and *keep* the commitment. We live in a society today that is very noncommittal. I reach out to people who need friendship by discovering what their needs are and meeting those needs—whether it's fresh cookies, a little note, an encouraging word, a telephone call, a time to shop together, taking care of a child so there can be some freedom for the parents—the list goes on and on. The way to reach out to others who need friendship is to have a mind-set that is ready to minister to the needs of others.

I know of a man who never gives the impression that he is bothered, rushed, or not interested when he talks to me. In fact, he was talking with a friend who stated that he and his wife would be going out of town and were having trouble getting someone to take their teenage children to school, pick them up from school, make sure they had groceries, etc. My friend responded, "I'll take care of them." That's giving in friendship, responding to needs in a Christlike way.

Friendship. It's love, it's action—willing to risk, willing to follow through, willing to respond to needs.

♦ FRIENDSHIPS WITH NON-CHRISTIANS
JILL BRISCOE

Many unbelievers are absolutely super people, and I think we should build friendships with non-Christians. These should not be evangelistic relationships—friendship for the sake of a scalp—but friendships because we genuinely love these people.

When you have unbelieving friends, though, you need to ask yourself, Is this friendship enabling me to stay close to God, or is it taking me away from him? If you begin to see that your friendship with a particular non-Christian is taking you away from the Lord, you will have to do something about that.

How Feelings Affect The Way I Relate to Others

ROBERT SCHULLER

The way we feel about ourselves is going to strongly affect the way we relate to others. I don't think it's possible for us to love others if we don't have a healthy affection for ourselves. We can't ever escape what psychology calls projection—seeing our own qualities in other people. We are all in the business of projecting all of the time whether we're conscious of doing so or not. It's an important adjustment mechanism.

If I feel insecure I'm going to be quickly threatened. If I have a tendency toward neurotic self-pity I'm going to consider myself victimized and will head off in life with a chip on my shoulder and a persecution complex. And if I don't have high self-confidence—belief in my own capacity for being a wholesome, beautiful person—then I'm going to project that lack of positive feelings on others and suspect that they are all dirty, crooked, and out to get me.

So it's terribly important that we have powerful, positive feelings about ourselves, because how we feel about ourselves unquestionably colors our interpretation of others. We may even measure God by how we feel about ourselves. I don't believe it's possible for us to truly believe in the God of forgiving love or to really accept salvation by grace through faith until we have an affirmation of our own value and worth.

A lot of Christian teachers and preachers are angry people. You can sense the anger in their tone of voice, in the words they choose. If you look at their faces you can see the wrinkles around the eyes, the tightness of the lips, and you realize that they're angry or afraid of something. When you listen to these preachers make proclamations about the nature of God and his personality, you think that God must also be an angry person.

However, I know God best when I keep my eyes on Jesus. Jesus is the incarnate Son of God. He is God in the flesh. If I want a picture of God, then I have to picture Jesus. The Word says that Jesus was angry only a couple of times, and that's when he saw human beings using the authority of religion and their high positions to exploit people's guilt and shame for commercial purposes, such as by selling animals in the temple at inflated prices. He was not angry with people simply because they were imperfect. In fact, he made a special point of calling the imperfect people—the ones that the "good" people looked down on—to him.

We have to be careful not to project our own faulty sense of self-worth upon God and then consequently think that he holds the same low view of us that we hold of ourselves. We must keep going back to the Bible. What does God think of us? What does Jesus—who shows us what God is like—think of us? If we are to love our neighbors as ourselves, then it stands to reason that we first must love ourselves and see ourselves with caring eyes—exactly the way God views us.

◆MAKING PEACE WITH OTHERS
YFC EDITORS

Resolving conflict is important. Jesus himself said, "Blessed are the peacemakers, for they will be called sons of God" (Matthew 5:9).

Because we are human beings, conflict is inevitable. We have different ideas and opinions about everything imaginable. As believers, we have a responsibility to obey what we know is right, but times may arise when we need to make peace with someone. How should we go about doing so?

First of all, realize that no matter how much you feel the other person is at fault, *you* have a responsibility to initiate the peacemaking. Don't wait for the other person to come to you. Before actually going to the person, spend time in prayer, asking God to give you the right words and attitude, regardless of how the other person responds.

When you go to the person, focus your words on yourself and your part in the problem: What am *I* doing to contribute to this problem? What can *I* do to help solve it? If needed, ask for forgiveness.

From then on, you need to act differently toward that person. That may take some doing because you don't feel any different. But part of peacemaking is living your words in your actions.

RELATED ARTICLES
Chapter 27: **Sharing Christ with Family and Friends**
Chapter 27: **The Bridge to Communication**

CHAPTER

27

Sharing Our Faith

- ✓ How do we share our faith with others?
- ✓ How can we overcome the fear to witness?
- ✓ How do we win the right to be heard?
- ✓ Why should we witness? Is it really necessary?
- ✓ Just what should we say?

Witnessing

✍ JAY KESLER

The New Testament teaches three distinct levels of communication. First and most obvious is the *proclamational* level. This is the verbal sharing of the gospel's truths in propositions or statements of fact. "All have sinned and fall short of the glory of God" (Romans 3:23). "The wages of sin is death, but the gift of God is eternal life in Christ Jesus our Lord" (Romans 6:23). "It is by grace you have been saved, through faith—and this is not from yourselves, it is the gift of God—not by works, so that no one can boast" (Ephesians 2:8, 9).

These are statements that, along with many others, make up the content of gospel preaching. They are familiar, they are generally understood by people in our culture, and they have become the centerpiece of biblical witness.

The New Testament, however, does not stop with proclamational witness. It also teaches the *relational* level of communication. Jesus demonstrated this level in his discussion with the woman at the well (John 4) and by his relationship with Zacchaeus (Luke 19). In both situations, Jesus sought to find common ground with these people. He surprised the woman by asking her for a drink, and then he talked with her about her background and her religious hopes. He went to Zacchaeus's house for a meal, allowing himself to be accused of associating with questionable people. Jesus thus built relational bridges that carried the content of his message.

The third level of biblical communication is the *incarnational* level. That is where the Word becomes flesh (John 1:14). We read in Philippians 2:6-10 about Jesus' Incarnation—how, though he was God, he did not claim his rights but became a man and lived among us, humbling himself further to become a servant and then a sacrifice. This fleshing out of the gospel is what we mean by incarnational witness: our life itself carries the content of the gospel. We don't talk about love; we love. We don't talk about forgiveness; we forgive. We manifest the fruit of the Spirit: "love, joy, peace, patience, kindness, goodness, faithfulness, gentleness and self-control" (Galatians 5:22, 23). A person with these qualities carries the gospel message in his person wherever he goes.

These three levels of communication require increasing maturity. That is, it takes less maturity simply to speak the words of the gospel than it does to build relationships in the name of Christ, and incarnating the gospel requires the most maturity of all. When we are witnessing, however, we will be most effective if we reverse the order—first living the gospel and then building relationships, thus earning the right to be heard.

Unfortunately, many people get the idea that witnessing for Christ means standing on the corner yelling at passersby, or obnoxiously breaking into people's conversations at inappropriate times and with a judgmental spirit and know-it-all attitude. This is surely not a climate that aids a verbal presentation, however.

Our witness is effective only if the Holy Spirit has opened the door for us. I have learned to follow these rules in witnessing:

1. First attempt to build a relationship with the person, constantly praying that the Lord will allow you to live the gospel in his presence by practical acts of charity and sincere interest in him as a person. This can happen even in relatively short contacts such as during an airplane trip.

2. Then pray that the Holy Spirit will open the door and cause the person to inquire about the gospel.

3. Begin where the person is rather than where you are. Allow the other person to tell about his experience, how he feels about God, how he feels about his own life, what questions he has had about God.

4. Be sensitive when you give your verbal witness. Verbal witness is threatening because it is so intimate and personal. Do not barge into someone else's

soul. Seek common ground; identify with the other person as a fellow sinner.

5. Present the gospel at a depth that is related to the amount of time you have with the person. The amount of truth one can convey during a plane trip is considerably smaller than the amount one can convey over several years of shared coffee breaks.

Whenever we witness and on whatever level, it is vital that we avoid taking a holier-than-thou approach. We must not put ourselves up as a standard; none of us is good enough for that. Jesus is the only holy and righteous one. We are not telling the person to be like us; we are telling him that together we are lost and through Christ we can be saved.

It is as if we are all lost in a terrible, dense swamp, and one of us has found a path that leads to safety. When we witness, we are telling others how they too can find this path to safety. Our verbal witness is much more effective when we learn to express it in terms of one beggar telling another beggar where to find bread.

Why Evangelize?

LUIS PALAU

People often ask me, "How does God's sovereignty fit into evangelism? If God knows everyone who is going to be saved, why should I bother sharing the gospel?"

Evangelism is part of the sovereign plan of God. He could have used some other method to bring people into his family, but God chose evangelism as his method to bring sinners to eternal life. Evangelism therefore in no way contradicts his sovereignty.

God knows who is going to be saved because of his foreknowledge—he would not be God if he did not. But we evangelize because, first, he commanded us to. In the words of Jesus, "All authority in heaven and on earth has been given to me. Therefore go and make disciples of all nations, baptizing them in the name of the Father and of the Son and of the Holy Spirit, and teaching them to obey everything I have commanded you. And surely I will be with you always, to the very end of the age" (Matthew 28:18-20). Sometimes when a person asks me why I am preaching at a conference, I say, "Because the Commander-in-Chief told me to come here."

The second reason is love and compassion for our fellow human beings. We are limited by time and space, so, unlike God, we cannot foresee who will accept the Savior. Because we have received so much, we should tell others what they are missing without Christ. We may not always know someone personally, but we do know the Lord and can tell others about him.

We testify to the Good News—how good it really is—and offer it to others as a free gift of God.

♦ WITNESSING OUT OF WEAKNESS
CALVIN MILLER

We can't wait to share Christ until our lives are perfect, or we would never share him at all. No Christian ever has his Christian life totally together. We share Christ simply because it's right to share Christ. When we run across a person who doesn't know the Lord, we know he is dealing with lots of problems now, and he is certainly going to have problems in eternity. We share with him because he needs to find Christ, not because we have won some great spiritual victory or because things couldn't be better between our own selves and the Lord.

♦ WITNESSING AND THE GIFT OF EVANGELISM / YFC EDITORS

Is there a difference between being a witness and having the gift of evangelism?

All believers are called to be witnesses; only some have the gift of evangelism. This gift reveals itself in a certain effectiveness and drawing of people that every Christian does not obtain.

But as witnesses for Jesus Christ, all believers are called to share their faith with others by taking advantage of the opportunities given by the Holy Spirit. It's not enough for us to just be good examples; we are definitely called to *tell:* "Always be prepared to give an answer to everyone who asks you to give the reason for the hope that you have. But do this with gentleness and respect" (1 Peter 3:15, 16).

Every believer can tell what Christ is doing in his life. You can share your faith in letters to friends and in conversations with people with whom you have built a relationship. You can use materials from Friendship Evangelism or Evangelism Explosion. Your local Christian bookstore carries tracts, books, and Bible study materials that can help you share your faith with others.

Most important, you need to continue to grow spiritually and stay in tune to the Holy Spirit as he opens opportunities for you to share your faith. Remember, you are simply telling. The Holy Spirit will do the rest in the life of your listener.

Ways to Witness
WILLIAM BRIGHT

Witnessing is an overflow of one's life in Christ. The apostle Paul wrote, "For Christ's love compels us" (2 Corinthians 5:14). So before we can fulfill the Great Commission to go and make disciples of all nations, we must keep the great commandment, which is to love. We love God with all our heart, soul, mind, and strength. Then, compelled by his love, we love our neighbors and our enemies, and we tell them about Jesus. We do that as an expression of the will, by faith.

Paul, in Colossians 1:28, 29, wrote that he preached Christ, "admonishing and teaching everyone with all wisdom, so that we may present everyone perfect in Christ. To this end I labor, struggling with all his energy, which so powerfully works in me." Likewise, everywhere we go we are to tell anyone who will listen about Christ. The Spirit-filled person is aware that Jesus Christ is living within him, walking around in his body. So as we get on our knees every morning to acknowledge Christ's lordship, we should invite him to seek and save the lost through us.

Wherever I go, if I am alone with a person for a couple of minutes, I begin to talk about Jesus. I find there are a lot of "Ethiopian eunuchs" along the way. I got on a plane the other day bound for New Jersey and I was seated next to a young engineer from Oxford. As we talked, he said he wanted to become a Christian. He prayed aloud, and I prayed with him. He was so excited. God had put us together.

I got off the plane in New Jersey, and a porter was waiting for my luggage. I gave him a "Four Spiritual Laws" booklet and asked if he was a Christian. He said no. I asked him if he'd like to be. "I sure would," he replied. He read for a while until he got to a little prayer in the booklet and an explanation on how to pray. The prayer read, "Lord Jesus, I need you. Thank you for dying on the cross for my sins. Come into my life. Forgive my sins. Change my life. Make me the kind of person I should be." I asked him, "Does that prayer express the desire of your heart?"

"It sure does," he answered.

"Let's pray," I suggested, and we did. Again, he was very grateful that I had taken the time to introduce him to the Lord Jesus whom he had wanted to know for a long time.

I went on to Washington, D.C. During the taxi ride to the hotel I asked the driver, a student from Ethiopia, if he was a Christian. He replied that he went to church, but he didn't know Christ. I asked him if he believed Jesus is the Son of God. He said yes. "Do you believe he died for your sins?" Again he answered yes. "Do you know how to receive him?" I inquired. His answer was no. So I asked, "Would you like to?"

He did, so we pulled over to the side of the road, where he prayed, inviting Jesus Christ into his life. I went through the steps of receiving Christ and prayed for him. As we continued driving, I was reminded of the passage in Acts where Philip taught an Ethiopian about Christ. I shared the story with him and said, "You're a twentieth-century Ethiopian."

"I've been looking for God for years," the driver replied, "but I haven't known how to find him."

A couple of days later I was in California. Two men came to our home to do repairs. One was from Czechoslovakia. As I talked with him, I learned that he was very interested in God. While we were talking, the other man asked my wife what we did. She told him we were in Christian work. A half hour later he asked, "How does a person come to know God? I want to know God. I've been looking for God and I can't find him."

My wife told me about the man's inquiry, so we sat down together with the Bible. I explained to him the four spiritual laws. He said he wanted to receive Christ, so we knelt and prayed together. When we got to our feet, he said, "My wife would like to know God, too."

"Take all I've given you," I told him. "Tell her what I have told you. And you lead her to Christ."

In each case, I take the names and addresses of those who receive Christ and send them letters and literature. I have found that wherever I go, if I really walk in the light as God is in the light, the Holy Spirit will lead me to people whom he has prepared. I don't have to argue or badger or browbeat or high-pressure. The One who came to seek and to save the lost lives in me. If I am filled with the Spirit who came to glorify Christ, he will use my lips, my heart, my hands, and my feet to do whatever he has to do if I'll let him, to reach out in love to others.

♦ WHAT TO SAY IN WITNESSING CALVIN MILLER

We need to get over the idea that witnessing is a set of words or a plan. The best way to witness is by the way you live. All witnessing has a verbal dimension, of course. If you are living a model life, others may be so motivated that they will come up and say, "I like the way you live. I'd like to know why you live that way," or "I'd like to accept Jesus." Then you will need to have something to say. But the Christian life comes first.

Not that there's anything wrong with having a plan or a set of words to use. In fact, I teach witnessing plans to my church members. But remember that a witness is one who has seen an important event as well as one whose words are important. Most people, even if they have had a life-changing experience with Christ, feel uncomfortable sharing Christ without a plan, so we give them a little schema to make them more comfortable. Still, when people respond to such a presentation, it is usually because they have already seen the effects of Christianity in someone's life.

Witnessing is most effective when it is the natural consequence of our joy in Christ. The best witnesses I have ever known needed no plan. Some of them were so new in Christ they had not had the time to learn one yet. But they were bubbling over, much like a girl who has just gotten engaged. She doesn't have to take a class to learn how to share her good news or how to show her engagement ring to others. She flashes the diamond and excitedly brags about her fiancé because she is full of joy. She is in love. And that is also what happens when we fall in love with Christ.

♦ LIGHT IN A DARK PLACE / LUCI SHAW

We have a very good friend who lived with us for four years—Grace McFarlane, a wonderful pianist and a remarkable Christian. She was invited to Dallas one year to participate in the Daley Competition. People come from all over the world to play in this piano competition. And Grace was one of the finalists.

The world of music can be extremely amoral, power hungry, and corrupt. The personal lives of many musicians are a shambles. So we prayed for Grace before she left for Dallas. My husband said in his prayer, "Make Grace a light in a dark place."

Grace said that the whole time she was in Dallas, she saw herself as a light in a very dark place. She modeled herself on what light does—it's visible, it shines out in every direction, it warms people. Other people at the competition saw the light in Grace. They said to her again and again, "You're different from these other people. We can see something in you, but we don't know what it is. What is it about you, why are you different?" And she was able to witness to three different people, two of whom were led to the Lord.

◆ FIVE STEPS TO FAITH / YFC EDITORS

When you want a few steps to share in order to tell a person how to accept Christ, the following is helpful. These are taken from "Your Most Important Relationship," a brochure written by Youth for Christ/USA and Campus Crusade for Christ, International.

1. God loves you and created you to have a personal relationship with him (Psalm 139:13, 14; John 3:16; John 17:3).

2. Your sin keeps you from having a personal relationship with God (James 4:17; Romans 3:23; Isaiah 59:2; Romans 6:23).

3. Only through Jesus Christ can you have a personal relationship with God (John 14:6; 1 Peter 3:18; 1 Corinthians 15:3-6).

4. You must personally respond by receiving Jesus Christ as Savior and Lord (Ephesians 2:8, 9; Acts 3:19; John 1:12).

5. Your trust in Jesus Christ begins a lifelong relationship (Hebrews 13:5; Colossians 2:6, 7).

To Whom Should We Witness?

CALVIN MILLER

When we light a candle in a dark room, we don't say, "Shall we light just a section of the room?" No, we leave it free to shine where it will, however far it may reach. Likewise I don't think we should restrict our witnessing to certain compatible people. We should let God select the people we witness to.

In the original Greek, the Great Commission doesn't really say "Go into all the world" so much as it says, "Since you are going into all the world anyway, as you carry on your normal pattern of life, preach as widely as you can. Preach the gospel to everybody!" God doesn't want anyone to perish (2 Peter 3:9)—the bus driver, the girl who serves ice cream cones, or anyone else we may pass in our daily lives. There is always space to care about others, and sometimes there is a proper moment to share our witness.

I've never believed in standing up in a public swimming pool or theater and starting to preach. Jesus said we should be "as shrewd as snakes and as innocent as doves" (Matthew 10:16) in our approach to others. We need to pick our witnessing moments carefully. Tact makes our words more effective.

How can we tell if a person is open to hearing the gospel? Remember that the Holy Spirit is the illuminator. John 16 says he will "convict the world of guilt in regard to sin" (v. 8). We are not trying to convict the person; the Holy Spirit is.

You can't always tell that it's OK to go ahead and witness just by looking at a person's face. Sometimes people will listen politely as we share Christ, but they are forcing their attention. The key indicator of readiness for the gospel is the eyes. The eyes have been called a window to the soul. If the eyes sparkle, if the eyes say yes, then we should share Christ.

If, on the other hand, we detect hostility, we should not press on with our witnessing. We should find a way to retire graciously from the conversation and maybe even from the other person's presence. If people don't want to talk to us, that is certainly their right. If it's just the gospel they don't want to talk about, then we need to find a bridge into something they do like to talk about, as long as their conversation doesn't offend our discipleship.

We need to be willing to wait for the right time to present the gospel. The time will come when people's ears will be ready. Perhaps they will have undergone a heartache or a great blessing, a bereavement or a joy. Something will arrest their attention and prepare them to hear the gospel.

I've always been amazed at how God often places those who are ready to hear near us. I sat down on the airplane recently next to a young man with whom I had no interest in talking. It was not his fault; I was just tired from a long meeting I had been conducting in a distant city, and I didn't want to talk to anyone. I was trying to pull a book around my face and shut out the world when I became aware that this young man was crying. What could I do?

I began talking with him and learned that the previous day his whole family—mother, father, and sister—had been killed in a car accident. This was a young man who, he told me, had never had much time for God. But now he was ready to hear. I told him that there was someone who cared about him—Jesus Christ. Flying along at thirty thousand feet I opened my Bible and shared with him some great passages of Christ's comfort and care. And then he received Jesus as his Savior.

God sends people to us at the right moment. If we can be alert to those moments, how God can use us!

♦ WHERE TO BEGIN PREACHING THE GOSPEL / CALVIN MILLER

What does it mean to preach the gospel in all the world? I believe it begins with the world at hand, our neighborhood. This is not really limiting. People we touch here touch people in the next neighborhood who touch still other people in a kind of human chain of relationships that wraps around the world. We live in one little corner of the world, but if we're really faithful in that corner, then it affects the whole world.

When Jesus said farewell to his disciples, he told them to be his witnesses first in Jerusalem, the city they were in; then in Judea, their country; then in Samaria, the country next door; and finally "to the ends of the earth" (Acts 1:8). They were to start at home. I've always loved the little observation, "There's no use taking a lamp to Indonesia that won't burn at home."

◆ CLEARING OUT DEBRIS / JAY KESLER

One often has to listen to a lot of perversions of the gospel and clear away a lot of debris before being able to lay out the real gospel. A man once spent half an hour telling me about the faith as he understood it from a relative, who was some sort of religious fanatic.

After he had finished, I said, "I'm glad you told me about the God you don't believe in, because I don't believe in that God either." Then I began to tell him the gospel message about a God who loves us so much he came to earth and experienced life among us in the person of Jesus Christ, going to the cross to take care of our sins.

When I had finished, the man said he didn't realize it was that way. He thought God was up there just waiting to zap us for being bad.

◆ WHY DO WE NEED MISSIONARIES?
YFC EDITORS

All Christians are missionaries because all Christians are to share with others the good news about Jesus Christ. Just because God is all-knowing does not excuse us from sharing our faith with a needy world. Why? Because *we* don't know who will believe and who won't, because God has chosen to work in the world through the witness of believers, and because he commands us to be witnesses (Matthew 28:19).

Sharing Christ with Family and Friends
ADRIAN ROGERS

Often I hear people say that it's hard to witness to a close friend or a family member, and I think, That's tragic. These people ought to be the ones most easily witnessed to. If we find it difficult to witness to close friends and family, it's because they know so much about us, and unfortunately, most of us haven't lived a consistent Christian life in our home or with our friends. If we had, it would be much easier to witness to these people. Many of us can give a better witness to a stranger than to a close friend. It ought to be just the opposite.

We need to practice genuine love with our family members. Loving them means doing things for them such as helping with the dishes, giving a scarf or a necktie when you come home from a trip, giving sincere compliments. Let them see that you really care.

We need to clear the slate. When we have shown love to our family, we then need to go to each of them individually and say something like this: "Bill, I have something I want to say to you. You know I'm a Christian, but you also know I haven't lived as I ought to live around this house. God has convicted me of that, and I've asked him to forgive me. I also want to ask you to forgive me. Bill, will you please forgive me for . . . ?"

He's probably never thought about the fact that he needs to forgive you. He's probably so used to hearing you put him down that he's shocked by your newfound humility. Very likely he'll say, "Yes, I forgive you."

So you say, "Thank you very much. I've just not been the Christian I ought to be." Now this isn't a time to witness to Bill; this is a time to live the Christian life faithfully by showing him love. Then at the precise moment when he sees a victory in your life, and when God opens the door, you're going to be able to witness to him. Preparing the way and then waiting for God to act is so vital, and yet so potent with those with whom we walk and work and live in close relationship.

We need to see our friends and family not as objects to be manipulated for Christ, but as persons for whom Jesus died. We need to see them as people to whom we can show genuine Calvary love. Love never fails.

If we do these three things—practice genuine love, clear the slate, and believe that God will then give us the right opportunity for witness—we will be able to share our Lord with those closest to us.

♦THE BRIDGE TO COMMUNICATION
YFC EDITORS

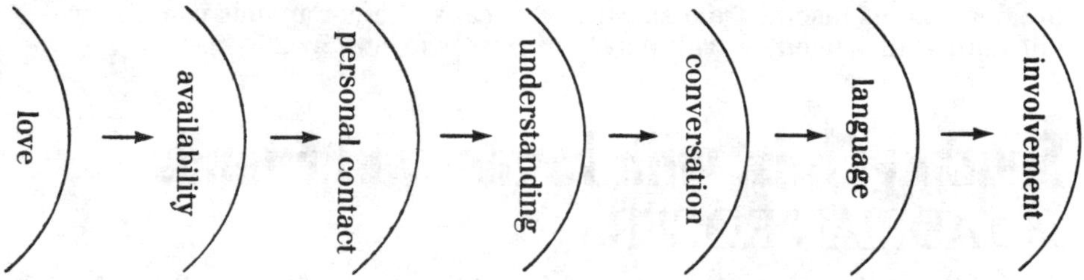

The steps to communication are logical, progressive, and true of any spiritual plan for witness. Take a look.

Love. Your communication will never get off the ground unless the motivating force behind it is love—not your love, but Christ's love working in you and out through you to your friend (2 Corinthians 5:14).

Availability. It will cost you something to be accessible to your friend. It will mean time and effort on your part to be where your friend is. In all probability, he will not come to you—you must go where he is. Jesus went where the people were. Read John 3 and notice verse 4. He was available, and you must be, too!

Personal contact. The effort to have a continual personal encounter with your friend is essential to communication. You must knock yourself out to make a daily contact with him.

Understanding. It takes a lot of effort and concern to grasp why and how your friend lives and acts the way he does. He may have different standards than you do, or he may have a whole different philosophy of life. You'll have to accept him as he is and be patient and kind as you learn to understand him.

Conversation. It takes two to carry on a conversation, and your relation to your friend must never be a monologue. Your interest in him should be genuine and reflect itself in your conversation.

Language. Language is the vehicle for conversation. Words are the means for expression. In presenting Christ, learn to express yourself in words that can be understood by your friend. Avoid cliches.

Involvement. Be willing to be genuinely and sincerely interested in the activities of your friend and become a part of him—as long as you don't violate your own convictions.

♦ BUT I'M NOT PERFECT ENOUGH
YFC EDITORS

Many people try to use the excuses, "But I'm not perfect enough yet," "My friends know my sins," "I don't want to push my religious views on others," in order to keep from witnessing.

As far as "pushing" your religious views, it depends on how you present Jesus Christ to the person. If you had found a doctor who gave you fantastic medical help, wouldn't you tell about him to someone else who had a similar problem? We don't hesitate to brag about the terrific gas mileage in our new car, but we hesitate to talk about the difference faith in Christ has made in our lives. Why?

That leads to our other excuses. We're terrified of being labeled hypocrites. How can we talk about Jesus when we know we're still imperfect in so many areas? The key to witnessing is to tell how Christ has worked in *you.* Just because every area of your life isn't perfect doesn't mean you can't tell how Christ has worked in other areas. You won't be perfect until Christ comes again. In the meantime, keep growing, and keep telling about the One who is helping you grow and change.

The Hidden Mission Field in Our Churches
✍ EVELYN CHRISTENSON

In every denomination, in every church, there is a hidden mission field. There are many people who have their names on the church rolls but don't have a relationship with Jesus Christ.

We are not to judge who is and who is not a Christian—that is the Lord's job. But Jesus said, "By their fruit you will recognize them" (Matthew 7:20). We can be fruit inspectors. If church members are not growing in Christ, if they hate everyone and do not love, if there is no fruit in their lives, they may not be Christians.

I find that up to three-quarters of the churchgoing people who come to my seminars are praying out loud to make sure of their relationship with God. These are people who are striving to change, and yet they are not sure if they know Jesus Christ.

This happened in Australia at a seminar sponsored by a woman's Bible study group. Five hundred out of a thousand women at the seminar prayed out loud to make sure they had a relationship with Jesus Christ. Afterward I met with the executives of this group. They were astonished, because most of those who prayed out loud to receive Christ had been coming to the Bible studies for years. The leaders told me, "If you have taught us one thing, it is that we have not made it clear in our study materials how to find Jesus Christ.

We have let these people study the Bible, assuming they had a personal relationship with Christ."

The same is true of our churches. One of America's largest denominations estimates that 30 percent of its members are not Christians. Other denominations estimate that as high as 70 percent of the members are cultural Christians: church members who went to Sunday school and participated in the youth group and went through all the steps, but never came to a personal relationship with Jesus. This is a major reason why church members do not grow. They don't know Christ as their Savior.

How should we reach this hidden mission field in our churches?

1. *Inspect, but don't judge.* The only one who has the right to judge is God. Our job is to challenge people to grow. But we must not exclude people simply because we don't think they know Christ. If they claim to know Christ, we must take them at their word.

2. *Give people an opportunity to accept Christ.* In our services, in our Bible studies, in our Sunday school classes, we should periodically explain the basics of salvation and give people who are not sure of their relationship with God a chance to repent and believe.

3. *Challenge those who claim to know Christ.* We should not settle for second best in our own spiritual growth or in that of those around us. In small groups and in prayer fellowships, we can hold one another accountable to the high calling God has given us.

4. *Above everything else, love.* We are to love both Christians and non-Christians. We are to meet their needs whether they have a relationship with the Lord or not.

♦ GROWING THROUGH WITNESSING
NORMAN GEISLER

When I became a believer, what most helped me get on the ball spiritually was the influence of my youth director. He plunged me immediately into witnessing and evangelism—and when I say immediately, I'm talking about the day after I got saved.

Monday night we went calling door to door, Tuesday night we had street meetings, Wednesday night was prayer meeting, Thursday night was jail service, Friday night was rescue mission, and Saturday night was Youth for Christ. Sunday night, of course, was church. I didn't have time to backslide!

That church held to the philosophy that even God can't steer a parked car. You have to get going before God can direct your life. So in spite of my inexperience, I was sent out to witness. I met people who knew more than I did, and they challenged me.

Once on skid row, a drunk staggered up to me and said, "You're not supposed to be doing this witnessing." He took my Bible and flipped it open to a verse where Jesus said, "Go and tell no man." I just looked at the man. I couldn't believe it. There it was in red letters—Jesus seemed to be saying I shouldn't be doing what I was doing. So I went home and got out my concordance and checked with my pastor to be sure I was doing the right thing. In fact, I had to do that repeatedly as questions came up. Witnessing forced me to grow.

Witnessing to non-Christians will force anyone to grow. If you don't grow, you'll fold up and quit. I chose to get into the Word and grow.

♦ USING THE BIBLE IN WITNESSING
CALVIN MILLER

I believe in Scripture memory. I do a lot myself, and I teach it to my congregation. But effective Scripture memory grows out of a passion for Christ, not out of a need for a witnessing tool.

Very few people say, "I need to witness today. I think I'll memorize some Scripture." People who love the Bible, however, will be reading along and suddenly a passage seems to leap out at them. A great truth suddenly apprehends them. They feel tremendous joy. So they dwell on the passage, and finally they have it memorized. They didn't even work at memorizing it. Their learning of Scripture wasn't mechanistic. It grew out of their affection for Christ.

♦ ARE ALL THOSE OTHERS LOST?
JAY KESLER

Often the question is put to us, "You mean, then, that all people who are not Christians—all Muslims, Jews, and Hindus—are lost, and that only those who know Christ are saved?"

Our tendency is to answer this by saying, "Yes, only through Christ can people know God." This is theologically true, but it is not the best way to state our belief. It sounds "holier than thou."

A better way to state the case is this: "Yes, all Muslims, all Jews, all Hindus, and all Christians are lost. The good news is that any one of us—Muslim, Jew, Hindu, or Christian—can be saved if we put our faith and trust in Jesus Christ."

The point is not that some people are good and others are bad. The point is that we are all lost—but some of us have found a way out.

The Powerful Effect of Being Saved
✍ RICHARD OWEN ROBERTS

A genuine work of God in our lives is going to have a very powerful effect. If the effect is absent, we might question whether God has truly worked in us yet.

Sometimes we jump to conclusions and assume people are in the kingdom before they have made the necessary commitments. Suppose, for example, Nicodemus had been told that because he had seen miracles and believed, he was now a Christian. He could have said, "Swell. I'm in," and gone on from there—but no magnificent change would have occurred in his life. Jesus, however, did not rush him. He dealt with him with great compassion, love, and tenderness, and he didn't let him suppose himself to have reached this tremendous objective before he actually did so.

All Christians engaged in the work of evangelism, as I am, need to be absolutely sure they are not counting converts prematurely because they personally need affirmation. We may hasten people into a decision before they are ready in order to be able to say, "Here's another convert I've added." We need to be freed of our need for affirmation that leads us to get in the way of God's grace. Part of the genius of Jesus, which made him such a remarkable vehicle of divine grace, is that he was free of the pride that requires human affirmation.

If a person has been led to believe he is a Christian before a true work of grace has occurred, there will be no lasting effect. This is part of the immense problem the church faces today. Some thoughtful, involved persons estimate that over half the people who claim to be born again are unregenerate. Entire denominations are acknowledging this problem. Many church members, if required to give a testimony of what Christ is currently doing in their lives, would have to say, "Well, nothing that I'm aware of." This is because they have been hastened into believing they have arrived when in fact they have made but the smallest beginning.

People who have truly been touched by God's Spirit are quickened and regenerated. They hear the Word, and faith takes root. They're convicted of their sin, and they repent and turn away from it. They turn toward Christ in absolute faith. As Paul wrote: "If anyone is in Christ, he is a new creation; the old has gone, the new has come!" (2 Corinthians 5:17).

A man called me on the phone one day and told me he wanted to join my church. "I don't recall your name," I said. "Have I ever met you?"

"No," he told me. "I've never been to your church." I responded that it seemed quite remarkable that someone would want to join a church he had never been to. He asked if I'd be willing to come over to his house to talk with him and his wife, so I went right away. When I got there I asked why he wanted to join the church.

"A very touching thing happened," he said. "Last Sunday I brought our children to your Sunday school. The director of the children's department was moaning because the pianist had called in sick. She said she didn't know what she was going to do without a piano. So I said to her, 'I play the piano a little. Perhaps I can help.' I sat down at the piano and did my best to play the children's songs. They brought me back to my childhood. When I got home I said to my wife, 'We're missing something. We ought to be part of the church.' So we'd like to join your church."

"Well," I told him, "We have a rule in our church that you may consider peculiar. Membership in our church is limited to those persons who can give credible evidence of regeneration. Can you give credible evidence of regeneration?"

He looked at me. "To be honest with you," he replied, "I don't even know what that term means. I'm a lawyer. I know what *credible* means, and I know what *evidence* means. I think I know what *regeneration* means, but I don't know what *credible evidence of regeneration* means, all put together like that."

So I told him it was evident that he wasn't prepared to join the church. He got indignant for a moment and said, "I thought churches were looking for members!"

I looked at him seriously. "My impression is that this is not some little passing thought in your mind," I said. "It came quickly, but it's very real and earnest." He agreed. "Well, I happen to have a little booklet in my pocket," I told him. "I want to ask you to master it."

"What is it?" he asked.

"It's the Gospel of John. May I ask you to master it?"

"What do you mean?"

"I want you to read it and read it," I told him, "and do everything it says. When you have done that, I want you to call me back. Are you willing to do that?"

"Oh, absolutely," he said. "Give it to us and we'll be glad to do that."

About three weeks later, my phone rang. It was the lawyer. He asked me if I could come over immediately. Something had happened. When I got to his home, I discovered that he and his wife had been gloriously converted. They were now ready to join the church.

A few weeks after that, he heard me preach on the text, "If anyone is in Christ, he is a new creation" (2 Corinthians 5:17). After church, he invited me to his home for dinner. When I got there, he took me on a tour. It was a lovely home situated on a bluff overlooking the Willamette River near Portland, Oregon. We stopped at every window. He told me about this bush and these flowers and this tree. Looking out on the river, he described the scene on the other side. Then we went into the living room and sat down.

"I liked your message this morning," he told me, "but it was incomplete. You mentioned lots of things that become new when a person becomes a Christian, but you never mentioned new eyes."

"What do you mean?" I asked.

"I'm fifty years old," he said. "All my life I've lived for money and women. That's all I ever saw. Since I became a Christian, I see trees, I see flowers, I see sunsets. I see things I never saw before."

That's the effect of a genuine work of God in our lives. We see life with new eyes. We have different goals, different motives, different purposes. It is an experience worth waiting for.

♦ CONFRONTATIONAL EVANGELISM
HOWARD HENDRICKS

Much of what we do is confrontational evangelism, yet studies have shown that only 10 percent of people in any church are good at the kind of evangelism where you sit down next to someone and start sharing your faith. That leaves 90 percent of the members of many churches feeling very guilty. Look at ways of sharing the faith that the other 90 percent can do well.

◆ WORDS AND WITNESSING / CALVIN MILLER

Some people say they can't witness because they have a hard time with words. But I've noticed that people who have a hard time with words don't have trouble with all words everywhere. Usually they are comfortable with some friend or family member, and with that person they can talk freely. It's best to forget whether words come hard or easy and major on something entirely different—relationships. It's hard for anybody to walk up to a stranger and begin witnessing. It should be. We need to make friends first, to get close enough to the person so that our witnessing flows out of our concern for him or her. When our relationship is solid, the words will not be difficult.

◆ SOWING THE SEEDS / OSWALD HOFFMAN

I went fishing with a youth worker one day and asked him why more lay people don't witness to their faith. He thought about that for a little bit and then said, "Maybe it's because they think they have to convert people, and they're afraid they're going to fail."

It's our business to sow the seeds, not to harvest the grain. We don't have to worry about failure when we sow. A farmer doesn't sow one seed for every plant he wants. He sows thousands of seeds because he knows not every seed will grow into a plant. Sowing is vitally important—if the seeds aren't sown, there won't be any plants. Our job is to sow the seed. We can let God worry about the harvest.

RELATED ARTICLES
Chapter 1: **How Does a Person Become a Christian?**
Chapter 1: **What Is a Christian?**
Chapter 26: **Friendships with Non-Christians**

CHAPTER

28

How to Change for the Better

✓ Should we try to change others?
✓ How do we know if we're changing?
✓ How do we make changes that will last?

Seven Methods of Change

✍ EVELYN CHRISTENSON

For a Christian, change is a way of life. When we receive Christ we are accepted and justified by him. But we do not become like him instantly. We go through a process of change to become the people God wants us to be.

1. *Reading God's Word changes me.* The Bible is the only book where the author is always present when I read it. God changes me when I read the Scriptures daily. I read devotionally until God speaks to me. This waiting is important. I need to give God a chance to speak to me. But listening is not enough. When the Lord points out something to me, I interact with him. I ask him, "What do you mean by that? How can I apply that? Why do I need to apply that?"

So I read until God says stop. When God stops me at Luke 23:9 with "[Herod] plied him with many questions but Jesus gave him no answer," I pray, "Lord, show me when I have been defensive. Show me those times when I wanted to have my rights." I wait and let God bring to my mind where I have fallen short. Then I pray, asking him to help me to apply to my life what I have learned. I also write things down—what I have learned, what I have prayed for, how God has answered.

2. *Reading the Scriptures in a group changes me.* When I read God's Word on my own and then come together and interact with others in a small group, my learning is broadened. I see where and why God stopped other people in their reading. As we share together, we help each other. Reading in groups can happen in Sunday school classes, Bible study groups, prayer fellowships, or wherever we gather with other Christians.

3. *Studying God's Word changes me.* When I dig deep into God's Word and study it, I change. If I only read God's Word and don't study it, I run the risk of going off on a tangent. When I study I ask God to remove my preconceived ideas so that I can look at the Scriptures without the nontruths I have picked up.

Use a commentary and an atlas so you can study accurately. Remember that study involves observation, interpretation, and application. Don't jump right in and interpret without spending time observing what the Bible really says. After observing and interpreting, apply what you have learned from the Bible. Figure out how to take the truths you have learned and make them a part of your life. Application is where change starts to happen.

4. *God changes me when the Holy Spirit recalls the Scripture.* When I don't have a Bible, the Holy Spirit recalls the Scripture I have tucked away through reading, interacting with others, and studying. "The Counselor, the Holy Spirit, whom the Father will send in my name, will teach you all things and will remind you of everything I have said to you" (John 14:26). That's the role of the Holy Spirit.

We need to do more than just read or study or even memorize. As Psalm 119:11 says, "I have hidden your word in my heart." When we hide God's Word, we apply it until it becomes a part of us. All day long the Holy Spirit can use the Scripture we have tucked away to change us. He brings to our minds exactly what we need at a certain time. It's like our mind is a computer and the Holy Spirit is a supernatural operator. He comes along and touches the recall button, and we remember the verses we need to know.

5. *God changes me when I ask him to.* I often pray, "I am weary, Lord; I have sinned. I am not close to my goal of being like Jesus. Change me." Then God reaches down and takes my un-Christlike attitude and gives me a Christlike attitude. But he will not force me to change. I have to be willing. Sometimes my prayer needs to be, "Lord, make me willing to be made willing." But I know that when I ask God to change me, he will.

6. *God changes me when other people pray for me.* "Carry each other's burdens" (Galatians 6:2). I can feel the power in my life when other people pray for me. Their prayers change me. Sometimes I don't even know they are praying. I love to get notes from people that say, "What happened to you on January 1? God told me to pray for you." I look back and find that, yes, God

alerted that person to pray for a reason. But more often people pray for me because I have shared my needs with them. I forfeit wonderful prayer support when I don't admit I have any needs.

7. *God changes me when I pray for other people.* I can't pray for someone and be angry with that person at the same time. I can't gossip about someone and still pray for him or her. I am a different kind of person when I am praying. I see other people's needs, and I get my mind off myself. When I pray for others I am participating in an activity that Jesus and the Holy Spirit also do.

These seven methods of change make me a different person. I can measure my growth by looking back and seeing how I am different now. Am I more like Jesus today than I was a year ago? Are my reactions more like Jesus' reactions this year than they were last year or five years ago? Are people seeing more of Jesus in me?

When we take inventory we need to remember that when we grow in Christ, we are like a baby learning to walk. The first step is a long way from running down the street. We don't grow overnight. We grow by taking one step at a time.

Making Spiritual Changes That Last

HUDSON T. ARMERDING

Spiritual changes usually aren't made until there is a real need for them. People don't come to Christ initially until they have a sense of sin and a need for forgiveness; and they don't grow in Christ without a sense of inadequacy or frustration that drives them to want more than they have of the things of the Lord.

Sometimes spiritual change is triggered by subjective emotions. A person is not satisfied with his relationship with the Lord or with his fruitfulness, or manifestation of spiritual qualities.

Sometimes spiritual change is induced by circumstances. One time I was in my office, feeling very frustrated because I was behind in my work. My secretary came in and asked if I would greet some visitors who had just come. I greeted them, but with bad grace, because I hadn't wanted to be interrupted. When this incident was over, I went back into my office, and suddenly realized how insensitive I was becoming to people. I told the Lord I couldn't continue the way I was going. I needed to make some very basic changes, or a crisis like this could erupt again and destroy a friendship.

Sometimes God allows us to do foolish things so we will see the poverty of our lives and thus want to make changes, whether developing a new life-style or growing closer to the Lord.

In order to make spiritual changes, a person must first engage in careful self-analysis. Look at the mundane things, such as health habits. This may seem strange to some, but I found I needed to address the issue of adequate rest, diet, and exercise. I needed to cut down on the number of cups of coffee I drank, and discipline myself in other ways as well to improve my physical health and strike a balance between physical and intellectual activity. It may not sound very spiritual, but our bodies and our emotions affect our receptivity to God's blessings.

Next, look at your schedule and your commitments. In the Bible, we see that God expects us to work six days and rest one day. If we don't, we tend to get irritated, frustrated, and strung out. Review your schedule, leaving adequate time for rest and renewal.

Third, establish an order of priorities. Too often the most important things get crowded out. Whether you're a busy executive or a parent with children to look after, it's easy to feel controlled by circumstances rather than being in control.

When I saw that I needed to make some changes, I decided to back off from some of my heavy work responsibilities. For example, I decided to be away from home no more than two weekends a month, and I would go to evening meetings no more than three nights a week. In addition, each week I'd take a half day to do in-depth work away from the office. And at least once every three months my wife and I would try to go away by ourselves for a three-day weekend to get some quality time together.

At home, we decided to find a time for family worship when we wouldn't be harassed by phone calls and conflicting appointments. We ended up having worship right after the children got up in the morning—that was the one time we could be together, and it was good to start the day with God before everything else crowded in.

In our family, we learned to say no to some things and yes to others. This gave us the time to do what we really felt was important. I can testify that the quality of my life has increased significantly since I began making some of these decisions several years ago.

When you are making strategic decisions, it's important to enlist help. At home I tried to enlist the help of my wife and children, and in the office I had the help of the support staff. I have learned that people are more enthusiastic about supporting decisions they help make. Since my family and I often shared these time-management decisions, we all felt ownership of them.

I also learned that having a support group is very important—a group with whom you work and to whom you are accountable. Alcoholics Anonymous works on that principle: recovered alcoholics surround the new person and call him at the right times. In a much less dramatic way, believers who are making changes in their spiritual lives need support, either from family or friends. We need people with whom we can meet for study and prayer, people who will shore us up and help us have expectations we can realize. We also need friends who will confront us in love when we're wrong. Paul recounts in the book of Galatians that he did this with Peter.

Finally, and most important, we need to realize that God is more interested in our change and growth than we are. With every overture we make toward him, with every effort we make, we can confidently expect his blessings in response.

We don't have to try to battle our way into heaven on our own. Every time we even take a faltering step, God encourages us, cheers us on, and strengthens us in our efforts. God's Spirit works within us to develop the qualities he wants us to have. The Lord does the work as we subject ourselves to him for the refining process.

Developing Programs for Doing God's Work

DAVID AND CHERYL ASPY

We have given our lives to Christ. We have looked for his will for us, and we feel called to fulfilling it in a particular way. From the parable of the talents we know that God expects us to be good stewards of the gifts he has given us. Good stewardship, we know, involves investing our talents so that they multiply. It isn't sufficient just to protect and preserve our gifts; we are to bring God more than he gave us. But the task looks enormous. Where do we begin?

It is important to begin each phase of our Christian life with a prayer that God will lead us and give us his wisdom. With trust in God as our base, we feel safe as we move out into the world to do God's will.

An old proverb says that a journey of a thousand miles begins with a single step. Insofar as possible, we should plan this beginning step—and all the steps that follow it—to increase the probability of arriving at our destination. Surely there will be surprises along the way. We will win some battles we expected to lose, and we will lose some we expected to win. But a well-conceived plan will still increase the possibility that we will succeed in doing the work God has called us to do.

Planning does not take away from our reliance on God. He gives us all our gifts, including our intellect. The God who planned the universe and outlined human history made it possible for us to dream, plan, and carry out our plans as well. In pursuing our goal of doing God's work, then, we should do our best to leave nothing to chance.

God calls us to do very different kinds of work. Some of us are called to a profession, such as medicine or the ministry. Some are called to an attitude, such as hospitality or generosity. Some are given gifts that enrich the church—teaching, music, administration. No matter what we are called to do, though, we will follow the same procedure for reaching our goals. It is not a complicated procedure. Let's see how it would work if my goal were to increase the amount of reading I do.

1. *Diagnose your present situation.* Diagnosis is always the first step in planning. In this case, it is a simple procedure. For a week or two I can keep a record of what I read. During this time, I do not try to read any more or less than usual. I simply go about my regular routines, jotting down magazine articles and book pages I read in the course of the day.

When I have completed the diagnosis, I may have learned that I read two magazine articles and twenty book pages in a typical week. Let's say I decide to concentrate on reading books. I will then summarize my diagnosis. *Starting Point:* read one-tenth of one book a week (twenty pages).

2. *Establish a target.* Now I am ready to determine where I want to go. It is not usually helpful just to say, "I want to read more." The target I choose must be specific so that I can tell when I hit it. It must also be within the realm of possibility. If I have a full-time job and a family, there is no point in setting the goal of reading five books a week. Perhaps I will state my goal like this. *Target:* read one book a week (two hundred pages).

3. *Close the gap.* Obviously there is a gap between where I am now and where I want to be. Procedures created to close gaps between our present state and our goals are called programs. Programs are step-by-step statements that permit us to move to our goal by making one small gain after another until the goal is reached. They make connecting links between our present state and our target. They eliminate the gap between where we are and where we want to go.

Each step is like a rung in a ladder. Each accomplishment brings us a little closer to our goal. Our actions become meaningful as we pursue our goals. A program to increase the amount of reading I do might include the following steps.

Starting Point: Read one-tenth of one book a week (20 pages).

Step 1: Take a speed-reading course at the community college.
Step 2: Read three-tenths of one book a week (60 pages).
Step 3: Read one-half of one book a week (100 pages).
Step 4: Read seven-tenths of one book a week (140 pages).
Step 5: Read one book a week (200 pages).

Goal: Read one book a week (200 pages).

Now if I follow the program, I will get to the goal. But what if I fall off the ladder? Then I ask myself why, and I make whatever changes are necessary to help me continue to follow it. Maybe my steps were too big. I may need to go from reading twenty pages a week to reading thirty pages a week rather than jumping to sixty pages. This means my program will take longer, but it may make it more likely that I will be able to complete it. The important thing is that I am using my talents to increase my talents. I am following the lesson Jesus taught in the parable of the talents.

Let's summarize the steps we can use to accomplish God's will for our lives:

1. Pray for God's blessing.
2. Diagnose your present situation.
3. Establish a target.
4. Create a step-by-step plan to take you from where you are to where you want to be.
5. Revise your plan as needed to keep yourself on course.

All Christian programs should give God the glory for allowing us to be about his work. By planning for our spiritual growth, just as we plan for growth in other areas of our lives, we can move closer to becoming the servants God would have us be.

What Difference Does Being a Christian Make?

JOAN H. YOUNG

So now I'm a Christian. I'm going to heaven, but what difference does that make to me today? The Bible says, "If anyone is in Christ, he is a new creation; the old has gone, the new has come" (2 Corinthians 5:17). But all too often, Christians and non-Christians appear very much the same, thus adding extra weight to the question, What difference does being a Christian make?

After we accept Jesus and his death as the payment for our sin, God does not force his way into our lives. He will only work in us as much as we let him. Although being a Christian should make all the difference in our attitudes and actions, unless we choose to follow the principles of living in the Bible, there will be no outward difference at all.

James had a lot to say about people who do not allow God to work on their attitudes and actions after they become Christians, and none of it was complimentary. He said, among other things, "What good is it, my brothers, if a man claims to have faith but has no deeds?" (James 2:14).

But what is the positive side? You can be actively interested in seeing a difference in your life. Jesus said that there are two basic commandments: to love God with your whole being, and to love other people as much as you love yourself. For most people, the highest priority is something more like looking out for number one, personal gain, acceptance, popularity, or even perhaps fulfilling some private vendetta.

The biggest change in our attitudes should be that love becomes our number one goal. This is not remotely possible unless we let the attitude of Christ fill and control our minds. Our human nature is selfish. It requires God's nature to love, but the wonderful news is that he promises to give us his nature as we learn to let him do so! There are so many Scripture references supporting this idea that it would take the whole page to list them; it's not just a minor theme that we can afford to overlook. For example, Ephesians 4:23, 24 says, "Now your attitudes and thoughts must all be constantly changing for the better.... Clothe yourself with this new nature" (TLB). Then the next fifty verses list specific ways in which our attitudes and actions are to change. Just when you are almost done reading this list, and feeling that no one could ever be good enough to do all those things, you get to 6:10. Paul was getting ready to close this letter, and he said, "Last of all I want to remind you that your strength must come from the Lord's mighty power within you" (TLB). You were right—no human nature is good enough. But we have God's power within us!

How much power is available to help us do what is right? Even if we are really willing to do the right things in a tough situation, isn't it sometimes just too hard? That often makes up the substance of our excuses, but the truth was pointed out by Paul, again in Ephesians: "I pray that you will begin to understand how incredibly great his power is to help those who believe him. It is that same mighty power that raised Christ from the dead" (1:19, 20, TLB). So much for that excuse.

Another way we try to dodge the issue is when we compare ourselves to other people. We think, Well, look at what *that* person does. I'm not so bad. This is a dangerous trick of Satan. We are always to compare ourselves to God's standards for our lives, not to other people's standards. Paul referred to some people like this in 2 Corinthians 10:12, 13. He said, "Their trouble is that they are only comparing themselves with each other, and measuring themselves against their own little ideas.... Our goal is to measure up to God's plan for us" (TLB). Can we say that this is our goal? Even the great prophets Isaiah and Daniel fell on the ground and realized how imperfect they were when they saw God's standard (see Isaiah 6:5 and Daniel 10). But God did not leave either one of those men lying in the dirt. Daniel was lifted up and an angel said, "God loves you very much!" Isaiah was told, "You are pronounced 'not guilty.'" This is exactly what God is saying to you and me through Jesus Christ.

How should our attitudes and actions change when we become Christians? Our new attitude is to be an overwhelming motivation of love. As for our actions—if love is our goal, our actions *will* change. We can open our Bibles almost anywhere to discover some specific actions that God recommends. But we will never accomplish this through our own nature and power. We must let God's nature become our own. It's summed up in Galatians 5:24-26. "Those who belong to Christ have nailed their natural evil desires to his cross and crucified them there. If we are living now by the Holy Spirit's power, let us follow the Holy Spirit's leading in every part of our lives. Then we won't need to look for honors and popularity, which lead to jealousy and hard feelings" (TLB). How's your motivation?

Making a Difference

✍ DAVE VEERMAN

As a family, we have been memorizing Bible verses together and will tackle about one a week and go over them at dinnertime. Kara, who's ten, and Dana, six, usually do better than Mom and Dad. One evening Gail and I were relaxing after dinner when we heard the girls arguing in the bedroom. "I hate you," one screamed. And the other responded in kind. Instead of running back to intervene, I decided to try an experiment and called out, "Kara." It got quiet and she said, "Yes?" "What is our Bible verse for this week?" I asked. Very sweetly she responded, word perfect, "First John 4:11: 'Dear friends, since God loved us as much as that, we surely ought to love each other too'" (TLB). Then with hardly a pause, the fight resumed with all its intensity. Undaunted, I repeated the process with Dana, but with the same results. They had learned the right words, but not their application.

The interaction with my daughters illustrates a problem all too obvious in our society: the lack of Christians who are putting into practice what they have read and memorized. We know a lot of truths, but we haven't allowed the *Truth* to change our lives.

Lest you think that this is an exaggeration, consider the following. Christian record and book sales are at an all-time high, church attendance is growing, and preachers pack the airwaves. At the same time, divorce, crime, suicide, drug usage, child abuse, abortion, and other terrible problems are becoming epidemics. As religion has become more visible and acceptable, so has sin. There yawns a widening gap between what we say we believe and what we really believe. According to a recent Gallup poll, only 56 percent of people in the eighties admit that religion is important in their lives. It was 75 percent in 1952.

The solution to this problem begins with you and me. We must take God's Word seriously and apply it to our lives at home, school, work, in the neighborhood and marketplace. We will only make a difference in the world as we allow Christ to make a diffference in us.

RELATED ARTICLES
Chapter 11: **Lord, Change Me**
Chapter 22: **Staying Open to Change**

SUBJECT INDEX

AUTHOR INDEX